CRUSADE TEXTS IN TRANSLATION

Volume 29

About the volume

The publication of this new translation of the *Jérusalem* and the *Chétifs* allows readers to take a complete view of this poetic trilogy about the First Crusade as the author originally intended. It makes accessible to readers the central texts of one of the key epic cycles of Old French literature which is of unique interest because of its portrayal of relatively recent events. It also gives readers an insight into the process of transforming history into legend, which arguably is of wider interest than just the history of the First Crusade.

About the series

The crusading movement, which originated in the 11th century and lasted beyond the 16th, bequeathed to its future historians a legacy of sources which are unrivalled in their range and variety. These sources document in fascinating detail the motivations and viewpoints, military efforts and spiritual lives of the participants in the crusades. They also narrate the internal histories of the states and societies which crusaders established or supported in the many regions where they fought, as well as those of their opponents. Some of these sources have been translated in the past but the vast majority have been available only in their original language. The goal of this series is to provide a wide ranging corpus of texts, most of them translated for the first time, which will illuminate the history of the crusades and the crusader-states from every angle, including that of their principal adversaries, the Muslim powers of the Middle East.

About the translators

Carol Sweetenham is an accomplished translator of medieval texts on the Crusades. Her previous publications include: *Canso d'Antioca*, with Linda Paterson (2003); *Robert the Monk's History of the First Crusade* (2005); and *The Chanson d'Antioche*, with Susan Edgington (2011).

*This book is dedicated to
Professor Linda Paterson
with grateful thanks.*

THE *CHANSON DES CHÉTIFS*
AND *CHANSON DE JÉRUSALEM*

Crusade Texts in Translation

Editorial Board

Malcolm Barber (Reading), Peter Edbury (Cardiff),
Bernard Hamilton (Nottingham), Norman Housley (Leicester),
Peter Jackson (Keele)

Titles in the series include

Mary Fisher
The Chronicle of Prussia by Nicolaus von Jeroschin
A History of the Teutonic Knights in Prussia, 1190–1331

Peter Lock
Marino Sanudo Torsello, The Book of the Secrets of the Faithful of the Cross
Liber Secretorum Fidelium Crucis

Susan B. Edgington and Carol Sweetenham
The *Chanson d'Antioche*
An Old French Account of the First Crusade

Denys Pringle
Pilgrimage to Jerusalem and the Holy Land, 1187–1291

Carol Sweetenham
Robert the Monk's History of the First Crusade
Historia Iherosolimitana

Damian J. Smith and Helena Buffery
The Book of Deeds of James I of Aragon
A Translation of the Medieval Catalan *Llibre dels Fets*

Martin Hall and Jonathan Phillips
Caffaro, Genoa and the Twelfth-Century Crusades

Keagan Brewer
Prester John: The Legend and its Sources

The *Chanson des Chétifs* and *Chanson de Jérusalem*
Completing the Central Trilogy of the Old French Crusade Cycle

Translated by

CAROL SWEETENHAM

ASHGATE

© Carol Sweetenham 2016

All rights reserved. No part of this publication may be reproduced, stored in a retrieval system or transmitted in any form or by any means, electronic, mechanical, photocopying, recording or otherwise without the prior permission of the publisher.

Carol Sweetenham has asserted her right under the Copyright, Designs and Patents Act, 1988, to be identified as the translator of this work.

Published by
Ashgate Publishing Limited
Wey Court East
Union Road
Farnham
Surrey, GU9 7PT
England

Ashgate Publishing Company
110 Cherry Street
Suite 3-1
Burlington, VT 05401-3818
USA

www.ashgate.com

British Library Cataloguing in Publication Data
A catalogue record for this book is available from the British Library.

Library of Congress Cataloging-in-Publication Data
Names: Sweetenham, Carol, translator.
Title: The Chanson des Châetifs and Chanson de Jâerusalem: Completing the Central Trilogy of the Old French Crusade Cycle / translated by Carol Sweetenham.
Other titles: Chanson des Châetifs. English
Description: Farnham, Surrey, UK, England : Ashgate Publishing Limited ; Burlington, VT : Ashgate Publishing Company, 2016. | Series: Crusade Texts in Translation ; 29 | Includes bibliographical references and index.
Identifiers: LCCN 2015022686| ISBN 9781409445197 (hardcover : alk. paper) |
Subjects: LCSH: Crusades – First, 1096-1099 – Poetry. | Epic poetry, French – Translations into English. | Chansons de geste – Translations into English. | Chanson des châetifs. | Chanson de Jâerusalem. | Epic poetry, French – History and criticism. | Chansons de geste – History and criticism. Crusades in literature.
Classification: LCC PQ1441.C57 E5 2016 | DDC 841/.1 – dc23 LC record available at http://lccn.loc.gov/2015022686

ISBN: 9781409445197 (hbk)
ISBN: 9781409445203 (ebk-PDF)
ISBN: 9781472406132 (ebk-ePUB)

Printed in the United Kingdom by Henry Ling Limited, at the Dorset Press, Dorchester, DT1 1HD

Contents

Abbreviations   *vii*
Preface   *ix*

PART I: INTRODUCTION

Introduction: From Antioch to Jerusalem by way of Oliferne   3

1   The *Chanson des Chétifs*   7

2   The *Chanson de Jérusalem*   23

3   The *Antioche*, the *Chétifs* and the *Jérusalem*: the Central Trilogy of the Old French Crusade Cycle   35

Editions Used and Principles of Translation   51

PART II: TRANSLATIONS

Plot Summaries   59

La Chanson des Chétifs   67

La Chanson des Chétifs: Selected Variants   147

La Chanson de Jérusalem   173

PART III: APPENDICES

Table of Rhymes by Laisse Number   357
Table of Names and Places   359

Bibliography   *415*
Index   *429*

Abbreviations

AB	*Analecta Bollandiana*
B	*Byzantion*
BDBA	*Bien dire et bien aprandre*
C	*Crusades*
DR	*Dublin Review*
FMLS	*Forum for Modern Language Studies*
EHR	*English Historical Review*
GRLM	*Grundriss der Literatur des Mittelalters*
H	*Hesperia*
HR	*Historical Review*
JCWI	*Journal of the Courtauld and Warburg Institute*
JMH	*Journal of Medieval History*
MA	*Moyen Age*
MGHS	*Monumenta Germaniae Historica Scriptores*
MS	*Medieval Studies*
OFCC	*Old French Crusade Cycle*
R	*Romania*
RF	*Romanische Förschungen*
RR	*Romanic Review*
RHC Occ	*Recueil des Historiens des Croisades: historiens occidentaux*
T-L A.	*Tobler, Altfranzösisches Worterbuch: bearbeitet und herausgegeben von Erhard Lommatzsch*
V	*Viator*

Preface

The *Chanson des Chétifs* and the *Chanson de Jérusalem* form part of the wider cycle of texts known as the Old French Crusade Cycle. Together with the *Chanson d'Antioche*, they form a central trilogy at the heart of the Cycle which portrays the First Crusade as a symbol of God's support for Outremer and part of His divine plan. This volume therefore forms a companion volume to *The Chanson d'Antioche: an Old French account of the First Crusade*, which Susan Edgington and I published in 2011. The two are designed to be read together, and as such I have not repeated in this volume analysis and references covered in the first volume.

I am most grateful to Professor Emanuel J. Mickel and the University of Alabama Press for permission to use the Alabama editions of these two texts as the basis for my translation: I have benefited immensely from the erudition of both editors, Geoffrey Myers for the *Chétifs* and Nigel Thorp for the *Jérusalem*, not to mention Professor Mickel himself. It was Nigel Thorp who originally suggested that it might be a good idea to translate the *Jérusalem* alongside the *Antioche*, and I hope he will be satisfied with the result.

First and foremost, thanks are due to Susan Edgington for reading and commenting on the entire translation: it is much the better (and pruned of a certain amount of irrational exuberance) for it. I am very grateful to Professor Linda Paterson and Professor Malcolm Barber for reading the text and improving it with their comments. Many of the ideas in the introduction were tested on colleagues in the British Branch of Société Rencesvals, the Society for the Study of the Crusades and the Latin East, the Medieval Chronicle Society and the Crusades seminar at the Institute of Historical Research: I have benefited greatly from their input. I should also like to thank Andrew Buck for reading the section on twelfth-century Antioch and providing comments and references; Thomas Asbridge, Jonathan Phillips, Marcus Bull and Peter Francopan for helpful discussions; and Philip Bennett for insightful comments which made many puzzling elements fall into place. It goes without saying that any mistakes are entirely mine. I am grateful to the unfailingly helpful staff at the Taylor Institute, the Bodleian Library, the History Faculty Library and the Sackler Library in Oxford. And as ever my editor John Smedley has demonstrated admirable patience and support.

Finally my thanks yet again to my long-suffering family for tolerating my absences in the twelfth century. In particular I should like to thank my husband Philip for skills in computer combat the equal of any twelfth-century warrior, and my children Oliver and William for support, insights and not complaining too much during a very hot week in Jerusalem.

I have dedicated this volume to my former supervisor Professor Linda Paterson, without whom I should never have found my way to the Old French Crusade Cycle and from whom I have learnt an incalculable amount.

PART I
Introduction

Introduction
From Antioch to Jerusalem by way of Oliferne

The *Chanson des Chétifs* and the *Chanson de Jérusalem* form part of the central trilogy at the heart of the thirteenth-century cycle of poems known as the Old French Crusade Cycle. The trilogy focuses on the events of the First Crusade, arguably the only Crusade perceived as successful, which is treated as an exemplum for later potential Crusaders. It comprises the *Chanson d'Antioche*, which takes events from the preaching of the Crusade to the siege, fall and battle of Antioch; the *Chanson des Chétifs*, which serves as a link between events at Antioch and the triumphant conclusion of the Crusade; and the *Chanson de Jérusalem*, which describes the siege and fall of Jerusalem and the subsequent battle of Ascalon.[1]

The Cycle was composed well after the events it describes. It survives in full in nine manuscripts, although not all contain the continuations after the *Jérusalem*. The manuscript used as the basis of the Alabama editions of the *Chétifs* and the *Jérusalem* is B.N.fr. 12558. This is a well-written manuscript with miniatures, probably to be dated to the mid-thirteenth century and produced in Picardy or Luxembourg. Whilst we cannot be precise on dating, the surviving manuscripts are largely thirteenth century.[2] The *Chanson d'Antioche* shows signs of an origin

---

[1] The complete Cycle is edited in the ten volumes of the Alabama edition: *The Old French Crusade Cycle*, (eds) J. A. Nelson and E. J. Mickel, 10 vols (Tuscaloosa, 1977–2003). The *Chanson des Chétifs* is volume 5: *Les Chétifs*, (ed.) G. M. Myers (Tuscaloosa, 1981). The *Chanson de Jérusalem* is volume 6: *La Chanson de Jérusalem*, (ed.) N. R. Thorp (Tuscaloosa, 1992). The *Chanson d'Antioche* is volume 4: *La Chanson d'Antioche*, (ed.) J. A. Nelson (Tuscaloosa, 2003). The *Chanson d'Antioche* has received more attention than any other text in the Cycle. There are two modern French editions: *La Chanson d'Antioche*, (ed.) S. Duparc-Quioc, *Documents rélatifs à l'histoire des croisades* 11, 2 vols. (Paris, 1976–78); volume I *Edition*, volume II *Etude*; and *La Chanson d'Antioche: chanson de geste du dernier quart du XIIe siècle*, (ed.) and transl. B. Guidot (Paris, 2011). The *Antioche* is also the only text to have been translated: into modern French by Bernard Guidot, and into English by Carol Sweetenham and Susan Edgington, *The Chanson d'Antioche: an Old French account of the First Crusade*, Crusade Texts in Translation 22 (Farnham and Burlington, 2011).

[2] Detailed studies of the manuscripts can be found in Duparc-Quioc, *Etude* pp. 43–80, and Myers in vol. I of the Cycle, *La Naissance du Chevalier au Cygne* (Tuscaloosa, 1977); summarised Sweetenham and Edgington pp. 36–9.

in Picardy at the beginning of the century.³ There are no precise indications for dating either the *Chétifs* or the *Jérusalem*, but given the manuscript tradition an assumption of early thirteenth century would not be too wide of the mark for either.

The Cycle is first and foremost a work of literature. In form it comprises a set of linked *chansons de geste* written in rhyming alexandrine laisses and using all the topoi of the genre: extravagant description of Saracens, innumerable single combats between knights and an obsessive focus on the details of weaponry and battle, all written in heavily formulaic language.⁴ Whilst the *Antioche* is close to two near-contemporary sources for the Crusade, Albert of Aachen and Robert the Monk, the same cannot be said of the *Jérusalem* which is devoid of historical content beyond the broadest outline of events.⁵ The *Chétifs* is entirely fantastical both in content and approach: there is no evidence for dragons, child-snatching monkeys or the near-conversion of Corbaran to Christianity in any source for the Crusade.

The modern student of the Crusades might therefore be forgiven for wondering why, as a thirteenth-century fictional take on events of over a century ago, either work is worth reading. The answer is precisely because that is what it is. The three texts together set out a coherent view of the First Crusade as a successful path to redemption and salvation, and therefore an example for later Crusaders to follow. The Crusade was transformed from a historical event to an event with mythological status alongside the cycles of Charlemagne, Arthur and the heroes of antiquity and the Old Testament.⁶ As such it was a source of entertainment, edification and emulation. The trilogy at the heart of the Cycle is the driving force of this approach, and a precious window into thirteenth-century self-perception and motivation.

---

³ On Picard influence in the language of the text in B. N. fr. 12558, see the comprehensive study by Guidot, pp. 39–90. On manuscript origin in Picardy see Duparc-Quioc and Myers as above. On the dominance of Picard characters see Sweetenham and Edgington pp. 34–5.

⁴ First argued in detail by R. F. Cook, *Chanson d'Antioche, chanson de geste: le cycle de la croisade est-il épique?* (Amsterdam, 1980). More recent analysis in Guidot, pp. 107–30; Sweetenham and Edgington pp. 63–85.

⁵ The historicity or otherwise of the *Antioche* has been strenuously and even viciously debated since the nineteenth century. For a summary of the debate see Sweetenham and Edgington, Introduction, chapter 2. For analysis of the parallels with Latin source material see Sweetenham and Edgington pp. 15–24; Duparc-Quioc, *Etude* chapter III.

⁶ As witness the promotion of Godfrey of Bouillon to the ranks of the Nine Worthies alongside figures from the Old Testament and Classical Antiquity such as King David, Julius Caesar and Alexander: *Chivalry*, M. Keen (New Haven and London, 1984) pp. 121–4. Already in the middle of the twelfth century Suger had episodes from the Crusade portrayed in the royal abbey of St Denis: 'The twelfth century crusading window of the Abbey of St Denis: *Praeteritorum Enim Recordatio Futurorum Exhibitio*', E. A. R. Brown and M. W. Cothren, *Journal of the Courtauld and Warburg Institute* 49 (1986) pp. 1–40.

Chapter 1 of the Introduction examines the *Chétifs* as a text in its own right, discussing its composition, source material and dating. Chapter 2 examines similar issues for the *Jérusalem*. Chapter 3 discusses the two texts as part of the central trilogy and the role they play in the Old French Crusade Cycle.

Chapter 1
The *Chanson des Chétifs*

The *Chanson des Chétifs* is an intriguing text which sits at the heart of the Old French Crusade Cycle. It follows immediately after the (relatively) realistic account of the siege and battle of Antioch in the *Chanson d'Antioche*, and leads to the similar rigours recounted in the *Chanson de Jérusalem*. In contrast to its companion texts it tells a fanciful tale featuring a dragon inhabited by a devil, a lubricious Saracen lady not in the first flush of youth, a child kidnapped by wild animals then robbers, and more besides. The heroes are the band of knights taken prisoner at the start of the Crusade at Civetot in the disastrous defeat of Peter the Hermit's army. The story undoubtedly provides some fantasy and light relief in the midst of slaughter, siege and starvation. But there is more to it than meets the eye.

The content of the *Chétifs*

The text comprises three episodes with little apparent linkage other than that they concern a distinct group of characters – the *chétifs*, a group of nobles taken captive at Peter the Hermit's defeat at Civetot – and their relationship with the Saracen leader and victor at the battle of Antioch, Corbaran.

The first episode follows on directly from Corbaran's defeat at the battle of Antioch, during which the son of the Sultan of Persia, Brohadas, was killed. Corbaran is duly arraigned for treason. He is required to fight a judicial duel, with one Christian champion prepared to fight two Turkish champions. One of the *chétifs*, Richard of Chaumont, agrees to do so in return for the liberty of all the *chétifs*, under heavy pressure from Corbaran's mother who makes her penchant for nice young knights and in particular Richard of Chaumont obvious. He fights the two Turks, Sorgalé and Golias, and unsurprisingly wins. Corbaran is reconciled to the Sultan. The relatives of the two Turks attempt to ambush him and the *chétifs*, but are defeated. Corbaran sets out for his city of Oliferne.[1]

The second episode concerns Corbaran and the *chétifs* only tangentially. They lose their way in a storm and come upon Mount Tigris, which is inhabited by a terrible dragon called Sathanas. Ernoul of Beauvais, on a mission to the Sultan on behalf of King Abraham, loses his way and is eaten by the Sathanas though it considerately leaves the head for purposes of identification. Ernoul's brother Baldwin then climbs the mountain and kills the dragon; Corbaran arrives close

---
[1] Laisses 1–51.

behind and discovers the dragon's treasure. The Sultan then arrives too. All are reconciled and return home.[2]

The third episode takes place after the return to Oliferne. Another of the *chétifs*, Harpin of Bourges, rescues Corbaran's child nephew successively from a wolf, a monkey and a band of robbers. Corbaran arrives guided by three saints in the guise of white stags and the child is rescued.[3]

The *chétifs* at long last are able to leave Oliferne for Jerusalem. On the way they meet and defeat soldiers sent by Cornumarant, son of the King of Jerusalem. They return to Jerusalem in time to join the siege although their role there is not particularly emphasised.[4]

The *chétifs* themselves constitute a somewhat disparate group. They consistently comprise Richard of Chaumont, John of Alis, Fulcher of Melun, the Bishop of Forez and the Abbot of Fécamp, and Harpin of Bourges. Richard of Pavia is sometimes mentioned. Baldwin of Beauvais and his brother Ernoul feature in the central episode but not elsewhere. They are clearly seen as a freestanding group within the crusade army. They are the central focus of the first main episode in the *Antioche*, the defeat at Civetot, which leads to their capture. They do not feature in the *Antioche* once taken captive for obvious reasons. More intriguingly they do not feature prominently in the *Jérusalem* after their return to the army, and some are not referred to at all.[5]

The text is more coherent than this summary makes it sound. There is a clear narrative line which takes the *chétifs* from their captivity in Oliferne to rejoin the crusade in Jerusalem: Richard's willingness to fight in the judicial duel leads to the release of the *chétifs*, who then travel back with Corbaran to Oliferne before taking their leave of him and heading for Jerusalem. The story also charts the evolving relationship between Corbaran and the *chétifs*. They begin as his captives, treated harshly and put to degrading work in his prisons. The judicial duel reverses the relationship, with Corbaran forced to seek help from his captives: ill treatment gives way to mutual respect and increasing dependency. When the *chétifs* climb the mountain to help Baldwin, Corbaran follows. In the third episode Harpin rescues Corbaran's nephew. When the *chétifs* leave for Jerusalem it is with Corbaran's blessing and splendid arms and treasure. During this process Corbaran becomes increasingly drawn towards Christianity although he stops short of actual conversion: this will happen later in the Cycle in *La Chrétienté Corbaran*.[6]

---

[2] Laisses 52–103.
[3] Laisses 104–27.
[4] Laisses 128–39.
[5] Thus neither Harpin of Bourges nor Fulcher of Melun appear at the battle of Ascalon.
[6] *La Chrétienté Corbaran* in vol. 7 part 1 of the Cycle, *The Jerusalem Continuations*, (ed.) Peter R. Grillo (Tuscaloosa, 1987). Duparc-Quioc argued that the *Chrétienté Corbaran* was in fact a second half of the *Chétifs*, completing it by the conversion of Corbaran: *Le Cycle de la Croisade* (Paris, 1955) p. 84. However it is never found alongside the *Chétifs*, and only in three manuscripts amongst the continuations; and central characters such as

That said, it is hard to deny that the text is something of a patchwork. Each of the three episodes gives prominence to a different *chétif*: Richard of Chaumont in the first, Baldwin of Beauvais in the second and Harpin of Bourges in the third. As Myers notes, the hero of the second episode, Baldwin of Beauvais, is not mentioned at all in the first or the third.[7] The prisoners are freed at the end of the first episode, and again at the end of the second episode. This rather episodic approach was clearly felt to be an issue by those who wrote the text down. It is much more unstable than the two texts with which it forms a trilogy, the *Chanson d'Antioche* and the *Chanson de Jérusalem*. It has more and longer variants: additional episodes are inserted in many manuscripts, with nearly 500 lines added to ms B describing a combat with the pagan Chainan and nearly 1,000 lines in B and I describing Sathanas' mother's intervention.

Potential source material

The origin of at least part of the text is very clearly explained. At the start of the Sathanas episode the author explains:

> 'Li boins princes Raimons ki la teste ot colpee,
> Ke Sarrasin ocisent, la pute gens dervee,
> Anthioce en remest dolante et abosmee,
> La terre fu perdue que Franc ont conquestee,
> (Onques puis par nul home ne fu si grant gardee,)
> Bien doit s'arme ester salve et devant Deu portee –
> Ceste cançons [fist faire] de verités provee.
> Li dus Raimons l'estraist, dont li arme est alee;
> Cil ki le cançon fist en ot bone soldee,
> Canoines fu Saint Piere, de provende donee.
> Tant con li clerc verqui fu li cançons gardee,
> Et quant il dut morir et l'arme en fu alee,
> Al Patriarce fu cele cançons livree:
> Si conme Bauduins a la ciere menbree,
> Ki de Bialvais fu nés, cele cite loee,
> Conbati al serpent al trenchant de l'espee,
> Por cou que son frere ot l'arme del cors sev[r]ee.

Baldwin of Beauvais and Richard of Chaumont are absent. It would not have been hard for a later redactor to pick up and develop these themes. See 'Les rédactions de la *Chrétienté Corbaran*, première branche des continuations du Cycle de la Croisade', P. R. Grillo, *Au Carrefour des routes d'Europe: la chanson de geste. Xe congrès international de la société Rencesvals, Strasbourg 1985* (Aix-en-Provence, 1987) pp. 585–600.

[7] G. Myers, '*Les Chétifs*: étude sur le développement de la chanson', *Romania* 105 (1984) pp. 63–87.

> Fu d'els deus la bataille et fors et aduree;
> Ainc d'un seul crestiien ne fu tele esgardee,
> Et par cele miracle qui la fu demostree,
> .VII. mil caitif et plus de gent desbaretee
> De l'ost Pieron l'Ermite et prise et amenee,
> Par paienime fu vendue et acatee,
> En buies et en grifes mise et encaanee,
> Ki les labors faisoient a le gent desfaee,
> [Par icele] bataille fu garie et salvee'.[8]

There is a further reference shortly after in the text.

> 'Li bons princes Raimons, qui ceste estoire ama,
> Fist ceste cançon faire que rien n'i oblia.
> Dex ait merci de l'arme qui l'estorie trova!'[9]

This is relatively clear. The Prince Raymond killed by the Turks can only refer to Raymond of Poitiers, ruler of Antioch, who was killed in 1149.[10] Raymond was the second son of William IX of Aquitaine who of course had a pedigree in the Holy Land from his participation in the abortive Crusade of 1101. Raymond was invited to Antioch to fill the power vacuum which had been left by the death of Bohemond II in 1130 and which had then been compounded by the deaths of Joscelin I of Edessa and Baldwin II of Jerusalem, two likely sources of support. The nobles in Antioch in concert with King Fulk of Jerusalem invited Raymond to come to Antioch to marry Alice's daughter Constance, a child of seven. The prospective ruler travelled out in disguise. When he arrived he faced, according to William of Tyre, the hostility of Alice (whose sister Melisende was married to Fulk of Jerusalem); the need to win over the Patriarch, Ralph of Domfront; a Byzantine Emperor in the form of John Komnenos who was keen to restore Byzantine influence in Antioch, with the Antiochene nobles having suggested that his own son should marry Constance; and pressure from the Muslims under Zengi. It is a tribute to Raymond's political as well as military skills that he managed to out-manoeuvre Alice (there is some suggestion that she thought he was intending to marry her rather than her daughter), bring the Patriarch onto his side, reach accommodation with the Byzantines and fight off Muslim pressure.

---

[8] *Chétifs* lines 1666–91.

[9] *Chétifs* lines 1778–80.

[10] For events in Antioch during this period see in particular J. Phillips, *Defenders of the Holy Land: relations between the Latin East and the West 1119–87* (Oxford, 1996), pp. 44–72, 100–103; Bernard Hamilton, 'Ralph of Domfront, Patriarch of Antioch (1135–40)', *Nottingham Medieval Studies* 28 (1984) pp. 1–21; Thomas Asbridge, 'Alice of Antioch: a case study of female power in the twelfth century', in *The Experience of Crusading*, (ed.) P. Edbury and J. Phillips, 2 vols, (Cambridge, 2003) vol. 2 pp. 29–47.

He was, notoriously, suspected of being too close to Eleanor of Aquitaine during her visit in 1148–49. In the aftermath of the Second Crusade Antioch came under increasing pressure from Nur-ad Din; and after some initial success Raymond was killed in battle at Inab in June 1149. In the words of Jonathan Phillips, 'the relative self-sufficiency of Raymond's rule compares well with Jerusalem's almost annual intervention in the north between 1119 and 1135, and is testimony to the Prince's military strength and skill'.[11]

We know nothing about the canon of St Peter's at Antioch: there is one reference to a canon, Osmond of St Garou, in a charter of 1140 by Raymond.[12] St Peter's was an early church in Antioch, partly subterranean and known as a burial place for martyrs.[13] There is nothing out of the ordinary in a cleric producing or being asked to produce a work of literature: Raymond of Aguilers, chaplain of Raymond of St-Gilles, produced an account of the First Crusade; William of Tyre and Jacques de Vitry were archbishops. What is striking is the implication that the work existed as a recognised artefact in its own right and which could be passed on to another owner after the death of the author: we find parallels to this in the troubadours and the *chanson de geste*.[14] It must have pleased its commissioner since he gave its author a stipend; there is no suggestion that this came from wider performance of the work. It is also striking that the work was given to the Patriarch: this suggests both that there was a recognised work to be given and that it was seen as important enough to the church in Antioch to be worth preserving.

We cannot say for certain which Patriarch is referred to.[15] Given the *terminus ante quem* above, it is unlikely to be Bernard of Valence who died in 1135; Raymond came to Antioch in 1136. It could be Ralph of Domfront, who was Patriarch 1135–40 before his deposition and was a bitter enemy of Raymond. However the

---

[11] Phillips, *Defenders*, p. 103.

[12] See G. Bresc-Bautier, *Le cartulaire du chapitre de St-Sépulchre de Jérusalem*, (Paris, 1984), 176–83. I am grateful to Andrew Buck for this reference.

[13] C. Cahen, *La Syrie du nord à l'époque des croisades et la principauté franque d'Antioche*, (Paris, 1940) p. 130.

[14] Compare for example the reference to the *Canso d'Antioca* in the *Canso de la Crozada* lines 1–3. *La Chanson de la Croisade Albigeoise*, (ed.) E. Martin-Chabot, 3 vols, (Paris, 1931–60); reprinted and translated H. Gougaud, *Chanson de la Croisade Albigeoise* (Paris, 1989); referred to as *Canso de la Crozada*; *The Canso d'Antioca: an Occitan epic chronicle of the First Crusade*, (ed.) and transl. Linda Paterson and Carol Sweetenham (Aldershot, 2003). For troubadour texts as artefacts see for example William of Poitiers IV.43–6: 'fait ai lo vers, no sai de cui;/ Et trametrai lo a celui/Que lo.m trametra per autrui/ Enves Anjau' ('I have composed the song though I don't know whom it's about; and I will send it to someone who will send it via somebody else for me to Anjou'): G. A. Bond, *The Poetry of William VII, Count of Poitiers, IX Duke of Aquitaine*, (New York, 1982).

[15] For Patriarchs of Antioch see B. Hamilton, *The Latin Church in the Crusader States; the secular church* (London, 1980) pp. 18–51.

very strong likelihood is that this refers to Patriarch Aimery of Limoges.[16] His uncle, Peter Armoin, was castellan of Antioch and an ally of Raymond. Aimery was a powerful figure who worked closely with Raymond, and took over power at the emergency caused by his death in 1149. His longevity and influence (he was to live until at least 1187) meant that he was one of the few Patriarchs to be known outside the Holy Land.[17]

The reference is clearly linked to the Sathanas episode: there is no indication that it applies to the text of the *Chétifs* more generally.[18] It is worth noting that it comes near the beginning of the episode, clearly marking it out as a separate part of the text. This part of the text is also distinguished by a number of assertions of truth:

'Segnor, or escoutés glorieuse cançon;
Onques tele n'oï nesuns crestiiens hom,
Ne ne fu tels cantee des le tans Salemon;
Molt est bone a entendre, car mius valt de sermon'.[19]

Given that it is no more fantastic than any other part of the *Chétifs*, this suggests that the author regarded it as particularly important. There is no particular reason to disbelieve the explanation. Indeed the similar explanation in the *Antioche* about the origins of that text is, as far as we can tell, pretty accurate.[20]

All this suggests that the author saw the Sathanas episode as distinct from the surrounding material, and a text with a clear identity and history of its own. This is supported by the non-appearance of Baldwin in the rest of the text.[21] There is no particular reason to disbelieve what the author tells us: that this text had its origins in Antioch at some point between 1136 and 1149 and was commissioned by the ruler of Antioch. We cannot however argue that it is evidence for the composition

---

[16] On Aimery's career see Hamilton, *Latin Church* 38–51; also Hamilton, 'Aimery of Limoges Patriarch of Antioch, ecumenist scholar and patron of hermits', in *The Joy of Learning and the Love of God: studies in honor of Jean Leclercq*, (ed.) F. Rozanne Elder, Cistercian Studies series 160 (Kalamazoo, Michigan and Spencer, Massachusetts, 1995) pp. 269–90.

[17] Hamilton, *Latin Church* p. 49: 'during his long tenure of the Patriarchate Aimery became throughout the Western world the best known religious leader in Frankish Syria'.

[18] U. T. Holmes and W. M. Mcleod, 'Source problems of the *Chétifs*, a Crusade chanson de geste', *Romanic Review* 28 (1937) pp. 99–108.

[19] *Chétifs* lines 2473–6. See also lines 1581–2; 1762–4.

[20] See Edgington and Sweetenham, Introduction p. 15.

[21] Myers, 'Développement', pp. 63–9. He points additionally to inconsistencies in the text, though these are found elsewhere in the Cycle (for example *Antioche* laisses 371–2, where a supposedly secret interview takes place shouting from the battlements) ; and to the fact that the Baldwin episode is inserted between two laisses with the relatively rare rhyme –ue.

of the *Chétifs* as a text per se in Antioch in the 1140s: the reference applies only to the Sathanas episode.

Even so this makes it a rare survival, one of our few pieces of evidence for literary and intellectual culture in the principality of Antioch and more generally in Outremer.[22] We do have some limited evidence specifically for a literary culture in Antioch. Walter the Chancellor produced his *Bella Antiochena* in the 1120s describing the events leading up to and following the defeat at the Field of Blood.[23] Stephen of Antioch translated the *Liber regius* of Ali ibn al-Abbas in the 1130s. Patriarch Aimery himself exchanged manuscripts in a way which suggests that he understood Greek and actively engaged in debate with the Orthodox church.[24] More generally Raymond himself was the second son of William IX of Aquitaine, famous as the first troubadour and indeed for composing entertaining songs about the vicissitudes of the 1101 crusade.[25] And there is certainly evidence for at least some level of cultural mixing, for example Greek and Latin clergy leading worship in the same churches. The mixing continued into the thirteenth century with for example a French/Coptic phrase book which survives from the thirteenth century, or the Armenian Nerses Lambronac translating the Rule of St Benedict from Latin into Armenian.[26] So there is nothing particularly surprising in the commissioning of such a work.

The verb 'estraire' implies that the text was drawn or translated from an existing work: either meaning is possible.[27] It is specified that the story was well established: 'cançon d'estoire de grant ancisserie'.[28] It is also suggested that it was

---

[22] S. B. Edgington, 'Antioch: Medieval City of Culture', in *East and West in the Medieval Eastern Mediterranean I: Antioch from the Byzantine Reconquest until the End of the Crusader Principality*, (eds) K. Ciggaar and M. Metcalf (Leuven, 2006), pp. 247–59; C. Burnett, 'Antioch as a Link between Arabic and Latin Culture in the Twelfth and Thirteenth Centuries', in *Occident et Proche-Orient: contacts scientifiques au temps des croisades*, (eds) A. Tihon, I. Draelants & B. van den Abeele, (Louvain-la-Neuve, 2000), pp. 1–78

[23] *Walter the Chancellor's 'The Antiochene Wars': a translation and commentary*, T. S. Asbridge and S. B. Edgington (Guildford, 1999).

[24] See R. Hiestand, 'Un centre intellectual en Syrie du Nord? Notes sur la personnalité d'Aimeri d'Antioche, Albert de Tarse et Rorgo Fretellus', *Moyen Age* series 5 vol. 8 (1994) pp. 7–36.

[25] Orderic Vitalis, much quoted: *The Ecclesiastical History of Orderic Vitalis*, (ed.) and transl. M. J. Chibnall, 6 vols (Oxford, 1969–80), hereafter OV; X.21, vol. 5 pp. 342–3.

[26] For mixing of population in Outremer see M. Benvenisti, *The Crusaders in the Holy Land*, (Jerusalem, 1970), pp. 17–18; J. J. S. Weitenberg, 'Literary contacts in Cilician Armenia' in *East and West in the Crusader States: context – contacts – confrontation*, (eds) K. Ciggaar, A. Davids and H. Teule, *Orientalia Lovaniensia Analecta* 75 (Leuven, 1996), pp. 63–72 at pp. 68–9.

[27] See footnote at laisse 56 for further discussion.

[28] *Chétifs* line 1618.

a written source: 'li escris le tesmoigne qui ja nen ert fausés'.[29] We do not know what such a work would have looked like or what language it would have been composed in let alone whether it was a *chanson de geste*. French culture remained dominant in Outremer: it could have been in Old French or even Occitan.[30] There are other examples of clerics composing in the vernacular although Latin might have been more likely.[31] The subject matter has little in common with other contemporary *chansons de geste* or vernacular texts. If we take the references in the *Chétifs* at face value, the text was written down; and this in turn presupposes that it was in a language accessible to a Western author.

The symbolism is obvious, almost heavy handed. The hero is called Baldwin in common with the kings of Jerusalem. Baldwin II is described in near-hagiographic terms by Walter the Chancellor as saving Antioch after the Field of Blood; potentially the work might refer to hopes of Baldwin III continuing to support Antioch. Equally the name might be a later addition by an author for whom the name Baldwin was synonymous with Jerusalem. The equation between a dragon or serpent and the devil goes all the way back to the Book of Revelations, 'hic serps anticus qui diabolus est': this is underlined by naming the dragon Sathanas, although we cannot be sure at what point this entered the text. This and the connection with St Peter's at Antioch and subsequently the Patriarch all point to some kind of ecclesiastical, maybe allegorical text in which a king called Baldwin despatches a dragon called Satan.

As well as symbolism the text draws on a strong cultural substratum. It has been described as similar to the Byzantine epic of *Digenis Akritas*, which enjoyed a vogue in the 1140s.[32] Antioch was linked particularly closely to the Byzantine

---

[29] *Chétifs* line 1792.

[30] C.f. D. Jacoby, 'Society, Culture and the Arts in Crusader Acre' in *France and the Holy Land: Frankish Culture at the end of the Crusades*, (eds) D. H. Weiss and L. Mahoney (Baltimore and London:, 2004) pp. 97–137 at p. 114: 'the cultural orientation of the Latins settled in the Frankish Levant was shaped by their strong bonds with the West and by their determination to maintain their collective social identity. The members of the Latin nobility expressed their affinity with the nobility of the West in social behaviour, rituals, attitudes, mentality, the French they spoke as well as in the courtly literature and legal treatises they read and composed in that language'.

[31] For example Ambroise, *The History of the Holy War*, transl. M. J. Ailes and M. Barber (Woodbridge, 2003), Introduction 2–3; the Occitan troubadour the Monk of Montaudon, (ed.) Michael Routledge, *Les poésies du Moine de Montaudon* (Montpellier, 1977).

[32] *Digenis Akritas: the Grottaferrata and Escorial versions*, (ed.) and transl. E. Jeffreys (Cambridge, 1998). This is a Byzantine romance involving the kidnapping of a princess, the conversion of her kidnapper into a dragon, her abduction by a lion and then a combat with 45 robbers and more, which coalesced in the middle of the twelfth century from earlier material. See also Jeffreys, 'The Comnenian background to the "romans d'antiquité" ', *Byzantion* 50 (1980) pp. 455–86, which argues for cross-cultural influence of Byzantine and Western literature around the visit of Eleanor of Aquitaine, with a revival in interest in Byzantine novels and romances in the 1140s; P. Magdalino, 'Byzantine literature: the

empire, and there is nothing unlikely in some degree of interaction. Equally the resemblances are not particularly close. The themes of the hero climbing a mountain to fight a dragon, combat with a dragon and the dragon's treasure are universal: they recur in Norse mythology with Siegfried and Fafnir, and indeed in Japanese and Chinese mythology.[33] There was a particularly strong Armenian influence in Antioch, and plenty of evidence of cross-cultural fertilisation.[34] The saints referred to show both Byzantine influence (the text contains the only reference to St Nicholas of Myra in the whole trilogy) and the influence of Antioch itself: saints Barbara and Leonard are mentioned only here in the central trilogy and both had churches in Antioch.[35] Antioch lay in the shadow of a mountain and was under threat both from Byzantium and Zengid Syria; the resonances of a combat in mountainous terrain are clear. But we cannot tie down the ancestry of this particular story more precisely.

We do not know for certain how this text came from Antioch to the West. We can surmise from the description that it had a clear identity: it is described almost in terms of a commodity which can be bought and sold. There is also evidence of cultural interchange between Antioch and the West: as Ciggaar argues 'the Frankish colonies formed a multinational society, the centre of crossroads which connected Jerusalem, Acre, Antioch, Cyprus and Constantinople with far-away France and with the Arab world'.[36] There were links between Antioch and the West through figures such as Aimery of Limoges and Eleanor of Aquitaine.[37] More specifically an embassy was sent under Bishop Hugh of Jabala in 1145 seeking help against the forces threatening the settlers in the East: the theme of captivity would have been a powerful motivator for the nascent Second Crusade.[38] So

---

twelfth century background', in *Digenes Akritas: new approaches to Byzantine heroic poetry*, (ed.) R. Beaton and D. Ricks (Aldershot and Vermont, 1993) pp. 1–14 similarly points to an efflorescence of interest in the mid-twelfth century. For Digenis Akritas as slayer of 400 dragons see A. Frantz, 'Akritas and the dragons', *Hesperia* X.i (1941) pp. 9–13.

[33] On dragons see *Dictionary of literary themes and motifs*, (ed.) J.-C. Seigneuret, 2 vols, (New York, Westport and London, 1988) pp. 400–406 at p. 404: 'The dragon was always seen as the devil'. St George, patron saint of the Crusaders, and St Margaret of Antioch both famously overcame dragons.

[34] .Weitenberg, 'Literary Contacts in Cilician Armenia'.

[35] Cahen, *Syrie du Nord* p. 131.

[36] 'Manuscripts as intermediaries: the Crusader states and international cross-fertilisation', K. Ciggaar, *East and West in the Crusader states* pp. 131–51 at p. 151.

[37] For an example of events in Outremer being commented on in the West see L. M. Paterson, 'Syria, Poitou and the *reconquista* (or Tales of the undead)', in *The Second Crusade*, (ed.) J. Phillips and M. Hoch (Manchester, 2002) pp. 133–49, arguing that the famous *vers del lavador* of Marcabru is related to the death of Baldwin of Marash.

[38] Otto of Freising's *Chronica sive Historia de Duabus Civitatibus*, (ed.) A. Hofmeister (Hannover, 1912), pp. 363–4. I am grateful to Andrew Buck for this suggestion.

there is nothing inherently improbable in the text making its way to the West and eventually to Picardy.

None of this is definite evidence. But we can construct at least some kind of picture. During the 1140s Raymond commissioned a text from a canon of St Peter. The text drew on folklore and religion to provide a near-allegorical Christian picture of victory over the Devil in the form of a dragon by a Crusader. It generated considerable income for its author, which suggests it was much performed or at least appreciated. On the author's death the rights transferred to the Patriarch, presumably as head of the Church and maybe too reflecting Aimery's literary interests. At some point it made its way to Western Europe and was eventually incorporated in the *Chétifs*.

The provenance of the other two episodes in the *Chétifs* is not given. However they play rather different functions. Their only common feature is that, unlike the Baldwin episode, they feature the same cast of *chétifs*.

The Richard of Chaumont judicial duel functions on a number of levels within the text.[39] It is central to the plot: by assisting Corbaran the Christians give him a reason to end their captivity and indeed help them on their way to rejoin the Crusade. The crusade begins, embarrassingly, with the defeat of its evangelist Peter the Hermit and the captivity of key Christian figures. In plot terms the author of the Cycle therefore needed to find a way of returning them to the crusade and hence restoring their honour. This would be possible only if Corbaran had a good reason to release them. As the main Saracen leader Corbaran also needs to be removed as an opponent. The entrusting of the Sultan's son Brohadas to Corbaran in the *Antioche* provides a pretext for this element of the plot, which comes to fruition in the judicial duel. A further unifying thread is provided by Corbaran's mother Calabra, whose partiality for Richard is embarrassingly evident but who here, as in the *Antioche*, gives Corbaran sound advice. The difference is that in the *Antioche* he does not follow her advice and loses; here he does, and gains. Victory in the duel also evokes the concept of judicial duel as a way of establishing the rightness of a cause. Richard's victory over the Turks makes it clear that Christianity is the dominant religion. The defeat of Islam in battle is counterpointed by its defeat at judicial level.[40]

There is some hint of a possible source for Richard of Chaumont's duel. The thirteenth-century Cistercian universal historian Albericus Trium Fontium comments that:

'Dum quidam de nostris irent pabulatum inter Antiochiam et Hared, capti sunt ex eis 12 nobilissimi ab illis de Hareth et in Perside transmissi, quorum fuit unus Arpinus comes Bituricensis et unus Richardus de Calvomonte; qui postea fecit

---

[39] See R. Bartlett, *Trial by Fire and Water: the medieval judicial ordeal*, (Oxford, 1986), pp. 103–26 for the significance of trial by battle.

[40] Bartlett 103–26 on ordeal by battle: 103, 'as an ordeal in the most fundamental sense of the word, it was supposed to reveal the judgement of God'.

duellum in presentia Soldani Persidis contra duos Turcos pro Corbaranno et ita seipsum et socios suos liberavit. Predictus autem comes Arpinus in reditu Rome obiit. Idem comes Arpinus, crucesignatus, comitatum suum vendiderat et ex tunc reges Franciae tenent immediate civitatem Bituricas et castrum de Duno'.[41]

This suggests that some anecdote about Richard was current, whether as part of an earlier *chanson de geste*, a sermon exemplum or in some other form; and that this was associated with material about Harpin of Bourges.[42] However it is not clear from the description whether this is a reference to the *Chétifs* itself or to its underlying source material. Either way there is nothing unusual in clerics drawing on such material: the thirteenth-century Cistercian Caesarius of Heisterbach for example makes abundant use of popular stories in his collection of sermon *exempla*.[43]

There is little evidence for a Richard of Chaumont at or near the time of the Crusade: Riley-Smith tentatively identifies him as Richard of Chaumont-en-Vexin, brother of Walo the Constable who died on crusade and was brother-in-law to Hugh of Vermandois.[44] Ms G of Baudry of Bourgueil refers to a Hugo de Calvo Monte during the defence of Antioch.[45] Duparc-Quioc has identified evidence of a tradition about Richard of Chaumont killing two Saracen giants, Estugalas and Golias.[46] This would have provided the raw material for a plot device. The description is different enough from the *Chétifs* to suggest that it is not a reference to the text as we have it; it refers to material to which both the author of the *Chétifs*

---

[41] 'Whilst some of our men were out foraging between Antioch and Hared, twelve of the highest ranking amongst them were captured by the inhabitants of Hared and sent to Persia; one of these was Harpin count of Bourges and one Richard of Chaumont, who subsequently fought a duel in the presence of the Sultan of Persia against two Turks for Corbaran and thus freed himself and his allies. The aforementioned count Harpin meanwhile died on his return at Rome. The same count Harpin was a Crusader who had sold his countship, meaning that from then on the kings of France held the city of Bourges and the castle of Duno directly'. Albericus Trium Fontium, (ed.) P. Scheffer-Boïchorst, *Monumenta Germaniae Historica, Scriptores* XXIIII, p. 807; my translation.

[42] For discussion and examples of how stories about individuals could be preserved and transmitted see N. Paul, 'Crusade, Memory and Regional Politics in twelfth-century Amboise', *Journal of Medieval History* 31 (2005) pp. 127–41.

[43] W. Purkis, 'Crusading and Crusade memory in Caesarius of Heisterbach's *Dialogus miraculorum*', *Journal of Medieval History* 39 (2013) pp. 100–127.

[44] J. Riley-Smith, *The First Crusaders, 1095–1131* (Cambridge, 1997) pp. 231, 240; see also J. Riley-Smith, *What were the Crusades?* fourth edition, (Basingstoke and New York, 2009) pp. 75–7 for discussion of the role of Hugh of Chaumont-sur-Loire on the Crusade. Walo's death is described in detail by Robert the Monk: *The 'Historia Iherosolimitana' of Robert the Monk*, (eds) D. Kempf and M. J. Bull (Woodbridge, 2013), V.6–7 hereafter RM.

[45] Baudry of Bourgueil III.6: *Baldric of Bourgueil, Historia Jerosolimitana*, (ed.) S. Biddlecombe (Woodbridge, 2014); hereafter BB.

[46] Duparc-Quioc, *Cycle* pp. 81–8.

and Alberic had access but in different forms. The concept of trial by duel was well established and could have been drawn on in general by the author.

The Harpin of Bourges episode by contrast adds nothing beyond an additional reason for Corbaran's gratitude when he is already won over. There is no explanation of why Corbaran has suddenly acquired a nephew or why this should matter. The *chétifs* are already at Oliferne, and the episode serves only to delay their return to the crusade: it does not advance it in any way. In terms of structure the only function is as a balancing episode with that of Richard of Chaumont. However it does have a plot function insofar as it ties Corbaran even more closely to the Christian cause by giving him a further cause for gratitude. It could also be argued that it provides a personal counterpart to the judicial victory in the first episode. Possibly too there is a counterpoint to the Brohadas episode: Corbaran lost Brohadas for whom he was responsible, but his nephew is saved through divine intervention. However neither of these is stressed in the text.

There is no obvious source for this episode. Tales of children kidnapped by wild animals and/or robbers are a staple theme of folklore. The episode of saints turning into white stags may have some reminiscence of the white warriors who rode to assist the Crusaders at the battle of Antioch.[47]

It is however striking that the hero of the episode is Harpin of Bourges. Harpin mortgaged his lands in order to participate on the crusade of 1101. He was captured and held prisoner in Cairo. He was ransomed by the Byzantine Emperor. He returned to Europe by way of Rome, where he visited the Pope, and ended his days as a monk in Cluny. The story is told in detail in Orderic Vitalis and briefly referred to by Albericus Trium Fontium; both Guibert of Nogent and Albert of Aachen mention his captivity.[48] Whilst Orderic largely drew on the account of Baudry of Bourgueil for his description of the crusade, he had access to first-hand eyewitness material through his own networks and visitors at St-Evroul. He also preserves anecdotes and episodes in a level of detail which suggests that they had taken on a life of their own, the most striking example being the narrative of Bohemond's captivity. Orderic does not preserve this particular aspect of Harpin's

---

[47] See e.g. *Gesta Francorum et aliorum Hierosolimitanorum*, (ed.) R. Hill (Nelson, 1962), hereafter *GF*, p. 69; *Chanson d'Antioche* laisse 358. Walter the Chancellor I.6 comments that at the victory of Tall Danith in 1115 the billowing white banners made the Persians believe that white-clothed knights were helping at the battle. More generally the episode is reminiscent of legends about St Hubert.

[48] OV vol. 5 pp. 324, 344–52; Guibert of Nogent, *Dei gesta per Francos* (ed.) R. B. C. Huygens, CCCM 127A (Turnhout, 1996), hereafter GN, p. 316; Albert of Aachen, *Historia Ierosolimitana: History of the Journey to Jerusalem*, (ed.) and transl. S. B. Edgington (Oxford, 2007), hereafter AA, IX. 6.See J. Shepard, 'The 'muddy road' of Odo Harpin from Bourges to La-Charité-sur-Loire', in *The experience of Crusading* vol. 2: *Defining the Crusader Kingdom*, (eds) P. Edbury and J. Phillips, (Cambridge, 2003) pp. 11–28; G. Constable, 'The three lives of Odo Arpinus: Viscount of Bourges, Crusader, monk of Cluny', *Crusaders and Crusading in the twelfth century*, G. Constable (Guildford, 2008), pp.215–28.

experience. But clearly Harpin had become being held captive by Saracens and subsequently released. So he was an obvious candidate as hero of an episode in a *chanson de geste* describing captive Crusaders.

There is a further link between Harpin and the *Chanson des Chétifs*. Shepard argues that Harpin became prior of the Cluniac monastery La-Charité-sur-Loire no later than 1103. This monastery was entrusted with the care of the monastery of Kibotos, which was probably built in 1096–97. This is of course the Civetot which saw the defeat of Peter the Hermit's army and where the *chétifs* were taken prisoner. So there is an obvious association between Harpin, captivity and Civetot.

The compilation of the *Chétifs*

A *chanson de geste* about captivity is not the most obvious choice for an epic cycle about the heroism and success of the First Crusade. There is a clear narrative logic to redeeming the captives: but it would have been quite possible to construct the Cycle without referring to them at all. Most sources for the crusade pass lightly over or ignore altogether this aspect; there was no obligation in the source material itself. So why these particular captives and why the deliberate focus on imprisonment?

If we look at the group of *chétifs* themselves, none are independently attested on crusade. However Myers has pointed out that, according to the Catalogue of Abbots of Fécamp, the Abbot of Fécamp before the First Crusade was called Jean d'Alie and he did indeed make a pilgrimage to Jerusalem with none other than 'Richardo de Callido monte' and was taken prisoner.[49] This does show that there was an association between these two characters and captivity in the Holy Land, but it is unclear whether the catalogue can be taken as historical confirmation or whether it drew on legendary source material which we also find in the *Chétifs*. Harpin's captivity in the Holy Land was well known. There is no independent evidence of the existence of Richard. There is evidence of counts of Meulan called Fulcher in the late eleventh century; and there were links between Fécamp and Italy, so it is not impossible to have a character from Pavia. There is no evidence on whom the Bishop of Forez might have been, or Baldwin and Ernoul of Beauvais. So there was some association of some of the *chétifs* with captivity. However none of these links are specifically with the First Crusade: some are earlier and Harpin was taken captive in the Crusade of 1101. In other words, the characters were famous for being captives and for associations with the Holy Land at various times, not specifically for their participation in the First Crusade: to quote Myers, 'quatre, cinq ou même six captifs à la recherche d'un capteur'.[50]

---

[49] Geoffrey Myers, 'Le Développement des *Chétifs*: la version Fécampoise', *Les Epopées de la Croisade: première colloque internationale, Trêves 6–11 août 1984, Zeitschrift für Französische Sprache und Literatur* Beiheft 11 (Stuttgart, 1987) pp. 77–82.

[50] Myers, 'Developpement' p. 85.

Arguably a number of layers of experience are at play. Firstly, the failure of the crusade of 1101 and the subsequent captivity of a number of the participants were well known and stood in sharp contrast to the success of the initial crusade. Orderic comments famously that William IX, one of the participants, produced songs about his experience.[51] Harpin was of course one of these. So captivity could not simply be ignored as a concomitant to crusade.

Secondly, much of the fighting force at Antioch had been taken prisoner after the Field of Blood defeat in 1119. Walter the Chancellor was one of these, and his account of the horrific treatment of the captives by Il-Ghazi has a vividness which leaps off the page 900 years later: '[He] sprang up, drew his sword and set out into their midst, to walk around in a circle and fix each in turn with staring eyes' before beheading captives at random until distracted by the gift of a wonderful horse.[52] Like the *chétifs*, many of the nobility in Antioch were singled out after the defeat and carried off to Aleppo by Il-Ghazi's son.[53] Walter is clear that he has described the experience in detail because it was too significant to be forgotten: 'That miraculous thing which happened to the prisoners in prison I am spreading abroad for the compassion of people living now and as a written memorial for people in the future'.[54] This provided a sharp counterpoint to the victory at Antioch on the First Crusade and the victory of Tall Danith in 1115, and was unlikely to have been forgotten by the time Raymond commissioned his text in Antioch some 20 years later. Walter's chronicle was known beyond Antioch: it is found in several manuscripts alongside the accounts of Raymond of Aguilers and Fulcher of Chartres.[55] The city retained a sharp and painful memory of what defeat and captivity meant.

More generally captivity was a dominant theme in the history of Antioch. Its first ruler Bohemond was held captive for some three years. The fighting and ruling classes of Antioch were decimated and led off as captives after the Field of Blood defeat. So it was a theme with heavy resonance for the crusader state. And more generally it was an ever-present danger in Outremer: 'it is no coincidence that captivity forms one of the principal literary themes in the epic poetry inspired by the First Crusade'.[56] A story which depicted captives in effect turning the tables on their captors, escaping, earning their gratitude and bringing them to the point of conversion was likely to play well in a precarious political climate. Whilst none

---

[51] See above: OV X.21, vol. 5 pp. 342–3.

[52] *Walter the Chancellor's 'The Antiochene Wars': a translation and commentary*, Thomas Asbridge and Susan nB. Edgintonn (Guildford, 1999); hereafter *Bella Antiochena;* II.15; II.6–7 for the terrible treatment of prisoners after the battle.

[53] *Bella Antiochena* II.7, II.13.

[54] *Bella Antiochena* II.15.

[55] J. Rubenstein, 'Putting History to Use: Three Crusade Chronicles in Context', *Viator* 35 (2004) pp. 131–68.

[56] A. Murray, *The Crusader Kingdom of Jerusalem: a dynastic history 1099–1115. Proposographica et Genealogica.* (Oxford, 2000) p. 109. OV XI.26, vol.6 109-27 for capture of Baldwin and Joscelin by Belek.

of this adds up to direct source material, it provides a context for the concept of captivity as part of the wider story of the crusade.

Putting all this together might suggest the following biography for the *Chétifs*. Narratives of captivity existed already and from an early stage which counterpointed the story of success on the First Crusade. A specific narrative had been produced in Antioch, probably at the behest of Raymond of Poitiers, which described in heavily symbolic terms the conflict of Christians against evil; Antioch itself was haunted by the shadow of captivity, both from its first ruler and from the events of 1119. At some point this text made its way from Antioch to the West: we cannot be specific about how or when. Meanwhile anecdotes were also circulating about figures such as Richard of Chaumont and Harpin of Bourges, who were thus sufficiently well known to be used as key figures. At some point these strands were brought together into a specific text whose central theme was captivity and its implications in the context of the First Crusade. We cannot be sure at what point and by whom this was done. It could have been by the compiler of the Crusade trilogy, or the compiler could have drawn on an earlier compilation.[57] Neither can we say what form the text would have taken or what language it might have been in. What we can say with confidence was that the author of the trilogy made use of his pre-existing material, however it may have been configured, to produce a text which sat literally and figuratively at the heart of the trilogy.

The format and structure of the *Chétifs*

The form and style of the *Chétifs* are similar to those of the rest of the Cycle. It is written in rhymed alexandrine laisses using the normal formulae of the *chanson de geste*. There are no particular features of language or style to mark it out as different from the surrounding texts.

What is striking however is the structure and length. It is much shorter than the *Antioche* and *Jérusalem*; the shortest version is 3,900 lines (ms B.N. fr 12569) and the longest 5,444 lines (B.N. fr 786), with an average length of around 4,000 lines. In B.N. fr 12998 it has 4101. This compares with the 9,554 lines of the *Antioche* and the 9,891 of the *Jérusalem* in the same manuscript. In other words it is less than half the length of its two companion texts. It functions as the central and smallest panel of a triptych of texts describing the Crusade.

The text is composed of five distinct elements. There is a linking prologue covering the first 280 lines describing the anger of the Sultan at what he sees as Corbaran's responsibility for the loss of his son Brohadas. The first episode, the judicial duel, covers the next 1,250 lines. The Baldwin of Beauvais episode covers the next 1,800. The final section of the text, the rescue by Harpin of Bourges, is

---

[57] Myers, , 'Développement' pp. 84–90 argues that there were three stages: the Richard of Chaumont episode, the addition of the Harpin episode by a second author and the later addition of the Baldwin episode by a third author.

much shorter at some 550 lines. There is then a linking epilogue of around 250 lines which takes the *chétifs* back to Jerusalem. The episodes thus form a triptych framed by two linking passages. The Baldwin of Beauvais episode lies at the heart not only of the *Chétifs* but at the heart of the entire Crusade trilogy.

The manuscript tradition suggests that scribes and redactors found the text puzzling. Clearly it was perceived as having an identity of its own as a text. The thirteenth-century Spanish compilation of Crusade epic known as the *Gran Conquista de Ultramar* translates the B.N. fr 12558 version virtually word for word.[58] In B.N. fr 12558 its beginning is marked by a miniature as is the case for each branch except the *Jérusalem*. It was also seen as an integral part of the Cycle: it is found with the *Antioche* and *Jérusalem* in all manuscripts except Hatton 77, which preserves a fragment of the first episode: in other words it is seldom found in isolation from the rest of the Cycle. Equally it has longer variants than either of its companions, with a number of additional episodes in some manuscripts: in particular ms F adds another fight for Richard of Chaumont, ms B adds some 500 lines about the Breton knight Chaïnans, and mss B and I have nearly 1,000 lines extra about the mother of the monster Sathanas. This instability suggests a perception that the text was episodic and seen as slightly out of line with its companions.

Conclusion

The *Chétifs* is, literally, at the heart of the Cycle. It is the central panel of the triptych of the Crusade; and the episode in which Baldwin kills the dragon is at the centre of the panel. Language, style and manuscript tradition all suggest that it was an integral part of the Cycle from the beginning. In plot terms it plays an important function: it redeems the captives of Civetot from the shame of imprisonment, restores them to Jerusalem in time for the taking of the city, and removes the main adversary Corbaran by bringing him to the point of apostasy. It also carries heavy symbolism: Corbaran is defeated and the supremacy of Christianity emphasised legally through judicial duel, spiritually through the combat with the dragon, and socially through the saving of Corbaran's nephew. The central symbolism however is that of the dragon, whose defeat plays out in symbolic terms the victory of the Crusaders. There is no obvious one source for the text. The author is clear that his central episode came from Antioch itself; it is likely that he gathered material for the other two episodes from material about people linked generally with crusades and captivity and used them as the heroes for his text.

---

[58] *La Gran Conquista de Ultramar*, (ed.) L. Cooper, 4 vols (Bogotá, 1979). The *Chétifs* is translated at II.207–62.

Chapter 2
The *Chanson de Jérusalem*

The *Chanson de Jérusalem* has customarily been seen as the poor relation of the central Crusade trilogy: 'une copie ... parfois servile' of the *Chanson d'Antioche*.[1] It lacks the vivid historical detail of the *Antioche*: indeed it contains hardly any material which was not common currency in the sources for the Crusade. Its structure is a close copy of the *Antioche*, and it contains many of the same characters and topoi. The sequence of single combats is repetitive, and it lacks the colour and verve of the *Chétifs*. The relative lack of variants compared to the *Antioche* and *Chétifs* suggests that it did not attract much contemporary attention; and its one modern edition compared to three for the *Antioche* says much the same about the interest it evokes (or not) now. Yet it is crucial to the Cycle. The story of the Crusade needed to be completed. The interest lies in how that completion happened and what it tells us about the perception of Crusade and the role of the Cycle.

The relationship between the *Jérusalem* and the *Chanson d'Antioche*

The *Jérusalem* falls into a number of blocks:

Laisses 1–17: the return of the *chétifs* in time to help the Crusaders fight off a Saracen attack.
Laisses 18–30: march to Jerusalem
Laisses 31–132: events of the siege of Jerusalem
Laisses 133–44: fall of Jerusalem
Laisses 145–213: skirmishes around Jerusalem which is put under siege by the Saracens
Laisses 214–72: battle of Ascalon and victory of the Christians
Laisses 273–81: the aftermath

There is an obvious parallel here with the structure of the *Antioche* insofar as the storyline permits. Both texts begin with a description of the *chétifs*: the *Antioche* describes their capture at Civetot and removal to prison in some 550 lines, whereas the *Jérusalem* begins with a description of about the same length of their triumphant return. Both have a lengthy description of the siege, some

---
[1] A. Hatem, *Les poèmes épiques des croisades: génèse – historicité –localisation* (Paris, 1932) p. 269.

3,500 lines in the *Antioche* and a similar length in the *Jérusalem*. The fall of both cities is narrated in some 500 lines. Events during the subsequent respective sieges by Saracens are recounted at considerably greater length in the *Jérusalem*. The preliminaries to the battle and the battle itself take around 1,800 lines in both texts. There is finally a short section on the aftermath. In sum, the structure of the two texts runs in parallel as far as the author could manage given that there was no equivalent of the other two main episodes in the *Antioche*, the taking of Nicaea and the battle of Dorylaeum.

Within this overall framework there is a strong similarity between the two texts. Episodes and plot devices from the *Antioche* reappear in the *Jérusalem*. In both texts there is a Saracen leader and his son, who is sent to summon help: Garsion and Sansadoine in the *Antioche*, Corbadas and Cornumarant in the *Jérusalem*. The Saracens take refuge in the Tower of David in the same way as in the citadel in Antioch, and are granted free passage out for surrendering it.[2] Peter the Hermit plays the same role of describing the Christian forces to the Saracen leader as does Amidelis in the *Antioche*.[3] The intervention of a heavenly army led by saints is a decisive feature in both battles.[4]

Themes and motifs from the *Antioche* also consistently reappear in the *Jérusalem*. There is a detailed description of setting up the siege which parallels that of setting up siege round Antioch.[5] The marching out of the squadrons for the final battle is described in similar detail.[6] Both have a description of the Saracen leader's marvellous tent.[7] In both the Saracens play chess before the battle.[8] Godfrey repeats his feat of slicing a Saracen and his horse in half.[9] The intervention of saints led by St George is repeatedly invoked.

The same characters also recur. All the leaders of the Crusade reappear from Antioch despite the fact that some were not there historically (Bohemond, Hugh of Vermandois, Stephen of Blois and Baldwin).[10] The St-Pols, the starring figures of the *Antioche*, reappear though with less prominence; so do other Crusaders such as Rotrou of la Perche and Roger of Rosoie.[11] Cornumarant in effect combines the roles played by Sansadoine and Corbaran in the *Antioche*. The heroes of a number of anecdotes in the *Antioche* – Eurvin of Creel, Gontier of Aire, Raimbaut

---

[2] *Antioche* laisse 371; *Jérusalem* laisse 141.
[3] *Antioche* laisses 315–28; *Jérusalem* laisses 217–22.
[4] *Antioche* laisse 358; *Jérusalem* laisse 265.
[5] *Antioche* laissses 127–39; *Jérusalem* laisses 45–51.
[6] *Antioche* laisses 315–28; *Jérusalem* laisses 217–22.
[7] *Antioche* laisse 210; *Jérusalem* laisses 176–9.
[8] *Antioche* laisse 299; *Jérusalem* laisse 209.
[9] *Antioche* laisse 162; *Jérusalem* laisse 206.
[10] Bohemond was in Antioch; Hugh and Stephen were both in Constantinople; Baldwin was in Edessa.
[11] See Table of Names for references.

Creton and Wicher the Swabian – reappear in different contexts, suggesting that the author remembered their prominence and sought to recreate it in the sequel.

It is therefore fair to say that to a large extent the *Jérusalem* does follow the lead of the *Antioche* in terms of length, structure, event and character. But it is far from being a 'copie ... parfois servile'. To some extent this reflects the fact that there is only so much violence a narrator can do to a well-known story like that of the First Crusade. The Crusaders could hardly set off twice on the same Crusade; the Emperor Alexios was firmly out of the picture after his refusal to help at Antioch; and there was no story of treachery at Jerusalem equivalent to the treachery which led to the fall of Antioch. So it is hard to see how actual events could have been changed to accentuate the parallels other than a general dualism of siege followed by battle.

However the two texts do in fact show differences. The *Jérusalem* contains a number of striking episodes outside the normal run of descriptions of battle and Saracens which are not paralleled in the *Antioche*. Godfrey shoots down three kites with one arrow as a symbol that the city will fall.[12] The engineers of the siege tower are named as Nicolas and Gregory.[13] There is a complex exchange of correspondence with bluff and counterbluff using carrier pigeons.[14] In a particularly vivid episode Baldwin takes refuge in a reed bed and is attacked by leeches which worm their way in through the links of his chain mail.[15] A hermit tells them where to find wood for siege machines.[16] Thomas of Marle is first into the city, flung over the ramparts in rather unlikely fashion from the points of spears.[17] God signals who is to be the King of Jerusalem by a miraculous episode of lighting candles.[18] A dove lights candles in the Sepulchre on the eve of battle, and brings a message to Godfrey that the rest of the army is on its way to save him.[19] After the battle the Saracen dead are gathered in by devils whilst a lion gathers up the Crusade dead.[20]

Some of these episodes are based at least loosely on fact. Thus other sources describe advice from a hermit on how to take Jerusalem.[21] Raymond of Aguilers also refers to messages being carried by pigeon.[22] Baldwin did indeed have a narrow escape from the Saracens.[23] Others are purely fictional.

---

[12] *Jérusalem* laissses 57–9.
[13] *Jérusalem* laisse 69.
[14] *Jérusalem* laisses 89–94. See note for more on the use of carrier pigeons on crusade.
[15] *Jérusalem* laisses 126–7.
[16] *Jérusalem* laisses 130–31.
[17] *Jérusalem* laisse 138.
[18] *Jérusalem* laisses 151–6.
[19] *Jérusalem* laisses 212–13.
[20] *Jérusalem* laisse 277.
[21] AA VI.7; *Le 'liber' de Raymond d'Aguilers*, (ed.) J. H. and L. L. Hill (Paris, 1969), hereafter RA, p. 139.
[22] RA pp. 135–6.
[23] AA IX.5; compare Fulcher of Chartres II.19–20: *Historia Hierosolymitana* (1095–1127), (ed.) H. Hagenmeyer (Heidelberg, 1913), hereafter FC. Ibn al-Qalanisi

The *Antioche*'s strong emphasis on Crusaders from the North East of France is less marked in the *Jérusalem*. The St-Pols father and son who star time and again in the *Antioche* do reappear but on fewer occasions. Enguerrand, who died of illness at Ma'arrat-an-Nu'man, is given a more glorious death in the battle of Ascalon.[24] It is striking that the two siege engineers who feature prominently, Nicolas and Grégoire, are from Arras.[25] They feature in no other source and we cannot say whether they are a later addition or an echo of some local tradition. Thomas of Marle, whilst mentioned a few times in the *Antioche*, is elevated to a major hero in the *Jérusalem*, swearing fealty to the Tafur king and entering Jerusalem first by somewhat unorthodox means.[26] The Tafurs are transformed from the bloodthirsty cannibals of the *Antioche* into key players, with the King given the honour of crowning Godfrey and mentioned repeatedly as a mainstay of the army; in a comic counterpoint they also deceive the Saracen envoys about the numbers in the Christian army with a variant of the old school photograph trick.[27]

There are some inconsistencies between the two texts. In particular Stephen of Blois flees ignominiously in the *Antioche* in an episode recounted with vicious glee: he forces some of his men to carry him away in a litter under pretence of illness, then leaps out and runs away as soon as he is out of sight of the army.

---

specifically refers to him taking refuge in a reed bed: *The Damascus Chronicle of the Crusades*, selected and transl. H. A. R. Gibb (London, 1932) pp. 55–6.

[24] For his death at Ma'arrat-an-Nu'man AA V.30; *Jérusalem* laisse 243 for his fictional death in the battle of Ascalon.

[25] *Jérusalem* line 1895.

[26] *Antioche*: at Nicaea laisse 50; at Antioch laisses 126, 139, 253, 355, 360–61; also 72, 122–3. In the *Jérusalem* he appears repeatedly, with particular prominence as the first Crusader into Jerusalem (laisses 75, 138), being tossed in from the lance points of his men; as doing homage to the King of the Tafurs (laisse 136), cleaning out the Sepulchre and the Temple with Robert of Flanders and Godfrey (laisse 142) and killing one of the Sultan's sons at the battle of Ascalon (laisse 242). The poet was clearly well aware of his record of violence and eventual excommunication and death at the hands of his suzerain: they are foretold at laisse 38. Suger: *Vie de Louis VI le Gros*, (ed.) H. Waquet (Paris, 1964). Chapter 7 pp. 31–3 for his eviction from his castle of Montaigu; chapter 24 pp. 173–9 for his condemnation by the Council of Beauvais; chapter 31 pp. 251–3 for his death and inability to receive Communion. Thomas was 'virum omnium quos novimus hac aetate nequissimum' ('the most infamous man of his time we have come across') according to Guibert of Nogent, *Autobiographie* (ed.) and transl. E.-R. Labande (Paris, 1981), pp. 328–9.

[27] In the *Antioche* the Tafurs are always described as cannibals, either actually or as a threat: laisses 174–5 for actual cannibalism, laisses 138, 177, 326 for references. In the *Jérusalem* they are still referred to as cannibals e.g. at laisse 184 where they gnash their teeth at the Saracen envoy to make the point that they enjoy eating humans, but play a much more extensive and heroic role. See my article 'The Count and the Cannibals: the Old French Crusade Cycle as a drama of salvation' in *Jerusalem the Golden*, (ed.) S. B. Edgington (Woodbridge, 2014) pp. 307–28 for more detailed discussion of how this change of role underpins the message of Crusade as redemption.

However he is referred to as back at Jerusalem.[28] Wicher the Swabian is killed at the battle of Antioch, but miraculously resurrected in the *Jérusalem*.[29]

The conclusion from this is that the *Jérusalem* does to a large extent take its lead from the *Antioche*. The structure is as similar as the course of events would allow. There is a deliberate repetition of episodes and motifs in a way familiar from cyclification of *chansons de geste*.[30] But the *Jérusalem* contains episodes and characters of its own. There is to some extent a mirror image effect: the crudely comic behaviour of the Tafurs in the *Antioche* becomes heroism and a leading role in the *Jérusalem* but with enough reference back to ensure consistency; the heroism of the St-Pols in the *Antioche* is matched by the heroism of that unlikely candidate Thomas of Marle in the *Jérusalem*. The *Jérusalem* is written as a reflection of and a companion to the *Antioche*, drawing on its events and characters and to some extent blurring them in the process. But it is more than a simple copy.

The relationship of the Jérusalem to historical sources – or not

We have a number of accounts of the fall of Jerusalem and the battle of Ascalon written at the time or shortly afterwards. There are two first-hand accounts, the anonymous *Gesta Francorum* which is likely to have been written by a soldier initially in Bohemond's army, and the account by Raymond IV's chaplain Raymond of Aguilers. Fulcher of Chartres was a contemporary but was not at Jerusalem; he was at Edessa as Baldwin's chaplain and his account is therefore based on Raymond and the *Gesta*. The *Gesta* was adapted by four authors in the decade or so after the Crusade: Robert the Monk, Baldry of Bourgueil, Guibert of Nogent and Peter Tudebode. Albert of Aachen's account was drawn from eyewitnesses though he was not himself on Crusade. Ralph of Caen wrote an account glorifying the role of Tancred. Later accounts are based generally on one or more of these, although often supplemented with other material: Orderic Vitalis for example uses Baudry's account but adds in material from eyewitnesses and other probably oral sources.[31]

---

[28] *Antioche* laisses 233–4, 284–5; *Jérusalem* laisse 222.

[29] *Antioche* laisses 362–3; *Jérusalem* laisses 114, 116. In fact he died near Jaffa of illness in 1101: AA VII.71. He is referred to in other sources such as Metellus of Tegernsee, *Expeditio Hierosolymitana*, (ed.) P. C. Jacobsen (Stuttgart, 1982), pp. 125–8: see P. Knoch, *Studien zu Albert von Aachen* (Stuttgart, 1966) pp. 123–5. This suggests that he had an active posthumous life in legend.

[30] *Cyclification: the development of narrative cycles in the chanson de geste and the Arthurian romance*, (ed.) B. Besamusca et al. (Amsterdam, 1994).

[31] Peter Tudebode, *Historia de Hierosolymitano Itinere*, (ed.) J. H. and L. L. Hill (Paris, 1977), hereafter PT.

The Christian army arrived before Jerusalem on 7 June 1099.[32] It was an emotional moment. However fervour quickly gave way to practicality. Speed was of the essence. The Christians had marched to Jerusalem at speed, leaving major cities such as Tyre untouched; this made them vulnerable to attack. An assault needed to be launched as soon as practicable rather than a long siege as at Antioch.

Jerusalem was under the governorship of the Fatimid Iftikhar ad-Dawla. At the sight of the Crusader army he expelled Christians from the city, poisoned the surrounding wells and sent to Egypt for aid. Heat and thirst quickly became a problem for the army. On 13 June they launched a first assault following the advice of a hermit on the Mount of Olives; clearly he was somewhat lacking in military expertise since the assault failed within hours. One casualty was Raimbaut Creton, whose hand was cut off as he tried to grip the wall from his siege ladder. This made clear the need for more siege engines; the material for these came from foraging expeditions and the timely arrival of ships from the West. Thirst continued to be a problem and there were desertions. Early in July the news came that a large relief army had set out from Egypt. This intensified the sense of urgency. Providentially perhaps the priest Peter Desiderius had a vision of the dead Bishop Adhemar of Le Puy, who prescribed a fast of three days and a barefoot procession round the walls of Jerusalem. By now the siege towers were ready, and the assault began on 14 July. The first step was to fill in the ditches so that the towers could be brought up to the walls. On the following morning, 15 July, Godfrey's forces succeeded in entering Jerusalem. The Muslims fled towards the Mosque of al-Aqsa and the Temple, but were unable to put up a defence. Iftikhar retired to the Tower of David and subsequently received safe passage from Raymond in return for the Tower and a large amount of treasure. The taking of the city led to appalling massacre of Jews and Muslims alike, with the Crusaders according to several sources actually riding in blood. The Crusaders meanwhile made it a first priority to worship at the Holy Sepulchre, then met on 17 July to begin negotiations about how Jerusalem should now be ruled. Raymond of St Gilles was first offered the crown but refused; it was then offered to Godfrey, who declined to be King but accepted the position of Advocate of the Holy Sepulchre. On 1 August Arnulf of Rohes was appointed Patriarch.

The Franks might now be in command of Jerusalem, but the situation was precarious. Dissensions surfaced between the leaders. An embassy arrived from Egypt to reproach the Franks for their conquest; and it was soon known

---

[32] The following account is synthesised from the above accounts. From the innumerable accounts available from modern historians I have used in particular C. Kostick, *The Siege of Jerusalem: Crusade and Conquest in 1099* (London, 2009), who gives a comprehensive summary of events. I have also drawn on S. Runciman, *A History of the Crusades* vol.1, 3 vols (Cambridge, 1951); T. Asbridge, The First Crusade: a new history (London, 2004); C. Tyerman, *God's War: a new history of the Crusades* (London, 2007); G. Lobrichon, 1099: *Jérusalem conquise* (Paris, 1998); and B. Kedar, 'The Jerusalem Massacre of July 1099 in the Western historiography of the Crusades', *Crusades* 3 (2004) pp. 15–75.

that a large Egyptian army commanded by no less than the vizier al-Afdal was marching towards Ascalon. Perhaps fortuitously, another relic came to light: a fragment of the True Cross which had been the most significant relic in the Church of Jerusalem and was now forcibly handed over to the Franks. Godfrey called on Robert of Flanders, Robert of Normandy and Raymond IV to help fight off the invaders, with help from Tancred and Eustace. Early on the 11th the Christian forces assembled at Ibelin, a few miles beyond Ramleh. On the 12th they launched an attack on the Egyptians and routed them. The vizier sailed back to Egypt. The plunder was immense, including the vizier's standard which was captured by Robert's Normans. Robert of Flanders and Robert of Normandy took ship for the West at the end of August, and Raymond left for Syria.

In the most general terms this is approximately the order of events we find in the *Jérusalem*: abortive assault, an embassy from the besieged Saracens to the Sultan of Egypt, advice from the hermit on the Mount of Olives, successful assault, massacre followed by immediate worship at the Sepulchre, envoy from the Egyptians, victory in battle and escape of the Sultan by sea. The emphasis on siege engines, the problems of thirst and the importance of the relic of the True Cross also mirror reality.[33]

However the *Jérusalem*'s account of events is full of inaccuracies. There are a few omissions, notably the arrival of ships with equipment, the vision of Peter Desiderius and any request to Raymond IV to assume the kingship of Jerusalem (he is in the *Jérusalem* the only leader not to be asked). There are far more additions and changes. To pick out the most obvious, Baldwin, Bohemond and Hugh of Vermandois and, to a lesser extent Stephen of Blois, are all wrongly placed centre stage: in actual fact Baldwin was in Edessa, Bohemond in Antioch and Hugh and Stephen back in Constantinople at the time. Thomas of Marle and the Tafurs receive far more prominence than in the sources. There are two abortive assaults rather than one, and the hermit advises them on the final successful assault rather than, as in the sources, on the first and abortive attack. The leaders are shown leaving before the battle of Ascalon rather than afterwards and heading in the wrong direction, to the Sea of Galilee rather than taking ship for the West. The battle of Ascalon is agreed in formal terms rather than being a dawn ambush.

The text also has as referred to above a number of picturesque but unrealistic episodes. Godfrey shoots down three kites with a single arrow as a sign that the city will be taken. There is a complex exchange of message and countermessage by pigeon post. Thomas is flung over the walls of Jerusalem from the lance points of his men. A cloth used to clean the Temple restores sight to a blind man. A miraculously lit candle marks Godfrey as the future King of Jerusalem. Just before the battle of Ascalon a dove lights the Crusaders' candles and brings a letter telling

---

[33] See Duparc-Quioc, *Cycle*, pp. 18–30; N. Thorp, 'La Chanson de Jérusalem and the Latin chronicles', *Epic and Crusade: Proceedings of the Colloquium of the Société Rencesvals British Branch held at Lucy Cavendish College, Cambridge, 27–28 March 2004*, (eds) P. Bennett, A. Cobby and J. Everson (Edinburgh, 2006) pp. 153–71.

them that their former colleagues are returning to help in the battle. A horde of beaked monsters are put to flight by the Tafurs in the battle. After the battle the Saracen dead are taken by devils and the Christian dead are laid out by a lion. The size of Cornumarant's heart astonishes everyone.

A further distancing from reality is given through the use of the stylistic and topical conventions of the *chanson de geste*. Around one-third of the text describes the activities of the Saracens. There is no attempt at any realistic portrayal of Islam. The Saracens are a mixture of menace and figure of fun. They have extravagantly luxurious possessions, typified in the description of the Sultan's tent. They worship the gods Apollon, Mahomed and Tervagant, and have idols of them which work by trickery and necromancy. The names are the usual mix of fantasy, allusion and abuse. The large majority can be paralleled from other *chansons de geste*, and there are a great many of them. There are innumerable descriptions of single combat in a form familiar from many other *chansons de geste*, tempered only by the odd reference to Turkish arrows.

It is therefore hard to see any particular historical source for the *Jérusalem* beyond the knowledge generally available of the course of events. The resemblances with Albert of Aachen and the translation of passages from Robert the Monk word for word which characterise the *Antioche* are entirely absent.[34] We cannot say whether the odd stray detail such as the names of the engineers Nicolas and Grégoire represents eyewitness testimony. The absence of detail reflecting any particular source supports the case made above: that the *Jérusalem* was written as a companion piece to the *Antioche* reflecting its course of events as far as possible and drawing on what was generally known about the Crusade. It is hard to quarrel with Duparc-Quioc's judgement: 'l'auteur, pour des fins pratiques ... a utilisé avec la plus grande fantaisie les données historiques qu'il a pu connaître et rendu ses sources méconnaissables'.[35]

The relationship between the Jérusalem and any poetic predecessors

Huge volumes of speculation have been built on the *Antioche*'s one reference to a work by Richard le Pèlerin: whilst this should probably not be taken at face value, the evidence that there was some kind of earlier poetic depiction of the Crusade both in the *Antioche* itself and in other contemporary texts is reasonably compelling.[36] The *Chétifs* also makes clear reference to preceding source material in the Baldwin of Beauvais episode, although as discussed above it is not obvious

---

[34] See Duparc-Quioc, *Etude*, for detailed analysis; Edgington and Sweetenham, Introduction pp. 15–24 for summary of scholarship and discussion.

[35] Duparc-Quioc, *Cycle*, p.30.

[36] *Antioche* lines 9013–14. Edgington and Sweetenham pp. 9–15 for discussion of earlier poetic sources.

what form this might have taken. By contrast there is no such evidence for a predecessor to the *Jérusalem*.

There are three kinds of evidence for such predecessors. The first is references within the text itself. *Chansons de geste* often refer to some form of predecessor or previous author: the *Chanson de Roland*, famously, alludes to a mysterious 'Turoldus' and *Girart de Roussillon* is ascribed to a monk called Sestu.[37] There is no such evidence for the *Jérusalem* other than the odd formulaic reference such as 'si con oï conter' in describing the preparations for battle.[38]

The second kind of evidence is stylistic. At the risk of over-generalisation, early *chansons de geste* such as the *Roland* or the *Chanson de Guillaume* tend to have shorter laisses, greater density of formulae and to be written in assonanced decasyllabics.[39] The *Antioche* retains traces of such form at three points: the disposition of forces at Nicaea, Adhemar's attempts to get each leader to carry the Lance and the marching out of the squadrons for the battle of Antioch. Each has a run of short laisses with a high degree of formulae.[40] These are probable indications of preceding *chanson de geste* style material: there is less similar material in the *Jérusalem*, although laisses 42–52 on setting up camp at Jerusalem show a characteristic run of short repetitive format.

The third is references and/or quotations in other texts. The Occitan romance *Flamenca* for example gives a massive (and self-parodying) list of all the songs sung at the wedding of Flamenca and Archembaud, though clearly those particular guests had no desire to hear about the Crusades.[41] What does give an insight into other versions of the Crusade Cycle is the Spanish universal chronicle the *Gran Conquista de Ultramar*.[42] This preserves large sections both of the *Antioche* and of its Occitan counterpart the *Canso d'Antioca* although not in an identical version. It also preserves large sections of the *Jérusalem*, though again not in an identical form to the text we have.[43] The basis of the *Gran Conquista* for events at Jerusalem and Ascalon is the Old French adaptation of William of Tyre's account known as

---

[37] *La Chanson de Roland*, (ed.) I. Short (Paris, 1990), line 4002: 'Ci falt la geste que Turoldus declinet'; *La Chanson de Girart de Roussillon*, (ed.) W. M. Hackett, transl. M. du Combarieu de Grès and G. Gouiran (Paris, 1993) lines 23–6.

[38] *Jérusalem* line 8133.

[39] For references and discussion see Introduction to the *Antioche*, pp.66–7.

[40] Edgington and Sweetenham, Introduction pp. 68–9.

[41] *The Romance of Flamenca*, (ed.) M. E.Porter, transl. M. J. Hubert (Princeton, 1962), lines 593–710.

[42] *La Gran Conquista de Ultramar*, (ed.) Louis Cooper, 4 vols (Bogotá, 1979).

[43] The resemblances between the two texts were noted by Gaston Paris in the nineteenth century and have been analysed several times. See G. Paris, 'La Chanson d'Antioche provencale et la Gran Conquista de Ultramar', *Romania* 17 (1888) pp. 513–41; 19 (1890) pp. 562–91; 22 (1893) pp. 345–63; G. T. Northup, 'La Gran Conquista de Ultramar and its problems', *Historical Review* 2 (1934) pp. 287–302; Duparc-Quioc, *Cycle* pp. 45–55; more recently N. Thorp, 'La Gran Conquista de Ultramar et les origines de la Chanson de Jérusalem', *Les épopées romanes*, GRLMA II.1.2 fasc.5 (1986) pp. 76–85.

the *Eracles*, which provides the framework and much of the detail.[44] However, it is interspersed with extensive sections from the Jérusalem, some verbatim and some with different details. It also contains some elements which are not found elsewhere.

The account of events at Jerusalem starts at II.260 of the *Gran Conquista* and runs to III.78. Parts are translated literally: thus III.11 translates literally lines 1449–53. Some parts are abbreviated: thus III.29 keeps the same order of marching out for battle but summarises it heavily. Some details are changed: thus II.261 transfers a comment by Bohemond to Tancred, and III.1 gives a speech by Bohemond to Robert of Normandy; perhaps more startlingly at III.42 Thomas of Marle's dramatic entry into Jerusalem is changed into a normal entry using the siege ladder and he follows the Tafurs. Some material is not found in any source: for example at III.47 the Occitan Crusader Aicart of Montmerle is resurrected to kill the doorman of the Sepulchre who insulted him, Jean Ferret. At III.71 the leaders are asked in turn to stay behind and guard the city but all refuse: in the *Jérusalem* it is simply stated that the city was guarded by the Bishop of Forez with a skeleton force.[45] At III.75 there is a different account of the battle of Ascalon. Most intriguingly of all, there is another reference to that shadowy and much-debated figure Richard le Pèlerin: 'cuenta Ricart el Pelegrino, que escrivió esta ystoria per mandado del príncipe Remonte de Antioca, que después que el mensajero del alférez Abdalla se partió de Iherusalem, el rey Gudufre con su cavallería se aparejaron para yr [a] aquella batalla de Rames'.[46] This comes at III.71, in the middle of a run of material only loosely resembling the *Jérusalem*.

Clearly there were different versions of the *Jérusalem* available. Thorp inclines to the view that the *Gran Conquista* preserves an earlier version perhaps written for Raymond of Antioch in the 1140s, and Duparc-Quioc also regards this as evidence for an earlier poetic version. To be this precise puts too great a strain on the evidence. We can be clear from the *Gran Conquista* that there were different versions of the text, but we cannot conclude definitively that they were earlier. The references to Richard link him clearly with Antioch, but we cannot be sure that this is not simply an extrapolation from the *Chétifs*. At most we can say that there was a different extant version which may or may not have been a predecessor: the evidence is inconclusive.

---

[44] William of Tyre, *Chronicon*, (ed.) R. B. C. Huygens, CCCM 63, 2 vols (Turnhout, 1986), hereafter WT. *Eracles*, RHC.Occ 1–2.

[45] *Jérusalem* laisse 223.

[46] 'According to Richard le Pèlerin, who wrote this story on the instructions of Prince Raymond of Antioch, when the messenger of the emir Abdalla left Jerusalem, King Godfrey and his cavalry prepared themselves to ride out for that battle at Ramleh'; my translation. The other reference to Richard in the text at II.152 associates him with St Peter at Antioch, which is not found in the *Antioche*'s reference at lines 9013–14.

Other source material

We have evidence for other material on which the compiler might have drawn. John France has published a manuscript compiled in the late twelfth century in Ripoll containing a unique account of the Crusade and other material.[47] This does not show particularly close resemblance to the *Jérusalem*. But it shows that other accounts were available drawing on source material which was in circulation.

There was also a liturgy of the liberation of Jerusalem which was produced in a first form before 1149 drawing on Fulcher of Chartres and Raymond of Aguilers, and revised for the fiftieth anniversary of the taking of the Sepulchre in 1149. This would have formed a further potential source.[48] And much of the detail of places would have been familiar from itineraries of the Holy Land, which had existed since the fourth century.[49]

It is therefore difficult to ascribe the *Jérusalem* to any particular source. The author's starting point in terms of structure and approach was the *Antioche*, which provides the framework for this half of the triptych; however there are some inconsistencies. The actual events of the Crusade are recounted in the barest outline, with considerable confusion and some key elements missed: this argues for an account based on dimly remembered general knowledge rather than any one source and augmented with other material such as itineraries and liturgy. To this the poet added a considerable amount of imagination and abundant use of the conventions of the *chanson de geste*. There is no convincing evidence of any predecessor, and this suggests that the text was custom written for a particular purpose: to act as a companion to the *Antioche* and mirror it as closely as it could.

Conclusion

In effect the *Jérusalem* functions as the other half of a diptych to the *Antioche*. The narrative arc is the same. The *Antioche* begins with the Christian forces setting out on Crusade: in the *Jérusalem* this is paralleled by the arrival of the *chétifs* from Sarmasane. The text rises to a first crescendo with the taking of Jerusalem, in the middle of the text like the taking of Antioch. The climax in the *Jérusalem* is the battle of Ascalon, which parallels the crucial battle of Antioch.

Its textual function acts as the climax of the trilogy recounting the story of Crusade and its redeeming power. In the words of Hatem, 'la *Jérusalem* est avant

---

[47] J. France, 'An unknown account of the capture of Jerusalem', *English Historical Review* 87 (1972) pp. 771–83.

[48] A. Linder, 'The liturgy of the liberation of Jerusalem', *Medieval Studies* 52 (1990) pp. 110–31.

[49] J. Wilkinson with J. Hill and W. F. Ryan, *Jerusalem Pilgrimage 1099–1185*, (London, 1988).

tout un monument elévé à la gloire des croisés'.[50] It was written for that purpose using an existing fund of knowledge about the Crusade alongside extensive use of the topoi of the *chanson de geste* and possibly some local tradition. There was no provable predecessor text and the *Jérusalem* was written to complete the trilogy drawing on the *Antioche* as the obvious source.

---

[50] Hatem, *Poèmes épiques*, p. 351.

Chapter 3
The *Antioche*, the *Chétifs* and the *Jérusalem*: the Central Trilogy of the Old French Crusade Cycle

The Old French Crusade Cycle

The Old French Crusade Cycle is a set of *chansons de geste* written during the thirteenth century which takes the events of the First Crusade as a nucleus and develops from them both a fanciful prehistory of the Crusade based on the legends surrounding Godfrey of Bouillon, and a scarcely less fanciful post-history which in some versions continues all the way to the siege of Acre.

The Cycle falls into three broad sections. The first might be entitled the 'histoire et chevalerie de Godefroi'. It comprises a number of texts: *La Naissance du Chevalier au Cygne* in two versions known as the *Elioxe* and the *Béatrix*, the *Chevalier au Cygne*, *La Fin d'Elias*, the *Enfances Godefroi* and the *Retour de Cornumarant*. Between them the texts set out Godfrey's genealogy going back to the legendary Swan Knight and pointing towards his ultimate fame as the first ruler of Jerusalem.[1] Whilst the material is referred to at the end of the twelfth century by several authors, we cannot date the texts more precisely than the first half of the thirteenth century. There is no named author other than a couple of references to a shadowy 'Renaus'.[2]

The heart of the Cycle lies in the trilogy of texts describing the First Crusade: the *Chanson d'Antioche*, the *Chanson des Chétifs* and the *Chanson de Jérusalem*. These put the First Crusade firmly at the centre of events. The *Antioche* has a detailed reference to one Graindor de Douai:

'Cist novel jogleor qui en suelent canter
Le vrai commencement en ont laisié ester.
Mais Grainsdor de Douai nel velt mie oblier
Ki nos en a les vers tous fais renoveler'.[3]

---
[1] See E. J. Mickel, 'Imagining history in the *Enfances Godefroi*' in *Echoes of the epic: studies in honor of Gerard J. Brault*, (eds) D. P. and M. J. Schenck (Birmingham, Alabama., 1998) pp. 175–87; Introduction to *Enfances de Godefroi* and *Retour de Cornumarant*, OFCC vol.3.
[2] *Enfances Godefroi* line 2412; *Retour de Cornumarant* line 1487.
[3] *Antioche* lines 12–15.

It is not clear whether he was author, *remanieur* or commissioner of the text and whether his role extended beyond the *Antioche*. What is clear is that there is a controlling intelligence behind the three texts responsible for an ambitious narrative conception.

The third part of the Cycle comprises a number of texts which continue the story to the fall of Acre and beyond: *La Chrétienté Corbaran, La Prise d'Acre, La Mort Godefroi* and *La Chanson des Rois Baudouin*, with further continuations in some manuscripts. These are not found in all manuscripts and the selection is different in each manuscript. They survive in two versions, one mid-thirteenth century and one from around 1300.

Cyclification of *chansons de geste* was a well-known phenomenon: the heroes would acquire both pre and post history extending to their families and descendants.[4] This is exactly the process we see in the Cycle. Godfrey is no more prominent in the central trilogy than any other leader; he is credited with cutting a Turk and his horse in half, but ends the text having to be rescued from his fight against Corbaran by his comrades.[5] However as the thirteenth century wore on, interest in Godfrey increased; by the end of the century he had become one of the Nine Worthies, the only figure from the post-Carolingian era to gain this distinction.[6] This reflects the increasing preoccupation with retaking Jerusalem: as its conqueror and first King (the subtleties of Godfrey's actual position as Advocate having been long forgotten), Godfrey became an increasingly significant and mythologised figure.[7] His ancestry was portrayed as part of the divine plan which ultimately led to the taking of Jerusalem.

It is likely that at least part of the Cycle was composed in north-eastern France. Graindor de Douai, if we are to believe that connection, was obviously a Picard. The large majority of the manuscripts come from that area and there is little evidence of its diffusion outside, although plenty of the subsequent legendary status of Godfrey. Godfrey himself was Duke of Lorraine and Lord of Bouillon. The St-Pols who play such a prominent role in the *Antioche* are from Picardy. More tenuously the emphasis on genealogy and dynasty reflects contemporary preoccupations in this area.[8] And the literary experimentation evident in the form of the text could reflect the ferment of literary experiment in Arras in the early thirteenth century.[9]

---

[4] M. Heintze, 'Les techniques de la formation de cycles dans les chansons de geste' in *Cyclification*, (ed.) Besasmusca, pp. 21–58.

[5] *Antioche* laisses 162, 262–5.

[6] Keen, *Chivalry* pp. 121–4.

[7] See Edgington and Sweetenham, Introduction pp. 43–4 for discussion and references.

[8] G. Spiegel, *Romancing the Past: the Rise of Vernacular Prose Historiography in Thirteenth-Century France* (Berkeley and Los Angeles, 1993).

[9] M. Gally, 'Poésie en jeu: des jeux-parties aux fatras', in *Arras au Moyen Age: Histoire et Littérature*, (eds) M-M. Castellani and J-P Martin (Arras, 1994) pp. 71–80.

We should not look to the Cycle for an accurate depiction of historical events: the only text with any link to actuality is the *Antioche*. Its interest lies in the mythologisation of the events of the Crusade and their presentation as a cycle of *chansons de geste*. The conventions of the genre are all present and correct: single combat with lance, depiction of Saracens as a mixture of villainy and ridicule, emphasis on divine support and a circumscribed role for women. What marks it out is that it uses these conventions to depict events which were certainly not contemporary but were not far off living memory. Other poems did describe contemporary events using the form of the *chanson de geste*, notably in Anglo-Norman and Occitan: but none were to turn them into a whole heroic and legendary cycle.[10] The Cycle stands alongside the *matière* of other medieval poetic cycles defined by Jean Bodel as the *matière de France*, the *matière de Bretagne* and the *matière d'antiquité*.[11] All had in common that they described past glories in a universe of nostalgic glamour. The lost kingdom of Jerusalem stood alongside the lost mythical or semi-mythical glories of Charlemagne and Arthur. Unlike them however Jerusalem still existed and could, in theory, still be regained. So the First Crusade acquired significance as the only crusade to take Jerusalem: it became simultaneously an evocation of the past and an exemplum to follow. Godfrey as its first king became equally significant.[12]

The composition and structure of the central trilogy

We do not know precisely when the central trilogy of the Crusade was compiled, by whom or when. Interestingly the average laisse length in the *Antioche* is the shortest of the three at 25.6 lines; the *Chétifs* average length is 29.5 and the *Jérusalem* 35.2. Applying the rough rule of thumb that the shorter the laisses, the older the poem, this supports the hypothesis that the *Antioche* makes the most use of pre-existing poetic material, the *Chétifs* some, and the *Jérusalem* little if any.

---

[10] For example Jordan Fantosme's account of the wars against the Young King: *Jordan Fantosme's Chronicle*, (ed.) R. C. Johnston (Oxford, 1981); the Occitan *Canso de la Crozada* and the rather later *Guerra de Navarra: Guilhem Anelier de Tolosa: Guerra de Navarra: Nafarroako Gudua*, II (eds) M. Berthe, R. Cierbide, X. Kintana and J. Santale, 2 vols (Pamplona, 1995). For discussion of verse and vernacular historiography see P. Damian-Grint, *The New Historians of the Twelfth-Century Renaissance: Inventing Vernacular Authority* (Woodbridge, 1999).

[11] As famously defined by Jean Bodel, *Chanson des Saisnes*, (ed.) A. Brasseur, 2 vols (Geneva, 1989), vol.1 lines 6–42.

[12] See J. Richard, 'L'arrière-plan historique des deux cycles de la croisade', *Les Epopées de la Croisade: première colloque internationale, Trêves 6–11 août 1984*, *Zeitschrift für Französische Sprache und Literatur* Beiheft 11 (Stuttgart, 1987) pp. 6–16 for discussion of how the First Crusade and Third Crusade acted in different ways as catalysts for the poetic depiction of the Crusade.

We can however be clear about the purpose of the trilogy. The first 200 lines of the *Antioche* act as a prologue to the entire trilogy with a very clear message. God suffered for humankind in Jerusalem and the Crusade was to seek vengeance for him:

> 'De la sainte cite vos vaurai conmenchier,
> U Diex laissa son cors pener et travellier
> Et ferir de la lance et navrer et plaier;
> Mais li jentius barnages qui Dieu ainme et tint chier
> En ala outre mer por le sien cors vengier'.[13]

It is clear that the goal was Jerusalem:

> 'Huimais pores oïr de Jursalem parler
> Et de cels ki alerent le Sepucre honorer'.[14]

The Crusaders suffered terribly, but were rewarded by God:

> 'Por Deu lor convint tos mainte paine endurer,
> Sois et faims et froidures et veller et juner;
> Bien lor dut Damedeus a tous gueredoner
> Et les armes a cels en sa glorie mener'.[15]

The audience should emulate them and seek to liberate Jerusalem, mindful of the example set out in the song:

> 'Ceste chançon doit on cier tenir et amer,
> Car tant maint bon exemple i puet proudon trover'.[16]
> 'Nostre Sire vos rueve en Jhersalem aler,
> Le deffaee gent ocire et afoler ... .
> ... Li bon baron de France ne vaurent arrester,
> En estranges païs s'alerent deserter,
> La devinrent salvage por lor armes salve..
> Ki la puet par bon cuer son cors por Deu pener,
> Jhesus li rois de gloire nel vaura oblier,
> Ains le fera en glorie hautement coroner'.[17]

---

[13] *Antioche* lines 35–9.
[14] *Antioche* lines 16–17.
[15] *Antioche* lines 24–7.
[16] *Antioche* lines 4–5.
[17] *Antioche* lines 128–9, 138–143.

The author is very clear that there are other versions, but they do not have the right beginning and hence the right motivation:

'Cist novel jougleor qui en suelent canter
Le vrai commencement en ont laisié ester,
Mais Grainsdor de Douai nel velt mie oblier
Ki nos en a les vers tous fais renoveler'.[18]

The *vrai commencement* is 'la geste de la mute Pieron'. This, and possibly more, was recounted in a previous work:

'Oï l'avés chanter en une autre chançon,
Mais n'estoit pas rime ensi com nos l'avon,
Rimee est de novel et mise en quarregnon.
Mais cil qui le rima n'i vaut metre son non
Por cou que tels l'oïst quin françast le grenon'.[19]

Put together this tells us that the author – whether Graindor or whether commissioned by Graindor, and who might therefore be referred to as 'Graindor' – has written a new version of the Crusade which starts with Peter the Hermit and his forces and culminates in the taking and defence of Jerusalem. This is part of the divine plan in avenging Christ's suffering, and those who participate in the divine plan will be rewarded in Heaven.

Whilst we cannot be more precise about dating than the early thirteenth century, the fall of Jerusalem had led to a reassessment and new presentation of the First Crusade: 'by the late twelfth and early thirteenth centuries, there existed a view of the First Crusade ... that was directed to potential leaders of the Crusade movement, and a more flexible body of images living in poetry, sermons, letters and treatises that could be molded to contemporary arguments ... the emphasis is on rewards for participation and on the overcoming of obstacles. Martyrdom and sacrifice form motives for going. History serves to point up the success of the First Crusade and to list its heroes, thus providing a link to the heroic past'.[20] This is exactly what we see in the central Crusade trilogy.

The purpose of writing is to justify the Crusade and encourage listeners to help retake Jerusalem. Between them the *Antioche*, the *Chétifs* and the *Jérusalem* describe this vision.

---

[18] *Antioche* lines 12–15.
[19] *Antioche* lines 78–82.
[20] J. M. Powell, 'Myth, legend, propaganda, history: the First Crusade 1140 – ca. 1300', *Autour de la première Croisade: actes du colloque de la SSCLE, Clermont-Ferrand, 22–25 juin 1995*, (ed.) M. Balard (Paris, 1996), pp. 127–141 at pp.136–7, 139).

Putting the trilogy together: (i) the 'chétifs' and accounting for defeat

The author faced two problems in compiling his Crusade trilogy, both stemming from inconvenient truths of the First Crusade. The first of these was that the Crusade started with defeat and captivity. In both Albert and the *Antioche* the genesis of the Crusade is ascribed to Peter the Hermit: Peter visited the Holy Sepulchre, had a vision of God ordering him to go to Rome and persuaded the Pope to launch the Crusade.[21] Whatever the truth of this account, it is historical fact that Peter was the first to reach Asia. Almost as soon as the Byzantines had ferried him and his somewhat ramshackle army across the Bosphorus he was attacked by the Turks at Civetot. His soldiers were wiped out or taken captive and Peter barely escaped with his life.[22] Fulcher of Chartres comments that heaps of bones were visible on the battlefield a year or so later.[23] This inglorious start to the Crusade needed to be explained in a context where God signified divine approval through success.[24]

The second inconvenient truth is the difficulty the Crusade ran into after the taking and holding of Antioch.[25] Bohemond was determined to hold on to Antioch. At least some of the other leaders, notably Raymond of St-Gilles, were equally determined that he should not. Unable to agree, the army spent several months locked in dispute. An attempt to solve matters at a summit meeting failed: in the acerbic words of Robert the Monk, 'all spoke in favour of reconciliation without any suggestions as to how it was to be achieved'.[26] The rank and file became so disillusioned that they took matters into their own hands. The army finally moved on towards Jerusalem, but different leaders went different ways. The unity of purpose of the Crusade had disappeared. This difficult period also needed to be explained; it is no coincidence that at least some of the sources give little detail on events.

The author invented a brilliantly original solution to these difficulties. He put the *Chétifs* at the heart of the trilogy with significance at a number of levels. Structurally the text bridges the awkward gap between Antioch and Jerusalem, switching the focus completely away from the main Crusade. We leave the crusading army victorious at Antioch; we next see them setting up camp around Jerusalem. The *Chétifs* acts as a hinge between the two, at half the length and with three symmetric episodes. And it elides the manoeuvring for power which would have undercut the exemplary message of the trilogy.

The text also has a twin plot function. The *chétifs* return in triumph to the Crusade in time to take the Holy City, bringing much needed reinforcements.

---

[21] AA I.2–5; *Antioche* laisses 15–17.
[22] See e.g Runciman, *History* pp. 121–33; Asbridge, *First Crusade* pp. 100–103.
[23] FCI.9.
[24] Thus e.g. RM IV.8: success in foraging is an indication of God's favour.
[25] See J. France: 'The Crisis of the First Crusade: from the defeat of Kerbogha to the departure from Arqa', *Byzantion* 40 (1970) pp. 276–308.
[26] RM VIII.8.

And they leave in their wake a grateful Corbaran on the verge of conversion to Christianity: the Christians' key opponent is thus neutralised.

But there is a deeper layer of significance. It would have been quite open to 'Graindor' to pass over the captivity of the *chétifs* lightly, or indeed not to mention it at all, in line with the approach taken by many of the chronicles. On the contrary, he lays heavy emphasis on it. There is no doubt about the bravery with which the *chétifs* fight the Turks. This is emphasised at the start of the *Antioche* through *laisses similaires*.[27] In particular the phrase 'al puy de Civetot' is repeated insistently, in a way which is reminiscent of the *Roland*'s 'halt sunt li pui'.[28] It is clear that defeat, like Roland, is against overwhelming odds. But it was a defeat which, with better planning, need not have happened, as the text is at pains to point out.[29] And 'Graindor' stresses the shamefulness both of the process of being taken captive and the subsequent treatment. The *chétifs* are put to work on Saracen hard labour, given some of the most degrading work available. They are chained and ill-treated.[30] 'Graindor' also makes it clear that the captives are not ordinary soldiers: they are a group of nobles and clerics. So their captivity is all the more shameful: in the words of Yvonne Friedman, 'the captive ... was the classic antihero, the failed warrior'.[31]

The process by which the *chétifs* extract themselves from captivity and return to the Crusade becomes a kind of redemption. At the start of the text they are so miserable that death seems the only solution. Their valour wins them Corbaran's gratitude, his mother's favour, their consequent release and Corbaran's active support in helping them return to the Crusade. In response Corbaran, the arch villain of the Antioche, becomes their ally and, more than that, ready to convert to Christianity. The *chétifs* have redeemed not only themselves but their enemy. They can return to the Crusade absolved of shame in time to help in the glorious capture of Jerusalem.

The message is clear. The redeeming power of the Crusade is so strong that it can wipe out even the crushing shame of defeat and captivity; it leads to true salvation. Jerusalem was, literally on maps of the era, the centre of the earth.[32] 'Jerusalem loomed large in all spheres of life, ranging from international relations to personal

---

[27] See in particular laisses 26–8; 31–3.

[28] See *Antioche* lines 558, 572,622; particularly 730, 748, 759 where the phrase starts three *laisses similaires*. *Roland* lines 814, 1830, 2271.

[29] *Antioche* lines 373–6.

[30] *Antioche* laisses 33–4; *Chétifs* laisses 11–12.

[31] Y. Friedman, *Encounter between Enemies: captivity and ransom in the Latin kingdom of Jerusalem* (Leiden/Boston/Köln, 2002), 1. See also J. Dunbabin, *Captivity and Imprisonment in medieval Europe c.1000 – c.1300* (London, 2003).

[32] The classic T-O layout showed Jerusalem at the centre of the three continents of Europe, Asia and Africa. See the Hereford Mappa Mundi and the Ebersdorf map: P. D. A. Harvey, *Mappa Mundi: the Hereford World Map*, (Hereford, 2010); *Magnificent Maps: Power, Propaganda and Art*, P. Barber and T. Harper (London, 2010) pp. 76–80.

salvation'.[33] The Holy Sepulchre and Jerusalem were near-synonymous.[34] It was particularly important therefore that Crusaders who had begun their journey under the cloud of defeat reach Jerusalem and the Sepulchre. This in turn underlines the messages with which the *Antioche* begins: that Crusade is the road to salvation and the heroism of the First Crusade is both the proof and the example to be emulated. It thus becomes apparent why 'Graindor' puts the *chétifs* so prominently both at the start of the *Antioche* and gives them their own text at the centre of the trilogy. Far from being picturesque light relief, they are at the heart of the message of crusade as redemption.

There is a further level of allegory. The text lays heavy stress on how the *chétifs* are led away in chains, flung into prison and the ordeals they undergo there. This could not have failed to evoke the image of sinners in chains being led by devils to Hell.[35] It would also have evoked parallels with the apocryphal Harrowing of Hell by Christ and rescue of sinners, a theme already found in the *GF*.[36] The *chétifs* thus become a proxy for all humankind, redeemed by Christ from Hell and in return recovering Jerusalem to redeem the shame to Christ of its loss, a theme very clear in Crusade preaching.[37]

This in turn sheds light on why 'Graindor' chose the three particular episodes which form the *Chétifs*. The episode at the heart of the *Chétifs*, and hence the heart of the entire trilogy, is the defeat of the Sathanas by Baldwin of Beauvais. The significance is clear. A Christian knight defeats a serpent called Satan. In other words, the allegorical conquest of evil is at the very heart of the trilogy, forming a spiritual counterpart to the defeat of the Saracens and the near-conversion of Corbaran. This could only have happened if the *chétifs* had already gained a measure of liberty from their captivity. The judicial duel is a plot motor which makes this possible. But it also suggests that the Christians defeat the Saracens by divine right: their victory in the battle is a proof of their moral superiority.[38] The function of the third episode is less clear. It does not take the plot forward: the *chétifs* are already free, Corbaran is their ally and it merely serves to delay them at Oliferne. Structurally however it provides symmetry in the text. It provides a social and emotional counterpoint to the judicial episode of Richard and the spiritual episode of Baldwin. And it provides a counterweight to the loss of Brohadas: the

---

[33] S. Schein, *Gateway to the Heavenly City: Crusader Jerusalem and the Catholic West (1099–1187)*, (Guildford, 2005), p. 7.

[34] C. Morris, *The Sepulchre of Christ in the Medieval West: from the beginning to 1600* (Oxford, 2005).

[35] See for example the portal of St-Trophime in Arles; slightly later from around 1240 the remains of the rood screen by the Master of Naumburg in the Dommuseum at Mainz.

[36] GF 2: 'dicentes sese Christia unanimiter sequi vestigia, quibus de manu errant redempti tartarei'.

[37] See for example RM's account of Urban's speech, I.1–2.

[38] Bartlett, *Ordeals* pp. 115–16.

infidel Corbaran was unable to protect the Sultan's nephew, whilst the child here is saved by a Christian knight through the power of God.

The author thus knits a range of source material together skilfully to create a whole. The choice of Peter the Hermit as the catalyst for the Crusade meant that the initial defeat at Civetot had to be justified. 'Graindor' chose not merely to justify the defeat but to put it at the heart of his trilogy. The captivity of the *chétifs* and their subsequent liberation, near-conversion of their enemy and triumphant return in time to help take Jerusalem are central to the message of crusade as redemption, and indeed structurally at the heart of the trilogy. This is illustrated through three episodes which not only move the plot on but provide three different angles on it: judicial, spiritual and social. The divine plan which began with Titus and Vespasian taking Jerusalem can thus be fulfilled with the crusading army going on to take Jerusalem in triumph.

Putting the trilogy together (ii): creating a climax at Jerusalem

The *Jérusalem* as argued above bears no strong resemblance to any particular source. The highlights of siege, fall and battle are recounted in terms which reflect little more than general knowledge of the order of events and recast them as a standard *chanson de geste*. There is no evidence of any predecessor text and no reference to one. What is interesting here is not the eclectic use made of source material but precisely the failure to use existing source material. The author could have used any of the numerous accounts available in the various chronicles. However that was not what the trilogy needed. Instead he focused on the creation of a text to serve as climax to the trilogy loosely built around a recognisable framework of events.

This accounts for the fact that, as set out above, the main source for the structure and content of the *Jérusalem* is the *Antioche* itself. As in the *Antioche* extensive use is made of the conventions of the *chanson de geste*, particularly description of single combat and portrayal of Saracens, to bring colour and deal with gaps in the narrative. The interest lies in the way the author uses his material and changes events to bring his narrative to its triumphant conclusion.

Central to the text is the doctrine set out at the start of the *Antioche*: the Crusade as part of the divine plan. Christ is shown on the Cross prophesying to the thief Dinas:

> ''Amis' dist il, 'encore n'est pas li pules nés
> Ki me venra ocire les paiens deffaés
> Ki mes commandemens ont tos jors refusés,
> Dont sera essaucie sainte Crestïentés
> Et ma terre conquise, mes païs aquités;
> D'ui en mil ans sera baptisiés et levés
> Et s'ert li sains Sepucres requis et aorés.
> Ausi me serviront om ses aie engenrés,

Il ierent tot mi fil, g'iere lor avoués,
En paradis celestre sera lor iretés'.[39]

The concept of the Franks as God's divine people chosen to carry out his will and recover Jerusalem was as old as the Crusade itself. Robert the Monk's *Praefatio* for example quotes Psalm 33 to make the point; and it is explicit in the title itself of Guibert of Nogent's account, *Dei Gesta per Francos*. Guibert sets out the history of the Crusade as part of wider world history. Baudry of Bourgueil makes the point explicitly: 'Ex Dei tamen dispositione factum nequaquam dubitamus, qui *disponit omnia suaviter*; nec casu fortuito permittit vel unum passerem ad terram cadere. Si enim Alexios imperator advenisset Turcosque superasset, triumphus gentis suae non exercitu Dei ascriberetur'.[40] Universal histories later in the century such as Otto of Freisingen show the Crusade as part of the wider plan for God's universe.[41]

But events at Jerusalem are overlaid with elements of wider significance: the plan for the end of days and the final coming of Christ. The doctrine of the Apocalypse set out in pseudo-Methodius sets out how one power will expel the Arabs from Christendom, then surrender the crown to God at Jerusalem; this marks the end of earthly rule and the advent of the Antichrist, who will then be defeated by Christ and bring God's reign.[42] The shadow of the Antichrist hangs over contemporary writings on the Crusade: for example the supposed letter of Alexius to Robert of Flanders invokes the coming of the Antichrist as a consequence of invasion by the Turks.[43] At a time when Jerusalem had been lost and there were no imminent prospects of recovery, the doctrine of the Apocalypse had all the more significance: Jerusalem would be recovered because it must be recovered as part of the divine plan.[44] So taking – and keeping – a vow to go on Crusade was more than a matter of individual salvation; it helped deliver final salvation for humanity.

One of the key preoccupations in the *Jérusalem* is thus to show the redemptive power of Crusade for all those who complete their vows. This is what underlies

---

[39] *Antioche* lines 171–81.

[40] BB III.13: 'we should have no doubt whatsoever that this was done by the will of God who *arranges all things for the best* and who does not allow even one sparrow to fall to the earth by blind chance. For thus if the Emperor Alexius had in fact come and conquered the Turks, the triumph of His people would not have been ascribed to the army of God'.

[41] *The Two Cities: a chronicle of universal history to the year 1146 AD by Otto, Bishop of Freising*, transl. C. C. Mierow (New York, 1966). The eight books of Otto's history stretch from the founding of Rome to the Antichrist and the Last Judgement. His account of the Crusade repeatedly refers to God's intervention, for example at the fall of Antioch (VII.2).

[42] Schein, *Crusader Jerusalem*, pp. 146–9; J. Rubenstein, *Armies of Heaven: the First Crusade and the quest for Apocalypse* (Philadelphia, 2011).

[43] Text in H. Hagenmeyer, *Die Kreuzzugsbriefe aus den Jahren 1088 – 1100* (Innsbruck, 1901), pp. 130–36; for translation and references Sweetenham, *Robert the Monk's History* pp. 215–22.

[44] Schein, *Crusader Jerusalem* p. 157.

the surprising appearance of leaders who in fact had left the Crusade some time previously: Bohemond, Baldwin and Hugh. All needed to reappear at the taking of Jerusalem to be redeemed. Similarly Enguerrand's death is placed in the battle of Ascalon rather than, as in actuality, during the siege of Ma'arrat'an'Nu'man. It is for the same reason that it is so important for the *chétifs* to be released in time to participate in the taking of Jerusalem: the shame of their captivity can be wiped out by victory.

This emphasis on salvation is also what underlies one of the more startling aspects of the text: the complete transformation of the Tafurs from barely human cannibals to the heroes of the hour. In the *Antioche* they are described in a manner reminiscent of devils and the author spares no detail in describing the relish with which they engage in cannibalism.[45] In the *Jérusalem* their cannibalistic activities are evoked to frighten onlookers and provide consistency, but they do not engage in cannibalism:

> 'Le messagier regardent, molt le vont resquignant.
> Et li rois des Tafurs vait les iex roëllant,
> Sovent bee la goule, molt vait les dens croissant'.[46]

They are repeatedly shown as heroes, leading in combat and carrying out arduous duties. The King of the Tafurs is shown as a leader on a par with the other leaders, often associated with Peter the Hermit, leading the first abortive assault on Jerusalem and given the honour of crowning Godfrey King.[47] In other words, even the outcast and barely human can be redeemed through the power of Crusade. We might wonder tentatively if this explains the prominence given to Thomas of Marle, notorious even by the standards of the age for violence and evil behaviour: even he could be redeemed by the power of Jerusalem. Only those who do not fulfil their vows are beyond redemption: and that is the role of Stephen of Blois, who memorably flees in the *Antioche* and appears only fleetingly (by mistake?) in laisse 222 before the final battle.[48]

However there is a wider canvas than merely personal salvation. The *Jérusalem* is also concerned to show the playing out of God's plan by adding a number of symbolic episodes. Before the battle of Ascalon the Saracens try to distract the Christians by laying out a large amount of treasure: the Christians are unmoved. Attempts to bribe in this way are one of the four wiles of the Antichrist, referred to for example in the supposed letter of Alexius.[49] The horde of beaked monsters

---

[45] *Antioche* laisses 174–5, underlined by the use of *laisses similaires*.
[46] *Jérusalem* lines 7301–3, a performance staged for the benefit of the Saracen envoy.
[47] *Jérusalem* laisses 78–9, 156.
[48] See 'The Count and the Cannibals' for a more detailed exposition of this argument. For Stephen laisse 233–4 in the *Antioche*; laisse 222 in the *Jérusalem*.
[49] R. Emmerson, *Antichrist in the Middle Ages: a study of Medieval Apocalypticism, Art and Literature*, (Manchester, 1981), p. 131 for bribery as one of the wiles of the

fought off by the Tafurs in the battle is reminiscent of the birds who feed on the flesh of men in the final battle in Revelation.[50] It also returns to themes which have appeared earlier in the trilogy. The candlesticks referred to a number of times are reminiscent of the seven candlesticks, and the saints riding to the rescue robed in white are similar to the white riders of the last battle.[51]

Against this background the full significance of the episode of the dragon at the centre of the *Chétifs* becomes clear. Structurally this episode is at the very heart of the trilogy. Its provenance is carefully described. The symbolism of the dragon, 'hic serps antiquus qui diabolus est' is clear.[52] He is defeated by Baldwin of Beauvais in the same way as Satan, the dragon, is defeated by St Michael and his angels, and subsequently cast into the lake of fire and sulphur; to underline the symbolism the dragon is called Sathanas, and St Michael appears to Baldwin.[53]

The trilogy thus sets out a clear vision for the Crusade as the fulfilment of God's plan for the universe against an implied eschatological background. This is not to argue that there are not inconsistencies. There are. Once the *chétifs* have returned to the Crusade we hear nothing about them until the very end, and then not in all manuscripts. Although the author is careful to mention Baldwin and Ernoul of Beauvais at the outset of the *Antioche*, they are lost from sight in the rest of the *Chétifs*. The St-Pols are much less prominent in the *Jérusalem*. But none of this detracts from the narrative sweep of the whole.

Why write the Cycle in the form of a chanson de geste?

Although originating in the eleventh century in something approaching its recognised form, the *chanson de geste* remained popular into the fourteenth century judging by the number of manuscripts written then. It was a consciously archaising and stylised approach which brought particular resonances. *Chansons de geste* depict a violent and largely masculine world where combat dominates according to a particular set of ritual. The enemy is often though not always Saracen, again depicted in accordance with a set of stereotypes. The events depicted are as a rule centuries in the past, whether going back to the reign of Charlemagne or to other feudal lords such as William of Orange or Raoul of Cambrai.[54]

Antichrist. The apocryphal letter has a similar theme of Saracens using treasure as a distraction.

[50] Revelation 19: 17–21.
[51] Revelation 1:12; 18: 11–15.
[52] Revelation 12:9.
[53] *Chétifs* lines 2492–505.
[54] An enormous amount has been written on the *chanson de geste*. For starting points see D. Boutet, *La chanson de geste* (Paris, 1993); F. Suard, *La Chanson de Geste* (Paris, 1993); *La Chanson de Guillaume*, (ed.) and transl. P. Bennett (London, 2000); *Raoul de Cambrai*, (ed.) and transl. S. Kay (Oxford, 1992).

There is some evidence for poetic material at or shortly after the time of the Crusade using the conventions of the *chanson de geste*: a similar run of material describing events in the Saracen camp appears in the *Gesta Francorum* and its derivatives virtually word for word, suggesting that it was a well-recognised and popular description.[55] We do not know what was contained in this tradition, what genre it was written in or even for certain whether it was in Old French. What we do know is that it contained topoi associated with the *chanson de geste*; that if we believe the *Antioche* itself there were earlier versions in Old French;[56] and that there was an Occitan poem in the first third of the twelfth century.[57] So there was a well-recognised poetic foundation on which the trilogy could be built.

However by the time the Cycle was written other genres were well established. Vernacular verse historiography had been produced throughout the twelfth century.[58] By the start of the thirteenth century vernacular prose historiography was also appearing, and was used for other accounts of crusades such as Robert de Clari's and Villehardouin's accounts of the Fourth Crusade.[59] So to use the *chanson de geste* format made a specific statement about the way the author wanted the text to be received.

By definition the *chanson de geste* was a backward-looking genre. It was about past glory and heroism. To use its format cast the protagonists in epic mould, the equivalents of Roland and Oliver or other heroes. The comparison is drawn on occasion in the trilogy: at Enguerrand of St Pol's death for example the author compares the mourning for him to the mourning for Roland.[60] But the mere use of the format was enough. The resonances are obvious in a work designed to be exemplary. The audience are invited to engage with the exploits of their ancestors in 1095, and those in turn are linked to the heroes of epic legend, creating a continuum of heroism in which contemporaries are invited to take their place. Not only will going on Crusade bring salvation: it will also bring kinship with past heroes.

The format of the *chanson de geste* also tells us something about the intended audience. Even when *chansons de geste* started to be written down as a matter of course in the thirteenth century, they had their roots in oral performance and

---

[55] *GF* 53–6; RM VI.10–12; GN 212–16; PT 93–6.

[56] *Antioche* lines 78–82.

[57] Geoffrey of Vigeois, *Chronica Gaufredi coenobitae*, (ed.) P. Labbé, *Novae Bibliothecae Manuscript librorum: Rerum Aquitanicarum praesertim Bituricensium uberrima collectio*, II, (1657), pp. 79–342, I.30.

[58] Damian-Grint, *New Historians*.

[59] Robert de Clari, *La Conquête de Constantinople*, (ed.) and transl. P. Noble (Edinburgh, 2005); Geoffroi de Villehardouin, *La Conquête de Constantinople*, (ed.) E. Faral, 2 vols (Paris, 1961). It is interesting that, whilst not creating a specific literary genre, Crusades seem to act as a spur to literary innovation.

[60] *Jérusalem* line 9700; see also line 7581 in the context of Turkish attacks.

continued to be performed.[61] We know little about actual performance, but the material in the texts themselves suggests that there was plenty of scope for humour, drama and exaggeration, perhaps not unlike a modern mummers' play. Whilst the references to an audience in the text form part of the topoi of the *chanson de geste* and should not necessarily be taken literally, these were texts to be performed which continued to attract an audience.[62] As a way of reaching a military and not necessarily literate or Latin-speaking audience, the power of the *chanson de geste* is obvious.

So there was no inherent contradiction in using the *chanson de geste* format to depict events which, whilst not within living memory, were relatively recent compared to Charlemagne. The relative archaism of the form, its heroic resonances and the potential for engaging performance all made it the ideal vehicle to engage its audience: men of fighting age who could judge the fine details of a single combat and could be persuaded to take the Cross.

Conclusion

The trilogy is a carefully constructed triptych in which the theme of divine salvation at a personal level through Crusade and the Crusade as part of God's plan for the salvation of mankind are played out. These themes are set out by Christ on the Cross in the prologue of the text, the '*vrai commencement*': this explains the importance of the *commencement* and the emphasis the author places on it. The author deliberately dwells on the initial failure to provide a concrete illustration of the power of Crusade to redeem. Divine support for the Crusade as part of the plan is played out in similar terms both at Antioch and at Jerusalem; and at the very heart of the text is the symbolic defeat of the Devil and the salvation of mankind.

The author chose his source material eclectically to underpin this narrative. He used a pre-existing text for much of the description of events at Antioch. He put at the heart of the text an episode which is likely to have originated in Antioch in

---

[61] Also a topic of huge scholarly debate. The majority of manuscripts are thirteenth century or later: J. Duggan, 'The manuscript corpus of the Medieval Romance epic', in *The medieval Alexander legend in Romance epic: essays in honour of David J. A. Ross*, (eds) P. Noble, C. Isoz and L. Polak (New York, 1982) pp. 285–311. On oral roots J. Rychner, *La chanson de geste: essai sur l'art épique des jongleurs*, (Geneva, 1955). On performance we know that works were sung for entertainment see Lambert of Ardres, *Chronique de Guines et d'Ardres*, (ed.) D. C. Godefroy-Ménilglaise (Paris, 1855), p. 217; transl. L. Shopkow, *The History of the Counts of Guines and Lords of Ardres,* (Philadelphia:, 2001) p. 130; Orderic Vitalis describes the clerk of Hugh of Avranches entertaining the household with stories from hagiography, the Old Testament and the *chanson de geste (*OV vol.3 pp. 216–17). For evidence of performance as opposed to simply singing, see D. Alonso, 'Estilo y creación en el Poema del Cid', *Ensayos sobre poesía espanola* (Buenos Aires, 1946) pp. 69–111.

[62] See for example *Jérusalem* lines 73, 469, 882–4, 9883–91; innumerable examples of oral formulae.

the 1140s in a different context, and added to it material about trial by combat and folkloric themes attached to characters who were famous for going on Crusade and being held captive, even if not this particular Crusade. He wrote the *Jérusalem* based on this material to complete the picture.

In doing so he constructed a powerful and coherent narrative over some 22,000 lines. The narrative arcs of the *Antioche* and *Jérusalem* correspond: the *chétifs* are defeated at the start of the former and return in triumph at the start of the latter, to progress through corresponding sequences of siege, fall and triumph in battle. Meanwhile the *chétifs* provide a consistent thread throughout: they are taken captive at the start, virtually convert the Saracens and slay the dragon in the middle, and are given the final honours in the battle of Ascalon where Baldwin of Beauvais kills the Saracen leader Cornumarant.

The trilogy of *Antioche – Chétifs – Jérusalem* thus reveals itself as a powerful piece of Crusade propaganda, and one giving an insight into the preoccupations of the age.[63] At a time when 'the vehement reaction to the fall of Jerusalem [might] be compared in its intensity with the response to its conquest by the First Crusade',[64] the trilogy provides a vernacular counterpart to ecclesiastical preaching full of entertainment, glamour, gore, drama and humour with a serious underlying purpose. There must have been considerably worse ways to while away a wet Picard day.

---

[63] See R. F. Cook, 'Crusade propaganda in the epic cycles of the crusade', *Journeys towards God: pilgrimage and crusade,* (ed.) B. N. Sargent-Baur (Kalamazoo, 1992) pp. 157–75.

[64] Schein, *Crusader Jerusalem* p. 185.

Editions Used and Principles of Translation

Editions

Both translations use the only modern editions, those in the Alabama edition of the Old French Crusade Cycle. These reflect all extant manuscripts and give comprehensive lists of variants.

The only previous edition of the *Jérusalem* was by Célestin Hippeau in 1868 and was full of errors and omissions.[1] The first edition of the *Chétifs* was again by Célestin Hippeau in 1858, who published fragments amounting to around half of the text; an edition prepared in the 1920s as a dissertation by Lucy Wenhold is available but overtaken by the Alabama edition.[2] Both nineteenth-century editions are partial and not adequate for modern scholarship; they are not considered further here.

Variants

The *Jérusalem* variants are short and add little to the main text; I have therefore not translated them. However the variants to the *Chétifs* introduce more varied material and are longer. Some of them simply elaborate the text with more detail: Appendix 3 for example is found in one manuscript and adds extra dialogue between Corbaran and his mother. Others however add significant new material. I have translated the three which do: Appendix 4, which is in six of the manuscripts and describes a magic spell cast by Calabra; Appendix 7, which is only in ms B but describes a somewhat Arthurian combat with the giant Chaïnans; and Appendix 12, an addition of nearly 1,000 lines describing the *chétifs*' battle with the mother of Sathanas and found in two manuscripts. This level of variation in itself suggests that the text must have presented a degree of mystification to medieval transmitters and scribes: clearly it was felt legitimate and perhaps necessary to add substantial material to make more sense of it. By translating the most significant variants, which in themselves are getting on for half as long as the text itself, I hope to give some flavour of this *mouvance* in the text.

---

[1] *La Conquête de Jérusalem, faisant suite à la Chanson d'Antioche, composée par le Pèlerin Richard et renouvelée par Graindor de Douai au XIIIe siècle*, (ed.) C. Hippeau, 2 vols, (Paris, 1868; reprinted Geneva, 1969).

[2] *La Chanson du Chevalier au Cygne et de Godefroid de Bouillon*, (ed.) C. Hippeau, 2 vols, (Paris, 1874–77). The *Chétifs* is published as an appendix; Hippeau used B.N. fr,1621 of which he edited around two-thirds. *The Chanson des Chétifs: an Old French Crusade Epic*, L. Wenhold (University of Chapel Hill, North Carolina, 1928).

Translation

The translator of literature faces challenges not posed by more factual translation. 'The translation of literary works ... has a feature that distinguishes it from all other translation tasks. We like to believe that a literary work is unlike all others – it is unique ... and essentially just itself'.[3] In other words there is no right way of translating a literary text. Literature aims to create an aesthetic and emotional effect in a specific context at a specific time. The translator is always going to be an unwanted third in the relationship between author and audience. 'What translators do is find matches, not equivalence, for the units of which a work is made, in the hope and expectation that their sum will produce a new work that can serve overall as a substitute for the source'.[4] In other words, the translator is in the game of finding a way of conveying the meaning of a text in a way which will match with the experiences and perceptions of a modern audience to create an effect akin to that which the original text would have created had they been able to read it.

The *Jérusalem* and the *Chétifs* present several layers of challenge to the translator. They are heavily fictionalised thirteenth-century accounts of events which happened a century previously, tailored to the preoccupations of a Northern French audience under pressure both to maintain their status and to regain the lost possessions in the Holy Land, and written in a consciously archaising and formulaic style. There is not much match between this and the needs of a twenty-first century audience with a largely academic interest in the text.

The texts are first and foremost *chansons de geste*, written in that idiom and using the topoi and formulae of the genre. There is no equivalent to this in English literary form: alexandrine laisses are not an English metre. Nor is there any modern stylistic equivalent. If pressed one might opt for the *bande dessinée* or the Hollywood action blockbuster. Neither however being at the disposal of the literary translator, I have therefore opted for English prose, the latter on the basis that the alexandrine laisse serves as a convenient format for narrative rather than an intricate piece of poetry in its own right. I have sought to strike the classic balance between accuracy and readability: the translation needs to be close enough to the text to be of use to students and scholars, but not so close that it is incomprehensible to a modern mindset.

Inevitably this leads to some compromises. On the one hand, I have sometimes changed the word order to make sentences run more smoothly and inserted or removed a few conjunctions. I have also changed some tenses to the past tense to give consistency to an English reader: the Old French shifts tenses sometimes mid-sentence, and I have kept this where I feel it is specifically required by the sense. Where the text uses two or three synonyms to make the same point, often dictated by the rhyme, I have sometimes shifted syntax to avoid awkwardness

---

[3] D. Bellos, *Is that a fish in your ear? The amazing adventure of translation* (London, 2012), p. 308.

[4] Bellos, *Amazing adventure* p. 320.

and very occasionally dropped a word. I have also inserted a few words in square brackets where the Old French is elliptical enough that the meaning would not otherwise be clear.

On the other hand I have had to recognise that these are thirteenth-century texts and some elements will seem awkward and unfamiliar to a modern reader. Firstly, some of the language does not read across well. Some of the idioms are problematic. A favourite of the author's is to say 'ne vaut une alie'. This is a sorb apple, not something commonly found in supermarkets.[5] Rather than opt for a modern equivalent like 'as useful as a concrete lifebelt' I have preferred to retain the medieval phraseology because that is what was familiar to the author. Another issue is insults or oaths: whilst basic concepts of rudeness such as parentage, girth and general villainy have not changed some of the language has, and these are inevitably going to sound stilted.

Secondly there are differences in material culture. Modern English simply does not have enough words for the panoply of medieval weaponry, for example the difference between a misericord and a dagger. A few words are untranslatable because they have no modern equivalent; for example 'enarmer' to describe the process of putting one's arms through the straps of a shield and getting it into position.[6] Where I think specific reference to material culture would help I have explained this in a footnote, for example silk decorated with a circular pattern ('roellee'). Units of money and measurement are particularly difficult because there are no equivalents and because the modern terms have resonances of their own. For money I have kept the Old French and explained equivalence in a footnote; for distances I have changed to modern equivalents, such as 'around six feet' for 'deux toises'.

Thirdly there are differences in customs and values which can be translated but have no modern resonance. There are frequent oaths and Christian references such as 'qui Dex doinst enconbrier' and 'se Jhesus n'en pense'. These are not verbal embellishments: they are central to the belief system of the text and therefore have to be translated literally despite a stilted effect. Similarly the subtleties of a feudal society need to be reflected: 'v cens mercis et gres' sounds odd to a modern ear but is the appropriate way for an inferior to greet and thank a superior. Some of the terminology around rank and status is particularly problematic. A particularly difficult term is 'baron', which I have translated as a rule meaning

---

[5] The botanical name is *sorbus torminalis*. The fruits are the size of a small cherry and need to blet before they become edible. See Richard Mabey, *Food for Free* (London, new ed. 2012, pp.134-35.

[6] For weapon terminology in the OFCC see D. Nicolle, 'Armes et armures dans les épopées de croisade', *Les épopées de la croisade: première colloque internationale, Trêves, 6–11 août 1984, Zeitschrift für Französische Sprache und Literatur*, Beiheft 11 (Stuttgart, 1987), pp. 17–34.

'lords' but on occasion more specifically 'leaders' or 'barons'.[7] Also difficult is the distinction between 'Franc' and 'Franceis': here I have followed the lead of the text by translating respectively 'Franks' and 'French'. The deliberately negative and misleading portrayal of Islam offends modern sensibilities but reflects those of the early thirteenth century and cannot be ducked by the translator.

Fourthly and finally, the conventions of the *chanson de geste* itself can lead to a stilted effect. One of the topoi is that the text is being performed rather than read: so the first person interjections by the narrator, 'oissies', 'a mon escient' need again to be translated literally. Formulaic style and repetition are fundamental to the style of the *chanson de geste*, stemming from the conditions of performance: not to reflect them would do violence to the style. So where phrases like 'al pui de Civetot' are repeated to incantatory effect in the Old French, I have retained this in English. Similarly the demands of rhyme and metre mean that filler phrases such as 'por l'or de Montpellier' or 'cheval d'Orkenie' appear frequently; again I have retained them as an integral part of the text.

Two particular terms have a significance all of their own in the text: *chétifs* and . They describe two groups who arguably counterbalance each other in the text: the aristocratic captives and the ruffianly followers of the King of the Tafurs. They are at opposite ends of the social scale: yet both end up redeemed through the power of Crusade.

For obvious reasons the word '*chétifs*' is central to the text which bears its name. Its central meaning is that of a captive. Around these are connotations of shame, defeat and low status.[8] The *chétifs* here are captives, literally; they are losers because they have suffered the shame of defeat; and at least at the start of the text they are the underdogs labouring in Saracen prisons with no obvious means of escape. There is no word in modern English which comes close to this lexical field. The Old English and Shakespearean 'caitiffs' is close, but brings an unwanted air of archaism with it.[9] The very modern English 'losers' captures much of the meaning but is a bit too reminiscent of a football crowd. With some reluctance I have therefore retained the Old French *chétif*.[10]

Similar considerations apply to the word '' or '*ribalts*'. This means a general hooligan and ruffian. In a military context it acquires additional overtones both of

---

[7] J. Flori, 'Lexicologie et société médiévale: les "barons" de la première croisade (Etude des termes "baron", "barnage", "barné", baronie" dans la *Chanson d'Antioche*)', *Actes du XIe congrès international de la Société Rencesvals, Barcelone, 22–27 août 1988*, (Barcelona, 1990), pp. 245–73.

[8] For modern French see *Le Grand Robert de la langue française*, P. Robert and A. Rey, 9 vols, (Paris, 1985), vol. 2 p. 549: 'chétif' is glossed as 'de faible constitution ... . sans valeur'.

[9] *Measure for Measure* II.i: 'O thou caitiff! O thou varlet! O thou wicked Hannibal!'

[10] Not completely without precedent in modern English however. See the Alan Clark Diaries: *In Power 1983–92*, 3 vols, (London, 1994) vol. 2 p. 285, entry for Sunday 4 March: 'G. Howe is behaving "poorly", *chétif* and unsupportive'.

a mercenary and those at the bottom of the social scale, scrounging a violent and deprived existence on the fringes of the army. In some texts they are blamed for behaviour the rest of the army would rather disavow: thus in the Occitan *Canso de la Crozada* it is the '', also described as 'tafurs' and 'arlot', who are responsible for the sack of Béziers and the murder of its inhabitants.[11] In the *Jérusalem* these forces are led by the King of the Tafurs and clearly overlap with, if not being identical with, the Tafurs. Again there is no term in English which comes close, and I have chosen to retain the French term *ribalt*.

There are a few references to *jongleurs* in the text. Again this is a key concept which has no modern English equivalent and I have chosen to retain the Old French.

With some misgivings I have also used the terms Crusade and Crusaders. These would certainly not have been recognised by those on the First Crusade and did not pass into general currency until much later.[12] I have used them here for the convenience of a modern audience.

To quote Bellos again, 'when we say a translation is an acceptable one, what we name is an overall relationship between source and target that is neither identity, nor equivalence, nor analogy – just that complex thing called a good match'. My aim has been to provide a good match to encourage modern readers to venture into a thirteenth-century universe.[13]

---

[11] *Canso de la Crozada*, laisses 20 and 21.
[12] C. J. Tyerman, *The Invention of the Crusades* (Basingstoke and London, 1998) pp. 49–55.
[13] Bellos, *Amazing Adventure*, pp. 335–6.

PART II
Translations

Plot Summaries

The *Chanson des Chétifs*

Prologue (laisses 1–8)

Corbaran of Oliferne, the leader of the Turkish forces defeated at Antioch, returns to the capital of his overlord the Sultan of Persia at Sarmasane. He was entrusted with the safekeeping of the Sultan's son Brohadas. However Brohadas was killed in the battle and his body has been brought back with great ceremony. The Sultan is furious and accuses Corbaran of treachery. The King of Nubia stands up for him unsuccessfully. Corbaran's uncle Brudalans suggests that Corbaran should be brought in front of the Sultan to plead his own case: this is done.

Episode 1: the judicial duel (laisses 9 – 51)

This episode focuses on Richard of Chaumont. Corbaran has been condemned to a judicial duel. He must bring one Christian knight to fight two Turkish champions to prove Corbaran's innocence. Back in Oliferne the Christians taken prisoner at the battle of Civetot are suffering under harsh treatment in captivity. Calabra, Corbaran's mother, has something of a weakness for Richard of Chaumont. She recommends him to Corbaran as the ideal champion. Richard agrees to fight on condition that all the *chétifs* are freed. Corbaran accepts. The *chétifs* are promptly freed from prison and well treated, particularly Richard whom Calabra is eyeing up as breeding stock. An extra two laisses describing Calabra's divination with a magic cloth are inserted after laisse 24 in most manuscripts. Corbaran then returns to Sarmasane with Richard and the *chétifs*. A last attempt to avoid the duel fails. Richard slays both his opponents, the Turks Sorgalé and Golias. Corbaran and the Sultan have a tearful reconciliation.

The relatives of the dead Saracens however do not share in the general rejoicing. Sorgalé's relatives, led by Lyon of the Mountain, want to avenge his death. They leave Sarmasane and set an ambush for Corbaran. Meanwhile in a parallel attempt at vengeance Arfulan, one of the sons of Golias, tries to assassinate Richard at a banquet. Having failed, he too leaves to set an ambush for Corbaran and combines forces with Lyon of the Mountain. Corbaran leaves Sarmasane. However he is forewarned in a dream about the ambush. His men duly attack and defeat the rebels. He and the *chétifs* return to Sarmasane to recover.

The Cainan episode is inserted after laisse 40 in manuscript B, immediately after Arfulan's attempted assassination of Richard.

Episode 2: the defeat of the Sathanas (laisses 52 – 103)

This episode focuses on Baldwin of Beauvais. Corbaran and the *chétifs* make another attempt to leave Sarmasane and again things do not go according to plan. This time they are caught in a whirling storm and lose their way. They find themselves at the Mont Tigris. This is the home of a terrible dragon called, symbolically, Sathanas.

Meanwhile King Abraham, in whose domain Mont Tigris is to be found, is due to send his annual tribute to the Sultan. He too has Christian captives. One of them is Baldwin's brother Ernoul who is given the mission of delivering the tribute. Ernoul sets out with a donkey loaded with treasure. He loses his way near the mountain, and is attacked and eaten by the Sathanas.

Baldwin was near the mountain at the time with Corbaran and hears Ernoul's screams. Despite Corbaran's reluctance, Baldwin insists on going up the mountain to avenge his brother, carrying a talisman given to him by the abbot of Fécamp. It is a hard climb. When he reaches the top he finds the Sathanas. With the aid of the talisman he is able to kill the beast, exorcising the demon inside it.

The bellows of rage as he attacks are enough to convince Corbaran that Baldwin too has been killed. The *chétifs* are not so convinced. They leave the wounded to guard the camp and make their way up the mountain. Corbaran reluctantly follows. At the top they find not only a live Baldwin but a dragon's lair full of treasure.

Meanwhile an army led by the Sultan is approaching. This is in response to a call from King Abraham for help against the Sathanas. Corbaran sees the army from the mountain and is sure they are the hostile force of Arfulan and Lyon. Once he realises who they are there is general rejoicing. Baldwin's feat is recognised. Corbaran continues on his way to Oliferne with the *chétifs* and the Sultan returns home to Sarmasane.

The 'Sathanas mère' episode is inserted after laisse 99 in manuscripts B and I, at the point where Corbaran and the Sultan meet.

Episode 3: Corbaran's nephew (laisses 104 – 28)

This episode features Harpin of Bourges. Out for a ride, he passes a group of boys enjoying the cool of the river. They are watched by Corbaran's nephew. At this point a wolf appears, snatches the boy and disappears into the forest. Harpin follows.

A large monkey seizes the boy and climbs a tree with him. He spends the night there. Harpin spends an equally uncomfortable night under the tree, warding off an attack by four lions by invoking St Jerome. The following morning the monkey tries to get away but drops the child in the attempt and Harpin rescues him.

The boy's trials are not at an end. A band of robbers now descend, seize him and attack Harpin. When Harpin explains who the boy is, matters worsen: the robbers are no friends of Corbaran, whom they claim has exiled them and taken their lands, and they are delighted at the opportunity to lay hands on his nephew. However Corbaran has been guided to the lair by three white stags: these are St

George, St Barbara and St Domitian in disguise. The robbers retreat into their surprisingly luxurious lair. Corbaran negotiates for the return of his nephew and the robbers make their peace with him.

Epilogue: the chétifs rejoin the Crusade (laisses 129–39)

Corbaran loads the *chétifs* with gifts and they receive a special farewell from Calabra. They agree to make their way to Jerusalem to help the Crusaders and to see the Holy City. They make their way there via the Red Cistern, meeting en route a force of 140 Turks on a mission from Jerusalem to seek help from the Arabs. There is a fight and only one Turk survives. He makes his way back to Cornumarant, and the King of Jerusalem, to tell him the news. The king is playing chess but soon stops on hearing the news. He and their 50,000 Saracens in Jerusalem prepare to fight.

The *Chanson de Jérusalem*

The journey to Jerusalem (laisses 1–30)

This section acts as a link to take the Crusaders to Jerusalem, to provide a context for the return of the *chétifs* from Oliferne and to introduce the key Saracen figures of the poem Corbadas and Cornumarant. The Crusaders arrive at Jerusalem but suffer an initial attack from Corbadas, the King of Jerusalem, and his son Cornumarant. The poem opens with the Crusaders first seeing Jerusalem from afar. They are however immediately attacked by Corbadas and Cornumarant. The *chétifs* appear on the horizon. The main army at first thinks they are Saracens and help is summoned from Raymond of St-Gilles. However Godfrey rides up to the newcomers and quickly establishes who they are: there is clear symbolism in it being he who welcomes them back. In the ensuing battle the leading *chétifs* Richard, Harpin, Baldwin, John of Alis and the Bishop of Forez all display their skills in combat. The Saracens retreat and the Crusaders regroup at La Mahomerie.

Bohemond now arrives. He carries out a night raid to seize the herds from Caesarea and Haifa. The Saracens fight back with reinforcements from Ascalon and Jaffa. The Crusaders are pushed back to Lydda: appropriately St George, who has a basilica there, appears with an army of saints and angels. The inevitable Christian victory follows, and the celestial intervention cements the reintegration of the *chétifs* into the Crusade. It is stressed that Bohemond shares out the plunder.

The siege of Jerusalem (laisses 31 – 129)

The Crusaders look out over Jerusalem, and Peter the Hermit describes the city. There is initial enthusiasm for an immediate assault by Peter, Thomas of Marle and Robert of Flanders. Bohemond counsels against; Tancred for; Hugh points out that siege machines will be needed; and Godfrey agrees, already playing the role of leader. The Crusaders set up camps all the way round the city, one leader at each gate, and agree how supplies should be shared.

Corbadas seeks aid from Cornumarant, who is dismissive of the Christians' chances of success. In a noteworthy exploit Godfrey shoots down three kites, impaling them on a single arrow. Both sides see this as a presage of the fall of the city. A night-time sortie by Cornumarant is fought off by Harpin.

The first assault takes place the following morning. The engineers Nicolas and Gregoire set up mangonels and the Crusaders are blessed by the Bishop of Mautran who wields the Holy Lance. There is a description of the heroic entry Thomas of Marle will later make into Jerusalem and his encounter with a Bedouin woman. Godfrey gives a squadron to the *chétifs* and the King of the Tafurs leads the first assault. He is wounded and healed again in double quick time. The main attack is launched and St Stephen's Gate is damaged. The first up into Jerusalem is Gontier of Aire, who in the Antioche captured the fabulous horse Faburs; his hand is cut off and he falls down. The siege tower is set on fire. Clearly the tide is turning against the Christians and the first assault is called off.

The siege continues with skirmish and counter-skirmish. Bohemond ambushes a supply convoy led by Garsien, who converts to Christianity; those who do not apostatise are killed by the Tafurs and their bodies catapulted into Jerusalem. Corbadas maltreats 14 prisoners. Lucabel suggests that carrier pigeons should be sent with a message seeking help. All but three are shot; falcons force them to the ground, where the Christians change their message to one saying that no support is required. Ysoré intercepts the pigeons and says he is sending help anyway; the Bishop of Mautran sabotages this too. This plunges Corbadas into despair.

There is now a second attack, led again by the Tafurs. This time Enguerrand of St-Pol is first up the ladders but is fought back by Cornumarant. The Normans and Bretons also fail. In a bizarre swap Wicher the Swabian and Eurvin of Creel are hooked up onto the battlements and throw Malcolon and Ysabart of Barbais down from the ramparts. Eventually Ysabart and Malcolon are set free in return for Wicher, Eurvin, the 14 prisoners and a large ransom. The Saracens burn the ladders, battering ram and siege towers.

In an echo of Sansadoine's mission in the *Antioche*, Cornumarant slips out at night to seek help from the Sultan, pursued by Godfrey. They make contact with Baldwin of Edessa. There is a fight with the Saracens led by Cornumarant and Orquenais. Outnumbered, Baldwin tells his forces to hide in an old fort whilst he shelters in a reed bed. This turns out to be a bad move as the reed bed is infested with leeches which wriggle in through his chain mail and bite him like pepper. Cornumarant sets fire to the reeds and Baldwin is saved by divine intervention and the arrival of Godfrey. Cornumarant reaches the Sultan at Hamadan and is promised a relief force.

The fall of Jerusalem (laisse 130 – 144)

The Bishop of Mautran tells the Crusaders of a hermit on the Mount of Olives who can give them good advice. As indeed he does, telling them where to find a supply of timber to make new siege machines. There is a fresh attack on Jerusalem in which the Tafurs are prominent; Thomas of Marle swears homage to their king to ensure he is allowed to join in the first assault. Night falls and the attack is abandoned. The Tafurs mine the wall. The following day is a Friday. The Crusaders break through the wall. As prophesied earlier, Thomas of Marle is flung over the ramparts from the spear points of his men and meets a woman who prophesies his later death at the hands of his lord. The Crusaders now let the rest of the army in and a massacre follows. The only ones to escape buy protection from Raymond of St Gilles in the Tower of David, reminiscent of the Saracens who sought refuge in the citadel at Antioch.

Godfrey, Thomas and Robert of Flanders make it a priority to purify the Holy Sepulchre, restoring sight to a blind man with the cloth they used. The Saracen corpses are burned, plunder ensues; and Corbadas surrenders his redoubt in the Tower of David in exchange for safe conduct.

The defence of Jerusalem (laisses 145 – 213)

The Bishop of Mautran suggests that it is time a king was elected. Godfrey initially declines. So do Robert of Flanders, Robert of Normandy, Bohemond and Hugh. In some desperation the bishop suggests a fast and vigil. In a ritual reminiscent of the lighting of the Holy Fire in the Church of the Holy Sepulchre, each candidate is to hold a candle: the one whose candle is lit by God should be king. At midnight Godfrey's candle is struck by lightning. He is crowned by the Tafur King with a crown of leaves.

The barons now decide to return to the west despite the remonstrances of Godfrey. Only the Tafurs, Raymond, Baldwin and Eustace remain. The others proceed to the Lake of Galilee, then receive a divine message telling them to return to Jerusalem and help Godfrey. Meanwhile Cornumarant returns from Hamadan and joins up with his father at Barbais. The Saracens launch a first attack on Jerusalem: Raymond of St Giles is captured and Baldwin captures Cornumarant. There is a further battle where intervention by the saints gives the Christians enough time to escape back into Jerusalem. The Sultan's army is now on the move. Godfrey catches Marbrin and envoys come to negotiate a release: this provides an opportunity to intimidate the Saracens by using the Tafurs in rotation to form an endless procession. Cornumarant is now released in return for Raymond.

The Sultan now moves his army up to the plains of Ramleh. He attempts to tempt the Crusaders out with a display of treasure, a motif familiar from Revelations; Godfrey forbids the Christians to touch it and the stratagem fails. In further skirmishing Peter the Hermit is taken prisoner and brought before the Sultan. The Sultan's doctor cures his wounds and Peter pretends, under some pressure, to apostatise. This inspires the Sultan to demand that Godfrey too should convert: he sends a messenger with a very expensive horse in another and futile attempt to distract the Christians. Godfrey repeats the Tafur trick with the envoy. He reciprocates the demand for apostasy by demanding that his captive Marbrin apostatise; on his refusal there is a single combat with Godfrey, who receives two blows unharmed then repeats his feat from the *Antioche* of cutting horse and rider in half. A further attack on Jerusalem is thwarted when night falls. Godfrey spends the night in vigil in the Holy Sepulchre: in something of a repetition of the previous miracle, a dove lights the candles and is found to be carrying a letter announcing the return of the other Crusaders.

The battle of Ascalon (laisses 214–74)

In a move more reminiscent of thirteenth-century warfare than the First Crusade, a time and place is fixed for battle with the Sultan; the plains of Ramleh on the following Friday.

The day of battle dawns. The marching out of the squadrons is described to the Sultan by Peter the Hermit in much the same way as Amidelis describes them to Corbaran before the battle of Antioch: in order Godfrey, Robert of Normandy, Robert of Flanders, Hugh, Bohemond and Tancred, Rotrou of La Perche, Stephen of Blois with the Count of Vendôme and Stephen of Albemarle, and the St-Pols march out. Jerusalem is guarded by priests, women and old men with the Bishop of Forez. The Sultan in turn leads out an army of a somewhat exaggerated five million. The battle begins with Godfrey killing the son of the Sultan, then becomes a series of single combats by the leaders and by Thomas of Marle. Enguerrand is killed and avenged by his father. The Tafurs put to flight a horde of beaked monsters. Holy relics help hold the Saracens off and turn their Greek fire back on them.

The Sultan now arms and fights back. Corbadas is killed by Bohemond and Lucabel by Tancred. Cornumarant, enraged by the sight of his father's body, massacres the Christians. The relics again come to the rescue. The focus moves to Richard of Chaumont and Baldwin of Beauvais in battle. The Count of Vendôme is killed. Baldwin of Boulogne kills Cornumarant.

Disaster looms for the Christians. It is averted by the arrival of the inevitable army of saints led by St George, which rescues Peter the Hermit. The Saracens flee, firing their tents; God shortens the night to aid the Christian pursuit. Peter kills Salehadin. Baldwin and Raimbaut Creton are cut off near Acre and rescued by Godfrey.

The battle is won. The Crusaders acquire the treasure; Enguerrand is buried to huge lamentation from Hugh; and as before the plunder is distributed to rich and poor.

The aftermath (laisses 273- 81)

There is a council. The dead need to be disposed of: devils have taken away the Saracen corpses and a lion has assembled the Christian ones. The castles and towns around are garrisoned by Crusaders. A service is held for the dead and a post-mortem carried out on Cornumarant. The size of his heart amazes the Christians. He is then buried with honours outside Jerusalem.

The author comments that the story of the conquest of Jerusalem is at an end. Another volume will describe the capture of Acre, Tyre and Tiberias.

La Chanson des Chétifs

1

So Corbaran ran away across all the plains of Syria, taking only two kings along with him and carrying Brohadas, son of the Sultan of Persia. The noble and brave Duke Godfrey had killed [Brohadas] with his shining sword in battle outside Antioch.[1] The kings had not left him there; they wrapped him up inside a deer hide and put him on a Hungarian mule. They fled towards the Black Mountain, giving Edessa a wide berth and crossing the Euphrates without ship or galley. My lords, that is a river blessed by God which comes and flows and takes its origin from Paradise, from which the Lord God expelled Adam for his foolishness.[2] Once they reached the other side with its lush grass, they lifted the youth down from the good Russian mule and laid him down on his back on the flower-strewn grass. By God! How the brave King of Nubia mourned him. Corbaran of Oliferne wept over him, shouting and crying; whilst the King of Falerne sobbed bitterly, overcome by grief and hitting himself about the head.[3] Together the three of them presented a picture of complete despair. Corbaran wrung his hands and tore at his beard, lamenting him eloquently from the depths of his grief. 'Oh splendid youth, what a terrible end to your life! What will your gentle and beautiful mother do? Take her own life once she finds out, that is what she will do. She will kill herself from grief unless there is someone to kill her first. And your father the Sultan, our overlord, will have us all hanged when he realises you are not coming back'. He collapsed in a faint across the corpse, his face congested; once he came round all he could say was: 'I know for sure that neither Mahomed nor Termagant – let alone his magic – are worth one rotten apple. Anyone who worships you and prays to you is a miserable loser. Any god who forgets to look after his own men is completely worthless and has to be rejected as not worth even one sorb apple.[4] Now that God of the Franks really is a powerful lord. He looks after his people and helps them

---

[1] In the *Antioche* the Sultan of Persia had entrusted Corbaran with his son Brohadas; Brohadas is killed at Antioch and the Sultan's grief provides a plot motor for the trilogy.

[2] Biblical reference emphasising the position of the Crusade within the divine plan.

[3] Some element of parody: Saracens are figures of fun. But ritual displays of grief are found both in *chansons de geste* and in medieval real life: compare e.g. *Roland* lines 2415–22, where 20,000 of Charlemagne's knights swoon at the news of the defeat of Roncevaux and the whole court weeps bitterly. It is worth remembering that *chansons de geste* were performed rather than read, and Saracens could be made figures of fun by such exaggeration.

[4] 'Ne vaut une alie' is a standard phrase for saying something is worthless; a favourite of the author's, chosen to fit the rhyme. See p. 53 note 5 for discussion of what a sorb apple is.

properly'. 'Too true', said his companions. 'Our religion is a failure. All our gods put together are not worth as much as one sorb apple'.[5] 'It wouldn't take much to make me believe in Jesus, the son of Mary' [said another].

2

So the three kings had dismounted in the meadow above the waters of the Euphrates, as I have explained, a holy river blessed by God. When they had finished mourning over and lamenting their lord Brohadas for his shrewdness and bravery and considerable generosity, they lashed him on a dromedary. The three kings, heavily armed, got back on their horses, which were fed and watered; they made their way straight towards Sarmasane, spurring on and making such good speed, as if hurried on their way by demons and devils, that within the space of one month they reached the Silver Bridge, which they passed and pushed on to the capital city Sarmasane. There they found the royal Sultan with his forces. All the Turks of Coroscane had assembled there to celebrate in style the feast of St John, whom they held in great honour.[6] Corbaran made his entry in the middle of the service. He laid down the youth's body and took off his armour in the very centre of Sarmasane under the branches of a pine tree. More than 20,000 Turks came crowding up to him, desperate to hear what had happened. They hurried Corbaran in front of the royal Sultan. On seeing him the Sultan addressed him in these words: 'Well, my noble friend Corbaran, what has kept you? Have you brought Bohemond along with you? Godfrey of Bouillon and the noble Tancred? Robert of Normandy, whose praises everyone sings me? Thomas of La Fère with his pennon raised? Lord Hugh of Vermandois in all his pride? What about all the nobility of Christendom, each one chained round the neck?' 'Well no, my Lord, not quite. By Mahomed, we have had a terrible time of it. We are completely defeated, finished and in disarray. The French nobles were all assembled in front of Antioch in orderly ranks, each one splendidly armed and helmeted. By Mahomed, even if you had been there with all your soldiers, and had with you all those ever born, and the dead had been brought out of their graves, their onslaught still couldn't have been borne or resisted. They chased us so hard, not turning aside for a moment, that we only managed to escape with the greatest difficulty. I have brought back your son Brohadas with me, dead. You can see him lying over there, under the branches of that pine'. When the Sultan heard this, he nearly went mad. He seized a finely shaped and feathered sharp dart. In his rage he took careful aim and flung and threw it viciously straight at Corbaran. The king ducked to the right next to a striped marble pillar and the dart whistled past his ribs. It struck a pillar with such force that it made a dent six inches deep. Had it hit [Corbaran] he would have been

---

[5] Standard topos in the *chanson de geste*: Saracens reject their gods for perceived failure. Compare *Roland* lines 2580–91.

[6] This is the 24th June. It is not clear why Saracens should venerate St John in particular.

dead on the spot. The emir fainted dead away. Four kings in crowns hoisted him up by the arms. They went over to mourn the youth where he lay on a marble slab.

3

The Sultan mourned his son Brohadas to the full, and so did the counts and the marquis and the King of Damascus. There were plenty from the race of Judas with him, and the high-ranking lords from his abundant entourage. He spoke of his grief in no uncertain terms. 'Listen, my lords', he said, 'I am the picture of complete misery. See, here is my handsome son lying dead beneath those sheets. Take them off him so I can take him in my arms and see his body for myself: that way I will know whether this is really true. I cannot bring myself to believe that he is dead or defeated'. A Turk called Dionas went forward and uncovered the body which lay beneath the sheets. When the Sultan saw it, he fell over backwards in a dead faint. Two kings picked him up, one from Euffras and the other one called Solins, son of Dinas. Once the Sultan had recovered his grief was unbounded. He lamented as follows: 'Apollon! Sathanas! You are hopeless gods and you are cowards! Look what a bad job you have done of looking after this, my son! As long as I live you will not be getting any more golden crowns from me and you will not be worshipped anywhere in my kingdom. All the gods know, and so does lady Pallas, that now the image of Aeneas is killed and defeated; and in my turn I shall die for him as is only fitting and proper.[7] May Mahomed bring evil on the one who struck those blows. I shall never be happy again, but spend my life a miserable and broken man'.

4

The Sultan saw his child and began to weep, tearing his hair and tugging at his beard. He collapsed in a dead faint over the body, completely overcome by grief. Nobody could do justice to the grief shown by the sweet-faced Queen Eublastris. Had you been there, you would have heard the grief of princes and emirs. You would have heard howls of misery in the valley of Sarmasane, with women and girls, poor knights and squires lamenting the young man they all loved so much, his shrewdness and his bravery and indeed the generous gifts he used to give them, horses, palfreys and cloaks to wear: they were not easily going to get another lord like that. They had the body anointed with very rich unguent and wrapped up in a golden shroud; then they had it carried to the place right in front of Tervagant. Had you been there you could have seen how the incense-burners smoked and the chandeliers, candles and lamps glimmered. The light illuminated their Mass

---

[7] A very rare classical reference in the trilogy. The meaning appears to be that Brohadas is like Ascanius, the son of Aeneas though there is no obvious parallel to this situation.

beautifully. The offertory was so big that nobody could count it all. You might have seen more than 7,000 bezants being flung down into the square to clear a way through the crowd. They had the body laid to rest in front of Tervagant, and had a superbly rich tomb cast for it in gold and silver. The Apostolic Caliph began a sermon: 'Let anyone who already has ten wives give some thought to procreating – that is how we will increase our numbers to fight the Christians. The children who result will be a redoubtable force. Let me tell you: they will avenge us on the Franks, those accursed people who want to prove our religion wrong'. No need to ask whether the Sultan was sunk in grief; had you been there you would have heard him in agonies of lamentation for his child Brohadas, weeping and wailing. 'Handsome son', said the emir, 'who will be able to rule this whole kingdom which should have been yours once I am gone? It is Corbaran who has orchestrated your death to deprive me of my heir! If he cannot defend himself from this accusation in a trial and through such reparation as is judged by my peers, I shall have him burned to ashes and scattered in the wind!' Queen Eublastris had the captives summoned from hard manual labour dragging ploughs along. 1,700 were thus released; she had them led along to the Temple of Solomon for the soul of the child she loved so dearly.

5

The cries died down and the noise abated. The Emir of Persia got to his feet and made a loud proclamation, his voice being heard clearly. 'My lords', said the Sultan, 'let me come straight to the point. By Mahomed my god, to whom you all pray, it is Corbaran who has betrayed all my people and left them dead, sold them for money and treated them appallingly. I rue the day I accepted his love and affection – he held my whole realm in stewardship for me. If he cannot defend himself against the great crime [of which he is accused], I shall have him burned alive in a cauldron of boiling water or hanged on high, make no mistake. He cannot be audacious enough to contradict me given that he is responsible for the death of my powerful force of knights, and of my son Brohadas whose soul has departed, and for the destruction and utter defeat of my huge army'. The powerful King of Nubia replied to this effect.

6

The powerful King of Nubia replied to the Sultan: 'By Mahomed, noble sir, you are wrong about Corbaran! I watched him laying about him with his Saragossan sword so hard that not one plank of his shield was left intact; I watched his tent and pavilion brought down in the fighting. Turks, Hungarians and Persians, the best of the Saracens and Samaritans all met their end there; you have lost part of what was best in your kingdom from the city of Antioch all the way to Jerusalem. Now you need to pray to Mahomed and your god Tervagant to defend you from a greater loss this year. All these Christians here are exceptionally brave. When they put on their mailed hauberks and unsheathe their swords forged by Wayland, their blades cut more cleanly than any knife from Cordoba.[8] Not even 30 Turks would be enough to make one of them turn tail and flee'. 'Silence, you son of a whore!' was the Sultan's response.

7

The Sultan spoke, very out of sorts. He was highly upset about his losses and had gone pale. 'Alas, King of Nubia, what were you on about? Are you telling me that even a well-armed Christian would not retreat as much as a couple of yards if faced with 20 Turks? If that is so, then all the lands as far as the Frozen Sea will be theirs. Let me tell you the truth about how things have worked out. Antioch was taken suffering from famine: a Turk betrayed it to them early one morning. They came to seek my help – that is proven truth. So I assembled my Turks from all across my dominions, and gave command to my counsellor Corbaran. Now it appears that [the whole army] has perished and everything has gone horribly wrong and my son Brohadas has had his head cut off and Red Lion has been decapitated.[9] Pagandom is a shameful laughing stock: by contrast Christendom is thriving and respected – that villainous race whom we have never feared before. It is my belief that he [Corbaran] is the one who has betrayed us and sold us and handed us over. If he cannot put up a sufficiently good defence in front of me I will exact justice in accordance with my powers and have him hanged or boiled to death in a big cauldron'. The Sultan's words were listened to with rapt attention; all the pagans were silent and backed away discreetly with the exception of the noble Brudalans: he spoke up with robust common sense.

8

Brudalans was very noble, courtly and eloquent; he got to his feet and spoke very persuasively. 'My lord', he said to the king, 'in your generosity have my nephew Corbaran summoned before you. He will be well able to defend himself against these accusations'. The others chimed in in support: 'Yes, sire, do! If he runs away from your court then let him be brought back as of right; any other action would be foolishness'. 'Go and bring him here', replied the Sultan. One of those present went running off to find Corbaran, who was ready and waiting. The king gave him a hard stare. 'Listen to my side of the story, sire', said Corbaran. 'By rights

---

[8] The Norse figure Wayland the Smith. He is referred to in this capacity in other *chansons de geste*: compare e.g. *Raoul de Cambrai* line 489.

[9] A summary of the events recounted in the *Antioche*. The city was betrayed by Datien. Red Lion, one of the main Saracen leaders, is killed by Robert of Normandy at laisse 357 of the *Antioche*.

I deserve high honours from you. It was at your command that I went far off to unknown lands and found myself up against the Franks in battle. It so fell out that I was defeated and your son Brohadas found his death; that is a grievous loss which can never be made good. By Mahomed my god and in good faith, my grief was all for you and I wish I had died then and there. I am being arraigned by you for mortal treason. I give you my pledge and you can be completely assured that I will clear myself of this charge. My champion will not be of our faith but a Christian who will fight alone against two Turks of high reputation and valour to prove that I am innocent of the charges brought against me'.

9

These were the words of Corbaran. He was desperately upset, terrified that he was going to die and petrified by the sharp and finely crafted dart which had been thrown. He said to his sovereign the Sultan: 'I used to be your close companion. I have been on the receiving end of trouble and numerous blows for your sake. This is the reward I get for all my pains: I should have been struck down by that dart had Mahomed so wished. But now I ask you to give me leave for long enough for me to be trusted to go to the Holy Sepulchre and back.[10] There I shall seek out some of those I fought and I shall bring back a particularly brave specimen. Meanwhile you will hunt out from your lands two carefully chosen Turks – the strongest, bravest and noblest to be had. My champion will fight them; let it be lawfully demonstrated that I have always shown you loyalty. But if he fails to leave them cowering and defeated on the field of battle, let my land be confiscated and I myself hanged by the neck'. The Sultan replied judiciously: 'I give you my solemn word that there will be no double dealing. If your champion can overcome the two Turks and leave them defeated, he will be allowed to leave a free man and go back to whence he came. Meanwhile you will be absolved and freed from my displeasure. Let the day be fixed six weeks hence'. A hubbub rose in the room. People said: 'Corbaran, you are totally mad. You will be utterly confounded'.

10

So the terms were accepted and the day fixed on which one Christian would fight against two armed Turks. Corbaran proved himself wise and honourable by handing over hostages to the Sultan. Then he confirmed the Sultan's wishes: 'If the Christian wins, he will not be attacked but will be allowed to go as a free man back to where he came from. You will be absolved and pardoned for your sins by Mahomed'. Corbaran took his leave and did not hang around; he took the two kings of Nubia along with him. They mounted their swift eager warhorses and galloped

---

[10] Corbaran presupposes that the Crusaders have already taken Jerusalem though he left them at Antioch.

eagerly all the way to the splendid city of Oliferne where Corbaran was acclaimed as king and lord. His arrival in the town was met with great rejoicing, with drums played up and down the streets; Mahomed was worshipped and celebrated that day. As Corbaran went into the hall ready to climb the stairs, he met his adoring mother; her name was Calabra, niece of Josué, and she was expert in necromancy and the casting of lots. She was old and shaggy, a good 200 years of age. She flung her arms round Corbaran, welcoming him with a shower of kisses and hugs: she had been waiting impatiently for him. 'My handsome son', said the old woman, 'I know what has been happening where you have been. You were lucky not to have been killed at the court by a razor-sharp dart which was flung at you. If Mahomed hadn't been at hand, you would have been a dead man'. 'Madam', said Corbaran, 'that is indeed the case. But how on earth do you know all this so quickly?'[11]

11

'My handsome son', said Calabra, 'I can see from your expression that things are not going well between you and the noble sovereign the Sultan. He is angry about what he has lost and his heart aches; he is angry about his men and angrier stillabout his child. Now you are on your way to the Sepulchre to find a Christian who will fight two Turks at the emir's court. But your quarry is full of captive Christians. If you need one, why look any further afield?' This advice was to Corbaran's liking. The old woman stood immobile on the hillside. She had a wide forehead and iron-grey hair; there was a hand's breadth between her eyes; there was no wiser woman all the way to the Orient. She held a cane which was made of ivory with two golden buttons, one in front and one behind, where she could loop a strap when she was riding.[12] They rode up to the prison with 30 knights. They called for the gaoler, a despotic type called Faramon. He lashed the captives with his heavy strap. They wept and wailed, lamenting bitterly and crying: 'In God's mercy, why are we still alive?'[13] Picture the scene: the gaoler sidling up to the lady. 'Faramon, come forward!' she ordered. 'Goodness me: what on earth is the matter with those captives?' 'Well, Madam, I beat them because they were annoying me. Yesterday when they were working on that wall in front of you on that old postern in front of that fast-flowing river, they killed one of the masons with the sharp

---

[11] This reminds us that Calabra has powers of divination. The dialogue is reminiscent of the similar episode at laisses 277–83 of the *Antioche*.

[12] The Old French appears to say 'flesh of children', which sounds highly unlikely; there are several variants which suggests that the scribes were also uncertain about the meaning. Susan Edgington suggests that Myers' reading 'car d'enfant' should be taken as 'cor d'elefans' which makes considerably more sense even though hypermetric and which I have adopted. Ivory croziers are well attested: see for example the twelfth-century St Nicholas crozier of the Victoria and Albert Museum.

[13] The author lays stress on the humiliated state of the *chétifs* to make the point that they can be redeemed even from this level of abjection.

end of a hammer because he was applying a bit of discipline and making them sweat'.[14] 'That is of no concern to me', said Calabra. 'In the name of my god Tervagant, bring them over there for me in front of Corbaran. He wants to talk to them and tell them what he wants'. 'My lady', said Faramon, 'your lightest wish is my command'. He went back over to the quarry and addressed the prisoners as follows: 'My god, what a bunch of pathetic losers and captives you are. This is your last day on earth. Corbaran has come from the mighty city of Antioch where he took a relieving army for the noble and royal Sultan. That was where Saracens and Persians, Hungarians and Bulgars and Paulicians went to their deaths. So did Brohadas, son of the emir, and Red Lion who was such a supporter of ours; my lord Corbaran left in full flight. He has sent me word via his mother that he wants you all brought; if you ask me he intends to exact vengeance on you. You will be strung up at the archery butts to serve as target practice for children and the best of the Turcoples and anyone else who can string a bow properly; and after that you will all be burnt to a crisp in a roaring fire'. At this count Harpin (who had previously fought so hard that blood had streaked his body from head to feet), lord John of Alis, Fulcher of Melun and the noble-hearted Richard of Chaumont said: 'We no longer want to live under these conditions. We shall go to martyrdom contented, joyful and happy. May God receive our souls as he rightly commands, because our bodies will suffer horribly as we die'.[15] Faramon bent down to raise the barrier and unlock the jail. The prisoners shuffled out. The Germans sang the *Kyrie Eleison* as they walked; the clerics and bishops recited the *Miserere*; and the rest said the *Te Deum Laudamus*. They had fetters on their arms which made it hard to move; each had a heavy shackle hanging round his neck and the chains of their fetters dangled from their belts. They made their way out past the large palace in a line, terrified they were going to die and have their heads cut off. The Saracens watched and went pale.

12

So our captives were brought to the palace chained together in a long line.[16] They had shackles on their arms which heavily restricted their movements; their

---

[14] Recounted in laisses 135–6 of manuscript B of the *Antioche*. The scene of captives working in quarries and an overseer being killed has some resemblance with the story of Moses: Exodus 2:11–16. Other texts compare the Crusaders to the Israelites: see e.g. RM I.1, II.16, IV.8, VI.12.

[15] Martyrdom for death on Crusade was promised on the First Crusade and is a standard topos. See e.g. *GF* 40, 'in caelum ascenderunt et candidatam stolam martyrii receperunt'; H. E. Cowdrey 'Martyrdom and the First Crusade', *Crusade and settlement: papers read at the first conference of the SSCLE and presented to R. C. Smail*, (ed.) Peter Edbury (Cardiff, 1985) pp. 46–56.

[16] The souls of the damned going to Hell are also routinely depicted in this way: see e.g. the portal of St-Trophime at Arles and the carvings by the Regensburg master in the

shoulders were bowed under the weight of carrying so much iron; and their skin and flesh were chafed by the bonds. They had gone through so much suffering that they were all half-dead with hunger and loss of liberty. Ah God! There were so many valiant knights, noble bishops and clerks in holy orders, all brought there from the mountain at Civetot when Peter the Hermit's army was defeated.[17] None had breeches or shirt; they were in a wretchedly poor state. They were bald because their heads had been shaven. Without shoes or hose their feet were in a terrible state, split down to the bone and with gaping wounds and sores. Let me tell you this: no man ever made by God could have looked at them and not felt pity. Terrified of their coming death, they all had their heads bowed. When Corbaran saw them in this state, he wept in compassion.

13

Corbaran of Oliferne acted in a most praiseworthy fashion. Tears pricked his eyes as he looked at our Christians; he tore his hair and beard because he had no idea where he was going to find this Christian who would fight two Turks and thereby save his life. His lord the royal Sultan, who had arraigned him for mortal treason, wanted to cut off his head because he simply could not bring himself to believe in his heart that a race had been born which could achieve such a victory, destroy such a huge army and defeat such a prince. The fact that Corbaran was right could not be ignored even if he never uttered the significant words which had terrified the Sultan. Corbaran said to his mother:

'I have no reason to hang around here. I shall go to Antioch to negotiate with Bohemond and with that author of noble deeds Duke Godfrey; I shall throw myself on the mercy of Robert of Normandy.[18] If one of those three comes to fight my case for me and win the battle, I will swear a solemn oath heavily guaranteed and backed by hostages; I shall have myself baptised as a mark of my respect for him; and I shall restore Jerusalem where they long to go and along with it the Holy Sepulchre they are so desperate to liberate'.[19]

---

cathedral at Worms. To depict the *chétifs* in this way underlines the message of redemption through Crusade: they are implicitly compared with the dead liberated by Christ in the Harrowing of Hell, and the text in fact underlines their nearness to death.

[17] Recounted at laisses 17–34 of the *Antioche*, and the first key episode in its account.

[18] Bohemond and Godfrey were obvious heroes to pick: Bohemond because of his renown as a Crusader and Godfrey as the first Advocate and later legendary hero. It is less obvious why Robert of Normandy should be singled out; this may reflect particular attention given to him in some Anglo-Norman sources for the Crusade. See Table of Names to the *Jérusalem* for references and discussion.

[19] The reference to baptism lays the groundwork for a later part of the Cycle, the *Chrétienté Corbaran*. See Introduction for further discussion. Here the author is clear that the Crusaders have not yet reached Jerusalem.

14

'My handsome son', said Calabra, 'do you really want to abase yourself like this? I'd rather have you plunge a large steel knife into me than hear you betraying your rightful lord in this way or renouncing Mahomed to worship Jesus. Now, why don't you take all these captives, have them unchained, properly dressed and given something to eat? If there should happen to be one amongst them who was proud and resolute enough and whose god would be capable of helping him to do battle for you, offer him a guarantee: they will have their liberty and a reward of a good palfrey and swift warhorse each plus 100,000 bezants of your purest gold'.[20]

15

'Madam', said Corbaran, 'let me tell you what I think. These captives in front of you are not worth as much as a glove. They are scrawny and pathetic; some are swollen with hunger; and they are as shaggy as beasts you might turn out to pasture. One small child on its own would be a match for twenty of them'. 'My handsome son', said the old woman, 'there is still one who has something about him. Yesterday he used the sharp end of a big hammer to kill a mason who was harassing and insulting him. Now in my view he has a proper heart about him'. 'Madam, which one is he?' 'Look, over there, the tallest one. He looks to me like a brave and determined knight except that he has spent too long behind bars and is pale because he has been ill and chained up'. Corbaran called the knight over and he came. He took off the knight's chain and heavy fetters, sat him down next to him and addressed him as follows.

16

Corbaran called him over and addressed him as follows. 'What is your name, my friend?' 'My lord, I will tell you straight away: I am called Richard, born in Chaumont, which belonged to King Charlemagne.[21] I was on my way to the Holy Sepulchre to seek mercy and forgiveness, and to see the grave of Christ, the place of His Resurrection and the holy Temple of Solomon. I was taken during the defeat of Peter the Hermit's army; your men brought me here and now I am your prisoner. I have served squires and pageboys repeatedly, cutting their grass and taking it back to their homes, and I have carried your stones, your lime and your sand. In return I have been struck over and over with rods and sticks, and had razor-sharp whips hit me and endless goads stuck into me all over my ribs

---

[20] I adopt the variant reading of 'iront' rather than 'riront'; the large number of variants on this line suggest that the scribes were equally puzzled.

[21] As elsewhere in the Cycle, the royal Carolingian antecedents of the Crusaders are emphasised: see e.g. laisse 300 of the *Antioche*, where he is identified as Godfrey's ancestor.

and my sides. Now I see our judgement approaching and I know we are all to die; to honour Jesus Christ, who suffered [for us], I would not shrink from being burnt to charcoal'. 'My friend', said Corbaran, 'nobody is expecting quite that of you. Let me explain to you what I need and why we are talking. I was at Antioch taking help to Garsion, with 700 times 60,000 knights and Red Lion, not counting the footsoldiers.[22] There we came upon the Christians, brave as lions. The princes and nobles took up arms against us: Robert of Normandy with Robert the Frisian, and the handsome-faced Thomas of La Fère, and Everard of Gournay and Droon of Moncy, Payen of Camelli and Gerard of the Donjon, and Roger of Rosoie who limps with one heel, Raymond of St-Gilles with Hugh of Vermandois, and the proudest set of noble followers ever seen; indeed there were so many princes that we cannot name them.[23] They flung our enormous army into complete disarray, and I turned tail and spurred away. I sought out the Sultan in his pride and villainy. I told him my news: my reward was to be treated as a coward; he tried to kill me with a dart without further ado. I had no choice in the matter: I was to set up a combat with one Christian so well armoured that he could take on two Turks and the Islamic religion. If you can do this in the manner described, you and your companions shall leave here free men: I shall have you conducted to the Temple of Solomon'. 'My lord', said Richard, 'this sounds pretty improbable. Someone who can defend himself against one person is much admired. Never mind: if you are happy we would like to take time to consider. We captives you see before you will consider the matter and let you know our views tomorrow morning'. 'Your request is granted', said Corbaran. That night they all ate to their hearts' content; their chains were taken off and their fetters removed.

17

Now day was fading and night approached. They were so terrified of death that not one of them slept. Richard was in the midst of them and spoke up. 'My lords, give me your advice in the name of God who never lies. Corbaran is asking me to do something unheard of. The royal Sultan hates him and came within a whisker of killing him: he flung a dart at him but missed. [He wants] an armed Christian beloved of God to fight two Turks or as it might be Arabs, showing his strength and bravery in a fight to the death. He is asking me to do it with my burnished steel sword. If I come out victorious, he has sworn to me on oath that all of us here will be freed: he will take us to the Temple built by Solomon'. When they heard this, the prisoners quivered with joy. They cried out in unison at the tops of their voices:

---

[22] Hugely exaggerated numbers are a staple of the *chanson de geste*: in the *Roland* the Kings Torleu and Dapamort bring together a force of 1.5million: lines 3216–19. 42 million is steep even so. See Jean Flori, 'Un problème de méthodologie; la valeur des nombres chez les chroniqueurs du Moyen Age (A propos des éffectifs de la première croisade)', *Moyen Age* 99 (1993) pp. 399–422.

[23] Familiar names from the *Antioche*.

'Richard, do battle – God will show us his mercy! If you do not, we are all dead men'. Richard acquiesced as any brave man would. Blessed be the mother who carried and nourished him, and the father who engendered him.

18

Count Harpin took up the argument. 'Richard, you come from noble stock. We have been in this impregnable prison for a very long time. We have suffered so much bad treatment; we have been persecuted; we have suffered so much from hunger and thirst, and felt it acutely. We are thin and weak, at the end of our tethers with being prisoners. My lord, noble knight, bring an end to our sufferings! For God's sake agree to join combat with the Turks. On the body of St Simeon, if you were not such an outstanding man and hadn't been the first to be called upon, I would not let anybody other than me do it'. Richard replied with measured eloquence: 'Ah! Harpin of Bourges, you have the heart of a lion; we have no better knight in this prison. If it be the will of God and the Virgin we shall join in battle, and I will fight to my utmost to save us all. May God who suffered on the Cross help me in this!' Harpin of Bourges heard this. He scowled. Full of the pride of a warrior, he gripped a stick so hard that he snapped it in two and sent the splinters flying. His heart leapt with emotion. If at that point he had been sitting fully armed on a Gascon warhorse, the Persians and Slavs would have had to pay dearly before being able to take him captive and throw him back into prison .

19

The *chétifs* were absolutely delighted at Richard's agreement to act as Corbaran's champion. Night drew to an end and dawn rose. Corbaran and his mother did not hang around. His mother marched up to Richard and asked him point-blank whether he had come to a decision on the combat. Richard replied that he would indeed do it: he would take on the two Turks for him, deliver him from the wrath of the Sultan and remove the threat to his life and possessions. Goodness me, Corbaran was absolutely overjoyed to hear this. He seized Richard and kissed him seven times. Undoing his cloak, he tied it round Richard's neck with silk fastenings. Richard promptly untied it and gave it to Harpin. Calabra took another cloak and tied it round his neck. Richard untied it immediately, passing it this time to lord John of Alis. He said to Corbaran that he would not wear any furs or ermines no matter how many he was given unless all his beloved companions had one: only then would he declare his loyalty to Corbaran, and his deep gratitude if Corbaran were to honour them thus. Corbaran called for his head chamberlain and ordered him to dress them in luxurious fabrics. The chamberlain returned [with robes] and dressed them finely. Morning had come and it was getting close to midday; a sumptuous meal was being prepared. The king demanded water and it was brought to him. Once he had washed, he asked Richard to be brought to dine next to him.[24] But Richard demurred, saying that if it pleased Corbaran he preferred not to be next to the king but would take his chances with his companions. The king took his seat. He gave strict orders that Richard was to be served whatever took his fancy, and so were his companions without exception.

20

The king sat himself in the place of authority at the highest table with all his retinue. Richard meanwhile took his seat elsewhere surrounded by all his companions. Corbaran's mother did not waste a moment. Tightly laced into a patterned silk gown and carrying a cane with a silver head, she had a whole succession of small dishes sent from one end of the table to another; she had them brought wine and spiced mead, white bread rolls and dishes to accompany them.[25] Lord Harpin of Bourges ate like a trencherman; so did Richard of Chaumont, who knocked back the drink: as you will appreciate they both needed it desperately. Neither did the other companions hang back. When they had eaten and drunk their fill, the butlers and servants took away the cloths.

21

So now the *chétifs* had eaten and drunk; they were clad in silk and luxurious cloth and very rich robes: this was thanks to King Jesus who, as He was hanged on the Cross to suffer for us, delivered them from captivity and brought them to safety. Richard had a tunic sewn all over in gold; the coat with its collar and feathers and jewelled tassels of beaten gold were worth a good thousand pounds of fine silver bullion. He had equipment prepared, bridle, saddle and shield; Corbaran of Oliferne had a warhorse with a flowing mane led to him by the bridle. Count Harpin said to him: 'What are you waiting for? Get on this horse and show us what you can do!'

22

Harpin of Bourges said to him: 'Richard, don't keep us waiting. Just get on this horse and try its paces! Remember France, that bounteous country. May God grant that we all return there safe and sound to see our families, who are desperate for

---

[24] A strict etiquette governed who sat where at the table: see P. Hammond, *Food and Feast in Medieval England* (Stroud, 1993) p.116; T. Scully, *The Art of Cookery in the Middle Ages* (Woodbridge, 1995) p.172. Being invited to sit next to Corbaran symbolises the high regard in which the *chétifs* are now held compared to their previous abjection.

[25] A mark of favour: the best dishes were for those at the top table and often failed to make their way further down the hall; Hammond, *Food and Feast* p. 135.

our return'. Now imagine Corbaran addressing Richard as follows: 'Richard, son of nobility, mount straight away so that I can see how well you can manoeuvre your horse, carry your shield and manipulate your lance. If you acquit yourself well I shall hold you in even greater esteem and will be more certain of winning my case'. 'My lord', replied Richard, 'I shall do as you wish'. He leapt onto the horse without bothering with the stirrup; he had powerful shoulders, a well-built body, a good seat and a proud expression on his face.[26] The packhorses were loaded down below the city. The ladies, girls and young knights compared notes with each other: 'This knight was carrying stone, lime and mortar with only quarter of a loaf a day to eat. Now there is no finer knight on the road. He will take them on in battle if the gods can come to his help'. Imagine the scene: girls and ladies and young men, all crowding after him in numbers too large for me to describe. They all stopped underneath an olive tree. Richard pricked the horse on with his spurs of pure gold: in response the warhorse leapt more than a quarter of the way across the field. Anyone who saw him displaying his banner, carrying his shield and manoeuvring his lance could be in no doubt that he was a noble knight. Once he had turned he came back, galloping to a halt beneath a mulberry tree.[27] 'My lord', exclaimed Corbaran, 'that was magnificent! This is just what I needed to help me win my case'. Corbaran's mother flung her arms round him and attempted to drag him off to her room; it was just the right place for a bit of seduction or some intimate discussion with a young lady. This was because she wanted an heir from him. This was not something Richard would have contemplated even if he were to have his head cut off as a result. She gave him a sword with a pommel of pure gold: it used to belong to King Herod and was the one he used to slaughter the little Innocents before his wife's eyes; it was an excellent weapon which achieved notable feats.[28] Calabra led him away to relax, offering him innumerable opportunities to wash and bathe; he spent virtually a whole month taking his ease.

23

Richard and the *chétifs* spent a month there and carried out penance as noblemen should. They had ten priests with them and an abbot from Blois; the bishop of Forez confessed them frequently, and they fasted two or three days each week. Corbaran had some 300 horses from Arabia and Turkey which had galloped all the way across the plains of Oliferne. The three who won the race were as white as snow. He presented them to Richard, hardly choosing the worst. He picked out one of the white horses, strong and sturdily built, a swift Arab [breed], strong and

---

[26] Not using the stirrup is an indication of his prowess.

[27] Standard manoeuvre to demonstrate prowess: Paterson, *The World of the Troubadours: medieval Occitan society, c. 1100 – c.1300* (Cambridge, 1993) p. 77.

[28] Herod is one of the most notable medieval villains of the Old Testament and it is appropriate for a Saracen to have his sword. The reference also roots Richard's subsequent victory firmly in the wider landscape of the divine plan.

tall and fiery. [Richard's] equipment was crimson with shimmering decoration. Lashing on their equipment, they set out to do battle; they were weeping with sheer fear and nobody was making any boasts. May God, King over all, accompany them on their way!

24

They took up their order of battle on a Tuesday morning. Corbaran was leading some 500 Turks from the lineage of Cain and of no mean appearance, dressed in silk and miniver and ermine. The *chétifs* rode by another route and entered Sarmasane through the Gate of Blood. The descendants of Cain took up separate lodgings; Corbaran took over the mansion of Hodefrin, [and] our captives were assigned a large marble palace. They were assigned two seneschals, Salatré and Rogin, 30 young attendants and a nice polite young man who served them bread and wine for dinner. When the Sultan heard of this he bowed his head, and so did the noble *almustadin* of Spain.[29] All of them prayed to Mahomed, Tervagant and Jupiter to make the battle turn out to the shame of the Franks and the honour of the Saracens.

25

Corbaran entered his lodgings on a Thursday evening, assigning to our captives a palace of considerable size. They were well looked after by squires and sergeants. When the Sultan heard this, he was cast into utter misery. The following morning they mounted as day broke. The king and emirs went to the mosque and made offerings of more than 3,000 bezants that day. [Meanwhile] the abbot of Fécamp sang Mass for Richard, and the bishop of Forez preached a proper sermon and said the kind of prayer appropriate to a learned cleric: 'Just as it is true that God created mankind and the first was Adam, Lord; just as You spent more than 32 years on this earth; during which Judas sold You (grasping coward that he was) and You suffered pain and torment on the Cross; during which Longinus struck You with his sharp lance and blood and water flowed out and ran down it; he rubbed it into his eyes, which were sightless – now he sees more sharply than any bird flying – he looked at the Cross and saw You there, he begged for mercy and truly repented and you pardoned him in his humble nobility; just so, noble Lord, as I am a whole-hearted believer, be there on the battlefield – help Richard and leave the two Turks skulking in defeat'.[30] A Turk was listening to this who could understand

---

[29] The author uses a number of terms to denote Saracen noble rank. None have any resonance in English or relationship to Arabic society and I have kept the terms unchanged or translated as 'emir'.

[30] The first of several such prayers in the two texts. The *prière du plus grand péril* is a standard feature in the *chanson de geste*; knights in danger enumerate events from the Bible

perfectly well and went off to report to the emir Soliman. When the emir heard this, he scowled all over his face. 'Well, lord Mahomed', he said, 'carry out your commands. Now I shall see which of the two gods is the more valiant'.

26

The day for the battle was a Friday.[31] Corbaran mounted and so did 20 Arabs, princes and emirs from the hated race; he led Richard and Harpin and John of Alis, in fact five Christians all carefully chosen. Goodness me, they were well dressed – you could not have taken them for beggars! They had cloaks of silk and velvet fastened at their necks. They climbed all the stairs of the venerable great palace. Corbaran took Richard by the right hand and addressed the Sultan as follows: 'King, I offer to fight for you before midday. Look at my Christian. He is a seasoned warrior and will defend me against two warriors chosen from amongst the very best you can find in this whole country to prove that I did not sell your men; I did not carry out acts of treason; and I did not take gold or silver from the army at Antioch. On the contrary, we fought hard with our burnished spears, with bows and arrows and feathered darts; we tossed Greek fire at them so we could burn them alive, and indeed their lances had caught on fire and the varnish was sizzling on their shields when the bishop of Le Puy appeared on the scene fired with enthusiasm, fully armed on his warhorse and with the cross on his chest. He flung it into the fire. The wind swung round completely. It put out the Greek fire and blew it back on us. It generated so much smoke that we were completely disoriented and could not see each other until past midday.[32] There was terrible slaughter in front of my standard, and the princes you put into my charge were amongst the dead. There was heavy fighting where your son fell, and before he could be sewn into a deer hide I took more than 100 blows on my dark shield'. 'I don't believe a single word you're saying!' said the Sultan. 'You shall have your combat, believe you me. Sorgalé of Valgris and Goliath of Mecca, brother of Longinus, go and arm yourselves. You have beheaded and killed plenty of Christians in your time. If you are both defeated by a Frank and my religion comes out the loser, I don't know what I shall do'. Corbaran made his way back to the lodgings of the *chétifs*. He instructed John of Alis to arm Richard, and Harpin of Bourges helped willingly. They put on

---

as part of a prayer for help. See Sister Marie Pierre Koch, *An analysis of the long prayers in Old French literature with special reference to the Biblical –Creed – Narrative prayers* (Catholic University of America, 1940). The strong emphasis on Longinus looks back to the theme of the Vengeance of Christ with which the trilogy begins: see laisses 8–13 of the *Antioche* and discussion in Sweetenham and Edgington, Introduction pp. 32–3. Longinus is evoked consistently in the central trilogy of the Cycle.

[31] An auspicious day for Crusaders in the Cycle: the great victory at Antioch is also unhistorically placed on a Friday (it was in fact a Monday); *Antioche* laisse 305.

[32] There is certainly a reference to fire in the *Antioche* at laisse 359, but no description of Greek fire and flames turning back on the enemy.

him a strong and well-woven white hauberk; they set a Saragossan helmet on his head, and buckled a sword with a shining blade round him: Corbaran's mother had hoarded this for a long time before giving it to Richard on the occasion when she had him sitting by the hearth in her private apartments and he joked with her. They hung a strong curved shield round his neck, bordered with azure blue and richly ornamented with silver, bearing a golden cross as a token of Lord Jesus Christ. They brought his chosen mount up to the steps of the palace: it had been selected from all Oliferne and there was not a finer one anywhere in Lutis. The saddle and its pommel and cantle were of ivory. The girth was done up and the bridle put on; and Richard swung into the saddle without using the stirrup. He settled down behind the shield and swung it round on the horse. He stuck the heavy spurs so far into the horse that blood spurted out on both sides, then streaked through the roads like a swift falcon. He struck the stones so hard that fire was sparked, lighting up all the road and the palace. The Sultan looked at him in utter horror. No wonder he was scared: Richard would have been a tough proposition for anyone seeking to take him on.

27

Sorgalé armed himself at the command of the Sultan. He pulled on soft comfortable boots, a mailed hood and hauberk whiter than any summer flower. The Sultan scrutinised him closely. They enclosed his head in a helmet from Saragossa and buckled a sword on his right side; and he did not omit the dagger, honed to a fine point and with a glittering tempered blade. He hung a sturdy striped shield around his neck made of elephant bone and with a border of sinew; when it was struck with a lance the head made no impact. Once the Turk had fully armed himself, they led a fresh warhorse up to the steps; the steed had no mane.[33] It was equipped with an excellent saddle and bridle; the saddle's pommel and cantle were intricately worked in ivory, and the saddle cushion and saddle cloth were of dark brown silk with a circular pattern.[34] The Turk mounted without needing the stirrup. He was big and strong and well able to fight two men at once. If only he was a Christian![35]

28

Goliath armed himself without further ado. He put on soft comfortable shoes, a strong and all-enveloping mailed hood and a hauberk whiter than a wild rose

---

[33] 'Aufaine' is not attested as meaning anything other than Saracen; the translation is slightly free.

[34] An ivory saddle may sound unlikely but the Metropolitan Museum of Art in New York has early medieval examples.

[35] Standard topos: compare, famously, *Roland* line 3164 of Baligant: 'Deus! quel baron, s'oüst chrestïentét'.('God, what a lord he would be if he were Christian')

flower; the Sultan held him in high esteem. He had a helmet of toughened leather laced onto his head. This Turk had never had any truck with shield and lance He took up instead his bow and quiver, which he had long experience in using; there was no better archer anywhere in the realm of the pagans. He never shot at anything without damaging it or putting an arrow right through it if he had made up his mind to do so. At his belt was strapped a feathered dart for throwing, arrows and missiles, everything he could possibly need. He carried a pike and a sharpened mace with steel nails. He buckled on a sword with a hilt of pure gold which was a good foot longer than any other knight carried; and he picked up a dagger which he intended to stick into Richard's heart if it came to a face-to-face struggle. When the *chétifs* saw him so proud and arrogant, you might have seen them embracing and kissing the ground, beating their chests and begging God: 'Glorious Lord and Father, who judges all, guard Richard from injury and death today!' The bishop [of Forez] and abbot [of Fécamp] began to chant a holy prayer from the Psalter. When Richard of Chaumont saw his adversaries, he laid himself in a cross on the ground and prayed to God: 'Father, Alpha and Omega and Lord of all. You became flesh and blood in the most venerated lady the Blessed Virgin Mary to free all those since the first man Adam who have gone down to Hell, unable to avoid their fate no matter how saintly they were or how much they loved and worshipped You. You took pity, Lord, and did not want to leave them there. You went to Jerusalem to speak to the people. You preached Your message. But Pilate and Barabbas could not agree. So they had You tied to the holy stake and beaten and struck. You suffered this, Lord, to thwart the Devil; You allowed Your sacred body to be tormented on the Holy Cross and Your noble blood to flow from Your right side, and the stones of Calvary to be shattered into pieces. Your blood flowed all the way to Golgotha. The very earth cried out and shook; the animals refused to eat; and the birds stopped singing and flying, remaining mute with sadness and wrath. Longinus, the one who struck You not knowing Whom he guarded, rubbed the blood into his eyes and they were opened; he saw the sky and the earth, and Your wounds bleeding; he begged You for forgiveness and You gave it, pardoning him Lord, from which he gained mightily. Just one knight asked for Your body, Joseph, one of Pilate's soldiers. He had served for seven years and sought no reward other than to take Your body down from the Cross, wash and tend it, anoint Your wounds and lay Your body in the Sepulchre.[36] You arose on the third day and went immediately down to Hell to help Your friends who loved You above all else. You released Adam and Eve his wife, Noah and Abraham and the gentle Abel, and Jacob and Esau, [Jacob's] dear son Joseph and Moses the prophet, who was flung into the fish pond at birth tightly wrapped in grass and reeds in a deep basket to ensure he did not drown by the one who consigned him to the water. The daughter of Pharaoh had come down to bathe whilst two sisters of the child were watching on the riverbank. The proud-faced queen found him there and had him brought up, tended and fed. Later he was to cause her father the Pharaoh much grief when

---

[36] Joseph of Arimathea.

he was appointed as God's messenger. As it is true, Lord, that You sent out Your holy Apostles far and wide to preach throughout the world, to spread the word of Your Holy Gospels, and You gave them the gift of language so that they needed no interpreter – just so, guard me against injury and defeat; let me kill these two Turks with my steel sword; and thus free Your captives who adore and worship You, Glorious Lord and Father'.[37]

29

Now all three are armed and make their way to the site of the battle, down in a field near the Quinquaille river; the sea comes up to it all the way along the shore. The Sultan had had it fenced in by a combination of strings and cords and skins sufficiently firmly fixed that if someone galloped up to the edge his horse would be kept in the arena.[38] They led the three there. There was only one way in and out; the field of battle was guarded by 30 African kings. The nobles went to see which sword would cut best. Meanwhile the Sultan dismounted in the shadow of a pine tree. He summoned Corbaran to be brought for talks with him, although whatever he might say he thought it would not be of much use. 'Corbaran, let us reach agreement and put an end to this. Surrender yourself to my mercy, body and soul. I assure you categorically that I will be reasonable'. Corbaran made it clear that this cut no ice with him. 'King, see for yourself the brave knight I have here: look how well his equipment sits on him and how skilfully he uses it. Anyone who gets on the wrong side of me should be very afraid! Moreover he is not one of the host of barons assembled at Antioch who did not put the value of your Turks at as much as a farthing. This one is in my service with my other prisoners. Come on, set them at each other without further ado: I have no worries about his god letting him down'.

30

When the royal Sultan realised that Corbaran was not inclined to listen, he was bitterly sorry he had insisted on setting up the battle. He handed over his hostages to Corbaran, who took them away. He summoned 14 kings from amongst his best: they swore faithfully by Mahomed to superintend the battle loyally in accordance with custom. Then he had the field of battle guarded – imagine how extravagantly – by getting on for 500 Turks, all part of the plan. They led the three combatants

---

[37] This long prayer comes at a key moment in the text. Richard is about to fight a battle which is not only crucial to Corbaran's future but to the release of the *chétifs* and their eventual rejoining of the Crusade. The prayer is important not only in marking this but in the comprehensive recounting of Old and New Testament narrative, underlining the status of the Crusade as part of the divine plan. See note to laisse 11 above for references to Exodus and comparisons of the Crusaders to the Israelites.

[38] The combat is described in terms of a jousting match. Bartlett, *Ordeal* p.110 for clearly marking out the place for a judicial ordeal, and the associated formalities

to the lists, and stationed Richard some distance from the two Turks.[39] The two of them held a hasty consultation, saying to each other: 'Listen to me, partner in arms. Whichever one of us he attacks, the other one should move quickly to ensure that he does not go for both of us at once; that way we will conquer him more quickly and easily'. The *chétifs* were up high in the main stand. The bishop of Forez raised his arms towards God: 'Glorious Lord and Father, who saved the human race, we came to seek You out in the East, noble lord, to see Your sepulchre and Your shrine; that was when Corbaran captured us and held us in a long imprisonment. We have suffered numerous agonising tortures on Your account. If it be Your pleasure, give us our reward today. Let it be Your command that the outcome of the battle is for Richard to conquer the Turks valiantly'. At these words the Holy Spirit descended and gave Richard a huge lease of energy. He urged on the warhorse with his silver spurs and made for Sorgalé, who was crouched beneath his shield awaiting him. Goliath of Mecca fired an arrow which struck Richard very hard in the neck of his hauberk and went on to cut a hole through the chain mail wounding him right across the flesh of his neck. Richard felt the wound and saw the blood on his hauberk; he invoked God: 'Omnipotent Father!' and shouted out the great name of Jesus at the top of his voice. He made straight for the archer at top speed, and landed such a powerful blow on him that it split and ripped the mailed hood where it hung down his back. He struck him in the heart with unerring aim such that the saddle bow behind him was shattered and split, sending him tumbling from the horse like it or not. The Turk staggered round in his dying throes, yelling and screaming, then fell full length; devils carried off his soul to the torments of Hell.[40] So one was down; Richard defended himself against the other. Sorgalé spurred in the bay, which sped forward. Seeing an undefended spot he struck Richard in the thigh, slashing through the leather and saddle pad so that the horse felt the shock. Imagine them both locked in hand-to-hand combat! Each readied his lance for use.

31

When they twisted away from each other and broke apart, they both had their lances. They both turned accordingly and moved some distance apart at an equal pace. However Richard, wounded as he was, feared that some trick would be played because he had been injured. But the Sultan, far from doing such a thing, imposed a short break; he would not play a dishonourable trick for 14 cities.

---

[39] Literally an 'arpent'. This generally refers to acreage rather than distance; it is attested in the latter meaning but the exact length is not clear. Tobler-Lommatzsch I.547: *Altfranzösisches Worterbuch: Adolf Toblers nachgelassene Materialien/bearbeitet und herausgegeben von Erhard Lommatzsch*, 11 vols, (Berlin, 1925–2002), hereafter T-L.

[40] Standard description of single combat. Devils taking the soul of Saracens are a similarly common topos: P. Bancourt, *Les Musulmans dans les chansons de geste*, 2 vols, (Aix-en-Provence, 1982), hereafter Bancourt, at vol.1 pp. 349–52.

Richard looked up to Heaven, gaining a second wind. He had a good seat on a horse and was exceptionally well equipped; he had a long handsome face and was a proud and much feared warrior. Blessed the hour in which he was born: he brought honour to his family every day of his life. Richard spurred on his horse and so did Sorgalé. They landed heavy blows on each other's striped shields with the sharp lance heads almost reaching their ribs. The Turk's lance shattered, the hilt smashed; Richard had him at his mercy, being the stronger of the two. Now something extraordinary happened thanks to God: the warhorses clashed heads, and the swift white horse smashed so hard that he broke the neck of the bay from Castile.[41] The warhorse collapsed, unseating Sorgalé, whilst Richard was spurring so hard that he rode right over him. The Turk jumped to his feet and pulled out the sword at his side; he picked up the shield by its straps and brandished it four times.[42] 'Come on, Richard', he swore in Mahomed's name. 'If you get down here with me I will count you a truly noble man. You would be a terrible fool to strike me'. Here he said something which would be his downfall: 'I give you the God you believe in as your help'. Richard replied with some restraint: 'Saracen, you won't ever be giving me my God. Neither you nor your family believe in him and love him. If he comes to my aid, you will suffer for it'. Before the Turk could even turn towards Richard, the latter leaned from his horse and knocked him sprawling in the field so that his bejewelled helmet fell from his head. At this a roar went up through the city. Even so the Sultan kept his word on not stopping the fight, his conduct beyond reproach.[43] It was cried at the entry to the battlefield that no man should go onto it, not even a crowned king; and if anyone did, they would be strung up from the gallows.

32

So the Turk was on the island bearing shield and sword. He was very noble and brave, one of the most impressive people in the land; and he was so full of the rage of battle that he had gone pale. Richard spurred his horse without further ado, and landed a massive blow on the striped shield so that the shaft went a good five feet through. The Turk took off his shield and flung it onto the field; this meant Richard lost his lance which had stuck in the shield and had been broken off near the guard. The Turk picked up his shield again, put the strap across his neck and whipped out his sharp sword: it was honed to a razor-sharp edge, more than a steel sickle. He came for Richard so hard that he pushed him back the whole length of a staff onto the island, where there was a palisade next to the water, so that Richard was unable to dodge him or turn.[44] The Turk gave him such an enormous blow from behind

---

[41] Making the point that God intervenes physically to help the Christians.

[42] Literally 'moller', to shape or mould; possibly putting it in front of him?

[43] The Sultan's honourable behaviour is in sharp contrast to the treachery of which Saracens are generally accused: see Bancourt vol.1 pp. 281–9.

[44] Bartlett, *Ordeal* p.110 for use of islands as neutral territory for judicial battles.

down onto his helmet with its golden cross that he sent the rim with its garnet flying into the field. The sword slipped down onto the shield round his neck cutting it down to the buckler; he sliced so much off his opponent's shoulder that, if it had been pork, you could have convinced yourself to buy it. The Turk recovered immediately and went for the horse with a staff, striking right into the middle of its chest. The warhorse stumbled, feeling the shadow of death. Richard dismounted from the golden saddle as the good warhorse fell dead beneath him, mouth gaping. When Richard felt the sword and saw the grass covered with blood, his head slumped forward in pain. The Turk looked at him in high delight, shouting to Richard: 'That got you, didn't it! You won't last long against me. Renounce your God: your life is in peril'. Richard did not say a word: he was choked with anger. The news was carried to the royal Sultan: 'Sorgalé has done it. He has attacked so hard that he has disembowelled what is a good horse, and the Frank is on foot and losing colour. If Sorgalé can land a good enough blow with his sword, the Frankish religion will be shamed and ours acknowledged in no time'. 'Silence, you fool!' said the Sultan. 'You are getting much too far ahead of yourself. The Turk is not going to withstand the Frank for long. That was never destined by Mahomed; I have observed our religion for a long time [but] today will be its downfall'.[45]

33

And so there was Richard on foot; he had lost his horse, and drawn his sword with golden inlaid patterns, wrought to a fine sharpness and with a pommel of crystal. He struck Sorgalé as any good knight would. The latter had his shield in front of him. The blade struck down through his helmet which was decorated with a branch of coral, knocking off the jewels and floral ornaments and enamel [decoration]; the hood of the hauberk was about as much use as a curtain.[46] The blow took with it some of his ear above the main vein, the strap and buckler and leather of the shield all the way down to the spurs.

34

The Turk was in agonising pain and spoiling for revenge. He saw his ear lying cut off on the flower-strewn grass, and his blood flowed down over his body in a tide of crimson. He held his drawn sword, wrought and glittering and razor sharp, so that it threw a greenish glitter against the sun. Be under no illusion: Richard was terrified of him. He made the sign of the cross in defence against the sword, saying: 'Adonai! One and only Holy Spirit, do not forget me. God, all-powerful Royal Father, come to my help'. The Turk struck Richard mercilessly

---

[45] The concept of divinely inspired victory is underlined by the Saracens themselves.
[46] Elaborately ornamented arms and armour are standard in the *chanson de geste*: see e.g. *Roland* line 1263 for a crystal buckler and line 1326 for a helmet set with carbuncles.

down through the Syrian-made helmet (which he slashed right through) and the hood of sewn fabric, so that a flap of his scalp and hair fell down onto his ear. 'Richard', said the Turk, 'you were pretty stupid to think you could escape my glittering sword. Attacking me is the height of madness. I have shown my valour in innumerable battles. Corbaran will be hanged and his lands seized: there is no way you are going to secure the release of the captives'. 'That is a matter for God, the ruler of all', said Richard. 'If he chooses to help me, your foolish bravery will not help one bit. We will know which way things are going by the time we reach compline. I shall make the emir of Persia weep for you if God, the son of the Blessed Mary, decides it should be so. You will have no head or helmet left'. Sorgalé was furious at these words and rushed ferociously at Richard. He smashed a blow down onto his helmet, which glittered and reflected. If the sword had not slipped away to the left that would have been the end of the battle. The impetus of the blow took the sword right down to the soil of the battlefield. Richard paled at such a mighty blow; he looked up to Heaven and humbled himself before God.

35

'Saracen', said Richard, 'I can vouch for the excellence of your sword: I have been on the receiving end. You have wounded my shoulder; and you have cut right through my shining helmet, my hood, my scalp and my hair, that much is apparent. I shall be truly sorry if I cannot take revenge now because I can see that I am losing blood. I am not the least bit scared of your strength; if I were you I would flee right now'. With a brave heart Richard held his sword drawn: it was the one given to him by Calabra, Corbaran's mother, who had long had it as one of her most precious treasures; it had been forged by a Jew in the deserts of Abilant. The Turk did not have a shield; he held his blade across in front of him to parry the coming blow. Richard was a skilled swordsman and struck him twisting away, sending his arm flying from the chest complete with iron gauntlet and glittering sword. 'As I fight with you in this field I know for a fact that God is watching over me as part of his divine plan – that is abundantly plain'. Sorgalé's response was not that of a coward. He had a dagger hanging at his side, filed to a sharp point and wrought to a good cutting edge. The Turk pulled it out and ran towards Richard, intending to plunge it into his heart. But Richard managed to deflect the blow as he rushed forward; the white hauberk he wore did not protect him at all, because the blow sliced off a good hand's-breadth of flesh on the right of his chest. You can be quite sure – take it from me – that if God had not saved him, he could not possibly have avoided death.

36

Now listen, my lords, in the name of God the eternally truthful, how Jesus brings glory to a man who repents and converts him as soon as it is his pleasure. When the

Turk saw that Richard had not fallen, he addressed him civilly asking for mercy. 'Richard', he said, 'hear what I have to say. I thought I was going to kill you, but your God has preserved you. I have served and worshipped my own god for a long time, but today he has completely failed me and shamed me and my lineage. I believe in Mahomed about as much as the rotting corpse of a dog.[47] Instead I believe in Jesus Christ, who was born of a Virgin, who came down to earth and met death on Mount Calvary, where Longinus struck his side with the Lance, making the blood flow; the stone split and fell apart, hard as it was, and he lay in the Sepulchre and was resurrected'. 'Your beliefs are exactly right', replied Richard. 'Let me assure you for definite that if you were to be baptised now, your soul would go to the flowery plains [of Heaven] singing for joy'. With that the noble lord picked up his helmet, which had fallen to the grass. He held it so that it filled to the brim with water. Making the sign of the Cross over him, he blessed him in God's name and poured the water on his head so that it splashed out. Then he picked a blade of grass and split it in three; he gave it to the Turk who chewed and swallowed it, accepting it in the full Christian faith.[48] 'Now cut off my head with your shining sword', he said. 'I do not deserve to live for a single day longer for all the gold in the world, such is the misery in my heart'.

37

'Saracen', said Richard, 'you have done exactly the right thing in denying, defying and turning away from the Devil. Take down the visor from your white armour overlaid with gold and I will cut off your head with your very own sharp sword. That is how I and my companions will be delivered: it is simple fact that things have to be thus. I take no pleasure in doing this, but it is at your request'. 'That is what I want', said the Turk 'and it is my destiny. I have no wish to live even as long as this evening for all the gold in the world or my own ancestry. My ear has been cut off; my arm has been slashed from my body; and my family would despise me as a result. But if you cut off my head I will be redeemed; you and your companions will reach the Sepulchre; and both I and God will pardon you'. By God, Richard certainly shed bitter tears of grief! He took the Turk's sword and lifted it high, then he cut off the Turk's head with his very own sword, though you can be assured he was heartbroken at having to do it. God be thanked – he had won his trial by battle. Sorgalé's family were bitterly upset, and made great public show of their grief. Now picture the guards placed round the field of battle helping Richard take off his white hauberk overlaid with gold. They all vied to bring him off the island and gave him safe conduct to the lodgings assigned to the *chétifs*. The *chétifs* wept with joy when they saw him. In their delight they

---

[47] A metaphor particularly (deliberately?) offensive to Islam.
[48] A communion with three blades of grass was an acceptable substitute for the Host in *chansons de geste*. See W. Sylvester, 'The communions, with three blades of grass, of the knights-errant', *Dublin Review* 121:23 (1897) pp. 80–98.

smothered his hands with kisses, and reverently kissed his eyes and face. All burst into tears: clerics, bishops and abbots, rich and poor and valiant knights. Corbaran certainly did not consider him to be of low status. He marched up to the noble Sultan and addressed him as follows, laying his demands on the line in front of all the nobility: 'Your Majesty, I was the victor on the field of battle. Give me back my hostages'. The royal Sultan acted very nobly: he gave them all back willingly and without any argument. He flung his arms round Corbaran's neck and pronounced his forgiveness for the death of Brohadas which had angered him so deeply. And he gave him back all his lands and dominions, and the seneschalcy of his kingdom. Corbaran then sought his leave to depart.

38

'My lord', said Corbaran, 'give me leave to return to my capital at Oliferne'. 'Not until you have eaten', said the Sultan. He issued orders for water. One hundred splendid young men came running with basins of worked gold. Once the king had washed and wiped his hands, he sat down on some folded silk on his folding stool. Corbaran sat next to him, radiant with happiness. They ate together in the most perfect amity, and you must imagine the number of delicacies brought to the table. But before they see the sun go down on that day [the Sultan] will have terrible trouble and problems from within his own ranks unless the Lord Who forgives sins turns His attention that way. Lyon of the Mountain was deeply grieved at the decapitation of his uncle Sorgalé. He marshalled his family, who were enraged. Once they were mustered they numbered more than 10,000. They marched out of Sarmasane in serried ranks. If God does not extend them his friendly protection, Richard and the *chétifs* will all have their heads cut off!

39

The noble and royal Sultan sat down to dine, with Corbaran next to him as a mark of his special favour. The *chétifs* were seated separately on benches at an exquisite table resting on three supports.[49] The table was gilded all over and fashioned from elephant bone. The borders were of gold with splendid jewels; hyacinths and topazes and flame-bright chrysolites to a value of 100,000 bezants surrounded them.[50] Butlers, servants, and noble young sons of emirs swarmed up and served our Franks with a sumptuous meal. But if the Lord who suffered pain and torture

---

[49] Rather than a trestle table, which would have been put up for the general household: Scully, *Art* p. 169. For examples, though not this elaborate, see the Kunstgewerbemuseum in Berlin.

[50] Standard luxury and exoticism for descriptions of Saracens. See O. Söhring, 'Werke bildender Kunst in altfranzösischen Epen', *Romanische Forschungen* 12 (1900) pp. 491–640.

does not remember them, they will be in mortal fear of losing their heads before the sun goes down in the evening.

40

Richard and the *chétifs* sat down to dine at a very valuable table with supports. Goliath had an extremely proud son, who was tightly laced into a golden tunic; he was well seen at court and was the butler's nephew. As he served in front of the Sultan, he looked across at the Franks. Thoughts started to revolve. 'I am beside myself with anger!' he said to his uncle. 'That big knight killed my father. I have every cause to avenge myself. I will stab him with this steel knife even if it means I have all my limbs cut off'. He seized the handle, ready to act.[51] His uncle restrained him and talked some sense into him. 'Handsome nephew', said his uncle, 'do you really want me exiled, strung up from the gallows and banished from the kingdom? Let me tell you something you would do well to heed. If you start doing anything stupid in this noble palace, all the gold in Spain would not be enough to save you from the Sultan's verdict of death'. He took the knife off him and called over a knight who was his cousin and a great friend. 'Can I ask you to remove my nephew and put him to bed? He has had too much to drink'. The young man was incensed at this.[52] Accompanied by 30 young men, all related to the devil, he made his way to his lodgings and had his warhorse saddled. 'My lords, now let us see who will come to my assistance. Anyone who will help me avenge my beloved father will enjoy my friendship as long as I live'. 'We cannot leave him in the lurch!' they all replied. They fanned out across the city to find their families. They put on their hauberks, laced up their steel helmets, and strapped on their swords with hilts of pure gold. They marched out of Sarmasane on the main road; crossing a stretch of water to the other shore, where there was a deep marsh next to an old path. That was where the wicked villains set up an ambush. Lyon of the Mountain was the first to notice. He summoned a messenger and told him that there was a plot to kill and behead Corbaran. When Arfulans heard this, he said to the messenger: 'I shall kill Richard if I can possibly engage him in combat'.[53]

41

So there were Sorgalé's family lying in ambush, and Goliath of Mecca's family concealed. May God protect Richard and Christendom! The Sultan had no idea

---

[51] The relationship between uncle and nephew is frequent in the *chansons de geste*. See W. O. Farnsworth, *Uncle and Nephew in the Old French chansons de geste: a study in the survival of matriarchy*, (New York, 1913).

[52] Drunkenness is of course forbidden in Islam. Sansadoine is similarly insulted in the *Antioche* at laisse 203. See Bancourt, *Musulmans* vol.1 pp. 443–5.

[53] These three laisses mark the importance of the Saracen counter-attack by an overlapping structure: each refers to the feast but linked with a different stage of the action.

what was going on; had he realised he would have meted out justice to his lords and killed and liquidated 150 on the grounds that they had attacked those to whom he had granted his favour.

42

The noble and royal Sultan rose, having dined. Once the tablecloths had been removed he called for wine. 1,000 noble young men wrapped in ermine [a line appears to be missing here]. The wine was brought to the Sultan in lidded cups and gilded jugs. Spices and pepper and spiced mead were mixed into the translucent wine in the jugs. When the king had eaten and drunk his fill, he called for Corbaran and said: 'Look! This rich vessel of gold is worth more than two cities put together. The noble Judas Maccabeus had it set with precious stones. The Queen of Sheba had it in her Treasury.[54] Take this cup and the wine as a token that I no longer have any ill feeling towards you even over the death of Brohadas, which caused me immense grief; and that henceforward you will be one of my intimates, seneschal and bailiff over all my nobles'. 'My lord', said Corbaran, 'how can I ever thank you enough? I shall return home. I have stayed here too long already. Be gracious enough to grant me your leave to go'. 'It shall be as you wish', replied the Sultan. 'I commend you to Mahomed and Jupiter. May he who rules Hell not forget you and from Paradise protect you so that you do not end up in Hell'. With these words Corbaran bounded down the steps. He led away the *chétifs* marching in formation. Richard was welcomed into the palace by the Sultan and offered him the pick of his rich treasures; however Richard did not accept even two *deniers*. He left together with Corbaran, who marched them to their lodgings in tight ranks. They put on their hauberks, settled their helmets and strapped their swords to their left sides. The *chétifs* marched out of Sarmasane, pennants aloft, riding in tight formation. 'Listen to me a moment, my lords', said Corbaran. 'Last night I had a dream which has left me very uneasy.[55] In my dream a large bear attacked me the other side of this ford. His eyes were as red as glowing coals and his claws as sharp as razor-edged knives. Accompanied by 1,000 leopards all coloured scarlet and 700 bear cubs all freed from their chains, he fell on me like a madman. Over on the right down there were grouped 700 vicious wild boars, tusks protruding from their jaws and as sharp as a meadow sickle. They picked Richard out of all the armed men and fell on him. He defended himself as a stout knight should. Lord Harpin of Bourges fought alongside him. They killed 700 with their sharp swords'.

---

[54] Again set in the frame of reference of the Old Testament.
[55] Dreams are routinely used to foreshadow the future in *chansons de geste*. Compare Charlemagne's dreams of Roland's fate in *Roland* laisses 185 and 186. Here the significance is emphasised through two *laisses similaires*. The dreams look ahead to the attack by the families of Sorgalé and Goliath.

43

'My lords', said Corbaran, 'I am very frightened and the dream I had has left me deeply troubled. It seemed to me that I was in the thick of the battle. The leopards attacked me so violently that they tore our flower-patterned shields to shreds. They killed my precious horse beneath me. There was so much commotion and the sound of drums around me, so much striking of sword on sword and cries and weeping that even the best of my family abandoned me'.

44

'My lords', said Corbaran, 'I must tell you that Lyon of the Mountain is of a very noble line. He has ordered all his men and prepared them for battle: he is mad with his determination to fight us', 'My lords', said Corbaran, 'do not hang back. Each one of us is fighting to save body and soul.

45

'Listen, Corbaran', said Harpin of Bourges. 'We have more than 50 knights, all well reputed in [their native] land of France, Christians in the misery of captivity. Be gracious enough to lend me a horse, and another to lord John of Alis. You can have confidence in them should the need arise'. 'Sire, lend him the horse', said Richard of Chaumont. 'By my head, willingly, given how highly you praise them'. Corbaran had 30 horses brought to the road, swift and rested, ready saddled and bridled. He called Richard over and said to him, 'Here you are; take these horses and share them out. Give your companions those of your choice to use them to best effect where you see fit'. Corbaran gave them hauberks and helmets, nielloed swords and striped shields.[56] Once they were armed, just imagine the sight of them all mounted! Each of them galloped out down on the meadows. Corbaran was in high delight seeing them thus armed. Richard came to the *chétifs* and addressed them as follows: 'My lords', he said, 'a moment's attention. If the pagans attack, defend yourselves stoutly'. 'You have no need to tell us that', they replied. 'Whether we all end up dead or taken prisoner, we are all of one mind: better death than back to captivity'. Trees were growing on the riverbank. They cut maces from them which were impressively squared off. Those with no weapons picked up stones to use in slings. Corbaran rode forward and came to the ford. When they had all crossed to the other side, Lyon – who had seen them – ran towards them, accompanied by 10,000 armoured men. Corbaran was terrified at the sight and said to his men, 'Make sure you strike hard! If I escape alive without

---

[56] Niello is silver inlay. Such ornament on weapons was already commonplace in the Viking era: *Vikings: life and legend*, (eds) G. Williams, P. Pentz and M. Wemhoff, (London, 2014), pp. 102–3, 137

being killed, know that your services will be rewarded'. At these words they urged the horses on, giving them free rein, and fell on [the enemy].

46

The ambush was launched from the woods on the river bank; there were more than 10,000, each with lance raised and horn bow ready to fire feathered arrow. Lyon of the Mountain had a good strong helmet; he was seated on a chestnut charger. By God, it carried him out such a distance that no bird or falcon in flight could have kept up, going more than a bowshot out beyond all the others. He shouted out loudly in a clear carrying voice: 'Corbaran of Oliferne, now you will have to face up to what you did. You will pay dearly for the death of Sorgalé'. When Corbaran heard this he did not hesitate. He grabbed his shield by the armstrap and balanced his lance, which had a pennant attached to it by three studs of fine gold. They spurred confidently towards each other, and each struck the other on his striped shield so that the lances splintered, the stronger being shattered. Corbaran of Oliferne took his sword in his hand and struck Lyon such a blow down through his helmet that he sent the largest of the jewels flying. The sword went down onto the top of the shield and cut all the way down to the buckler. Neither the mailcoat nor the fastened leg armour could stop the blade slicing off flesh from his thigh. Corbaran shouted out very proudly: 'Lyon of the Mountain, so much for your arrogance! By Mahomed, it was a bad day for you when you plotted treachery. You can be sure of this from past experience: if you escape from here [with your life] the Sultan will have you strung up by your handsome little neck'. Lyon went pale when he heard this.

47

Lyon of the Mountain was furious, angry and upset to see his own blood. He urged the horse forward with the spurs at his ankles. Grasping his gold-hilted sword in his right hand, he struck Corbaran on his ridged shield and sent the flowered ornaments and jewels from it flying. The blade struck the shield at the neck and sliced it apart all the way down to the buckler: neither the mailshirt nor the fine chain mail could stop a flesh wound being inflicted, which hurt him badly. 'Give in, Corbaran!' he yelled at the top of his voice. 'Your head will be cut off in revenge for the death of my uncle. When you leave here you will never be happy again. Before sunset this evening every single Frank will be taken hostage over your body'. The *chétifs* were disconcerted by this. Now Corbaran will be avenged in my opinion.

48

Lord Harpin of Bourges was sitting fully armed on his charger. He heard the two kings hurling abuse at each other. He decided to take on Lyon of the Mountain. For the last three years he had had no opportunity to bear arms, but even so he had no trouble lowering his lance now. He struck Lyon on his pure gold shield, splitting and shattering it and ripping the chain mail of the hauberk so that blood came spurting out from under his arm. He sent him flying onto the bank of the river at the full length of his lance. Then, as a knight would, he pulled out his sword and was on the point of cutting off his head when more than 1,000 archers loosed off their arrows at him, which put him off his stroke. More than 700 feathered steel arrows fixed themselves in his shield and hauberk – may God, Guardian of all, protect him! Harpin took Lyon's horse and turned back towards his own lines. Meeting Corbaran on the way, he said to him: 'Here is a prize for you. Do with it as you wish. But you might want to ride it. Join the battle without delay!'

49

Corbaran of Oliferne took the swift horse: he would not have given it back for its weight in gold. He addressed his leaders and men in measured tones: 'My lords, noble and brave knights that you are, now do your best. If I can make my escape, I will give you so much from my own wealth that I will make even the poorest amongst you rich and prosperous'. 'It shall be as you please', they all replied. 'We shall not fail you as long as we live'. Lyon had remounted his handsome white horse and got his leaders and men into an excellent order of battle. Imagine just how extraordinary and dangerous this battle was. The Saracens engaged with volleys of arrows, showering down darts and javelins, and iron clubs were thrown by each side at the other. Now you are going to hear about a battle with a great deal to boast about, in a first-class song – provided of course there is someone to sing it to you.[57] There has never been such a battle since the time of Moses. You might have seen innumerable lances breaking, mailshirts and glittering hauberks ripped, countless Saracens bellowing and Turks yelping.[58] 700 of them fainted dead away on the verdant grass, and devils immediately carried off their souls. I couldn't give a bezant if the Turks all kill each other. Yet may He Who was born of a Virgin in

---

[57] Self-referential; oral formula of the type common in *chansons de geste*. Whether or not the song is actually being performed, the convention is that it is being sung to an audience. See Rychner, *La chanson de geste, passim*.

[58] The Old French 'glatir' is the term used for hounds giving tongue and more generally yelping. The Saracens, as often in the *chanson de geste*, are compared to dogs: this is of course particularly insulting to Islam. Compare *Canso d'Antioca* line 321 on the Saracens guarding the tent: 'ans larco coma chas': *The Canso d'Antioca: an Occitan epic of the First Crusade*, (ed.) L. M Paterson and C. E. Sweetenham (Aldershot, 2003).

Bethlehem when the angel appeared to the shepherds in glory redeem our Franks and lead them to salvation.

50

At a place where a hill sloped up from a ford, the battle with the descendants of Mahomed was in full swing. They were launching so many missiles that nobody could fail to be impressed; and the sound of their pipes and drums was so loud that the drumbeat and the tones could be heard a good couple of leagues off. Here comes a pagan known as Arfulan, brother of Sorgalé and nephew of Red Lion. He galloped up at full tilt on a Gascon warhorse. 'Where is Richard of France, descended from Charlemagne?[59] He has killed my brother and that is mortal treachery. I will make you pay the price for that today if I possibly can! I will slash your head off below your chin and hang up your torso to give my footsoldiers some target practice'. Corbaran heard this noisy altercation and came spurring up. 'Arfulans, what are you seeking from the noble Richard? His Majesty the Sultan accused me of mortal treason and told me to find two champions whatever anyone might say. If it is battle you want, let it be between you and me'. 'I could ask for nothing more', replied Arfulans. They spurred on their horses and sped towards each other, raining prodigious blows on each other's shields; indeed so much so that the lances shattered and splinters flew everywhere. The blows made the sand fly up around them. The villainous Saracens jumped off their horses to fight on foot, going hard at each other with drawn swords. Lyon's household surrounded them and seized Corbaran, who could not fight them off, and they were on the point of cutting off his head. A shiver ran down the spine of the *chétifs* when they saw this. They rushed to Corbaran's rescue, those on horseback spurring at top speed [and those on foot running as fast as they could], all yelling at the tops of their voices 'Montjoie! Charlemagne!'.[60] They laid about them in the press of battle. Had you been there you would have seen dazzling swordplay, innumerable stones thrown and sticks wielded! Corbaran mounted in a state of wrath; the king pursued him and aimed a crossbow at him. I couldn't care less if the Turks kill each other but may God protect our Franks, in mortal peril amongst the infidels.[61]

51

It was a large battle and everybody fought it well. The Turks and Persians rained down blows. Lances were broken and shields pierced, most participants receiving

---

[59] Explicit link to the Carolingian past.
[60] The parentheses render a line supplied by Myers from manuscript D on the grounds that A and C have missed a line.
[61] Literally 'the people of Noiron'. 'Noiron' combines reference to Nero with reference to blackness.

body blows; the din of horns and bugles was considerable. Our French gave a good account of themselves, decapitating 700 Saracens. Young and old gave themselves excellent new equipment from the weapons of the pagans they had left lying dead. Meanwhile Arfulans fled, soundly defeated, along with a thousand disgruntled and enraged Saracens. There was not a single one who had not sustained a body blow or had a limb of some kind chopped off. News of this reached the Sultan, which upset and angered him. He had them summoned and they appeared before him. Without so much as giving them the time of day he launched into a furious tirade. 'Sons of whores! Boys! Infidel Saracens! You have completely shamed me, and dishonoured my religion, and betrayed my gods Mahomed and Cahu. I will not let a morsel of food pass my lips until you are all hung by the neck'. And without further ado he had them all hanged from the branches of a leafy oak tree. Then he sent Corbaran a message of friendship and companionship: he did not know whether or not he was guilty of treason and therefore he should defend himself with lance and shield, or undergo trial by ordeal of water or fire. Corbaran of Oliferne was happy to take him at his word. He and the *chétifs* descended from their mounts to go and rest after a hard day's fighting. Then they remounted and rode without stopping. Thus Corbaran took his departure, having won on the field of battle, but with an injury from a dart honed to a fine edge. He held Richard in great esteem as one of his intimates.

52[62]

So off went Corbaran, the victor on the battlefield, but having sustained an injury which made his face repeatedly turn pale, and having lost so much blood that his whole body ran with sweat. He had conceived a great liking for Richard, who had overcome the two Turks with drawn sword and got Corbaran's fief back for him. They were riding together along a wide and lengthy road. But they had hardly gone any distance when the weather took a turn for the worse. A storm of wind suddenly descended from a cloud and whirled around, so dense and all-encompassing that they could no longer see clearly. They veered off left and lost their way. Beneath the slopes of Mount Tigris, covered with mossy stones, they saw a little-used track overgrown with greenery and ivy and they spurred off down it. The sun burned down on their skin. Our men were making their way into the land of Abraham, a king of infidel Saracens. On the sharp crags of Mount Tigris lived a large and powerfully built beast. It was 30 feet long and as much across. Its neck was the length and thickness of a large mace; if it went after someone it could kill them with a single blow. Its claws and teeth – this is no lie – were as long and sharp as a tempered javelin. Its hide was so tough that no drawn sword could

---

[62] This is the beginning of the Sathanas episode, which is at the heart of the Crusade trilogy. The importance of the arrival at Mount Tigris and the Sathanas are marked by three *laisses similaires*, 52–4. The storm and leaving the path symbolically mark an exit from (relative) reality to fantasy.

injure the terrible beast; its hairs were longer and sharper than tempered blades. A devil inhabited it and often sent a shudder through its frame. It ate men, women and animals; it had inflicted such devastation on its surroundings that not a single plough was in operation. My lords, noble as you are and absolved from your sins, listen to me: this is not a fantasy, a lie or a fairytale.[63] Once Corbaran sees his aged mother and his aunt Maragonde, whitehaired and shaggy, a great miracle by God will be witnessed.[64]

53

Corbaran rode on with his entourage, Richard and the *chétifs* following in line; they made their way round the flanks of Mount Tigris. They were suffering from the wind, the dust and the heat, and the sun burned down on them painfully. They rode across the expanses of the wasteland until they reached the land of Abraham, a king of the Saracens much harassed by the serpent. On the bare rocks of Mount Tigris lived this extremely vicious beast. It was 30 feet long, tall and strong. Its hide was so tough that no burnished sword was sharp enough to pierce it. No man could say for sure what colour it was: indigo and dark blue, blue and green as well, black, crimson and yellow with a tawny skin. It had a very large head and hideous ears, which were bigger than a flower-painted shield and with which it could cover itself when life became too much for it. It had a long thick tail, and believe me when I tell you it was some nine feet long; anyone who received a blow from it was not long for this world. It was inhabited by a devil which gave it reckless courage. When it was angry it kicked up such a racket that you could hear it two leagues off. On its forehead was a glittering jewel which you could see better than a lantern at night. No man or woman could come within two and a half leagues of the mountain without meeting a very sticky end. There was no activity within three days' ride: the people had fled towns and castles. Now listen, my lords: by God the son of the Virgin Mary, you are going to hear a song telling a story with a long pedigree. Once Corbaran sees his great and venerable city, and his mother Calabra rejoicing in her wisdom, and his aunt Maragonde who is shaggy and white-haired, God will bring about a great miracle. This is how Baldwin from the joyous land [of France] (a companion of Richard and sworn to him), in the strength and support of God, fought the serpent with his burnished sword. God, who has power over all things, ensured a great feat.

---

[63] Assertion of truth; these tend to be used in particular for miraculous events. See P. Damian-Grint, *The New Historians of the twelfth-century renaissance: inventing vernacular authority*, (Woodbridge, 1999) pp.152–3.

[64] Not in fact described later unless it refers in general terms to the killing of the Sathanas.

54

Corbaran rode with his noble company, Richard and his companions following him. They spent the day riding down a track next to Mount Tigris which was elderly and in poor repair but not ancient, covering ten leagues at a fast pace. It is no lie to say that they struggled to see each other, the wind and dust causing them considerable difficulty. The sun burned down on them so hard that every single horse had sweat dripping from its flank or croup. Richard was riding a mule with a felt saddle which had been accorded him to lessen the jolting.[65] The wound in his side made by Goliath with a broad arrow had opened up; he was pale with the loss of blood. Our forces made such quick progress that they entered the land of Abraham, a Saracen king renowned far and wide. On Mount Tigris two crossbow shots away they found an orchard with branches in full leaf. [Beneath a tall tree with broad leaves they found a spring which was relatively new.][66] Corbaran descended from his felt-saddled mule along with 10,000 Turks from his household and the 140 captives from noble France. It was a beautiful clear day without a breath of wind; the heat was oppressive although it was past nones. Once they had dismounted they took their supper and drank the water they had been desperate for. They ate together, with meat being brought. The horses grazed on the grass, which was crisped hard with no moisture. In a recess in the rocks of Mount Tigris lived a much feared beast. Its talons were more than a yard long, as razor-edged as a sharp javelin. It had completely devastated the surrounding countryside; the land went unploughed and no measure of wine was produced; whilst any man or beast would be devoured instantly. Now listen, my noble lords: you are going to hear a splendid song; indeed when it is properly sung I do not know of a better one.[67] The good Prince Raymond, he who had his head cut off and was killed by the Saracens, those mad bastards, leaving Antioch grieving and desolate and the land conquered by the Franks lost (never again was anyone to be able to hold onto so much land) – may his soul find salvation and be carried up to God! – was the one [who had this song composed] : it is of proven truth. Duke Raymond, he whose soul has left his body, found it and took it from its source;[68] the composer of the song, a canon of St Peter, was well rewarded for it and received a stipend. The song was kept as

---

[65] A practical tendency the author shows elsewhere. The description of constructing a deerhide ladder at laisse 239 of the *Antioche* is a prime example.

[66] Myers inserts these two lines from C, arguing that A has missed them.

[67] 'Enluminé' generally means illuminated in the sense of a manuscript. However it is attested more generally in the sense of splendid or magnificent: T-L III.447–50. The author marks the beginning of a particularly significant episode by his emphasis on the quality of the song.

[68] Raymond 'estraist' the song. The meaning is well attested in a literary context as to abstract or translate from a source: T-L III.1437. Compare e.g. *Cligès* 22–3, 'de là [an ancient book in Beauvais] fu cist contes estrez/Dont cest romanz fist Crestiens': *Cligès*, (ed.) and transl. O. Collet in *Chrétien de Troyes: romans*, intro. J.-M. Fritz (Paris, 1994) pp. 291–494.

long as the cleric lived; when it came to his time to die and his soul left his body, this song was handed over to the Patriarch: it told how the renowned Baldwin from the famous city of Beauvais, fought the serpent with his sharp sword because it had separated his brother's soul from his body. The battle between the two of them was hard fought; no such battle has ever been seen by any Christian. It was by dint of the miracle which took place there that 7,000 captives or more defeated in Peter the Hermit's army, taken and led away to be bought and sold in the land of the pagans, fettered and chained in shackles and working as slave labour for the infidels, were saved and reprieved; that was the result of that battle.[69]

55

Corbaran was lying on the grass beneath the tree; his people were exhausted and he had taken a pounding. The day was at an end: the sun had set, the wind abated and the heat eased. 'My lords', said Corbaran, 'we have lost our way and none of us is on the right path. I am feeling rather unwell and not at all comfortable; and Richard is badly injured – he is weakened because he has lost so much blood and you can see it in his pallor, which upsets me. We shall remain here for the moment in this beautiful orchard. Have your tents put up; you will stay here until day breaks tomorrow'. Ah God! These words delighted our French and the pagans too, many of whom were injured. Corbaran's tent was erected and firmly staked, with a golden sphere and eagle raised above it. The tent was very rich, of swathes of brown silk with embroidered green silk spread out on the grass, inset and slashed with birds and animals. The ropes which held it down were of silk, and the quilted outer cover of fine and costly velvet. The king went to sleep in it, racked with anxiety. Our French were lodged off at one side; their horses browsed on grass which was soft beneath their feet. 'My lords', said Corbaran, 'some quiet please and listen to me. Make sure that none of you take off your arms today; do not disarm yourselves in case you are taken unawares. See Mount Tigris. That is where the serpent Sathanas has taken up residence. He is so dreaded that no writing or letter could tell you how many people he has killed, devoured and swallowed; he has laid waste this country and brought it to its knees. If the serpent comes to find you, show him no mercy: ensure you receive him with iron and steel and plunge your drawn swords into him; if you do not, you are signing your own death warrant'. 'Do not be too downhearted, my lord', said Harpin. 'If the serpent pays us a visit, the world will be avenged'. 'By Mahomed', said the king, 'that would make me happier than adding four cities to my fiefdoms',

---

[69] This unusually elaborate description of the origin of this part of the text marks its importance and explains its role within the Cycle. A similar account of the origin and purpose is at the end of laisse 56. For more detailed discussion see Introduction, chapter 1.

56

The day was at an end, night was coming down and the wind had dropped; a beautiful bright star rose and shed its light all around. The king's household bivouacked for the night until the following day dawned. Corbaran was exhausted and glad of a rest; so was his proud household after the rigours they had undergone [But] none took off their shoes or undressed; they lay on the grass with their weapons to hand and none took off their armour. At this point I am going to leave the king and his stay in the orchard to one side; he was not there for long, as I shall proceed to relate. Instead I am going to tell you about Abraham and how he hunted the beast; it was the ruin of all his lands and domains, so that nobody could plough or earn their living. He attacked it four times, with notable lack of success; few of the 15,000 Turks with him came out alive. When Abraham realised that he was getting nowhere, he reported the serpent to his emir the Sultan and asked for help as his liegeman. The Sultan responded by sending him 60,000 Turks; he set them on the road to Mount Tigris and accompanied them in person. They were well armed as he had commanded. But before they could reach their destination, Jesus brought it about that the Sultan got himself killed by a single Frenchman; this was greatly to the honour of the word of Our Lord.[70] Let everyone realise without a shadow of a doubt that, through the happenings God brought about, 7,000 captives and more were released from prison. Now anyone who pays attention will hear a song better than any nobleman has ever heard. My lords, the story about to be sung to you is true. It recounts how Baldwin, who loved Jesus so truly that He sent His Holy Spirit to guide him, managed to kill the serpent which ate his brother, an excellent knight by the name of Ernoul. A pagan took him away with him from the army of Peter the Hermit, a rich emir with a very large fief. He owed tribute to the Sultan and sent Ernoul along with a donkey heavily loaded with rich silks. After this adventure you will hear all about what happened, how deeply the army of Our Lord loved Jerusalem and how it was taken and who conquered it. But first I am going to tell you how Ernoul met a sticky end: he set off as a messenger but never returned. It was the good Prince Raymond who, being very keen on this story, had this song composed to ensure it was not forgotten. May God have mercy on the soul of its composer!

57

My good Christian lords, listen to me for the sake of God! Corbaran of Oliferne was resting in the orchard, where he and his companions had set up camp; he was delighted to rest because he was exhausted. The royal Sultan was riding to meet him with his noble entourage, a good 60,000 armed knights with crossbowmen and good experienced archers. Imagine them making their way towards Mount

---

[70] Presumably a different Sultan; Corbaran's overlord successfully reaches Mount Tigris with reinforcements later in the text.

Tigris. But before they managed to reach it – listen in God's name! – such a great marvel came to pass that you will never hear one more striking; this is not a lie but absolutely true, written down by a witness who can be trusted implicitly.[71] My lords, on the day I am telling you about there was in the land of the pagans a man who had been taken captive; along with many others he had been taken prisoner when the army of Peter the Hermit was defeated. He was bought and sold throughout the pagan realm. Each captive was locked into chains and fetters. They were put to work in whatever way came to hand, carrying huge stones to walls and ditches, [or] dragging ploughs like yoked oxen from morning until the sun went down in the evening; anyone who did not work hard enough was beaten and whipped until their sides and their ribs were cut open. My lords, a rich and very powerful Turk had one of these in prison, as I shall proceed to tell you; he was called Ernoul, born in Beauvais, and was a brave and respected knight. But as you well know, having heard it many times, no man on this earth no matter what his ancestry can avoid being captive once he is in the hands of the Saracens. A Turk confined him in prison, one with extensive lands, castles and towns beneath and royal cities; he held all these from the royal Sultan. Each year he gave him a large quantity of gold and silver on the feast of St John, the widely renowned saint, which is observed and celebrated by Turks and Persians.[72] On that day the rich and royal Sultan was presented by the noble Turk with a sturdy packhorse loaded with rich silk clothes and silk with a circular pattern. He called his captive over to him, as you are going to hear. 'Ernoul', said the Turk, 'a moment's attention please. You have been a good ten months in my court; you are brave and sensible and eloquent. I would like you to go to the noble and royal Sultan for me. Pass on my greetings and protestations of friendship, and give him this large and heavily laden donkey on my behalf. Do not hang about once you have given him the present. On your return you will be well rewarded: I will never again put you in prison as long as I live – on the contrary you will be my friend, companion and part of my inner circle. You will often accompany me to woods and rivers; moreover I will give you my sister if you want to have her, and rich holdings which will pay you well, giving you horses and experienced steeds'. Ernoul's heart skipped a beat on hearing this. He was so overjoyed that he flung himself at [the Turk's] feet and would happily have kissed him when he rose to his feet. 'Ernoul', said the pagan, 'you are noble and experienced; let me warn you as a friend. Do be careful not to go near the lofty Mount Tigris because it is haunted by the evil presence of the desperately feared Sathanas. Even if you had 1,000 armed Saracens with you, not one would come back alive – they would all be devoured. The mountain houses a hideous and malevolent beast. It has laid waste the surrounding area, the countryside and the cornfields. No man can go within at least four leagues of it on any side without meeting his death. Make sure you pass the mountain on the left and not on the right'. 'My lord', said Ernoul, 'it shall be as you command'. He

---

[71] Assertion of truth underlined by reference to an unnamed but trustworthy witness.
[72] The same feast day is referred to at laisse 2.

buckled his sword on his left side and took up a Turkish bow with feathered bolts, then set off on his way with the presents lashed [on the donkey]. It did not take him long to get on the road – but within three days journey the time for him to die will have come. No man born of a mother will be able to save him – but he will be properly avenged, as you will hear if the story can be trusted and you listen to me. Ernoul loaded up his gold and set off; as Jesus wanted in His holy mercy, he rode for three days. The fourth day arrived. The sun rose on a fateful day for him: never again would he see evening or sunset but would be horribly tortured in a terrible storm. A cloud blew up: it was a magic cloud which stopped him seeing anything, with the air swirling around; unable to keep his sense of direction he strayed and, losing his way, wandered off into the desert.[73] He was heading for Mount Tigris and did not stop until he reached it. At midday the darkness lifted; the surrounding cloud broke and the sun rose, swiftly followed by the greatest heat imaginable. Ernoul was appalled to see the mountain. He made to turn back, but was already too close; the Sathanas was eyeing him narrowly and bounded down the mountain. It hadn't eaten for more than five full days or slaked its thirst. Mouth gaping wide and hideous as sin, it came running madly towards Ernoul.[74] The nobleman saw it coming and was terrified. 'Alas!' he said, 'I am a poor unfortunate captive! I shall never again see Beauvais where I was born, captive as I am, or my wife and children who want me back. Handsome brother Baldwin, you will never see me again – you will not lay eyes on me nor I on you, which makes me even more miserable. Lord and Holy Father, in Your holy generosity, and beautiful Lady Mary the Virgin, do not forget me! Saint Nicholas, come to my aid! Have mercy on my soul. My days are at an end'.

58

Ernoul saw the serpent coming towards him with gaping jaws, looking like a devil; it was intent on devouring Ernoul and consuming his soul. He was quite sure he was going to die, you can be certain of that. He invoked Lord God, who can pass judgement on all. 'Glorious Father God, mighty counsellor over all; Lady Mary the Virgin, allow me to address my prayers to you. [I invoke] He Whom you bore, who can judge us all; when we all plead our cause at the Great Day of Judgement and great and small alike have no intercessors. He will display His wounds and cause them to bleed, and raise His arms with the nails up to the Cross just as happened on that day: I can vouch for this. [And I invoke] the suffering the Jews inflicted on Him on the Cross when He was crucified on the Mount of Calvary to free us, poor weak captives, from Hell. On that day all will tremble, dukes and

---

[73] Corbaran has a similar experience.

[74] A standard depiction of the jaws of Hell is a monster gaping wide to eat souls: see for example the wall paintings at North Leigh in Oxfordshire and Holy Trinity, Coventry: R. Rosewell, *Medieval Wall Paintings in English and Welsh Churches*, (Woodbridge, 2008) pp. 74–5. Laisse 58 makes the comparison explicit.

princes, and the rich and poor will have nobody to speak for them; the holy men and women who love God will tremble just like olive leaves. As soon as any one of them closes his eyes and blinks his last You will reward each as he deserves, Lord God. By God, nobody will be able to ease the pain of those whom You consign to eternal punishment. Conversely those You choose as your companions will be so overjoyed that nobody can encompass the joys which await them. The father will be unable to help his child, the lover his beloved or the husband his wife. As all this is true, God, which You hear me proclaiming, have mercy on my soul I implore You. God, consummate Lord, I implore You to have mercy on my soul: the body is past judgement'.[75] He picked a blade of grass and began to cross himself. He began to eat it in place of the Body of Our Lord in order to secure his aid at the great day of judgement.[76] He brandished his sword forged of steel, and prepared his Turkish bow with which he was well skilled at defending himself; fitting an arrow into it, he shot it at his diabolical adversary. The arrow met its target but with little effect: the [beast's] hide was so tough that it could not pierce it; the arrowhead could not get through it or even damage the hide any more than if it had been made of hard-to-sculpt marble. The steel arrow was shot so hard that the shaft and head were broken and shattered.

59

As Ernoul came to the end of his prayer he called on God and confessed his sins; in the name of the Body of God and in very truth he ate the blade of grass, chewed it and swallowed it. He fired a long broad-headed arrow which shattered into pieces as it hit the hide of the beast. The Sathanas neared him with jaws gaping wide. Ernoul saw it coming towards him. He drew his sword and struck it in the face, but to little effect: he could not make as much as a pennyworth's impact, and the sword bounced off as if it had hit a steel anvil. He struck [the beast] with such determination – this is absolutely true – that the sword broke despite being well set in its hilt. The Sathanas seized him instantly and flung him up the hillside more than the length of a lance; landing heavily on the ground he broke his thigh. The Sathanas rushed on him with its mouth wide open. With one snap it seized Ernoul between its teeth; and it smashed the donkey with its large square tail, killing it with a single irresistible blow. Seizing the donkey in talons which were sharper than a sharpened dart, it flung the donkey over its shoulder and set off, not stopping until it reached the mountain. Ernoul cried and shouted as hard as he could: 'Holy Lady Mary, crowned Queen, have mercy on my soul! What a sad

---

[75] The reference to the Last Judgement and the Harrowing of Hell again draw the parallel between the redemption of the *chétifs* and the redemption of humanity. *GF* 2 had already made the connection: 'dicentes sese Christi unanimiter sequi vestigia, quibus de manu erant redempti tartarei'.

[76] See note to laisse 36 for communion with blades of grass; emphasised by repetition in laisse 59.

fate! Alas! Those at home will never know that a serpent ate me and devoured my flesh'. Corbaran heard this from the leafy wood.

60

Good Christian lords, listen in the name of God. That vicious beast showed its hideous strength that day. Along with the donkey and the presents lashed onto it, [the Sathanas] seized Ernoul in its teeth honed to razor sharpness, sticking them right through his body from one side to the other. It dragged them up the mountain with no possibility of escape. Ernoul was shouting out, 'Help me, God!' The noble and wise Corbaran of Oliferne heard the cries and leapt to his feet, calling the French and Turks to him. 'My lords', said Corbaran, 'listen carefully. I heard a man shout out twice. I do not know whether he is pagan or Christian, but either way nobody could fail to take pity on him'. 'My lord', replied his men, 'that may well be the case'. 'Whatever help he may need he is clearly terrified. He is most likely a captive who has escaped, I suppose. He has seen the serpent which has everyone living in terror'. Baldwin was plunged into grief and anger when he heard this, and approached Corbaran in a state of high emotion. 'Take pity my lord, in the name of God Who was hanged on the Cross. As sure as God was born that was my brother I heard'.

61

The Sathanas turned away without further ado and staggered up the mountain with its burden of the captive and his already dead donkey; blood streamed from [Ernoul's] mouth. He was shouting at the top of his voice: 'My lord St Nicholas! Holy Lady Mary! I am mortally wounded. I shall never see the city of Beauvais again, or my noble wife named Aalais, or my two noble sons Gillebert and Gervais, or my brother Baldwin – alas, who will ever love him better than I!' And these words were his last. His soul left his body: may God grant him consolation. Baldwin heard him and heaped imprecations on God. He ran up to King Corbaran at full pelt. 'My lord, by the mercy of God who created priests and lay alike, I want to go straight away to take on the wicked and vicious Sathanas – he has killed my brother and I have just heard his cries'.[77]

62

Baldwin was racked with grief, believe you me. He was very brave and noble and resolute. He came to Corbaran and implored him most persuasively: 'My lord, by the mercy of God Who rules all – the sky, the earth as the world turns, woods

---

[77] Laisses 60 and 61 have a similar structure, cutting in a near-cinematic montage between the Sathanas and the *chétifs* waiting below.

and rivers and lush grass – may He grant you lands and fiefs. My king, give me a hauberk and a Syrian helmet, two sharp swords both highly wrought, a dart to fling and a strong flowered shield. That will allow me to go and fight that reviled beast who killed my brother and has broken my heart'. 'My friend', said Corbaran, 'that is a stupid idea. Stop right there. All your bravery will avail you nothing against the serpent. Even if you had every single inhabitant of Tabarie with you and they all accompanied you up into those bare cliffs, not one would reappear alive. The royal Sultan of Persia would not be able to take it on even if he had every last person from Romanie with him! The mountain is formidably dangerous with its desolate rocks. No horse or steed from Orcanie has ever managed to climb it – or any donkey, camel or Syrian mule.[78] A pagan born in Asconie once told me that beyond this mountain, huddled beneath the bare rock, there used to be an ancient city: it was rich, wealthy and well supplied. But its inhabitants fled because of the terrible beast'. 'My lord', said Baldwin, 'this is a strange and wonderful tale I have heard. But I shall still take any road I can with Jesus' help'. 'By Mahomed!' said the king, 'you will not go if I have anything to do with it. We ourselves have been very foolish in camping here yesterday evening. The moment dawn comes up my tent should be bundled up. My lords, let us get under way without wasting a moment, and hurry back to Oliferne. I am terrified of the serpent which kills our people'. Baldwin was not at all happy to hear this. 'My lord, in God's mercy, you cannot just go! By the loyalty I owe my men, and my sweet wife to whom I have sworn my troth and whom I have left grieving and miserable on account of me, either I or the serpent will meet our end'.

63

'My lord', said Baldwin, 'let me implore you by God, and by the Lord who makes bulrushes flower, [and brings] wine and cheese and dew in May, Your Majesty, give me a hauberk to protect my back and a jewelled helmet to tie onto my head, two sharp swords and a dart for me to throw, and a strong striped shield to hang round my neck. I shall make my way up Mount Tigris on foot, all by myself, with no warhorse or brown or bay steed. So strong is my trust in God and St Nicholas, and the noble St James whose altar I have kissed, and the true Sepulchre which I want to embrace, that if I find the serpent and take it on in combat, I shall have no trouble conquering it in God's name. If you so wish I will give you my solemn word that either it will kill me or I will kill it. With God's consent I shall happily put it to death and lighten my heart for the brother it took away from me. I shall never know a moment's happiness until I avenge him and will not go back to the land of France until I do'. 'My friend', said Corbaran, 'I shall do as you wish. You will not accept my advice: I shall not insist on it. But at least stay here tonight for your own good. I shall call my entourage to give me advice, and if they think it is a good idea I shall let you go there; I shall supply you with very high quality arms;

---

[78] Orcanie for the sake of the rhyme, as often with epithets.

and I shall explain the reasoning to Richard and the others'. He summoned his men together beneath a holly bush. 'My lords', said Corbaran, 'do as I command. Richard and Harpin, I am in need of your advice'. 'And I shall give you good advice', said Harpin of Bourges. 'Give Baldwin arms, in the name of St Nicholas'. Corbaran replied: 'Give me your opinion and I shall listen; and if I so decide I shall follow your advice willingly'.

64

This is what Count Harpin said. 'Noble king, give me your attention. I shall give you the best advice I can in all loyalty. In my opinion you stand to lose nothing from this; give Baldwin all the weapons he wants, good quality and fit for purpose, as soon as possible. Then he will be able to go off and fight the evil serpent who has killed so many pagans so cruelly. I place such trust in God on whom the whole world depends, in the Father and the Son and in holy baptism [that I am sure] he will kill the serpent – it is not much longer for this world. We will be overjoyed and so will all our families'. 'Let it be so', replied Corbaran. He had the army's weapons brought to Baldwin, more than one hundred hauberks and helmets and swords. 'Choose whatever you would like, my friend', said Corbaran. 'This is certainly a rich gift, my lord', replied Baldwin. He raised his hands to God in delight, and was about to fall at Corbaran's feet when he grasped him and lifted him up with an expression of his good wishes: 'My friend, may He who made the heavens come to your aid and bring you back to us safe and sound. No man living in this century has dared to take on such a dangerous enterprise'. Baldwin bowed and turned towards the [heap of] weapons. He picked out a hauberk as white as the flower on the shoot of a vine; the chain mail was made of refined gold and steel and silver, and the King of Beniventum had had it forged and put together. Getting to his feet, Baldwin took it in both hands and flung it over his head in one swift move. Harpin laced the neck protector tightly on his head. His companions were in tears because of the high regard they bore him, surrounding him in communal grief. Baldwin picked up two swords with silver hilts. They laced a helmet firmly on his head, and did not forget to supply him with a sharp dart for throwing. He called the bishop of Forez to him cheerfully: 'Your worship, address me in the name of Almighty God. I am going to take on the evil serpent in a fight. A man facing such peril needs to approach it in a reverent spirit: I want to make my confession to you in private'. 'It shall be as God commands' said the Bishop. Baldwin took him to one side, down next to a wild rose. He repented to God the sins he had committed. Laying himself on the ground in the shape of a cross, head towards the East, he prayed to Lord God, the King of Bethlehem to give him strength and courage against the evil serpent. 'Baldwin', said the Bishop, 'your intentions are admirable. I grant you this penance, that if you ever return to Christendom, you do not fail to attack the Saracens who have inflicted such grievous harm on us in the very place where God and the Holy Sacrament are worshipped'. Baldwin was delighted to hear this: it was a penance which would guarantee his soul against harm.[79] 'Baldwin', said the bishop, 'you are a very brave man. Get back down on the ground and confess your sins to God'. 'Your worship, I want nothing but to make amends to Him for my sins'. The bishop made the sign of the Cross over him with great fervour, giving him advice from the Holy Spirit to ensure that God helped him to the full that day.

65

'My friend', said the bishop, 'you are brave and noble, and what you are undertaking today is extraordinary. Remember God Who was hanged on the Cross. May He give you strength and courage and preserve your life so that you can return from this Mount Tigris having killed the serpent with your two burnished blades; may you [live to] see the city where Jesus was dragged along, beaten and insulted, struck and spat at. You are to serve in the Temple for a year and 15 days.[80] May Jesus and His Holy Spirit be with you'.

66

The bishop of Forez heard Baldwin's confession and laid a penance on him for his sins. The most holy Bishop gave him good advice to ensure that Jesus in his glory would extend him every help that day. The bishop called the king's seneschal over and asked him for a loaf of bread; he brought him one. The bishop took the shield Baldwin would carry up the mountain and laid the loaf on it; he sang a mass in the name of the Holy Spirit; then he administered Communion. The bishop called for the abbot of Fécamp. 'My lord abbot', said the Bishop, 'in God's name listen to what I have to say. Here is our companion. He badly needs the help of Him Who gave us shape and form, and Who fasted in the desert for 40 days. I have given him my advice; he will take yours'. 'My lord', said the abbot, 'I shall be delighted to advise him. Our Father Lord God Who created the whole world, Who established the heavens and the earth and the [oceans] and pardoned Mary Magdalen for her sins will help him to be victorious in battle'. 'Amen, God and Holy Father', they both cried.

67

The bishop left having given Baldwin counsel. Baldwin the lion-hearted remained. He asked the abbot of Fécamp to hear his confession. 'Your worship, I thank you

---

[79] An implicit reference to the importance of the *chétifs* reaching the Holy Sepulchre to find redemption.

[80] A reference to the Order of the Templars, founded in 1119. Harpin of Bourges, another *chétif*, did indeed join the order: see Jonathan Shepard, 'The muddy road'.

in the name of God Who shaped Lazarus. I ask your pardon for the sins I have committed. It is my duty to go and fight the evil Sathanas who has inflicted such destruction on this land that nobody, pagan or Turk or Slav, dares to enter it. I implore the Lord Who suffered in his passion that, if I am devoured, my soul may find salvation'. 'Baldwin', said the Abbot, 'you have a truly noble heart. Lord God and St Peter the Holy Father who lies in the Gardens of Nero will grant you pardon whatever may happen to you'. Filled with a spirit of devotion, he gave Baldwin a document which contained the 99 names of God and was nearly as long as a portrait.[81] 'Baldwin', said the abbot, 'let me give you this document. Carry it into battle and you will be sure not to come to harm'.

68

Baldwin was extremely brave and shrewd and strong. He took in his hand the document the abbot had given him. The abbot addressed him in words of encouragement. 'Do not delay: carry the document round your neck on your chest. If you have faith in it, it will protect you well; you cannot be killed as long as you wear it on you. I have safeguarded it ever since it was first drawn up and have never yet given it to any man born of woman. When you find yourself in desperate need, shout the mighty names of Jesus at the top of your voice. Go, take up your weapons and arm yourself'. 'Your worship', said Baldwin, 'I shall do as you command and make myself ready'. He put on the finely worked hauberk and laced a valuable helmet on his head; it was a gift from Corbaran, that highly generous king, and could not be dented by iron or steel. A strong round shield was then brought to him; he hung it round his neck and did not find it cumbersome. Richard gave him a well-feathered dart which he weighed in his hand and sized up. Had he wanted a horse he could have had his pick; but one could never have got up Mount Tigris and he had to go on foot even though that would be tiring. 'Your Reverence', he said to the bishop, 'in the name of God do not forget me. Utter the most fervent prayers you know; pray for me, Lord Abbot, when you receive alms. And you too, my friends, all weeping for me, I implore you in the name of God Who was hanged on the Cross all to stay together and not to move from here until the moment at which you are certain I am safe or eaten or devoured. If I do come out alive I shall be back quickly'. 'Surely you can have no doubt on this score', they replied. 'If it be the will of God and His names, we will wait for you here until Jesus in His glory and His holy bounty has delivered you from the danger you are going to meet'. 'My lords', said Baldwin, 'I am worried. If any of you has a grievance against me and has been injured or upset by something I have said, I beg you in God's name to forgive me. You do not know, noble friends, if you will ever see me again; and I do not want to die with something on my conscience'. They all cried with one accord, 'May God be our witness that we all pardon you for whatever wrongs you may have done us!' 'My lords', replied Baldwin, 'God

---

[81] Islam recognises the concept of the 99 Names of God; less known in Christianity.

thanks you for this'. He kissed them one by one, then turned and left in tears. His departure provoked an outburst of grief. Hands were wrung and hair torn, abundant tears shed and sighs uttered. Not one single Turk or Frenchman was unaffected. Even Corbaran was upset. He sat down on the grass and had his Turks called. 'My lords', said Corbaran, 'mark this well. This man from France is completely mad; he is so brave that I cannot see how he cannot be deranged. He is making his way to the mountain and will not come back down from it once he has gone up'. Then he had second thoughts and said, 'I have been talking like an idiot. The God this man believes in is a very powerful one; see how He has released these others from prison and will lead each one of them to immediate salvation'. Overcome by grief, he stretched himself full length on the grass.

69

Once Baldwin had armed himself and embraced all his companions in turn, he turned and left. He did not prolong his departure, leaving everyone in tears. All of them prostrated themselves on the ground looking east; they called on Jesus in His glory and recited the holy litany of revered saints. Meanwhile Baldwin took his leave without delay. At the head of a disused path which led to Mount Tigris he found a path cut into the mountain; it had been excavated at the orders of a rich and famous king before God had ever been born, seen or His coming announced. It was a habitual haunt of the serpent, who had smashed it up. It was hedged in on all sides by hawthorns and thorn bushes, which grew thickly on the mountain. I can tell you for certain that nobody came out at the other end of the path without being torn to shreds. Baldwin raised his right hand and crossed himself in the name of Jesus. Then he entered the path, commending himself to God. He climbed up and up, becoming so exhausted and so weighed down by his weapons that he was dripping with sweat, thanks to the heat and his nervousness. He stopped and leaned on a rock, looking down on the mountains and the valleys, the fords and the ditches, the steep precipices and threatening ravines. Toads and worms and snakes creeping out of their lairs and the great snake basking in the sun all infest these mountains and render them uninhabitable. 'Ah God!' said Baldwin, 'in Your holy pity and by Our Lady the Virgin Mary, offer me your aid. Ah, noble St Nicholas, take pity on me. Lord God, come to my help so that I do not get attacked and eaten and devoured by this serpent. God, where is this serpent who is so dreaded, who killed my brother and plunged me into grief? No man of such worth had ever come up here before'. He needed to rest five times before reaching the summit of the mountain. By the time he was halfway up the going had become so hard that he had to go on hands and knees. You can take it from me that he was having a very testing time.

70

My lords, listen in the name of Almighty God to how Lord God in His glory by his command gave Baldwin courage and valour. He went alone to find the beast which 10,000 Saracens of pagan stock would not have dared to attack because it had reduced so many of them to grief and misery and parted souls from bodies with no time to confess. Baldwin, by contrast, climbed the mountain without succumbing to fear, driven on by grief for his brother. Now the time was at hand for him to take revenge on the dragon. He was up on the mountain, dripping with sweat. He had not gone far across the summit before he happened on the mosque.[82] Around it he saw breathing holes and the ground churned up.

71

Baldwin was up on the mountain, worn out by his exertions. He looked down and saw ravines, high peaks and valleys, caves and precipices and desolate rocky landscape. He called on God and Saint Nicholas: 'Lord God in glory, Who created the whole world, and established the heavens and the earth and the sea surrounding them, You shaped the first man, Adam, with Your two hands from the soil of the earth at your command, and pulled his wife Eve from his rib. Once You had created them You entrusted Paradise to their care; You granted them all the fruit in it except one which You forbade. Adam could not keep away from it; and this had serious consequences because it was the work of the Devil who had him firmly ensnared. He was precipitated from grace by his wife Eve. From then on they lived in pain and put on clothes; You sent them and their descendants down to Hell. They were there for a long time; where You visited them. You released your friends from Hell. You came down from Heaven to Earth because You loved us so greatly. You sent the holy angel Gabriel to announce to the Virgin that You would be conceived and brought to fruition inside her; God, how great was the joy to come from Your plan. The Virgin carried You to her great happiness until the time came for You to be born. You were born in Bethlehem under the star You put in the heavens. The shepherds all rejoiced at the light You sent. When the two kings, Melchior and Jaspas saw it along with the third king, their companion Balthasar, they went to seek You in Bethlehem to where you led them. They found You there at the Virgin's breast. In their arms they carried gold, frankincense and myrrh which they presented to You, and You signed them with the cross. This was a sign that You would become Three in One on Mount Tabor, where you ascended into Heaven. When the three kings returned, You protected them from Herod by sending them a different way. The Virgin nourished You with not a single problem until You were old enough to be able to play with other children. They called

---

[82] As a dragon inhabited by the Devil and depicted in diabolical terms, it is appropriate within the poem that it should live in a mosque and moreover one built by an exceptionally wicked Saracen who was Herod's brother; emphasised by repetition.

You Jesuiel, and You often came to blows with them. You lived on earth for 30 years, showing Your power, protecting and healing the deaf and the outcast. You entered Jerusalem on the fine day of Easter riding a donkey through the Golden Gate and leading the little colt and its mother.[83] You began to address the wicked Jews, announcing a new religion to them which You explained and foretold, noble Lord. The Jews refused to believe You and so did their chief Pilate. Then, noble Lord, they seized You and tied You up, for which the traitor Judas was rewarded with 30 deniers. Never was such a deed purchased at such a price. They beat You tyrannously until they were exhausted, lashing Your ribs and Your arms with knotted cords; they drew blood and You suffered horribly. They inflicted terrible suffering on You on Mount Calvary, where You carried the Cross on Your own shoulders; there Malcus and Jonatas hanged You from the Cross, and Longinus struck You – whose sight You restored, opening his eyes with Your precious blood. Your blood soaked down through the stones right to Golgotha; the stones cracked and broke into smithereens. The whole world was racked with Your anguish, all the birds and all the beasts: this is completely true, My Lord. In the shadow of the fear of death You invoked Your Father. 'My God', You cried, and invoked the Holy Spirit. You sought out death for our sake and took Your place in the Sepulchre. The [holy] women came to seek You but did not find You. Mary Jacobi, the other Mary called Salome and Mary Magdalen – whom You addressed first – came bringing You unguents, myrrh and aromatic herbs. They came to the Tomb and went straight to the stone, where they found the holy angel You had sent them, God. 'Whom do you seek?' said the angel. 'Jesus of Nazareth', [they replied]. 'My Lord is arisen', said the angel Gabriel. Weeping they heaved the stone aside with their arms, but did not find him: You had gone down to Hell. The women turned and left. You broke open the gates [of Hell], Lord God, and released Adam and his wife, Noah and Abraham, Moses and Jonah, Jacob and Esau, and Joseph Your well-beloved; Your holiness cleared Hell out. The following day You encountered Mary Magdalen. She was completely overwhelmed: You comforted her. You came to Your Apostles and showed Yourself in their midst: You said 'Peace be with you', and signed them with the Cross. All of them recognised You straight away other than the Apostle Thomas. To him You showed Your wounds and addressed him; he placed his hands in the wounds and they came out covered in blood; he fell at Your feet and You raised him up. Noble Lord, You give Your blessing to all those who believe truly that You suffered for us and that after that You came back to life. You gave Your doctrine to Your holy Apostles, Lord God, teaching them a whole range of languages. You commanded them to go out and preach throughout the whole world. As it is true, God, that You did all this, and saved Susanna and rescued Daniel, so too protect me against the evil Sathanas!'[84]

---

[83] In fact Palm Sunday.
[84] This long and elaborate prayer sits at the very centre of the text and hence the trilogy. It marks the importance of Baldwin's quest and sets it firmly within the divine context.

72

Once Baldwin had finished his prayer, he briefly signed himself with the Cross in the name of God, son of the Virgin Mary; he commended himself to God, Who commands all things. Then without further ado he headed for the mountain. He climbed up onto a stone covered in moss, and saw mountains and valleys and the wasteland, the fearsome ravines and the expanses of desert – and the mighty serpents which lived on the mountain, slithering through the rocks and kicking up a huge din. It is hardly surprising that he was terrified. Looking to the right, he saw the mosque which had been built back in the mists of time by a Saracen, Gorhan of Esclavonia, one of the most villainous Saracens who ever lived, at the time of wicked King Herod; it was where he kept his prisoners under lock and key. When this king had died, [the mosque] had fallen into disuse until it was occupied by the beast which devastated the surrounding lands. For a good 200 years, whatever anyone may tell you to the contrary, it did no harm to anyone and killed nobody until the hour in which God decreed that it should be possessed by the Devil, who gave it a new boldness; and the defeat of Peter the Hermit's army, which was routed and cut to ribbons and led off into the lands of the pagans to live amongst the hated race, was all at the behest of God who forgets no sinner.[85] Up on the mountain, Baldwin shouted at the top of his voice: 'May God curse you, you foul creature! I cannot see you: where are you lurking?' The beast was asleep, its stomach pleasantly full; it had eaten all of Ernoul except his head and ears.

73

Baldwin of Beauvais was a valiant knight; he was richly armed, his helmet glittering with gold bands and flashing jewels; his hauberk strong and his helmet stout, and the shield hanging lightly from his neck. The heat of the sun was causing him considerable discomfort; it had heated up the iron [of his armour], which was very painful. He climbed up onto a rock and saw the ravines, mountains and valleys, echoing clefts, plunging precipices and brooding cliffs; and he saw the huge serpents coiling through the rocks, toads and worms and tortoises and whistling adders. It is hardly surprising he was frightened, brave knight though he was! Looking to the right past two owls,[86] he saw the mosque built by King Gorhan, one of the wickedest kings who ever lived. He was brother to King Herod who massacred the children. He had his prisoners brought here in innumerable numbers and killed at his command. 'Where is the Sathanas who killed my brother

---

[85] The events preceding Baldwin's heroism are explicitly described as part of the divine plan.

[86] Myers suggests that the reading of D, 'chasans' (oak trees) may make more sense. The owls could however be guarding the spot. Owls were associated with death, which is highly appropriate here. Variants suggest that the scribes were less than sure about the meaning.

and plunged me into grief?' cried Baldwin. 'If I cannot even see you I shall be furious; I am truly sorry that I ever came here. The powerful King Corbaran gave me good advice, and so did the bishop of Forez and the abbot of Fécamp. I shall never see the warrior Harpin again, or Lord John of Alis, or Fulcher of Melun, or the noble and honest Richard of Chaumont, or my other companions. May God come to their aid! I am terrified of death. Help me, O God!' Then he checked himself and said, 'I have been talking like an idiot. May the Lord Who has power over everything stop me in my tracks. If I do not come back down from this wasteland alive, at least I shall have struck so ferociously with my steel sword that the Saracens and Persians would be amazed to see me. Even Corbaran and the powerful royal Sultan would blanch to see me landing blows like this'.

74

My lords, listen to a glorious song; no Christian has ever heard one like it and nobody has sung like this since the time of Solomon. It is highly edifying to hear, much better than a sermon: [it tells how] Jesus in His glory and by His salvation, saved the noble Baldwin from death when he fought with the evil Sathanas. Drawing on the strength of God he took such a revenge on it as you will be able to hear in the lines of the poem. But before he managed this – let us be honest – his blood streamed down him to his spurs and his whole body was covered in blood. He made his way up a cleft in the mountain and climbed up onto a boulder with a rounded top. At the top of his voice he called out the following: 'God, where is the serpent? Why can I not find it? True God, show it to me in Your holy name'. The serpent was asleep on the other side of a staircase. As God wished and by his blessing, picture St Michael appearing in the shape of a dove.[87] He announced the following in the name of the Holy Spirit: 'Do not lose heart, my friend; nothing but good will come of this. He Who pardoned Longinus and raised up Lazarus to life from the dead will come to your aid. If you place your trust in Him you will find Him a fine companion. As soon as you come to the Temple of Solomon, you will release 7,000 Franks from captivity who are held under duress by the pagans. They were brought here from the army of Peter the Hermit. They have implored God so earnestly that He wants you to save them for Him'. When Baldwin heard this he looked up, and sat down on the staircase overcome by joy.

75

Baldwin sat down and the angel departed. His heart was full of joy, believe you me, because of the holy message sent by Jesus: he now knew for certain that God would help him. He stood up and signed himself four times with the Cross,

---

[87] St Michael is of course typically portrayed defeating the Devil in the guise of a dragon; he is also found at the Last Judgement.

commending himself to the great name of Jesus. And as he wandered he came on the beast. When the serpent caught his scent, it woke up, leaping immediately to its feet. It flew into a rage at the sight of Baldwin. It stretched itself out in anger and made itself look hideous: it made all its long sharp bristles stand on end, staring at him proudly in all its foulness. It covered itself with its ears, and scratched its nails so hard on the bare rock that it struck sparks from it. God delivered a great miracle. The beast had gobbled down so much of Ernoul that it was nearly bursting. It had devoured his body but left his head untouched, leaving it lying on the rocks, and strangled his donkey.[88] Baldwin's heart missed a beat when he saw it, and he hurried to pick it up. The serpent surged up and rushed at Baldwin with its mouth gaping wide. Now may God who made the world come to his aid! If God who made and created all is not mindful of him, he will not last long: but God will come to his help. Now you can hear about how he fought.

76

Baldwin was very brave and a bold knight. He saw the serpent coming, huge and strong, rushing towards him with its jaws gaping wide. The nobleman saw him coming but was not at all concerned. He raised his hand, made the sign of the Cross on his chest and, grabbing his dart, started to call out at the top of his voice: 'Father God, Jesus Christ, I conjure you, beast, in the name of lord St Denis and the Lord who was killed for us on the Holy Cross when he was struck by Longinus. I conjure you in the name of all the blessed saints: St George of Ramleh, the noble St Maurice, St Peter the Apostle who guards Paradise, the noble St Lawrence who was grilled alive for God, St Leonard who releases captives, St Nicholas dearly beloved of God, the noble St James who is worshipped in Galicia and the noble St Gilles whom I have revered in Provence, and all the Apostles who serve God, and the Holy Cross on which His body was hanged, and the revered Holy Sepulchre where He lay dead and alive, by the heavens and the earth in their place – you will not have the power to conquer me or to devour and destroy and hurt my body'.

77

Once Baldwin had conjured the serpent in the name of Jesus in glory, king in majesty, he moved towards it without further delay and flung his well-made feathered dart at it. Listen to this miracle, brave and noble Christians! The hide and skin of this accursed beast was so tough that he was unable to make more impression on it with his sharp dart than if he had flung it at a stone staircase. Let me tell you for certain that he struck it so hard that the head and the haft of the dart were smashed to smithereens. It was possessed by the Devil, which had thoroughly taken it over it and made it strong and very cruel. But God in

---

[88] Essential for purposes of identification.

his great piety cast the Devil out. When the Sathanas realised that he had been expelled, it let out a great howl of anger which echoed right round the mountain. Corbaran and his men were terrified, hearing it clearly in the leafy orchard. The king called his men around him. 'My lords', said Corbaran, 'did you hear that? I heard the serpent bellowing and yelling. We have been stupid to hang around for so long; we should make ready to depart immediately. We are not going to see our bold Frenchman again; I don't think he can have been able to hold out for long. The Sathanas has killed him, slaughtered him and devoured him'. At this our Frenchmen burst into tears on account of Baldwin, whom they had dearly loved. Richard and his entourage were devastated. 'Alas, noble companion and all that is good about you! We have been through so much suffering together. You will never see your city of Beauvais again, or your wife or your extensive family'. 'Things have turned out badly for us', said John of Alis. 'I am all too aware that we have made a bad mistake. We shall never command any respect in a decent court or get a hearing from any nobleman if we allow ourselves to be disconcerted by such an insignificant event. We should have gone up with him. But there is not one of you who is not strong enough to fall in with my suggestion if he so wishes. Before evening falls let us climb the mountain to see this so-powerful serpent. I will take it on with my sharp sword. Leaving Baldwin breaks my heart'. 'I agree with all this', replied Corbaran. 'I will definitely go with you, taking 400 armed Saracens along with me, each one carrying a lance or a good feathered dart'. Our Frenchmen were overjoyed when they heard this. They fell at Corbaran's feet in gratitude. 'My lords', said Corbaran, 'you have shown me signal honour since the day when you helped me escape from the thick of battle in my combat with my kinsman Sorgalé and you helped me onto a fresh warhorse. Let me make it clear: that has put you firmly in my favour. Once you are back from the Holy Sepulchre, I will give you so much from my wealth that you will be counted rich'. 'That is highly generous, my lord', replied the Christians. 'Your mercy on us will be well rewarded'. 'By the Holy Trinity', said the abbot of Fécamp, 'we should get under way to help Baldwin, our particular companion'. 'That is quite right, Your Reverence', said the bishop [of Forez]. 'I have an inkling he is still alive'.

78

'My lords', said the bishop, 'let me tell you to look at this King Corbaran who holds us in his power. He is very powerful and a great lord, and we must carry out his commands to our utmost ability. If he allows us we will go up the mountain and take on that hated beast in combat, and help Baldwin if he is still alive'. 'In faith', said Corbaran, 'I will not stop you doing this. Indeed I will go up with you and form part of your company. I will not fail you in your hour of need'. He called Morehier and Bruiant of Orcanie. 'You will accompany me to the great wasteland, taking 400 Saracens with us. We shall not take those who are injured: they will be responsible for guarding the deserts of Orcanie'. The Saracens agreed and each one acceded to the request: they made a battalion of 400. They set out towards Mount Tigris. But before they got up as far as the bare rock, God the son of the Virgin Mary arranged things so that an amazing host of pagans came up, Saracens and Persians from as far off as Tabarie. It did not take long for the news to reach Jerusalem, with God's blessing: he who believes in God had achieved a truly amazing feat.

79

Pagans and Saracens together and our own Frenchmen did not hang back: they went up the tall mountain at a good speed. But before they reached it they were to suffer so badly that not one would have come back alive from the pagan army if you ask me had it not been for our Frenchmen. Their presence acted as a protection for them that day because God came to their help as part of His plan. I do not want to add further to the song: I shall say no more about how these made their way, but will turn to Baldwin and his resolute bravery, fighting painfully on the mountain against the Sathanas, which was bringing him to the edge of despair. The dart he flung at it was of no avail. The serpent kept on mounting close attacks. If the Lord who is king of the East and was born of the Virgin Mary in Bethlehem does not come to his aid now, nothing remains to protect him from being killed. The Sathanas looked at him balefully; its ability to defend itself was truly amazing. It would have been impossible to find a man who could hold out for long enough or mount an attack on it. Baldwin ran towards it, enraged. It slashed at him with its talons, which were very sharp, on the left and split his shield. His hauberk could not protect him against this. As the stroke followed through it ripped and tore the chain mesh and ripped the flesh on his ribs beneath, tearing it off all the way down to his hips so that the bone poked through – if the story is to be believed. By Almighty God, it is hardly surprising if the nobleman staggered and was overcome by fear. He invoked the name of Jesus loudly. He brandished one of his swords which had a silver cross on it, intending to strike a blow: the Sathanas seized it and bit it in half, then immediately made as if to gulp it down. Here God who rules the world made an impressive intervention: he made Baldwin's sword grow inside the beast's throat so that it nearly cut through the chest.

80

Now keep quiet and listen to the feats which God performed along with St Nicholas and the angel Michael and the noble St Gervais. Baldwin stuck the tip of the sword into [the beast's] palate so that blood gushed out of its mouth. So that meant he could defend himself from the slashing talons since he no longer had to worry about the teeth. Now may the Lord who created clergy and laymen come to his help! Baldwin looked [the Sathanas] in the eye; he had never felt such joy, and could not have felt more delighted even if he had been offered the fief of Edessa.[89] The serpent tried to stick in its talons and gaped wide; Baldwin called on all the names of God together.

81

As Baldwin ran through the names and conjured the saints and their miraculous attributes, King Jesus carried out a superb miracle for him. The Devil flew out of [the beast's] mouth without enough time to take his leave or the power to stay any longer. The barons saw him in the form of a crow. The Sathanas staggered and nearly fell over because the Devil had come out of it. It had devastated and laid waste the surrounding countryside, killing Saracens young and old alike. When the raging serpent came across Baldwin, it thought it could beat him on the rocky shelves. It slashed down into his helmet with its talons, knocking it from his head and snapping the laces, and inflicted four wounds which streamed with blood. But the nobleman stood firm, as anyone should for Jesus. In my view he would have been overcome and killed if it had not been for God remembering him and coming to his aid, along with St Michael the angel and his power. Baldwin brandished a sword which had been forged four times and very skilfully sharpened, tempered and honed. He faced up to [the Sathanas] resolutely, ran towards it and landed a huge blow on it with the beaten blade above his ears, but the skin was not even broken because it was tougher than forged steel. The steel sword bent and nearly broke. Baldwin stayed on his feet and fell back. 'Ah God!' he said, 'this is certainly a tough beast. There has not been one like it since God was born'. I will tell you about the enemy who had come out of the serpent. He had flown down and descended on Corbaran's people. He stirred up such confusion where he landed that no Turk or Frenchman was not overwhelmed. A tempest arose which wreaked such havoc that even Corbaran was left lying prostrate in the desert along with Balan of Orcanie and his companion Morehier. In my opinion it was the biggest tempest anyone had ever seen. When the abbot of Fécamp came spurring up, he blessed them and absolved them in the name of God, and the bishop [of Forez] greeted them courteously. The Devil turned and ran to the river. Nobody knew what became of him: he disappeared from the scene. The tempest abated and they all stood up.

82

The tempest abated and the heat began to build. They all clambered up, scrutinising the bare rock. The pagans and Saracens, those infidels, would soon have been in torment if it had not been for our honourable race of Frenchmen: He who made the heavens and the dew rescued [the infidels] for their sake. 'My lords', said

---

[89] Reminiscent of Baldwin of Boulogne, who did gain the kingdom of Edessa.

Corbaran, 'this is proved beyond doubt. It is because of you that we are saved in this desert. When we return you will be richly rewarded and I shall have you brought to the honoured land'.

83

Corbaran of Oliferne boldly climbed the high mountain without a moment's hesitation, accompanied by his favourite Morehiers and by Balan of Orcanie, along with 400 Turks from his household of liegemen; Harpin of Bourges, Lord John of Alis, the abbot of Fécamp from Normandy, the bishop of Forez (may Jesus bless him), Fulcher of Melun and Raymond of Pavia [were all with him]. The company of God numbered more than 60, all armed to the teeth and ready for battle. A narrow path led up the bare rock, through a grim ravine which made them distinctly apprehensive. They went in single file, which perturbed them. This was the site of a highly heroic feat of King Corbaran. As you know, God the son of the Virgin held him in high favour. He was baptised in his ancient city, and along with him 20,000 pagan Turks.[90] His mother, the white-haired Calabra, was deeply upset by this, so much so that her life was at risk. She declared the greatest war ever heard of, which raged right across the realm of the pagans: and Corbaran himself was besieged by a mighty army in his ancient city of Oliferne. Now you are going to hear a song which will not be a disappointment: nobody has ever composed, sung or heard anything quite like it. I am going to tell you about Baldwin of deathless memory, who sought out the serpent with his shining sword. The battle between the hateful beast and brave Baldwin – may God help him – lasted from the chimes at midday right through to compline.[91]

84

My lords, noble and brave knights, now listen and you can hear about an amazing and desperate battle: you will never have heard anything quite like it in your lifetime. Listen to how the brave warrior Baldwin sought out the serpent with his sharp sword. He rained blows on it, in front and into its sides and behind, but its hide was so tough that he could not hurt it or do as much as a bezant's worth of damage to it. The serpent reared up, but with the sharp sword stuck across its jaws by Jesus' command it could not use its teeth to defend itself. The serpent had a long, thick, heavy tail, and slammed it into Baldwin's glittering golden shield; it sent him spinning round three times and nearly knocked him off his feet; and it sent the shield flying from his neck. If the wicked [serpent] had followed through on its attack, Baldwin would never have seen the powerful King Corbaran again,

---

[90] This looks ahead to the *Chrétienté Corbaran*. The reference could have been inserted by a later compiler.

[91] Further emphasis on the importance of Baldwin's exploit marked by oral formula.

nor the brave warrior Richard of Chaumont. But the strength of our redeeming Father in Heaven and the Holy Spirit did not forget him, and the angels in the sky offered him comfort. Baldwin picked up his shield from the massive rock; he took his sword in his right hand and ran towards the serpent. The battle was so hard-fought until sundown that no cleric could describe it, nor could any *jongleur*'s song suffice.

85

Baldwin of Beauvais was a daring warrior, because he was beloved of God Who extended His protection to him. He did not hesitate to pick up his shield again. The serpent had damaged it and knocked it about. He held his sword with its shining blade in his right hand. The angel comforted him, much to his joy. Filled with rage he pursued the serpent. The Sathanas was having problems running because it had lost so much blood and was weakened as a result, and because the Devil had left its body. It turned on Baldwin, enraged and vicious. It tore his curved shield with its talons, piercing it in 10 places and ripping it away from his neck, tearing the strap which was of dark-coloured silk. The talons met his white mesh hauberk, leaving the links broken and displaced behind them. It was only because God protected him that they did not rip into his flesh. The serpent was on the point of trapping him between its two feet, and he could not long have avoided death had it not been for God and the Holy Spirit holding him, along with the most holy angel who placed himself in front of Baldwin.[92]

86

The battle was a great one, hard and long fought. Believe you me, this is the truth; no Christian had ever seen a harder one. Listen to the demonstration God made of his strength! Baldwin ran straight for the beast, sword in hand and taking it head on. The jaws of the Sathanas gaped wide open because of the sword which had got stuck in it, going right through the palate and handicapping the serpent so badly that it was exhausted and unable to get its breath. Baldwin pressed his attack in sheer terror of the serpent. Jesus ordained in the power of His name that the beast should faint from sheer loss of blood. When Baldwin saw this, he looked up to the heavens. Even if someone had given him a whole valley full of gold he could not have been happier about the course of events. He went straight forward without hesitation and plunged the blade of the sword into the beast's throat. He rammed it in with such enthusiasm that it went right into the beast's vital organs and out the other side, stopping only when it reached the rock-hard heart. As it could not penetrate there, the blade came out elsewhere, slicing through the liver near the spine. The beast collapsed sprawling on the ground and died then and there,

---

[92] Presumably the Archangel Michael, referred to above at laisse 74.

commending its soul to the devils of Hell. Baldwin retrieved his sword, which was drenched in blood, and retreated into a cave in the cliff. The wound in his side had bled so much that he was struggling to see and his head drooped; he had gone pale from loss of blood, and collapsed in a faint on a wide flat stone.

87

Baldwin lay in a dead faint across the stone ledge. When he came round he got back to his feet. He looked all round him, and saw the head of his brother lying on the mound, on a wide stone with moss on top. He recognised it from the cast of the features, the long beard and the distinctive chin. He flung himself down beside it and burst into a storm of tears. 'Alas, my brother', he said, 'your sons and your wife are wasting their time waiting for you back at home. You will never see them again, noble baron's son'. He tore at his beard and moustache.

88

'Alas, my brother', he said, 'how prudent you were, how wise and generous; how full of good sense your heart was, and a model of noble behaviour. When you crossed the Arm of St George with me, you unburdened your concerns from your heart to me. You would never return or come back once you had seen and met pagans and looked at the land where Lord God was born and the Holy Sepulchre in which his body was laid. When I remember this, my brother, I am overcome with sorrow; as you are dead, my friend, it seems wrong that I am still alive'. He picked up the head and cradled it in his arms, showering it with kisses and washing it with tears from his eyes. Now picture Corbaran coming up the mountain with his 400 Turks, all heavily armed sergeants. Harpin and his company came behind them. Every last one was completely exhausted, dripping with sweat from anxiety and anguish; the burning heat of the sun had worn them out. As each one of them made his way up the rock, Baldwin – who had got to his feet – heard them. Nobody ever experienced such joy from the day he was born. 'Ah, God! Noble Lord', he said, 'may you be worshipped'. Seeing his companions, he looked into their faces: you do not need to ask whether his heart rejoiced to see them. 'Ah God, noble King in glory, all praise be to You because now I can see the people I most wanted to see coming here. I would never have been able to make my way down from this rock: I am in too much pain, too badly hurt and wounded. But God the King in glory has brought them here'. 'Your arrival is very welcome', he said to his companions. 'All of you have suffered to get here. May Jesus, King of Heaven ensure you get your reward'. With these words picture them coming up to him. The bishop of Forez and the abbot of Fécamp kissed him full on the face in transports of friendship; then they looked at the wounds in his side. Not one of them failed to be concerned at the sight; and they were all the more delighted he had come out alive. Baldwin saw the king and went to his feet: he made to kiss them but was raised up.

89

The powerful King Corbaran sat down next to Baldwin along with the bishop of Forez and the abbot of Fécamp, the brave and noble Richard of Chaumont, Harpin of Bourges and John the Norman.[93] They looked at the wounds the noble [Baldwin] had on his sides, and not one of them did not marvel at them. Baldwin, in terrible pain, fainted away in the midst of the Saracens in front of our Frenchmen. They looked over to the side near the clefts in the ground and saw the beast. It was enormous, a good 30 feet long by our guess. It had long tough hair, like the Devil. Its talons and teeth were sharply pointed. Its blood was running down its back, blacker than pitch boiling on a fire. You should imagine Saracens and Persians round it, inflicting more than 1,000 blows with their sharp swords. None of them made as much impact on it as the value of a glove or were able to inflict as much as four *deniers*' worth of damage on it. In fact several, I do not know how many, broke their swords. 'By Mahomed, my lords', said King Corbaran, 'I am well aware how great is the strength of your God. He has more power than Tervagant, Mahomed and Apollon in whom I believe. If it were not for the royal Sultan and my mother the magician Calabra, I would get myself baptised; she would be broken-hearted if she knew, and not all the gold in Damascus would save me from her plunging a knife into my side'. 'My lord', said the bishop, 'our religion is a powerful one'. The blood drained from the Saracens' faces when they heard this. If God, the Heavenly Redeemer, did not come to their aid, the words powerful King Corbaran had just uttered were going to be dangerous ones, because they would lead the Emir Sultan to declare war on them and besiege the rich city of Oliferne. The land around it and a good part of the surrounding countryside within 10 days' journey would all be laid waste.

90

'My lords', said Corbaran, 'let me suggest that we go and see the mosque where this devilish creature used to live'. 'We agree', they replied. The whole company moved off in short order. Now let me tell you what they found, the blessing of God be upon you: red gold, white silver, Russian silken cloths, silk from Almeria and fabric from Esclavonia. There was enough to load up 30 Syrian mules. 'My lords', said Corbaran, 'we do not want to leave all this lying around'. But before they could come back down from the bare rocks even the best of them would be wishing he was anywhere but there even for all the gold in Hungary.[94]

---

[93] Not mentioned elsewhere: probably John of Alis. Norman fits the rhyme.

[94] The Sultan's arrival is marked by three *laisses similaires*. The references to Hungary, Besançon and Biés are formulaic to fit the rhyme.

91

'My lords', said Corbaran, 'let us take possession of all these riches and make our way back to those who are awaiting us – I to my Saracens and you to your companions. We will share the gains equally with them and go back to Oliferne together. My mother will be overjoyed when we get there. She will listen to the story of our adventures even though she already knows how we have got on.[95] If you wish to stay we shall have a most enjoyable time'. 'My lord, we are happy to follow your commands without demur', they replied. But before evening falls and the sun goes down, even the best of them would rather not be there even for all the gold in Besançon.

92

'My lords', said Corbaran, 'do not wait to be asked – take some of this treasure which is tied up into bundles; if you can carry it you will find it of great use. Wealth enables many men to be waited on hand and foot, their every wish granted, and their every bodily need honoured, met and respected'. They bundled up the riches ready to be transported. The serpent which had given them such a hard time had collected it all; it had taken it from the people it had devoured, ambushing them on their way from fairs and markets. The abbot of Fécamp, however, good and learned cleric that he was, did not want to take any of it, and neither did the other clergy. Indeed he reprimanded them, saying: 'You should not take any of this. You know full well that it has not come from God'. Most of them retorted, 'You are talking nonsense. Only a fool would leave such a treasure after winning it'. But before any of them could make it back to our own people, not even the best of them would want to be there even for the city of Biés.[96] Corbaran stood up and walked forward. He saw the army of the royal Sultan spread out across the plain below, more than 60,000 pennons raised aloft. Corbaran was appalled at the sight. Both pagans and our Frenchmen were horrified: you can be sure they all thought that it was Arfulans who had found them out and his noble barons who had followed them there.

93

Corbaran of Oliferne, hero of many brave feats, looked down from the cliffs towards the right and saw the army of the royal Sultan swarming across the rocks. They numbered more than 60,000, each on a fine warhorse; not one of them was without a mailed hood and a strong steel helmet, a good sharp sword and a good

---

[95] As we saw in laisse 10.
[96] As Myers comments, it is not clear what city this might be and it is there to fit the rhyme.

dart for throwing, and a strong round shield which was decorated with pure gold. In front of them rode more than 10,000 archers: there were crossbowmen and numerous lightly armed troops carrying Greek fire in brass pots to throw: they intended to burn and destroy the Sathanas.[97] Corbaran looked down onto them from his high vantage point; he pointed them out to our *chétifs* (may God help them!) and also to the Turks Brulant and Morehier. 'My lords', said Corbaran, 'I need you to advise me. You see down there the wide plain full of massed ranks of Saracens. That is the great dynasty that I live in fear of, the relatives of Sorgalé who are hardly my best friends. We were sorry to see the death of Sorgalé of Allier, and of Goliath of Mecca who carried out so many heroic feats. I do not want to hide the truth from you: we are all dead men. There is no way we can defend ourselves against such a mighty force. It is Baldwin who has got me into such a difficult position. We are dead men, noble lords, and it is all his fault. None of us will be able to help each other. Alas, lord Mahomed! What plans I had! I was going to adorn your ribs and your sides with pure gold! Why on earth did you make me turn aside from the right path and climb up to wander in this desert place?' 'In God's name, do not lose heart', said the abbot of Fécamp. 'He Whose place is to judge the world can easily come to your aid'.

94

'My lords', said Corbaran, 'let me just say this. I made a big mistake in climbing up this mountain. Don't be surprised if I am terrified: I see my death on the horizon and I cannot get away from it. I know full well I cannot escape and you will all die, which grieves me profoundly. Alas Lord Mahomed! I shall never see them again, Richard and his companions whom I left behind in the orchard. Our enemies are heading for them and I cannot help them, aid them or advise them. Mahomed, what shall I do? Alas, my noble lord bishop, how can I fight this? I want to die with honour: I shall not remain here. When I left her, my mother said that I would find myself in great difficulty of this kind. But she lied to me: I shall never come out of this alive'. 'Noble king, my gracious lord, I have some sound advice for you', said the abbot of Fécamp, a man of great integrity. If you choose to do what I suggest, worship Jesus Christ who makes the bulrushes grow, wine and corn and dew in May, I can tell you for certain that he will come to your support; and if you pledge yourself to God and St Nicholas you and all the rest of us will be protected against death: I know this for a fact'. 'I shall accede to this', replied Corbaran. 'I want to beg God in His mercy to protect us, and His mother Mary of whom I have heard,

---

[97] The Naval Museum at Haifa preserves small earthenware pots for Greek fire; these would have been both cheaper and more practical, since they would smash when thrown and spread the fire. Possibly the fire was brought in brass pots for protection and decanted when ready for use; or clay pots could have been carried inside brass pots. See J. R. Partington, *A History of Greek Fire and Gunpowder* (Cambridge, 1960) p. 22 for Greek fire carried in copper pots.

who nurtured God inside her – I believe this and I will invoke Him; He was born of her and I shall be saved through Him; I shall go to seek Him in Jerusalem, where he was put to death, and will serve Him in the Temple for a year and more. Let all of you hear what I have to say. I shall make this gift. If I come out of here alive, I shall have myself baptised'.[98] By God, clerks and lay alike were overjoyed. I am not surprised at just how delighted they were.

95

As the valiant Corbaran lamented over his imminent death and his men whom he had left behind in the leafy woods, his fear – this is absolutely true – gave God the opportunity to plant a wonderful thought in his heart, which he told the bishop immediately. He would believe in God, author of heavens and dew, sea and earth, fresh and salt water, Who took on human form in the womb of the Virgin Mary. Our people were delighted to hear this. By God! How many pious tears, and how many affirmations of faith heard in fear of death. He pledged to the bishop and his clergy that, if God brought them back to their own country safe and sound, they would receive baptism through the renewal of faith. Corbaran looked down the valley and saw the host of the royal Sultan making towards him. 400 Saracens came spurring ahead of the main force at great speed, each wearing a helmet, and did not draw rein until they reached the spring. There they found those of our people who had remained there. Richard and his companions were terrified. They seized their weapons, each buckling on his sword, and made preparations to defend themselves.

96

My lords, good Christians as you are, listen to me in God's name and I will tell you about those who were left in the orchard. They readied themselves to fight. Now imagine the Turks who had ridden ahead of the main force, not drawing rein until they reached the spring. Frightened of the serpent, they had all armed themselves to the teeth. They asked our men: 'Tell us straight away, who are you people resting here? Are you Saracens or are you Christians?' A Turk skilled in languages replied: 'We are amongst the closest associates of King Corbaran. The king has gone up Mount Tigris taking 400 Saracens with him to fight with the serpent who is so feared. Our friend and protector has left us here, and we are astonished that he has taken so long. We hope that the Lord Who makes the corn grow, the vines flourish and the meadows grow green will bring him back to us'. 'So is it really the case that Corbaran has gone up into the crags?' they asked. 'Yes it is, by Mahomed: have no doubt on the subject. And whom do we have the

---

[98] The text carefully stops short of Corbaran actually accepting baptism; this is saved for the *Chrétienté Corbaran*.

pleasure of addressing?' 'We are the men of the Sultan who has numerous castles. He has summoned his men from the realms of Persia: more than 60,000 are riding with him. The mountain will be under control for a long way around: and if the Sathanas is found there he will be killed or burnt with Greek fire and reduced to dust. 'May God be worshipped!' said Richard of Chaumont. The pagans watered their horses at the spring and slaked their own thirst. Then imagine them making their way back, spurring over pebbles and sand. They reached the royal Sultan. 'Our lord, you do not know half the marvellous things we are going to tell you. Listen and marvel. The noble King Corbaran of Oliferne has climbed up to the crags to find the serpent who haunts them. He is fighting at this very moment, and you will never see him again if Mahomed does not use his great power on his behalf. Lord, you must come to his help'. The Sultan nearly went mad when he heard this. 'Get ready to help him', he said to his men. 'I would not want his death for 14 cities. I shall never know happiness again if he is injured, or feel contentment in my heart if he is eaten'. The pagans fanned out across the surrounding countryside. Imagine how quickly they made their way to the start of the path, and all rushed to be the first to make their way up. Corbaran saw them clearly, and said to his men: 'My lords, whatever shall we do? Our enemies are coming to seek us out. Get ready to defend yourselves; if you do not you will lose your heads'. 'You need have no fear of that', they replied. The abbot of Fécamp, a man of great goodness, and the admirable Harpin of Bourges said: 'Anyone who does not defend himself properly should be proclaimed an infidel, who will not see the land where Jesus was made to suffer or the revered Sepulchre where His body was laid'.

97

Corbaran saw the Turks making their way up the path, strung out one behind the other and climbing as fast as they could. They were heavily armed so that they could attack the beast, and were carrying Greek fire to burn it. They were desperate to come to Corbaran's rescue and happy to suffer on his account. Corbaran heaved a sigh on seeing them; I have to be honest and say he was terrified of dying. 'Don't fail me!' he said to his men. 'Take up position at this pass and defend it stoutly: this is where we shall make our stand to save ourselves'. At that you might have seen his men all seizing their weapons. The bishop of Forez started to pronounce a blessing on them and to encourage them to raise their spirits. They were ignorant of the joy which awaited them.

98

Corbaran was in a terrible state, desperate to defend himself; they took up position in the pass, putting their shields in front of them. Now imagine the Persians and Saracens coming on them. 'Who are you up there?' they cried at the tops of their voices. 'Are you King Corbaran, the friend and intimate of the Sultan?' 'Who are you down there?' replied Corbaran. 'If you are coming to do us harm, come up and find us'. 'You have no need to worry', they replied. 'We have not come here to attack you but to help all of you with our utmost strength. We are the Sultan's men along with the emir. The Sultan is waiting for you beneath that leafy pine. He has come down with your companions: King Abraham is there, and Jonas and Fabus. Come and talk with them: do not hang about'.

99

'My lords', said Corbaran, 'tell me the truth. Is it really the case that the Sultan of Persia has made his way to that leafy grove down there?' 'Yes it is', said the Turks, 'you can be sure of that. There are 60,000 pagans with him. They have come to seek out the serpent and take its life. We have climbed up into this rocky wasteland for your sake. The Sultan has sent us to your aid, to come and help you against the loathed beast. We are carrying Greek fire to scorch and burn it'. Ah God! These words sent our people into transports of delight; not all the gold in Romania would have pleased them as much. They scrambled down the bare rock together, not forgetting the rich treasure. They arrived in the meadow full of green grass, where the Sultan and his numerous company awaited them. Those terrible bastard Saracens were cock-a-hoop about the death of the proud serpent.

100

The Sultan was overjoyed at the sight of Corbaran. He flung his arms round his neck and showered him with kisses. Both Arabs were overcome by delight. They sat down at one side under the branches of a pine tree. Then the Sultan asked Corbaran, 'How did you get here?' 'My lord', said Corbaran, 'we were in a dreadful state. We lost our way before three days had passed and had no idea where we were. We reached the mountain. When I looked up at those crags I realised that I was scared to go up; I was terrified and so were all the Christians with me. We heard the serpent whooping with delight over one of the *chétifs* it had managed to catch. I had with me a brave Christian, indeed the bravest knight I have ever seen. He was the brother of the *chétif* taken by the serpent. He killed the beast with his sharp sword'. The emir was delighted to hear all this: he had never been so pleased in his life.

101

The emir commanded that the knight who had killed the serpent with his own sword should be sent for. Corbaran stood up straight on his dais. He made his way down the slope to the Christians and came to a spring which ran away down a channel with the water crystal clear above the pebbles. The *chétifs* were sitting next to it. They were hardly in a positive frame of mind: they were concerned that Baldwin might have suffered a mortal injury. Corbaran greeted them in the name of the divine Holy Spirit.[99] 'May He Who created hill and dale watch over you. Baldwin, noble friend, get onto this horse and put on this silken cloak. The royal Sultan is asking for you: he wishes you nothing but good'.

102

Baldwin mounted although he was in terrible pain and suffering badly from the wounds he had received. He had not yet had time to wash; he was covered with the blood that had streamed down his body and which had soaked his mailed hauberk right through. The hauberk had been ripped apart from the head right down to the side panel; that was the work of the serpent which had gone for him with its sharp vicious talons. The Frenchman called to Lord Harpin of Bourges, 'You are to come with me, and so is Richard the Norman'. 'We shall do as you command', they replied. Corbaran led them through a grassy meadow to where the Sultan could be found with King Abraham. The emir was delighted to see them. He embraced Baldwin, beaming all over his face, then said: 'Christian, you are a brave and valiant man. I shall never again be after you as long as I live. You have taken revenge on the huge serpent which was devouring all our men and women and children'. He called for his seneschal, whose name was Faramans: 'Give Baldwin 20,000 of my bezants on my behalf, two Arabian horses and two ambling mules so that he can return home rejoicing and happy'.[100]

103

The emir summoned a pagan called Salatré. 'You are also to give presents from me to the good knight Richard, the one who killed Sorgalé and Chapoé's brother Goliath of Mecca, so that he is aware of my generosity. Give him a free choice of horses and palfreys, and as many high-quality weapons as he wants – for the companions who have come with him too so that they are recognised for their friendship with those two. Let all the *chétifs* be released from prison in my realm and return to their homes safe and sound'. 'That is well said, my lord', responded Corbaran. 'Let those in my realm receive the same treatment'. King Abraham added, 'I shall not stand in the way. My captives will be released too'.[101] Our Frenchmen were delighted to hear all this. As soon as they had tied up the loose ends, they got under way without further ado. Each returned to his beloved homeland. The Sultan returned home with his noble entourage, and the army he had assembled dispersed

---

[99] Despite being a Saracen.
[100] The mason at the start of the text is also called Faramans.
[101] The *chétifs* secure release and redemption not only for themselves but for other captives.

back to its home. News went out all across the kingdom that the serpent who had laid everything waste was dead. Those who had abandoned it – this is quite true – all returned eagerly to their original lands, repopulating the land which had been repeatedly laid waste. Corbaran returned along the direct route, a well-made road, with Richard and his companions, well-beloved by God. They rode at high speed, spurring ahead and making their way up hill and down dale, and did not draw rein until they reached Oliferne. The people came flooding out from the city to meet them, falling over themselves in their eagerness to hear the news. Nobody born of woman could possibly describe the joy and happiness they exhibited.

104

Corbaran of Oliferne, white-bearded, and our men Richard and his companions, now free, did not draw rein until they reached the city. The inhabitants came pouring out to hear about the wonderful events which had taken place. Corbaran's elderly white-haired mother came out to meet Richard and greeted him elaborately, kissing his bare hand four times. They entered the city by the Damascus Gate, which was decked with silken cloths and hangings extending all the way up the main street. The populace, even the meanest, strewed the earth with reeds and bulrushes.

105

People and nobles alike entered Oliferne. Richard and the *chétifs*, true believers, rode in fully armed on the horses they had captured from the pagans, sorrel and black and chestnut. The whole main street of the noble city was richly decked with carmine silk; light was reflected off the silk and purple fabric. The children celebrated enthusiastically. Had you been there you would have heard the music of 1,000 pipes, drums and vielles playing tunes. The noble young soldiers flourished their swords whilst noble young women flaunted themselves, walking along and singing in twos and threes or four or six together. The women of the town rode alongside the *chétifs* while in an excess of joy the richest Turks spread their furs and ermines on the ground for them to ride over.

106

Lord Harpin of Bourges and his companions took off their armour together. Corbaran's mother did not wait but ordered water to be brought immediately. She sat them down for a banquet and had more bread and wine and pepper brought than they could eat. When they had eaten and drunk their fill their minds turned to their pilgrimage. They burst into tears and, heaving sighs, went to find the king straight away. 'Your Majesty, grant us leave to depart as you agreed with the noble Richard, who put himself forward to do battle against those two Turks in front of all your retinue and retrieve your position. He saved all of us from certain death by cutting off their heads with his blade inlaid with silver'. 'My lords', said Corbaran, 'that was indeed the case. I shall be delighted to grant you leave to go, and will have you given safe conduct from my country. You have served me well and you will not suffer for it'.

107

'My lords', said Corbaran, 'a moment of your time. I should like you to stay here with me for eight days, eating at my table and drinking with me. Once you are feeling recovered from your wounds, I will give you leave to depart with assurance of my true friendship. I will give you so many presents from my own possessions that you cannot but be grateful to me: horses, palfreys and experienced warhorses, tents and shelters against rain and storms, and silk cloths and fabrics for you to wear. I will designate a force of 1,000 well-armed Turks to accompany you'. 'I thank you most fervently, noble Corbaran, if this is how you intend to treat us', replied Count Harpin. 'Yes', said the king, 'you will not be let down'.

108

'My lords, listen to what I have to say', said Count Harpin. 'The king is graciously granting our wish. Go and rest quietly; have no fear, God will show us His mercy. Meanwhile I am going to take a ride out by those springs on my palfrey: I am feeling a bit in need of a change of air'. 'That makes me anxious, my lord', said John of Alis. 'Whether you need a ride or not, that is what I am telling you, in faith'. Count Harpin, the French count, mounted, taking no retinue with him. He hung his shield round his neck and carried a spear, buckling on his sword. The count left through the Gate of the Ravine, which is down in a grove. Now listen to the amazing thing which happened to the faithful count that day: I am not lying.

109

My lords, God bless you. Listen and you will hear about the greatest marvel ever – it is all true, believe you me. As the count went out by the gate, a child was bathing next to fishponds in a meadow on the left flank of the mountain. He was the son of a rich man with extensive lands. There was a young man there born in Turkey; he was a nephew of Corbaran by his sister Florie, who was the lady of Fondefle and all of Syria. The old woman loved him as well as her own heart and life. The master whose job it was to teach and chastise him had left him under an olive tree with white leaves. Dozing beneath his cloak he was watching a boat and the children playing in the glinting waters of Cordie. The worse for him! Poor thing, he has no idea what will happen to him before nones are over. A huge lion made its way down from the crags. The Arab peoples there called him Papion.[102] He ran up to the child, seized him and ran off with him clasped across his jaws. The child howled and screamed.

110

My lords and noble knights, listen to the amazing events which befell this child whom the enormous lion carried off in his jaws: the pagans called the lion Papion.[103] Count Harpin saw this and came spurring up as fast as his horse could carry him, lowering his spear. The beast made off without fear, across the sharp vicious mountain rocks. Harpin chased him for seven whole leagues. Unless the Lord who is king of the East thinks to help him, the count will try in vain to retrieve the child. Those who had been bathing at the spot were appalled. They made their way back to the city in a state of great agitation, all yelling at the tops of their voices that a huge lion had carried off Corbaran's nephew. Terrified, the Saracens and Persians all leapt up and flung themselves onto their horses. They swarmed out of Oliferne, spurring on at top speed and took up the chase through the thickest part of the forest.

111

The city was in uproar. Its inhabitants, who had slept through the heat of the afternoon, were in a state of agitation. The news reached the elderly queen. Meanwhile two Turks reported to Corbaran that a wild beast had come rampaging down the valley and carried his nephew off in its jaws. 'Alas!' said Corbaran, 'what a cruel twist of Fate!' He tore his hair and pulled at his grey beard. His mother was beside herself: she tore her tunic and sweeping robe, flung herself onto her horse and set off in pursuit through the thick branches of the forest.

112

Meanwhile the lion was making a rapid escape, carrying with it the child of high lineage. Every so often he put the child down on the ground then picked him up again. Count Harpin was spurring in pursuit, and had followed his tracks for a good seven leagues. He might have had to do so for the rest of his life had it not been for an extraordinary monkey which came out of the undergrowth. It saw the

---

[102] For the word 'papion' see Jacques de Vitry: 'sunt ibi papiones quos canes silvestres appellant: lupis acriores, continuis clamoribus de nocte ululantes' ('there can be found papiones, which they call woodland dogs; they are more vicious than wolves and howl continuously through the night'): *Histoire orientale: historia orientalis*, (ed.) and transl. J. Donnadieu (Turnhout, 2008), LXXXVIII pp. 351–2.

[103] *Laisses enchaînées.*

child being carried off and and immediately took a fancy to him It confronted the savage lion at a narrow defile and took the child from it by force.

113

The Count saw the two beasts turn on each other, snapping and fighting. The great lion tired first and left the mountain, tired and dripping; it could no longer put up a fight against the monkey. Harpin watched it beat a retreat. Sitting on his horse, he spurred ahead with all his might. He could see the child on the ground weeping bitterly, but could not get to him fast enough. Instead he saw the monkey pick him up under one arm and climb a tree. Even a squirrel would have found it hard to shin up. The Count came to the foot of the tree and dismounted.

114

So there was the Count under the tree, in a state of some perturbation. He had tied his horse to it by the reins. He was tired out, dripping with sweat and at the end of his tether He could see the monkey up in the tree with the child between its feet, sitting between two branches and leaning comfortably against the trunk. It is hardly surprising that the child was terrified. 'Ah God!' said the count, 'Holy Virgin Mary, give me your counsel in your holy mercy. Alas, why did I abandon my companions? I have got so far away from them in this wild land that I no longer know where I am and evening is drawing in'. While he was lamenting in this way, imagine four lions coming out of the undergrowth and converging on him. If the Lord Who pardons our sins does not spare him a thought, he will be eaten and devoured in short order.

115

The count saw the lions making for him, and you can be sure he was terrified he was going to die. 'Ah God Who allowed Longinus to strike you with the Lance and willingly died on the Cross to redeem Your holiest souls from Hell, Baal, Elisha and the martyr Abel, Noah and Abraham to serve you – as all this is true, God, do not let me perish!' He drew his sword, his companion in many feats, and made a ring round himself which he marked with the sign of the Cross in the name of the Holy Spirit, in such a way that his horse could lie down in it. He loudly invoked the great name of Jesus in his terror of death, something I do not dare tell you. The result was that the lions, determined as they were to attack him and devour him and his horse, were not able to get to him or his horse because God, protector of all, showed his great power.[104]

---

[104] Reminiscent of Daniel in the lions' den; often depicted, for example in a twelfth-century carving of Daniel in Worms cathedral. Also evokes the Biblical image of the Devil

116

The count saw the lions surrounding the circle, patrolling round it, yawning and lunging with their claws. But God, salvation of all, showed his great power by ensuring that they could not get to Harpin or his horse. The count, dismounted, thought about his situation. He conjured the lions in the name of St Jerome, who took a thorn out of the lion's foot when he was in too much pain to walk.[105] As soon as the lions heard him invoke St Jerome, it was enough to make them turn tail and run away immediately. Now night fell and it began to rain. Ah God! What an amazing thing he saw now, with serpents and beasts passing him. A bowshot away was a freshwater lake where they were all going to drink, because (as I have been told) there was no other water fresh enough to drink within seven leagues. The Count was in such discomfort that he was on the point of giving up when the monkey started to make its way down the tree with the child tucked under its arm; it wanted to carry him back to the monkeys' lair to have some fun with him. The monkey jumped down to the ground. Harpin speared it and the child, to his great delight, broke free. You can imagine the monkey's consternation. It leapt around trying to get the child back. But the count defended him stoutly with his shining sword.

117

The monkey was old, large and powerfully built; it had amazing arms shaggy with age, big feet and a large head; it was powerful and strongly built; its ears were hairy and his teeth sharply pointed.[106] May God, all-powerful in Heaven, protect the count! He wore neither hood nor hauberk; instead he was clad in a rich cloth adorned with beaten gold. The monkey made three leaps. It reached him with the fourth, leaping at least three feet above his head. Had it not been for Harpin's shield, which he flung over his head in a fit of strength, the monkey would have grabbed his hair. As it was he was forced to his knees. The monkey grabbed his shield and leapt on it; it ripped apart the strongly glued joints with its teeth, and the gilded buckler and the feather above.

118

The monkey grabbed the shield. It pulled off the buckler, ripped it to pieces and tore apart all the nails; it chewed the gold-painted border. Then it turned back on the count, jaws gaping in fury. Harpin seized the child. He slashed at the monkey

---

as a roaring lion seeking whom he may devour: 1 Peter 5:8.

[105] Apocryphal story about St Jerome, often depicted in art.

[106] Monkeys were seen as ugly and analogous to Satan: *Bestiary: Manuscript Bodley 764*, presented R. Barber (Woodbridge, 1999) pp. 48–9.

with his sword and sliced off its arm at the shoulder – this is quite true – and wrapped the child in the skirt of his garment which was ornamented with fur. The monkey retired hurt, slinking away furious and in pain from its wounds.

119

So now the monkey retreated, badly injured; its arm had been severed at the shoulder. It left a trail of blood flowing from it and made for a tree, which it sheltered under to recover. It licked the blood from its wound to make it better. The count picked up his shield, which was in a terrible state, ripped apart, split and the nails torn out. He hung it back round his neck and mounted his horse. Taking the child in his arms he retraced his footsteps and took a well-used path. His horse was in a bad way. Ah God! There was not much to give it that night: no barley or oats and nothing for it to drink. The count took an old path which was frequented by serpents and beasts. He made his way through the wild desert and defiles which hung over the path, making slow progress up hill and down dale. His surcoat was torn by the wild roses, the leather of his shoes ripped and torn so that blood was drawn in several places. Coming down from a hillock he found himself in a valley which had some grass, enough to be valuable. He slackened the gilded rein on his mount and slid down from the exhausted warhorse to let it graze on the grass it desperately wanted. But alas! Why did he dismount there and not push on? He was spotted by some people who came threatening to kill him with sharp knives. 'Ah God!' said the count, 'in your blessed goodness, Holy Lady Mary Who bore in your womb Our Father, Jesus Christ, Salvation of the world; and Lord St Nicholas, who comes to the succour of orphans and widows who sing your praises – save me from death and bring me home safe'. Whilst he lamented thus, imagine the following coming down the valley towards him: some ten cowardly and infidel pagans; with them 20 camels and ten bullocks which they had stolen; and three pack animals loaded with expensively embroidered silks. As the first streaks of dawn appeared at daybreak, they had put to death five merchants by chopping off their heads. Terrible cries echoed round the fortifications; they chased after them on foot and on horseback, but without running a single one to earth in the vast tract of desert from where they had come.

120

It was on a Tuesday in the month of February that the thieves swarmed down from a crag, chasing camels and bullocks in front of them, beasts of burden and priceless silks. All five were well armed, each mounted on an excellent warhorse; they had hauberks, spurs and bows of horn, sharp arrows and darts to throw. All of them were noblemen and high-born knights; Corbaran had had them all exiled from his domain, disinherited and forcibly banished. All five were murderers, robber barons and grave robbers: murder came more naturally to them than eating and drinking. May God who brings succour to all confound them, because they are going to make life very difficult for the count. They fell on him before he could defend himself, just there where he was sitting under an olive tree. When the count saw them coming he was filled with dismay. He ran to his horse but let go of the child, who was immediately seized by the five in a most unfriendly way. Harpin had undone the bridle and this slowed him down considerably. By the time he was able to mount his swift warhorse the Saracen archers had surrounded him from all sides. May God, the judge of all, consign them to perdition! They spoke to him loudly and insultingly. 'And who might you be then, sir? Leave your horse right there. Don't try and take it away if you know what's good for you, or you will be cut to ribbons'. 'Ah God, judge of all!' said the count. 'As You allowed Yourself to be beaten and crucified, tied to the stake and Your side pierced, so defend me, noble Lord, from injury!' He covered himself with his shield and struck the first blow at the oldest of the five brothers. With his steel sword he sent the man's head flying in front of him so that it smashed into the cliff. The brothers were enraged at the sight. Imagine how they stabbed and struck and threw things at him. The mountains are high and the passes forbidding; the noble lord defended himself – may God keep him from harm.[107] Anyone who saw him wielding sword and shield would have no doubt about what a valiant knight he was. The Turks rained arrows on him from their bows of horn, wounding his horse in more than 30 places.[108] Count Harpin positioned himself against a large rock and dismounted. The wicked Saracens – may God be their downfall! – attacked him viciously. He defended his position, his back to the wall. None of the Turks was brave enough to get within striking distance.

121

So now Count Harpin was trapped against the rock, his horse wounded in more than 30 places with sharp arrows and feathered darts. It fell dead beneath him, leaving him even more desperate. He hauled himself a short way up the rock and got himself into a position he could defend. Ah God! How the Turks surrounded him! They rained arrows and well-made feathered darts on him, javelins and darts and crossbow bolts weighted with lead. His shield was pierced, split and knocked into holes; and he himself was wounded in the side by a sharp dart so that the scarlet blood ran down. The noble lord defended himself vigorously, killing two

---

[107] Compare *Roland* line 1830 'halt sunt li pui e tenebrous e grant'. Harpin is implicitly compared to Roland.

[108] Turkish bows are routinely referred to as being made from horn. For an interesting analogy see John Wesley Powell describing bows made of sheep horn by Native Americans: 'these are soaked in water until quite soft, cut into long thin strips and glued together; they are then quite elastic'. *The Exploration of the Colorado River and its Canyons*, J. W. Powell (reprinted London, 2003) p. 319. The Islamic Arts Museum in Kuala Lumpur has some good examples.

of the thieves with two pointed stones. This put fresh heart into him: he cried out 'By the Holy Sepulchre!' at the top of his voice, calling on the noble St Nicholas. 'Alas, Richard of France, I shall never see you again! Lord John of Alis, companion and friend, I wish you were here with me now with all your weapons and fully recovered from your wounds – just think how we should be able to fight off these Turks then!' The oldest remaining brother addressed him. 'Who are you, sir? You have killed my brother and left two of my companions dead. Such a great loss will never be made good; they were excellent thieves and stole large amounts of treasure. I will not let another morsel of food pass my lips as long as you still live: you will have your head cut off with your own sword!' 'Saracen, you lie', replied the Count. 'Just come here and feel my sword. You will be a brave man if you dare to do so and can boast to the entire world'. 'On my head', said the thief, 'you are certainly arrogant. Tell me who you are: do not try and hide your identity'. 'I should be happy to if you could just stop beating me and give me some space', said the count. 'I shall tell you if you want to know'. 'You will have plenty of time for respite', replied the Turk. 'I will not let a morsel pass my lips until you have been cut to ribbons'. 'In faith', said the count, 'you will end up very drunk then. I believe in Jesus Christ Who was hanged from the Cross. My name is Harpin and I am a Frenchman. I am a noble count from Bourges and recognised as its lord, but because I had no son or daughter to be my heir, I sold my lands for hard cash. The most noble king of France, my overlord, bought it from me for a generous price of 30 pack animals loaded with pure gold and silver. No greater treasure trove could be found in France than what the king gave me to fulfil my vow.[109] I was in the army of Peter the Hermit, which you have heard about: I was in the rout at the mountain of Civetot, where I along with many others was taken captive and bound hand and foot. We were taken off to prison in Civetot, 50 French knights of good standing and 140 other captives, bishops and abbots. We carried out hard labour under orders, carrying large rocks to the ramparts and moats and dragging carts like oxen under the yoke all day until evening fell and the sun set. Then each of us was shackled in a vast subterranean room; we stayed there all night until day broke. But each one of us was delivered in an unexpected way, and I and my companions gained our liberty'. 'And just what was this unexpected way? Tell me more', said the thief. 'Since you are so keen to hear about it I will tell you', said the count. 'You have heard all about the siege of Antioch. Bohemond and Tancred, the count of Normandy and brave Thomas [of Marle], and the noble and wise lord Hugh of Vermandois, and their noble forces, bishops and abbots, attacked it with considerable force. The king [of Antioch] sent sealed letters appealing for help to his liege lord, the Sultan of Persia. The Sultan brought together a force of 30 royal kings and the nobility of 30 kingdoms; when they were all assembled their numbers were counted; they totalled 3,000,000, all armed and drawn up outside Antioch. Holy Christendom took them on and killed just about all of them; the only ones

---

[109] This is accurate. Harpin did indeed mortgage his lands to the King of France to go on Crusade. See Jonathan Shepard, 'The muddy road'.

to escape were Corbaran and two of the kings. Corbaran made his escape reduced to despair; the two kings were with him, all three of them broken men. When he returned to his lord he found himself in deep trouble, on trial for causing the death of so many others. The Sultan accused him of having wilfully betrayed them, selling them out and leading them to their deaths. Corbaran defended himself vigorously. He declared a challenge, putting up one Christian against two armed Turks: Richard, one of my companions pledged and sworn to keep faith. One Turk was Goliath of Mecca; the other was called Sorgalé of Valgris. Richard fought them, with God on his side. He cut off their heads, seasoned warrior as he was. As a result everyone gained their freedom; I and my companions were released from captivity. Yesterday morning I was riding my horse outside Oliferne to the spring in the fields. This child here was found down there: he is Corbaran's nephew by his sister. The child was carried outside Oliferne by the king and laid down to sleep under two leafy trees. A huge and savage lion came roaring up and seized the child. The hue and cry was raised. You can imagine for yourself the storm of grief for the child, with people weeping bitterly and tearing their hair'. 'So much the worse', replied the Turk. 'I will not eat another morsel until he is cut to ribbons because I mortally hate him and all his family'.

122

This is what the Turk said to the count. 'If I manage to take you, I shall cut off your head – have no doubt about that – because you killed my brother and I am deeply upset. I have made up my mind I am going to kill this child because his uncle Corbaran is a mortal enemy of mine. He took my inheritance and banished me from the country, and took my lands and fiefs. I will fight him by any means at my disposal. I do not have a castle, fortress or enclosure to call my own other than a rather good cave inside a dark-coloured rocky cliff. It was hollowed out with chisels, hammers and picks. I fear no man born of woman'. The count replied with considerable sagacity, 'You would be very stupid to kill the child. You shall have your land back and good allies to boot. I made a solemn promise and pledge to God that I would not surrender as long as I remained alive. Now I beg help from Him Who was killed for us on the Holy Cross when Longinus struck Him with the Lance'. With that they resumed the fight, with arrows flying and lances thrust hard. Harpin defended himself as a brave knight should. Now listen to the miracle that Jesus Christ brought about. Corbaran was riding out with 500 Arabs; as he searched the desert he found a place which had been trampled, the monkey's arm and traces of feet. They followed in the tracks of the horse. Suddenly three pure white stags with branching antlers walked out onto the road in front of Corbaran: imagine the scene. Corbaran followed them up hill and down dale. My lords, they were St George, St Barbara and St Domitian. They climbed all the way up to the rock where the count was sitting. He had fought so hard that he was exhausted, and he was so weakened by loss of blood that all he could do was wait for death or capture. When King Corbaran fell on them they were taken completely by surprise; they leapt onto their horses and the count was free. They took the child with them and made their way to the cave. The struggle lasted all the way to the cave. 90 of them stayed with the count, all highly delighted to find him still in one piece.

123

The king was delighted that the count was still alive. They were all in the cave, which turned out to be a place full of wonder. There were five chambers filled with the glint of pure gold, hung with silken cloths and curtains and carpets with embroidered borders. In them were a bevy of beauties dressed in brocade, silk and ornaments; their children were with them playing. The king attacked the Saracens ferociously to drive them out. They defended themselves with bows of horn, sharp swords and daggers.

124

The cave was well made and richly decorated, covered with gold mosaic with inlaid pictures. There were five chambers, each large and spacious; each one had a chimney to let out the smoke and fumes.[110] Abundant supplies of bread and corn, wine and flour, and meat both fresh and salted had been laid in. There was fresh water to drink that ran together into a cistern hollowed out in the rock; when it rained on the rock it drained down into it. The king attacked them fiercely at the entrance and they defended themselves, each brandishing a sword; they would not have given a peeled apple for the attack.

125

The king was very upset and angry, in a towering rage because his attack was unsuccessful. 'I have been chasing you for days, you sons of whores', he said. 'I am delighted to have your bodies in my power at last. I am going to hang or drown every last one of you'. 'That would be a terrible sin', they replied. 'By Mahomed, you are making a mistake in attacking us. Chasing us off our land and taking it away from us so you could have it was the wrong thing to do. You can hardly be surprised we have fought back and retaliated by seizing your property. We've got your nephew. If you love him that much, give us back our fiefs and lands in exchange. We will serve you punctiliously every day. We will give you four pack animals loaded with bezants, and 1,000 folded silken cloths embroidered with

---

[110] An occupation with practicality the author shows elsewhere. This also indicates the level of luxury in the cave: medieval dwellings without chimneys smelt permanently of smoke.

pure gold. Alas, noble lords – implore the king on our behalf'. 80 Saracens fell prostrate at his feet, all begging, 'Your Majesty, have mercy!'

126

'My lords', announced Corbaran, 'this is what I think. Neither Tervagant my god who has power over all, nor all the gold and silver in Byzantium would be enough to persuade me to grant these people their lives and lands. But I would do it for this princely child. The trouble is that I am quite sure they will not give him back to me in one piece. So let them come out of the cave, and they need have no fear that I will not give them back their lands in exchange for the child: I will give them back everything because I love him'.

127

When Corbaran offered these terms, the brothers in the cave exchanged glances: all of them burst into tears of joy and delight. They seized the child and handed him over to the king. He took the child, delighted to have him back, and covered his face with affectionate kisses. Those in the cave ran and fell at his feet, begging him for mercy. Corbaran raised them again, pardoned them, gave back their lands and inheritance and handed them the seneschalcy. The brothers did not hang about. They immediately loaded up four pack animals with beautiful work in pure gold and 1,000 silken cloths embroidered in gold made in Greece. The king called Harpin straight over and put all the gold and silk into his keeping. 'My deepest thanks', said the count, 'for trusting me to look after this treasure'. 'Let me tell you this', said Corbaran, 'you know you will not lose as much as one *denier*'. Then they mounted their warhorses, swung round and rode all the way to Oliferne without drawing rein. The townspeople came out to meet them, eager to hear their news. When they saw the child they went wild with joy. Believe you me: the count was the subject of universal adulation, honoured even by the richest. Richard and the *chétifs* did not wait to be asked: they came straight up to the count and asked him, 'My lord, what happened? How have things gone?' 'Pretty well, my lords', he replied. 'You find me in one piece. Now let us make our way to the Holy Sepulchre if that is what God has destined for us'.

128

Corbaran's mother did not hang back: she came rushing up to the count, flung her arms round him and showered his eyes, face and hands with kisses. 'My lord', said the queen, 'I realise you have brought the child back to me, and that is a great achievement'. 'My lady', said Harpin, 'now I want my side of the bargain as you promised Richard'. 'You shall have it', replied the queen. She took gold and bright silver from her own wealth and had it presented to Harpin of Bourges. Even the poorest received clothing, and each had as much treasure as he wanted. Some received 1,000 bezants, some 80 and some 100; she rewarded all who were there richly. To Richard she gave 1,000 silk cloths and a fast steed, a rich tent to protect against storms and wind, and a packhorse laden with vessels. She summoned an emir, Escanart, the son of Florent. 'Take these captives home in safety. I entrust them to you on your faith and on your promise'. 'Your lightest wish is my command. You need not worry about a thing', replied the emir.

129

'My lords', said Richard, 'what shall we do, in God's name? Shall we go to pray at the Holy Sepulchre, or shall we return to the army and the lords in it: Robert of Normandy, Robert the Frisian, the handsome Thomas of La Fere, Lord Raymond of St-Gilles and Hugh of Vermandois, Bohemond and Tancred and Lord Raimbaut Creton, Pagan of Camelli and Gerard of the Keep, Roger of Rosoie with the limp, the brave-hearted Aimery of l'Aitrus, Eustace of Albemarle son of Count Otto, and the noble lords from the kingdom of Charlemagne. If God loved us enough for us to join them, we could help to take the city of Jerusalem and many wicked Saracens would lose their heads'. 'By the holy Ascension, what on earth are you saying, noble Richard?' said Harpin of Bourges. 'Don't you want to see the Temple of Solomon and the venerated Sepulchre, or the holy mount where God suffered death for our salvation? We have suffered so badly from hunger and thirst, lost so much and experienced so much misfortune. If I am not to see the ramparts and proud castle and the city where Jesus was resurrected from the dead, it will kill me in this kingdom so far from home. If God were to grant us the inestimable boon of being there, I would reverently kiss the Sepulchre and the holy Temple and the Confession[111]; then I would not care about my mortal body because my soul would have received salvation'. At this shouts went up all around: 'Yes, Harpin of Bourges, let us make our way to the Sepulchre!'[112]

130

Corbaran was a nobleman whose word could be trusted, and held to the truth of the Saracen religion. He armed all our knights richly with white hauberks, helmets and shields bordered in gold, and sharp swords with blades honed to a fine edge. Then

---

[111] It is not clear what this is. Myers suggests it is an imaginary shrine in Jerusalem: however that seems slightly odd given how well known the main pilgrimage sites were. There is no manuscript authority but it is tempting to wonder whether an original reading might have been 'et ferai confession'. Ms T shares this uncertainty, giving the reading 'que fonda Salemon'.

[112] The need for the *chétifs* to complete their journey to Jerusalem is underlined.

he called them together before him and addressed them as follows: 'My lords', he said, 'a moment's attention if you please. I shall give you safe conduct to wherever you want to go. You will carry my authorisation and letters of introduction with you. Give my greetings to the King of Jerusalem, my lords: he is my lord and each of you will be treated with great respect and well looked after. As for the noble and wise Cornumarant his son, you need have no worries: as soon as he sees my letters he will have you taken to wherever you want to go'. 'Our humblest and deepest thanks', said Count Harpin. The bishop of Forez and the abbot of Fécamp called Corbaran to one side. 'Your Majesty, tell us what you plan to do', they said privately. 'Do you intend to keep without reneging the solemn oath you swore to God in the desert that you and your whole city would convert to Christianity?' 'I have thought it over', replied Corbaran, 'and I will convert within the next two years. I do believe in Jesus and his power. But I cannot do as I wish just yet'. And so they returned to our Franks with honour, giving fervent thanks to the king and his lords. Queen Calabra paid them great honour. With the speeches concluded each Frank mounted, and they left Oliferne rejoicing and resplendent. Corbaran and his mother rode a good stretch of the way with them, a good ten leagues, before turning back. Meanwhile our *chétifs*, delivered by God and released from misery in his great goodness, rode on their way. Those whom God helps will never be lost. Conversely it is only those who despair of him who are wretched in their captivity.[113]

131

Our noble pilgrims rode on their way rejoicing, making their way through vast tracts of Saracen territory. They passed by Armenia and its Armenians, and the Turkish dependencies of Joriam and Pateron. They made their way all the way down the Bacar valley for 15 days, finding it full of bread, meat and wine, dates, figs and other garden fruit. They entered the wasteland before Haleching, a very strong castle held by the Saracens; they passed by Hamelech straight to the castle on the coast. They reached the River Jordan on a Saturday morning and bathed in it, kissing the fine marble where God was baptised by his cousin John.

131 a

When our brave pilgrims had finished their bathe, the emir called Lord Richard the Norman and Harpin of Bourges for a word. 'My lords', he said, 'we will go no further. We turn back here, and leave you to your own god'. Our barons commended them to Almighty God. Then they mounted their horses and made straight for Jerusalem without delay. On the rocky hillside at the Red Cistern they

---

[113] A further implicit reference to the Harrowing of Hell.

met 140 infidel Turks on their way from Jerusalem to seek help from the Saracens of Arabia and King Corbaran.

132

Dawn was rising on a Sunday. Richard and the *chétifs* heard Mass in the garden of the prophet Abraham beneath the crags, the place where God the Son of the Virgin fasted for 40 days and nights according to Holy Scripture. They mounted their horses without further ado and made straight for Jerusalem. At the Red Cistern, beneath a rocky hillside, they met 140 pagan Turks coming from Jerusalem to seek aid from the Arabs of Arabia and the king of La Berrie. The people of Jerusalem were all in a ferment. They had heard the news in the city that Bohemond and Robert of Normandy, lord Hugh of Vermandois and a sizeable force, and Raymond of St-Gilles with a large number of knights were all making for them. They had taken Antioch and garrisoned it strongly. They had taken the great Gibel, Margat and Valenie, Beirut and Sidon in Syria, Carcloie and the March all the way up to Saphoria.[114] The army of Jesus had made such good progress that they had reached the mosque only two and a half leagues from Jerusalem. They had fixed tents and pickets and set up camp. Gold and silver glittered and sparkled all around: the army of Jesus was well lodged. But before the evening comes and compline is sung, let me assure you that Richard and the *chétifs* will stand in sad need of help from Robert of Normandy in the well-defended valley of Josaphat where the Mother of God died and was buried. When Duke Godfrey and the lords of Jesus with him had caught up with their quarry, there was an almighty battle and a ferocious attack.

133

Richard and the *chétifs* rode all the way across the plain, armed and on their warhorses, and made their way alongside a valley. Lord Harpin of Bourges sat armed on his horse. By God! Just imagine how he looked, sword buckled at his left side, shield hung from his neck, helmet of crystal, spear clasped in his right hand and silken pennon topped with a golden cross of Our Spiritual Father. He called all his companions together and addressed them as follows: 'Noble and faithful knights, the Turks are bearing down on us. We are all stout men. Let us make sure that not one of us is held up by chest-strap or girth. My lords, remember how much pain and grief these infidel Turks have given us'. At this all shouted, good and bad alike: 'Come on, Harpin of Bourges, ride across that plain! God willing, those Turks will rue the day they came here!'

---

[114] See Myers, Introduction pp. xxii-xxxi for discussion of topography: as he comments 'it is at the same time exact and vague' (p.xxxi).

134

Richard and the *chétifs* rode ahead at full speed; so did the most noble bishop of Forez, Lord Harpin of Bourges carrying the pennant and Richard of Chaumont carrying a very richly ornamented flag. Now imagine the Turks pouring down off the hillside. Those in front challenged them: 'Who are you? Do you believe in Mahomed, Margot and Apollon and in Jupiter Baraton?' 'I don't need this kind of catechism', replied Count Harpin. He brandished his spear and protected himself with his shield: all the *chétifs* spurred forward. There was a great clashing of lances: the shafts smashed into a shower of splinters. Those proud villains of Turks attempted to defend themselves, but our *chétifs* fell on them as noble lords should; drawing their swords, each picked out an enemy, and sent his head flying over the top of the shield. Out of the whole 140 none got away alive bar one single man, God curse him. He spurred to Jerusalem at top speed and pounded in through the Golden Gate all the way to the keep. He told what had happened so vividly that, if the Lord Who suffered for us does not accord them His protection, Richard and the *chétifs* will be dead men to the last with no hope of escape, I assure you.

135

It was a massive battle and the Franks gave a good account of themselves. The one Turk who did escape was terrified. He clattered all the way up the main street of Jerusalem to the Tower of David without drawing rein. The king was playing at tables, surrounded by a retinue of emirs, princes and infidels. The messenger shouted out in terror: 'Alas, King of Jerusalem, do not think I am about to tell you lies. I do not know how but an army fell upon us, armoured from head to toe and impervious to crossbows and sharp arrows alike. Your emissaries are lying dead on the grass at the Red Cistern beneath those rocky cliffs'. The blood drained from the king's face as he heard this. He pulled at his white beard in rage. Hair was torn, beards tugged and clothing ripped and torn apart as they cursed the land which had given birth to such a race.

136

The king heard the news and it was not to his liking. He was appalled at his loss: his face changed colour, and hair was torn and beards pulled. Imagine Cornumarant on his felt-saddled mule, holding a stick stripped of its bark in his hand. He yelled for the messenger. 'Tell me, by God, who were these people you met?' 'My lord, they are Franks, a race of infidels who cover themselves with armour from head to foot and have no fear of crossbows or feathered arrows. An evil fate has left your messengers lying dead on the grass by the Red Cistern'. 'Are they really human, by God? Give me your honest opinion'. 'Yes, and I would estimate their numbers at some 4,000'. The messenger was petrified; this is proven fact, He told the full tale of the valour of the 190. Cornumarant listened attentively to what he had to say, and then immediately uttered a war cry. 'All lords to arms now, without delay. I wish to challenge for my land, which I have held for a long time'. He ordered a drum to be beaten on top of the square tower. The pagans, those filthy sons of bastards, armed themselves: when ready they numbered 50,000. So now unless the Lord Who was struck whilst tied to the holy stake on a square pillar accords them His help, Richard and his companions will find themselves facing a sticky end.

137

Cornumarant had certainly heard the news, but there were only 4,000 Christians and his heart leapt at the prospect. He thought they were Franks from the beautiful city of Antioch. He was having a very pleasant time in the mosque. The women were singing inside and there was a choir of virgins. Cornumarant pledged to his beautiful beloved that he would go and strike a Frenchman full in the chest. He ordered his horse to be saddled swiftly. Three noble young men from Tudela brought him his arms and a new shield. He armed himself under the admiring gaze of a bevy of young ladies.

138

The proud-hearted Cornumarant armed himself. He put on a white hauberk with a double layer of rings, the chainmail whiter than hawthorn flower. He had his helmet laced on above his visor: it was encircled by a band of gold very elaborately worked and set with many jewels when it was made by Malachi, a Jew who did not enjoy God's favour; he spent seven full years expurgating his sins. He hung his shield from his neck: it was painted with a checkerboard pattern, and a very rich carbuncle was set into the pure gold buckler; there was a picture of Mahomed in the right hand quarter.[115] He made sure not to forget his bow and quiver, the latter full of arrows which he had had dipped in poison. He took up his sharp-pointed lance which could not be broken; on the contrary it could be bent right round on itself. He leapt onto his warhorse, the fastest in the whole pagan kingdom: it could cover 12 leagues without being caught. If the Lord of all does not accord them his protection, Richard and his companions are all going to have their heads cut off.

139

Inside Jerusalem the Saracens were arming themselves: there were 5,000 of them descended from Cain. They were banging drums and blowing pipes, creating a great din. They swore to Mahomed and their god Apollon that if they could find any Christians they would make short work of them: they would hang them all like

---

[115] Not of course permissible in Islam.

servants. Now let us hope that God remembers Richard and Count Harpin and the other *chétifs* coming down the road: if not, they are in imminent danger of death.

THE END

La *Chanson des Chétifs*: Selected Variants

The Alabama edition gives a dozen variants on the text of manuscript A. Some of these simply expand existing material or supply further description of single combats, and I have not translated these. Three however do bring significant additional material. Appendix 4 describes a piece of magic by Corbaran's mother. Appendix 7, which runs to some 500 lines, describes a challenge to Corbaran by a Breton knight who is defeated by Harpin of Bourges in a combat with fencing staves. The longest variant is Appendix 12 which is nearly 1,000 lines. This describes how the *chétifs* take on and defeat the mother of the Sathanas, an even more terrible serpent, in an episode uncannily reminiscent of Grendel's mother. I have translated these three variants to give some idea of the significant *mouvance* around the text. I have also translated the short laisse found at the beginning of the *Chétifs* in all manuscripts and which serves as a link from the *Antioche*.

Introductory laisse

My lords, the author who made these verses and cast them in rhyme now wants to bring an end to his tale until it is told afresh on another occasion. So now I am going to tell you all about the infidels. Corbaran fled, head bowed, lost in thought and distracted, the blood drained from his face. His people had been defeated, routed and killed, whilst Brohadas had met his end when his head was cut off. Corbaran had him carried in a bier hoisted high onto the backs of four warhorses who carried it each day, draped fittingly in a rich silken cloth.

Appendix 4

Six of the manuscripts (D, B, O, G, E and T) add these laisses. The only manuscripts not to have them are A, C and F. So it is hard to know whether the variant formed part of the original redaction; as Myers points out, Calabra never actually shows Corbaran the cloth, and it is hard to know whether this represents lack of continuity by the original author or a later addition not followed through.[1] The two laisses come after laisse 24, just before Richard's single combat. Myers points out that

---

[1] Myers, edition p.151.

there is a precisely similar piece of divination in the *Moniage Guillaume*.[2] The average length of laisse is 18 lines, shorter than other variants.

1

Corbaran's mother was a very wise woman; there was no greater German in all of Germany.[3] She had a good six inches between her eyes, and knew more about divination than any cleric about stories.[4] She came up with an extraordinary marvel to be demonstrated to the brave Richard [of Chaumont] if he could defeat the two Turks and force them to submit. She took a green silken cloth made in Agoant. On one side she wrote the names of Mahomed and Tervagant, Apollon and Jupiter, Cahu and Balsinant, in fact all the gods worshipped by the Turks she could think of.[5] On the other side she wrote Jesus of Bethlehem just as the tyrants did when they hung Him on the Cross, and His mother the all-powerful Queen, and John the Apostle dearly beloved of God. She climbed to the highest pinnacle of a tower.

2

Corbaran's mother climbed up a tower, clutching the silken cloth on which she had written the text for divination. She invoked Mahomed and Apollon, and called on God, Our Father and King that if Richard was to be victor in the forthcoming battle and kill the two Turks chosen as champions by the Sultan, the image of Jesus should appear on it. She raised her hand and let the cloth drop. It floated up into the air, turning over as it did so. Now listen to the miracle which God performed! The cloth split in two. The image of Mahomed separated itself from one part and made straight for a dunghill. Meanwhile the image of Our Father Jesus Christ flew up into the air without touching the ground. The old woman came running and stared at it. She took the green cloth, folded it carefully and put it away reverently in one of her jewel boxes, with the intention of showing it to her son. Here I shall cease telling you about this old lady and her clever device, and tell you instead about how Corbaran sought lodgings.

Appendix 7

This episode is found only in manuscript B. It comes after laisse 40, resuming at line 1287 in laisse 42. It is reminiscent of episodes in Arthurian literature where a champion comes into the hall and demands a combat: famously for example

---

[2] *Le Moniage Guillaume: chanson de geste du XIIe siecle*, (ed.) N. Andrieux-Reix (Paris, 2003), lines 2959–3026.
[3] She is not referred to as German elsewhere.
[4] Bancourt vol.1 p. 72 for width between eyes.
[5] Mostly familiar but Balsinant is found only here: Moisan vol.1 p.206.

Sir Gawain and the Green Knight. It is no accident that the adversary is referred to as Breton. The episode is in effect a doublet of Richard's combat with the two champions: Harpin fights a self-appointed champion in just the same way to vindicate Corbaran from an accusation of treachery. Average laisse length is 51 lines.

1

I am going to leave these to one side for a moment and focus on the *chétifs*, may God be with them. They were sat down eating in the Sultan's palace at a table elaborately carved with a chequered pattern. They were lavishly fed, no two ways about it. But as soon as they got up from the table they heard some news which left them seriously concerned that their heads were about to be cut off, make no mistake. In front of them was a Breton making his way through the court area. His name was Cainan and he cut a fearsome figure.[6] In front of him one of his squires carried two round wooden shields which he had had covered with leather, and two fencing sticks made of medlar wood. To ensure they could not be mistreated or damaged he had them baked hard in a big furnace; the sticks were so big that no living man, no matter how brave, could possibly have wielded them; he was the only one able to make use of them, and he was so strong that they did not give him a *denier*'s worth of trouble. Let me tell you something about how he looked. He was broad-shouldered and of large girth; he had a paunch like the dewlap of a plough ox. His neck was coarse and thick, with a large nape; his mouth was large and flat, making him look like a devil. His nose was small and flat like a monkey in a tree; his eyes burned as red as coals in a brazier, and there was a full hand's width between them. His hair was as black as a mulberry from a mulberry tree.[7] His head was large and bulky, a fearsome sight. He had big legs and arms, and huge fists. From the moment the Devil was with him, he granted mercy to no man. He stopped in front of the Sultan and addressed him as follows. 'Emir of Persia, you are not exactly impressive. The man sitting next to you at table was responsible for getting your men beheaded by the French; he sold your son Brohadas whom you had entrusted to him to the French, he cannot deny the fact and in return they gave him more than 23 pack horse loads of gold and silver. He actually helped them behead pagans himself. As for those who took refuge inside Antioch, they would not have been killed within the year even if they had had their feet and hands tied and despite beingin such a reduced condition that they couldn't help themselves; they are weaker than children for want of food'. A well respected Saracen spoke up: he was Corbaran's cousin and held him in high esteem. 'My noble lord', said the Turk, 'you have said enough. Nothing you say is worth even a *denier*. The French are extremely brave and determined knights who do not give as much as a viburnum leaf for our men. If 100 of them were to fight 1,000 of ours on the

---

[6] The name Cainan is found elsewhere: Moisan vol.1 p.283.
[7] 'Meure' can be a blackberry or a mulberry: TL VI.265–7.

battlefield, not as many as four would get away in one piece because they would kill and slaughter every last one. As a token of this look at the warrior Richard, eating at this table with these *chétifs*. He fought with two men on behalf of the noble Corbaran. One of them was Sorgalé, who had many feats to his name; the other was the proud Goliath of Mecca, the best archer in all pagandom. Richard killed them with his burnished steel sword'. The Breton nearly went mad when he heard this. 'I hope you suffer', he said to the Saracen. 'If he did kill them there is nothing so surprising about that: They were under a spell and unable to help themselves any more than if they had been tied up with ropes. All those double-dealing French cast spells'.

2

The Breton stood on the paved floor in front of the Sultan and spoke loudly to the Sultan. 'Noble king, listen to me. Those two Turks who were horribly killed were so under the spell cast by Richard that they were completely unable to help or defend themselves. It is true – all the French are necromancers. And King Corbaran whom you see in front of you has sold the entire armies of the Orient to the French. And he got your son Brohadas killed. I know for a fact that he is guilty of deceit. He is wicked and treacherous. May Mahomed kill him! If you would not hold it against me, I should land such a blow on him in front of all his men that he would never betray you again. And I would kill the *chétifs* in horrible ways. If anyone tells you that I am lying to you in any way, watch me take up his shield in front of you, and this foursquare heavy staff: the challenger can come and defend himself against me in battle and before evening falls I will show him three such blows in single combat such as nobody has ever seen in my view. Nobody would be brave enough to receive the blows without moving because I would reduce him to a bloody pulp'. Corbaran was frightened when he heard these devilish words. He would have preferred to be anywhere but there for all the gold in the Orient; he was terrified of the Breton and his boldness. Richard and the *chétifs* were in great consternation. If Richard had not been so badly wounded in the neck he would not have hesitated to show his skills in single combat. But he was in a very bad way from his injuries. Cainan spoke loudly in front of all, saying to Corbaran: 'You are in a difficult situation. If you do not defend yourself before evening falls, I shall have you strung up from the gallows and decaying into holes in the wind as befits any traitor who lies to his lord and sells his people for gold and silver. And I shall string all these *chétifs* up too: their spells are of no good to them now and will be of no more help to them than a vine branch'. When Corbaran heard this he was seized with terror. The Sultan glared at him angrily, sure that the Breton was not lying to him in any way. He called for Corbaran and said to him loudly: 'By my God Mahomed whom I see in front of me, if what this man whom I see in front of me says is true you have deceived me completely with your spells.[8] If

---

[8] Lines 115 and 116 end with the same hemistich: most likely eyeskip by the scribe.

you cannot defend yourself I am going to make you suffer before the day is out'. When the *chétifs* heard the emir talking like this, none of them were brave enough not to be scared. They invoked God, the Ruler of the world: 'Benevolent Lord and Father Who rules the heavens, keep us safe today as part of Your divine plan from this evil devil in front of us. We think he must be an emissary from Hell, sent by his master to torment us'. Cainan stood there on the paving, planted angrily on his two feet. He addressed the Sultan in a towering rage. 'My lord, by Mahomed I am astonished that you have not already hung this stinking traitor. If you give me permission, he will soon be properly dead and I shall kill all these *chétifs* as well'. 'Corbaran', said the Sultan, 'you have made serious mistakes. If what this man says is true, you have made serious mistakes.[9] You should be hung like a thief in the wind. Anyone who betrays his lord must die in agony'. Corbaran's heart nearly burst in two with grief when he heard this. He responded most humbly to the noble and royal Sultan: 'My lord, by Mahomed in whom I believe, I have never plotted any kind of treachery towards you, nor taken gold and silver for any of your men. You can be absolutely sure that this champion is lying. I have never had the slightest desire or wish to deceive you'.

3

Cainan stood tall and cut a redoubtable figure. He addressed the noble and royal Sultan again: 'My lord, by Mahomed who has power over all, I am frankly astonished that you can put up with having lord Corbaran next to you at dinner. There is no worse traitor all the way to the Red Sea. He sold your men to the Christians, who killed them and beheaded your son Brohadas: surely that must bother you. He was completely wrong in taking money for this. He is a traitor and a liar: he should be killed, and has deserved death by daring to deceive you. Have him strung up from the gallows. That would be just the right thing for a lord to do: that is how one should rid oneself of villains. Anyone who betrays his lord should suffer for it. If there is anyone who wants to fight this accusation on his behalf, let him come and take up shield and staff and I will teach him all about fighting with staves. You will see me strike three such blows as no champion has ever experienced no matter how much trouble he were to go to. Anyone who comes to me will be able to boast that he has no chance of escaping that day without a great deal of pain. I shall have all the limbs cut off these *chétifs*; they will not find their spells much use'. As he said these words he turned on Corbaran; he ripped at his silken surcoat and tore it apart from top to bottom.[10] The blood drained from Corbaran's face at this. He was so terrified of his diabolical adversary that he was unable to utter a word: no need to ask just how terrified he was that he was going to die. Our renowned captives looked on. The bishop of Forez broke the silence, saying to his companions: 'We should be maddened at seeing the man who is to

---

[9] Again eyeskip in the second hemistich of lines 135 and 136.
[10] To make the point that he is challenging formally.

free us from our hard captivity and take us back to our own people being treated in this way by one solitary Saracen. Is there really not a single one of us, renowned as we are for our exploits, who dares stand up to him and say even a word?' When Harpin of Bourges heard the bishop's words, he leapt to his feet like a wild boar. He undid his cloak and dropped it on the floor, standing there in his surcoat of silken cloth. You would have to go a long way before you could find even one knight who seemed brave enough to deal with a fight. He came and stood in front of his companions and swore by Our Lord Who brings salvation to all that even if someone were to give him 1,000 marks of pure silver he would still rather go and kill the Saracen. Indeed he was now desperate to show off his fighting skills: better to suffer death with honour than slip away in shame. 'Even if the Saracens kill me, we cannot escape if they kill Corbaran. And if Jesus is willing to give me His aid in freeing us so that I can kill and destroy this champion, we can still return to France rejoicing. I learnt to deal blows as a young man: you could not find any man able to better me in wielding shield or staff'. 'My lord', said the *chétifs*, 'may that God save you Who allowed His body to be tortured on the Cross'. With that Harpin advanced straight away. He stopped in front of the royal Sultan and said to the champion: 'You talk too much. You should not be maligning and criticising Corbaran. He is a noble and loyal man and much to be admired.[11] You are entirely wrong in branding him a traitor. I am going to take you to task no matter who might be upset by that: I am going to make you sorry before evening falls'.

4

'You are behaving very badly, sir', said Harpin. 'Go on, pick up your shield, don't hang about. I want you to show me just how good you are at single combat – and I will show you just how good I am too if you think you can cope. I intend to leave you in such a state before the end of the day that no decent court will ever honour you again'. Cainan nearly lost his mind when he heard this. 'You are a total lunatic if you think you can just turn up and fight me', he said to Harpin. With that exchange each flung his shield across his body and positioned the large staves of medlar wood. Now listen to a battle if you want – it is the most ferocious ever fought by two champions. When the emir saw them ready to fight he had the tables carried out of the way and got up from supper.

5

The emir Sultan left his supper where it was whilst the two champions seized their shields. Both of them were raring to show their mettle. Harpin was noble and wise, brave and bold. He did his practice strokes as an experienced man should. Cainan watched all this and sniggered. Then he came forward snarling with rage, staff in hand and shield in front of body. He aimed a blow with an extremely good swing

---

[11] The variant goes further than the *Chétifs* in praising Corbaran.

aiming to strike Harpin across the face. Harpin saw the staff coming and protected himself with his shield. Cainan landed a blow on it, which unfortunately left it damaged and broken. Harpin was terrified when he felt the blow land. He invoked God, King of Paradise. Then he raised his staff and turned towards him, and made it his business to pay him back with heavy blows. He struck his shield so hard that he damaged it. They fell on each other like mortal enemies. The battle between the two chosen barons was ferocious. No man born of woman had ever seen two men more skilled in wielding shield and staff. However it was not an equal contest between the two of them. Cainan was tall, heavily built and strong. Harpin looked like a puny weakling beside him, but knew how to fight skilfully. They advanced towards each other, shields in front of bodies; they attacked each other with their staffs, giving each other a run for their money. Now may God, King of Paradise, remember Harpin: if Jesus does not think of him, he is going to end up in a pretty poor state.

6

Now the two champions are busy fighting. They advanced on each other, as angry as lions and slamming blows into each other's shields. The whole palace rang with the noise. The emir Sultan swore that by Mahomed he had never seen such a combat in judicial ordeal between two men since he first put on his spurs. The fight between them lasted for a long time. They rained blows on each other more thickly than a smith or mason. Now may God in His holy name remember Harpin!

7

The battle in the magnificent palace was a fierce one. The two knights battled each other hard. They battered each other's shields with their medlar wood staves, smashing and damaging them more with each blow. They made the whole great palace ring with the din, and the noise could be heard all the way through the town. The champions rained blows on each other more thickly than a smith in a forge hammering the hot iron on an anvil, desperate to inflict injuries on each other: the shields of both were holed and battered through. Cainan hefted his medlar wood stave and aimed an enormous blow down on Harpin's cap designed to disable him. Harpin leapt backwards in anticipation of the blow and covered himself with his shield, in fear of his diabolical adversary. The villain landed a hard blow foursquare. The blow went down towards his hips, straight at the top of the thigh near his waist; it tore his clothes, pierced his flesh and nearly broke the bone. The impact of the blow on Harpin was so great that he was forced to his knees on the ground. Our barons were dismayed at the sight. They called on God, the Father in justice, to defend Harpin against injury and death. The bishop of Forez saw the lord yield and began an elaborate prayer. 'Lord God and Father, Judge of all' he said, 'Who created Adam and his wife Eve; You gave them Paradise as their home, Noble Lord, and gave them dominion over everything in it except one apple tree of which You forbade them to eat. But Eve did eat and then through the wiles of the Devil tempted Adam to eat, which he should not have done; they had to leave Paradise immediately and found themselves to be naked with no clothes. They covered their shame with fig leaves and from that day on had to earn their own living. Since that day no man or woman has died without being sent to Hell no matter how much they love the Lord. This was the path on which all found themselves for 2,000 years and no saint, male or female, was able to save them. You took pity, God, not wanting to leave mankind in this position. You came down to Earth to help your friends. You took shelter in a virgin who carried You for nine months without suffering at all. You were born in Bethlehem under a star and were laid in chaff alongside the animals.[12] The three kings came and sought You out, each from his own kingdom. The princes offered You gold and incense and myrrh and You accepted them without demur; then You sent them back to their own country. You protected them against Herod, who was having them watched. He was furious at not being able to get them into his power. He had small children of less than two years old sought out all over his kingdom and ordered them all to be beheaded; they numbered 33,000. They are known as the Innocents and they worship you. He thought he had had Your head cut off as one of them, but You were well able to defend Yourself against such a fate. Then You travelled through the land to preach to the people, teaching Your word for 32 years and more. Judas sold You, worthless wretch that he was, to the Jews who judged You harshly; the price they gave him was 30 deniers of silver. They led You to the stake and lashed you to it, where they beat You and reviled and insulted You. They hung You on the Cross to suffer, attaching Your feet and hands with great nails. Longinus struck You with the steel lance and pierced Your side; the blood flowed down all the way to his hands on the apple-wood shaft. Before then he had been unable to see, so I have heard. He rubbed [the blood] on his eyes and saw clearly. Then he knew that You were God and Judge of all. He begged You for mercy. You did not have to be implored twice; You pardoned him immediately without hesitation. When You were taken down from the Cross, You were laid in the Holy Sepulchre and guarded against thieves. On the third day You rose again, True God, without delay. You took the path straight to Hell and smashed the doors open by main effort; You released your friends who worshipped You and who had served You loyally without wavering. As all this is true without a word of a lie, now defend Your knight Harpin against injury and damage and against being killed by this evil diabolical adversary so that we can still kiss Your Sepulchre in transports of joy'. With that he finished the impressive prayer.[13]

---

[12] 'Esclairier' is not attested in this way but clearly refers to light; I have surmised the star.

[13] As on similar occasions in the *Chétifs*, a climactic moment is marked by a long prayer emphasising divine support for the Christians as part of the divine plan.

8

The bishop of Forez finished his prayer and Harpin of Bourges got to his feet. He was wounded in the thigh and in great pain.[14] Cainan cried to him: 'You coward, now we shall find out just how your evil God will come to your aid! How can He help you when he allowed Himself to be killed? The emir Sultan will still hang you and all these *chétifs*; not one will escape with his life. And as for Corbaran, he will meet a grim end. None of your enchantments will serve for anything'. When Harpin heard this he invoked God and humbled himself most sincerely before him. God heard his prayer and came to him. Harpin's courage returned and his resolve doubled; he pulled his shield towards him and put it on. He immediately rose to his feet and squared up to the champion. Seizing the staff, he raised it high, sized up his enemy and aimed it up from below. Cainan saw the blow coming, hoisted his shield and put it in front of his head where he expected to receive the blow. Harpin saw this: he made a feint and aimed the blow down from above, following through and hitting Cainan hard. He struck him in the temple full on. He broke his leather helmet, shattered his head and slammed the medlar wood stave down into his skull so that his brains were sent flying. The Breton felt the blow and let out a mighty cry which could be heard all the way through the town. Harpin stepped forward and knocked him with the shield so hard that he fell to the ground at the feet of the Sultan who was terrified. He made such a noise as he fell that the whole palace and tower shook. The coward lay prone and his soul left his body. Harpin was overjoyed to see this and all the *chétifs* praised God. Harpin came up to the Breton and cried in his face: 'You lying there have suffered a terrible fate in front of the emir, and he is petrified'. Then he went and seized his feet and dragged him off through the palace all by himself. John of Alis leapt to his feet and went to help him. The lord strained every muscle and with a huge effort flung [the Breton] out of a window onto the dung heap. Then he marched up to the Sultan and addressed him as follows: 'Listen to me, my good lord' said Harpin. 'I have killed the devil who was threatening us and tore King Corbaran's surcoat. If you want to render him justice, you should not hold him guilty of any evil because that has never been his intention. He is acquitted by right by Richard of Chaumont, who defeated the two Turks. It is quite clear that he was helped by justice and by Our Father God, Who has no love for villains. Anyone who acts like a villain will not come to a good end and will find the day come when he has to repent'. Then the Sultan replied, swearing by his gods that he would never again from that day believe Corbaran was untrustworthy; he would give him his favour every day of his life and would not be separated from him as long as he might live. Then he came up to Corbaran and spoke to him, forgiving him all the malice and hatred. He granted him power over his lands beneath him and gave him the seneschalcy. Corbaran accepted this and thanked him. 'Corbaran', said the Sultan, 'listen to my words. I shall never feel hatred in my heart towards you again; your orders will be carried

---

[14] Like the Fisher King of Arthurian romance.

out all through my domains. Anyone whom you hold in esteem will have nothing to fear; those you do not will have to answer to me'. 'My lord', said Corbaran, 'your lightest wish is my command'. The bishop of Forez rose to his feet and brought hot water to Harpin of Bourges, who was delighted to be able to wash. John of Alis passed him a white towel to dry his hands. Then he went to sit with the other *chétifs*. They were delighted to see him and gave him a hero's welcome.

9

So you have heard all about the deeds of Harpin and how he took on and killed the champion. Now I am going to tell you about the relatives of Sorgalé who were ambushed in a stand of trees; the [relatives of] Goliath of Mecca had hidden and they were well equipped to fight. May God protect Richard and Christianity! The Sultan knew nothing of this and had no idea it was going on; but he dealt out justice to the acclaim of his lords. The malefactors were hung and met a painful end as their punishment for attacking those whom the Sultan had taken under his protection. The noble royal Sultan was overjoyed and embraced Corbaran of Oliferne repeatedly. He called for his sergeants and ordered wine to be brought. 100 nice young men with [robes] trimmed in ermine snapped to it and brought the wine in lidded cups and gilded pitchers, with spices and pepper, mulled wine, wine with herbs and spiced wine mixed with the clear wine in the pitchers. They brought it to the Sultan and presented it to him, and the emir drank enthusiastically.

Appendix 12: the 'Sathanas mère' episode

This variant is found in manuscripts B and I after laisse 99. It is inserted in the middle of Corbaran's meeting with the Sultan. It is clearly written as a reprise of Baldwin's killing of the Sathanas. Average laisse length is 64 lines.

1

But before long the army will be so terrified that all, even the bravest, will wish they were in Hungary rather than here.[15] The serpent was asleep in the mosque, right in front of Mahomed in a smooth niche next to a beautiful polished fountain; she had been asleep for two days. Nobody has ever heard of such a splendid beast: her son the Sathanas was not worth a sorb apple and all his strength was worth about as much as a rotten apple compared to her. Ah God, what a disaster when she woke up! She reared up with lightning speed, raising her head and stretching herself so violently that the room shook. When the serpent moved off, she bellowed and shrieked so much that the mountain resounded with the din for a league and a half around. The royal Sultan's people were so scared that even all the bravest amongst

---

[15] Hungary for the rhyme scheme; similarly Russia below.

them would rather have been in Russia. The emir saw his people in confusion around him. He called them together and addressed them immediately as follows: 'My lords', said the Sultan, 'I am petrified. I have no idea what is bellowing and shrieking like this, and it feels as if the mountains and fields around us are reeling under the impact'. 'My lord', said Moradanz, 'I can tell you the answer. This is the mother of the serpent, may Jesus curse her. I don't think we are going to get away without a fight'. The Sultan's blood ran cold on hearing this. Nobody could possibly express how terrifying he found the prospect of death; he would much rather have been back in his great vaulted tower. Nevertheless he pulled himself together and rallied his men.

2

When the emir heard his people saying that it was the serpent he had heard crying out, the redoubtable mother of Sathanas, he was nearly demented with anger and foreboding. He immediately had Corbaran of Oliferne summoned. 'Corbaran', said the Sultan, 'tell me the truth: has the serpent which caused me so much trouble been killed?' 'My lord', said Corbaran, 'I can tell you for a fact that Baldwin killed it with his sword of shining steel. You and everybody else need have no doubts on that score'. 'So what is all that noise then?' said the noble Sultan. 'What is making such an almighty noise that the whole world seems to be falling apart? I am not going to pretend that I am not terrified. Take it from me, I would rather be at Haifa on the coast'. 'My lord' said Moradier, 'I can tell you what is happening. The noise you have heard is the serpent's mother. She is looking for her offspring but cannot find him anywhere. The plain truth is that if she finds him dead you will see her come rampaging down that hill at the other end of the valley. If she makes for us, I have to be honest and say that we will not get away without fighting an almighty battle. Anyone who escapes with their life will owe Mahomed homage every day of his life, serving him and loving him and rejoicing at the prospect'. The Sultan nearly went mad when he heard this. He bent down to the ground to pray, then got up and started to think. He swore to Mahomed, the God he worshipped, that if he could not overcome and kill the serpent 'I will not want to wear a golden crown on my head any more. If 60,000 men were not enough to kill the serpent, what are our chances of ever being able to take France?' 'Men, everyone to arms!' he called. 'Let's make sure that if the serpent comes it does not leave in one piece'. Picture the horses being untied and harnessed, helmets tied on and shields hoisted on arms, Turkish bows of horn restrung and retensioned, darts and javelins of horn seized and grabbed, crossbow bolts put in quivers, Greek fire being lit in bronze pots, all the panoply of Turks and Saracens preparing for battle. They surrounded Mount Tigris on all sides. Even so, before the sun can go down even the best of them would have preferred not to be there even for a thousand pounds of pure gold. My noble lords and Christian men, would you like to hear the best song anyone could sing? The mother of Sathanas whom you have been hearing about and who guarded the palace with its many pillars had been sleeping for two whole days, may God destroy her! She had had nothing to drink or to eat, and this did not do much for her temper. When she awoke she looked all around, and soon realised that her treasure had been taken. She nearly went mad with fury. She was so angry that her talons scored the marble deeply enough to make chips fly from it. She uncoiled herself so violently that the whole palace shook. Imagine her rubbing up against the embrasures in her fury, smashing about and knocking things flying with her feet and tail, bellowing and yelping and crying , foaming at the mouth with rage, spitting flames and fire from her mouth so that the whole palace was in flames so that anything made of wood promptly caught light and burnt, sending sparks flying all over the mountain. Impatient to be on the move, she swung round and left in fury, knocking things out of her path as she went; she went off in search of her treasure, determined not to stop searching until the moment she found it. Now Christians and Saracens alike need to be on their guard: take it from me, if she catches them no shield or hauberk will be strong enough to stop her ripping the entrails from 7,000 of them.

3

My noble lords and honoured freemen, now listen and you will hear an excellent song: indeed it is the best ever sung. There is not a shred of untruth: this is proven truth – the history bears witness to that and it has never been falsified. That terrible serpent the mother of Sathanas, and her son the broad-headed serpent, had wreaked such devastation on the land that not a single settlement or town remained intact for more than a day's ride around; all the people had fled and gone elsewhere; none of the land was ploughed and neither vines nor corn grew. The two of them had killed, slaughtered and eaten so many people that not even the best informed could say how many. The serpent and his mother whom I am telling you about had feet harder than a steel anvil. The renowned Baldwin of Beauvais killed the Sathanas with his sharp sword blade thanks to God who created heaven and dewfall. His mother, a crested serpent, watched over him; she went in search of her treasure, terrified it might have been lost. She is the ugliest beast ever to be described. Let me tell you just what she looked like. She was the length of a lance thrust head to tail. She had big ears, each one as wide as a fleece and which she used to cover herself when in difficulty: this meant she could range up hill and down dale without having to worry about rain or hail, cold or frost, Turkish bows and arrows or speeding crossbow bolts, spears, Danish axes, maces or swords.[16] She stood on sturdy legs;[17] she had long wide feet and a commanding stride with sharp talons more vicious than a sharpened sickle, an ell wide and long. No man under heaven could possibly withstand her! Her teeth were as long and sharp as a sharpened

---

[16] This feature is referred to a number of times in the variant. It is reminiscent of the Pannotii, a mythical race who could cover themselves with their ears. See John Block Friedman, *The Monstrous Races in Art and Thought*, (New York, 2000) pp.18–19.

[17] As Myers comments, the word 'empecolee' is not attested elsewhere.

bradawl; they could have bitten through a lump of rock as easily as a sickle through a sheaf of grass. Her legs were thick and blacker than a blackberry. Her hide was covered with prickles like steel bradawls. Her head was large and wide with a broad forehead; her eyes glittered like lit candles. The tail swishing behind her was a good 12 feet long – this is absolutely true – and so powerful at the end that in truth it was harder than a tempered anvil; no matter how tough a wall or building it would collapse under a single blow. She had two large feathered wings which enabled her to fly nimbly and get about in the air. She was protected on the chest by a shield against which a crossbow bolt was about as valuable as a *denier*. She had a crest all the way along her spine which was harder than steel and crimson in colour; a blow from a weapon was about as much use against it as a peeled apple. The tongue in her mouth was so poisonous that any man or beast who got a whiff of it would not be able to escape death with the most horrible torments before he had got even a league away.[18] She had a devil ensconced in her body which had set itself up so that when the serpent was angry she swelled up with flames which belched out of her mouth like a blazing furnace. She had wreaked such devastation on Abraham's domains that she had not left intact any kind of property worth a *denier* throughout the land. She had killed, slaughtered and devoured so many people that they would have sufficed to populate a large city.

4

The crested serpent, mother of the wicked serpent which the lion-hearted Baldwin had killed, went searching far and wide over the mountain for the treasure close to its heart and which Corbaran and his companions had taken. She was beside herself at being unable to find it. After covering the mountain she flew over scrubland of wild roses and sharp-thorned gorse. The serpent's gaze lighted on her offspring, lying covered in blood next to a bush: the lion-hearted Baldwin had killed it – it had devoured his brother and this was his revenge. The Sathanas was lying next to a rocky ledge: the sword was still sticking out of his eyelids and blood was gushing from his mouth. When the serpent saw him, she gave a huge shudder. Her cries of grief were so extreme that the valley rang with them for miles around; her teeth snapped together so hard that chips flew off them. She ran at full speed to the mosque. She shattered Mahomed's arms and chin, striking him four blows with all the strength of her tail, and crushed him under her heel.[19] Then she smashed up the palace with its dark terraces. Any attempt to withstand her was not worth as much as a button. She shrieked and bellowed at the top of her voice, making the mountain resound for a league around. She rampaged across the whole

---

[18] A well-known feature of dragons: Jacques de Vitry, *Historia Orientalis* LXXXIX pp.366–7.

[19] This refers to an idol of Mahomed. Islam of course has no such idols. The serpent reflects the frequent *chanson de geste* topos of Saracens destroying idols who have failed to protect them: see Bancourt vol.1 pp. 514–18.

mountain. She came across Ernoul's donkey and tossed it down her throat; then she ate two pigs and a lion for good measure. She came raging back to the serpent. Now listen to the greatest marvel you have ever heard. She opened the mouth of her offspring with her talons and stroked him with her thick tail; she wanted to get him to stand up and come back home, but she could not get him to move or to say a word: Baldwin had dealt him such a blow that he would never again harm a squire or a page. When she realised this the serpent went as black as coal with rage. In sheer fury she ripped him apart from the teeth to the lungs and hauled his liver and kidneys from his body. Then she turned and left, bellowing like a dragon. Now the pagans, French and Esclavons need to look out for themselves: if God does not have mercy on them and grant them his blessing, they will have no means of protecting themselves from death and destruction – in fact they will be in such a terrible predicament that their arms will not be worth as much as a spur to them. There is nowhere they can flee to get away from the serpent even if every last man of them went as far as Capharnaum. Even if it were the will of Our Lord who suffered for us that they were all new-born babes, I still do not think one of them would escape if they were not helped by Him Who pardoned Longinus, and suffered death on the cross for us and lodged St Peter in the Gardens of Nero, and indeed raised Lazarus from the dead, and sat down as God to dine in the house of Simon. May he protect our Franks from death and captivity and bring them rejoicing to the Temple of Solomon: they are indeed in great danger from the race of Nero.

5

The mother of Sathanas was beside herself at finding her serpent mortally wounded. Baldwin of Beauvais, distinguished for his goodness, had slaughtered him, killing him with his steel sword. She was also grief stricken at the loss of her treasure. The devil had guarded it for the last 60 years; she and her son had amassed it and heaped up inside a vault all those they had put to a horrible death in the process and the [remains of] the women and children they had devoured. Corbaran's men had taken all that away. And if God does not take pity on them that will turn out to have been a bad move: they will have paid too high a price and their doom cannot be averted. Before evening falls they will all have been devoured, burnt to a crisp, slaughtered and poisoned. Even the best man there would give the gold from a whole city not to be; any attempt at defence will not be worth a *denier* coin. The crested serpent was on the warpath. She gave such a furious cry that the whole mountain rang with it from one end to the other; the pagans were terrified at hearing it. She shot flames out of her mouth which lit up everything around, setting all the bushes and scrub on fire. The emir Sultan was in the leafy orchard, with Corbaran sitting next to him. They both looked up towards Mount Tigris and saw the fire roaring down towards them. Every single Saracen was trembling with fear! They all ran down the meadow to take up arms; once armed they were a fighting force of a good 60,000, Turks, Almoravids, Persians and Esclers; they had plenty of crossbowmen and archers. Corbaran of Oliferne looked up towards the mountain, and saw Mount Tigris well alight. He looked back towards his lord and addressed him as follows. 'My lord', said Corbaran, 'let the horns be sounded and your men all prepare for battle. The mother of Sathanas has found her son – the vilest beast ever talked of – dead'. 'You are absolutely right', replied Moradier. 'We have already described the sheer power of the vicious serpent whom Baldwin killed in revenge for it slaughtering his brother: compared to his mother that was worth a *denier* coin – she threw such flames and sparks from her mouth that you could see the whole of Mount Tigris up in flames! Anyone who comes out in one piece will only do so because he has shirked his responsibilities'. The blood drained from the Sultan's face as he heard this. He would have given a full mark of gold to be anywhere but there. The Saracens and pagans were so terrified that they were unable to think straight. The infinitely good abbot of Fécamp and the bishop of Forez went to one side with the brave and determined Harpin of Bourges and with Richard of Chaumont who killed Sorgalé and fought against Murgalé. Baldwin of Beauvais was badly injured, exhausted by the huge battle he had fought and with badly injured limbs and body having killed the Sathanas with his steel sword. The barons carried him away on a striped shield, face and body drenched in blood, careful to make sure he was comfortable. Our French came flocking round. Nor did they forget Corbaran of Oliferne. His men and Turks were assembled round him, and every single one believed in God the King of Majesty. Once they had all assembled the bishop of Forez talked to them as follows: 'My lords, I beg you in the name of God and his dignity that you should all take care to have made your confession properly; we are at risk of all being eaten alive. But if you die having confessed you will be saved'. At this the *chétifs* and pagans cried: 'Your Reverence, we all believe in God for absolute certain, and in the Virgin Mary who carried Him in her womb'. They fell to their knees and made confession of their sins. Then [the Bishop] told them not to lose heart but to defend themselves stoutly knowing they had professed their belief in God: if they truly believed they would not be killed or put to shame by the wiles of the Devil. Baldwin of Beauvais promptly rose from his sickbed; so did Richard of Chaumont despite his injuries, and the other barons were armoured and carrying their weapons. Had you been there you would have seen innumerable renowned knights, hauberks and helmets and striped shields, sharp lances with the pennon laced on, noble warhorses piebald and plump, good swords and feathered darts, Danish axes slung from necks, crossbow bolts and feathered quarrels. The emir Sultan was not exactly reassured to see that the *chétifs* had split off from his army. He called repeatedly on Mahomed to bring him back safely to Persia and promised him 100,000 marks of gold.

6

The emir was perturbed and his army was in terror. Every last one wore a helmet. 100 horns were all sounded simultaneously to call the host together: the blare of the oliphants and bugles was so loud that you could have heard the mountains and valley all around echo with it. The emir's host gathered around him all equipped and ready to defend him, every last one armed head to toe. You might have seen plenty of good crossbows wound for use, but they will do about as much good as a peeled apple. Corbaran took his people to one side and, calling his *chétifs* together in front of his tent beneath a branched sapling, addressed them as follows: 'My lords, I call on you in the name of God who made the heavens and the dewfall not to slacken your efforts today until this serpent has been finished off. You can take it from me that I have every confidence in you'. All our *chétifs* shouted as one: 'We will not fail you, my lord, as long as we can hold out!' And with that the crested serpent came into view on Mount Tigris on the blocks of the cliffs, shooting fire and flame from her mouth which set the desert which stretched all around on fire. Not a single toad or viper or tailed snake stayed put, or toad or lizard or curve-shelled tortoise: all of them fled the fire in terror. Each made such a din that you could have heard it from half a day's ride away. The animals streamed down from the mountain into the valley and plunged straight into Corbaran's army. They inflicted a fair bit of damage on the Saracen army: the pagans killed them, raining down a shower of stones and killing more than a shipload of the vermin. Now imagine the serpent storming down the hillside, ablaze with fury and rage. Praise be to God and the honoured Virgin that she did not make for our *chétifs* first but turned on the forces of the Sultan. Now there will be a battle with a hard fought combat! The pagans and Saracens, that godforsaken race, let off volleys from their bows and crossbows. Crossbow bolts and javelins flew even more thickly than dew; innumerable arrows were shot sharpened to a razor point and made entirely of tempered steel with barbs. In the first encounter with the dragon they landed 1,000 blows from darts, maces and innumerable lead clubs, sharp pikes and innumerable good swords. But all this had about as much impact as a peeled apple because the serpent's hide was harder than a tempered anvil: any blow landed on it shattered the weapon. The serpent lost her temper, raised her tail and rained down blows on the misguided pagans. She killed a quartet at the first blow, slashing through them like a fast scythe setting out for a day's scything in thick grass. No hauberk or strong round shield could protect them from having the monster gulp their blood and rip out their entrails. No shield or helmet or hauberk, no matter how tightly crafted, or round shield even with four layers of leather was able to resist being torn apart under the monster's talons. With its teeth it tore open large numbers of chests and entrails, slashing chests and legs in two. It killed 10,000 from this army. The Turks did not dare to wait [to be attacked]. The serpent struck terror into their hearts because it had defeated their entire host and they could not hold out against its mad anger. The serpent cut right through the middle of them. It had surfeited itself on their blood to the point where it nearly burst; it had gorged itself on the blood of the Saracens and eaten so many that it was totally intoxicated. It belched a great cloud of smoke out of its mouth which was so disgustingly foetid and poisonous that the Saracen army fell over in a mass faint. A good half of them were killed and eaten; the remainder were in such a bad way that they were lying around in heaps of three and four with their mouths open. The serpent went back up the mountain, not pausing until it reached the summit; it did not rest until it was there, on a plateau at the top of the mountain four lances' length wide. There it lay down to sleep, mouth gaping wide open. It covered itself completely with one of its ears, meaning that it did not have to worry about rain or frost. Day ended and it was evening again; the moon shone brightly and the stars rose. The bishop of Forez called our people together. The abbot of Fécamp came straight away, and the other *chétifs* were there in a trice. The Bishop set out a proposition. 'My noble lords', he said, 'let me tell you what I think. You are the army of Our Lord: do not be downcast because [you have every reason to feel] happy with new reserves of strength and completely confident. The serpent has flown up to the top of Mount Tigris. We do not have to worry about anything before tomorrow because the beast has eaten and is completely full. If you were to fall in line with what I am about to propose, we would ride away as soon as the moon has risen, spurring on our way at full speed and not stopping until we reached Oliferne. Once we were there, we would not have to worry about this maddened beast any more than about a peeled apple. In fact you have seen a significant miracle: the serpent has killed and devoured the forces the Sultan brought with him, and I have never seen so many disposed of in such a short time! My lords, let us depart; we have stayed too long'. The blood drained from Corbaran's cheeks when he heard this, and he called the bishop over for a private word. 'My lord, for the mercy of God who made the heavens and dewfall, please can you find it in yourselves to suffer for a bit longer? Believe me, I would rather have my head cut off than see the Sultan's reaction to the scene in this meadow. He is my lord by right and I have pledged fealty to him. I came to this land to destroy the serpent: I have made a poor job of delivering on that pledge. If I do not confess my sin my soul will be damned to perdition and, unless God deems otherwise, taken off to Hell if I have not helped him against the savage beast.[20] I will send to find out whether his soul and body have parted company; I would not abandon him for my whole realm. Come with me, good and honourable people'. 'Yes', said Harpin, 'by the grey in my beard you can be sure we will pay proper attention to your words'. With that they immediately mounted their horses and went to see the Sultan, ambling along the road and not stopping until they had arrived in his presence.[21]

---

[20] Corbaran has not in fact converted to Christianity at this stage but speaks as though he has. The writer of the variant may be reading across what happens later in the Cycle in the *Chrétienté Corbaran*.

[21] Ambling does not have the leisurely connotations of the modern word. It was a pace where a horse had two legs on one side on the ground at the same time, and gave a smooth gait good for covering distance.

7

Corbaran of Oliferne was very brave and noble. He was richly armed – you can be sure of that; his hauberk was white and his helmet glittered, the blade of the sword buckled at his side shone; a round shield was slung from his neck which had a pattern of blue foliage; the strap was of coloured and lacquered silk; and a jet black lion was painted on it; his lance was strong and stiff with a dark pennon attached to it; and he rode a swift and willing warhorse. He took Harpin and the *chétifs* along with him as well as the abbot of Fécamp and holy clerics, the bishop of Forez and John of Alis, and good 400 Turks, Persians and Arabs. Richard went along with them despite being wounded in the face; and so did the brave Baldwin of Beauvais. They went to see the emir, who was lying in the meadow covered with flowers, completely knocked out by the breath of the beast. He was lying face upwards towards the sky and looked as if his spirit had departed his body. Picture how Corbaran and the King of Lutis called to him and addressed him as follows: 'My lord, how do you feel? Have you taken much of a beating? By my god Mahomed, you are in a terrible state. You will certainly not be happy if you have been killed in this way. You came here to Mount Tigris to help me with the evil Sathanas, who has been killed; Baldwin, the marquis of Beauvais, slaughtered him in revenge for the death of his brother'. The Sultan heard Corbaran and said to him: 'My friend, I am not actually dead but too ill to recover. The serpent breathed right into my face and now my whole body has swollen up: there is no way I can come out of it alive'. The abbot of Fécamp said: 'My lord emir, I can guarantee that if you decide to grant the God of Paradise the freedom of the *chétifs*, men and women, I can say a single word to you and you can be sure of a complete recovery'. 'I consent', said the emir. 'I solemnly pledge and, just as you say, grant Jesus Christ the liberty of all the prisoners, important and insignificant alike, whom I can find anywhere in my domain. I will give them so much from my own riches that not one will need to beg, and I will send them all to their home country'. At this the Bishop made the sign of the Cross over him and he leapt up. He then had all his men blessed by God: no more power for infidels or the Antichrist!

8

'My lords', said the emir, 'I will not make any secret of my views. Your God is very powerful and his deeds impressive, such as making sure his people survive great danger unscathed. You must serve him and adore him to the best of your ability. I intend to free large numbers of captives because of my love for him'.[22] 'My lord', said Corbaran, 'we should all get ready to move off – we really do not need to hang around here any longer. If the serpent's mother decides to come back and uses this path to come back down from the mountain, not all the gold in the world would be able to save you from her inflicting huge damage on us. She has

---

[22] The Sultan similarly speaks as if he has already converted to Christianity.

killed two sections of our army most effectively. And let me tell you for a fact that if she comes back not a single one of our forces or your forces will escape with their lives'. The emir paled on hearing this. 'Corbaran', said the Sultan, 'let me give you my views. I do not want to pretend to you that I do not place great trust in the French: they have a particular God who carries out prodigious feats and has delivered them from enormous peril. If we want to move off, let us get on and lash [the burdens on the pack animals]. But I will be straight with you: I am leaving with reluctance'. 'My lord', said Corbaran, 'I agree and will comply'. So they immediately got their equipment loaded up and lashed on; Corbaran had his tent struck so it could be transported. But before the sun could rise and start to shine, even the best of them would rather not have been there even for 1,000 bezants of pure gold. Before dawn just as day was breaking, the serpent woke up, God bring her misfortune! She remembered about Sathanas and flew into a fury; and she remembered the enormous treasure she used to guard which Corbaran had carried away by his men and put in a heap in front of his tent. The crested serpent began to shriek with such fury that she made a piece fall off the mountain. Franks and pagans alike heard it, and could not but be frightened. Even the bravest of them could not help trembling with anguish and fear, their faces going pale and working with terror. They seized their horses ready to saddle them up, and they had put on their bridles immediately; they did not want to leave their tents and pavilions behind even though all they wanted to do was flee and save their lives. But the serpent swooped on them before they could mount, making straight for King Corbaran. The men in charge of the pack animals scattered in all directions, dismounting in disorder with each man for himself, and they did not stop until they reached the Franks from France. They by contrast are going to hold out for as long as possible, and you will not see them act in a cowardly fashion as long as a couple are alive: they are determined on death or captivity. The crested serpent was very much in evidence but nobody dared to go to the rescue. Sathanas' mother saw the treasure heaped up on a carpet with a circular pattern woven in Outremer. Corbaran of Oliferne had had it gathered there, having it all ready so that he could have it carried away. But now someone has come who intends to get it back. As soon as the serpent saw it, she knew exactly what to do. She went straight to the treasure without hesitation, took it in her mouth and gulped it all down. Now you will hear about the greatest marvel you have ever come across. As I have heard it told, ten oxen would not have been capable of transporting the treasure without their legs giving way under the strain – but for her it weighed as much as an olive branch. She reared up in front of our army. Now may God save them; she is going to give them a huge fight. Now may God, the salvation of all, guard them: anyone who can escape will certainly be in his favour.

9

So the serpent got under way, jaws gaping wide, and heavily weighed down by the treasure she was carrying off; no more flames or fire came from her mouth. God had never delivered such a miracle: our whole army would have been attacked and set on fire, killed, destroyed, and poisoned to death if it had not been for the fact that the monster had not got its breath back, and that was how Our Lord saved them this time. Moradier found her right in front of him in the meadow. He was well armed with lance and sword, green helmet laced on his head, shield slung round his neck, grasping his lance with its pennon attached. He had no chance to evade her or turn tail. The serpent saw him and went for him hard, giving him such a blow with her left foreleg that she slashed his chest entirely from his body. A huge din rose from the Saracen army when they saw this; the whole area around rang with horns and bugles so that it seemed as if the mountain was sliding down into the valley. The French came spurring up yelling 'Montjoie!', whilst the Saracens shouted 'Damascus!' at the tops of their voices. They reached the serpent and surrounded her, raining down blows from swords and lances, sharp halberds and razor-edged axes, and maces made of iron or oak sharpened to a point. But this had about as much impact as a peeled apple because the monster's feathery covering was harder than a tempered anvil. When the serpent realised this was going on, she became maddened with rage and fury. She struck out at the pagans with ferocious abandon, cutting a swathe of death and destruction through their army and leaving the whole area strewn with dead bodies. John of Alis gave his horse its head and couched his lance with its pennon tied on. He went to attack the serpent head on. But the blow did not even penetrate its flesh any more than it could have punched through a rock terrace, and the lance splintered all the way up to the grip. John made to turn tail and make his escape, but he could not pull the horse round quickly enough to escape the talons of the evil serpent. They went right through his hauberk and hooked him out of his gilded saddle. She flung him, fully armed as he was, dangling across her back, turned tail and carried him off. The noble lord yelled out at the top of his voice: 'God of truth, come to my aid on such a terrible day! Holy Lady Mary, crowned queen, protect me from having my body eaten and devoured and my soul forced out. Alas, Harpin my companion, this is a sad way to go. If you don't help me I am a dead man: Richard [of Chaumont] is injured and bleeding from numerous wounds, whilst Baldwin has 20 injuries across his body. So if you and God do not come to my aid, it is the end of me and I will never return to my home country. Let me tell you this for certain: if you had been seized and ripped to shreds by a beast, even the most horrible ever to walk this earth, I would have chased after it all day until the evening and come to your rescue with my sharp sword. But now I do not think I will ever see my wife again whom I left half-mad with grief at my departure. Alas! What a sad destiny for my beloved children!'[23] He raised his right hand and made the sign of God and the Cross of salvation. He implored the revered [Heavenly] queen not to allow the crested serpent any power over him and to protect him from injury and harm. Count Harpin heard this appeal to use his strength to help John very clearly. He

---

[23] Parallel to Ernoul of Beauvais in the *Chétifs*. This gives Harpin a reason to attack the dragon in the same way as Baldwin of Beauvais.

swore to the royal Virgin in high emotion that he would rather have his head cut off than fail to help his countryman John. He would never recover from the shame of having harboured base thoughts (unless it was God's will) just because he was frightened to die.

10

Count Harpin was enraged that the serpent had carried off John of Alis. He kept shouting out to remind them to come and help him in the name of God, King of Paradise. Seeing his plight, Count Harpin could barely contain his anger. He would have thought himself worth not even a Paris coin if he did not take steps to help someone in such a parlous situation.[24] He spurred up to Corbaran in a high state of emotion, shouting for his friend the Bishop and that honourable man the abbot of Fécamp, Baldwin, Richard and the other *chétifs*. 'My lords', said the Count, 'listen to what I have to say. That cruel serpent has done us a serious wrong in carrying off Lord John, one of our good friends. He sailed here with me from our home country; he is godfather to one of my cousins and son of another. I would be put to shame if I did not help him and every Frenchman would make hay with my reputation. I prefer to die with honour rather than live as a coward. Corbaran of Oliferne, noble and powerful king, let me beg you in front of Franks and Arabs alike to make your way home to your own country. I do not want any of you hurt on my account. Take Baldwin with you because he is seriously injured. By my faith in Jesus of Paradise, I would not leave here for an emir's treasure if I cannot pursue the beast all the way to Mount Tigris. By Our Lord who was hung on the Cross on Mount Calvary and struck by Longinus, if I can find this beast I will not stop to consider my options – either I will kill her or she will kill me. As for you, my companions, I throw myself on your mercy: if I have ever wronged you in word or deed, forgive me now so that it does not get put into the balance on the great Day of Judgement before Jesus Christ Our Lord'.[25] The *chétifs* replied, 'Do not worry – we all forgive you willingly and do not bear any grudges'. The emir of Persia said: 'Harpin, you are a rash man. I don't know what possessed you but you have made a ridiculous pledge. Even if every man between here and the gates of Lutis had put on a white hauberk of chainmail, not a single one would come back alive. She has killed and destroyed us all; she has inflicted devastation on more than 60,000 brave knights whom I brought here. She has dealt out terrible wounds and killed many. If you seek her out, you will not return alive'. Then he thought again and said: 'And yet I have spoken like a coward. If the God he believes in comes to his aid and he trusts in Him, he will not be shamefully defeated; after all Baldwin killed that Antichrist the serpent. His God and the Holy Spirit helped him; this one can do just the same without injury'.

---

[24] See T-L VII.271 for other examples of this usage.
[25] Again similar to Baldwin: see laisse 68 of the *Chétifs*.

11

Harpin of Bourges said: 'Noble and renowned knights, I commend you all to God, King in Majesty. I am going after John; I have already delayed too long. Pray for me in holy charity, my lord Abbot; and you, noble lord Bishop and my valued friend, pray to Our Lord to have pity on me'. Both Baldwin of Beauvais, of proven courage, and Richard of Chaumont cried out: 'We will go with you and will not turn back!' 'No you will not, in the name of holy charity', said the Count, 'you are both too badly wounded. Instead make your way together to the wonderful city of Oliferne, and make sure you take it gently since you are wounded'. The barons were overwhelmed by grief at hearing this. Every last one of them solemnly pledged, and Corbaran and the Sultan took the same oath, that they would not leave the meadow until they knew for certain what had happened to Harpin and the brave vassal John of Alis and whether they would return together or both be eaten alive. The bishop of Forez heard Harpin's confession, absolved him graciously of his sins and gave him the Host as a symbol of his strong faith. He gave him his stole, explaining that if he were able to get it round the neck of an infidel the latter's strength and power would disappear because infidels carried out the Devil's work. 'You can be sure of my deep belief in Jesus and His dignity', said Harpin of Bourges. 'I will kill the serpent without turning and fleeing, or I will bring her back chained like a bear'. He got to his feet and prepared for battle: he put on his hauberk, laced up his bejewelled helmet and buckled his sword on his left side. His iron leg-guards were as white as a meadow flower. Then they brought him a dappled warhorse and Harpin leapt into the saddle without using the stirrup. He hung a strong shield with a buckler round his neck, with a strap of heavily worked silk; three of the names of God were painted on it which the Bishop had written when he consecrated Harpin. He had presented him with a sharp spear, the pennon having God in Majesty on it, surrounded by an embroidery of the Twelve Apostles and the most holy Virgin Mary beloved of God. He took the stole from the ordained Bishop and put it round his neck draped over his jewelled helmet, and displayed the Abbot's beneficent inscription on his chest. His companions kissed him, all weeping in sympathy; they all prayed to God the King in Majesty to bring the Count back in good spirits and in one piece. Once Harpin had taken his leave he turned and left, setting out across the meadow on his quest to find the great serpent. Now, noble and renowned lords, let me tell you of a great miracle. The serpent had fled, having swallowed the treasure and carrying off John of Alis slung across her back; she had covered him entirely with one of her ears. The sign of the Cross had protected him and ensured that the long sharp spines of the serpent did not rip him to shreds and that he was not poisoned by her breath. She arrived at Mount Tigris but did not climb it, and it was a good thing that she did not. A wood had been planted on the left of the hill full of aromatic pines and olives; indeed there was not a single kind of tree under the sun which was not represented there in abundance, whether fruit tree or some other kind; this is true. Miracle, the daughter of Triboé, had planted it. There was a room which had belonged to Methuselah who according to scriptural authority lived for 900 years; he subsequently left it to his nephew Joshua.[26] The paving tiled floor had been laid and sealed with gold, with precious stones and enamelled inlay. No man on earth had ever seen a palace of this magnificence. That was where the hideously cruel serpent made for. And Harpin, full of determined courage, followed her; he would not give up until he had found John.

12

The crested serpent came to the palace, and put down the heavy load she had been carrying. She decided to devour John, which would have been the end of him. He cried out: 'Come and help me, St Nicholas! God, help save me from certain death! Help me, Holy Lady Mary and St Gervais![27] I shall never see you again, Baldwin of Beauvais, or my true friend Richard of Chaumont. I don't think I will ever set foot in France again. Ah, Harpin of Bourges, valiant knight that you are, what are you doing? I had never thought that for all the gold in Marcais you would have failed me in either war or peace.[28] Harpin, I have always been assiduous in your service. If you do not help me now I do not see how we can remain friends. Jesus, King of Glory, if he is still alive do not abandon me!' Now imagine Harpin spurring along as fast as he can go, his whole heart furiously bent on saving John of Alis.

13

The serpent entered Joshua's palace and spat out the gold from her mouth onto the paving. Then she whipped round madly, intending to gulp down John in one mouthful. But that was not God's plan, nor that of the revered Virgin. John had the excellent idea of retreating up the mountain. Down at ground level he moved backwards steadily, gripping the beast next to her eyes so that she could not retreat or turn: even a slight shift in position would have jeopardised him. The serpent kept on twisting and turning about, thinking she could kill him on the paved area; but she did not stand as much as a *denier*'s chance of doing this because the lord stood his ground: far from forgetting the mother of God, he invoked her constantly. 'Come to my aid today, you who are crowned Queen. Ah, Harpin, noble and renowned man, you had sworn your loyalty to me. I have kept you faithful company. I shall never see you again, or my fellow countrymen either'. Now picture the scene. The Count comes spurring into the paved courtyard on his horse, meeting the enraged serpent in mid-air. He struck her a mighty blow with his sharp lance, but her hide was so tough that it made no more of an impact than

---

[26] Genesis 5:25–7 says that Methusaleh lived 969 years. Miracle is not found elsewhere. Triboé is a common Saracen name; Moisan vol 2 p. 939.

[27] St Nicholas of Myra. Also cited together at laisse 80 of the *Chétifs*.

[28] Marcais is a fictional city: Moisan vol.2 p.1236.

if it had struck a wall. Harpin struck so hard and with so much anger that the lance splintered in his hands. The serpent swung round, flinging out her foreleg and following after the horse to attack it. She smashed its shoulder, its chest and its entrails. The spirited warhorse with the chestnut flank fell dead to the floor of the paved courtyard.[29] Harpin of Bourges leapt from it brandishing his sword. Now may God, maker of the skies and the dewfall, be with him! John of Alis caught sight of him and his face changed: take it from me, he could not have been happier if someone had presented him with a towerful of gold. The noble lord found a new lease of strength and recovered his energies. Putting his hand to his side, he drew his sword. With the hilt he rained more than 100 blows onto the beast, smashing them down on her forehead. But he did not manage to do even a *denier*'s worth of damage. The dreadful serpent opened her mouth wide and jetted out flames and foul smoke; both barons had their faces burned. My lords, now listen to this amazing miracle! The beast had eaten so much that she was ready to burst with all the Saracens she had eaten. Thanks to the power of God she lost her balance and fell out of the air, being too bloated to right herself. She had a devil inside her which afflicted her and goaded her on until she was more or less upright again. But in the meantime Harpin had grabbed the stole, swiftly unwinding it from round his own neck; he went straight up to the serpent and put it round her neck. The devil came out, half dead, in the disguise of a crow which was blacker than pitch. As it left the room it made such a commotion that it nearly demolished the whole place; as it was it knocked down a large section of it, nearly killing the hideous serpent and causing her much grief.[30] She was so weakened that she fell to the floor. She would not have been capable of moving from the spot for the full tower of gold. Since the evil spirit had left her she no longer breathed fire; the flames were extinguished. Now God had tamed her and brought her under such control that she was more docile than a sweet little lamb; she will never again harm any living creature. This great miracle should be remembered and told publicly in front of people of all kinds. It was through the events of this adventure that 30,000 and more captives who had been bought and sold by the pagans and endured terrible suffering were delivered in this way and brought to salvation in Jerusalem.

14

My lords and noble gentlemen, now listen and I will recite a song which is well worth hearing. It is absolutely not a lie, take it from me; it is the truth as set out in writing. Harpin bound the serpent with his stole; it had laid waste and devastated all the surrounding land, killed and slaughtered and mistreated innumerable people, fought them to a stand and devoured and gobbled them. As for the difference between her and her son who lost his life, killed by Baldwin with his sharp sword, no cleric or man living could begin to recount the evil they wreaked on the pagans.

---

[29] Formulaic licence: it was previously dappled.
[30] Compare laisse 81 of the *Chétifs*.

Through the power of God she was tamed so that she would never again show any flicker of pride or foolish behaviour. John, perched up on her ear, did not dare come down: he was terrified she would gulp him down. But when he saw she was safely secured by the stole, he gave praises to God, son of the Holy Virgin Mary. He shinned down quickly without holding on, brandishing his drawn sword in his right hand. He greeted Harpin in the name of the son of the Holy Virgin Mary: 'Noble and splendid count, may God come to your aid, Glorious in His Heaven, the son of the Holy Virgin Mary, and may Jesus Who rose from death to life be your help. You have truly helped me against this foul beast, as of course you should do for someone who is your close associate. I am astonished that she is no longer in a state of raging fury'. Harpin of Bourges, whom God had supported, said: 'You should realise that she is no longer possessed by a devil. We shall take her along with us, not stopping all the way to the army. The emir of Persia will be amazed to see her; so will King Corbaran and the emir of Alie, and King Abraham and all the pagans; they will be talking about it all the way to Almeria, the Dry Tree and Tiberias'. 'It shall be as you command', said John of Alis. Harpin tugged at the beast and she rose, then fell to her knees right in front of the lords, apparently full of affection for them and fawning at their feet.[31] Harpin helped her up and steadied her with his hand, but her pelt was so rough that he nearly got cut open. John of Alis was delighted to see all this. He called to Harpin immediately: 'My friend, we should definitely not leave this treasure here. It would be sound common sense, not stupidity to carry it away with us. We could ensure fiefs and land for many by sharing it out between our company which is awaiting us down there, full of concern'. They both immediately loaded up their gains, carrying off the gold and leaving none behind. They lashed it onto the beast, no magic involved; three Syrian mules could not have carried as much. They loaded innumerable Pavian silks from the polished vaulted room of the palace, and innumerable rich silk coats from Almeria. The beast was very tall, long-backed and sturdy and well built; its neck was some seven feet long.[32] Harpin leapt onto it without grabbing for support. He sat in front, cradling the stole. John of Alis mounted next to him. Once they were both on board they each said',May God help us not to fall off in this meadow'. The serpent was strong; she did not bend or buckle even under 100 Russian silk cloths. The barons turned and got on their way. They left the vaulted chamber immediately and made their way across the waste land at a great pace. Corbaran of Oliferne glimpsed the beast; so did the emir Sultan and his household. They were so terrified they were going to die that their blood ran cold. They were on the point of taking flight when Harpin of Bourges yelled at the top of his voice: 'My lords and noble barons, there is nothing to be frightened of; you have no need to defend yourselves or be scared'. When the Franks and Saracens heard these words, not

---

[31] This is not unlike images of St Margaret of Antioch, who is shown with her foot on a fawning dragon. See for example the cycle of frescoes at Battle church in East Sussex: Rosewell, *Medieval Wall Paintings* 65–6.

[32] Taking 'torse' as 'toise'.

all the gold of Almeria could have made them happier. They went surging forward to meet them and dismounted on the green grass. They kissed Harpin of Bourges' face, then John of Alis as he bowed down before God, the abbot of Fécamp with his seat in Normandy, the bishop of Forez and the other lords. They all clustered round the beast with its load. None of them had ever seen anything that big in their lives. They praised God at the sight. That day many high-ranking men were casting covetous glances on what she had.

15

There was great rejoicing in the meadow below the Tigris for that stout vassal Harpin of Bourges and John of Alis the renowned vassal, because God had kept them in one piece and given them good fortune. They looked at the serpent they had brought with them, and scrutinised the enormous treasure bound onto its neck and the abundance of silk cloths. They praised God, the King of Majesty. Now they are going to go to Oliferne: that is their plan.

La Chanson de Jérusalem

1

The villainous [Saracens] were arming themselves ready in Jerusalem. There were 50,000 of those foul villains, defending the Temple of Solomon.[1] Richard and the *chétif*s were riding towards them at high speed: arguably they were going to their deaths, no two ways about it. But God, King in glory and Ruler of all, will come to their aid and protect them: anyone who trusts in Him will receive nothing but good. Our lords were at La Mahomerie. Godfrey of Bouillon, the count of Normandy and Robert the Frisian, the handsome Thomas of La Fère, Pagan of Camelia and Gerard of the Keep, the limping Roger of Rosoie, the noble-hearted Aimeric Alaitrus, Steven of Albemarle son of Count Otto, and 10,000 seasoned knights – no rabble there – had all split off from the main army. Imagine the scene: full of mailed hauberks, green-sheened helmets being laced up, shields with lions on, beautiful flags and rich pennants. They sped on over the sandy earth until they saw the Tower of David with its dragon flag, the Gate of St Stephen and the Lion Cemetery. Overcome with emotion, they bowed down at the sight of Jerusalem.[2] You can imagine the storm of weeping, tears flowing down faces and chins. By God! Just picture all those noble lords biting and kissing the stones and earth around them, talking to each other and saying: 'Jesus, who suffered for us, passed this way with his Apostles and all his companions.[3] It has been our fortune to have suffered so much from attacks, hunger, thirst and misery, wind and storms, snow and ice – at last we can see the city where God suffered and died for our salvation'.[4] Then each swung into the saddle of his horse and rounded up livestock from the surrounding lands. They rode without stopping from the valley of Josaphat to Mount Sion and as far as the Pool of Siloam. There was a

---

[1] The *Jérusalem* uses the standard insults to describe Saracens. There is an extensive literature on portrayal of Saracens in *chansons de geste*: for starting points see N. Daniel, *Heroes and Saracens: an interpretation of the chansons de geste* (Edinburgh, 1984) and *Islam and the West: the making of an image* (Oxford,1993); the comprehensive catalogue of motifs by Bancourt; M. Bennett, 'The First Crusaders' images of Muslims: the influence of vernacular poetry?', *Forum for Modern Language Studies* 22 (1986) pp. 101–22; J. Tolan, 'Muslims as Pagan Idolators in Chronicles of the First Crusade', in *Western Views of Islam in Medieval and Early Modern Europe: Perception of Other*, (ed.) D. R. Blanks and M. Frassetto (New York, 1999) pp. 97–117; S. Loutschitskaya, 'L'image des musulmans dans les chroniques des croisades', *Moyen Age* 105 (1999) pp. 717–35.
[2] A dramatic start to the poem with the first sight of Jerusalem.
[3] The theme of 'imitatio Christi' is explicitly stated.
[4] As recounted in the *Antioche*.

steep hill up beyond Bethany where God raised the corpse of St Lazarus. They had collected so many animals that they could not be counted: camels, donkeys and large numbers of fat sheep.[5] They went straight towards the hill of the Mount of Olives. If they can make it to a safe place without losing large numbers of the animals they will have deserved a lot of help from God. But you can be sure of this: before evening, if God Who suffered for us does not accord them his help, not even the best of them would want to be there for all the treasure of Sanfon.

2

The Franks had collected together large numbers of animals. They retreated smartly through the Valley of Josaphat to St Mary where the Mother of God died and was buried. The King of Jerusalem had the signal given for an assault by a brass horn used to rally the pagans, called Galie by the Turks and pagans. Up on the Tower of David with its glittering eagle, the horn's custodian blew it so hard that it could be heard for five leagues round, including by the army at La Mahomerie. The King rode out with a huge mounted retinue from the Golden Gate blessed by God, with his son Cornumarant and a large company, 50,000 of those depraved pagans, riding fully armed on warhorses and steeds from Orcanie. Intent on recovering their animals, they launched a vicious and determined attack so vigorously that if each Christian had not defended himself body and soul with good sharp spear and well-forged sword, he would have lost his head without question. Believe you me, this was a major fight with 10,000 of our men against 50,000 of theirs whatever anybody else may tell you.

3

The French had assembled large numbers of livestock. They rode back to the Valley of Josaphat, and the inhabitants of Jerusalem rode out to deliver battle. Pagans and Saracens were all spoiling for a fight. There were 50,000 of them, all hating God. They played drums and pipes and some sounded horns of brass so that the hills and valleys echoed.[6] They plunged into the fray to regain the livestock, and our noble Christians withstood them firmly. It was blisteringly hot and the French were desperate for water.

---

[5] The animals are strongly emphasised in several laisses. Compare *GF* 94 for capture of large flocks of animals at a similar point.

[6] Reminiscent of Isaiah 49:13, 55:12. RM IX.24 describes the hills ringing with the noise of victory at Ascalon.

4

The battle in the Valley of Josaphat was extensive. The men from Jerusalem issued out and plunged into the thick of battle to get their livestock back. The French welcomed them with lances and darts, plunging them in so hard and so accurately – I am not exaggerating – that the lances shattered and sent splinters flying everywhere. Imagine swords biting into those glittering helmets, ripping apart hoods, shields and protective barriers. By God! The companions of Judas pressed them so hard that the Franks were struggling to put them off their stride. But Duke Godfrey swore by St Jonah, Count Robert of Flanders by his lord St Veas, and Stephen of Albemarle by his lord St Thomas that they would rather die in the city of Arras than let the Turks and Saracens defeat them on this battlefield and have the pagans take back the ewes and fat sheep. Then the duke invoked St Andrew of Patras, and Robert invoked the Holy Sepulchre and also St Nicholas: 'Strike on, noble lords! This is no time for frivolity. Anyone who believes in God should not hang back: do not give the race of Caiaphas anything to boast about!'

5

My lords, that was a very hard fought day when the Franks took the livestock out of the great valley where St Mary, the mother of the Creator, died and was buried, and all the angels carried her up to Heaven to the presence of Our Lord.[7] The pagans pressed our people hard, hemming them in by shooting with bows and arrows. Imagine the scene: many expensive warhorses being shot at, and lots of princes and counts laying about them in the thick of battle with their swords gripped in both hands. The sun was blazing down and it was blisteringly hot. Most of those fighting were in a terrible state: the noble knights were so desperate for water that in their distress the Christians were drinking the urine, blood and sweat of their horses.[8]

6

It was a bitterly fought battle with much blood shed. By God! King Cornumarant and his father Corbadas, the old grey-haired warrior, pressed them so hard that had you been there you would have seen horses and steeds knocked off their feet,

---

[7] The valley of Josaphat was where the Virgin supposedly died and was taken up to Heaven: there is no account in the Gospels but an abundance of accounts in apocrypha. The abbey of St Mary of the Valley of Josaphat commemorated her: D. Pringle, *Churches in the Crusader kingdom of Jerusalem: an archaeological gazetteer*, 4 vols (Cambridge, 1993–2009) vol. 3 pp. 287–306.

[8] Thirst is a recurrent theme in Crusade sources: see e.g. RA 139, AA VI.6. In part this is sheer realism: Jerusalem in June is very hot. But there is also a measure of symbolism: the thirst of the Crusaders is slaked by the redemption of Christ the *fons vivus*.

dragging their entrails through the valley in their death throes. Those who lost their horses were indeed unhappy men: they were trapped in the fray on foot like sergeants. The French defended themselves with good sharp spears; when the lances had splintered they drew their swords and slashed Turkish heads, ribs and sides so that the battlefield was covered with blood and brains. The Duke looked over towards the Mount of Olives – and saw our *chétifs*, armed and on horseback.[9] It was Richard and his companions, their green-sheened helmets glittering, wearing white hauberks picked out splendidly in gold, sitting on fast and spirited horses, stout shields hung from necks and grasping lances, flags of silk and fine fabric billowing: they looked truly brave warriors. My lords, it was Richard the noble knight, Harpin and his God-fearing companions, fresh from captivity in the city of Oliferne whose lord was Corbaran, and freed by Jesus. They had been there for three years and 15 days.[10] Jesus secured their release and it was at his behest: anyone who believes in God can be sure of this. There were 190 of them. They had suffered terribly: each was brooding, lost in thought beneath his helmet. This battle was so fierce that our Franks were in dismay: it was hardly surprising that they were beginning to lose heart. By contrast the pagans were in buoyant mood, sure the reinforcements were pagans. 'Radiant redeeming Father and Holy Lady Mary, who carried within you the Saviour of the world, come to our aid now!' said Duke Godfrey.

7

My lords and brave noble knights, now listen to how the French fared at their hour of need. The Turks were attacking them, shooting from their bows of horn, pressing them so hard with their razor-sharp arms and vicious darts and steel swords that they pushed them back to the Gate of St Stephen, sinking their steel swords into their helmets and killing their horses with their finely worked stilettos. Many horses were dragging their entrails behind them; and those who lost their horses were in a terrible state. The livestock had been gathered on the slope of a hill, and the combat there was particularly hard fought with the Christian princes and lords. No cleric could tell you or any *jongleur*'s song do justice to the violence of the pagans as the Christians tried to defend themselves. There was no knight or prince, powerful as he might be, who was not terrified of losing his head. 'Forward in the name of the Holy Sepulchre!' they cried at the tops of their voices. Imagine Robert the Frisian spurring forward; he came to speak to the duke of Bouillon. 'My lord Duke Godfrey, this is what I think. Do you see that squadron riding towards us which has stopped by that hillside? In my opinion those are Arabs. They are a proud, determined and warlike people. If we are to lose our livestock now

---

[9] The author emphasises the desperate nature of the battle with three *laisses similaires* in order to underline the opportune arrival of the *chétifs*.

[10] This is reasonably accurate. The Peoples' Crusade failed in 1096 and the siege of Jerusalem was in the early summer of 1099.

and have demeaning songs made up about us, I personally by God the Redeemer would rather be dead'.[11] 'Lord God', said the Duke, 'do not let today be the day the Turks get these spoils: not a single sturdy donkey, not a camel or mule or jenny, bullock or elephant or goat or sheep, not as much as a single bleating lamb. Let us send two messengers at top speed to that wise knight the count of St-Gilles, and to Bohemond and Tancred our friends and the noble Christian barons, asking them for help in the name of God the Redeemer. If they do not come to our help quickly they will see us losing ground – in fact they will not see us alive again!' With these words they exchanged glances of sympathy: many of them were in tears crying for sheer pity of each other because they were terrified they were going to die.

8

'Whom shall we send to tell the count of St-Gilles about our plight?' said Godfrey. 'Aimeric Alaitrus and Fulcher of Chartres: they have a high reputation and are good knights', replied Thomas of La Fère. You should have seen Fulcher launch a solo attack on these Turks, slashing and laying into them with his sharp sword![12] I am not going to downplay his achievements: I can vouch for him plunging it in so viciously and energetically that more than 7,000 lost their heads. 'That man is a hero!'[13] cried the princes. 'May God grant him a long life. Let's come to his help'. Aimeric turned and rode all the way down the main road, not drawing rein until he reached the Christian army at its base in La Mahomerie. He gave his message to Lord Raymond the prince, Bohemond and Tancred who prized his services, and the noble lords (God give them wisdom). 'My lords, by the Holy Sepulchre, your services are needed in battle! You must come and help urgently because our men are in dire need. No knights have ever been in such danger, and the army cannot hold out much longer where it is. It was an amazing miracle that one person was able to get away. But anyone who trusts in God should not despair!' When the lords had heard what the messenger had to say, passing on the words of the Duke and the barons, you might have seen many a brave knight come to avenge God reduced to tears: bishops, abbots and noble princes, noble maidens and gentlewomen all in transports of grief unable to stop the tears coursing down their bodies: they were lamenting the lords they held so dear. You can imagine those lords in floods of tears – this is quite true – putting on double-ringed hauberks, strapping on their swords, lacing up their green-sheened helmets glittering with pure gold under the rays of the sun, seizing strong shields and good steel swords and well-made blades [with hilts of] ash and apple-wood, and letting their beautiful silken flags billow. When they were armed each one swung onto his swift and spirited warhorse

---

[11] C. f. *Roland* line 1466: 'Male chançun n'en deit estre cantee' ('no evil song must be sung about our prowess').

[12] According to RM V.12, VI.2 Fulcher was first into Antioch.

[13] The Old French term is 'vassal terrier', a minor member of the nobility who held lands from his lord.

without using the stirrup. If the pagans at the Gate of St Stephen outside the main walls – cowardly smooth-tongued villains! – do not watch it, I think they are going to pay a heavy price. No drawing of swords or thrusting of lances is going to save them, and they are going to die with no hope of escaping their fate.

9

Aimeric Alaitrus dismounted in the camp right in the middle of the tents for the young women. He gave Lord Raymond of St-Gilles, Bohemond and Tancred his news: it was not good. 'Alas, noble lords! Come without delay and assume command! The battle outside Jerusalem is hard fought. We have definitely suffered terrible losses of many men and horses in the valley of Josaphat. 10,000 horses are lying there with their entrails spread around them. The French are so desperate and in such need of water that they are drinking the urine and blood of their animals'. 20,000 Franks wept, hand pressed to face.[14] Then they all put on hauberks and helmets, buckled on their swords, saddled up, and 60,000 rode out of their quarters. You might have seen women and girls filling buckets, pots and dishes with water and coming out of their quarters; the companies looked splendid.[15]

10

Our brave knights left their lodgings: princes and barons trusting in God, women and girls carrying water, clutching it against their chests and necks, across the boiling hot sand. Quite a few of them had no shoes, and blood flowed from their feet and heels. They praised God, redeeming Father, for the pain caused by the sharp stones which cut into them; they walked along praising him for the suffering they endured. Bohemond and Tancred rode along in front, in floods of tears, hands pressed to face, fervently praying to God in glory in his all-encompassing power to save the Duke, and Count Eustace and the young Baldwin, and Robert the Frisian, Robert the Norman and the valiant-hearted Thomas of La Fère and Eufroi of Buison, Wicher the German and the noble lords so beloved of God. 'Ah God!' said Bohemond, 'I hope I live long enough to find myself alongside the duke with his sharp sword, and find him safe and sound and very much alive. I have every intention of landing so many blows of my steel sword on these infidel pagans that those who do manage to escape with their lives will look back with regret every day they live'. 'My lord', said Tancred, 'what are you waiting for? Get riding at top

---

[14] A classic gesture to convey anxiety and suffering: see for example the queen from the Lewis chessmen in the British Museum and compare *Moniage Guillaume* lines 2988–9.

[15] The first reference to a theme which will appear repeatedly and goes back to the description of the battle of Dorylaeum in *GF* 19. The *Antioche* refers several times to the theme: laisses 99, 327, 353. Water was crucial in battle. The author uses it as a leitmotif to evoke combat, sometimes with mildly salacious overtones: see laisses 10, 17, 105, 135.

speed! We don't want to wait to get to the Saracens. By my faith in the Glorious Almighty, I shall land such blows with my sharp sword that anyone I attack will be a dead man!' So they rode out together in the name of the Redeemer, lances resting on saddles, gonfanons hanging, shields and arms glittering with gold and silver glinting in the sun: horses and arms made a fine spectacle. They left the tents and pavilions standing where they were under the guard of the sick and small children. The women carried water [in pots] hung round their necks and clutched to them. At this point I am going to turn my attention from the help on its way to that brave fighter, the duke of Bouillon, much favoured by God. He looked down the slope into the valley and saw our *chétifs* riding towards them. He urged his horse towards them and when he was near enough addressed them as follows: 'Hoy! Who are you? Do you believe in God, son of the Virgin Mary, glorious and all-powerful? Or do you believe in Apollon, Mahomed and Tervagant, Margot and Jubin, Jupiter the god of thunder, and all those wicked idols whom the Persians worship?'[16] Richard, who was out in front very richly armed on a piebald warhorse, replied; Harpin of Bourges was riding along listening and the other *chétifs* followed on behind: 'And you, sir, who are you? Are you talking about God? That is something we have not heard for a good three years, Gospel, Psalter or sung Mass. Know that we believe in the King of Bethlehem and in the Holy Virgin who bore Him. Now tell us, noble sir, whom you are looking for. Tell me your name: I am most keen to know'. 'You shall know it straight away', replied the Duke. 'My name is in truth Godfrey of Bouillon, and we have come from beyond the sea to seek the Sepulchre. Here we are busy fighting the pagans, Saracens who go around yelping and do not believe in God the Redeemer. Now tell us who you are and where you are riding in such a hurry'. Richard replied immediately: 'We were held captive by the powerful King Corbaran. We escaped by the will of Jesus. We have suffered so many pains and torments that nobody could possibly tell you of them or any *jongleur* do them justice in his song!'

11

There was great rejoicing when the Duke heard that they believed in God the incarnation of truth, the Son of the Virgin Mary Who redeemed us all. I can assure you that he was overjoyed and so were the other *chétifs*, you can be sure of that. 'I thank you, noble knights', said Duke Godfrey. 'Just see how the Turks, Persians and Arabs are laying into us, those Saracen people who curse Jesus and refuse to acknowledge that he was born of a Virgin, that he suffered death and rose again. Our men are on their last legs defending their faith. The enemy have killed our horses and we are much weakened. Help us, my lords, by God Who is eternal truth, and by the death He suffered for us on the Holy Cross when He was nailed

---

[16] Apollon, Mahomed and Tervagant are the classic trio of pagan gods familiar from other texts. See e.g. *Roland* lines 2696–7; 'Apollon', M. Zink, *Mélanges René Louis: la chanson de geste et le mythe carolingien* (St.Père-sous-Vézelay, 1982) pp. 503–9.

to it on the Mount of Calvary and He spilled His blood'. All the *chétifs* shouted out in unison: 'Help us, Holy Sepulchre! See, we are saved! Ah, God, how You have filled us with joy! What shall we do, noble lords? We are being too defeatist. God will not favour anyone who does not attack Turks today'. They flung themselves into the battle, absolutely delighted. Spurring on, each one seized his shield, sharp lance and well-forged sword. Each fought well as a brave man should; the pagans were under pressure from one end to the other. Imagine a vigorous battle: everyone was striking Persians, or Turks or Arabs, piercing their shields and tearing their hauberks, ripping open chest and heart and their other innards so that each one of the 50 took down his man, and so did the other 140 *chétifs*. Had you been there you would have seen wholesale slaughter, people yelling, strong shields smashed and gaping, hauberks wrenched apart, heads cut off, chests sliced open down the middle, and viscera and innards spread across the grass. John of Alis, companion of Richard and one of the *chétifs*, made for the battle brandishing his spear and struck an emir, splitting his shield down the middle, piercing it and breaking his mailed shirt: the emir was the son of Barbais and emir of Ali. John sliced his chest and heart down the middle. The Turk fell to the ground on top of his flowered shield; his soul left his body and was seized by devils. John took his swift Arab warhorse and quickly gave it to one of his companions from amongst the *chétifs*, who took it with alacrity. He swung quickly onto the horse's back not bothering with the stirrup; then he rode into the press of battle brandishing his bright steel sword and struck a pagan emir. He struck down right through the middle of the helmet as far as the teeth; the emir fell dead to the ground like a slaughtered piglet.[17] His soul fled his body and was snatched by devils.[18]

12

Lord Richard of Chaumont did not hang around. He spurred on his swift warhorse, wielded his lance with its pennon, and struck a Turk full on in the front of his helmet so that he smashed right through the mailed hood; he aimed his good sharp spear right through his body. The Turk fell dead to the ground on the boiling-hot sand and his soul went off to the fetid realms of Hell. Richard cried out at the top of his voice, 'Lords, strike hard! My lords, now is your chance for revenge on the Saracens who put you through so much hardship. May God, the redeeming Father, confound them!'

---

[17] The meaning of 'souci' is unclear here. The line has numerous variants, suggesting that scribes too were unclear. The metaphor is clearly some form of splitting: Susan Edgington suggests the metaphor may be a suckling pig split open for the table. Recipes for suckling pigs refer to spitting them and splitting them open for stuffing though neither metaphor quite works here: Harleian mss.279 and 4016 in *Two fifteenth century cookery books*,(ed.) T. Austin, (Oxford, 1888; reprinted Woodbridge, 2000), pp. 40, 82.

[18] Another common topos: Saracens are portrayed as diabolical and emissaries of Satan, often referred to as 'aversiers'. See e.g. RM I.3, III.1, IX.20; *Guilluame* line 3202.

13

Lord Harpin of Bourges was sitting armed on his warhorse. He urged it on with spurs of pure gold. By God! How well he was armed with a double-ringed white hauberk, a green-sheened helmet set with jewels, and a quartered shield with a lion as white as a wild rose. He brandished his lance with its sharp steel blade, with the pennant of rich crimson silk laced onto it, and struck a Turk on his shield ornamented with pure gold so that he split it, ripped the mail of the hauberk, and – following through the thrust – left the Turk dead on the path. The body lay dead on the ground; he had met the end he deserved. Devils and demons carried off the soul.[19] Harpin of Bourges started to shout: 'Help us, Holy Sepulchre! Strike away, noble lords!' He struck so hard with the spear that it shattered. In a rage at seeing it broken, he quickly drew his sword of burnished steel and struck a Turk with it on the upper part of his helmet in such a way that he sliced through his mailed hood and the cap underneath. The Turk sprawled dead on the sandy ground. 'So much for you, you wretch!' he said, 'may God make you suffer!' Anyone who saw the baron laying into the Saracens, slashing and wounding with his sharp sword, would not have exchanged him for any knight. Anyone he attacked was a dead man with no hope of escape.

14

Baldwin of Beauvais was a brave knight. By God! How well he was armed on his fine steed! He wore on his back a white chainmail hauberk; the links were whiter than lily flowers. He had laced on a green-sheened helmet with burnished gold, the golden circle round it all set with jewels. On top was a topaz from the river of Paradise. The powerful King Corbaran was very fond of it; he had given it to Baldwin because he considered him as a close friend for killing the serpent on Mount Tigris which had devastated the country. And he had buckled on Baldwin his sword with its burnished blade. Abraham, old and white-haired, had given it to him; a Jew had forged it on Mount Sinai and he gave it to Baldwin as a prized vassal.[20] He brandished his spear with its dark tempered blade, with a gonfanon of dark silk tied onto it; golden ribbons tied it to his fist and his chest. He struck out in the midst of the pagans scything hrough them and struck an emir called Copatris. He was a native of Baghdad, where he held large estates; his father Justamar had sent him to help the King of Jerusalem on behalf of his country and to help him to defend himself against our lords. Baldwin struck him on his curved shield, splitting and breaking it above the gold buckler, and breaking and splitting

---

[19] Saracens are classed with the damned, whose souls are also taken away by devils: see for example the Doom painting in Holy Trinity, Coventry, where enthusiastic devils lead away cheating alewives to Hell: Rosewell, *Medieval wall paintings* pp. 74–5.

[20] In the *Chétifs* Corbaran gives Baldwin armour and weapons including a sword, but none with this pedigree: laisse 64.

the refined gold mailshirt. He slashed through his spine, his heart and his chest. The Turk toppled from the saddle dead to the ground; devils carried his soul off to Hell for eternity. Baldwin cried: 'Father God, Jesus Christ, come to our help in Your mercy!' He struck so hard with the spear that he broke it into pieces. His lance failing like this put him into a fury. He drew his sword coated with refined gold and plunged it into the flowered helmet of a Turk, slashing and breaking right down to the teeth; the Turk was left lying dead on the ground in a clearing. Then he went off and struck another. In all he killed 14, all so efficiently that none escaped. Having this noble man amongst the Arabs was rather like a lion in a fold of ewes. The pagans went pale and yelled: imagine them completely defeated.

15

Lord John of Alis had no intention of hanging around. By God! How well he was armed on his Syrian steed. He had put on a mailshirt glinting with gold, a present from Corbaran and the King of Nubia. The chainlinks were whiter than a lily flower; it was strong and so robust that no stiletto or falchion would be able to rip it. He laced on a green-sheened helmet made in Byzantium; the circlet round it was of gold and a large number of jewels glittered in it. He buckled on his burnished, well-forged sword and spurred on his horse, brandishing his lance; a pennon hung from it of silk which fluttered in the wind, and the laces of fine gold fell down to his feet. He made for a Turk and struck him mercilessly, landing such a strong blow on the flowered shield that he split it right apart and ripped open the chainmail, slicing open his heart and liver with the steel blade and leaving him dead on the scrubland. 'Take that, you coward, and God's curse on you!' he said. Devils carried off the Turk's soul back to their abode. The noble knight shouted at the top of his voice: 'Strike on, noble lords! Do not hold back! May God help us today! Blessed Virgin Mary!' Count Robert of Flanders, the count of Normandy, the brave Thomas of La Fère, Duke Godfrey who placed a profound trust in God, Count Eustace who should not be forgotten, Baldwin his brother, Achard of Byzantium and the noble lords of the rich land of France all saw Richard and Lord John of Alis, Fulcher of Melun and Rainald of Pavia, Harpin of Bourges and their large following, the abbot of the rich monastery of Fécamp and the bishop of Forez laying into the pagans and killing 10 of them with his strong spear. The other *chétifs* did not hang back either. They all laid into the Turks together; they were just like a lion maddened by hunger, going for the middle of the sheepfold; that is just what our *chétifs* did to the pagans. You can be sure that when our barons saw this they laughed with sheer joy and happiness, and God laid His noble hand on them in blessing.

16

It was a densely fought battle with considerable bloodshed. Picture the battle: Lord Robert the Frisian and the handsome Thomas of La Fère, Duke Godfrey (God's mercy on him), Pagan of Camelia and Gerard of the Keep, Roger of Rosoie with the limp, Fulcher the vassal and Eufroi of Buison, and the noble lords of Charlemagne's kingdom all laying vigorously into the Turks. Every last one was killing Turks and Slavs. Meanwhile Harpin of Bourges, Richard of Chaumont, Lord John of Alis and all their companions were likewise busy attacking the forces of Mahomed. The bishop of Forez was mounted on a Gascon steed.[21] Ah! Just imagine him armed in a chainmail hauberk, with a green-sheened helmet and a shield with a lion on, and a sharp sword buckled round his waist. He clasped his spear from which there hung a gonfanon made of Almerian silk with a lion painted on; it was topped with a golden cross to show the rightness of his cause, and the golden laces hung down to his spurs. The *almançour* Faraon loomed up in front of him: he was a nephew of King Corbadel from beyond Carion, a very rich lord with extensive lands. The bishop struck him so forcefully that he broke through his shield and the chainmail hauberk. He sliced open his chest, liver and lungs, his heart in his chest, spleen and kidneys, knocking him dead to the sandy earth.[22] 'Take that, you wretch!' he said. 'Make that your confession!' Seizing the horse, he swung into the saddle, which was made of refined gold worked by Solomon; the bridle, chest strap and elaborate studs were worth a lot of golden *mangons*, take it from me.[23] Duke Godfrey said to Robert the Frisian: 'That man deserves a prize – let us go and help him out.' Just look at the Persians and Slavs massing for the attack, shooting arrows at him and making a din.' The Turks and Persians came swarming round the body which was lying on the sandy ground. Our French fell back the distance of a crossbow shot. The battle was over and the Turks lamented bitterly: truly nobody could imagine the depth of their grief.

17

The pagans made a terrible din. The bishop of Forez had brought an end to the battle by killing such an eminent emir. Richard and the *chétifs*, on the right side of fortune, had won the battle without a shadow of a doubt. The Turks and Persians and infidels swarmed thickly around the emir. Hair was torn and beards tugged, richly worked helmets ripped undone, clothes slashed apart, chests beaten and faces scratched: the display of grief was indescribable. Imagine Cornumarant wielding

---

[21] The bishop of Forez fights in battle like the classic battling cleric, Archbishop Turpin in the *Roland*. See T. Reuter, 'Episcopi cum sua militia: The Prelate as Warrior in the Early Staufen era', *Warriors and Churchmen in the High Middle Ages: essays presented to Karl Leyser*, (ed.) T. Reuter (London and Rio Grande, 1992) pp.79–94.

[22] A slightly literal approach to single combat, typical of the author's practical bent.

[23] A *mangon* is a gold coin worth two bezants: T-L V.1054–5.

his sword: he would have plunged it into his heart if it had not been forcibly taken from him. Picture how many noble wives came running and how many noble girls wept, hair in dishevelled disorder. To the accompaniment of much lamentation and mourning they carried their dead into the city through the Gate of St Stephen, which they shut off with a great iron chain. Our renowned Frenchmen left the scene driving their flocks of livestock: they had certainly paid a heavy price for them. The count of Normandy was grasping his sword in his fist: he had struck so many blows in the battle that his hand had frozen in position, with the handgrip so tightly held that he could not unclench his fingers until they had held his hand in hot water and massaged it with oil. They found Bohemond and his well-armed men on a mound half a league off. The women brought water to assuage the army's thirst: plenty of the soldiers were foaming at the mouth, believe it or not. People came thronging round the *chétifs* to hear the story of their adventures: they were listened to with the greatest attention. Many tears were shed. The army returned to La Mahomerie: our people were well looked after that night.

18

Our barons returned to La Mahomerie. The livestock was shared out with rigorous fairness according to who held the highest rank, but even the poorest were in tears of joy. The whole of the army was fed and satisfied. The count of Normandy was still holding his sword: he had stuck so many blows in the battle that his hand had frozen in position. He had it soaked in hot water just below boiling point, and once it had been sufficiently soaked it relaxed: he was truly grateful to be able to put his sword down.[24] The mass of the cavalry was so exhausted that they did not set up pickets that night but lay down in the meadow fully armed. The only bed they wanted was the bare ground: they were not after sheets, or pillows made of oriole and magpie feathers, but used their shields as beds and slept in their hauberks. Bohemond rose at the depths of midnight. He was uneasy, genuinely, because he was not with the other lords and Duke Godfrey and his company in the valley of Josaphat attacking the vile pagans who believe neither in God nor the son of the Virgin Mary. He put on his great chainmail hauberk and laced his Pavian helmet on his head with its circlet of refined gold glittering and glinting; he buckled on his well-honed bright sword and hung his great flowered shield round his neck; he took a spear decorated with a flag made of a rich silk from Syria with a cross of gold which glittered and glinted. He rode out away from the army with a retinue of 10,000 knights. Without delay he made straight for Caesarea to look for the mounted force, collecting plunder as he rode across the plain. They rode all the way down the solitary valley to Haifa without delay. The Turks of

---

[24] The heroism of Robert of Normandy is emphasised by the use of *laisses similaires*. This is the first of several occasions in the text where his heroism is emphasised more than his actual achievements justified: see 30, 141. See Table of Names for other references and discussion.

Caesarea, those infidel villains, were lurking about half a league from Merle above the Tower of Moskes in the middle of the wasteland. They rode out for battle – curse them, by the body of God! If God the Son of the Virgin Mary does not accord His help, bringing their livestock could turn out to have been a very bad idea. If the Lord Who rules all does not accord His help, they will not be going back to their quarters. The pagans and Saracens from that prosperous city immediately put ten messengers into a galley and sent it to Ascalon to get help and support. They raised their sails, and the wind pushed them along faster than a speeding arrow. They reached Ascalon before tierce. The galley arrived in port alongside the fleet and they anchored next to the strong and ancient fort.

19

The messengers disembarked from the rich galley, each wearing a silken robe from Caesarea. They came to the emir to deliver their request. Picture the scene: hordes of Turks yelling and lamenting, tearing their hair and their fur cloaks. 'Alas, lord emir, you noble and respected man! Now the nobles of Caesarea are seeking your help. A race of degenerates has gone off with their livestock, people who have no fear of lances or arrows because they are completely covered with armour'. On hearing this the emir stood up on his dais and had his drum set up on a great chest. He was armed and fiercely proud to look at. When he had his drum beaten on the highest tower, there was not a Saracen whose heart did not quicken at the sound.

20

When the emir heard what those from the galley had to say and their message about the French and the concerns at Caesarea, he had his drum beaten and his horn sounded at full blast. He was armed: his shield was made of bone edged with precious stones from the Robanos river; the hauberk he wore on his back was richly worked. The emir Fanios issued from Ascalon accompanied by 20,000 wicked outlaw Saracens. If they attack us the battle will be never-ending.

21

Bohemond and Tancred had laid an ambush facing Caesarea down in a valley with a small brook. There were large flocks of ewes and goats, camels and donkeys and bleating lambs. The Turks from Caesarea pursued the strongest and fastest along the sandy shore, instilling more fear into them than larks pursued by a falcon. Our barons made their way up above Mirabel: they found a most beautiful altar at St George of Ramleh served by Syrians from Nazareth.

22

Our barons arrived at St George of Ramleh – Bohemond, Tancred and all their companions with just about all the great flock of livestock, ewes, goats and large numbers of fat sheep, camels and bullocks and lots of donkeys. They dismounted, prayed and beat their chests as a sign of their contrition; they invoked God by his holiest name and the valiant lord St George, begging forgiveness for all their sins. Whilst they were engaged in worship in this way, picture the Turks from Ascalon riding along the sand, armed in various combinations on their steeds. The emir was riding armed on a white horse from Aragon, its neck and hindquarters covered by a green cloth; he was carrying the banner with flag and dragon, the golden laces falling down to his spurs. The pagans were riding in force and at full speed, thronging on all sides behind the emir. Had you been there, you would have seen plenty of mailed hauberks, green-sheened helmets laced on heads, shields with lions and rich shields with golden emblems embroidered into silk and green sigladon, Turkish bows of horn shooting at full pelt and arrows dipped in poison down to the feathers.[25] When our barons saw this they each swung into the saddle and swept up their shields, brave as lions.[26] Bohemond raised their morale with a sermon. 'My lords and noble knights', said the noble lord, 'we are all from one land and of one stock, sons of noble mothers and of one region. Here we have no castle or fort or keep we can call our own and retreat into. You can see these Turks coming to seek us out. They do not believe in God or in His Resurrection; they do not believe that He suffered death and pain to release us all from the prisons of Hell. Lord, let anyone who dies here have the same blessing as God gave the Apostles on the day of His Ascension. Anyone who dies here will receive true forgiveness on the great Day of Judgement and absolution.' As he came to the end of his speech, there were the Turks of Caesarea spurring forward: they combined with the forces of Mahomed's people who fought alongside the pagans of Ascalon. Imagine them all fighting to the death, hauberks of linked chainmail ripped apart, Saracens and wicked cowards dying left, right and centre, heads sent flying, chests and chins slashed: the earth was littered with dead [pagans] who will receive no pardon from God. The sandy earth was strewn with dead and injured. 4,000 Esclavons died in this charge: devils hastened to carry off their souls, which will be trapped forever in the prisons of Hell.

23

It was a fiercely fought battle with considerable bloodshed. The Turks gave them a lot of trouble from arrows and lance thrusts. You might have seen lots of shields pierced, mailshirts torn apart, hauberks ripped, Saracens killed and knocked flying and stumbling about, injured horses and swift warhorses with broken

---

[25] Sigladon is multi-coloured Oriental silk: T-L IX.644–5.
[26] One of the rare metaphors in the text: nearly all compare Crusaders to wild animals.

reins careering about. Ah God! How the minor nobles attacked. Bohemond took command, may Jesus help him. Imagine him waving his banner, sweeping up and down as fast as his horse could carry him, dodging and turning adroitly then plunging back into the midst of the Turks. Anyone he pursued was not going to get as much as a *denier*'s worth of protection from any white hauberk or strong coat of mail: he would still slide his spear into their body and send them flying dead. Imagine the Turks yelping and barking: 4,000 of them met their end down next to the river.[27] Those smooth-talking villains were on the point of flight, but the Franks did not know the mortal danger about to confront them. Looking to the right towards Golfier's castle, they saw a good 15,000 Turks from Jaffa coming down the main road and armed to the teeth. Seeing this fierce squadron reduced the Franks' morale considerably. Bohemond however reassured them and stiffened their wavering resolve. 'My lords and noble knights', he said, 'let me implore you for the love of God in glory and the true Sepulchre not to lose heart! Greet the Turks with iron and steel! Anyone who dies here will be rewarded by God with a place in Paradise, serving and taking his ease next to the Holy Innocents!'[28]

24

'My lords', said Bohemond, 'this is an unfortunate series of events. We would have had those men from Jaffa on the run if these new reinforcements hadn't turned up – the worse for them, I hope – making for us and laying about them at a fast pace. Look at the arrogant way they are approaching us. Anyone who gives them the right reception will have a chaste and pure soul and his deeds will be enough to take him in front of God'.

25

'My lords', said Bohemond, 'I will be straight with you. Anyone who receives death for God will be greatly favoured. God will lead him to celestial Paradise and he will be crowned alongside the Holy Innocents'. Imagine the scene: the Turks bringing the standard forward right in front of the French, planting it in the ground and raising it, all that pure gold and silver glittering and shining and the precious

---

[27] The Saracens are compared to dogs: another standard topos; Bancourt vol. 1 74–76 for animal comparisons. Compare RM IV.15, VI.8; *Canso d'Antioca* line 321, 'ans larco como chas'.

[28] The Innocents were the first martyrs. The reference recalls the promise that those who die on Crusade are martyrs and will be offered heavenly crowns. See *GF* 40 for an early statement of the belief, 'in caelum ascenderunt et candidatam stolam martyrii receperunt' (they ascended into heaven and received the shining white garment of martyrdom); H. E. J. Cowdrey, 'Martyrdom and the First Crusade', *Crusade and settlement: papers read at the first conference of the SSCLE and presented to R. C. Smail*, (ed.) Peter Edbury (Cardiff, 1985) 46–56.

stones glinting like firebrands. They fell on our lords with long sharp stilettos: shields and blazons were torn and holed, and swords bit into helmets. The French were crowded together without room to move. They planted their shields to serve as a fence – may Jesus save them! Bohemond could stand it no longer and broke from the ranks. In front of 5,000 Frenchmen (God grant them honour) he made for the standard and laid about him ferociously, toppling it by sheer strength and power. Picture the Turks yelping and shouting, sounding their horns and banging their drums! Furious, they raised it again by main force and made our Franks retreat by an acre and a half. If you had seen our barons taking a stand at St George and heard Bohemond yelling and shouting 'Holy Sepulchre, noble St George, come to our aid!' you would have been reminded of dogs harrying a wild boar when its legs go sprawling out from under it and the dogs move in for the attack: that was how the Turks were treating our Frenchmen.[29] In my view they would only be able to withstand the assault if God, Salvation of all, came to their help.

26

My lords and noble knights, listen and I will tell you how things went with the French in such dire straits, with the Turks harassing them by shooting from their bows of horn, attacking with sharpened sticks and throwing darts. Just like dogs hunting a wild boar when his feet sprawl out and they snap at his heels, that was how the Turks harassed our Frenchmen. You can be quite sure they would not have held out if God had not come to their aid by exercising His holy powers. There they were: St George spurring forward, St Barbara and St Domitian each on a warhorse, St Denis of France riding up on a white charger, St Maurice of Angers beloved of God, and a legion of angels flying like falcons.[30] They fell on the Turks like bellowing wild boars. Anyone they went after had no hope of escaping death. Each one flung Saracens or Persians or Turks or Bedouin or pagans in general dead to the ground. Our lords were overjoyed at the sight. Some who were lying on the ground injured leapt up again, picked up their shields and took up their sharp swords. St George gave rein in pursuit and struck the emir who ruled over Ascalon full in the chest, piercing right through his shield, ripping his hauberk and slicing right through his chest and his heart. He knocked him dead and bleeding to the ground with the force of his thrust. 'What on earth are these

---

[29] Another metaphor of wild animals, though here unusually vivid.

[30] As in the *Antioche* the saints intervene at a crucial moment. The white horse is reminiscent of the white horses of the Apocalypse, Revelation 19:11–14. See D. S. Bachrach, *Religion and Conduct of War c.300 – 1215* (Woodbridge, 2003) p. 178 for a similar description of St Lambert on a white horse; *Historia de expeditione Friderici imperatoris MGH SRG* 5 (Berlin, 1928) pp. 80–81 for white-clad warriors attacking the Turks on Frederick Barbarossa's Crusade; *The Deeds of Count Roger of Calabria and Sicily and of his brother Robert Guiscard*, transl. K. B. Wolf (Ann Arbor, 2005) II.33 pp.109–10 for St George riding to the rescue of the Normans at the battle of Cerami.

people – living demons?' said the pagans. 'Nothing is going to protect us against the blades of their lances. May Mahomed whom we worship destroy them!' They turned their backs and fled. Bohemond rode in pursuit, leading with St George; the nobles came spurring along behind, now landing sword blows on the Turks. The sandy plain was strewn with dead and injured. They pursued them closely all the way to the sea, where 4,000 drowned in the waves and devils carried off their souls immediately.

27

There was a fierce pitched battle with the diabolical adversaries at St George of Ramleh in front of the beautiful church which is there, ranging across the sandy plains around: these were Turks and Persians who have no love for God and refuse to believe that God took on flesh and blood in the womb of the Virgin Mary and was baptised. Bohemond pursued them indefatigably, closely followed by the other barons. Each landed blows on them with steel sword; anyone they attacked fell off his horse because St George was in front and ensured that the horse stumbled. They chased them all the way to the sea and 4,000 of them drowned on the beach: devils and demons carried off their souls. Imagine St George giving his horse its head, passing back and forth past Palagra on the coast, and St Barbara and St Domitian riding towards each other in jousting mode as if they were sparrowhawks. Bohemond shouted at the top of his voice: 'We are devoted to you, noble lord St George. I will endow your holy church: I will put in a bishop and 20 clerics who will sing Mass and carry out services, and read the hourly devotions from their psalters, and pray to God without ceasing until the end of the century.[31] My lords and noble knights', he continued, 'we must extol and worship God in His glory for ensuring our lives were not cut short. My lords, aim for their heads. Give them a close shave. Cut the pagans' heads from their shoulders and tie them to the tails of the horses. I will have them stuck up at Jerusalem right up close to the high walls to demoralise the pagans: that will really upset them.' Imagine the sight of our princes dismounting on the shore, unbuckling swords, unlacing helmets, leaving behind not a single hauberk or weapon, sharp swords or throwing darts, Turkish bows of horn and steel arrows – all equipment badly needed by our people in God's army. They dragged the Turks out of their hauberks and cut off their heads, tying them to the tails of their horses. They made bundles of the weapons and lashed them onto 15,000 pack animals with as many chests. And there they were, going back to St George and rounding up their livestock, then setting out down the road. May God, Judge of all, be their guide.

---

[31] The basilica of St George at Ramleh was one of the most significant in Outremer: Pringle, *Churches* vol.2 pp. 9–27.

28

Picture the sight of our barons at St George. There were 30,000 horses all loaded up with white hauberks and helmets and shields bordered with gold, sharp swords and feathered darts. They herded together the numerous livestock and set off down the wide and well-paved road. They passed above Mirabel and reached the army of God as the sun rose. Duke Godfrey came out to meet them along with the wise and noble Thomas of La Fère and Lord Hugh of Vermandois armed on his horse. 'Bohemond, where have you turned up from?' said Godfrey. 'Where did you get all that livestock you have with you? What is all that booty you have gathered?' 'My lord, we took it outside Caesarea. We found pagans in the plains around Ramleh and defeated them, God be praised. Let all the booty we have brought be shared out amongst everyone, split between rich and poor. Let anyone who does not have a horse be given one. There are white hauberks, green-sheened helmets and good steel swords'. By God, these were welcome words and he was listened to with rapt attention. 30,000 Frenchmen bowed to the lord to express their gratitude for these words. They dispersed to their quarters and went to their tents.

29

The princes and barons dismounted. They unbuckled their swords and unlaced their helmets, all spattered with blood and brains. Godfrey, green-sheened helmet laced on, kept watch all night until day broke. The bishop [of Forez] and abbot [of Fécamp] and all the noble clergy sang Mass and gave thanks to Jesus, saying and chanting the holy liturgy.

30

Bohemond, Tancred and a considerable retinue dismounted at their quarters. Their large force of cavalry and the noblemen who placed their trust in Jesus had suffered a hard time. Godfrey of Bouillon put on his great hauberk and kept watch until dawn rose. The bishop, the abbot and the noble clergy sang Mass and chanted the liturgy to 10,000 knights all from his retinue. That same day Bohemond divided the considerable spoils. Anyone who needed a fast horse or a mailcoat, a sharp sword or a strong flowered shield was given one by Bohemond – a truly princely act.[32] Even the poorest were laughing with delight. The large numbers of young men in the army set fire to the bivouacs, loaded up mules and pack animals, and they all set out straight across the wastelands for Jerusalem. The duke of Normandy, dark complexioned and brave, was in the vanguard.[33] After they had covered two and a half leagues, the main force dismounted and abased themselves in contrition in front of God.

---

[32] Bohemond displays the courtly virtue of largesse: Keen, *Chivalry*, pp. 151,158.
[33] The role of Robert is emphasised again.

31

The princes and barons dismounted. The toes of their hose had worn through and the fabric above their ankles was threadbare and in holes. Each led his horse with rein doubled over. They made their way over the sandy ground, which was very rough and painful to walk over. They reached Montjoie and sank to their knees: they bowed down towards Jerusalem overcome with emotion[34]

32

Our barons, the bishop and the venerable abbot made for Montjoie. The sound of loud Kyrie Eleisons rose up, and they sang 'Alleluia! Laudamus Te Deum!' Bavarians and Germans each sang their songs, loud Kyrie Eleisons which could be heard up in Heaven. Imagine the sight, by God, so many noble barons biting into the earth and kissing it, stones and sand! They addressed each other as follows: 'This is the ground trodden by Jesus, Who suffered death and blessed the Apostles and all his companions. We have suffered so much hostility, terrible hunger and thirst, huge losses, wind and storm and snow and ice – now at last we can see the city where God suffered and accepted death for our redemption'. Up and down the ramparts of the city were flying numerous flags of red silk, golden cloths and oriental fabrics. Pagans and Saracens, followers of Mahomed, thronged on the walls.

33

The French came to a halt at Montjoie and bowed down to the ground at the sight of Jerusalem.[35] They were overjoyed to see the city with its walls and battlements and strong castle. Princes and castellans, rich and poor and stout knights all alike dissolved into tears. They saw the Tower of David with the standard fluttering over it, the golden eagle glittering as if it were in flames, and the poles to hold it up raised by the Turks. It was 60 feet long and 30 feet wide; on it were written the tenets of the religion observed by those infidels, the cowardly and unbelieving Saracens. By God! There were so many rich fabrics of crimson patterned with circles, gorgeous flags of coloured silk and costly silks elaborately worked in gold that there must have been a good 1,000 marks' worth, all a-glitter with gold and silver. The men who set up siege there in force were brave and extremely tough –

---

[34] The Montjoie was a mountain top where the tomb of St Samuel was located. It gave the first sight of Jerusalem from the north and was sacred to all three faiths. It was customary to stop and pray there: Joshua Prawer, *The Crusaders' Kingdom: European Colonialism in the Middle Ages* (New York, 1972; reprinted London, 2001) p. 208. See Pringle, *Churches*, vol.2 pp. 43–5 for discussion of various hilltops with this name.

[35] The importance of arriving outside Jerusalem is emphasised by *laisses similaires*.

there was no water, no grass for grazing, and no spring nor source all the way from there to the Pool of Siloam, which in itself is salty and not good to drink.

34

My lords, this spring, known as the Pool of Siloam in Scripture, is very brackish. Buckets and jugs of it were brought to the army on donkeys and packhorses. The princes and lords willingly gulped it down – this is absolutely true. There was no question of them hankering after large private dining halls to knock back good wine in secret or eat plump capons and venison basted with bacon: no, they ate badly cooked and under-seasoned beef.[36] Their life was one of privation, effort and misery, suffering from hunger and thirst, snow and ice and topped off with fierce battles and hard fought skirmishes. Before the Holy City could be taken and conquered many hauberks were to be torn and shields punched in, bodies sliced open and hurt and injured, chests and entrails and heads sliced apart on both sides: this was absolutely the case. This is where a splendid song begins: nobody has ever crafted or sung a better one![37]

35

Lord Peter the Hermit mounted on his donkey, taking along with him the lords and princes and nobility to whom he was devoted; they went high up onto the Mount of Caiaphas. Peter the Hermit looked out over the city. He addressed the lords and princes as follows: 'I have already been inside this holy city, noble lords. You can see the Mount of Olives, where Jesus asked for a donkey and her colt when He was brought there. You can see the Golden Gate through which Jesus entered into Jerusalem, when the populace took off their cloaks of fur so that He could ride over them.[38] The Jewish children *strewed the road with* branches of olive and *palm*.[39] The city wept and the ground yielded beneath His feet, never to rise again. You can see the Praetorium where He was put on trial and Judas sold Him asking only 30 *deniers* before he strangled himself.[40] You can see the stake

---

[36] A rather startling insight into thirteenth-century customs. Seasoning was essential less to disguise the taste of rotting meat (which was as indigestible then as now) than to make palatable food stored for a long time and often monotonous: C.Spencer, *British Food: an extraordinary thousand years of history* (London, 2002) pp. 45–50 on use of spices.

[37] It is interesting that this reference comes 34 laisses in. It marks the beginning of the description of events at Jerusalem; of itself it is not evidence of a specific predecessor text.

[38] Fur in thirteenth-century France though probably not in first-century Palestine.

[39] The text drops briefly into the Latin of the Vulgate: 'sternebant in via' is in Mark and Matthew though the reference to palm leaves is not.

[40] Jesus was taken to the headquarters of the Governor to be put on trial. The Praetorium was a standard inclusion in medieval itineraries of Jerusalem: see *Jerusalem Pilgrimage 1099–1185*, (ed.) J. Wilkinson with J. Hill and W. F. Ryan (London, 1988) pp. 46–7.

to which He was tied and beaten and struck. I have seen Mount Calvary where He was led on the day He was crucified when Longinus struck Him, piercing His side so that the blood ran down over Golgotha. You can see the Sepulchre to which Joseph went. That noble lord asked for [the body of] his Lord; he had served Him for seven years and that was the only reward he sought – what a rich reward he received. And you can see the holy Temple founded by King Solomon, where the Apostles had gone when God consoled them saying 'Pax vobiscum' and gave them illumination. You can see the house where He addressed them in 90 languages which He taught them.[41] You can see Mount Sion, where the mother of Jesus Christ was taken up to Heaven when her time came to die. And here you can see Josaphat where she was taken; her tomb is there where she was laid. Now you should pray to Our Lady, whom God loved so dearly that His blessed angels took her up into heaven, because she bore His beloved son, Who loves us so much that the King Who created all pardons all our sins, from the greatest to the least in the army'. 'Amen, by God, noble lord!' they all shouted.[42]

36

Counts and barons, princes and marquis, bishops and abbots and nobles all dismounted in the scrub on the hilltop. They stretched out their arms towards God and cried at the tops of their voices: 'Jerusalem of the Nazarene, Lord God Jesus Christ, we have gladly abandoned our fiefs and our own lands, our rich wealth and grand homes, the pleasures of falcons and fur and ermine, and our noble wives whom we adored and our beautiful lands and our small children – all this to see the city where Jesus was betrayed, beaten and struck, hit and spat on, crucified on the Holy Cross where He died for us poor captives to release our souls from the grip of those enemies who had imprisoned us and all our ancestors! As it is true, God, that You were laid in the Sepulchre and rose again on the third day, let us take vengeance on all our enemies – these Turks and Persians and Arabs thronging along these walls of dark-coloured marble!' With these words they mounted their horses. They put on their hauberks, laced up their shining helmets and buckled on their swords and good sharp blades. They hung their strong curved shields from their necks. The gold and silver, sheen and varnish, blue and green shot with red painted onto the shields and the rock crystals set into the gold sent glittering beams flashing around: they all thought they had gone to Paradise. The flags of silk, fine

---

[41] The Old French says 'latin': this is not attested elsewhere in this meaning and I have used the term 'house' as in the Gospels. There is significant scribal variation here.

[42] This laissa draws on itineraries of Jerusalem. See Prawer, *Crusader Kingdom* chapter 11 for a description of the standard pilgrim route; *GF* for a contemporary example; a range of examples in Wilkinson, *Jerusalem Pilgrimage*. The theme of *imitatio Christi* is emphasised.

fabric and velvet hanging from lances and shining swords fluttered and billowed in the gentle breeze. Lord Peter the Hermit addressed them as follows:[43]

37

'My lords and noble knights, princes, barons and noble landowners, you bishops and abbots who know exactly how to carry out ecclesiastical rites, elevate the Host and give us the Body of Christ', said Lord Peter, 'feast your eyes on Jerusalem. Look at its walls crowded with people, its high towers of stone, lime and mortar, its strong doors reinforced with iron and steel. We must love and serve and obey God. Anyone who wants to win a glorious reward and go beyond all bounds to gain God's blessing must set out to fight bravely, force his way towards the city, attack its gates and set up siege around it, destroy its high towers and smash through its walls. We should not hang back: we need to press on. Everyone must use his strength and prowess to attack the city; we must not hang back. Anyone who dies in the attempt will be rewarded by God with a place in celestial Paradise, and will serve and take his ease alongside the Holy Innocents'.

38

The brave Thomas of La Fère spoke as follows: 'Glorious God, help me – I have no idea how we are going to be able to take this major city by force – it is so strong and powerful and heavily defended. It is surrounded by deep ditches and high ramparts; its walls are strong, thicker than a bowshot, and its towers substantial and higher than a crossbow can shoot. There is no spring, no forest or river, no cultivated land, no wheat and no fallow land. The land is deserted and covered with scrub. The army of God is in desperate straits, and water is at such a premium that you could charge 100 *sous* for a packhorse fully laden with it.[44] There is no water, and no woods or trees along edges of field which could provide the wherewithal to boil an iron pot or cauldron. But by the loyalty I owe Godfrey of Bouillon and Our Lord whom I love and adore, I would rather be dead, cut to pieces and laid on a bier than not attack this gate with all the force I can muster, wielding my sharp sword with both hands. None of those sons of the devil will be able to stand in the way. No prayer will save those who will die here – Jesus the true Judge of all will make the arms invincible!'

---

[43] Peter is given the honour of addressing the army on arrival at Jerusalem, underlining the importance of his role in the trilogy. The evocation of Biblical events marks a key moment in the text: here arrival at Jerusalem. Thomas of Marle is also given the honour of a speech.

[44] A *sol* was worth 12 *deniers*.

39

The count of Flanders added: 'If I have God's blessing, I wonder at the God Who rules over all, heaven and earth and the world as it turns, for coming to live here in Sinai.[45] This must be good cultivated land: incense must grow here, pepper and frankincense, galingale and ginger and blooming roses, and medicinal herbs which help ease the body. It is quite true to say that God never created a man who was so ill and infirm that he could not be restored to health and life by eating plants cultivated here. No city has ever been built in such a desert since God was born from the Virgin Mary. Here there are no forests or meadows, no springs or sources, no fishponds or places to fish. I prefer the large castle in the city of Arras, the wood of Arie and the wide hunting grounds of Niepe and the abundant fish I can take from my own fishponds to all this land and this ancient city. But by my loyalty to my beloved Clemence and the love I humbly bear to my son Baldwin, I would rather be dead and mortally wounded than fail to mount a proper attack on this noble gate where 100 rich cloths billow. I summon all of you, my knights, without delay: anyone who dies here will find his soul redeemed and passing to God, singing and all in white'.[46]

40

A council of the barons, bishops and pious abbots was called on the hills overlooking Josaphat. They could look down over Jerusalem, its walls and castle keeps, the silken cloths and fabrics and crimson pennants. Down in the city of those wicked Saracens they could see much coming and going as houses were emptied, gold and silver and bezants and *mangons* were carried; they saw the Temple founded by Solomon filling up with women, children and young boys.[47] 'Noble lords and knights', said Bohemond, 'all the cities we have conquered so far are as nothing compared to the one you can see now. The noble city of Antioch, ruled by King Garsion, was extremely well provided with water and fish, lush meadows and ample supplies, but in all the conquests we have made we never suffered as much as we did there'.

41

The next to speak was the bold and valiant Tancred. 'Alas, lord Bohemond, what on earth are you saying? When we were on the plains of Anatolia riding against the Arabs, it was your constant refrain – and you treated us to plenty of eloquent

---

[45] Not quite accurate; Jerusalem is not on the Sinai peninsula.
[46] 'Flori' refers to a white beard; I have taken it in a wider meaning.
[47] The Temple was one of the few spaces in Jerusalem which could accommodate large crowds: Pringle, *Churches*, vol.3 p. 400.

sermons on the subject – that if God allowed you to live long enough to see the city where Jesus was betrayed, beaten and struck, hit and spat upon and suffered death for us miserable wretches, you would eat stones with as much relish as if they were dainty cakes or fine white rolls or girdle cakes made with the best flour.[48] And look at you now – worrying your head about water. You have no need to worry. God will be on our side. Why should anyone who knows that he will come out of it safe and sound be a coward? That should be a reason to be brave. My lords', he continued, 'we don't need to waste time in council. Let us simply get on and attack all the way round the city with hammers and pickaxes. If the Turks open any gate or postern or attempt to make any sally out of the city, they will find themselves objects of ridicule. We would go surging in alongside our enemies: the bloodshed would go all the way to the holy Temple and the Sepulchre would be taken all the sooner'. On these words innumerable shields were seized, green-sheened banded helmets and good swords taken up. They all rushed down from the scrubland. 60,000 horns were blown so that the hills, slopes and scrub all rang with the sound. But as far as I can see this is going to be a painful experience if the Lord Who was hung on the Cross does not come to their aid – 10,000 of the best fighters are likely to meet their end.

42

Bohemond and Tancred, the duke of Normandy and the powerful Thomas, the brave and shrewd lord Hugh of Vermandois and the nobility, bishops and abbots all came down the hill. All holy Christendom was ready for the attack with hammers, hoes and sharp pickaxes. Imagine them all charging forward pell-mell in confusion. The households of the knights made straight for St Stephen, the place where the martyr was stoned with rocks and slingstones, battered and beaten. They streamed forward to the walls and ditches. Imagine the sight of Hugh of Vermandois on his armed warhorse, its flanks covered with a white surcloth which he had taken on the fields outside Antioch. 'Stop a moment, noble lords!' he cried. 'For the love of God in glory, just listen to me a moment! If you go up to the walls now, take it from me that we will suffer unsustainable losses'.[49]

43

Lord Hugh of Vermandois, count of Peronne and brother to the crowned King of France, continued: 'This city is stronger than Ascalon or the beautiful city of

---

[48] Reminiscent of the Temptation of Christ: Matthew 4:2–4, Luke 4:2–4.
[49] Hugh's wise advice is emphasised by a three-laisse structure: it is at the end of the first, fills the middle laisse and begins the third. It is further emphasised by Godfrey's endorsement.

Antioch, Durazzo or Avalon. If we do not have any siege engines we are wasting our time by attacking – in fact many brave people are going to lose their lives'.

44

Hugh le Maisné, count of Vermandois, added: 'Noble knights, do not be tempted to rash behaviour. We are all united as brothers of long standing: together we have suffered hunger and thirst, wind and storm, rain and snow, conquered lands and passed through difficult terrain. Look at Jerusalem: it is bristling with high stone towers and surrounded by Saracen walls. Without siege engines we have no chance of taking it. In fact you will see French, Angevins and Bretons, Scots and English, Provençals and Gascons, Pisans and Genoese all dying horribly. Let us get our camp set up first and do the sensible thing. I should like to have siege engines to overcome these Saracen walls; I cannot wait to possess these Greek palaces'.[50] 'He is right; that is what we should do', said Duke Godfrey, the duke of Normandy and Robert of Flanders.[51]

45

Duke Godfrey said: 'Listen, noble barons. The brave Hugh of Vermandois is giving us good advice and we would do well to heed it.[52] In the name of God pay attention and I will explain how we can set about taking Jerusalem. I will go and set up camp straight away on Mount Sion with those from my region and land. That is where I will have my richly worked tent set up, and we will guard that gate night and day. I shall have siege engines made so that we can breach the wall. Those villains inside will not be able to save themselves'.

46

Gerard of Gournay and Thomas of Marle said: 'And we shall go and set up camp in the valley of Josaphat, right next to St Peter of Galilee, the place he fled when his companion Judas had Jesus taken and led to Pilate. We shall have water from Siloam brought to the army on 30 plump packhorses carefully picking their way. We shall have the weak and cowardly sent away. We shall get engines made to

---

[50] It is not obvious why the palaces should be Greek other than to fit the rhyme, 'grigois'.

[51] Here Robert of Tiois to fit the rhyme.

[52] This run of short laisses mirrors the description of the Crusaders setting up camp round Antioch at laisses 127–39 of the *Antioche*. Thorp comments that the order is accurate except that it moves all the leaders one gate counter-clockwise and inserts additional camps: '*La Chanson de Jérusalem* and the Latin Chronicles' pp. 159–61.

smash down the walls: those devil-worshippers inside will not know how to save themselves'.

47

The count of St-Gilles said, 'And I shall set up camp right on the Mount of Olives. I shall have my tent pitched there and send out foragers through the lands of the Arabs. I shall make frequent expeditions down to the river. Whatever I gain I will bring back to the army and share it between rich and poor alike, keeping no more for myself than I give the poorest. I shall mount guard vigilantly on the noble Golden Gates for you and destroy pagans and Saracens in that quarter. I will have siege engines made so that we can break through the walls'. 'It was a fortunate day when you were born', said Gerard of Gournay.

48

'My lords', said Robert of Normandy, 'with God's blessing I shall pitch tents for my extensive retinue here at St Stephen. My men will press attacks constantly against this rich gate with its billowing silk banners. If the Turks come out to mount an assault, I will fling myself into the battle with the people of my region so ferociously, raining down so many blows with my sharp sword that we shall surge back inside with them, good idea or not. When evening comes and night closes in, I will put on my great hauberk and mount guard for you with 10,000 knights until dawn breaks. I will send foragers out all the way to Tiberias and share the results generously with rich and poor alike in the army of God – this is my firm intention'.

49

The brave-hearted count of Flanders said: 'And I shall set up camp at the Gate of David with the people from my region who are here. We will mount attacks on the Turkish gates morning, noon and night. When evening draws in I will mount guard for you with 10,000 armed men so that the weary can sleep in peace'.

50

'My lords', said Tancred and the noble Bohemond, 'we will set up our camp over towards Bethlehem and have our tents set up on the main route.[53] Whatever we

---

[53] According to AA V.44 it was at this point that Tancred captured Bethlehem. The town is some 10km from Jerusalem and setting up camp there would not have been much help in the siege.

gain we will bring back to the army of God and share out between poor and rich'. 'May God watch over such noble lords!' said the bishop [of Mautran].

51

Count Baldwin, brother to the duke of Bouillon and Count Eustace, said, 'Listen, noble lords. We shall set up camp at the Lion's Cemetery. We shall send out foraging parties towards the coast, to Jaffa, Tyre and all the way to Calençon and indeed as far as the gates of Acre before retracing our footsteps. We shall move towards Nazareth down the main road to Nablus with great determination; we shall bring back [water from] the Spring of the Dead to the army and share it out between poor and rich alike'.

52

Hugh of Vermandois spoke: he was responsible for many brave deeds, and the noble knights respected him a great deal because of his wise advice. 'My lords', said the count, 'I suggest we would do well to act as follows. Let us be sparing with bread and rations. We should not use packhorses to fetch water but send armed companies of noble knights who will help load and lash the water onto the animals. Once they have brought it back to the camp, let each prince appoint a trustworthy steward and get him to swear faithfully that he will share out [supplies] without taking so much as a *denier*, neither pure gold or silver, sterling nor any reward. Will you all agree to proceed in this way?' 'Yes, noble lord count!' they all shouted. The bishop of Mautran started to pronounce a blessing on them.

53

Now listen, noble and honourable lords, and I will explain how the confraternity was set up and agreed with the full agreement of princes and counts: they solemnly pledged, swearing by the saints, that they would abide faithfully by the agreement and that food and water would be equally shared.[54] The city was promptly put under siege. Imagine the scene: innumerable tents, pavilions and shelters, gilded pointed roofs, glittering golden finials and eagles brought to the camp. Now you are going to hear a splendid song – nothing like it has ever been crafted or so well sung – all about how the Holy City was taken and conquered and how the handsome Thomas of Marle, white hauberk on his back, helmet laced on, strong shield round his neck and sword in his right hand allowed himself to be tossed right into the middle of the infidels; the Bedouin woman, blacker than pepper, struck him with a sharp piercing blade and stabbed through his shield and his

---

[54] See J. Richard, 'La confraternité de la croisade: à propos d'un episode de la première croisade', *Mélanges offerts à Edmond-René Labande* (Poitiers, 1974) pp. 617–22.

gilded hauberk and left him tumbled to the ground before her on the path; but good fortune ensured that he recovered and saw the bloodstained slab of the Sepulchre where the body of Jesus Christ was laid; he turned away from the light and the gold and purple cloth.[55] The Franks surrounded the city of Jerusalem.

54

The Franks laid siege to the mighty city of Jerusalem. Imagine the scene: innumerable tents, pavilions and shelters, shelters staked out, golden finials glittering under the rays [of the sun]. Day was at an end and night had fallen. The city was under heavy guard that night with a great deal of noise and yelling and horns and flutes and the army of Our Lord being barked and yelped at. The King went up to the top of his heavily battlemented tower. He took Cornumarant by his cloak of fine fabric and went forward to a window carved from ornamented marble.[56] 'Noble son', said his father, 'these madmen have left their homes behind and sailed across the sea. My noble and gentle son, they are mounting a fierce challenge against our land. They have taken my livestock and my people are restive. Give me some reassurance, my son, and reassure your retinue'.

55

'My noble son Cornumarant', said King Corbadas, 'it is a good 200 years since the Greeks, Syrians and Armenians, Patarins and Georgians foretold that the Franks, whom you can see with your own eyes, would come and seek us out to avenge the Lord who was killed in this city.[57] He was beaten and struck and hung on the Cross. But it was the Jews who did this: it was to our detriment. The princes, counts and kings were deeply distressed. Titus Vespasian came to attack them and took vengeance on them: he was an excellent king.[58] My son, now you can see with your own eyes the French, Angevins and Bretons, Scots and English, Gascons and Provençals, Pisans and Genoese: they are so well armoured that they have no fear of Turkish bows or poisoned arrows or of any lance thrust. My son, give me your advice as it is your place to do: how shall I fight against these French?' 'Father', replied the young man, 'there is no place for despair as long as I can buckle on my sword from Saragossa, or carry my shield with its gold-embroidered strap, or strike with my blade or shoot a Turkish bow. We have 60 months' worth of provisions – bread, wine, meat, corn and stored grain. And we have such a strongly

---

[55] This looks ahead to laisse 138. The reference to a song relates almost entirely to Thomas of Marle rather than wider events.

[56] A leitmotif in the description of Corbadas.

[57] Patarins are heretics: T-L VII.477.

[58] This refers to the theme of the Vengeance of Christ with which the *Antioche* begins. See discussion in *Antioche* Introduction 32–3. The divine plan is given additional weight through its implicit endorsement by a Saracen.

fortified city with a strong mortared wall that there is no assault under the sun for which I would give as much as two nuts'.

56

'My father', said the young man, 'there is no cause to despair as long as I can buckle on my burnished steel sword or carry my shield or mount a warhorse. We are well equipped to face a siege of a whole year. We have a very strong city protected by lime and mortar. There is no assault under the sun for which I would give as much as a *denier*. The French will not be able to hold out here for long. Shortage of water will make them give up and leave, taking down their pavilions and striking their tents'.

57

The King of Jerusalem was in his tallest tower looking out from the main window carved from shining marble. He saw the French army setting up camp around him, pitching tents and pavilions, horses neighing and mules bellowing, young soldiers and apprentices practising swordplay, women and girls strolling around singing and the people of the Tafur king gathering round the walls. He cursed them in the name of his lord and god Tervagant: 'Ah, you losers, you make me sick!' he said. Imagine Duke Godfrey armed on his charger, the hardbitten fighter Thomas of Marle, Count Eustace and the young Baldwin; they were riding round scouting for places where they could set up the petrary.[59] While they were thus engaged, imagine three kites flying over the massive Tower of David; they soared above the top of the tower lunging every so often at two white doves.[60] The duke was carrying a strong, tautly strung bow: he let off an arrow with such a sure aim that he killed all three birds with one shot. They tumbled dead onto the standard which gleamed next to the synagogue of Mahomed and Tervagant. The duke was delighted and the French roared with laughter. Many of them knew exactly what this signified: it was an omen shown them by God. Corbadas pointed it out to his son Cornumarant. The wisest of the pagans were downcast, whispering their interpretation to each other: 'All of us in the city are going to be killed: there is no escape'. 'That is all too true and certainly how things look', replied the others.

---

[59] A petrary is one of several machines for catapulting stones at besieged cities. See John France, *Victory in the East: a military history of the First Crusade* (Cambridge, 1994) pp. 48–50. Baldwin is called 'l'enfant' at least partly for the rhyme.

[60] The first of the symbolic episodes inserted in the narrative; this underlines the future role of Godfrey. The miracle is acknowledged by the Saracens in succeeding laisses as a variant on the *laisse similaire*.

58

The King of Jerusalem saw the birds fall, shot with immense skill by the duke of Bouillon who fired a crossbow bolt right through the middle of all three. Corbadas had Lucabel of Montir called; he was stepbrother by their father and held great lands; he was seven years older than Corbadas, as white-skinned as a lily flower.[61] You could not ask to see a shrewder pagan or one better at distinguishing good from evil. The King of Jerusalem seized him by the sides of his robe. 'My brother, do you want to hear something extraordinary?'said Corbadas. 'I have seen three kites killed stone dead with one blow! Come with me to see them'. The two kings turned, full of curiosity, and made their way to the standard where Mahomed liked to sit, next to the synagogue where the King was accustomed to hold court, hearing pleas and granting audiences to impose his power. There they saw the birds lying dead on the ground. Had you been there you would have seen more than 7,000 Turks arriving and making the city shake to its very foundations.

59

People were thronging and eddying in the valley below Jerusalem. In front of the synagogue belonging to the mosque and next to the gleaming and glittering standard was an enormous crowd of pagans. The white-haired Corbadas drew himself up and addressed them in a voice which carried far and wide: 'My lords and noble Saracens! Mahomed must have forgotten us when he allowed the Franks to take my lands.[62] They have already taken Antioch and the well-supplied city of Nicaea. Radiman, a Turk from Valerie, tells me that the armies of Arabia and Persia were killed in the fields outside Antioch. The only ones to escape alive were two kings of Nubia and their lord Corbaran, who led and commanded them. They carried with them Brohadas, whose head had been cut off. Corbaran was then arraigned for the crime of treason at the accusation of the sultan. A very significant battle was fixed for one Frank to fight two Turks. That was a terrible idea, since the outcome of the battle was that the Frenchman killed the two Turks with his drawn sword. Our religion took a dreadful knock whilst Christianity rejoiced. For that reason and others they have fallen on us. And now they have set up siege all the way round my city, setting up camp and erecting their tents. Their army extends for a league and a half. If I do not get help and succour from Mahomed, this noble city is going to be ravaged and laid waste. And to make matters worse, my lords – and this is quite true – I saw a feat carried out today which made my blood run cold. Above my tower of polished marble were flying three kites in formation, when two white doves suddenly appeared. This was enough to put the kites on the

---

[61] Lucabel's white skin reflects his relatively positive portrayal in the text and his espousal of Christian teaching in laisse 60. Devils and Saracens are often depicted with black skin: see Bancourt vol. 1 pp. 67–72.

[62] A narrative reprise of the *Antioche* and *Chétifs* as a linking device.

attack: they flung themselves on the doves all three together. The Christians were making their way up next to the porphyry ramparts. One of them was carrying a bow with an arrow ready to shoot. He aimed the feathered arrow so accurately at the kites that it killed all three – that was a truly diabolical feat! Look at them lying here, one tumbled dead on top of another!' With that he bent down, picked them up and waved them in the air; the iron shaft of the arrow had pierced the heart and liver of each and the three were spitted as if on a spear. Lucabel told Maucolon the story: 'The one who managed this feat will become a great lord. He will become King of Jerusalem and it will be his to command. His dominions will stretch all the way to Antioch!' Maucolon bowed his head on hearing this; he was angered and his face darkened. Picture Cornumarant spurring up the roadway, yelling in ringing tones: 'Oi! King of Jerusalem, your people are asleep – why have we not mounted an attack on those Franks outside?' 'My noble son, do not be so stupid', said Corbadas. 'What I have seen today has profoundly disturbed me'.

60

Lucabel stood up. He was more than 100 years old. His beard was long and thick, his moustache long and wide, and his countenance was handsome and florid.[63] No mother had ever borne such a wise pagan, and he had been well taught and schooled by his masters. He called Malcolon and made his way over to him; Lucabel esteemed him highly, and he was one of his intimates. Holding hands they walked side by side, and the nobles assembled round them. Lucabel called: 'Corbadas, come here! You are the king and lord and ruler of Jerusalem; and my nephew Cornumarant is to follow in your footsteps. King, you are my brother and hold me in affection. You ask me for advice: I shall give it to you. Allow me until tomorrow morning and I will tell you the true meaning of the shot through these birds which you have witnessed'. 'Willingly granted, my brother', said Corbadas. 'But let me beseech you by Mahomed to consider coming to my assistance and make sure my city is well defended against the Franks – if they take it we shall all have lost everything. Their lord was manhandled and ill-treated, tied to a stake and beaten and nailed to the cross there up on Mount Calvary right opposite you. When He was taken down from the cross before evening fell, He was laid to rest in the Sepulchre. Now the Christians assert that it is true He rose from the dead on the third day. But let me give you my opinion on all this. If He was really the Lord of Heaven, He would never have got killed in this fashion or been so badly mistreated and manhandled'. 'Brother', said Lucabel, 'that was by His choice. Let me assure you that since I was born I have seen several miracles of His in various places: cripples raised up, the blind made to see, male and female prisoners released from prison and saved and protected by faith in many places'. 'My lord', said Corbadas, 'I think you are senile. You must be raving mad if you believe all this. Make sure you do not say anything further on the subject in my presence because you would

---

[63] Stock description. Compare Baligant in the *Roland* lines 2615–17.

instantly destroy the morale of my men'. 'We should indeed talk about something else', said Malcolon, 'and specifically about your son who is under orders to keep watch with 10,000 pagans: make sure they are all armoured. 'That is a sensible request', said Cornumarant, 'it shall certainly be granted'. The day had come to an end and it was night again. Corbadas entered the mighty Tower of David; his brother Lucabel accompanied him, the King Malcolon and many others. Imagine them leaning on the sills of their marble windows looking out at the French in their quarters and tents. They could see everything brightly lit by candles, and heard horns and bugles sounded in the camp. They cursed [the Christians] in the name of Apollon who makes the wheat grow. The king's son Cornumarant was not reassured, and moved quickly to arm himself; he summoned 10,000 Turks to stand guard over Jerusalem.

61

It was a beautiful clear night and the evening air was sweet. On a dark marble platform right in front of the holy Temple, Cornumarant armed himself along with 10,000 Arabs. He put on leg guards of white chain mail and a mailshirt with a hood of gold. On his head they laced a helmet from Saragossa which was done up with 12 buttons of gold. Then he buckled on [the sword] Murglaie with its burnished blade, forged by Matesalans on the island of Orfeis. Then they brought him Plantamor the Arab steed, who could run 20 leagues and not be out of breath. Let me tell you about his conformation and colouring. His head was delicate and as white as a lily flower; his ears were redder than a burning coal; his nostrils flared wide and his eyes large, limpid and attractive; his legs were strong and sturdy, his feet elegantly arched. His chest was wide and the front of it pitch black. On one side he was bay and on the other grey. His hindquarters were square and speckled like a partridge; his tail bright blue and his rump set high. What more can I tell you? When he was at full stretch not even the fastest greyhound could catch him. The saddle was made of ivory and the pommel polished and even; the metalwork in his bridle was exceedingly fine. The stirrups and harness were made of boiled leather. The noble Cornumarant leapt into the saddle. At his neck hung a green and dark coloured shield which he had had made by one of our *chétifs*. Then he seized the spear with its grip of willow.[64] He led forth 10,000 Turks, all armed to the teeth.

62

Cornumarant rode out with his men marshalled into ranks. They slipped out quietly from the Gate of David: but it will go hard with them before they can return! If God supports Harpin [of Bourges] in his audacious enterprise, even the best of them

---

[64] 'Calis' is not attested anywhere. I have tentatively translated as 'willow' on the basis of 'saule' and Latin 'salix'. There is a different reading in almost every manuscript.

would rather be anywhere else even for all the gold in Beneventum! Our barons, favourites of God, were in the army in high good humour over the duke's bowshot. They begged Harpin to keep watch that night until dawn broke; which Harpin willingly undertook to do with 500 brave knights. They made their way over to the Gate of David. Meanwhile St Stephen was under the watchful surveillance of Lord Richard of Chaumont, who did not exactly hang back in destroying Saracens and killing them in horrible ways; he had 500 valiant knights. At the Golden Gate were another 500 with John of Alis and Fulcher of Melun; beyond the gate where the ground slopes down was Count Stephen, lord of Albemarle with 500 knights all in the first flush of youth. That night the army of God was in great agitation.

63

That night the nobles stood guard over the army of God. There were 500 knights outside the Gate of David. Lord Harpin of Bourges began to pray: 'Alas, Jerusalem! May the Lord let me last long enough to go and kiss the Sepulchre inside the city and adore, embrace and worship the cross on which He allowed His body to be beaten and mistreated! My heart is filled with anguish when devils are there; may God grant me peace in it!' With that he leapt up onto his swift horse; with enormous strength he swung it round and held his quartered shield close to his chest. His proud heart was filled with hatred of the Saracens. Cornumarant set out at a smart pace, accompanied by 10,000 knights. They came out onto the sandy ground outside the Gate of David. They made for the army of God with lances ready to strike; but they were about to meet an unexpected reverse – not even 100 of Cornumarant's Turks would come out in one piece. Lord Harpin saw their helmets glittering and said to his companions: 'At last I have what I have been waiting for. See those pagans coming out [of the city]. Let us take revenge on behalf of God, who allowed Himself to be beaten and crucified for us. Do not make a sound; keep quiet and give them time to get some distance from the city'.[65] If you had been there you would have seen our forces tightly packed and moving agitatedly: they were keener to get at the Turks than a sparrow-hawk a lark. The Turks advanced so far – may God foil their evil plans! – that our Frenchmen saw them coming up close. By now they were a bowshot's length from the gate. At this Harpin broke the silence with a shout: 'Come to our aid, Holy Sepulchre! Strike hard, noble knights!' With this he pricked his horse forward with spurs of pure gold, and making for Gorant, son of Brehier, struck his shield. He pierced it and broke through it above the gold buckler, and tore apart the links of the hauberk he wore; burying the blade of the lance in the centre of his heart, he knocked him dead from the horse onto a dilapidated path. And the other companions did not hang back. They all lowered their lances, and each of our barons sent his opponent flying. Cornumarant gave his spirited mount its head and made for Harpin, landing

---

[65] The *chétifs* are given the honour of the first major skirmish of the siege. Harpin's comments underline the symbolism.

a blow full on him. He shattered his lance on the shield which protected Harpin's chest but was unable to knock him off his horse. He spurred past him, then drew his steel sword and sent two of our barons flying. 'Damascus!' he cried out to urge his people on.

64

It was a hard fought battle with much bloodshed. Had you been there, you would have seen a fierce and violent fight. However the pagan forces were simply too strong and our people retreated in disorder as far as a missile might be thrown, very hard pressed under a rain of Turkish arrows. They were forced all the way back to their camp. There [the Saracens] caught Richard and Fulcher of Melun, Anselm of Avignon and the young Baldwin, Roger of Rosoie and Pagan the Norman, and 14 others who were ahead of the others; they inflicted serious damage on [the Christians] with heavy lead maces. Count Harpin was appalled to see this. 'By God, help them! Forward immediately, knights! Those villainous infidels have captured our companions. We would not be cowardly enough to let them be carried off'. With that, they rounded on the Turks, each with drawn sword. But their efforts were not worth as much as a bezant. The French heard the din and began to arm immediately, but not quickly enough: their efforts were wasted. All our valiant barons would have been taken off had it not been for Richard of Chaumont, who came spurring up. Just like a goshawk makes for bleating lambs when it sees them from high up in the air, Richard galloped up to the Turks with a flourish: anyone he attacked was not going to escape alive. He immediately killed four with his sharp sword. Then he confronted the Turks who were taking our people away: you can be sure he did not waste time in fine words. He rode through cutting off their heads: this allowed the prisoners to break free whilst their captors took to their heels. Richard and his men rode in hot pursuit, leaving the ground littered with dead and injured. The army was in turmoil in front and behind. Why should I go to the trouble of naming each and every baron when so many were ready armed in such a short space of time that, even if all the Turks of the Orient had come and offered them single combat in battle, they would have been no more bothered by them than by a small child. At this you could hear horns and bugles sounding. A Saracen called to Cornumarant: 'Hey! King of Jerusalem! Where on earth are you? All your men have been killed and there are precious few still alive. You would be a fool to hang around – no father will be able to help his child. Look at the army of the French coming towards you and roaring at the tops of their voices'. Cornumarant heard this, mounted his charger and spurred straight towards Jerusalem. Richard and Harpin followed on his heels, but could not catch him all the way to the Orient. The Turk made for the Gate of David. He slipped past Richard who had nearly caught up with him, and struck him a mighty blow with his sword as he swept past, right down through the middle of his helmet, slicing it in half. Richard stumbled as he avoided the blow and the Turk overtook him: he was furious and declared that if he could not kill Richard he was not worth as much as a glove.

65

King Cornumarant was a noble lord, very valiant and brave and mounted on a swift horse. He gave Plantamor his head and bounded towards Harpin. He landed such a blow on his enamelled helmet that he sliced through it right down to the noseguard! If God, the Spiritual Father, had not come to his aid, it would have been all over for Harpin. The noble lord cried out: 'You cowardly heathen bastard! You will regret striking that blow! You will suffer for it!' He drew his sword with its golden hilt and made to strike the Turk, but with about as much effect as two sorb apples. Imagine the army spurring up hill and down dale. When Cornumarant realised what a difficult position he was in, he urged Plantamor on with his spurs, bounded towards the Gate of David and clattered into Jerusalem through the middle of the gates. It was to go hard with those who were trapped outside; not one of them, good and bad alike, was left in one piece. They pushed the bars across the Gate of David. The people were called together in front of the Temple, and young and old lamented together. Corbadas came running with the emir Malcolon, closely followed by the shrewd Lucabel. Had you been there, you would have seen more than 1,000 torches grabbed. Cornumarant cried out his orders: 'Protect the battlements, gates and wooden hoardings, the walkways and the walls![66] The assault will begin tomorrow morning! This evening I have suffered a mortal blow. Our worthless gods have proved themselves false and failed me in my hour of need. So I shall have them so soundly beaten with sticks and clubs, lead maces and batons and stakes that they will never think about dances and festivities again![67] Alas! Jerusalem, imperial city! You are so rich in buildings and gardens, beautiful quarters and splendid open spaces, pure gold and silken cloths, of fine fabrics and rich sigladon of indigo, crimson and blue'. He went crimson with emotion, and hordes of noble pagan women wrung their hands hard enough to break them. Lucabel cried: 'Get the mangonels ready for action! Do not despair, my noble lord Corbadas. We will eat raw flesh and hunting birds and gerfalcons rather than see Jerusalem fall. Multitudes of French will be driven back, huge holes ripped in their shields; masses of captives will be killed and wounded when they serve for target practice. We shall send for help to King Mariaglaus and King Darien, and Ferrals will come too; he will extend the empire all the way to Guinesbals!'

---

[66] 'Bretesches' are wooden hoardings which serve to deflect weapons and fire, and provide a shelter for soldiers to fire from: T-L I.1137.

[67] Standard motif: Saracens turn on their gods when they are perceived to have failed: see *Roland* lines 2580–91 where the Saracens destroy the image of Apollon, rip off Tervagant's carbuncle and throw Mahomed into a ditch. Sansadoine attacks the image of Mahomed at *Antioche* laisse 202.

66

'My lords', said Lucabel, 'do not lose heart. We will send a message to the noble Sultan. In response he will send us the most impressive host you have ever seen in the empire of the East or the Beton Valley. But now make for the wall and set up defences around the ramparts and wooden hoardings; let us prepare and if the French attack us we will defend ourselves stoutly'. 'Your lightest wish is our command', replied the pagans. With that they sounded 10 drums and a brass horn. Picture the scene: swarms of Turks carrying stones, crossbow bolts and stone blocks setting up defences all round the walls. Night came to an end and day broke. The Christian army – God's forgiveness be on them – was assembled. The princes, counts and lords assembled on a large sandy space outside the walls. The first to come was Godfrey of Bouillon; then Baldwin and Eustace [of Boulogne], Drieu of Monci; Lord Raymond of St-Gilles and along with him Raimbald Creton; Robert of Normandy and Robert the Frisian; Tancred, the son of the marquis with Duke Bohemond; Enguerrand of St-Pol and the black-moustached Hugh; Lord Thomas of La Fère and Gerard of the Donjon; Count Rotrou of La Perche, no lover of villains; the lion-hearted Thomas of Marle; Harpin of Bourges, Richard of Chaumont, the renowned Baldwin of Beauvais, Lord John of Alis and Fulcher of Alençon, and the pious bishop [of Forez] and abbot [of Fécamp]; the King of the Tafurs along with his companions to the tune of 10,000, as we shall come on to relate. Not one of them had enough money to afford a coat or mantle or cloak; they wore no shoes, hose nor cap; not a shirt on their backs nor hose nor shoes. The only jerkins they had were rags and tatters. They had hair which stood up in a shock on their heads; their muscles were burnt as if by wood or coal; they were tanned to leather by storms and blazing sun.[68] Their legs, feet and heels were in a terrible state. Each carried a stick or staff in his hand, a lead club or crossbow bolt and pike or stave, or a sharp halberd or a huge axe or a javelin. The King carried a razor-sharp scythe without any taint of lead. There was no pagan between there and the Gardens of Nero well enough armed to withstand a blow from theKing's scythe – he would find himself sliced right down to the lungs. The King wore neither silk nor sigladon but a sack which had been unpicked and had no shape; it fitted his body tightly though without much shaping around the shoulders.[69] It had a gaping hole in the middle and was torn all over; he tied it together with a web of ropes. His collar was attached with the point of a spur. He had a cape of leaves which was covered with buds.[70] The King was treated with great respect by our troops; each of our lords looked up to him. The bishop of Mautran pronounced a

---

[68] Hair standing on end is a feature of devils: see for example the tympanum of Ste-Foy de Conques. Brown leathery skin is a sign of scurvy, appropriate to such a poor section of the army; I am indebted to Dr Piers Mitchell for this information.

[69] Thorp suggests 'mohon' might mean 'fastenings' here, which is not however attested. Levy suggests a stump or shoulder and I have tentatively followed.

[70] Rather like the Green Man or wild man of the woods: see Block Friedman, *Monstrous Races* p.200.

blessing on them. 'My friends, may He who suffered His passion for us and raised St Lazarus from the dead protect you'. 'My lords', said the King [of the Tafurs], 'are you about to preach a sermon? Why don't we just get on and attack this holy city? We will not have tried very hard if we fail to take it'.

67

It was a beautiful morning, indeed unusually so. There was a sandy area with paths outside Jerusalem.[71] That was where the army of God assembled: palatine counts, French and Burgundians, men from Maine and Anjou, Lotharingians and Bretons, Gascons and men from Poitou. The King of the Tafurs did not lack in courage. He said: 'My lords, what on earth are we playing at? We are hanging back when we should be getting on and attacking this town and those bastard infidels. You are behaving like a bunch of weary pilgrims. By the Lord Who turned water into wine when He was at the marriage of St Archideclin, if there were only me and my brother companions in poverty here the pagans would find that they had never had such alarming neighbours'.[72] 'Be quiet, noble cousin', said Robert of Flanders. 'Something which hasn't been properly completed is not worth a Rouen coin; nothing can be well done if it has not been well finished.[73] If someone were to cover all the land between here and the river Rhine, he could not find so many poor but noble vassals as are gathered together in this army. May God grant them good fortune so that we can destroy the lineage of Cain and capture this city with all its marble palaces'. With that the count spurred forward to the shadow of a hawthorn tree; he looked on Jerusalem and bowed down repeatedly.

68

It was a beautiful clear day, fine and windless. Picture Duke Godfrey sat on his Castilian horse and his brother Eustace on a white one. They had two brass bugles carried before them. They stopped on a flat area outside the walls, and noble captains flocked around them. The bishop of Mautran held in his hand the Lance with which Jesus' all-powerful side had been pierced. He proclaimed loudly and impressively: 'My lords and honourable Christians! In God's name believe: it was in this city, full of marble, that Jesus Christ, Son of Mary, suffered death. Anyone who receives death in His name will be fed with living bread, and will be given eternal life without hungering or thirsting. Last night those dogs, sons of whores,

---

[71] The importance of the first assault on Jerusalem is marked by *laisses similaires*.

[72] The Marriage at Cana. The name Archideclin is a malformation of 'architriclinum', the dining room with couches which Romans used for meals. See Du Cange III p.250 for the Feast of Architriclin, celebrated shortly after Epiphany; John 2:1–11 for the Wedding at Cana.

[73] T-L VIII.1445: a 'romoison' is a small value coin originally from Rouen; used by extension to mean something insignificant or worthess.

attacked us. Thanks to God in glory Who made Adam and Eve, very few have escaped being caught on our hook. 7,000 are lying dead in the road which winds down this valley. If you are willing to believe what I say as your chaplain, let us fling them from Turkish catapults straight into Jerusalem over its towering walls, and then get on and attack the city today or tomorrow'. When our lords heard this they immediately pulled at their reins, shouting loudly: 'These words are not spoken in vain!'

69

Our lords shouted in unison: 'Get those mangonels set up without delay!' This was done to the accompaniment of loud whoops. The engineer Gregory, a native of Arras, set them up along with the noble Nicolas, a shrewd and expert man who hailed from Duras.[74] They set up their machines next to the Golden Gate. They loaded the bolts and angled the arms, attaching the weights held down by ropes. Each bolt was held in place by 10 cords. They battered the Turks inside the city, flinging missiles over the towering walls. Bowels and brains were sent splattering at each blow, and there were puddles of blood and entrails everywhere. The pagans wailed as one: 'Alas, lord Mahomed! How are you going to avenge us on these wretched *chétifs*, these sons of Sathanas who are determined to destroy us and turn us into defeated slaves, to smash our cities and pulverise our lands? The Caliph of Baghdad was all too accurate when he said that one day a race would come who would defeat us utterly!' At the sound of this lament imagine the powerful King Corbadas riding up together with the emir Lucabel, Malcolon and Butras; Cornumarant and his nephew Quinquenas also came. 'Alas, King of Jerusalem', said his son, 'what will you do now? Whose advice will you take to help you hold onto the city? If they manage to take Jerusalem with its regular layout, we have as good as lost Bilbais, Tiberias and Damascus. But before the Franks can take them, I will reduce them to such a state as they have never been in before'. 'Uncle', he said to Lucabel, 'when you carry out divination on the arrow which killed three birds, what will you tell me?' 'Noble nephew', said Lucabel, 'I shall tell you immediately but I know you will not like the answer'.

70

'My noble nephew', said Lucabel, 'I will tell you the truth. I know for certain you will not thank me for it, but I will tell you how things are since you ask. The one who killed three birds with a single bowshot will be King of Jerusalem and this whole kingdom; his power will extend all the way to Antioch'. Cornumarant

---

[74] The names of the engineers are not given in any other source; we have no way of knowing whether they are accurate or a later fictional embellishment. It is noteworthy that one is from Arras, close to Douai.

roared with laughter at hearing this. 'By Mahomed, you are raving mad', he said. 'We will not see that in my lifetime. As long as I am capable of buckling on my good steel sword you will see me riding out of the city time and again to launch sneak attacks on the Franks without warning'. 'My noble son', said Corbadas, 'you are talking nonsense. Going outside those walls is thoroughly dangerous; the Christians are far too powerful. So stay inside with your lords to defend Jerusalem: that way you will earn my good will. I am safe as long as you are with me'. 'My lord, those are your orders and so I will do as you wish', replied Cornumarant. They sounded a drum from the top of the great Tower of David, then blew a brass horn. The pagans gathered on the hill of Calvary, and in particular all the carpenters that could be found. In front of the assembled crowd he asked them to exercise their craft as assiduously as they could. The smiths were to make the arrows which would be aimed at the Franks, missiles and falchions and axes of tempered steel. Meanwhile the carpenters made hammers with ash handles, long sharp lances with firm grips, strongly bound by iron and steel and reinforced by strong brass from one end to the other so that they could not be damaged or chopped through by weapons. After establishing his sentinels [Cornumarant] drew up his army in ranks. They numbered 50,000 armed Saracens. The 25,000 climbed up onto the rampart; the French looked them in the eye and shouted 'Montjoie! To arms without delay, noble knights!' Which they proceeded to do immediately. Each hurried to arm himself in front of his tent, buckling his sword onto his left side; those who had good horses were hardly going to ignore them, mounting the moment they were saddled. Each prepared himself to the best of his ability.

71

So the Christians all armed themselves. They sounded horns, bugles and instruments of metal so that the sound rang round the hills and valleys. They prepared for battle on the flat ground outside the walls of Jerusalem. Picture Duke Godfrey, fully armed on his horse, covered entirely in armour right down to his spurs. Then came the duke of Flanders with silk pennant, and Lord Hugh of Vermandois with the royal flag; and the noble lords Bohemond and Tancred. Had you been there, you would have seen a fine collection of lords, a good 60,000 all armed and on horseback. They drew themselves up into ten squadrons to mount the attack. Imagine the sight of the King of the Tafurs with his 10,000 ragbag troops drawn up on a level sandy area; each held a hoe or stake or long-handled axe or pike of Poitevin steel; they carried hammers and flails, slings and catapults.[75] The bishop made the sign of the cross over them in the name of God and the Holy Spirit. 'My lords, launch the attack and may God protect you from harm! To anyone who dies for Him during the course of the day He will offer a place in blessed Paradise with St Michael the Archangel and St Gabriel'. The King of the Tafurs turned and made

---

[75] 'Gisarme' is a long-handled axe: Nicolle, 'Armes et armures' p. 17.

his way across a flat area. They halted in a valley outside St Stephen. Now you will hear all about the attack: nobody has ever heard of one like it.

72

The force assembled in front of Jerusalem was massive. You might have seen numerous armed princes: the renowned Godfrey of Bouillon, Lord Hugh of Vermandois carrying his standard, Robert of Normandy as black as pepper, the count of Flanders skilled at swordsmanship, and Bohemond of Sicily who only liked to fight infidel pagans. With them was the bishop, popular with our lords. Between them they drew up the squadrons. One was commanded by Raymond of St-Gilles, comprising 10,000 men from his own lands. They were armed as well as they could be for people living on the edge, suffering terrible hunger and many painful days. Their bodies were corrugated with the effects of wind and rain; their faces were pale and drawn. But they were proud, bold and determined: every last one swore by the power of reputation that he would rather have his head cut off than retreat as much as six feet in front of the pagans.[76] The bishop of Mautran raised his hand and blessed them in the name of the Lord who made the heaven and the dew. Count Raymond about turned, shouting his battle cry. He drew up his men in front of St Stephen's [Gate]. The King of the Tafurs was less than a stone's throw away. Now you are going to hear all about the attack and the hard-fought battle which followed, and a blessed song – nobody has ever sung a better one – about the fall and capture of the Holy City in which the body of God was harmed and injured, laid to rest in the Holy Sepulchre, and then resurrected on the third day. Those who decide to make the crossing and go to kiss the Sepulchre can count themselves happy men.

73

Our celebrated army was in front of Jerusalem. The bishop of Mautran was full of resolution and held a rod of maplewood in his hand. He most certainly did not wear silk or furs but a hairshirt next to his skin – this is absolutely true. He was deeply grieved at the thought that the Turks were using the Holy Sepulchre as a stable. He swore to God, the spiritual Lord, that if he could – this is the truth about him – he would not sing Mass on the table in the Temple until he had thrown out those who serve the devil.

74

The bishop of Mautran was in no mood for revelry. He and our barons were under battle orders. They drew up a battle line devoid of youngsters; on the contrary they

---

[76] The Old French term is 'ausne', an ell.

were all seasoned warriors, on foot without a single colt in sight. All of them had mail shirts and nail-studded hauberks; they carried large flags, not little pennants. Each one buckled on a sword with razor-sharp cutting edge. The bishop of Mautran blessed them all in the name of God and the holy Daniel with his hand on which he wore a bishop's ring. Count Rotrou of Perche led them down a shallow valley to Jerusalem surrounded by its fine ramparts. They stopped outside near a small garden and swore to God, the founder of Israel, that if they found pagans to attack they would annihilate them. The Saracens looked down at them, each hiding behind a battlement. You can be sure that every last one of them was armed with a mace or a flail, or a halberd freshly sharpened and set in a hilt with chains at the end, or a sharp dart decorated with niello, all ready to defend the town and citadel of Jerusalem. In time they will shed so much blood that it will run in enough of a river to turn a small mill. Down from Jerusalem came the sound of 1,000 flutes, drums and bugles, horns and pipes. Corbadas called to his brother Lucabel: 'Look at all those splendid fast horses outside the walls and those princes, armed lords and young soldiers. They are going to mount an attack on the walls regardless of crossbow bolts. They have no fear of steel hammers, pickaxes or mallets, and sinking a knife into them will have no impact. Let us go up that tower and see the combat; you will be able to see the mangonels hard at work'. With that they went into the tower, which dated back to the time of Abel, and leant against the embrasures chiselled out of the walls.

75

The King of Jerusalem went to lean out of one of the windows to watch the attack. Meanwhile our noble lords – God grant them salvation! – decided how best to draw up their columns. They split off a force of 10,000 knights, all with hauberk and helmet with cap [beneath] and a shield or round shield for protection. They entrusted them to Lord Thomas of Marle to lead, and to Hugh of Saint-Pol who was famous for various heroic deeds; Raimbaut Creton and Enguerrand of St-Pol were also with them. Just picture the pennants blowing in the wind, innumerable hauberks and helmets glistening and glinting. They went to station themselves outside the walls of Jerusalem. Imagine the noise of the bugles, horns and trumpets being sounded. Their plan was to launch a ferocious assault on the walls. The bishop of Mautran addressed them. 'My lords, may He Who allowed Himself to be made to suffer in this holy city in order to save His people protect you; and, if it be His will, may He give you victory today and allow His Holy Sepulchre to be liberated from the pagans – I have heard stories about the Turks turning it into a stable.[77] It should weigh heavily on all our hearts that the devil can exercise this kind of power over us. I tell you now that anyone who dies here for God

---

[77] Accusations of defiling the Holy Sepulchre were standard in Crusade rhetoric; this is mild compared to some. See e.g. RM I.1 and the letter of Alexius to the Crusaders translated in Sweetenham, *Robert the Monk's History*.

will receive a crown from the King who rules over Heaven, and will find rest there with the angels. I pardon here and now through God any sins you may have committed in word or deed'. He then had the Lance brought to him by which Jesus Christ allowed himself to be pierced and wounded. The Christians burst into tears at the sight and all cried out at the tops of their voices: 'Alas! Jerusalem! How worthy you are to be praised!' Then they said to the bishop, 'Even though you are exhorting us to launch an attack on the city, it may put up too much resistance'. 'My lords', said Godfrey, 'let me advise a bit of caution; do not launch an attack before you hear the horn give a signal'. The emir Lucabel was watching them closely from the lofty Tower of David, constructed of plain marble; he saw the Holy Lance rise so high that it looked as though it would go right up to the sky and tumble down onto the Tafurs. He was well aware beyond a shadow of doubt that the Tafurs were determined to be first into Jerusalem. But Thomas of Marle did something which made him renowned. He got himself lifted up on the points of some long spears and bodily flung up and over the wall. So I can tell you for certain that he was the first one in; if you want to listen I will tell you all about it, so give me your attention as I would like to tell you the story. Now you will hear an amazing song sung – no *jongleur* could sing you a better one – all about how Thomas of Marle had himself raised up on spear points, lifted up on lances and flung over the wall; he cut through the bars on the doors with his sword and went in search of the Holy Sepulchre.[78] With him were Robert, lord of Flanders, and the duke of Bouillon with the courage of a wild boar: may Lord God reward them for this feat! The emir Lucabel was next to a pillar; when he saw this, the colour drained from his face. He began to sweat with fear and anguish, knowing full well that the pagans could not hold out. He would have been delighted to make his escape if he could have sneaked off.

76

It was a Wednesday and the sun was beating down. The King of Jerusalem stood at a window and looked down from the lofty Tower of David at the French. He was accompanied by his close counsellor Lucabel. They looked at the French host, which was a wonder to behold. Our lords and bishops formed a squadron which numbered a good 10,000. Each had armed himself as strongly as he could. Godfrey had given the command to Baldwin of Beauvais and handed them all over to Richard of Chaumont; Harpin of Bourges would help lead them, and Lord John of Alis was part of the company. The bishop of Mautran raised his hand and blessed them in the name of God Who created the world. This squadron headed for the walls of Jerusalem and took up position outside St Stephen's. They all came

---

[78] Needless to say this feat is not attested in any other source, nor is Thomas the first into Jerusalem. The reference to a song is interesting: possibly some kind of ballad was current about Thomas. We know that such songs were sung on Crusade: RA 154. It could equally however be self-referential.

to a halt, but nobody moved to launch the attack until they heard the great horn give the signal to launch the assault. The King of Jerusalem started telling them all about his god Apollon and all his deeds, and swore by Mahomed that nobody would escape until everyone fell and worshipped at his feet. He would start by praying to Tervagant and to Apollon too, begging to be forgiven. He believed in the truth of his religion, misguided as he was: but before long he will see his walls flattened. Godfrey of Bouillon rallied our lords: 'My lords, let us get on with it – it will soon be midday'. The duke drew up another squadron which must have numbered a good 10,000. Each carried a pike or hoe or a spade or hammer to strike blows on the wall. Count Lambert of Liège led these people. The bishop blessed them and made the sign of the cross over them: 'My lords, may He Who created the whole world and sheltered in the womb of the Holy Virgin and fasted for 40 days in the desert protect you'. Then he seized the Lance in both hands and embraced it close to his chest. He spoke clearly at the top of his voice: 'My lords and noble Christians! In God's name, it is the case that anyone who avenges God today will receive a crown in His holy Paradise, and He will forgive all the sins you have committed!' At this the squadron wheeled about and began the advance. They turned to face the bishop in front of Mount Zion and each prepared to make an assault on the town. But they will suffer grave losses before they succeed: 20,000 are alive now who will be mourned – though anyone who meets his end there can die happy since God in glory will give his soul salvation. It was a beautiful clear day without a breath of wind. The princes hurried to dispose their columns as instructed. They discussed who should be first to launch the assault on the walls of Jerusalem and strike the first blow. 'The honour should go to the King of the Tafurs', said the count of Flanders. 'We granted it to him three weeks ago'.

77

So our Christians have drawn up their order of battle, taking along with them the infantry and the masses of footsoldiers. Nicolas and Gregory had set up their machine right in front of the Golden Gate, well concealed under protective coverings. They had made a shield of nails and leather and the archers would be concealed by it in such a way that the pagans would have no more inkling than a quail's egg that they were there, meaning that they could shoot at the Saracens whatever they might think about it. Anyone showing himself up on the ramparts would find his heart and entrails shot through. Arrows would fly more thickly than straws in the wind, with no protection unless God so chooses. I can tell you for certain that whilst the assault was in progress even the best soldiers would give all of Cornwall not to be there, because those in Jerusalem had massed for the attack. They were carrying Greek fire, which consumes everything it touches. They were wasting their time, as (if you ask me) much good it did them: they were all killed in the end even though they had the best of it at the beginning.

78

The King of Jerusalem was up in his tall tower. He looked down on the squadrons and saw how each was striving to leave the expanses below the city strewn with bodies. He cursed them in the name of Apollon, and gestured angrily to them that it was a bad week which saw their arrival. The noble lords – may Jesus lead and guide them! – gave the King of the Tafurs their firm promise that he could have the first go at attacking that day. The King took his turn to speak, and made his views abundantly clear. He swore on the body of Mary Magdalen that he would give the pagans a miserable time during their 40 days of service. Now forces who were most certainly not of humble birth joined the attack. Ah God! What a lot of sons of castellans, princes and lords from sovereign lands! With one breath they sounded 1,000 horns, then the main horn which blasted out over the ground outside the walls. The squadrons scattered out like water from a fountain, with the Lance of God leading the way. It was past midday and getting on for nones when our most outlandish forces in the army began the attack.

79

It was a beautiful clear day and the sun was shining. The *ribalts* launched the most damaging assault they could. They flung carefully chosen stones from their slings, and dug like moles with their hoes and shovels so that they filled the ditch – I tell you no lies – to a point where a large cart could have driven across it. The pagans rained down arrows from their bows of horn. 1700 of the rabble had bodies covered in blood, wounded in the head, the chest and the side: but even so not a single one retreated. They went straight to the wall as soon as they saw it. The King of the Tafurs was holding an enormous pike, and struck the wall with both hands like a true brave soldier. He had large numbers of his force with him, I do not know how many. Each one went at the job with a will, and they made a wide and tall hole in the wall. The Turks flung boiling hot water down on them and scalded 10 of them, to the discomfiture of the King. He ordered his people to retreat back into the ground surrounding the walls. Blood ran down him from 22 wounds. Now imagine two of our princes riding up to him on their warhorses and asking him how he was: 'My lord, you have been badly hurt: will you recover?'[79] 'My lords', replied the King, 'I am desperate for all of us to find ourselves inside Jerusalem. So may God allow me to stay alive and to kiss the Sepulchre from which he arose from the dead'.

---

[79] A shade of irony.

80

There was a huge battle round the walls of Jerusalem, with the Christians launching repeated assaults on the ramparts. Godfrey of Bouillon called out at the top of his voice: 'My lords and nobles, do your level best. Here is the city where God suffered death and lived again. This is the city for which we have stayed awake so many nights, suffered such hunger and such misery; our skin is burnt black by wind and storms. Now let us all do our best to fulfil our mission: nothing we have done will be worth as much as a sorb apple if we do not manage to take the city'. 'Ah God and holy Lady Mary', said the bishop, 'take pity on our lords who will have suffered so much for You'. Count Hugh of Vermandois heard these words and, taking the great horn, blew the signal for attack. At that imagine huge numbers of nobles lowering their lances for the charge, not drawing rein until they were outside the main gate. At the Gate of David, which is protected by a chain, Godfrey struck with his long sword until it shattered in his hands. He was surrounded by enormous numbers of knights. The Turks – God curse them! – fought back in defence. Large numbers of stones were smashed down, and blows rained down on our men with their helmets from Pavia. Anyone who was pursued was finding it no laughing matter: his head would be smashed in and his ears left ringing. King Cornumarant was up on the porphyry walls. 'Jerusalem!' he called out to his troops, who were in good heart. 'You are acting like fools, you weak Frenchmen! I wouldn't give as much as a rotten apple for your attack'. Duke Godfrey heard this and his blood boiled. He was holding a Turkish bow with an arrow ready to fire. He sent it winging straight towards Cornumarant. It cut through the links of his mailshirt and sliced open his flesh; it fixed itself in his left side. The Turk wrenched it out, enraged. He took his aggression out on Pagan of Beauvais, sending a crossbow bolt straight into his Pavian helmet: it smashed through the helmet, shattered his head and knocked him dead into the ditch. His soul left his body, and St Michael the angel gathered it up immediately and brought him straight in front of God: the bishop of Mautran commended him on his way.[80] Now they press the assault with fanatical determination. Had you been there, you would have seen immense slaughter, unimaginable noise from the horns and bugles, and so much din and shouting from the pagan forces that you could have heard it a league and a half away. St Stephen's Gate was broken through in seven places; however the Turks had strengthened its defences from the inside, placing great baulks of timber across it, so that this was one of the stronger parts of the defences.

---

[80] St Michael the weigher of souls. Compare the death of Roland: *Roland* lines 2391–6.

81

The ditch had been filled in opposite St Stephen's Gate to a length of some 30 feet.[81] That was the ground onto which they moved the siege engine, made of hides nailed together. They heaved and shoved it along until it was right next to the wall. They had nailed strong hides on it as a protective covering. 10 knights concealed themselves behind it; picture them clambering up. The head of the ladder was brought up against the wall. It was levered up with rods and lances until the top was leaned up against a battlement. The knights kept low and clustered together, not uttering a word. They numbered 1,500, all armoured and carrying halberds and large hammers set in hilts, axes and lead clubs and sharp spears, darts milled to razor sharpness and flails joined in the middle; the [Greek] fire was brought in brass pots.[82] May God Who was hung from the Cross protect those on the siege engine! Now you are going to hear about the biggest assault ever. A knight from Flanders called Gontier went up the ladder, a mad thing to do. He did not stop until he reached the top. The French pressed the attack from all sides, throwing javelins and weapons and firing feathered crossbow bolts. The mangonels were hurling large lead missiles. The wall had been breached and collapsed in seven places, and the wounded were strewn outside and inside. Many had fainted from the torments of thirst; that day many of our men slaked their thirst on blood, and some in desperation on the urine of their horses. Ah God! These Christians suffered so harshly from hunger and thirst and captivity that no cleric could possibly give it proper expression, no matter how skilled he was with words. Now listen to what happened to Gontier, who had gone up the ladder, and what became of that noble knight. He had got so far up the ladder that he actually had his hands on a main battlement. A Turk chopped his hands off with one blow of an axe. The lord toppled backwards to his death; a crown was placed on his head before God in Heaven.[83] Ah, God, what a terrible shame that he should meet such a premature end. A messenger went back to the army of Our Lord to tell them that Gontier of Aire had been killed. Count Robert [of Flanders] was devastated to hear the news. The attack was pursued with renewed vigour, but did not result in the holy city being taken. Greek fire landed in the siege engine and set it alight immediately in more than 15 places. The men inside came spilling out: they had had enough, and they could see that the engine was ablaze and that they would not survive if they stayed in it any longer. The Franks sounded the retreat: the assault was called off. The Turks came out onto the walls and blocked up the holes except where earth was piled up inside.

---

[81] Literally five fleeces; a fleece was approximately 6 feet.

[82] See Partington, *History of Greek Fire* pp. 10–32 for Greek fire; p. 22 for it being carried in copper pots, p. 29 for glass or ceramic pots.

[83] Gontier of Aire is one of the heroes in the *Antioche* to have his own anecdote, capturing a splendid horse: laisses 142–3. He is immediately rewarded with the martyr's crown.

82

The assault was called off and the army pulled back. The Franks regrouped some way off in a clearing. Many of our men were injured and in a bad way; it was no surprise that some had been killed given the ferocity of the assault and the combat. Some were fainting from thirst: they were drinking the urine of their horses and of the pack animals. Pools of blood lying on the ground were eagerly gulped down; anyone who found one drank willingly rather than with revulsion. Alas, by God! This was no place for merriment, jokes or laughter. Baldwin of Beauvais had been wounded in the chest; Harpin of Bourges in the face; Richard of Chaumont in the head; and John of Alis had been struck by a large lead club and was still completely dazed. The bishop of Mautran addressed them: 'My lords and noble Christians, in the name of God of Paradise do not lose heart. Stick together. You may all be missing your normal comforts, possessions or pleasures, but trust in God Who holds you as His sons. Each one of you will find eternal glory as His liegeman. At the great Day of Judgement you will all wear crowns. Make sure none of you goes back on his vow to avenge God!' The Christians all responded as one, shouting that they would rather fast for three or six days than fail to take Jerusalem, the city where God died and rose again – 'we shall liberate from the villainous Arabs the true Sepulchre where He came back to life!' A blessing on the hour when each was nourished and may the fathers who engendered them be recognised. Ah, God, these words put fresh heart into them! The day was at an end and evening fell. They spent the night on the battlefield: no furs or sables for them, cloths or sheets or silk or samite, but rather heads pillowed on shields, wearing their hauberks, and their swords wrapped at their sides all stained and blackened with blood and brains. That night the marquis Bohemond took sentry duty for them with 10,000 brave-hearted knights: every single one had accompanied him from his native land. They kept watch for the whole night until day brightened and the sun rose flooding the world with colour. The Turks got ready for a fresh battle with their enemies. They were terrified of [the Christians], afraid because they were pressing close and had made a breach in their wall which was thickly studded with crossbow bolts. Not one of them was courageous enough not to be perturbed by fear of them; despite which every last one nerved himself up to fight them off.

83

It was a beautiful morning and the sun shone from a cloudless sky. The Christians rose – may God come to save them! You can take it from me that they were desperate for water. Robert the Frisian, lord of Flanders, said: 'My noble lords, we need to think what to do'. 'Cousin, you are a true knight' said duke Godfrey. They gave orders to be passed all the way down the army for everyone to go down to the river and bring back water; they should put it in containers on the back of pack animals. When they heard this the Christians made ready. They drove 15,000 pack animals ahead of them. The noble duke Bohemond accompanied them to keep watch, accompanied by 10,000 knights. Meanwhile the sergeants and young knights went foraging for food, seeing whether they could find any in the Turkish barracks. The nobles got under way, keen to move off. Now listen to an adventure more amazing than any you have ever heard. They met a pagan king accompanied by 1,000 Esclers: his name was Garsion and he came from Acre on the coast. 4,000 pack animals were being driven in front of him, all camels and bullocks able to carry large burdens.[84] They had been loaded up with bread, wine and meat, and waterskins full to the brim of good fresh water. Cornumarant had sent a message by means of a dove carrying a sealed letter. There was no way out for King Garsion: such was the will of God to save His people. Bohemond spotted them making their way down a hill; he pointed them out to his companions and ordered them to keep quiet. He ordered all his barons into a dip. Our knights had their horses saddled up; each seized the strap of his bossed shield; swinging into the saddle straight away, they lowered their spears, being careful not to raise them in case the Turks saw them because of the fluttering of the pennons. However this was wasted effort because the Turks had no intention of fighting. Garsion spurred ahead with no idea of what lay in wait, accompanied by 10,000 Turks in a great hurry. He ordered the pack animals to be herded behind him. He and his companions spurred on desperately in their wish to be in Jerusalem before supper, hoping to slip in secretly and avoid the Christians. But Cornumarant will have nothing to boast of and neither will King Corbadas be able to brag to Lucabel. If the noble Bohemond can once catch him up he will send the King flying from his horse and bring him perforce captive to the army, along with all the food, enough for them to eat and drink for a full 15 days.

84

The pagan king rode along at the head of the army. They were in a steep valley next to the path. The pack animals followed along behind them. No better dove had ever left a dovecote: the Turks were lost and unable to save themselves. Bohemond rode out of the dip with his knights. Crying 'Montjoie!' he spurred on his horse, brandishing his spear with its apple-wood shaft. He struck King Garsion on his quartered shield, smashing it to splinters beneath the golden boss and tearing apart the mailed rings on the back of his hauberk. God was with him, though, since he was not actually wounded; he was knocked from his horse to the ground with the force of the thrust. Leaping up, the king grabbed Bohemond's stirrup, begging for mercy and imploring him: 'Noble lord, don't kill me – I want to be baptised. I will declare my belief in Jesus, Judge of the world, Who allowed Himself to be beaten in Jerusalem, tied to a stake and then crucified. I want to believe in Him – that is my wish'. When he heard this Bohemond made no further attempt to attack him; he ordered four of his men to keep him under close guard. The pagans were appalled at the sight; they turned and fled to save their own skins, but ran

---

[84] Not the same Garsion as the ex-ruler of Antioch.

into the pack animals behind them. Our barons rained blows on them mercilessly, splashing their arms with blood and brains. This made the pagans yell at the tops of their voices: 'Alas, Lord Mahomed! Come and help us! Take pity on our souls – they are in dire need!' With this imagine our people flinging themselves on them, killing and slicing them apart with their steel swords. They left the valley strewn with dead and wounded. Not one of the 10,000 escaped unscathed other than the 80 charged with keeping the horses to one side. These were obliged to tie the corpses onto the packhorses, lashing them with strong straps to keep them in place. Then they all set off down the main route, the footsoldiers driving the camels and bullocks along. The noble lords made such good progress that they reached the army of God as the sun went down. Had you been there you would have heard unbounded joy, hubbub and excitement – but also many noble women weeping with grief, and numerous princes and barons sobbing in sheer misery. You might too have seen the duke being hugged and embraced, kisses showered on his face and neck, and the women shrilling: 'Lord God, we have our hearts' desire. Ah, Jerusalem, most desirable of cities! God is allowing us to stay put here so that we can worship His body and make the sign of the Cross, adorn and purify His own true Sepulchre and set up a church there worthy of a lord. We will do all this if God is willing to come to the aid of those who have come across the sea to avenge His body. Our hearts are entirely at His service every single day'. Ah, God, these words did wonders for the morale of our people.

85

Now it was night; day had come to an end. Godfrey and Tancred stood guard for the army of God with 10,000 knights, all fully armoured, until the following day dawned. Our Christians rose all over the army, and the day brightened as the sun came up. The lords, beloved by God, all assembled and the spoils were brought out in front of them. They were split and shared equally across the army, each receiving what was appropriate to his bravery and merits. Nobody, poor or rich, was excluded from the army. The cry of 'By the Holy Sepulchre!' resounded. The bishop of Mautran addressed them. 'My lords', he said, 'a moment's attention please. Each of you has enough provisions for the next nine days. In the name of God husband them carefully and be careful how much you drink. The city will fall within that time'. 'It shall be as you command', replied the Christians. 'May the God Who was hanged on the Cross bring us victory'. The princes and barons sent for the prisoners, and the Christians ran off to fetch them; there were 140 incarcerated in heavy bonds. Their leader came first. He was not in chains; he was wearing a velvet [gown] with gold stars closely fitted to his body with flaring panels, embroidered thickly with gold in more than 30 places. He was wrapped in a silken cloak; its lining was grey with the sheen of a peeled reed, bordered all the way round with luxuriant sable and with crimson marten fur sewn in bands over it. The tassels were decorated with precious stones, and the ties were worth a good thousand *sous* in coins. The neck was fastened with an emerald. His hair was chestnut, cut short in a circle all round; his face was very handsome and fair-complexioned; his eyes were large and piercing; his chest was broad tapering at the sides; his legs were straight and his feet delicately arched; his hands were whiter than flowers in a meadow, neither too large nor too small; all in all he was a handsome specimen.[85] The King was aged 50 years old. Ah, God! What joy if he were a Christian! When he saw our lords he bowed low, greeting them in his own Saracen language. The duke Bohemond got up and came to meet him, took him in his arms and embraced him warmly. An interpreter was swiftly summoned, and through him they asked him what his views were on being baptised as a Christian. He replied that he had believed in God for the last two years. 'Ah God, may you be worshipped for this!' said Bohemond. The bishop of Mautran had the font prepared; then the King stripped off and was baptised on the spot, reborn through the water; however his name was not changed or altered. Then he proceeded to give the army a great deal of useful advice. The other Turks cried: 'See how you are killing us! There is not a single one of us who would not rather have his head cut off than renounce our allegiance to Mahomed!' When Duke Godfrey heard this he came forward. He handed them over to the *ribalts* who beheaded them and, once they had killed them, stripped them naked. They dragged the bodies out in front of Jerusalem and flung them inside using Turkish mangonels. They flayed the corpses and cut them open and salted them, then hung them up to dry in the wind. As for the heads, they impaled them on sharp sticks and stuck them in along the edge of the ditches.[86] Corbadas climbed up to the top of the lofty Tower of David. He leaned out of one of the windows, greatly distressed at what he had seen; the inhabitants of Jerusalem banged their drums in memoriam of the Turks who had been lobbed precipitately onto them. King Corbadas came down, descending the steps of the lofty Tower of David. An uproar went up throughout the city.

86

A huge uproar filled Jerusalem. Everyone howled and yelled over the Turks who had been catapulted into the city. When King Corbadas heard what had happened, he rushed down the stairs of the large ancient tower [of David]. He was accompanied by the white-haired Lucabel. They made their way down the main thoroughfare and found more than 1,000 pagans lying sprawled along the roadway, every last one minus his head. The King of Jerusalem heaped abuse on our people and cursed the land which gave them birth. Tearing his hair and

---

[85] Such descriptions of male as well as female beauty are a standard topos. For a comprehensive (and tongue-in-cheek) example of the topos see *Flamenca* lines 1584–1621.

[86] The implication is that human flesh is being dried for later consumption: for dried meat see R. Tannahill, *Food in History*, (London, 1973; revised 1988) pp. 180–81. This would have been particularly relevant on Crusade where neither salting nor smoking would be especially practical.

ripping at his beard, he said: 'Alas, you wretches! We shall never recover from this!' 'Do not lose heart, brother', said Lucabel. 'Look on the bright side and don't be dismayed; be of good cheer. Before the Christians can take Damascus or Tiberias, Tyre and Ascalon and the well-provisioned city of Acre they will be in desperate need of help'. Picture Cornumarant riding down the road. He was armed and brandishing his burnished sword; as a result of the blows it had struck it was damaged in seven places and splattered and soiled with blood and brains. There was no braver pagan in any Turkish land. The Turks reinforced the gate opposite St Stephen and blocked the holes with considerable skill; the defence was stronger than ever in this stretch. The square was full all the way to the holy Temple with Turks, pagans and Persians. Each was lamenting mightily, weeping and howling and crying out and cursing the French and all their companions.

87

The people of Mahomed stretched all the way down to the holy Temple, where they were lamenting mightily and weeping floods of tears. The King of Jerusalem tore his cotton jerkin, ripped at his beard and grabbed at his moustache. Lucabel and King Malcolon comforted him. Imagine Cornumarant trying to talk sense into him, 'My lord, why are you weeping? Are you worried about what is going to happen?' 'My noble son', said the King, 'I do not know how to say this. Let me tell you now: we are going to lose Jerusalem. The Christian lords have inflicted huge losses on us. I watched yesterday evening from up in this keep. Garsion was brought in tied up like up a farmyard mongrel, and with him more than 1,000 Esclers. They were bringing me provisions in great abundance. I saw him baptised; this is the absolute truth. Not a single one of his men escaped with his life: all had their heads sliced off above the chin. They flung the bodies to us in contempt of us and fixed the heads on sticks which they dotted around this patch of sand. I do not know whom to turn to if not you, noble son'. When Cornumarant heard this his face went coal black and he swore by Mahomed to stop at nothing in his revenge. He had his captives brought from prison, 14 of them and in very poor shape: they had neither mantle nor cape, surcoat nor breeches, nor shoes on their feet nor hose nor clogs.[87] They had been taken prisoner from Peter's army at the same time as Harpin [of Bourges] and Richard of Chaumont. Three of them were from the town of Sainteron, five from Valenciennes, three from Dijon and the remaining two from the castle of Bouillon: these were close relatives of Robert the Frisian and the lion-hearted Duke Godfrey, one being called Henry and the other one Simon. Each of the 14 was weighed down with a heavy chain wrapped round his neck several times; they had large chains on their arms and brass fetters. The King had them beaten so hard with a stick that blood ran down from their heads to their heels. Then he had them driven with a goad through the centre of Jerusalem

---

[87] See note to laisse 66. Here I have tentatively guessed at 'clog' as something approximating both a stump and footwear.

to the Temple of Solomon. They invoked God at the tops of their voices. 'Glorious Lord and Father, Who suffered the Passion, look down on us and grant us Your forgiveness, Holy Lord. Our bodies are going to undergo great suffering for you!' On the way they passed in front of the steps where the body of Jesus Christ was protected from thieves. Each fell to his knees and said a prayer. The Turks who had charge of them fell on them with enormous straps weighted with lead and tore their flesh open right down to the guts so that you could see all their lungs. But then God in his strength brought them salvation as you will be able to hear in the lines of this song.

88

Once the captives had been beaten and ill-treated to the point where no man created by God could have failed to take pity on them, the King of Jerusalem gave orders that they should be consigned to the dungeon of his prison; they were carried off there immediately at his orders. They did not carry them there but pushed and kicked them along one in front of the other. 'Keep moving, you losers!' they said. 'You have given us more than enough trouble. You are not worth one thousand of us. Now let us see how great the power of your God really is. If you do not all get killed and have your brains smashed out it will be a huge miracle and well worth the telling. After all, the dungeon is some four lances' length deep'. Now you are going to hear all about the great miracle that God performed: not one of them suffered as much as a scratch. God received them down [in the dungeon] without injury and each one found himself cured from serious wounds. Angels visited them there day and night ensuring that they had plenty of whatever they needed. They spent four weeks down there until Jesus decided that they should gain their liberty.[88] Now we shall leave their story there, and say nothing more of them until we take up the story afresh. The pagans assembled all the way along to the holy Temple, emirs and princes of high degree. Cornumarant rose, in a state of high emotion. He climbed onto a platform and spoke before them all. 'My lords, you know me as your rightful protector; the kingdom will pass to me from my royal father. But these evil Christians have devastated swathes of it. They have laid siege to us inside this city; they have launched assaults on it, shown their strength and battered down this entire wall, but only because it had not been banked up from inside. Well, [the walls] are mended and the holes blocked, the gates reinforced and the turrets secured, and all the walls protected from crossbow bolts: so their attack will not be worth even a *denier*. But we do not have much in the way of wine, oats or corn; the camels and donkeys have eaten their way through much of it as have the other animals because we have not been able to put them out to pasture. So we shall find ourselves forced into starvation'. 'My noble nephew, you are right', said Lucabel. 'I have already given you sound advice on several occasions, and I will do so now if you wish. My hair is white and I am old – indeed I go back to the time

---

[88] Reminiscent of St Paul in prison: Acts 14:6–10.

of Herod, when he beheaded small children with his razor-sharp sword. Wise and learned men have long prophesied that a powerful race would come and conquer our lands and our goods.[89] And now these men have forced their way into our land. They have conquered it far and wide, to the tune of four days' ride – that is the unvarnished truth. And in my view the prophecies have come true. Anyone who takes on the Franks would be a fool: they believe in a God who does all according to their wish'. When he heard this Cornumarant laughed uncertainly.

89

'My noble nephew', said Lucabel, 'I will not mince my words. I can see full well that our religion is dragging us down and putting us at a disadvantage. Get some eloquent letters written and some summonses prepared. We have 100 doves all ready to be dispatched.[90] We will hang the letters from their necks with silken threads. We will send them out to Damascus telling them that we are in a very bad way. Not a single man in Tyre or Tiberias should refuse to join the army. And if they do not come to our help they will find they have signed their own death warrant. None will escape, neither the best nor the worst; all will be cut to ribbons and slaughtered, and not even the bravest will [survive long enough to] need a doctor. Anyone who manages to capture Frenchmen is to burn them or fry them or boil them alive in water or pitch or wax. That is about the best way to defeat and demoralise them and chase them out of our lands as painfully and violently as possible'. 'You have made me feel considerably better about all this', replied Cornumarant.

90

'My noble nephew', said Lucabel, 'here is what I think. [The doves] know their way to all the castles around – they only came here from the dovecote a week ago. Get your letters written and sealed with wax; set out everything you want in them, begging them to come immediately to your assistance. Anyone who reads the letter must not keep it quiet but have it announced far and wide to princes and kings all the way to the Betean Sea. Make sure it is explained to the lord Sultan that he needs to take pity on his people in their suffering and on his strong and renowned city of Jerusalem under siege from those infidel Christians. If they take it by force – there is no doubt of this – our pagan kingdom will be destroyed, our

---

[89] Similar to the prophecies made by Calabra in the *Antioche*; as frequently the *Jérusalem* draws on its predecessor. Again the theme of the Crusaders being pre-ordained to conquer the Holy Land is emphasised.

[90] The use of doves to carry messages in the East is attested in RA 135 and AA V.9. See S. B. Edgington, 'The doves of war: the part played by carrier pigeons in the crusades', *Autour de la première croisade*, (ed.) M. Balard (Paris, 1996) pp. 167–75.

land laid waste and our belief in Mahomed overthrown and humbled. Let each of our doves have its head plucked as a symbol of the pressure the city is under.[91] Each dove should have its letter knotted round its neck and hidden in the feathers on its breast to make sure the French (those infidel bastards!) do not notice it. We will let them all fly off in a flock; each one will make its way somewhere and land so that these words will be spread far and wide. And on the assumption the letter is found, say in it that the recipient should write another and hide it in the feathers so that the dove can fly on with it. That way the city will get far more reinforcements and braver and fresher defenders'. 'I am happy with this recommendation', replied Cornumarant, 'and it shall be done as you suggest'.

91

King Cornumarant did not hang about: he had his letters written immediately. He did not hang back in setting out his thoughts and wishes. Faced with the Christians laying siege to Jerusalem by force and launching frequent attacks, he begged anyone who held the least regard for him to come to his help all the way from the east all the way to the Sultan in Babylon and King Abraham of the Silver Bridge. He summoned the king of the Asses, whom he counted as a kinsman. He told the powerful King Corbaran of his plight; Stephen the Black from the east; the emir Caucadras from the hills of Bocidant; those of Quenelongne and King Glorient, Murgalant of Audierne, Canebalt and Rubent and the King of Valnuble where no wheat ever grew. If the story is to be believed his subjects are blacker than the blackest pitch or ink, with not a speck of white on them other than their eyes and teeth; they live entirely on spices, wax and pepper and other useful herbs which grow in profusion.[92] Once a year they summon Saracens, pagans, kings and emirs all the way to the Split Tree for rejuvenation, but only those who come to their aid with all possible speed. [The Saracens in Jerusalem] did not hang about once the letters were written: they brought out the doves, a good hundred or so, and, hanging the letters from their necks, they immediately let them fly free from a promenade. Now may God remember our army in his plans, because if the doves make it safely to the various castles they will set in train a whole assembly which will bring suffering down on the army of God.

---

[91] The symbolism is not clear; possibly this implies that their heads were shaved as a sign of suffering.

[92] 'Sirre' is not attested in meanings other than wax, which is an odd thing to live on. Possibly a waxy or resinous plant? The description of the inhabitants is similar to *Canso d'Antioca* 316.

92

So the doves flew off above the heads of the army. The French caught sight of them and took a closer look, saying to each other and pointing their fingers at them, 'Look at all those doves! There have never been so many together. All have the fronts of their heads plucked'. The army was thrown into confusion and agitation rippled through the ranks. All our lords were in a green meadow on a slope outside the Golden Gate. They were busy sizing up Jerusalem, deciding how best to take it and with what stratagems and whether the mangonel would be of any use. With them was Garsion, whom God had turned into a Christian. They turned and looked up to the sky where they saw the doves fluttering swiftly past them, sent by God's mighty command. Garsion shouted: 'Noble valiant lords! Those are messengers being sent to the pagans! Each of those doves has a letter hung from its neck and is on its way to seek help – I know this for sure. If they can fly away without being killed they will bring the whole of the empire of the Orient down on our heads!' When they heard this our leaders shouted, 'Anyone who is a good shot will be rewarded with a bezant!' The army moved ready to attack in front and behind; the archers shot off arrow after arrow at the doves, and the men of the Tafur king lined up shots from catapults. What more can I say? They killed them all apart from three who made their escape, but those three carried out their mission as well as the whole flock could have done. The Saracens watched grimly, but rejoiced happily for those who did manage to get away. Duke Godfrey sat astride his warhorse; Lord Hugh of Vermandois on a skewbald horse, and Count Robert of Flanders on the swift black horse Mulberry. Each held a falcon. They turned and sped away, spurring after the doves who flew away as fast as they could manage, from time to time landing briefly. When [the three lords] saw that they were approaching the Mount of Olives they released the falcons who flew off noisily and circled the doves ready for the attack. However the doves took refuge crouched on the ground; they huddled up next to a hump and did not dare move a muscle.[93] Our leaders dismounted, picked them up and swung straight back into the saddle; taking their falcons back they turned round and rode back to the army of the Lord at Bethlehem.

93

Our lords dismounted in front of the main pavilion. The nobles came flocking round them. They removed the letters from the neck of each dove and gave them straight to the bishop of Mautran. The duke of Bouillon, the brave Robert and the valiant and wise lord Hugh of Vermandois each took the letter from his dove's neck. Then all the doves were properly fed and given water. They put them in a

---

[93] This would presumably have made it harder for the falcons to swoop in.

barrel with holes in, guarded by two men-at-arms who kept careful watch.[94] The bishop scrutinised the letters carefully and said to our lords: 'You will be amazed to hear what these letters you can see are saying. In them the King has summoned all the barons with lands surrounding the Dry Tree. But we have the letters, praise be to God!' The duke of Bouillon said: 'Here is an idea, my lord. Write three letters for us as quickly as you can, putting it out that Corbaran is telling all his vassals to stay at home and that he has plenty of forces: that will ensure they stay behind'. The bishop accordingly wrote as he was asked. They brought back the doves and attached [the letters] to their necks. They took them straight back to the Mount of Olives and put them in the same pace: and off they flew. None of them took a detour: they went straight to Belinas and into a house where they had perches. They were intercepted by a Saracen called Ysoré. Searching the doves, he found the letters and got a literate pagan to read them. They said that Cornumarant was in a strong position; that he was not concerned about the position of Jerusalem because it was well defended; and that the pagan should stay in the castles and fortresses on his own lands because the French were weak with hunger. The pagan's spirits rose on reading this. He hurried to have some other letters written. He sent greetings and friendship to Cornumarant. Within the next month or week he would assemble 10,0000 armed Turks who would help him fight off the Franks and secure his position; the wretches would be killed and torn limb from limb, their religion humiliated and Mahomed raised up. With that he took the doves and secured the letters on them, tying them round their necks and throats, and set them on their way back. They flew in convoy all the way to the French army, guided by God and kept on the right path by his divine will. Our leaders watched out for them and halted them, using mewed falcons to frighten them so that they settled side by side on the tents. The princes who had halted them gathered them up.

94

The doves had been recaptured and their letters removed. They gave the letters straight over to the bishop of Mautran, who unfolded them and read them. Without delay he wrote some more letters, in which the inhabitants of Damascus claimed that the Sultan was furious and deeply angered by King Corbadas; he had better make the best of things as no help would be coming his way. The bishop folded the letters small, tied them tightly onto the doves and sent them off to Jerusalem the following day. Corbadas rose as day broke; he ordered a drum to be banged to summon the pagans. The Turks assembled in an ancient square which ran in front of the holy Temple, many of them in a jolly mood. Lucabel and his nephew Malcolon were there, and Cornumarant was standing there too; he is not going to be very pleased at the news he receives.

---

[94] Typical of the author's interest in practical details, and an interesting insight into material culture.

95

The square in front of the holy Temple was swarming with Turks and pagans, infidels that they were. Imagine large numbers of beautiful Saracen women converging, each dressed in clinging silk robes, to hear the latest news. The white-haired Corbadas rose and made his way through the crowd to Lucabel. He handed him the letters and asked him to read them. The emir took them in his ungloved hand. His blood ran cold as he read the letters; the golden staff he carried fell to his feet. He said out loud in a ringing voice: 'By Mahomed! This is not turning out well. We have lost the help of the lord Sultan. This means double pain for us all: if Mahomed does not help us our city is lost'. At hearing this Cornumarant grabbed a mace and was about to smash it down on his uncle when it was seized from him.

96

Picture the scenes of grief in front of the holy Temple, with pagans and Saracens flocking in. The King of Jerusalem began to weep, tearing his hair and ripping at his beard. His son Cornumarant tried to comfort him. 'My lord', said the young man, 'do not distress yourself like this; you have nothing to fear as long as I am alive. You will see me riding out indefatigably, making sorties and attacking, killing and slaughtering the French. Every last one I catch will be beheaded. Go and set up your quarters in your tower; leave me to make arrangements for guarding Jerusalem. No matter what the attack you will not see a single Frank get in!' 'I am happy to agree, my noble son', said Corbadas. The King went off to the lofty Tower of David, and leaned out of the marble windows. He was accompanied by his intimate Lucabel, and the pair of them could look out and watch the ebb and flow of attack. Cornumarant ordered four horns to be sounded. At this picture the pagans getting ready and arming themselves, coming and going up on the ramparts, setting up mangonels and laying in stockpiles of stones and crossbow bolts (and coming and going on the ramparts). You could not have thrown a bean up there, or flung a stone or stick or pebble without striking the weapon of some Persian or Escler. I have never seen them in better order for battle, not least because they had not failed to supply themselves with Greek fire. Cornumarant ordered the principal horn to be sounded: at this picture the pagans lining up next to each other, standing close together. Now you can hear about a fierce attack: if our men remain on the spot they will be able to prove themselves.

97

It was a beautiful clear day and the sun glittered. Our barons saw that the Turks were so keen to defend Jerusalem that they were swarming all over the walls. They were all perturbed at the sight. The duke of Bouillon said: 'You look too cowed to me. We should not be doing anything other than mounting an assault every day to take this holy city where God lived and died. The Saracens have made us too nervous to go in. Have the horns sounded in the name of Jesus Christ and let us attack Jerusalem in force!' 'Blessed be the day that sees this!' replied the lords. 'My lords', said Count Hugh, 'listen and I will tell you what I think. Let us not launch all our forces into the attack simultaneously. Let each squadron be assigned a particular assault; while one attacks the dark-mortared walls the others will provide cover with their curved horn bows. When the first wave have got tired and lost their impetus, they can fall back and be replaced by another armed and armoured squadron. That means that we can launch the equivalent of ten attacks on one single place today. You can be sure this will inflict heavy losses on the Turks. And if we have managed to damage the wall with our catapult, they will not be opening any gates or posterns'. This was recognised as sound advice well worth following. Accordingly they ordered the bugles to be sounded, and you can imagine them launching the assault. Each was armed and equipped to the maximum. Picture the King of the Tafurs in the midst of a clearing with 10,000 *ribalts* all spoiling for a fight. They carried hoes and spades and large falchions and pikes, long-handled axes and maces and hammers of forged iron, razor-sharp daggers and sharp knives and clubs made of copper and reinforced with chains. Some were carrying slingshots and many had picked up pebbles. Many of them were still suffering from the wounds they had received in the previous assault. The King of the Tafurs had been injured in 30 different places, on head and shoulders and arms and chest, and had put dressings on his wounds. He carried a sickle forged from pure steel with a well shaped and turned ash handle. His head was protected by a helmet of boiled leather and he was tightly protected by his padded coat. He shouted at the top of his voice in front of our lords: 'My lords, I beg you in the name of God, the King of Paradise, to let us launch the first attack on these wretches who refuse to believe in the Resurrection of God! I will be your devoted follower for the rest of my life!' Our barons granted his request, but rather reluctantly given that all his men were completely without (conventional) weapons. The bishop of Mautran, sleek and well nourished, made the sign of the Cross over all of them in the name of God Who was hanged on the Cross.[95] Then he ordered them not to be so rash as to launch the attack before the great horn had been sounded.[96] The King of the Tafurs took his leave and turned away with his *ribalts*: imagine the sight of them en masse. The bishop of Mautran blessed every last one.

---

[95] A slightly pointed comment.

[96] This injunction is repeated a number of times, partly reflecting the use of *laisses similaires* but also underlining the danger of breaking ranks without adequate cover: compare Gerard of Melun in RM VII.15, where the title glossed to the chapter is unequivocal in condemning his foolishness.

98

After this our lords set up another squadron. All those in it were youngsters, men-at-arms and squires. [97]They made Enguerrand of St-Pol the pennant-bearer. These were determined to have first crack at the attack, but the King of the Tafurs had been given the privilege of starting things off. The bishop of Mautran started to pronounce his blessing on them. 'My lords, do not make any move to shoot arrows or throw any weapons until you have heard the noise of the great horn swelling!' Enguerrand and his lightly armed young men turned and went to take up their station in front of Jerusalem. They looked up at the sturdy walls towering above them and the holy Temple glistening in front of their eyes. To a man they bent and began to pray to God to let them enter the city and embrace and kiss His revered Sepulchre. [Enguerrand of St. Pol started off their prayer:] 'Make sure that when we launch the attack I do not see one coward. If I see every soldier flinging himself at the wall and scrambling up the ladder hand over fist I shall be a happy man'.[98] They shouted back, 'There is no need to beg us! If we can just get the ladders up against the wall, call us despicable if we do not go shinning up them!' The King of Jerusalem went and leaned out of a spacious window of marble and hard white stone; he cursed the French in the name of the diabolical Apollon.

99

Next our leaders set up a courageous squadron composed of Bretons and some Normans: there were a good 10,000 of them, brave and ready to fight. Their leader Count Robert put Joserant in charge of them with his cousin Thomas and Fulcher of Melun. The bishop of God the Almighty blessed them and told them that not one of them should move a muscle to attack until they heard the horn being blown at full blast. 'It shall be as God commands', answered the lords. They bowed to the bishop and turned away to take up their position in front of the walls of Jerusalem. They stationed themselves next to the other squadron and looked up at the city, its strong high walls and the holy Temple so beloved of God. The heart of every last one shivered in sympathy. They bowed down towards the city, tears streaming from their eyes, each thinking to himself and muttering under his breath: 'Alas, Jerusalem! How we suffer for your sake. May God grant us the mercy of entering your walls'. The King [of Jerusalem] was at a window framed with fine shining marble. He scrutinised our Frenchmen forming up into order the other side of the ditch ready to attack the town. He cursed them in the name of his

---

[97] The start of the successful attack on Jerusalem is emphasised by a run of *laisses similaires*. The *Antioche* similarly marks key moments, notably battle at Nicaea and the march out of Antioch against Kerbogha's force: laisses 54–62, 315–28.

[98] Old French 'charpentier': I have translated in a wider sense as those who inflict damage.

God Tervagant. 'Alas, you wretches! You arrogant bastards!' he said. 'The curse of my God Mahomed fall on you!'

100

Our leaders organised another squadron. This comprised men from Boulogne (may Jesus grant them his blessing!), Flanders and Burgundy, a race distinguished for its bravery. Together their formation numbered a good 15,000. Imagine the sight: numerous flags tied to poles, hauberks and helmets resplendent with gold. The good duke and the bishop who had oversight of them put Eurvin in charge to lead and guide them, Wicher the German who was no coward, and Lord Raimbalt Creton, scourge of the pagans: you could not have found three knights like this all the way to Romania.[99] The bishop who served God, the Son of the Virgin, made the sign of the Cross over them. Then he issued his orders, imploring them in no uncertain terms to ensure that none of them made a move to launch an attack until the great horn gave the signal. The barons assented, each agreeing; then they turned and drew up ranks all ready to fight. They took possession of the ground in front of Jerusalem. They looked across to the city, the walls of porphyry and the holy Temple glistening and resplendent near the Sepulchre where God died and rose again. Each of them bowed down with a humble heart. 'Alas, Jerusalem, ancient and holy city! What shame and misery that you are in the hands of the pagans! May God give us the strength to seize you and for us to enter your walls. The moment the ladder is up against the walls we will do our level best – I am determined to be first up, cry or laugh who will'. 'And I will be with you every step of the way', said Eurvin. 'I am spoiling for the fight', said Raimbaut Creton. 'If I can just get up there amongst the pagans, they will pay my burnished sword a high price'. The King of Jerusalem was up in the ancient tower looking down at our Franks as they made their preparations to attack the walls with their mossy stone. He cursed them all in the name of his god Apollon. 'Alas, you wretches! You cowardly bastards! By Mahomed my God, you are all a set of fools. Jerusalem is a strongly defended city. You have no chance of taking her! All you will get for your efforts is 20,000 men lost'.

---

[99] All these feature in episodes in the *Antioche* and are presumably picked out on that basis: Eurvin somewhat ingloriously as the owner of a donkey which is stolen and eaten (laisse 303); Wicher who cuts down the Saracen standard at the battle of Antioch (laisses 358–9) and is killed at laisses 362-63; and Raimbalt as the mass slaughterer of pagans on the bridge over the Orontes at Antioch (laisses 167–9). None are distinguished as commanders in the sources; their presence here again suggests that the author drew on the *Antioche* itself for much of his source material.

101

Our noble lords set up another squadron composed entirely of allies from Constantinople. There were a good 10,000, brave as lions; they were led by the dragon-hearted Estatin.[100] Imagine the innumerable mailed hauberks, the helmets of steel with no admixture of lead, the long lances and the crimson pennants. The Bishop made the sign of the Cross over them in the name of St Simeon. Then he issued orders for them to behave sensibly and not to attack the city where God suffered until they heard the sound of the great brass horn. Estatin, son of a nobleman, said he would comply. He led his people away at the double to occupy the sandy area in front of Jerusalem. They looked up at the city and the walls surrounding it and the holy Temple which used to belong to Solomon and is near the Sepulchre – I tell you no lies – where God died and came back to life. Each of them bowed down and prayed. 'Alas, you famous city!' they said. 'May God grant us the privilege of living long enough to conquer you, to kiss the Sepulchre with humility and to drive out those wicked Saracens!' The King of Jerusalem was up in the main keep and cursed our people in the name of the people of Mahomed. 'Alas, you wretches! You filthy Christian villains!' he said. 'You are courting disaster. You will all be killed and destroyed. Your God Jesus will not be able to save you. Mahomed, whom we worship, is very strong. He will avenge us on you like it or not'. 'That is true', said Lucabel, 'do not doubt what he says'.

102

Then our lords set up another squadron, the sixth. It was very well armed, the men ready to fight with spades and hoes and long steel poles for making holes in stone . They carried also innumerable blades, bows and swords and rich flags tied to their lances. They were from the renowned race of the French: their squadron numbered an estimated 20,000, all armoured. The famous Count Hugh of Vermandois assigned it to the command of lord Thomas of Marle. The bishop, famous for his virtue, blessed them with the sign of the Cross. Then he ordered them not to raise the battle cry to attack the walls, or make any noise or commotion until they heard the great horn summon them to battle. Lord Thomas agreed and bowed in acknowledgement. Then he raised the oriflamme and led his squadron away to take up the ground outside Jerusalem.[101] They looked up at the lofty extent of the city and the holy Temple with its huge paved area, near the Sepulchre with its shaped

---

[100] In real life Tatikios, the Byzantine envoy who accompanied the Crusaders as far as Antioch and was made the scapegoat for anti-Byzantine feeling. He was not at the siege of Jerusalem. Interestingly he is praised here: most sources including the *Antioche* criticise him virulently.

[101] The oriflamme was the banner of the Kings of France, kept at St-Denis: L. Hibbard-Loomis, 'L'oriflamme de France et le cri Munjoie au douzième siècle', *Moyen Age* 14 (1959) pp. 469–99. It is significant that Thomas of Marle has the honour of carrying it.

stone where God came back from death to life. Lord Thomas of Marle looked at it with adoration. 'Alas, you fortunate city', he said. 'I have endured endless hard days for you, suffering snow and frost, hunger and thirst and privation, my body darkened and burnt by blazing sun. And I am not alone; I am surrounded by people from many lands. May God let them achieve their wish and desire to take you in conquest as they have so long desired so that the Mass can once more be heard and sung at the Sepulchre. Ah God, how worthwhile will the suffering be and what a great fortune awaits the man who, out of all this army, gains the honour of being first into the city! By the Lord who made the sky and the dew, I would happily have my head cut from my shoulders and my body ripped into 20 wounds if I could get myself thrown in [over the walls] to be the first one in: I am determined'. At this he stared at the pagans. He shook his head; his heart swelled in his chest; his strength doubled. If he had been amongst them at the moment, he would have dealt such a blow that any Saracen would have had his head chopped from his body. The King of Jerusalem was up in his square tower looking down on our men, who, as he could see all too well, were ready to attack his city. The blood drained from his face. He let fly a huge volley of curses and bitterly blamed the land which had brought forth such a race.

103

Our own barons set up the seventh squadron. There were men from the south of France and many others, as well as Lotharingians and men from Marseilles; there were Gascons and Poitevins too on the flat area [outside the walls]. They numbered a good 10,000 and as many horses. The loyal-hearted Lord Raymond of St-Gilles gave the command to Bernard and Antelme of the Valley, lord Gerard of Blois, Guy of Poitiers, John of La Flèche and Robert the seneschal. Imagine the sight of all those hoes and stakes, hauberks and helmets with gold and enamel, innumerable iron blades and hooks and stones, and rich flags of silk and fine fabric. The Bishop made the sign of the Cross over them in the service of the divine God. Then he gave orders, to which they made no objection, that not a single one should make a move to throw weapons or mount an attack until they heard the great metal horn sound. They assented, then turned and made their way onto the flat ground outside the walls of Jerusalem to take up their stations. They looked up at the city, up on its hills and slopes and the holy Temple with its lustred decorations near the Sepulchre in which God was laid and where he rose from death to life without pain.[102] You might have seen many heads bowed and each one drenching his horse with tears. 'Alas', they said, 'holiest of mighty cities! Look at the misery and

---

[102] 'Esmal' is attested as meaning 'enamel'; it is not obvious why a wall should be enamelled but this may refer to Islamic tiles which have a high lustre. If as seems likely the Holy Temple is to be identified with the Dome of the Rock, the latter was covered with Byzantine mosaics at the time. The reference to enamel may just be for the rhyme or to convey a general sense of luxury.

destruction these pagans have inflicted on you. May God grant us the privilege of smashing our way through the walls so that we can dance and rejoice before the Temple and celebrate God in the mystery of the Mass'. The King of Jerusalem was up in his royal tower. He looked down and saw the French beneath him on the sandy ground outside his city, ready to knock down the walls, stones, decorations and all. He cursed them in the name of Mahomed who created a huge din. 'Alas you wretches!' he said. 'May Mahomed make you suffer. I don't give as much as a chest strap for all your attacks. My heart is brave enough to cope with anything you throw at me. I will gouge out your eyes with my spur then have you tied to the stake and used as target practice!'

104

Our lords put together the eighth squadron. It contained men from Apulia and also Calabria; all those from Sicily, a considerable number; and the Venetians distinguished for their bravery. Together they numbered some 20,000 if the source is to be believed. Bohemond and Tancred, whose squadron this was, put in charge Ernais and Arnold of Melun, Garin of Pavia and his relative Arnold; each of them had considerable lands and buildings. Imagine the sight of all those silver shields, hauberks and helmets and good quality equipment, and crimson shields catching the sun's rays. However they were all on foot together. They carried spades and hoes to dislodge the cement, long steel poles to land heavy blows, and blades with curved iron prongs to be able to drag things out effectively. The Bishop made the sign of the Cross over them in the name of God the Omnipotent Father. Then he told them, making it very clear what they should not do, that not a single one should make a move to attack until they heard the horn being sounded loudly. They assented and drew up their ranks in front of Jerusalem, waiting for each other. They looked up at the city with its fine walls and the holy Temple glittering and shining near the Sepulchre and the holy tomb where God came back to life – you can be sure of this truth. Each of them worshipped Him with a full heart, every single one in tears and heavy-hearted with sympathy for God and His birth. 'Oh city', they said, 'it was a bad day which saw these dogs defile you. May God grant us as part of His divine plan to be able to deliver you completely and be able to worship His body with the greatest veneration'. The King of Jerusalem was up in his wind tower.[103] He kept looking down at the squadrons and could see how keen they were to fight, desperate for the attack. He cursed them and all their works in the name of Apollon. 'Alas, you wretches!' he said, 'You are annoying me. You will be killed as painfully as possible in short order'.

---

[103] Wind towers are a common feature of Arabic houses: see for example the houses in Bastikaya in Dubai.

105

Our lords had the ninth squadron drawn up, but this one was not about throwing weapons or launching attacks.[104] The women who were on their way to worship at the Sepulchre all grouped together, saying to each other – this is quite true by the way: 'We made our way here all across the sea a long time ago, each one following her husband (may God guard him). Since then we have seen them go through endless suffering, batter down castle after castle and wall after wall, and convert many pagans to our faith. Now they have come to conquer the holy city where God allowed His body to suffer and be tortured, struck with the Lance and injured and wounded. Each of us must serve and love her lord, obey him and honour him in all. If they are suffering we must be part of it. So it will be a noble woman who allows herself to suffer today attacking the city and encouraging our forces'. They picked up stones and pebbles to be made into piles. What I am going to tell you is true, by God, and well worth listening to. Imagine the sight of the women coming and going, fetching and carrying water in pots and barrels; anyone who was thirsty could drink to his heart's content. They went to take up their position before Jerusalem. They started to scrutinise the city closely, and the holy Temple shining resplendently near the Sepulchre where God chose to come back to life. Each of them worshipped it, bursting into tears. 'Alas, O city', they said, 'you are truly wonderful. May God grant our forces strength to enter and kiss the Sepulchre to which we owe reverence'. With that you might have seen them bowing down in the direction of the city, each woman's heart full to bursting. The King of Jerusalem was leaning on a pillar in the great Tower of David in such a position that he could size up the French. He called out to the emir Lucabel: 'Do you know who those people are that I can see drawn up?' 'My brother', said Lucabel, 'let me tell you as it is. They are the wives of those wretches who are determined to destroy our religion, overthrow it and consign it to shame'. Corbadas shook his head when he heard this. 'I am going to have them taken to the emir Sultan to attempt a reconciliation with him', he said to Lucabel. 'He will be able to use them to restore his vast depopulated lands. He can have each one given to a prince or emir and will marry every one of them off as he wishes'.[105] 'My brother', said Lucabel, 'I suggest you don't pursue this train of thought any further. [Actually you are going to see these people throw down the walls of Jerusalem] and the Christian army force its way in as of right'.[106] When Corbadas heard this he was beside himself.

106

The French nobility – God grant them His mercy – had divided up their forces into nine squadrons; they made up the tenth from the nobility in God's army.

---

[104] The *Antioche* also has a squadron of women in the battle of Antioch: laisse 327.
[105] Common theme: Bancourt vol.2 pp. 58–65.
[106] Thorp inserts a line which he considers missing in A.

I couldn't possibly tell you the name of each one, and anyway you have heard them elsewhere in the song. I know for a fact that there were 1040, each of them splendidly armed. There was not one without a banner, ensign or pennant; they were all covered in armour right down to their spurs. They gave the command to the Duke of Bouillon and his cousin Lord Robert the Frisian. The two of them turned and spurred away across the sandy expanse and made their way to the King of the Tafurs with a message: 'My lord, you are to attack in the name of St Simeon when you hear the great brass horn sounded'. 'Blessed be God', replied the King. With that the princes turned and rode away, not wasting words. They gave orders to their squires and arrayed them so that they could do their bit after the King of the Tafurs. Then they made their way back to the Normans without stopping, and gave them orders to wait in reserve and to deliver their attack after the squires, putting their whole weight into the attack. Then they made their way back to the lion-hearted Flemish and the men from Boulogne, who were fighting alongside each other, and ordered them to attack after the Normans. 'We cannot wait!' said Raimbaut Creton. Then they came back past the counts, each holding a stick, and came to the highly renowned French, whom they told to mount a vigorous attack after the Flemish.[107] [Then they came to the Occitans, who comprised significant numbers of nobles, and ordered them to fling themselves into the attack after the French,] assaulting the city where God suffered and knocking down the walls, the stone and the blocks.[108] Then they granted them sweet absolution in God. Now you are going to hear all about the attack – you have never heard of one as fierce.

107

Our barons were armed and in front of Jerusalem. They had Nicolas of Duras summoned. Between them he and Gregory had constructed a siege engine with wooden hoardings and a framework nailed on, carefully made and reinforced with crossbars. It could shelter a whole force of archers, who would be able to shoot in safety against opponents up on the walls. However their attempt to take it up to the walls had not gone well because the Turks set the whole thing on fire with Greek fire; in fact it had been set ablaze twice. The ladders of tanned cowhide were ready. They had put poles down each side, tying them securely to the ladders to hold them firmly against the walls of the city. They gave one to each squadron. Nicolas and Gregory had mounted an iron-clad battering ram on wheels and beams. They took it along in front of the siege engine quite close to the gate, level with the ditch. But in terms of what it achieved it was not worth a penny. The Turks inside the city were watching all this carefully and fought back with another device. All those outside will be showered with Greek fire and most of them scalded with boiling pitch. God, the King in majesty, allowed all this to happen because He wanted His people to be put to the test and suffer grievously in their attempts to take his city

---

[107] It is not clear why each holds a stick: a badge of office?
[108] Thorp edits to avoid awkwardness in A.

because that was where His body had been so grievously treated, His side pierced and left bleeding and wounded: that was the significance He impressed upon them.[109] Now you are going to hear about a really fierce attack. The good Duke of Bouillon, resplendent in his dignity, took the great horn and blew it vigorously. The King of the Tafurs shouted a command and the *ribalts* ran forward. Imagine them slinging large numbers of pebbles rank upon rank and churning up the earth with picks and hoes. They did not stop until they reached the bottom of the ditch. More than 1500 flung themselves in and hauled themselves up hand over hand. Not put off by arrows, stones or crossbow bolts flying at them, they stormed up to the foot of the wall where they drew up ranks with great vigour. The King of the Tafurs scaled the wall but was to pay a heavy price: a Turk smashed a hinged flail down on him so hard that it knocked him unconscious from the ladder. However God was looking out for him and ensured he came to no harm: the men under cover of the siege engine were able to save him. Javelins and crossbow bolts fell like summer rain. King Cornumarant shouted his battle cry. It was a ferocious attack and a long one. The good Duke of Bouillon sounded the horn to signal a retreat, and the *ribalts* fell back dirty and bloodstained. They carried away the King of the Tafurs dripping with blood, the blow from the flail having smashed his nose and badly damaged his head and brains. They laid him carefully in a shield and put him into the care of two doctors, who soon effected a cure.

108

The *ribalts* made a good job of the first attack. The good Duke of Bouillon sounded the horn for the next wave. Imagine all those squires and young men attacking fiercely without a second thought! The squires leapt across the territory already churned up by the *ribalts*. They protected their heads with one shield between two; every single one carried a spade or mattock or hatchet. They piled rocks up against the wall. They set up their ladder next to the one which was already there and lashed them together, a sharp move. The brave Enguerrand of St-Pol was the first up, a pretty foolhardy thing to do. Stephen climbed the next one to be put up. Each ladder had five men go up it – may God come to their aid! They are going to have a terrible time before they come back down. The Turks were up top with ready-boiled pitch which they flung down onto them mercilessly. Where the pitch touched them it left their skin blackened to a crisp. Then the Turks flung down lots of huge stones onto them, smashing in the heads of every single one through their helmets. Enguerrand had 15 wounds on his body but still insisted on climbing up the ladder, fool that he was. Cornumarant was grasping a mace tightly bound with wide steel bands. He waited long enough for Enguerrand's head to appear and

---

[109] An explanation of the perennial problem faced by Crusaders: if they enjoyed divine favour, why was God's support not always apparent? See Riley-Smith, *Idea* pp. 112–13. The text comes full circle back to the depiction of the Crucifixion with which the *Antioche* starts.

for him to get level with the top of the wall; then he struck him a double-handed blow near his ear so hard that he smashed in his helmet from Pavia and crushed his mailed hood right into his head. There was nothing Enguerrand could do to stop himself being precipitated from the ladder. He tumbled down but did not die, knocking flying all those who had grabbed the ladder to climb up. Steven of Lucuel showed great bravery in climbing the other ladder, cry or laugh who might, followed by others to whom he gave a lead. The Turks were busy shooting and firing off missiles – may the body of God curse them for it! They had flung large numbers of stones down. Ysabars of Barbais reached out with his stiletto and threw it so skilfully that it struck Steven on his flowered shield; it pierced his hauberk and leather jerkin and went right into his body, knocking him and his companions flying from the ladder. This blow felled 15 of our men; all their souls went to the flowery fields of Paradise. King Cornumarant shouted at the top of his voice: 'By God, you wretched bastards, you filthy scoundrels! I wouldn't give as much as a rotten apple for all your assaults! Before you can swim back across the sea over there, the best one of you would give all the gold in Slavonia to be somewhere else. I will have you all thrown into the dungeons of the emir of Persia. My city will survive whether you like it or not!' The Duke sounded the horn and they called off the attack. Now the women came with their sleeves rolled up. They moistened the mouths of those who were thirsty and ensured they could drink their fill; this was of considerable help. Indeed it would have gone hard with the army if the women had not been there.

109

The squires had put up a good show in this attack, but the *ribalts* had done a rather better job in the first one.[110] Duke Godfrey sounded the great mountain horn; imagine that as the signal for the Normans and Bretons to break ranks. They followed in the footsteps of the *ribalts* across the ditch to fling themselves against the wall and break it down. They stormed up the slope and did not stop until they reached the wall, where they knocked down some six or eight feet. But this really wasn't of much use, not as much as a penny, because the walls were securely made with lime and mortar. The Normans raised their ladder by force up against the wall and lashed it tightly to the two others, but none of them were brave enough to go up it. They struck and poked at the walls with their long steel poles whilst those in the siege engine fired arrows up at the infidels, drawing blood from many heads and chests. 'Come on, gentlemen, up the ladder!' yelled our lords. 'Any one of you should be proud to boast that, if God gave him the privilege of approaching Jerusalem, he would bite the walls with his own teeth even if they were made of steel. Yet all we can see is you hanging back and refusing to climb!' 'Don't be such cowards!' shouted the women. 'Young men up in honour of your girls,

---

[110] This sentiment is repeated in laisse 110; the importance of the Tafurs is underlined.

husbands up in honour of your wives'.[111] At that you might have seen the Normans and Bretons find new heart: they did not wait to be asked a second time to climb the ladder. Joserans and Thomas were first up along with Fulcher of Melun, who was given the banner to carry. They were storming their way up. May God offer them his protection because the Turks were going to do them serious damage. They dragged a great baulk of timber up onto the wall; it took 30 Turks to hoist it up, each at a lever.[112] They tipped it over the walls to inflict maximum damage on our men. As it came down it knocked people flying; it killed seven of our men and did a lot of collateral damage. The arrogant Cornumarant started shouting at the top of His voice: 'Come on! Bring on some others! These ones are not worth talking about. Do you think we are all shepherds and peasants in here? By my god Apollon, who can pass judgement on all, you made a mistake in coming over the sea to challenge me for my fief. You will have to pay a very high price indeed to secure it!' The King of Jerusalem did not have much to be happy about; he had gone to prop up the walls in the Tower of David. The good Duke of Bouillon had the horn sounded, and the Normans and Bretons ceased the attack. They retreated as far as the shot of a hand-wound bow and the lords came to assist them. They assigned doctors to the wounded and had them carefully laid flat. Picture the sight of the women breaking ranks and running hither and thither, coming and going so that they could quench the thirst of those in need of water: you can take it from me that it was desperately needed in God's army.

110

The Normans had made a good job of mounting a fierce assault, but they had not done as well as the squadron of *ribalts*, who had been the first to punch large holes in the walls and had filled up the ditch with their hoes and stakes. They suffered terribly for it as they had no armour. It was a beautiful clear day and the sun blazed down. The great metal horn was sounded loudly. The brave-hearted Flemish and Burgundians got into the ditch with pikes and hammers. They scrambled up the sloping ground against the walls, each desperate to attack as soon as he could. The pagans defended themselves, firing heavy crossbow bolts which smashed through their brightly enamelled helmets. Arrows and missiles rained down in abundance. The Bedouin women catapulted stones at them, shouting to the pagans: 'Kill these infidels who want to stop us dancing and having any fun!'[113]

---

[111] Again the women are shown having a decisive influence on the course of events in the same way as their repeated water-carrying activities.

[112] The baulk is of 'celier'; it is not clear what this is. 'Cleee' is a timber rampart but it is difficult to imagine this being big enough to need 30 levers. Some sort of timber is clearly implied.

[113] There is a fair bit of scribal variation around this line, suggesting it caused some puzzlement.

111

It was a beautiful clear day and the sun shone, and the attack surged and the din grew. Wicher the German yelled at the top of his voice: 'My lords, do your best! Do not hang back!' The Flemish were full of the rage of battle. Each advanced. They had put up no fewer than four ladders. Lord Raimbaut Creton made his way up; Eurvin of Creel went up another; Wicher up a third without hesitation; and Martin grabbed the fourth with both hands. Now may God Who created the world extend His protection over them. Ysabars was grasping a grappling hook. He flung it at Wicher, and the hook caught in the collar of his hauberk. Danemons seized the elderly Eurvin and dragged him up helped by others. Raimbaut Creton saw this and was not happy at all. Brandishing his naked sword he thrust upwards and cut the feet off a Saracen. Pagan of Camelia smashed another. A giant Turk landed such a heavy mace blow on Raimbaut that he knocked him stunned from the ladder. Another Turk struck Pagan of Camelia and sent him flying, like it or not. Each of them tumbled to the bottom of the ditch. God showed his power with an amazing miracle: they landed so softly that they were not hurt at all. Cries sounded on all sides. The women lifted their voices, there with the army of God to conquer the city where God came back to life; He will give his favour to whoever avenges Him. When the duke saw what had happened to Wicher, he was convulsed with rage: he was dismayed that the Turks had captured him along with Eurvin whom he held in high regard.

112

The duke took the horn and sounded a call on it; then he blew it a second time and a third with all his might. That was to give the signal for a general attack: all were to launch an assault immediately. At this the French from the blessed land broke ranks to attack; so did those from Apulia, Calabria and many other regions. Had you been there, you would have heard the most almighty din, the land ringing with it for more than a league around. It was a very fierce attack with a ferocious mêlée. The men in the siege engine shot arrows more thickly than dew. The renowned Count Robert came down; so did the duke of Bouillon with his sharp sword. With them came Count Hugh carrying the flag; Robert of Normandy, black as pepper; and Tancred and Bohemond with their helmets. All the other princes spurred towards the ditch like a flight of falcons. However each of the ladders was in a poor state: they had been flung down into the ditch one after the other. This had greatly angered our men. They were going at the walls with pikes and hammers and chipping the stone away. The Saracens flung pitch down onto them from above and tipped boiling wax onto them. If it had not been for the shields they sheltered under, our men would have suffered severe burns. My lords, now let me tell you about an amazing miracle: how Wicher escaped and under what star, and Eurvin with him, from the mad infidels.

113

Jerusalem was a very strong city surrounded by high walls. The princes and lords attacked it ferociously. They brought their siege engine up close to attack with the battering ram, thinking they could knock down the wall: but much good it did them, because it was backed up inside by rubble and mortar. The wicked Turks had captured Wicher and Eurvin and were dragging them off to imprison them in the keep. But the lion-hearted Wicher seized the emir Malcolon, and Eurvins courageously seized the other one – Ysabar, King of Barbais. They flung them down from the wall willy-nilly. This was a prodigious feat, and ensured they did not get killed. Malcolon clutched the good duke of Bouillon whilst Ysabar ran to Robert the Frisian, begging him for mercy at the top of his voice: 'Noble lord, we beg you in God's name not to kill us! If you want to seek a ransom for the pair of us we will do anything you ask in full'. 'This is how you can save your skins', said the duke, 'give us back two of our men from captivity in exchange for you two'. 'That is really demeaning', replied the pagans. 'Better to be killed and beaten to death with a stick than to regain our freedom for such a low price. We still have 14 of your people in prison who came here as part of Peter the Hermit's army. We will give you back the 14 and the two in exchange; and moreover you will get an Aragonese mule. You shall have fine bezants with no admixture of copper or brass; five vermilion silken cloths and a green silken fabric. This whole region belongs to us; we swear on our faith to keep this bargain and guarantee it on our loyalty'. 'Indeed we do', said Malcolon, 'and on Mahomed, whom I would not renounce even if I were to be burnt to a crisp'. When the duke heard all this he looked down and chuckled secretly into his shield. 'Just listen to this madness!' he said to Count Robert. 'We certainly fell on our feet when we took these men prisoner. Sound the retreat straight away and let us fall back; we will renew the attack on another occasion. We will take the city at the pleasure of God and St Peter'.[114] 'Blessed be God' replied Count Robert. He sounded the retreat in clarion tones; the Franks dropped back from the din and swirl of the attack. They took the two pagans to their tent. A shiver ran down Cornumarant's spine when he saw this, and he scowled in angry discomfiture.

114

Eurvin of Creel and Wicher the German were up on the wall amongst the pagans. They wore shining white hauberks and their swords were drawn, splashed and stained with brains and blood. They struck about them fiercely in the rage of battle, but the force of infidel pagans was too great for them. Wielding large thick maces and hinged flails, big lead clubs and heavy millstones, they smashed down blows onto helmets and bodies. The brave-hearted pair struck them in turn: indeed they

---

[114] St Peter was of course the first Bishop of Antioch, and the main church there was dedicated to him: Cahen, *La Syrie du Nord* p. 130.

killed 15 Turks. Now may God watch over them! The evil Cornumarant bellowed at the top of his voice: 'Christians, surrender yourselves if you want to come out of here without losing your limbs. Your defence is hardly very impressive – I wouldn't give as much as a pair of gloves for it. Mahomed and Tervagant will be beside themselves with joy'. When our lords heard the King issuing these orders, they realised that all their fighting strength was not worth even two bezants; they surrendered to him under heavy pressure. The French made their way back to their tents, many feeling downcast. They headed for Godfrey's tent, which was tall and lofty with a finial of brightly glittering gold, taking with them two very apprehensive Turks. There was a multitude of our princes, too many for me to count. The two Turks were standing there, grey-haired, tall and strong, with large white eyes. They were fluent in Latin and the vernacular because they had learnt them a long time ago.[115] Each was in charge of 10,000 Persians; they were amongst the intimates of the emir Sultan.

115

The Turks were in the tent of dark-coloured silk. The princes and marquis of God's army assembled to hear what they had to say for themselves. The good Duke of Bouillon addressed them: 'Pagans, you should believe in God, Who was hung from the Cross, born of a Virgin, and died and came back to life: I shall be favourably disposed to you as long as I live'. The bull-necked Ysabar replied: 'By Mahomed, I may well be killed for saying this, but even if you were to give us enough gold to stretch from here to Paris, not a single one of us would convert to your religion. Our God is very powerful; he just happens to be asleep. If he were to wake up, take it from me that you would not be able to stay in this country for long'. The good duke roared with laughter at this. Now Garsion appeared in his grey mantle: he recognised the kings very well because he had been brought up alongside them. He made for them and kissed their faces, and sat them down next to him as all our barons watched. He said to the duke of Bouillon: 'These two prisoners you have taken are kings whose power extends all the way to the gates of Luitis. If they so wish you shall have Jerusalem – you can have my oath on it'. 'Shut up', said Malcolon, 'Handing the city over would be a terrible disaster. I would rather have both of us killed than let these people have the tower which David built or the Temple which his son raised on high. In exchange for us two what we will give is up to 16 captives, two mules laden with pure gold and velvet, and 1500 barrels of good strong wine as well as 200 packhorses laden with hard biscuit'. 'If I can be sure of this, you may go free and will not be harmed'. said the duke of Bouillon. 'You can', said Ysabars, 'I am under an obligation. Any agreement and promise I make with you will be kept'.

---

[115] A rare reference to the issues of communicating across cultures.

116

'My lords', said Ysabars, 'listen to me for a moment. I want you to be clear that you can take me at my word. Tie a rope round each of us and let us climb up the ladders onto the wall long enough to give orders to the pagans that you are to be given the possessions [we agreed] and your Franks freed from prison. If we show any signs of going back on the deal, tug us down and cut off both our heads and limbs'. 'We shall do as you suggest', said the duke of Bouillon, 'but I shall arm myself and come with you'. They led the kings to the Gate of David and erected a ladder; imagine the two pagans shinning up it. Each had a rope knotted round him; the duke of Bouillon followed close behind with drawn sword at the ready, the lettering visible on the blade, so that if the pagans took it into their heads to untie the rope binding them he could plunge the blade straight into their bodies.[116] He had an entourage of 10,000 French. Ysabars of Barbais climbed up onto the wall and called for Cornumarant: he came over to him. 'My lord', said Ysabars, 'you are my liege lord. I do not want to return to you or to anybody else until I have discharged my promise to the French. The 14 captives you have in prison, the two knights whom you detest, two Arabian mules with loads of silver and gold strapped to their backs and 200 packhorses laden with hard biscuits – that is the price you will have to give to get us back if you think we are worth it'. Cornumarant's heart missed a beat when he heard this. 'Ah, lord Mahomed, praise be to you!' he said. 'I wouldn't have wanted to lose these two for 14 cities'. He promptly declared a truce with our French until the sun went down. He turned and left immediately. Climbing the steps of the great Tower of David, he had the captives summoned from their cells. They were overjoyed that God had saved them. He had each one richly dressed and wrapped in rich silks and sat on mules with felt saddles. Eurvin and Wicher were richly equipped and sent on their way with the rest of the promised ransom. They drew back the bars on the gates of the Tower of David and set the French and their booty on their way. Then they closed the gate with its tight hinges and huge oak beams carefully shaped and reinforced; meanwhile the prisoners went on their way, liberated by the grace of God. Our lords were overjoyed when they saw them. Shouts of 'By the Holy Sepulchre!' went up on all sides. 'My lords', said Ysabars, 'I have kept my promise in all particulars'. 'Indeed you have', said the Duke. 'Go in the name of God, and may His will be done'. The Turks were unbound and you can imagine that they made a quick getaway up and over the walls into the city. Cornumarant kissed and hugged them. A thousand drums were sounded in the valleys down from the city, and Mahomed was worshipped in gratitude for the return of the two Turks. Meanwhile our lords made their way back to their billets and bivouacs. There was ample food for the whole of the holy army, and everyone had his fill of food and drink. Night fell again as the day came to an end. Bohemond and Tancred mounted guard over the army of the Lord with 700 knights all with green-sheened jewel-studded

---

[116] Swords with inscriptions are well attested: see Nicolle, 'Armes et armures' p.22 note 7.

helmets. However the Turks caught them out that night. They flung Greek fire into their siege engines, which were burnt and the battering ram went up in flames; the ladders too were burnt in the ditches, and no man could have prevented it. Many of the tents were burnt too. Now the pagans were stronger than ever, and you can imagine the anger and frustration this induced in our men. The Bishop of Mautran bolstered their morale. 'My lords and noble Christians, do not lose heart', he said. 'All this is happening by the will of God, who was hung on the Cross. If he so commands, you will take Jerusalem'. 'That is absolutely true', said the lords. They were left feeling happy and reassured that they were doing the right thing.

117

Now our Christians have ample supplies throughout the army. The Turks inside Jerusalem did not hesitate: they assembled in front of the holy Temple, coming and going. They brought the King of Jerusalem there accompanied by the grey-haired Lucabel and a large number of other pagans. Cornumarant rose and spoke a few words. 'My lords and noble Saracens, listen to what I have to say. You have served me well and I have held you in high regard. The French have laid siege to us; they are very determined. If they can, they will take my city by force, and frankly I would rather have my head cut off than have them deprive me of my inheritance so ignominiously. I am going to seek the help of the emir Sultan. He cannot but take pity on my plight. If I can secure his help, be assured that you will have me back here inside a month. You have plenty of bread and wine and corn inside the city, and the French outside are in a bad way – most of them have suffered severe wounds and exhausted themselves in their attempts on the walls, and they are in no state to mount another attack until they have recovered. Before then I will have brought all the forces of the Orient to you'. Corbadas heaved a deep sigh as he listened to his son. He tore his hair, ripped at his beard, and bitter tears streamed from his eyes. He fell down in a dead faint because he was so upset about his son. When he came round, he lamented loudly: 'Alas, Jerusalem! I have held you for so long, and now I am losing my son and all my inheritance for your sake. What of it if the whole Temple were sent up in flames by Greek fire, the city tumbled and the wall smashed down, and the great Tower of David with its banded marble battered in by innumerable crossbow bolts? I don't care what happens to me if my gods have let me down'. He was clutching a knife of razor sharpness, and would have plunged it into his heart if he had not been relieved of it. Cornumarant his son did his best to comfort him, raining kisses on his face and embracing him tightly.[117]

---

[117] Reminiscent of the scene in the *Antioche* where Garsion injures himself cutting off his beard and has to be restrained by his son, who is then sent as an envoy to seek help: laisses 189–94.

118

The King of Jerusalem was beside himself. He wrung his hands and tore at his hair, cursing Jerusalem, the Temple and everything which surrounded it and the Sepulchre of God which had given him so much trouble. His son Cornumarant called him firmly to his senses. 'Alas, my King and lord', he said, 'have you completely taken leave of your senses? You know full well that all these French are condemned to death. I shall have every last one of them brought to you bound as a captive, then have them thrown staggering into your prisons. I will bring the might of the empire to you all the way to the capital Mecca'. The King kissed Cornumarant on the face at hearing this; he embraced him and kissed him for joy. Cornumarant had however made him happy on a false premise.

119

'Noble King', said Cornumarant, 'do not worry yourself – I will go and seek help from the emir of Persia.[118] There will not be a single Saracen left in Almeria or all the way through the pagan kingdom as far as the Withered Tree; I will have assembled every last one for your army as long as breath remains in my body'. 'My noble son', said Corbadas, 'come here and give me your oath on it'. Cornumarant gave him his hand and pledged his word. 'May Mahomed give you his blessing, my noble nephew', said Lucabel. 'But how are you going to manage to get out of this well-defended city without those filthy Frankish bastards seeing you?' 'Let me explain my plans', said Cornumarant. 'In the early evening get our men armed and have them lead a skirmish from one side of the city whilst I leave from another part; I shall be fully armed and carrying my burnished sword, and I shall lead Plantamor my Nubian warhorse; with my large flower ornamented shield hung from my neck. I shall also carry a horn. Once I have made it to the waste ground I shall sound it at full blast; you will easily hear it and it will be a signal that I am safe and sound'. The Saracens all shouted as one: 'Cornumarant has a good plan: may God be with him!' Day waned and night approached. That evening Robert of Normandy was on guard duty for the army of God, with a force of 700 knights. The Turks and Saracens did not wait: they took up position in front of the Tower of David with 15,000 Turks ready to launch an attack. Cornumarant armed himself splendidly. He put on a mailshirt with a chainmail torso; he tied on a green-sheened helmet which glittered and glistened; he buckled on his sword with its gold handle, long and wide, razor sharp, smooth and burnished; they hung his shield of burnished gold round his neck; and they brought his Nubian steed Plantamor, Butors of Salorie leading him by the reins. Cornumarant leapt on and took the reins. Then he seized a spear and brandished it ostentatiously. He took the horn of Herod, which had a resounding tone that could be heard from a league and

---

[118] This mirrors Sansadoine's mission in the *Antioche*.

a half away. They unbolted the Gate of St Stephen and opened the Gate of David abruptly: the Turks streamed out to attack.

120

The Turks poured out through the Gate of David whilst Cornumarant left through the Gate of St Stephen. He paused until he heard the din of battle rising. The Turks fell on the army, shouting their battlecry; Robert of Normandy pushed them back effectively. Our men were armed and quick to respond: they all spurred towards the spot where the Franks were being attacked. The Turks fell back, retreating and closing the gate behind them: none lost his life. Meanwhile Cornumarant spurred on his Arab steed Plantamor straight through the middle of the army unopposed. He made his way across the waste ground. Two knights, armed and carrying weapons, happened on him. Once found they were quick to realise he was a Turk and challenged him loudly saying: 'You shall not pass!' Cornumarant heard them but did not retreat. He did not feel a single flicker of fear in his veins: he gave Plantamor his head, positioned his lance and struck one of the Frenchmen full on. He plunged the burnished spearhead right into his heart and knocked him off his horse with the full thrust of the lance. His companion saw red at this. He spurred towards Cornumarant and with a sure aim hit him in the middle of the shield and split it in two. However the mailshirt was so strong that no link broke. Cornumarant spurred on his Arab steed Plantamor, well aware that he should not hang around. He flashed past like an arrow out of a bow, and would have covered 60 full leagues before midday if he had not been prevented. The [second] knight cried: 'Mercy, Holy Sepulchre! Alas, you French lords, see how he is getting past you. If this Turk gets away you will pay a heavy price!' The good Duke of Bouillon heard his voice; without a moment's trepidation or hesitation he went spurring up faster than a crossbow bolt could fly. The moon was shining brightly, its rays pouring down. Godfrey reached the knight and found him gibbering.

121

It was a beautiful quiet night and the moon shone brightly. The duke of Bouillon gave his horse its head and galloped to the knight he had heard crying out. The knight came spurring to meet him, and explained to him that a Turk was getting away and was going to carry a message to the Sultan of Persia asking for reinforcements. 'He has just killed my companion in single combat; I struck him and broke my lance, but I didn't manage to unseat him from his horse and it wasn't enough to prevent his mission; he is getting his horse to go faster than an archer can launch a crossbow bolt when he has to shoot'. The duke was overcome at hearing this. He would have loved to chase Cornumarant, but had no idea which way he had gone. He started to shake with rage and frustration; he swore by the Sepulchre, where he hoped to worship, that he would follow Cornumarant for as long as it took to cut his head off. He rode after the Turk. May God come to his aid! The noble and valiant Cornumarant made his escape. Once he reached the waste ground he sounded his horn loudly enough for it to be heard in the army and in the fair city of Jerusalem. At this the pagans danced up and down with joy. The knight meanwhile came and cried: 'Alas, lord Bohemond, you were too slow off the mark. The good duke of Bouillon, whom you hold in great regard, is pursuing a Saracen but is not going to catch him'. Duke Bohemond listened and ordered a horn to be sounded. At this you might have seen the princes swinging into their saddles, seizing their lances and protecting themselves with their shields. Bohemond turned [and rode off] with his closest associates, asking the other knights to stand guard over the army. His entourage rode after him, determined not to turn back until they retrieved the Saracen, dead or alive. Now let us turn our attention from the barons for a moment, and also from the duke of Bouillon and his exploits: we shall come back to them in due course. Instead I am going to tell you about the proud Cornumarant. As he rode through the dawn across the waste ground he came face to face with Baldwin of Edessa at first light.[119] Baldwin was making his way to the army of God at Godfrey's summons. He was riding such a fine horse that you could not have found a better one anywhere in Persia. He rode at the head of a company of 300 young men wearing hauberks and helmets, fierce as wild boars. Baldwin of Edessa saw the Turk making his way down into a small dip through which his path led. He spurred his horse towards him, determined on a confrontation. Cornumarant felt a spark of fear seeing him and all his company riding behind him. Unsurprisingly he did not hang around: he spurred on the tireless Plantamor so hard that the rowels drew blood. Imagine the horse covering the ground faster than any bird or falcon could have flown. Baldwin shouted after him: 'You're not going to make it, you know. Provided God stops Prinsaut from stumbling I am going to drag you back to the army like it or not'. Imagine the sight of lord Baldwin spurring on the warhorse, his golden spurs glittering as he did so, and the Aragonese steed Prinsaut galloping at full tilt, leaping high in the air and skimming over the ground. Provided he managed not to fall he was gaining on the pagan. Before the sun could rise enough to gain any strength he had closed the gap to near enough to throw a bean. The pagan's horse was starting to sweat. Cornumarant saw this with consternation. As the horse galloped he massaged its ears, stroking them up and down with his hand; the animal was doing well not to collapse to the ground. His mount began to find its second wind.

122

The pagan carried on determinedly making his escape. Baldwin rode in hot pursuit, pushing his horse to the utmost. The two men had ridden right out of sight and

---

[119] Baldwin would inherit the Kingdom of Jerusalem from Godfrey; Cornumarant would have inherited it from Corbadas. It is appropriate that the two meet in combat. At the end of the poem Baldwin kills Cornumarant.

out of earshot. Prinsaut was gaining on Cornumarant faster than the wind chases a cloud, and ran him to earth next to a rocky pinnacle. Baldwin shouted to him at the top of his voice in a way which could brook no misunderstanding: 'Turn and face me, pagan! Time for you to suffer!' Cornumarant heard him and his heart leapt into his mouth. Seeing that Baldwin's entourage were some way back, he swung Plantamor round ready for combat. He thundered down on Baldwin faster than a falcon dropping from a cloud. Baldwin struck him hard and split his shield; his mailshirt was so strong that not a single link broke. He slammed the full force of the lance into Cornumarant's chest but did not dislodge him: the Turk retained his seat, and struck Baldwin with his tempered stiletto. Baldwin's shield was about as much use as a hemlock stem and Cornumarant struck and ripped his hauberk. The blade went all the way to Baldwin's body, and he cried out 'Come to my aid, Holy Sepulchre!'

123

When Count Baldwin realised he had been struck, he flew into a rage and drew his sword. Before Cornumarant could move quickly enough to draw his sword, the Count struck him so hard down through the middle of his helmet of beaten gold that he sent the flowers and jewels flying. He cut through the hood of the mailshirt, good quality though it was, and cut through his head as far as he could; if his blow had landed better he would have sliced the head in two. King Cornumarant struck him in turn with a blow worthy of a real man, smashing and splitting the shield round his neck and ripping through the fine links of the mailshirt, and coming within a whisker of killing him. Cornumarant yelled: 'Take that, you bastard! Did you really think I was so frightened that I was going to hide behind my shield for the sake of one single Frenchman? You made a mistake on the day you came across the sea to avenge your God Jesus, you and your pathetic infidel friends. You are wasting your time. You will all be utterly squashed if I can make my escape, every last one of you killed and destroyed, because I am going to the emir Cahu to get help. I will bring back with me all the forces of the empire as far as Arthur's Wood. The Franks will be flayed alive and their princes hanged!' When Count Baldwin heard the Turk say he was going to seek help, rage overcame him. 'Pagan', he said, 'do not wait but tell me who you are, may God have mercy on your soul'.

124

'Listen to me, pagan', said Count Baldwin. 'Tell me who you are: do not try and pretend'. 'Very well', said the Turk, 'on condition that you then tell me your name too'. 'All right', said Count Baldwin. 'Sir', said the King, 'my name is

Cornumarant and I am the son of Corbadas who rules over Jerusalem.[120] The fief is his, and after him will be mine; all his lands and castles will come to me. Now tell me straight away who you are, then do your worst. I certainly shall'. 'Pagan', said the Count, 'you are someone of very high rank. My name is Baldwin, if you can take me at my word. I am the brother of the valiant Duke Godfrey and the noble-hearted Count Eustace'. 'You have an impressive family', said Cornumarant. 'I know for a fact that Godfrey will be king [of Jerusalem].[121] Now, enough of talking: let us get down to the fighting'. He slung his shield across his arm and rushed forward. He was about to land a grievous blow with his sword when he saw Baldwin's entourage coming down a slope. He could see straight away that if he delayed he was lost; so he spurred Plantamors, who leapt forwards and galloped away faster than a bowshot. Baldwin did not hang back in his pursuit. Now may God protect him as part of His divine plan, because he will find himself in a very perilous situation before he returns.

125

Cornumarant rode off at great speed, turning for Barbais; Count Baldwin followed him at top speed on his Aragonese [warhorse] Prinsaut who had tremendous stamina. Now may God who made the heavens and the dew watch over him, because before he returns he will be injured, with more than 30 cuts. King Cornumarant met with his own side to the tune of some 10,000 men, all armed, who were riding through the waste land to defend their land. Orquenais rode in the lead bearing the battle standard. Cornumarant was delighted to see them. Recognising Orquenais, he shouted out his warcry, and the Saracens flocked towards him in consternation as they recognised their lord. His shield was holed, he held his sword drawn in his hand, and they could see deep cuts in his helmet and blood running down his head: every one of them was appalled at the sight. Without uttering a single word they made furiously for Baldwin: the King was in the lead, delighted at the helpful turn of events. Baldwin saw the whole place crawling with Turks, and was mortally terrified, you can be sure. He urged Prinsaut on and gave him his head. Cornumarant shouted to him: 'The game is up for you. You have ridden too far ahead and left it too late to turn back. Your head will be cut off before evening falls!' 'You will have to pay for it', said Count Baldwin. 'If God chooses to help me, I don't give much for your boasting'. Now picture his companions riding along the valley. No chance of a truce or any negotiations: each of them lowered his lance with its stiff pennant and made for the Turks full of the lust of battle. How many shattered lances and pierced shields ensued, how many mailed hoods were ripped and how many hauberks torn through. Saracens and pagans were left

---

[120] The Old French word is 'vassal': see T. Venckeleer, 'Faut-il traduire VASSAL par "vassal"? Quelques réflexions sur la lexicologie du francais médiéval', *Mélanges de linguistique, de literature et de philology offerts à J. R. Smeets*, (Leiden, 1982) pp. 303–16.

[121] Even Cornumarant affirms the eventual success of the Crusade.

gaping in death. Count Baldwin found a lance, taking it from the hands of a Turk who had been killed. He spurred towards Cornumarant, giving his horse its head, and landed such a blow on his striped shield that he sent him sprawling onto the ploughed land and seized Plantamor by the reins. He was just about to lead away the chestnut-quartered warhorse when Orquenais struck him with his sharp lance; 14 pagans followed suit, one after the other knocking his shield right away from his neck. But God came to save the Count in his renowned strength. He left Plantamor peacefully in the middle of the battlefield and struck a Saracen, Fanon of Valdoree. The Count sliced him in half all the way down to his entrails and knocked him dead from his horse into some bushes. A Turk grabbed Plantamor's reins and led him down the valley back to Cornumarant, who leapt immediately into the gilded saddle. The sun was blazing down relentlessly and the ground was baking hot, so much so that it was full of tiny cracks in some places. This caused great discomfort for our men: not one got to the end of the day without his face burned raw by the heat.

126

As the battle got going it was a large one: our men were unable to withstand the full force of the *mêlée*. There were only 400 of our knights compared to another 9,000 Saracen reinforcements as some who lived in the mountains rode down to help them. It is hardly surprising that they found this pretty alarming. Count Baldwin rallied his troops and gave orders to fall back to Jerusalem; however they were completely unable to find a way, path or track to get them there, and the Turks attacked them unconstrained, swarming round them and throwing weapons. Cornumarant cried: 'There is no way they will get out of here alive!' Count Baldwin was enraged when he heard this. He would have been quite capable of getting away from the Turks and outrunning them, but had no intention of leaving his men to be decapitated. The Count called them together and addressed them as follows: 'My lords and battle companions, do not despair! Let each one of you fight as best he can and sell his life dearly. Let us stick together as long as we can. If we can just manage to defend ourselves until nightfall, we need not fear them by as much as a *denier*'. With that they rode in close order round a rocky outcrop, and saw an old castle in the middle of a pond. The reeds had grown up tall, strong and thick, so closely packed that they were like a forest where one might go for pleasure. The earth between them was dry and the sandy banks were pitted with holes. Large numbers of leeches had sought out the shade there, hiding from the hot sun. They attached themselves in the hollow [stems] of the reeds, ready to go and cool off in the water when it rained. Anyone who went into the reedbed faced certain death. Baldwin of Edessa had no inkling that he needed to watch out for trouble. 'I should like to suggest that all of you go and take refuge in that castle', he said. 'I shall go and hide myself outside it in the reedbed. When the pagans come to stage an attack, I shall hasten back to the army of God to tell them what has happened. They will not catch up with me: my horse is too good for that'. 'We are happy to agree', said his companions. They lost no time in taking refuge in the castle, ready to be the target of the pagan attack.[122]

127

Baldwin and his men made their way back to the castle. They evaded the Turks, yelling 'Montjoie!' Pushing the Turks back a good acre, they then surged into the castle. Meanwhile Count Baldwin turned his horse about and, making for the reedbed, concealed himself in it. Now may God watch over him in His holy kindness! The leeches sensed him coming and played him a horrible turn.[123] They came swarming out of the crevices and the hollow reed stems. They sank their teeth into the flanks and ribs of his fine warhorse, clamping onto its hide in at least 30 places, whilst the horse swallowed many as it tried to bite them off.[124] The pagans launched a fierce assault on the castle mound whilst those inside defended themselves stoutly. The Turks did not stand as much as a *denier*'s chance of making any impact because there was only one entrance, the ditches were very deep and it was entirely surrounded by the reedbed where Baldwin was having a very unpleasant time. He had sharp-teethed leeches crawling all over him and slithering in through the chain mail of his hauberk. It felt as though he had been seasoned with pepper. They bit him in more than 200 places, sucking his blood from his veins. In fact it was amazing that they did not kill him, as indeed they would have done if God had not taken pity and come to his aid. Cornumarant called for Orquenais. 'There is one Frenchman who did not take refuge in that castle. He has pursued me and given me real grief, and his warhorse outpaced mine and wore it out. He is in the reeds, I am sure of it. Set them on fire and we shall soon smoke him out'. They hurried to do his bidding in evil determination. Before long the reeds had caught light and were well ablaze. Baldwin saw the fires and the burning reeds and was terrified he was going to die. He invoked Jesus: 'Father, Alpha and Omega at whose behest I was born, come to my aid now if You so choose. Help me and my horse get out of this situation – I am afraid they have bled my warhorse dry'. With that the leeches fell off immediately. Baldwin turned about, protecting himself with his shield and his sword glittering in his right hand. As soon as he emerged from the reedbed he spurred away, Cornumarant

---

[122] Baldwin did indeed hide in a reed bed, but not here and not on the First Crusade: the episode was after the battle of Ramleh. The reeds are found only in Ibn-al-Qalanisi: see *Damascus Chronicle* p. 56 and discussion in Introduction.

[123] The Old French says 'siffloi', whistling: I have taken it in a more widely attested meaning since leeches do not whistle, or indeed have teeth. The passage is startlingly vivid compared to the conventional topoi of much of the rest of the poem, and there is no parallel in the *Antioche*.

[124] Dangerous: AA VI.6 comments that some pilgrims choked to death after swallowing leeches in water.

caught sight of him and called to the pagans: 'Look, noble Saracens, he is getting away!' With that imagine hordes of Turks on his heels. They will suffer greatly before they return because they are heading straight into the arms of Bohemond and Tancred, Godfrey of Bouillon and the sturdy Robert of Normandy, and Count Hugh carrying the banner, and the noble barons beloved of God.

128

So Baldwin went spurring off, blood dripping from his ribs and his sides. His warhorse was bleeding too: this bothered him more because he was worried that it might fail beneath him – though that worry was unfounded because it carried on vigorously. Cornumarant meanwhile spurred on the swift Plantamor. As they came up to the waste land he was gaining on the Count, and in my opinion they were just about to join in combat when our lords saw him and made for him shouting. Cornumarant was thrown into total consternation. He flung both his spear and a parting shot at Baldwin: 'Go to the devil, Frenchman!' Then he gave his swift warhorse its head, turned round and sped back to the pagans, shouting to them at the top of his voice: 'My lords, prepare yourselves! Look, the French are spurring towards you! In my estimate there are at least 30,000 of them. Anyone who comes out safe and sound will thank Tervagant for it!' He spurred Plantamor and turned round, his sole aim to make it back to the East. The other pagans scattered and made their escape into the surrounding hills and mountains. Now imagine our princes riding up. They came upon a blood-soaked Baldwin. The Duke was astonished to see his brother and made to kiss him and talk to him Baldwin however shouted to him: 'Don't wait about – help all my men who are down in that valley!' The barons streamed off, seizing their swords. They killed and slaughtered every last one of the Turks they found attacking the castle [in the reedbed]. Those who had taken refuge in the castle came out beaming, overjoyed and delighted, rushed up to the princes and flung their arms round them. The lords looked at the huge reedbed all aflame and saw 100,000 leeches writhing on the ground, dying in large numbers in agony from [their burns in] the fire or crawling off into deep crevices. The lords looked at them then turned away making the sign of the Cross. They came up to Baldwin, who by now was on the verge of fainting and whose Aragonese horse Prinsaut was weak for lack of blood. The noble Count lay down on a hillside, and Prinsaut did not move an inch from the spot. Our barons came running down, all weeping. Godfrey seized his brother and raised him to his feet; he kissed him on the eyes and lamented his state: 'Alas, my brother! He who has brought you to the point of death has plunged me into grief. Alas, Jerusalem, how much we suffer for you. It is for you that I am losing my beloved brother'. The noble Thomas of Marle had a very powerful written talisman.[125] He held it above Baldwin's head and made

---

[125] The letter serves as a token. See M. Clanchy, *From Memory to Written Record: England 1066- 1307*, (Oxford, 1993, second edition), pp. 253–93 for the symbolic power of the written record: for example in 1193 the Abbot of Glastonbury physically placed a

the sign of the Cross – and the baron promptly leapt to his feet. The princes and barons were overjoyed. They lifted him onto a horse chosen for its comfortable ambling gait and had Prinsaut led along on the right at a gentle pace.[126] Count Baldwin went along telling them all about how he had chased King Cornumarant on his mission to beg help from the Sultan, and how the leeches had attacked him on all sides in the extensive reedbed. The barons found all this most entertaining. They retired to their tents exhausted, still determined to attack Jerusalem. They gave Baldwin some food, which revived him, and two sergeants were charged with looking after the Aragonese Prinsaut.

129

The company of Jesus came back to the army determined to mount an assault on Jerusalem. King Cornumarant overlooked nothing; he sent his messengers to the four corners of the waste land. He sent a letter to Dodequin of Damascus ordering him to provision his castles at Barbais and Tiberias. The King rode so fast across Syria that he was already past the Silver Bridge and on his way. In fact the Turk made such good progress – may the Devil be his guide! – that he arrived at the Sultan's kingdom of Persia. He happened on the emir and the King of Nubia in a field beneath Sarmasane, along with the emir Aupatris and Flanbaut of Orquenie, the King Calcatras, Abraham of Rusa, and the emir Sucaman who ruled Almeria. Each one had issued a summons to his army to attend because the emir Sultan had heard the news that the Christians had laid siege to Jerusalem: he needed to dispatch the pagan armies to the rescue. Imagine the sight of Cornumarant weeping and wailing and shouting. He flung himself off Plantamor and shouldered his way through the crowd. Catching sight of the Sultan, he threw himself abjectly at his feet, embracing his legs and kissing his hose. The white-haired Canabel lifted him up again. The Sultan addressed him to the point: 'Tell me, my noble and brave nephew Cornumarant, how are things at the great and well-equipped city of Jerusalem which your father Corbadas holds on my behalf?' 'By Mahomed, lord emir, the French have laid siege to it. They have surrounded it with a huge army and devastated our lands. Moreover they have knocked down the walls to a length of a lance and a half, and killed enormous numbers of our Turks. They are almost out of corn and oats: if they do not get help pretty soon they are dead men'. 'Noble nephew, you shall have help and my strength; such a great force indeed if I can get them all together that they will eat them all alive as if they were boiled meat. You shall have all your lands back in full. I intend to cross the sea in force to Pavia, and conquer France and Apulia and Romania'. That may well be his intention in an access of bravado, but he does not know much about the knights of God: they

---

charter on the altar as the clergy and people watched (p. 256). For written documents with quasi-magical powers see Paterson, *World of the Troubadours* pp. 201–02.

[126] A horse which ambles puts the two right feet down simultaneously then the two left feet; this is a more comfortable gait for an injured rider.

will take Jerusalem on Friday before the office of compline and give the lie to his words. My lords and faithful Christians, it is only right that I should tell you about the holy city which God granted to those who suffered terribly on His behalf. One morning Robert of Normandy arose. He consulted with the bishop of Mautran and the nobles on how best to set up the catapult.

130

Robert of Normandy got up one morning and had all the nobles in the army summoned. 'My lords', said the Count, 'please give me your attention for the love of God, and turn your minds to how best to take this holy city. Cornumarant has gone to seek help. There is no way you will be able to keep it once you have taken it with the whole empire of Persia coming here'. The bishop of Mautran, a well-schooled cleric, said to our lords: 'Listen to me, in the name of God! Last night God spoke to me. He told me that on the Mount of Olives there is a holy man who has spent the last 15 years shut in a rock. He is the key to taking the city. I urge all of you in the name of God to seek him out: when you return you will know how to take the city and smash through its walls'. 'My lord' said the barons, 'we shall do as you command'. They left their billets; imagine them setting off for the Mount of Olives. They looked everywhere but found no trace of any hermit; so imagine them coming back again. Actually he was there all along but this was the will of Jesus. They traipsed back to the bishop in a state of high dudgeon. 'Your reverence', said the barons, 'you spun us a fine story there. By our heads, you must think we are real fools and idiots sending us off to look for something about which you have no idea'. 'My lords', said the bishop, 'I have to agree. But come back with me; if you do not find him there you are all free to burn me on a pyre, but you all need to be barefoot and in your shirts'. 'We shall do as you ask', said the duke of Bouillon. With that they all dismounted from their well-rested warhorses. Each one stripped down to his shirt and the bishop made the sign of the Cross over them in the name of God. Picture them dressed just like pilgrims.

131

My lords, now listen to this glorious song all about how the city where God suffered [for us] was taken and completely liberated from Mahomed's people. A holy man lived right outside on the Mount of Olives: he saw the glory of God and bowed down in prayer.[127] The bishop sent our men to search for him. It was a Sunday which saw our lords make their way there, the day which saw Our Lord in prayerful procession with His holy Apostles. The French nobility – may God have mercy on them! – followed him that day all the way to the platform where the

---

[127] The hermit is attested in RA and AA: see introduction. The key role of the hermit is marked by a metatextual reference.

hermit lay prostrate deep in devotion. He called to our people, addressing them as follows: 'Listen to me, good Christians! May God have mercy on you! Tomorrow you will attack the city without a single death. Down there by Lord Gaston's castle you will find the timber to make the battering ram and a large catapult well nailed down on top. In the woods around Bethlehem you will find wood to make planks for the hoardings all around. Then you can attack the city with all your might! This means you will take it by humble means. That will be a symbol that God has no time for arrogance and villains'.

132

Once the hermit had addressed our lords, he blessed them in the name of God and they turned and left. The hermit had adjured them all strongly to observe the day of the Lord and do no work, to which they were happy to agree. So that day they held off any attack. The following Monday, as soon as day broke, they all armed and prepared. They ordered the army's carpenters to be assembled; Nicolas of Duras was a key figure along with the grey-haired Gregory. Our leaders went to the castle of Lord Gaston and found timber in a valley the other side of it which, once it had been planed, could be used to make the siege engine. It had been flung down and left there more than 30 years ago, and since then not a single inhabitant of the kingdom had abstracted one baulk and it had not been removed or taken away since that was what God wanted for his divine plan.[128] The leaders hitched their horses to the timber to the tune of 444 of them. Each was led back to Our Lord's army, dragging along one piece of timber after another; it was all thrown down in the space in front of the Gate of David. That was where the carpenters set it up and prepared it. They built a big battering ram with iron on the tip; then they built the siege engines which were reinforced in front with large crossbeams planed and lashed together. In the woods round Bethlehem they cut poles which they fixed on top of the engine, making plenty of holes for Greek fire. Nicolas and Gregory did a first-class job on the carpentry given that the previous time things had not worked out well. They lifted the engine up onto big wheels and rolled it along. Inside the city the Turks made an opposing engine which they set up right opposite the Christian one. But it will not do them a *denier*'s worth of good: before evening falls their engine will be elsewhere and its walls will have been broken and smashed. It was a Wednesday when all this was prepared. After compline that evening, when all was quiet, they took their engine up to the Gate of St Stephen right opposite the gate on the same level as the ditch. They protected it thoroughly in front with leather hides. They took turns to mount guard over it all night with 4,000 men until day broke.

---

[128] This is reminiscent of the stock of timber found by Tancred: in a startlingly graphic passage Ralph of Caen describes him overcome by dysentery, looking for a private spot and finding a stash of timber left by the Egyptians: *Radulphi Cadomensis Tancredus* (ed.) Edoardo d'Angelo (Turnhout, 2011), hereafter RC, 354–6 pp. 100–01.

133

My noble lords and knights, now listen to this glorious song which should be held in high esteem. It tells how Jerusalem was taken on this first attack.[129] On a Thursday morning when daybreak was imminent, the counts and princes got up throughout the army; so did bishops and abbots, sergeants and squires; and there were plenty of girls and noblewomen. The sun rose, and God made its rays burn. Now picture a lightly armed young soldier coming to give all our barons the news that Nicolas and Gregory had had the siege machine transported and erected opposite St Stephen, and a large catapult set up with the intention of smashing down and destroying the wall. When our barons heard this they all began to shout: 'Lord God, Holy Father, Who has dominion over all, may it be Your pleasure that we win Jerusalem!' And God granted their common wish. Godfrey of Bouillon did not hang back: he had the great horn blown aloud. This was a signal for those in the army to arm themselves: French and men from Berry, the seafaring Flemish, Normans and men from Ponthieu, Gascons and Poitevins and proud Lotharingians, Saxons and Welsh and warriors from Brabant, and men from Apulia and Romania who carried out many splendid feats. Picture the scene: masses of weapons glinting as they were waved around, and on the slope pennants and flags billowing in the wind and raised aloft to glitter in the sun. The force was huge and redoubtable: it covered a full league along the sandy ground [outside the walls]. Each of them had screwed up his courage to the maximum, and never had an army been more fitted to launch an attack. The King of Jerusalem went and leaned up against one of the windows in his splendid palace, looking down on our nobility: he was filled with blind rage. He raised his hand to curse them, and called down invocations on them in the name of Apollon, imploring him to make them suffer. At this imagine the Tafur king starting to shout: 'Where are all those reduced to destitution who need plunder? If they come to me now, they shall have a dozen *deniers*. Why? Because if God wills it so, today I intend to get enough plunder to load up seven mules!' So many people flocked to him that they must have numbered 10,000. They went to cut logs in the woods round Bethlehem which the King of the Tafurs used to make a large wooden protective cover; this was to be used as a shelter to batter through the wall and smash apart the stones, their lime and their mortar. And with God's help that is exactly what he did that day. Now you can hear all about a massive assault which gave no quarter and lasted all day until sunset.

134

It was daybreak on Thursday when our Christians all erected their siege engines, setting them up opposite St Stephen. For their part the Turks thronged onto the walls of the city. Each of them was comprehensively equipped to defend the place: they had heavy iron clubs and large forged hammers, crossbow bolts and

---

[129] The fall of Jerusalem is signposted by a reference to the poem.

curved bows of horn, and a brew of lead and pitch boiled together. Our battering rams were brought round in front of St Stephen, martyred in the name of God. In preparation for their assault from the scrub [around the city] the French raised a ladder up against the dark bronze of the wall, up against the tower built by David. A brave and determined squire swarmed up: he was the cousin of lord John of Alis. A Saracen sliced off both his hands at the wrist with his gleaming sword: unable to hold on, the squire tumbled from the ladder. Raimbaut Creton now climbed up, furiously angry. He got level with the battlements and sliced off the Turk's head. However there was only one of him and he retreated back down. The cry went up round the army that some of our men had already been attacked and wounded, and that a brave squire who had tried to attack had been killed. This sent a shiver up the spines of our barons. They had the trumpets sounded and the horns blown. The French heard the call to battle and launched themselves forward: the army advanced, each man afire with enthusiasm. And so a massive attack was launched on Jerusalem. The bishop of Mautran blessed our men, making the sign of the Cross over them in the name of Him Who was crucified, and clasping in his hand the Lance of Jesus Christ which pierced His beautiful body on the Holy Cross. He held it up in front of our men, and it had a big impact on morale: every single one pressed on eagerly towards Jerusalem. They smashed their way past the barbicans and the timber palings and crossbeams which the Turks had erected. Neither beam nor post was enough to stop them in their tracks, and they fought their way across the bailey all the way up to the main ditch. Meanwhile the catapult was ceaselessly firing at the wall, knocking apart the cement and the dressed stones. The Turks defended themselves desperately, each flinging sticks and stones, large rocks and thick stakes and firing off bolts of polished steel from their crossbows. The arrows showered down more thickly than hail or rain. The Turks threw down hot pitch and molten lead; then they set light to some Greek fire and flung it at our men in a volley of missiles so that the paint and varnish on their shields caught light. No hauberk no matter how strong or well made could protect them then, nor could any shield or leather jerkin or padded jerkin – they were burnt alive and nothing could save them. However the wind quickly swung round and back on the Turks, incinerating many of them up on the walls. This was the undoing of them all; as far as I know not one could have escaped alive had it not been for the fact that they all had vinegar to protect them, which sufficed to damp down and extinguish the fire.[130]

135

The assault was launched on all sides with great ferocity; men died in agony inside and outside the city. The women there had tucked up their clothes ready for action: every one of them, even the most noble, had her dress up at knee level. All of them were carrying water – a very sensible move – and some had filled their sleeves

---

[130] Vinegar was well known to be an effective means of extinguishing Greek fire: see Partington, *History of Greek Fire*, pp. 27–9; Jacques de Vitry, *Historia Orientalis* LXXXV p.341.

with stones. They all cried as loudly as they could: 'If anyone needs to drink, come and tell us in God's name and he shall have as much water as he wants in the name of the Virgin Mary! Let everyone fight to the death to defend body and soul: those who do will find themselves in the company of the angels enjoying eternal life in Heaven, where they will find their heart's desire'. Ah God! These words put heart into our men. 'By the Holy Sepulchre!' they all shouted in unison. They rode all the way to the ditch without drawing rein, more than a thousand at one fell swoop. Imagine the sight of Robert of Normandy spurring forward with the bold Duke of Bouillon, accompanied by Tancred and Bohemond. Count Hugh of Vermandois was brandishing his glittering sword; with him were Thomas lord of Marle, count Rotrou of Perche – no cowardice there, Steven of Albemarle sitting on his Syrian bay and all the other princes with their retinues. All of them stormed up to the gate, lances couched [to attack]. The Turks inside however mounted a stout defence. Huge numbers of arrows flew from Turkish bows, and large boulders were flung down to shatter; anyone on the receiving end found it no joke. Many heads were smashed in by stones from catapults. All our lords dismounted from their Syrian warhorses. Each took a steel pike or a heavy mallet or hatchet and smashed their way through the Gate of St Stephen by sheer force. They were on the point of getting in and seizing the city. However the Turks had another gate up on the walls, suspended by a chain: it was large and heavy and well armoured, firmly held up by a pulley. The Turks undid it from its fastenings and it fell with such a crash that the wall was shattered all across the ground. As it fell it took three knights with it, who were crushed down into the ground by it. St Michael received their souls and led them up into the presence of God.

136

Our nobles were much downcast by this. They had cut their way through to the Gate of St Stephen, but the Turks had let the other gate fall down. It took three of our knights with it, falling on top of them and crushing them into the earth; St Michael sang as he carried away their souls. Godfrey of Bouillon came running to the siege engine; he gave orders that the ditches were to be filled in with shovels then the engine taken right up next to the walls. The duke climbed up onto it and shouted at the top of his voice: 'Ahoy, noble lords and brave knights! For the love of God do not slacken your attempts to take the city: press forward as best you can'. The French found a second wind and renewed heart. They brought the battering ram up with such speed and force that they smashed it against the wall whilst the petrary flung enormous rocks. They knocked down a lance's length of the wall. The Turks and Saracens defended their position fiercely: they struck with large clubs and flung darts, struck blows with large iron hammers and threw stones – they were able to defend the walls to the chagrin of the Franks. They protected the walls with baulks of timber, and tipped down hot pitch, sulphur and boiling lead. Our men surged backwards, terrified of the molten lead, and the

Turks made them retreat two lances' length from the walls. Now imagine the King of the Tafurs and his rabble running up, dragging their wooden shelter with ropes. They were undaunted by any attack on them: they flung themselves down into the deep ditches and scrambled up the other side on hands and feet. They brought their shelter so close in that it brushed up against the wall, and erected it firmly above them such that they did not have to worry about crossbow bolts or stones being hurled. They dug away underneath it with spades and hoes and pulled the wall apart, taking out the cornerstones and prising apart the cement and the blocks. [The Turks, their attention distracted elsewhere, did not notice] because they were being attacked on 40 sides at once.[131] They defended themselves fiercely, fighting for their lives. Lord Thomas of Marle got off his warhorse and sought out the King of the Tafurs. He begged him to be allowed to form part of his assault, promising that he would become his vassal for his whole fief and would fight on his side against all comers. The King was more than pleased to agree. Thomas did homage to him then and there in the sight of everyone.[132] Pagans and Saracens raised a huge din to raise the morale of the Turks, yelping loudly. When they saw our men pressing in on them, they flung burning Greek fire at them. This set the battering ram on fire, to the great consternation of the French. It also landed on the siege engine and was in a fair way to burn when Duke Godfrey came spurring up and extinguished it straight away with wine which had turned to vinegar. This amazed our lords no end. The day was drawing to a close and the sun was setting. The French fell back from the attack. This was hardly surprising given their state of exhaustion. The women went amongst them quenching their thirst with fresh water which was badly needed: they were parched with thirst and several were fainting under the stress of it all.

137

This was a massive attack and deserves a full description. Before our men could conquer Jerusalem they had to endure huge pain and suffering. It was a beautiful clear day and evening was drawing in. The French retreated, unable to take any more. The good duke of Bouillon shouted: 'Alas, noble lords! This is no way to behave! I heard you all boasting on your way here that if anyone could bring you to Jerusalem and position you all the way round the walls, you would tear them apart with your teeth even if they had been made of steel. And now here you are, all too afraid to take the city. For my part, by the Sepulchre I intend to worship where the body of Jesus Christ was laid to rest, you will not see me abandon this siege engine until Jerusalem – for which we are suffering so much – has fallen and I can make my way in over this wall'. The barons were reduced to tears by this, saying to each other 'What a wonderful duke!' His words put new

---

[131] Thorp identifies a missing line here.
[132] An affirmation of the role of the Tafurs: one of the leading characters recognises their supremacy.

heart into the troops. That night not one man dared to go back to his quarters; they all stayed clustered round the siege engine to watch over the noble duke. Night fell again as the day came to an end. You might have heard horns blown inside and outside the city, the brass tones of trumpets, pipes and bugles; drums and tambours and flageolets being played; violins and flutes and vielles; Saracens and pagans wailing and ululating; and horns booming out in the mighty Tower of David. Torches were lit all the way round the walls; anyone listening would have heard it all with amazing clarity. They kept watch all night until daybreak. Meanwhile the rabble dug away all night until they had made a hole in the wall; then they blocked it up loosely, nobody daring to go through until the assault was launched. As soon as the sun rose on Friday morning the barons returned to the attack without delay. They flung themselves at the walls and the gate; the pagans defended themselves, on the edge of despair. The story I have heard is that at precisely the stroke of midday, the time at which Our Lord allowed His body to be raised on the true Cross to save His people, our people managed to bring a large section of the wall of Jerusalem crashing down.[133] The good duke of Bouillon put himself in considerable danger. He had the drawbridge of the siege engine dropped down onto the wall so that it was easy to come and go across it. The Saracens and pagans tried to cut it loose, but the duke of Bouillon was there and stopped them. Imagine him on the spot dealing out death and destruction, cutting off the heads of more than 20,000 pagans, starting to sweat from his efforts: he was a true wild boar in the combat. The King of the Tafurs came forward unable to contain himself any longer: he was desperate to be the first into Jerusalem. But lord Thomas of Marle is the one who will win all the attention by getting himself flung into [the city] from the points of spears.

138

There was a huge fight over Jerusalem. The good duke of Bouillon, renowned for his achievements, went head to head with the Turks with drawn sword, the blade splashed and soiled with blood and brains. Tancred and Bohemond went up onto the walkway protected by wicker shields with large numbers of our princes, each well armed. The Saracens threw their forces against them. The King of the Tafurs cried out to his people: 'In with you, gentlemen! The city has fallen!' Thomas of Marle saw that the Turks could not hold out. He stormed out of the ditch, his face smeared with blood, and reached the great square gate. A gap had been made in the wall where stones had been taken out. The noble lord cried out 'Marle!' to bring his men together. He had himself sent flying into [the city] from the spearpoints of 30 of his knights. That was an amazing feat which deserves high praise: it will be remembered down the centuries.[134]

---

[133] In fact at nine in the morning according to Mark 15:25.
[134] Thomas's feat has already been signposted at laisses 75 and 102. It is emphasised by use of *laisses enchaînées*.

139

There was a ferocious battle to take Jerusalem. The noble Thomas of Marle did something truly remarkable: he had himself raised up on the point of lances and flung over the walls into the city. Once he had landed on the walls he leapt straight to his feet and drew his sword, bounding down the slope to the gate. But he was not going to find it easy to get there. A Bedouin woman accosted him and landed a heavy mace directly on the top of his helmet and smashed it all in, strong as it was, sending him reeling unable to help himself. The Turks came swarming round to attack him and were on the point of beheading him with their drawn swords when the King of the Tafurs shouted: 'Help, by the Holy Sepulchre! Noble lords, enter [the city]! Jerusalem is taken and the Turks are defeated! You will soon see them dead and beheaded!' That was the signal for the rabble to fall on the pagans, sending them flying and tumbling dead one on top of another. Even so the Turks did not let up their attack on lord Thomas of Marle. The lord had a very valuable letter: as long as he had it on him he could not be hurt. Thomas did his utmost as his lust for battle welled up. Brandishing his drawn sword, its pommel of pure gold, he cut through the Saracens plunging it in as he went. He intended to seek a high price if he was to be killed. Anyone he attacked was not exactly going to need a doctor. Thomas saw the pagan woman gripping a steel dart, the same Bedouin woman who had brought him down. He approached her bent on a fight and she realised she was in trouble. She implored the noble lord out loud at the top of her voice: 'Please don't kill me, noble Frank. I want to foretell the manner of your death. No Turk or pagan will be able to wound you, and you will not come to any harm this side of the sea. It will be your lord who kills you and pronounces judgement on you'.[135] Thomas was filled with rage at her words, and struck her with his sword without a second thought, sending her head flying right over a rock. Imagine the din, the noise and the hubbub which arose. The good duke of Bouillon was up on the wooden shelter. He had ensured that the Turks were forced back from the walls. Indeed that day you might have seen the good duke inflicting bloody massacre. Thomas was at the gate slashing through the leather hinges, and the King of the Tafurs ran to help him. They began to raise the gate with a pulley until it was all the way up, then attached it with more than 30 of the rabble tying it with stout ropes. Then they went to launch a full frontal assault on the other gate and forced their way in, to their great delight. Imagine the scene: pagans being chased down the streets, killed and slaughtered, struck and impaled. The clergy began to give thanks to God with the '*Te Deum laudamus*', sung to glorify Him.

---

[135] As recounted in Suger's *Life of Louis VI*: see Table of Names for more detail. Clearly the author is well aware of Thomas's reputation, which makes his depiction as a hero the more puzzling.

140

It was a Friday, as those reading will find, that our Christian lords conquered Jerusalem.[136] They forced their way violently into the city at the same time as Jesus suffered for us. We are pretty sure that Thomas was the first in, having been raised up on lances. But the King of the Tafurs – if we can believe what we are told – had been the first to make an entry, all alone and with no companions. That was why Thomas swore fealty to him that same day, doing homage to him twice without demur. My lords, now listen to this glorious song. The princes and lords entered Jerusalem; so did the Flemish and the Normans, the French and the Burgundians. The pagans scattered left and right to find refuge. The duke of Bouillon went in hot pursuit, accompanied by Tancred and Bohemond, his brother Eustace and lord Raimbaut Creton plus plenty of others whose names we do not know. As they chased them down the streets they inflicted such slaughter that the blood and brains lapped around the fetlocks [of the horses].[137] The Saracens were crying out: 'Help, lord Mahomed! Have mercy on our souls and grant us your forgiveness, because our bodies are going to be destroyed. Alas, lord Cornumarant, we shall never see you again. Poor wretches that we are, we are waiting desperately for help'. Count Robert of Flanders went after Malcolon and sliced his head in half down to the chin with his steel sword. Ysabars was fleeing towards the Temple of Solomon when he was caught by Richard of Chaumont, who sliced him in half down to his lungs with his burnished sword. The pagans were wailing, yelling and ululuating like mongrels. Imagine all those beautiful pagan women dressed in quilted jackets in paroxysms of grief, crying at the tops of their voices: 'Alas, Jerusalem! It is not right that we should lose you like this. Apollon, noble lord, avenge us!' The King of Jerusalem was up in the main keep, next to a marble dais up in the Tower of David. He was wringing his hands, tearing at his silken [tunic], and tugging at his beard and moustache. He fainted four times one after the other. Lucabels picked him up and cradled him in his lap.

---

[136] Symbolic of Good Friday, though the city did in fact fall on a Friday. The battle of Antioch is also depicted in the *Antioche* as happening on a Friday even though it was actually a Monday: laisse 305. The Old French is clear that readers are referred to: 'si con lisant trovon'.

[137] RA commented famously that at the fall of Jerusalem 'equitabatur in sanguine ad genua, et usque ad frenos equorum' ('people were riding in blood up to their knees and it came up to the reins of the horses') 150. The Crusaders made a similar point in their letter to the Pope after the victory: *Letters from the East: crusaders, pilgrims and settlers in the twelfth and thirteenth centuries*, transl. M. Barber and K. Bate (Guildford, 2010) pp. 33–7. Reminiscent of the blood which flows in Revelation 14:20.

141

Jerusalem, strong and well equipped as it was, had fallen. You might have seen pagans fleeing down the streets, each doing his utmost to save himself. The Christians were killing them and inflicting massive slaughter: the road was awash with blood and brains. Robert of Normandy proved his worth that day; so did all the others and that is no exaggeration.[138] They unleashed huge bloodshed on the Turks and pagans. Some knew that their sister or wife or lady had fled from the slaughter in fear for her life. A large party of Turks fled towards the Tower of David; Raymond guaranteed their safety for a high price, a mule loaded up with genuine Syrian bezants: being bought off in this way was shameful. He granted them safe conduct into the Tower of David: anyone who heard the bargain could not but have found it criminal. The holy city was overrun that day; Saracens and pagans met a horrible and bloody death. A whole squadron was fleeing towards the Golden Gate, chased by their enemy Count Hugh on foot, without shield and brandishing his glittering sword, accompanied by large numbers of brave lords. They pursued the Turks all the way to the Golden Gate blessed by God, showing no mercy. They massacred them with their steel swords; every last one had his sword dripping with brains and the road was polluted with infidel blood. The Saracen women were in floods of tears, all crying and yelling as they cursed the land which had given birth to such a people. They fled towards the Tower of David, each leaving behind her wealth and her home. The rabble followed them and seized large numbers to have their wicked way with them, then robbed them of everything, hardly even leaving them their undertunics: this grieved Jesus, Son of the blessed Virgin Mary. What more can I say? The attack lasted so long that not one of the pagans survived other than those who had taken refuge in the Tower of David. The French nobility did not hesitate: each took possession of a house to live in with a cellar and a stone-built room.

142

By now the French were desperate for rest. Each seized a house or palace or cellar or great stone room or tower in front of a solar. They were all determined to seize booty, so much so that they nearly came to blows. The good duke of Bouillon did not waste his time; neither did Robert the Frisian famous for his many exploits, or the brave lord Thomas of Marle. These three had no intention of stabling their warhorses, grabbing houses or relaxing. On the contrary they ran to the Sepulchre to cleanse and beautify it, and to the holy Temple so dear to God. Each held a quarter of silken cloth in his hand. They went to kneel in front of the Sepulchre. They swept it clean of any dust, straw or filth, leaving neither soot nor splinter, dirt nor grime. Imagine the sight of the lords kissing the Sepulchre weeping for the pity of it, flinging themselves on it to embrace it, then going to the Temple to dress the altar where Jesus was offered up when He allowed Himself to be laid there

---

[138] Robert of Normandy is again singled out for less than obvious reasons.

They scoured the whole area below the cathedral clean.[139] Once they had done all this they made their way back to find somewhere to stay. They found a large rich palace outside the Temple [which no Frenchman had appropriated for himself] since God had designated it for the three of them to take their ease in.

143

Once the Duke had beautified and swept the Temple and arranged the altar, he and the two barons found a palace as yet unoccupied by any of our men right outside the door: this was because God had kept it aside safely for them. The keeper of the palace who had the keys was completely blind, unable to see any glimmer of light. He had locked and unlocked the Temple innumerable times. He knew all too well that our men had taken Jerusalem. When he heard the duke, he raised his voice as he begged for mercy. 'Do not kill me, noble Frank – I am ready to convert to Christianity!' On hearing this the duke approached him and flung the silken cloth he carried into this face. 'Here, keep this', he said. 'I have afforded you my protection'. The moment the cloth touched his eyes, a light went on in his head. His heart overflowed with joy. He told the duke that he had not been able to see for the last 30 years, and that now the silken cloth had restored his sight. The good Duke gave praise to God when he heard this tale. Then he took the cloth back and folded it up again. Each of them reverently held his section of it. The pagan led the Duke into the palace straight to his treasure: he unlocked it and signed himself and his wealth over to the duke. The duke accepted it and gave him protection. Then he was baptised in the temple of the Lord. The barons assembled together and gave orders to the other citizens to throw all the dead pagans out of the city, pile them up and burn them on a pyre. They got straight on with the job. They dragged the Turks out of Jerusalem, piled them into four heaps and set fire to each: the wind was in the right direction and they readily caught light. Meanwhile they buried our Christians with full honours, the Bishop of Mautran singing Mass over them. Then Bohemond blew the great horn and the French got ready to fight below Jerusalem, barons and princes comprehensively armed. They dragged their siege engine in front of the Tower of David, set up the petrary and sling. Inside the Tower of David, next to a panel of striped marble, Corbadas was leaning out of the main window which splashed light across the floor. He addressed the French, each of the barons and princes by name.

144

The King of Jerusalem was in a terrible state. He called for our lords and addressed them as follows. 'My lords', said Corbadas. 'Listen to what I have to say. This

---

[139] Literally cleansing the Temple from the ravages of the Saracens: see e.g. RM I.1 for rhetoric about the Temple being soiled by Saracen occupation.

tower is very strong, and you will have considerable trouble taking it. You can be sure of losing a good thousand of your men before you manage to get possession of it. My lords, let us be allowed to depart unharmed with all my household whom you see here. If you so order, I will hand this tower over to you but only if you give me a safe conduct'. Our barons granted his request. He descended the tower with Lucabel, his elder brother. The gates were opened and he led his people out numbering a good 7,400. They left Jerusalem: picture them making their way from it. The King set off on the road to Barbais tearing at his beard and pulling out his hair, lamenting non-stop that he was an unlucky wretch – if Lucabel had not been with him he would have committed suicide. So they all went on their way and may the Devil be their guide! The French lords, favourites of God, conquered Jerusalem and its striped palaces. All their equipment was brought inside [the walls]. The women went to the Temple. There was great rejoicing, with incense burning in houses and streets and sheets of cloth hung from on battlements and solars. The *Te Deum laudamus* was sung loudly by bishops, priests, clerics and abbots. Our Lord was fervently thanked and praised.

145

Ah God! What great joy there was on the day which saw Jerusalem taken and the great tower surrendered. Every last house, room and street in the city was hung with draperies and silken banners, with sumptuous curtains along them and stretched out above. The Bishop of Mautran said a Mass of absolution. That day the Host became the naked Body of God publicly on show to all. Ah God! Many tears were shed that day. After holy Mass the collection was taken up and handed to the bishop of Mautran: he shared it out amongst the poor and humble, not keeping back as much as the worth of a hemlock plant for himself. Then he blessed our people in the name of God Who made the clouds. Then the good people went back to their lodgings as objects of fear and respect. The princes held splendid court for eight days. As dawn broke on the Thursday morning, the nobles arose – may God love and support them.[140] They assembled in front of the holy Temple in a grassy expanse, a race never overcome or defeated in battle by infidel Turks; on the contrary they had smashed down plenty of towers to avenge God and taken many fertile lands in combat. They had mortified their flesh with pain and agony, some flayed with cold and hunger. No such people will ever be seen in this world.

146

Our revered forces were in front of the holy Temple, princes and barons and soldiers from many regions. The bishop of Mautran, clad in his stole and robes from singing Mass, held up in front of him the Holy Lance which wounded God

---

[140] Not quite accurate: the city fell on a Friday.

as He hung on the Cross, and was subsequently brought back to Antioch. He addressed our lords with the following proposition: 'My lords, you have taken this city. Now it would be a good idea to have a king to guard it and defend the surrounding countryside against the pagans'. 'You are absolutely right', replied the princes. At that the people shouted in unison: 'Let the city be given to the good duke of Bouillon, provided he is willing to take it on and the role suits him: then a crown of pure gold will be placed on his head'. The princes replied: 'You have made the right judgement. We concede everything to him because that is the right destiny'. The bishop of Mautran raised his hand, looked into the eyes of the good duke and bowed down to him. 'My lord, come forward: your virtue is well known. Receive this renowned city of Jerusalem where the body of Jesus was tortured and wounded for us'. 'My lord', said the duke, 'stop there. There are many princes here with high reputations. I am not going to take such a position before them when they have not even had a chance to refuse it. I wish the city to be offered to the others first'. The colour drained from the Bishop's face when he heard this. People burst into tears all round the square.[141]

147

The bishop of Mautran heard the duke of Bouillon refuse to accept Jerusalem. He summoned lord Robert the Frisian: 'Come forward, noble son of a baron. Accept Jerusalem and the walls which surround it, the city where God suffered and died for us'. 'My lord, I will not', said the count. 'Let me tell you that when I left Flanders, I promised the beautiful Clemence that as soon as I had been to the Temple of Solomon, and kissed and prayed at the Holy Sepulchre, I would come back and not seek any reason to delay. I cannot stay longer without breaking my word. If it were the will of God and St Simeon that right now I were back in my mansion at Arras, holding my son Baldwin on my lap and showering him with ten kisses at a go, even giving me all the gold from here to the Gardens of Nero would not be enough to keep me here'. The bishop kissed him on the chin when he heard this, and did not reply for a considerable time. Ah God! The weeping that was heard as they addressed a heartfelt appeal to God: 'Alas, Jerusalem, most famous of cities, just see how these princes shiver at the thought of taking you on. They are falling seriously short of their duties in not daring to accept you, the more so because they have suffered so much in the attempt. Alas, true Sepulchre, how we put you to shame!'

148

The bishop of Mautran went straight away to take up position on a dais of striped marble in front of the holy Temple. He addressed Robert of Normandy by name:

---

[141] A run of formulaic laisses marks the key moment of Godfrey's assumption of power.

'Come forward in the name of the God of Majesty, my lord, to receive the great honour of Jerusalem. You shall wear the crown in the Temple of the Lord, without question the high place of Christianity and indeed of the world. Jerusalem rightly has dominion over the whole world because it is the city where the beautiful head of God wore a crown. My lord, accept this charge in the name of holy charity. Your friends will be well protected and given high positions if you do'. 'My lord', said Robert, 'nothing could be further from my thoughts. I already have lands which stretch far and wide, and I have no intention of abandoning my fiefs and my inheritance. Moreover I have given a solemn pledge that, as soon as I have worshipped at the Sepulchre, kissed it with my lips and made an offering, I will set off home – that is what I promised. If at this moment I were at home in my city of Rouen, it would not matter if someone gave me all the gold between here and Gardens of Nero – there is no way I would return after suffering so much and undergoing the tortures of hunger, thirst and utter destitution. I have worn my hauberk for so long that my whole body aches; I am not made of iron or steel. By God! anyone who could go through what we have suffered here in snow and freezing conditions might do it for you, Lord – may you be thanked for your mercy – but would not do it for all the gold in a city. Let me assure you that I have gathered my palm leaves and prepared for my journey in the Garden of St Abraham. We will be on the move tomorrow as soon as day breaks'. The good bishop heaved a sigh when he heard this. Ah, God! how many tears will be shed now by poor and rich Christians alike.

149

The bishop of Mautran was on the paved court outside the holy Temple, which was thronged with people. He called for Bohemond without delay. 'Come forward in the name of God the Omnipotent, my lord, to receive into your keeping Jerusalem and the surrounding fief and elevate all your relatives to high office. You will be a happy man if you hold Bethlehem, which is the city where Jesus was in truth born of a Virgin and suffered torment. My lord, accept the crown and take over the city'. 'My lord', said Bohemond, 'I shall do nothing of the sort. Apulia and Calabria and the surrounding fief are mine. Antioch was given to me too in faith – though I have no desire to hold onto it and will happily cede it to Lord Raymond if he really wants to have it.[142] I really have no wish to be King of Jerusalem and command its fortifications, nor to inherit the lands in Syria. I have gathered my palm leaves in the Garden of St Abraham and wrapped them in silk picked out with silver thread. I and the companions here with me will be on the move tomorrow morning God

---

[142] Completely at odds with what actually happened: Raymond IV was expelled from Antioch by Bohemond despite a determined attempt to take it: see Asbridge, *First Crusade*, pp. 242–50. Since the author goes out of his way to make this statement, we may surmise that he knew the history and is underlining Bohemond's credentials as a disinterested participant.

willing'. The bishop was very downcast to hear this. By God! imagine the weeping and wailing.

150

The bishop of Mautran took up his position on a platform in front of the holy Temple, surrounded by princes and loyal barons. He addressed the brave hearted Hugh of Vermandois. 'My lord, in the name of the spirit of God, come forward to receive this royal city of Jerusalem. Here God suffered pain and death for us mortals'. 'My lord', said Count Hugh, 'I have been through too much. I shall never feel well as long as I stay in this country. The earth is so blisteringly hot with the force of the sun that I cannot bear it whether on foot or on horseback, and I can find no comfort either out on the battlefield or in lodgings. I have wrapped my palm leaves in strips of silk, prepared my staff and put iron on the tip of it.[143] I shall set off at cockcrow tomorrow morning. No man ever born could persuade me to stay'. The Bishop was heartbroken at hearing this. By God! Just imagine the weeping and wailing amongst the barons gathered on the court.

151

The bishop of Mautran was an eminent cleric. He took up position right in front of the holy Temple. With all our leaders as an audience, he shouted loudly: 'Ah, Jerusalem, today you bring shame on our religion! The Body of God was laid to rest in you when He was brought down from the Cross. All these people have been through agonies of hunger and thirst for you, and we went through terrible suffering to win you. But now not a single Norman or German wants to keep you. Everybody will be able to say that we have made a bad decision by allowing all our leaders to leave at once. Alas, God in Glory, what a situation to be in. Your religion is putting us to shame today'. At this the good Duke Godfrey burst into tears.

152

There was a huge assembly of our lords and princes in front of the holy Temple, all refusing to accept the fief of Jerusalem. Not one of our leaders was brave enough to dare defend it against the pagan hordes. There was weeping on all sides, because all of them were desperately upset. Everything they had worked for was set at nothing. They had taken the city by force, and killed and expelled the pagans. Yet now they were faced with going back home straight away because the city was not going to be defended by the Franks. The bishop of Mautran put matters in simple terms. 'Noble lords, I thank you in the name of God the Omnipotent. We have

---

[143] Making the point that the Crusade was considered a pilgrimage: Riley-Smith, *Idea* pp. 22–5.

overrun many territories by sheer force, including the city of Jerusalem and the lands of Bethlehem where God was born for us and spread His precious blood to redeem us. And He did not abandon us once redeemed; on the contrary He continues to give us His succour and aid. We should do the same for Him. We have taken Jerusalem and the lands of Bethlehem from those who insulted and mistreated Him: now we need a king to defend what we have won. Look: here are Duke Godfrey and Robert of Normandy, Robert the Frisian and Tancred the Apulian, Hugh and Bohemond. None of them wants anything to do with this. By God, my lords, what a set of cowards you are! May it please God to send us the forces for us to be able to hold onto the city robustly. Let us fast today in the name of God and in a spirit of reverence; and tonight let us come together with bare knees and bare chests on the bare pavement. Everyone without exception should carry a candle. The one on whose candle God kindles a flame will be made king, I guarantee. He will be king in lordly style and given a crown of gold or silver as he chooses'.

153

Our leaders heard a tremendous sermon. Not one of them would not have been persuaded in a fit of religious fervour to take off his silken robes and put on instead a hauberk, a hair shirt or linen or sackcloth in repentance. They fasted, taking only bread and water, and prayed to God to guard the city where He had suffered. Now, my lords, listen while I tell you about the good duke of Bouillon. He put on a hairshirt and hauberk, then his padded coat. It is the absolute truth that the Cordovan shoes he put on had no sole all the way from the heel to the toe. Then he sought out the bishop to have his confession heard, begging true mercy from God for his sins. The other leaders all dutifully followed suit, and the Bishop gave them all absolution.

154

When it was suppertime the knights assembled. A host of young men brought napkins for them all, water and barley bread, and [the bishop] who had sung Mass that same day for the great lords blessed it for them.[144] He broke the bread, crust and crumb, in the name of Jesus Christ, son of the Blessed Mary. The bishop administered Communion to himself three times first, then to the rest: nothing was left over. When they rose from supper each thanked God. They made straight for the Temple, led by [the Bishop] who was responsible for the see of Mautran. 'My lords', he said, 'do not be downcast if we suffer misery and pain – God suffered for us far more when He lived as man. Let us all keep vigil and beg for God's help.

---

[144] Barley bread was poor quality compared to the fine white bread knights would normally expect: Smith, *History of British Food* pp. 56–7. Suitable preparation for the vigil to come.

Each of you are to hold a candle of a pound and a half. None will burn – if God grants me His blessing – until God sends down a light for it'.[145]

155

The sun went down and day lost its brightness; the darkness of night returned. The noble warriors entered the Temple; they implored God to give them courage to keep control of the city in His divine honour, and to prevent those mortal villains from ever returning. Each lay prostrate on the ground and confessed his sins. 'Take pity on us, Lord God. Tell us this day whom we should appoint as lord of this great city by your command, which we fear to disobey'. The noble counts, bishops and abbots, great and small, were in agonies. All of them begged God earnestly to show them to whom he wanted to give the honour of ruling. There was not as much as a candle or a light in the whole Temple other than a single alabaster lamp on the altar which burnt unceasingly night and day. Our barons lay there desperately apprehensive. At midnight there was a blinding flash of lightening and a crash of thunder, followed by more and then several more again. Simultaneously a wind rose which made them all tremble. It blew the lamp out and plunged them into darkness, leaving our lords in a state of abject fear. The bishops, abbots and clerics were terror-struck. They started to sing the major litany, followed by other prayers and the *Veni creator spiritus*. Now imagine an almighty crash of thunder on the main tower which sent our lords fainting clean away. Then there was a flash of lightning, so bright that it lit the candle of the lord to whom God wanted to grant the kingdom and the fief of Syria to hold by his bravery.

156

Once the light of the candle was restored in full, our men recovered from their terror. They saw the duke's candle well and truly lit by the good grace of God. Our lords all leapt up shouting as one: they realised full well that God had listened to their prayers. The blood drained from the duke of Bouillon's face, and he heaved a huge sigh from the depths of his being. Tears welled up in his eyes and poured down his cheeks. He raised his head and said in the hearing of all: 'Alas Jerusalem, renowned holy city! It is my destiny to die for you if God does not grant me his favour and renowned strength. All I could wish for, if it be the will of Jesus, is to lose my life in the same place where He was wounded for us. I am the first to whom you have been granted, and I shall receive you in the hope that God will

---

[145] Reminiscent of the ceremony of the Holy Fire in the Church of the Holy Sepulchre each Easter where a candle miraculously catches fire. There was much consternation in 1101 when this failed to happen: see FC II.8. William of Malmesbury IV.379, vol.1 pp. 674–7 describes events in detail: *Gesta Regum Anglorum*, (ed.) and transl. R. A. B. Mynors, completed R. M. Thomas and M. Winterbottom, 2 vols (Oxford, 1998–99).

give me victory over the races he has deserted and guard this land and its regions against them. May Jerusalem be protected with great honour and her inhabitants securely governed'. Ah, God! this went down well with our lords. They ran to him holding out their arms; that day they embraced him repeatedly and wept tears of pity over him. The rank and file of the army cried at the tops of their voices: 'Our Lord, duke of Bouillon, famous as you are, blessed be the father who created you and the mother you carried you! Today you have raised and secured our people. Ah, Jerusalem! Now you will be properly defended by the best knight who ever put on a sword, and he will protect you against the pagans. Now you will be sought out from beyond the salt sea once the duke becomes King of the land of Galilee. God has done a good day's work today in lighting his candle for you!'

157

Our lords were overjoyed. They flung their arms round the good duke of Bouillon, and the bishops and abbots of the church carried him off to the Temple in a great procession. The King of the Tafurs was there with his entourage. He grasped the right of Godfrey's robe, and the princes and bishops all presented him devoutly at the principal altar, the same which saw God presented as a baby.[146] The bishop of Mautran pronounced a blessing on him. When they had sung Mass and chanted prayers, they brought the Duke with great rejoicing all the way to the Sepulchre. They installed him on the dais. Ah, God! How he was the centre of attention. 'My lord', said the princes, 'we shall crown you [king]'. However the duke responded eloquently. 'Be assured, my lords, that it is unthinkable that a crown of pure gold should ever be placed on my head. Jesus after all had a crown of thorns when He suffered for us; so my crown shall not be of gold, or silver, or brass'. Instead they had a branch brought from the garden of St Abraham (called spikenard on both sides of the sea) and that was what Godfrey of Bouillon had for his crown. He acted in this way for the honour of Jesus. 'Who shall put it on his head?' said Drieu of Monçon. 'Your highest ranking man, my lords', said the bishop. 'That would be the King of the Tafurs', said Raimbaut Creton. 'There is no other king here for certain. So he should be the one to crown Godfrey by right'. 'We are happy to accord him this favour', said the princes. The King took the famous crown and placed it on the head of Godfrey of Bouillon. The bishop of Mautran absolved him of his sins. The offering was massive, full of gold *mangons*. The noise rose to a crescendo as Godfrey was crowned king. The bishops and clerics sang the *Te Deum*. The nobles did homage to the King, each in order and according to protocol. Duke Godfrey said: 'Listen to me, my noble lords. See here the King of the Tafurs. He has declared himself my man. I want to receive Jerusalem from his hands because he was the first to enter, and that is why I commend him to you. I would not give as much as a button for anyone else other than God himself, in whose service we are'.

---

[146] Godfrey is presented implicitly as the successor of Christ, the earthly king of Jerusalem compared to the celestial one.

The princes replied, 'You have never prized anyone who was not worth it'. The King of the Tafurs took a rod in his hand and offered the fief and the kingdom to King Godfrey, then kissed his padded jacket in floods of tears. The two kings knelt to each other. The nobles who had pressed around dismounted and made their way back to their lodgings: there was no hint of treason. The King held court for eight days in the Temple of Solomon, sleeping at night in his residence in the Tower of David. On the ninth day the princes and barons prepared [to leave], carrying palm leaves and each with his staff; they planned to return home. Ah, God! What a lot of tears were shed that day. The King summoned them and addressed them as follows: 'My lords, you are leaving. I know perfectly well that is what you feel right for you. You are, though, leaving me all alone in this country, surrounded by vicious people who believe in Mahomed. We still have to capture all these castles round us – Acre, Tyre and Ascalon, all crawling with wicked Turks. If we lose this city again because of our sins, everything we have done will not be worth as much as one spur. So, by God and by His name, think carefully. Let us stay in this holy city together, and serve our Lord just as we are doing now. We will take the castles from their pagan occupiers, and anyone who dies for God will be truly pardoned'. The princes neither agreed nor disagreed; each stayed silent and refused to meet Godfrey's gaze.

158

The King stood in state in front of the holy Temple. He summoned his nobles and addressed them: 'My lords', said the King, 'in the name of God the Redeemer, I can see that you have made your preparations to leave. You have picked palms from the garden of St Abraham, and each of you has his [bags] packed and hanging [across the pack-animal]. It is quite clear that you want to depart and leave me all alone amongst the pagans. We still have not taken Tyre nor the powerful city of Acre, Damascus or Tiberias – two very powerful cities, Banyas or Ascalon, Barbais or Le Colant. No pilgrim will be able to go and bathe in the River Jordan.[147] If we lose Jerusalem again now, all our pilgrimage will not have been worth one bezant, and I would not give as much as one glove for everything we have achieved. So think carefully. Stay in this holy city to serve our Lord, conquering pagans and Turks. I know all too well that the might of the Saracen empire is making its way here from the east'. Our lords' faces darkened when they heard this, but not one announced that he would remain.

---

[147] A reminder of one of the key motivations of the Crusade: to make access to Jerusalem easier for pilgrims, who could thus follow in the steps of Christ: Riley-Smith, *Idea*, pp. 22–5.

159

The nobles were assembled in great numbers in front of the holy Temple. King Godfrey addressed the princes: 'My lords, I can see all too well that you are desperate to leave. I can see that you have already lashed together your palms and spikenard and loaded them up. Soon you are going to leave me all alone in this strange land. We have plenty of castles around us to conquer. If you lose this city because of your sins, everything you have achieved will not be worth even two *deniers*. So think carefully: in God's name stay here and serve our Lord in this city'. 'You must be joking', said the count of Flanders. 'My lord and King Godfrey, this is totally inappropriate. We are not all made of iron or steel and able to endure as much suffering as much as you seem to suggest. Speaking personally, all my ribs are broken. I have lain in my hauberk come rain and storm, and it has worn some 30 holes on me; my ribs and sides are covered with sores. And I may be in a pretty poor state, but the others here are in a very bad way. Every last one of them needs to rest. It has been a whole year since I saw clean sheets or ran a comb with soap through my hair. I take my leave of you; I have made all my preparations to go. And you could come with us if you so pleased'. 'Go in the name of God, noble lord', said King Godfrey. 'I would not leave just to get myself torn limb from limb! May God and the Holy Trinity be by my side'. At this point the King of the Tafurs cried out at the top of his voice: 'My lord, I will stay here with you, along with the 10,000 *ribalts* you see here, and you shall have the best help I and they can manage. I am your liege man and you are my lord'. 'I thank you most sincerely', said Godfrey. Then the count of St-Gilles approached him. 'Your Majesty, I will stay with you along with 5,000 armed men'.

160

So the army of Jesus rode off together. They made their way up the river valley and rode without stopping to Tiberias. Dodekin of Damascus launched an assault against them, attacking our forces with 15,000 Turks. The barons rode to meet them with lances couched, ripping and piercing in many shields, tearing many hauberks apart and splintering many lances. Saracens and pagans were killed bloodily and the ground was left strewn with the dead and injured. There were loud joyful shouts of 'Montjoie!' Each of our soldiers brandished a burnished sword, all of them stained with blood and brains. When they attacked the Turks they were as good as dead: the grass was stained crimson with the blood streaming from their bodies. Dodekin fled with his people in disarray. He did not draw rein all the way to Tiberias. He and his retinue streamed through the gate. They raised the drawbridge, barred the gates and went up onto the dark-stoned walls. Robert of Normandy shouted at the top of his voice: 'Dodekin, hand Tiberias over to us immediately! We will give you safe conduct out. If you do not leave, your life is forfeit'. Dodekin replied: 'I have no intention of surrendering. My lord Cornumarant entrusted this town to me, and I would be guilty of a crime in handing it over. I rule all this land subject to him. In the name of Mahomed, Frenchmen, I am not lying. The brave Cornumarant is on the move, bringing with him all the men of the kingdom of Persia. There is not one single Saracen left anywhere in the pagan realm. There are 90 kings alone without counting any of the other lords. Tonight they will set up camp down along the waste land, and their army will stretch two and a half leagues. Your God will not be able to give you any protection or guarantee of safety!' When our leaders heard this, they all shouted 'Montjoie!' With that, just imagine how ferociously they fell on the town. They cut off the barbicans, cut down the timber bars and filled in a large section of the ditch, digging up the earth with spades and hoes. They attacked the town vigorously but were nowhere near taking it. The barons and princes sounded horns to give the signal for the assault, and they all crowded up to the walls together at once. The pagans defended themselves desperately. Stones were flung and tossed on all sides. When our barons saw that the town [defences] had not been breached and that their assault was not worth a sorb apple, they gave the signal to retreat and abandoned the assault. They passed on, leaving Tiberias untaken behind them; having given up the attack they would not be mounting any further attempts. They rode without stopping all the way to Galilee. The day was over and night was near. Our men bivouacked above the Sea of Galilee, then went to see the table blessed by Our Lord, where He invited His apostles and household to eat with Him.

161

The French nobility set up camp, each bivouacking above the Sea of Galilee. Then they went to see the table where Our Lord sat on the day when His Apostles fed the multitude, a good 5,000 according to Scripture. You can be assured that, even though there were only five loaves and two fishes, 12 baskets were filled with what remained and everyone there ate to their fill. God did a great miracle that day, praise be to Him. One Frank pointed out the table to another and all of them were delighted. None of them undressed or as much as took off his shoes that night right through to when dawn came up. They were ready straight away and loaded up their pack animals. Just as everyone was ready to get under way, a dove was sent down to them by God, bringing them a tightly folded letter. It was handed to the bishop of Mautran. When he read what was written he was appalled. 'My lords, there is not a moment to lose!' he shouted at the top of his voice. 'Every last one of us needs to make for Jerusalem at top speed. Duke Godfrey is faced by a terrible peril which will lead to the death of many Franks if God does not have mercy on them!'

162

The bishop of Mautran did exactly the right thing. Once he had read the letter he burst into tears and said to our barons: 'We have to go straight back to help King

Godfrey in Jerusalem. There is not as much as one pagan between here and the Red Sea or a single Turk or Saracen capable of bearing arms whom Cornumarant has not dragooned into his forces. They are riding day and night non-stop. No man in God's creation could count how many of them there are or estimate the hundreds and the millions. There are 90 kings, all Esclers. In this letter Our Lord is calling your men for love of Him to endure this great battle of which there has never been the like! If you can manage to achieve this through your strength, the King will be able to maintain possession of Jerusalem. There is no need to be dismayed. You can take comfort from Him Who stooped to redeem you with His own blood. The way we conquered this land was through suffering, but none of that would have helped you even enter it without the support of Him Who is going to deliver you'. Count Robert of Flanders shouted: 'My lords, take courage! God wants to try your strength. We are not going to refuse to fight this battle. Let us see who is best at cutting off pagan heads. God wants us to go and liberate His Sepulchre'. When our Christians heard the explanation that they needed to turn round and go back to Jerusalem, most of them were not keen to agree. More than 30,000 said they would leave the army. The count of Normandy stood and faced them with lord Hugh of Vermandois and the noble Bohemond. 'My lords', said the princes, 'do you want to go back on your oaths and return home without us? God will not exactly be pleased if you do. So help me God, my lords, you should not even be thinking this way. You should be concentrating on finishing the task we set ourselves'. The bishop of Mautran then addressed them: 'My lords and noble Christians, let me command you in the love of Our Lord Who allowed Himself to be tortured, struck with the Lance and wounded and broken; laid to rest in the Sepulchre; rose again on the third day and went to break down the gates of Hell to free his followers from captivity; my lords, God suffered all this for the salvation of our souls. In the name of this Lord I implore you to pay heed to my words and do not demoralise the army and its lords: we should not be turning on each other'. When the body of the army heard this they stirred uneasily. Imagine those who had wanted to return having second thoughts. 'Sound the horns!' they cried at the tops of their voices. 'Any Saracen we can find is a dead man!' When the bishop heard this he began to thank God. At this you might have seen the army rejoice. Not a single man, sergeant or young soldier, was so cowardly that his heart was not emboldened to be as fierce as that of a wild boar. You might have seen the army of God full of new determination. Each seized arms to defend himself, under the leadership of Him Who gave Himself to suffer [for us].

163

The princes and barons armed themselves through the whole army of God. They all got ready, loading up their provisions and tying their armour into bundles. Had you been there you would have heard a multitude of horns and bugles singing out. They made their way straight back towards Jerusalem. But you can be sure of this:

before they ever get there, Jerusalem will be full of violent fighting with many Franks and many pagans wounded and killed. With that I am going to leave the army of God while they all get under way, and I am going to tell you how things stood for the valiant Cornumarant. He had ridden so hard through the day and night with his 100,000 Turks, all armed to the teeth, that they arrived at Barbais within the space of 24 hours. He came across his father in the fields outside the town, his men with him in a state of some demoralisation. Cornumarant came riding up, pennant fixed, a good acre ahead of his companions. Once he had glimpsed his father he recognised him for certain. He plunged his golden spurs into Plantamor and, spurring up to his father, he greeted him in ringing tones. Then he flung his arms round him and asked: 'My lord, tell me, how are you?' 'Let me tell you, my noble son', said Corbadas. 'I lost Jerusalem 11 days ago. The Franks had me at bay in the Tower of David. They brought up their siege engine, set up their petrary and sling. It did not take them long to smash down the wall of the Tower and leave my men destroyed, dead and ripped to pieces. I could not go on. I handed the Tower over to them and they gave me safe conduct out. They have crowned Godfrey of Bouillon king. The army has left and the barons have set out for home; there is only a skeleton force of knights left in the city. I, though, have lost all my land and my ancestral inheritance. If I had a good sharp knife with me right now I should have killed myself, by my God Mahomed!' Cornumarant comforted him on hearing all this. Taking him by the hand, he swore to him that he would fast until he had left the Franks for dead and taken Jerusalem back by conquest. He is going to find that a very long fast, his hauberk shredded and his body torn and bleeding. The valiant Cornumarant shouted out his battle cry, then took Herod's horn and blew it loudly. The people of Barbais came flocking out to meet him, complaining of the Franks who had brought destruction on them. 'Take heart', said Cornumarant, 'because I will avenge you to your heart's content for what they have done to you'.

164

The pagan hordes were making an almighty din. Cornumarant cried out above it: 'Father, you must ride out immediately and without stopping to meet the emir who is coming to your aid. He is bringing the biggest army anyone has ever seen. Christendom is dead and buried'. The emir swore by his long white beard that he would make the French barons pay for the death of Brohadas, whose head they had cut off: they would never see the sun, the light of day or the clouds again. His huge deep dungeon would be filled up with them, while the rest of the rank and file would be carried off into his deserts and harnessed up to drag ploughs; anyone who failed to put his back into it would be beaten raw with knotted cords. Their religion would be brought down to the dust. 'We shall win Jerusalem back from them, and Nicaea, and Antioch which we have lost!' Corbadas was overjoyed at these sentiments from his son.

165

'Your Majesty, do not lose hope', said Cornumarant. 'Go on the attack against the army and make them retreat; drive them back to take up position on the plains around Ramleh. I will ride on ahead to guard against the Christians. I am concerned that I may not find them in Jerusalem. I do not want a single one to escape with his life'. With that he took up the horn of Herod and sounded it; that was the signal for the pagans to fall in behind him. There were easily 100,000 Saracens and Esclers. They rode straight to Jerusalem without stopping, led by the noble and valiant Cornumarant. He ordered them to arm themselves in the Valley of Josaphat, to mount and to protect themselves with their shields. 60,000 were to stay behind in the valley while the other 40,000 were to ride ahead with him. They packed up the booty they intended to take with them. The lookouts raised the alarm so that it could be heard all the way to the shining city of Jerusalem. A messenger went to report to the Tower of David. King Godfrey heard the news and was filled with rage. 'Arm yourself immediately!' he said to Count Raymond. He ordered a trumpet to be blown from the roof of the Tower of David. At this you might have seen our men putting on their hauberks, saddling up and mounting their horses; each buckled on his sword with its glittering steel blade, and they slung their shields round their necks. They were fiercer than wild boars. They spurred ahead, swords in hands. They left the King of the Tafurs with orders to defend Jerusalem along with the revered Peter the Hermit. The King was the first to ride out. May God defend him, because if Jesus Who allowed Himself to suffer [on the Cross] is not mindful of him he will have a close brush with death before he returns.

166

The Saracens arrived at Jerusalem with their booty. The brave Cornumarant brought it along with 40,000 pagan soldiers. Imagine Godfrey riding up with his household, a good 4,000 all with lances couched. When they were within the length of a charge of the Turks they fell on them mercilessly. Numerous spearshafts were splintered, shields smashed, and feet and hands and heads cut off. The noble King Godfrey cried at the top of his voice: 'My lords, do your utmost! Help us, Holy Sepulchre! There is no way these pagan bastards are going to walk away triumphing over us!' With that he spurred on his horse, lance at the ready, and struck Cornumarant in the middle of his embossed shield, smashing through the golden buckler. However his mailcoat was so strong that not as much as a link gave way. He knocked him flying from Plantamor to the dusty ground, and would have sliced off his head with glittering sword had the Saracens not surged up all together in a company of 15,000. They shouted 'Damascus and Tiberias!' non-stop. Just imagine the noise and clashing: there was so much din and shouting by the Persians that you could hear it a good league and a half away. The Turks heard the noise back in the Valley of Josaphat and came racing out to join the fight. Our men were pushed back the length of a crossbow shot. Cornumarant got back onto his Nubian horse and sounded the horn of Herod to rally his troops. They attacked King Godfrey. Cornumarant gave Plantamor of Russia his head. He seized a lance from Randol of Aleppo and spurred towards King Godfrey, pennant lowered. He struck him with the lance on his ornamented shield and pierced it beneath the buckler, but did not injure him. The lance dragged sideways across his chest without piercing the hauberk, and the King had to work hard not to fall. He put his hand on his sword and drew it from its scabbard. He struck King Murgalant, the lord of Esclaudie. His helmet and mailcoat were no more use than a sorbu apple. The sword went right into his chest and he fell dead from his horse onto the green grass. Then he killed Danemolt and Flanbalt of Tornie, King Bricebalt, Carcan of Rousia, Estorgan of Aliie, Marbrin of Salorie, Brunamont of Valterne and Bruiant of Almeria, King Malcoué and the emir Galie: he left all 14 dead. Cornumarant's face darkened at the sight. He yelled 'Damascus!' and rallied his men. Innumerable arrows were shot from Turkish bows. The infidels launched attack after attack on our men and they killed each other ferociously. But there were simply too many pagans and things had got off to a bad start. The track was strewn with dead and fallen.

167

It was a very fierce battle with heavy losses; but there were so many pagans that the noble [Christian] knights could not withstand them. The Saracens pursued them hotly towards Jerusalem. Our men halted in front of the main gate and turned towards the Turks, killing a large number. Cornumarant cried: 'Saracens, forward! By Mahomed these losers will not not find themselves walking away free to boast they have triumphed over us!' Holding the horn of Herod, he blew it at full blast. The Saracens and pagans found a second wind and pushed our men back into Jerusalem. At that point our men suffered a great misfortune. The pagans captured the Count of St-Gilles and hurt him badly with blows from large lead maces. The battle was over. The Turks fell back and our Christians made a miserable entry into Jerusalem. They shut the gates; the Turks left them to their own devices, and King Godfrey got down from his warhorse. Imagine the King of the Tafurs coming up to him, and that valiant fighter lord Peter the Hermit. 'My lord', they said to theKing, 'how did things go? Did you manage to get the booty from the valiant Cornumarant?' 'In faith, God has forgotten me', said the King. 'The infidels have taken the count of St-Gilles. The rest of my life will be truly wretched'. 'Do not lose heart', said Peter the Hermit. 'By my faith in Jesus of Bethlehem, the Turks will not take him away if they find themselves hard pressed'. 'Those were my thoughts too', said the King of the Tafurs. 'My lords, arm yourselves without delay'. With that he blew a horn and his *ribalts* came running, each carrying an axe or a sharp halberd or a steel knife or a heavy club. They marched out of Jerusalem. The King rode in front; his brother Eustace sat on his skewbald horse and Count Baldwin on the swift Prinsaut. He carried his lance pointing up, pennant hanging, and rode ahead in front of all the others. He caught up with the Turks in the Valley of Josaphat. He shouted, 'You will not leave here in one piece, you bastards'. Cornumarant looked at him and knew who he was. He recognised Prinsaut very well from his spirited demeanour, and realised that it was the Frenchman who had pursued him when he went to get help from the emir Sultan. He could not hold himself worth as much as a bezant if he did not take him on in combat. He spurred Plantamor towards him, wielding his spear. Now the two of them will joust together in full sight of everyone.

168

When Count Baldwin saw the pagan making a feint, he positioned his lance and prepared to strike. Cornumarant did the same, determined to land a blow. Both their shields were pierced and split, and their ashwood lances smashed and shattered. They struck each other so hard and with such vehemence that they sent each other flying, like it or not. Before either of them could get back on his feet or regain his momentum, imagine Christians and Saracens flocking round. You might have seen a fierce battle, with one Saracen staggering and falling down dead on another and the wounded yelling, roaring and howling. Lord Peter the Hermit struck out ferociously: anyone he struck was beyond the help of any doctor. The *ribalts* fought hard, thoroughly determined to kill and defeat Turks and pagans. Had you been there, you would have seen a fierce battle unfold. The earth shook with the din of swordplay and the noise could be heard for a full league around. The Turks were forcibly pushed back by our men more than the distance of a crossbow shot, and fell back. Count Baldwin came running to seize Cornumarant. He grabbed him round his sides and grasped him tightly, wanting to protect him against the *ribalts*.[148]

169

When Cornumarant realised that the count had laid hands on him, he whipped out his glittering sword. Baldwin took it and flung it to the ground. Imagine King Godfrey spurring up enthusiastically along with his valiant-hearted brother Eustace. 'Don't think you are going to get away like that!' they shouted to Cornumarant. 'You aren't. You are going to be hanged in front of the Tower of David so that all your best friends can enjoy the show'. When Cornumarant heard this, he begged the King for mercy. He picked up his sword from where it lay on the ground and held it out to him; King Godfrey accepted it. Cornumarant stood up and gave his word as a captive. The King immediately had him mounted on a hack whilst Plantamor fled through a clearing and was caught by Arabs in the valley of Josaphat. When they saw that Cornumarant was not riding him, imagine

---

[148] Because he would be more valuable as a hostage than if the *ribalts* killed him.

how much they wept and wailed and lamented. 'This is a sad turn of events!' said King Sucaman. 'Cornumarant is a prisoner: the French have taken him. We should be sad cowards if we let them take him away'. The pagans sounded their horns and banged their drums, and rode out to battle spoiling for a fight. Meanwhile our noble Christians, blessed by God, had ridden straight back towards Jerusalem. Count Baldwin was sitting on his Arab steed Prinsaut, and the King of the Tafurs was leading him by the rein.

170

The company of Jesus made for Jerusalem, riding along tightly grouped in battle order. The *ribalts* went ahead of them, led and guided by their King and by Peter the Hermit with his white beard. King Godfrey and his knights were in the rearguard to defend them against the hated infidels. The Saracens fell on them abruptly, sounding their horns so loudly that the whole earth shook. King Godfrey put heart into his men, shouting 'Montjoie! Help us, Holy Sepulchre!' Count Baldwin brandished his glittering sword, and light glinted off the blade held by his brother Eustace. The three brothers swore by the son of the Blessed Virgin Mary that each would rather have his head cut off than flee as much as the length of a lance and a half to get away from a pagan. Picture King Sucaman shouting at the top of his voice: 'By Mahomed, Christians, you are acting like fools. We are going to get Jerusalem back before compline. Give us back Cornumarant or you are all dead men, because tomorrow the army from Persia will be here. It is the greatest anyone has ever seen or heard of. We are going to take back one of your counts, lord Raymond of St-Gilles. He will be hung tomorrow morning before we even find lodging for our army'. Baldwin's face darkened when he heard this. He spurred on his horse, giving it its head; he laid his hand on his sword and took it from its scabbard. He struck King Sucaman on his green-sheened helmet, slicing off the jewels and floral decorations, cutting down through the hood of his mailshirt. The steel sword glanced towards his ear on the right; he sliced it off and cut down through the flesh of his right arm and shoulder so that the fist and sword went flying into the meadow. The King tumbled to the earth onto the green grass. Hardly surprising that he feared he was going to die!

171

When King Sucaman realised that he had lost his ear, his arm, his hand and his tempered sword, he shouted at the top of his voice: 'Lord Mahomed, help me! Noble deity Apollon, see the blow I have taken! I will not be winning any more land or fiefs'. He shouted 'Damascus!' in a voice which could be heard far and wide. More than 20,000 pagans heard the warcry and cut their way through the press of battle by firing arrows from their Turkish bows of horn. The battle was hard fought. Innumerable spears were shattered and shields split, feet and hands and heads cut off; the ground was strewn with dead and wounded. The French rained blows on the infidels; so did Peter the Hermit with his white beard, the King of the Tafurs and the other rank and file; each of them did his utmost to attack the pagans. However the Turkish forces came spurring up. If Our Lord Who ascended in a cloud does not look to them, our forces are going to suffer badly, because the Turks have pressed them hard down the road. In fact the gate would already have been forced and the city taken had not King Godfrey made use of his tempered sword to defend it stoutly against the infidels.

172

There was a hard-fought battle outside the Gate of David. The cowardly infidels would in fact have forced their way in had it not been for King Godfrey fighting them off with his sharp sword at the gateway. Anyone he struck with his sword was sliced apart. He called out to his brother Eustace and his younger brother Baldwin: 'What are you playing at, brothers? Come on, don't act like cowards. We are reputed to be the bravest in God's army: do not fear death, go out and seek it!' These words put new heart into his brothers. 'By the Holy Sepulchre!' they shouted, 'Forward, gentlemen. These Saracens will rue the day they tried to triumph over us!' At that you might have seen the brothers killing and slaughtering the pagans as if they were taking their pleasure in a forest. They drove them back an acre from the gate. Picture the King of the Tafurs and Lord Peter [the Hermit] coming running, with the Tafurs and *ribalts* flocking towards them yelling; each carried an axe or a heavy mace, a knife or a large club with dangling chain, or a punch or pike or sharp bradawl. The King of the Tafurs wielded a large sharp scythe: he plunged into the midst of the pagans and inflicted such slaughter that he was completely walled in by dead bodies. Lord Peter the Hermit followed him, carrying an axe with a large blade; it was some eight feet long and sharper than a razor moulded by a blacksmith. Peter the Hermit hardly fought like a child: wherever he turned he cut down Turks, lopping off heads and arms and chests. Between them the King of the Tafurs and the grey-haired Peter and their valiant followers, all thrusting forward in unison, drove the Turks back more than the distance of a bowshot, chasing them all the way back to King Sucaman. The pagans did not try and dodge but fled, hotly pursued by King Godfrey and all the other princes who spurred after them. They left the earth covered with dead and wounded. Now may God spare a thought for our men as part of His Divine Plan. They had chased the Turks too far and lost their sense of judgement; they were going to find it hard to get back in one piece. The Saracens and pagans blew the horns and had rallied in the blink of an eyelid: there were a good 60,000 of the race of Tervagant.

173

There was a fierce battle outside the walls of Jerusalem. The Turks sounded their horns to rally their people; there were a good 60,000 of those diabolical people.

Imagine the sound of all those Turks baying and howling: they made so much noise and such a din that you could hear the noise a good four leagues away. The archers were in front to demoralise our men by firing their horn bows; you might have seen the arrows launched against our men more thickly than the snow which falls at the end of February. Those with javelins started to throw them, drawing blood from the heads or ribs of our men and forcing them to fall back more than the length of a crossbow shot. When King Godfrey saw his men forced back in this way, he nearly went mad with anger and fury. He grabbed his shield and drew his steel sword, determined in his rage to make them pay a high price, and flung himself into the mass of Turks. Imagine him laying about him left, right and centre. I can tell you this for certain: he did not land one single blow which did not kill a Saracen or his horse. The ranks thinned in front of him no matter which way he turned. The Turks scattered in front of him like larks in front of a sparrowhawk, not daring to come near him. But if Jesus, Judge of the world, does not assist him he is about to find himself in mortal peril. The Turks killed his horse beneath him. He leapt up from it, full of courage, grasping his shield and drawing his steel sword. Anyone who saw the lord slicing his way through Saracens, sending one staggering to his death on top of another one, could not have imagined a better knight. The King saw a horse loose in front of him: he grabbed it by the rein and swung into the saddle from the stirrup. St George and St Demetrius came to his help, accompanied by more than 300,000.

174

As soon as the King was back on his horse, St George came spurring up at top speed with the noble St Maurice armed and on horseback, St Demetrius and a number of others – there were more than 300,000, all as white as flowers in a meadow. St George said to the King: 'Come, my lord, ride on! These forces have come to help you. Now let us see what you can do. If you are a truly brave man, show us the proof!' With that he spurred his horse, turned and rode away taking all his noble companions with him. King Godfrey followed. The companions of St George shouted to the Turks. They lowered their lances and knocked the Turks flying: you might have seen more than 20,000 pagans unhorsed. Anyone who was there could have seen St George spurring through the meadows, St Maurice and St Barbara, pennants flying.[149] They flung more than 50 Turks dead to the ground whilst their companions put paid to a good 10,000. The Tafurs thrashed these to the ground. The pagans turned and fled and the battle was over. However King Sucaman had not been forgotten. He was brought out on an Arab horse led by his son Marbrin, who was greatly distressed at what was happening to him. They brought the Count of St-Gilles with them. Unless God intervenes he is going to have a very rough time. Anyway, the pagans fled; imagine them fleeing in disarray

---

[149] A repeat of the divine intervention at the battle of Antioch; see *Antioche* laisse 358. The saints are different, but there is the same emphasis on the whiteness of the forces.

all the way to the plains of Ramleh without drawing rein. They turned their horses and made a stand there. That was a fierce and difficult battle: many Saracens were killed and decapitated, and the fighting lasted until the evening. St George turned and came back bringing the King and all his men with him. They lashed the pagan weapons onto their horses and took away their plunder – thanks be to God. St George brought them safe and sound all the way to Jerusalem: imagine them riding in. They shut the gates and barred the doors. St George disappeared from their sight immediately. The King and the leaders disarmed. Then Cornumarant was sent for without delay. They put a strong shackle round his feet. 'Keep watch on Cornumarant', said the King to his brothers. 'It shall be as you command', replied Baldwin. The King went up into the Tower of David. The tablecloths were laid and food set out. The knights sat side by side in rows. There was an abundance of food and drink. The others similarly feasted at their lodgings in the city. That night they all rested well. Lord Peter (he of the beard) mounted guard over Jerusalem with a good 4,000 well equipped men, who kept watch all night until day dawned. The Turks lit their fires across the plains of Ramleh. 140,000 of them had managed to escape. That night they had beaten Raymond so severely that blood was flowing from 20 wounds; they had tied him up tightly and blindfolded him. The following morning as the sun rose the Turks seized their weapons and put on their armour.

175

Before the sun rose or day broke, the pagans had armed themselves and picked up their shields. They sent letters winging their way to Qualquere, beyond there to Calençon and to Caesarea. They sent to Acre and the surrounding region for Turks. They sent to Herod asking for reinforcements because they had been comprehensively defeated on the plains of Ramleh and Cornumarant had been taken captive in the valley of Josaphat. They also sent letters to Banyas. Those who went to Acre managed to assemble precious few Turks. There was not a single pagan or Arab in Carkarie, Caesarea or Acre who had not already fled. They found the castles completely empty and devoid of provisions. The inhabitants of Banyas had fled their houses and sent their wealth to Barbais and Damascus along with their wives, households and young children, their foodstocks and their animals. They heaped curses on the French. There was no Saracen brave enough not to be cowed by fear of them. As yet Corbadas had not left Barbais. When he heard the news, he declared himself the most wretched of men because the Saracens told him his son had been taken. He ripped out his hair and tore his face so that he was bleeding in at least 30 places. 'Death, where are you?' he said. 'Come and take my life. Alas Cornumarant, my noble and gentle son, my best friend, you were the best of all the Turks and Arabs, the bravest pagan who ever lived or died!'

176

When King Corbadas heard the news that his son had been taken, a cold shudder ran through his blood. He wrung his hands and tore at his beard. He cried at the very top of his resounding voice: 'Alas, Cornumarant, noble and brave son, I shall never see you again! Evil Death, come and put an end to my misery!' 'My brother', said Lucabel, 'do not lose your mind; let us go and join up with the army which is coming to reinforce us. The Christians will be killed and their religion trampled in the dust, and King Godfrey will be deprived of his head. There is not one Christian, no matter how much his lust for battle, who will have the determination to oppose Cornumarant'. With those words he sounded the horn to start the battle. Those inside Barbais came spilling out to meet the emir, guided by Corbadas. They met the Sultan's army around a league and a half away. From the first encampments at its head to the other end it stretched over a good seven leagues, and its tents reached two leagues from one side to the other. Corbadas spurred on his good mule from Russia and reached the tent of the Sultan, lord of Persia. The tent had been erected in front of a spring and was surrounded by a pleasant meadow. Let me tell you all about how the tent had been made: you will never have heard about such an amazing one.[150] It used to belong to King Alexander during his lifetime. Nobody could count the amazing works inside. Mahomed Gomelin made its intricately detailed work through necromancy and magic. All the stories from the beginning of God's creation were there, picked out in burnished gold, cunningly worked in pure gold with crystal and gilding: the heavens and the sun and the shining moon, pastures, rivers and land and the waves of the sea, fish and beasts, birds, the boisterous wind, and the vision of stars in waves through the firmament.[151] Like the abyss all four were firmly set on the marble stone with a strong foundation; the sea swelled all round; and the throne at God's command turned round more swiftly than a bird or magpie. God had not created a single creature which had not been portrayed in the tent, brought to life in gold and azure.

177

It was an extraordinarily rich tent: there had never been one like it. It had 30 panels made entirely of enamel which shone more brightly than a lighted candle. The

---

[150] The tent is deliberately compared to Alexander's tent as described in the *Roman d'Alexandre*: *Alexandre de Paris: le Roman d'Alexandre*, (ed.) L. Harf-Lancner (Paris, 1994) branch 1 lines 1948–2070; also branch 3 lines 2880–85. Such elaborate tents did in fact exist: see AA 336–7. They are something of a topos in the Cycle: there are similar descriptions in the *Antioche* 201 and the *Canso d'Antioca* lines 294–312

[151] This description reflects the intricate goldsmithing of works like the Altar of the Three Kings in Cologne cathedral, and the Guelph treasure such as the Kuppelreliquiar in the Kunstgewerbemuseum in Berlin.

Seven Arts were painted on them, holding a public debate about good and evil.[152] The panels were all made with exquisite workmanship. The settings around them were all of coral. All the tent pegs were of ivory and walrus task, many of ebony and several of emerald. The ropes were of imperial manufacture, more tightly woven and tough than iron or metal so that no arm of Poitevin steel could cut them. Despite all that each was so light that it weighed less than a cheststrap, and two horses sufficed to carry the tent and its ropes.

178

It was an amazingly rich tent and well worth describing. Mahomed Gomelin had had it cunningly worked. He had had a fine border set all the way round it with a row of topazes. He had an abundance of valuable stones set in balsam wood which had amazing properties I am going to describe to you.[153] Any man who saw them on a given day could not be put under a spell or poisoned by a potion or dangerous herbs and, provided his faith in God was strong, not wounded or injured. Mahomed had had it ornamented with 23 rows, more than anyone could ever have selected and bought because there were so many precious stones in them: emeralds and rubies to reflect light onto the tent and other fine gems which were so impressive that it was hardly possible to look at them full on. The tent was made of silk which was of such high quality that nothing could touch it: it was known as 'sidor'. Arachne wove the silk on a sand dune by the sea and was turned into a spider by Pallas [Athene]. Her whole task is to spin when she has to, drawing the thread from her abdomen: I can vouch for this. Gomelin had the tent pole cast from metal and gilded with 15 coats of the finest gold in Arabia.[154] Nobody could put his arms all the way round it. Mahomed had the precepts of Islam engraved on it. He wanted to impose himself and his religion by force, and thought he could have himself universally worshipped as a god. Our Lord had no intention of putting up with this. One Thursday Mahomed got drunk on some heady wine. When it was time to leave the tavern he came staggering out and saw a dungheap heaving in a public square. He went to sleep on it and couldn't get out again; according to the story I have heard he was suffocated by pigs.[155] That is why no Jew touches pork. They had Mahomed carried straight to Mecca to Salatré, a rich Jew who was skilled in carpentry, and had him sealed inside a magnetic coffin. It was between

---

[152] The Metropolitan Museum of Art in New York preserves similar enamel panels.

[153] Lapidaries formed part of medieval science and described the properties of jewels: see *Anglo-Norman Lapidaries* (eds) P. Studer and J. Evans (Paris, 1924).

[154] The tentpole is cast from 'sidorie' which is not attested; it may be a fictional metal whose name reflects 'sidor' from the description of the tent. T-L IX.627–8 attests as an exotic fabric though not a metal.

[155] A legend referred to elsewhere: see e.g. *Couronnement de Louis*, (ed.) E. Langlois (Paris, 1925) lines 850–52. Guibert of Nogent also refers to it: I.381–416, pp. 99–100.

earth and heaven, spinning in the air.[156] The Saracens go and visit it to this day, and it is worshipped by Persians and Esclers. Anyone who sees it is convinced that it must be flying and that Mahomed speaks through it to the pagans.

179

The Sultan of Persia's tent was staggeringly impressive. The finial on top of the tent pole was a glittering carbuncle whose rays could be seen from 15 leagues off. The image of Apollon had been set up above it complete with a stick in his hand to beat the French. Mahomed Gomelin had it lowered from its decorated pedestal of pure gold. 14 kings of Africa ran to embrace it. They set it up in the middle of the tent on a piece of costly silk. As the Sultan of Persia, watched, the Devil entered the image and all the pagans could hear him drumming and creating a din.[157] 'Come and assemble in front of me, pagans', said Satanas. 'I have something to announce. I am going to bring the Christian religion to its knees. Lord God can look after Heaven; the earth is mine to command. I have supreme power. I make all the decisions. Woe to any man I find who worships God – and if he does he will pay a high price. It is me who should be worshipped and served and receive your grateful thanks. I bring you the corn, the vines for harvesting the vintage, the potherbs and the flowers and the fragrant meadows'. When the pagans heard this they all went to prepare; more than 15,000 bowed down to him.[158] They said to each other sagely, 'It is only right to believe in a God Who comes to the aid of his people'. When they got back to their feet they made extremely generous offerings, some four packhorse loads of bezants I think. The Apostolic Caliph began to preach. 'Anyone who only has one wife can take two – or three – or four – or five! He needs to sleep with all of them and add to the population to protect our faith.[159] The French have come to take us on in our own lands, but the Sultan's command is that we should go and kill them!'

180

The Apostolic Caliph was right next to Mahomed. 'Listen to what we have to tell you', he said to the Saracens. 'It is the Sultan's command and we will make it quite clear to you. Every man must get busy procreating because the French have invaded our territory. The Sultan's order is that we should go and kill them. I think, though, it would be better if we took them alive so that they could go and repopulate

---

[156] See *Le Roman de Mahomed*, (ed.) and transl. Y. G. Lepage (Louvain/Paris, 1996) lines 1876–1965.
[157] For other examples of Saracen idols and magic see Bancourt vol.1 pp. 388–91.
[158] Although A reads 'aparellier' all other manuscripts give 'agenoilloier', to kneel down: that would make considerably more sense and is the reading I have adopted.
[159] Standard topos: compare *Antioche* laisse 223, and see Bancourt vol.2 pp. 655–9.

our deserts'. 'That sounds like a good plan', said the emir. 'We all agree!' shouted the pagans with one voice. Now imagine Corbadas coming into the tent with the shrewd Lucabel and the elderly Glorion. Each was wringing his hands and tearing at his padded jacket; in fact they were lamenting so much that nobody had ever seen anything like it. All three fell to their knees in front of the Sultan. Corbadas kissed his foot and his heel. Canabel, the brother of Nubion and the wisest man in the whole pagan kingdom, raised him to his feet. The Sultan addressed him: 'Tell me, Corbadas, do you have anything to say?' Corbadas was so abjectly cast down that he could not string two words together and could not have said anything for all the gold in the Gardens of Nero. 'My lord', said Lucabel, 'there is no easy way of saying this. As of yesterday we have lost his son Cornumarant. The French have incarcerated him in the depths of the Tower of David'. 'Say no more', said the Sultan. 'We shall have him back by tomorrow. All the French will be taken off as abject captives and we shall marry off their wives to the Turks!' Corbadas raised his eyes when he heard this, and said to the emir: 'If we do this, we could take France in revenge, the kingdom of Charlemagne ruled by King Philip, brother of Count Hugh'. The Sultan stood up and raised his hand. 'My lords', said the emir, 'I forbid any Frenchman to eat bread or fish or to drink wine or water or claret or any potion or sit or take oath or lie in his own house until Cornumarant has been freed from prison'. 'That is a powerful set of prohibitions by our emir for Mahomed's people'. The brother of Philip [Hugh of Vermandois], Robert of Normandy and the duke of Bouillon, Count Robert of Flanders known as the Frisian, Tancred of Sicily cousin of Bohemond, and the count of St-Gilles and the other leaders can all be certain that they will suffer for it if we take them! Each one will have his head chopped off and not a single one will be ransomed!' With that they had 1,000 bugles and 1,000 brass horns sounded. They struck their tents, lashing together the tent poles and loading up their linen, weapons and other equipment. The guides led them off down the route for Barbais. Once the army was en route – I am not going to lie about this – it covered the earth for some seven leagues. Their high quality horses neighed and so did the Aragonese mules; the elephants bellowed and roared; the greyhounds gave tongue; the mongrels barked; austers and falcons next to them called loudly. Mahomed led the way in front of Calcatras and Noiron, Danemons the Diabolical and the emir Corbon. One of them rode a serpent, the second a lion, the third a wriggling monster and the fourth a griffin. Canabels was seated on the offspring of a dragon, leading the elephant which carried Mahomed. The [pagan] deacons sang loudly at the tops of their voices, whilst the Persians and Slavs brandished their swords. The Turks were making so much noise that it could be heard ten leagues off.

181

The Sultan of Persia had a huge army. So many horns were sounded together in chorus that the mountains and valleys and earth shook. The din could be heard from ten and a half leagues off. The Sultan was seated on a throne made entirely of gold worked with fine Oriental craftsmanship. A silken cloth from Almeria formed a canopy above his head to ward off the heat burning down on him from the sky; 12 kings held it up in great state. The Sultan rode a mule which was piebald like a magpie. It ambled so smoothly that he did not even feel it moving beneath him; his hair was not ruffled and his silken robes did not twitch. He had put on a long robe made of silk which was deeper vermilion than a sorb apple and with speckled fur trimmings. The man who wore it was proof against problems with his hearing; he could not be poisoned by any evil spell nor suffer any wound or hut; the robe could lie buried in the ground for 1,000 years and not rot through. It was set with precious stones which glittered so brightly that they lit up the ground around them. The Sultan wore a shining yellow topaz round his neck: nobody who laid eyes on it on any day would lose his sight. His long white beard was spread out over his chest, flowing white as snow down to his belt. His hair fell down over his shoulders; it was gathered up and decorated with four pure gold threads and tightly fastened with jasper buttons. The hood on his head was worth more than Pavia, whilst his robe was worth Brittany and all of Hungary. More than 60 pagan kings surrounded the emir with drawn swords to ensure that no pagan could get within striking distance of him. The whole land was in ferment as far as Tyre and Acre, Damascus and Caesarea and all the way to Tiberias with the news that the Sultan was on his way with an army from Esclavonia. More than 100,000 Turks headed that way, riding to meet the Sultan with large forces. They presented him with rich gifts, abasing themselves before him and begging his pleasure. Now let us hope God, the son of the Holy Virgin, spares a thought for our men: it will not go well with them if help does not arrive soon. Let me tell you about the Turks from Ramleh. They drew up their battle order and made for Jerusalem, taking the route via St Stephen. Our barons came spurring out all together. Now there will be a ferocious battle, and the earth will be left strewn with dead and wounded.

182

The Turks raised their war cry in front of Jerusalem, and our barons came spurring out eagerly. King Godfrey called out to lord Peter, 'Sir, I beg you in God's name to guard the city'. 'I shall do so despite my own wishes', said Peter the Hermit. The King came spurring out, comprehensively armed. He came across Marbrin in the valley of Josaphat; this was the son of Sucaman, the valiant King whose arm and ribs Baldwin had sliced through.[160] [Marbrin] recognised the King as soon as he looked at him. A whole valleyful of gold would not have been enough to make him attack. He shouted for mercy the moment he saw him. King Godfrey seized him by the golden bridle fittings, making no promise as to whether he would spare his life or not. He handed Marbrin over to four knights with instructions to take him into Jerusalem straight away. When the Saracens saw this they turned and fled, not

---

[160] See laisses 170–71.

a single one raising his lance ready to attack. The Turks made their escape as fast as their horses would go, fleeing across the hillsides and mountains, each running for it for all he was worth. King Godfrey meanwhile led his men away and they all went back into Jerusalem. The Turks all assembled on a hillock, next to a ravine. They moaned to each other, strongly demoralised. 'My lords', said Alis, 'things have not gone well for us. We have lost Marbrin, the eldest son of Sucaman. And we have every reason to be upset about the valiant Cornumarant. Bring us that Frenchman so we can cut off his head!' 'No we will not, on my head', said the son of Malcoué. 'It would be far more sensible to get one of our men back in exchange for him'.

183

The son of Malcoué said, 'No we will not, on my head. If you follow my judgement, let us choose a messenger and send him straight back to Jerusalem. We will ask the King and his men for a truce. Then if he so requires we will give him back this Frenchman, but only if we get Cornumarant or Marbrin in exchange'. 'Let us hope Mahomed is with us', chorused the Saracens. They sent Margot and Fauseron and envoys to the King along with King Carbuncle, the brother of Red Lion.[161] Ten or so Esclavons went along with them, carrying olive branches and each brandishing a dove as symbols of peace and love. They came into the presence of King Godfrey and delivered their message. 'My lord', they said, 'you already know what we are going to ask. If you return to us the two Turks you are holding prisoner, you shall have back the count known as Raymond. If you do not agree we will hang him tomorrow, or at the very least cut off his head'. 'My lords, we shall take advice', said the King. With that he summoned his brothers and the other leaders. 'My lords', he said, 'advise me on what I should do. We should get the count back in exchange for one of these pagans'. 'Listen to our views', said Peter the Hermit. 'If it is God's will, we should not lose the count because of the Turks. If we can, let us arrange an exchange of one for the other. Consider the matter, noble King. We advise you strongly that if God were to bring him back to us, we would fight them'. The King came back to the messengers with his response: 'My lords, we will give you back Cornumarant or Marbrin, whichever you prefer, provided we get our man back. Moreover we guarantee you a truce until the third day from today'. 'We pledge ourselves to these conditions', replied the envoys. They took their leave of the King and spurred away. King Godfrey issued orders to his immediate companions, his knights and the *ribalts* – not many youngsters amongst them. He had them dressed in luxurious cloaks of ermine, some with silken tunics and several with siglaton. All carried batons or staffs. Once the *ribalts* were dressed up they looked every inch the part. They drew themselves up imperiously and glared fixedly like lions.

---

[161] Red Lion is a leading Saracen character in the *Antioche*, where he is killed by Robert of Normandy at laisse 377.

184

When the *ribalts* were dressed up they looked like thoroughgoing nobles; they had never put on such rich garments, but behaved like nobles and stalked about imperiously. Together with the knights they numbered 20,500. King Godfrey was a shrewd operator. He got all of them to pass in front of Cornumarant and Marbrin, the son of Sucaman, then to come back round through the door onto the paved courtyard. All of them went round some ten times on the trot, each changing his clothes each time. Take it from me, that was a remarkably cunning trick. Cornumarant whispered to Marbrin, making sure that none of the French could overhear him or listen in: 'An awful lot of knights have paraded in front of us. I never realised that there were so many assembled from the four quarters. They will put up a good fight against our eastern armies; I judge there must be a good 200,000 of them. That Godfrey is impressive. Wouldn't it be good if he believed in Tervagant and was given the Sultan's daughter for his bride? Then the Franks would not be able to withstand us because we would hold everything as far as the Silver Bridge. He would never come back because he would have become a believer – either that or he would have his head cut off without a doubt'. 'Be quiet and show a bit more courtesy!' said Marbrin. 'If the French hear what you are saying, we are in serious trouble. They will draw their swords and take vengeance on the pair of us'. The King promptly made the *ribalts* take off their rich clothes and put on their shabby ones again. They returned with clubs slung round their necks, strutting along proudly two by two in formation in front of the pagans. The King of the Tafurs was there and so was Peter. Each carried a sickle with a resplendent steel blade. The *ribalts* made horrible faces at the Turks, shaking their clubs and baring their teeth.[162] 'In Mahomed's name, anyone who places trust in these people would have to be a madman. They look like devils; they are absolutely hideous. Anyone they attack will really suffer. I think they must be devils or goblins or serpents.[163] They all look the same as if they were related'. 'These men eat ours!' said Cornumarant. When Marbrin heard this he was so terrified that his body and limbs all ran with sweat; he would not have wanted to be where he was for all the gold of the Orient.

185

The Saracens were absolutely terrified by the *ribalts*; Marbrin was so scared that he nearly lost his wits. The noble Cornumarant addressed the King, Baldwin of Edessa and Eustace the elder brother. 'My lords', said the pagan, 'on your honour,

---

[162] The author alludes to their cannibalism: this is exploited to terrify the Saracen envoys. For the ritual nature of cannibalism see M. Janet, 'Les scènes de cannibalisme aux abords d'Antioche dans les récits de la première croisade: des chroniques à la chanson de croisade', *Bien dire et bien aprandre* 22 (2004) pp. 179–91.

[163] Emphasising the liminal otherness of the Tafurs, who are depicted as barely human.

will both of us be exchanged for Raymond? We beg you in the name of your God, tell us the truth: do you intend us to live or die?' 'We have reached a view', said King Godfrey. 'One of you will be freed and we have given our word on it'. With that they went up to the palace. The pagan envoys brought Raymond and presented him to King Godfrey straight away. In return they asked for Cornumarant, and the King released him from prison and handed him over. Once he had surrendered him to the pagans, Baldwin of Edessa enfolded him in an embrace and begged him to have faith in Jesus in majesty. If he did he could have back his lands and all which was his by right. 'I can never agree to that', said Cornumarant. 'I would rather have my head cut from my body or each of my limbs sliced off rather than deny or refuse Mahomed!' King Baldwin wept with chagrin when he heard this. Cornumarant rose and asked permission to go. [King Godfrey commended him then to God; they observed the truce to the third day. Cornumarant mounted his horse and left the city.][164] The King and his two brothers went with him for a considerable distance. As he left them Cornumarant announced his defiance. He would never as long as he lived, he said, feel any kind of friendship for them; they could not expect any kind of trust or reliance because he would never harbour kindly feelings towards any Frank or the Christian religion. With that he left them, spurring his horse away, and the ten messengers went with him. The King and his brothers turned back. They had Marbrin taken down to the dungeons in the depths of the tower, but gave him plenty to eat and drink. The King and the barons were delighted to have got the count of St-Gilles back. They gave him plenty of baths and treated him with medicinal herbs until he was completely recovered from his ordeal.[165] They offered our Lord abundant praise and thanks, but were extremely concerned about the Persian army. And they had every reason to be apprehensive because it was the largest there had ever been – you can be sure this is true. They spent every night fully armed on watch over Jerusalem. Let us leave them there for the moment and not say anything more about them. Cornumarant had ridden away with his companions without delay. They had spurred on so fast that they met the imperial forces ten leagues out from Ramleh. The army of the emir Sultan was so great that it covered the mountains and surrounding land, and the valleys and mountains were thick with them. Nobody had ever seen such a great army since God formed Adam from clay and drew his wife Eve from his rib – that is the plain truth. There were easily 150 kings and emirs. The Saracens numbered 300,000; that was the number estimated by Caliph and Canabel.

---

[164] See Thorp's note on the text: some lines have got garbled and various scribes use different solutions to fill the gap.

[165] Raymond's captivity counterpoints that of Rainalt Porcet in the *Antioche*: unlike Rainalt however he is released and returned to the Christian army. The author could not bring Rainalt himself into his text as he was missing presumed dead in the *Antioche*.

186

The Sultan's army was encamped ten leagues from Ramleh. Nobody could possibly tell you how many tents and pavilions there were; they covered seven and a half leagues. The whole land was full of them, and the country glinted with finials and eagles. The Sultan's tent was down towards the waste land in front of a fountain in a meadow, and the land glittered from its impact three leagues around. The emir was sitting in great state on a folding stool of fine oriental craftsmanship, surrounded by 100 pagan kings. Imagine Cornumarant and his household spurring up. He swung out of the saddle of his Nubian warhorse; he entered the tent, with the crowd parting in front of him, and came into the Sultan's presence. He fell at his feet in an attitude of subjection, and was on the point of kissing his legs and his hose when the white-haired Canabel seized him and raised him to his feet. Corbadas gave thanks to Mahomed when he saw his son and said to the noble Sultan: 'You are truly powerful. Your commands are carried out throughout the world. There is no man alive who would dare to refuse your orders'. The army was overjoyed at the sight of Cornumarant; they worshipped Mahomed and made offerings. Once the celebration was in full swing Cornumarant spoke in ringing tones. 'By Mahomed, lord emir, I will not mince my words. All my men are killed and my army is in disarray. Jerusalem is in the hands of a great host of knights. I launched an attack on them on the day I arrived, having taken booty from the valley of Josaphat. The Christians drew up ranks and marched out; they gave us a fierce reception almost like madmen, with broken lances and shattered shields all over the place. I myself was taken and held captive; there is no other way to put it. And King Sucaman has lost his right arm, cut off by Baldwin's gleaming sword. No weapon is worth as much as a sorb apple compared to the blows inflicted by the French as they brandish their swords in front of their chests. When King Godfrey wields his sword and strikes one of our men on his green-sheened helmet, he slices down through him and his horse as if they were a branch of olivewood, severing soul from body so cleanly that he does not feel a thing. Marbrin is being held captive inside the ancient tower [of David]. We took one of their counts, Raymond of St-Gilles. I was handed over in exchange for him but they have hung onto Marbrin: if he does not apostatise he will find he is not long for this world'. The Sultan's blood ran cold when he heard this. He swore by Mahomed, whom he worshipped and adored, that the city would be put under siege the following day and the attack would continue as long as it was not surrendered. Cornumarant said, 'I have given my word that we will have a truce until the third day from today, and we will hold to it. I would rather be killed than see my religion worsted. Before we get to that point, their religion will be dragged in the dust and Godfrey's men so dismayed by the sight of our army that they will surrender to you and the city will be yours. We shall take them off as captives to the kingdom of Persia; you can use them to repopulate your wastelands and bring them back to life through the wealth they will generate. Our religion will be exalted and theirs weakened. Your word will be law throughout the kingdom of France; and if anyone refuses to obey your commands let his head be cut off instantly!' 'Well said, by Mahomed!' said the King of Nubia. With that they left things there as night was falling. The pagans went to their tents, banging enthusiastically on their drums. They created such a din with their drums and pipes and horns that it could be heard nearly all the way to Jerusalem. Now may God, Son of the Blessed Virgin Mary, come to the aid of our men: it will go hard with them if they do not get help quickly.

187

The army whooped it up that evening. There were lanterns lit all over the place, and the land flickered with the lights of bonfires everywhere so that the glimmer could be seen for ten leagues around. When dawn broke the following morning they struck their tents, lashed their provisions together, harnessed up and got everything ready. The Sultan ordered the whole army to arm itself and to march non-stop to the plains of Ramleh. At that the Saracens promptly took up their arms. More than 20,000 horns sounded a flourish, and the sound could be heard all the way to Jerusalem. The army of Our Lord was petrified with fear. The Persian army got under way immediately, covering seven leagues around. The Sultan was riding in full state on Maigremor, with a star on his forehead;[166] the horse had never broken into a sweat no matter how hard it was pushed and could cover more ground in hilly and mountainous country than other horses could in fields. Its hooves were tougher than any tempered sickle. It could run for 30 leagues without stopping while carrying a block of iron. The horse was draped in purple with a pattern of circles; the saddle was of ivory set with topazes and with numerous emeralds set in balsam wood; it shone more brightly than a lit lantern. The emir was very tall and had a broad forehead, wider than a good palm's width. His long grey beard flowed down his chest as far as his breeches, which were as white as flowers in a meadow. His hair reached down to his shoulders, drawn up and fastened with jasper buttons; and his head was crowned with a rich circlet worth a whole mine full of gold. The emir had put on a sweeping fur robe. I don't know that it is worth carrying on this description since there had never been a robe like it. It had been designed and made in the deserts of Abilant, where it was worked on by Pallas and Morgan la Fée with her.[167] The emir held a square rod which was covered with intricate patterning of the finest gold in Arabia and set all over with precious stones. It was pierced in various places so that when the wind blew through the gaps it made a sound more sweet than the best-tuned lute, and when it came out through any of them no song or note or voice could have sung better nor any melody sounded [sweeter]. As the Sultan rode along mint, balm and rushes and brightly coloured roses were thrown down in front of him. 150 infidel kings surrounded him, all with drawn sword, so that the pagans could not get within a

---

[166] The Old French could equally mean that he was ornamented with stars.
[167] A rare reference to Arthurian legend in the Cycle. Morgan la Fée was Arthur's half-sister.

crossbow shot. Saracens bowed down at every step he took and every last one pledged him his faith. The army was enormous when it was under way, winding through hills and mountains; it would have taken more than a day to get from one end to the other. Horns, bugles and brass instruments were sounded in unison so that the mountains rang with them and the valleys responded. So much dust was raised by the swift warhorses that the cloud could be seen from Jerusalem: this terrified the soldiers of Our Lord. And they could be forgiven for being so scared: it was the largest army anyone had ever seen. The emir swore on his flowing beard that he would not return home without having devastated France, and taken the Christians prisoner in chains; anyone who refused to embrace Mahomed would have his head cut off. But, if God so wills, his beard will be perjured. If God is with the princes of the land of salvation – who have already turned back towards Jerusalem and are already across the river Jordan – the Sultan's whole army will be defeated and the Saracen people conquered and killed. And now you are going to hear a splendid song: no *jongleur* has sung of this better.[168]

188

The emir rode ahead with his huge force. 150 kings headed things up, bringing their gods Mahomed and Tervagant and the emir Sultan's fabulous treasure. The Caliph called out Canebalt and Morgant and the old emir; his brother the *amulaine* and Tort the son of Aresne and King Gloriant; Calcatras the aupatris from the hills of Boccidant, the King of Caneloigne and his brother Rubant and the old Aerofle Cornumarant's uncle; Cernugle of Monnoigte and his brother Ataignant; Amindab of Rodes and Bondifer the tyrant. His company included the Moor of Moriant, Seong Oain the Fat from the deserts of the East, Butor and Damemont, Masarie the *amudant*, Galafre and Esteflé, Corbon and Suspirant and Marmoire and Sanguin, Ysabras the giant, Fabur, and Maucoe the brother of Solimant.[169] He also called out with them King Cornumarant. 'My lords', said the Caliph, 'listen to what I have to say. Order all your treasure chests to be brought out, the rich reliquaries of Arabian gold and your splendid vessels: that is my command. 10,000 pagans are to carry them ahead of us to Jerusalem, while you follow behind with 100,000 Turks. Once the French see the gold they will be desperate to get their hands on it; they will come swarming out to take it – and that will be your cue to come spurring over the horizon and cut their heads off straight away!'[170] 'By Mahomed, that is not a stupid plan', said Gondris. 'The Apostolic Caliph's proposition is a very attractive one'. With that the Turks hurried to undo their chests, dragging out treasure and silken

---

[168] 'Enluminée' literally means 'illuminated' as in a manuscript letter; here more generally the meaning of 'splendid'. T-L III.447–50.

[169] 'Amulaine' and 'amudant' are fictional Arabic ranks without French or Islamic equivalent: Bancourt vol.2 pp. 839–52.

[170] A similar reference is found in the supposed letter of Alexius to the West: see discussion in Introduction. The stratagem is typical of the Antichrist.

cloths and large reliquaries of glittering gold. The Saracens carried out armfuls in long processions, singing at the tops of their voices. The Azoparts surrounded them singing. All of this was a cunning plan by those cowardly villains. 50,000 Turks, all good archers, and another 100,000 carefully selected for their valour – not a single one without a good swift horse, a mailed hood and a good helmet and a sharp sword, a long tempered stiletto or a heavy lead club – all followed at a distance behind the emir's treasure. King Cornumarant acted as the pennant bearer, riding Plantamor swiftly through the defiles. The Turks rode forward at such ferocious speed that the metal of their stirrups bent beneath their feet. He brandished his spear with ostentatious pride, uttering imprecations against King Godfrey and Baldwin. Now may the God Who made Adam and Eve come to their aid: if the King and his men come out to the battlefield they will all be killed or taken, with not one escaping. Seeing a great deal of treasure which one covets can only have bad consequences.

189

The emir and his noble barons rode on; not a single one stopped until they reached the plains of Ramleh. Meanwhile the treasure was taken on ahead to Jerusalem. It was all laid out together opposite the Gate of St Stephen, who was killed in the name of God by being stoned to death with pebbles and rocks. The Juracop cried: 'It's here for the taking. Sing!'[171] They turned to each other and started to sing. King Godfrey went up onto the walls; so did Baldwin, Eustace and the brave Raymond, the King of the Tafurs and the bearded Peter [the Hermit], knights and *ribalts* alike: there was a huge throng all crowded onto the wall. The good King Godfrey addressed them: 'My lords, your attention please', he said. 'I implore you: not one of you is to dare go out of the city to get what you can see. The Turks are using their gold as the bait for a trap. Look carefully. They are laying an ambush not far off. Do not give them the idea that they can catch us by taking the treasure they have strewn around in front of the city. But if Jesus in glory were to have shown us such favour that there is a way of getting possession of it, then it would be split between you in equal measure'. The French replied: 'My lord, it shall be as you wish. Not one of us will break your ranks on pain of death'. When the King had bolstered their resolve, he went up into the Tower of David by himself. From there he saw pagans and Turks erecting their pavilions and tents. All the land he could see was covered with armed men. The King invoked God, in great anguish of spirit. 'Lord God Our Father', he said, 'take pity on the little army of Your people which has remained here to guard Your city where Your body suffered and the Holy Sepulchre in which You were laid. Lord God, if so be Your wish, do not allow it to happen that the Devil continues to be served and worshipped. But God, if it is the case that You want to suffer Your city to be taken by the infidels and Your people to suffer and die, then I beg You, noble lord, to listen to my prayer:

---

[171] Neither the name nor the apparent rank is attested elsewhere: a fictitious character.

allow my head to be the first one to be cut off, because I would rather be killed than be taken captive. Ah, where are you, you nobility of France? You have left me alone and undefended in this foreign land. I am pretty much alone against these infidels. You have left me so abandoned that you will never see me again. If the Holy Sepulchre is taken and shamefully surrendered, holy Christianity will be much the poorer as a result'. With this the King wept and tore his hair. God never made anyone born of woman who would not have taken pity on the King if they had seen him in that state.

190

Once King Godfrey had finished his lament, he said many things to God in private. Seeing the host of pagans surrounding his city, he made his prayer to God with fervent sincerity. Once he had finished it he buckled on his good sword; drawing it from the scabbard he brandished it in his hand. 'Sword', said the King, 'yet again I shall see you stained with the blood of dead Saracens. I shall go down fighting before I die if such be the pleasure of God and His mother, whose soul will be blessed'.

191

When King Godfrey had finished his speech he put his sword back in its scabbard after saying his prayer. Then he raised his hand and gave the sign of blessing. He bounded down the stairs of the keep and found his people in great consternation. 'My lord, what shall we do?' they asked him. 'If you tell us to we will go out for that treasure'. 'Gentlemen', said the King, 'please do no such thing, because the wicked Saracens are trying to trick us. If we once go out there, we shall never be able to get back in. Let us hold our peace and watch development. If the pagans attack us we shall defend ourselves stoutly for better or for worse'. The King of the Tafurs frowned when he heard this. He swore angrily by the body of St Simeon that if Godfrey did not let him out he would no longer accept his suzerainty, and that he was going out anyway, like it or not, even if he had to creep out like a thief. 'What, Devil take it, are we prisoners?' he said. 'Have the Saracens got us shut up in here? They are actually bringing us treasure and we do not dare to take it? If anyone wants to trust in me they can have the whole lot! We know full well we can only die one death, and we will suffer it for Jesus the All-Conquering so that we do not need to reproach ourselves before God. By saint Lazarus, let us get out there! Even if we end up all dead or all captured we don't care! If I have a horse which can carry me fast enough, I shall go and kill the Sultan in his pavilion. I don't care if I die since I shall have done a good deed'. 'And we shall all follow you!' shouted the *ribalts*. 'None of us will fail you because we are afraid to die! We would rather be killed than lose you!' 'You need to be reasonable', said King Godfrey. 'The truce is still in force and that would be treachery'. Whilst the Tafurs were creating all this noise and argument, picture Cornumarant spurring up with 100,000 Turks and Esclavons. They spurred right up to our people shouting at the tops of their voices: 'The truce is over! If you do not worship Mahomed you will all be killed or captured! We are going to have you led off into the depths of captivity, and the Sultan will have your Peter the Hermit hanged: not a single one of you will be ransomed'. 'If God so pleases, let us strike', said Godfrey. He shouted loudly: 'My lords, to horse! But I implore you in God's name not to pursue them'.[172] Raymond of St-Gilles sounded the great horn.

192

Lord Raymond of St-Gilles sounded the great horn, and the armies of Our Lord got ready for battle swiftly. Lord Peter the Hermit called to Godfrey, 'My lord, I am going to take up arms too in recognition of the love I bear you'. He put on his hauberk straight away, and King Godfrey laced up his helmet; however he did not put on iron shin-guards. He buckled a steel sword at his left. They brought a horse and he mounted; Count Baldwin handed him his shield and his brother Eustace his lance. Peter found it too light and flung it to the ground. He took up a large rod and sharpened its cutting edge, then picked up a sharp blade and put it into the sharpened end, swearing on the death of God that nobody else should carry it. Once armed he looked splendid. He rode with such pressing determination that the stirrups broke and the saddle split. 'My God, what a knight!' said the King of the Tafurs. 'It must be a century since he got on a horse, or put on a hauberk or jousted with a lance. He may be wearing arms but he won't be of much help to anyone'. Peter swore that in death's name he would; if he once attacked the pagans he would knock down so many that the noble Sultan himself would be amazed. Peter dismounted, saddled his horse again, and King Godfrey gallantly aided him. When Peter was mounted, he made the sign of the Cross over himself and cried at the top of his voice: 'By God, this much is clear: compared to those who get all the plunder from this battle, those who come off worst will have plenty to complain about'. Once he came back, he would have plenty to boast about, he said. Lord Peter was absolutely determined to prove himself and take Cornumarant, provided his horse did not fall: but without God's help he has no chance of returning.

193

The King and his household rode out of Jerusalem, leaving the city garrisoned with 200 knights. Covering the ground as far as their horses could run they flung themselves mercilessly on the Turks. Had you been there, you would have heard an almighty din from the pagans, such clashing of lances and swords that it could

---

[172] This would have broken the battle order and left the Christians vulnerable, exactly what the Saracens were trying to do by displaying the treasure. Possibly an echo of the herds loosed at Ascalon by the Saracens to try and distract the Crusaders?

be heard from two leagues off. Lord Peter the Hermit with his white beard was mounted on a good warhorse. He pricked it with his spurs, took up his shield by the straps and brandished his weapon. If you ask me, he is going to do something pretty stupid. When he moved his weapon went all over the place because he didn't know how to carry it raised upright. He grabbed it in both hands and lowered it again, couching it across his saddle in front of him. He pricked the horse beneath him with his spurs, and it bolted off at high speed; his Nubian warhorse was carrying him straight towards the treasure. Now may God, son of the Blessed Virgin Mary, watch over him. The pagans rode in front of him (may they be cursed, by the body of God!). Peter aimed his horse at them and spurred forward, followed the Turks and attacked them *en masse*. His weapon was very strong and did not get damaged at all. He killed 500 before it broke.[173] Those guarding the treasure fled towards the mountains in the direction of the waste land, hotly pursued by Peter – may God guard him! His spear splintered in the thick of battle and the foul pagan bastards killed his horse beneath him. Once on the ground Peter flushed with rage. He seized his sword immediately, flung the shield he was carrying down onto the battlefield and struck great two-handed blows with his shining sword. The hermit defended himself stoutly; he is not going to get any reinforcements because our men are a good half league off. Peter was surrounded completely by Persians.

194

It is hardly surprising if Peter was rather perturbed at finding himself surrounded by the race of the Devil; however he did not let himself get paralysed by fear of death but struck great two-handed blows with his steel sword. Seeing a rocky ledge he made for it and defended himself in front, though with no protection behind. Anyone who could have seen Peter slicing up Saracens, knocking one dead on top of another, could not have asked for a better knight. The pagans attacked him: there were a good 2,000, but not a single one was brave enough to get near him. When they saw the hermit inflicting such damage on their men, the fork-tongued pagans all fell back because they were scared of Peter's bravery, and the way he was looking at them as if he would like to gobble them up.[174] Now I am going to tell you about our men – may God help Peter! – and how amazingly brave they are in the press of battle. They make the earth beneath their feet shiver and shake with the clash of their swords, their cries and their din. Picture King Godfrey riding to the rescue, his brothers and the other warriors riding up and down the ranks with their swords looking for him; their ability as swordsmen made it clear just what good knights they were. The Turks were unwillingly forced from the battlefield; the Christians rained blows on them and they retreated by the length of a bowshot. They pursued them all the way past the treasure, but did not pick up as much

---

[173] Rather comic-book humour. Compare Rainouart's antics in the *Guillaume* cycle.

[174] Even though he is not a *tafur*. He is however shown in the company of the King of the Tafurs a number of times. The theme is developed further in laisse 198.

as one piece of it. When the Saracens saw this, they did not make any move to load it up but shouted their warcries. The archers turned. Picture the arrows sent from Turkish bows; our men suffered greatly as the Saracens drew their bows and flung their weapons; neither hauberks nor quartered shields were of any help in preventing them being wounded in the side and in the ribs. Gautier met his end in this skirmish; so did Godescal and Simon, Roger of Etampes, Achard of Montmerle and Ralph of Pevier, Guy of Aubefort and his brother Rainier; a lot of havoc was wreaked on our men on that occasion. When the King saw his ranks thinning, he thought he would burst with rage and anger. 'Jerusalem! Forward, men!' he shouted. 'Let every last one of you think about his life and put it on the line!' At that you might have heard the shouting and the din intensify. Anyone he struck with his sword on his banded helmet got cut in half right down to the neck. His brothers and all the rest struck with consummate skill; their swords were stained with blood and brains.

195

The skirmish was fierce and it was a ferocious battle. Picture the King of the Tafurs with his mob; each carried a mace, an axe or a sharp knife. The ruffian force fell mercilessly on the Turks. They sliced open their hearts and ripped at their entrails. They cut the Turks into smaller pieces than straw blown by the wind. The King of the Tafurs went to work ferociously, scattering them with his sharp sickle; anyone he attacked didn't even have time to yawn. So the Turks fled in front of him like a flock of ewes; not one was bold enough to confront him; not even the bravest of them would have waited to meet him for the whole realm of Cornwall. Cornumarant called to the emir of Escaille: 'By my God Mahomed, I don't think we can be worth anything because here is a body of men from who knows where killing our men and inflicting carnage. This must be some diabolical trick by the denizens of Hell!' When the emir heard this he bowed his head and was so frightened that he almost threw up. 'By Mahomed', he said, 'I am sure without a shadow of a doubt that we are going to end by being soundly defeated. It was a bad day when we ran into this band'.

196

When Cornumarant saw that the *ribalts* had arrived he shouted 'Damascus!' and drew his sword. He aimed Plantamor and spurred on, 20,000 infidels riding with him and bearing down on the *ribalts*. Innumerable arrows were fired from Turkish bows; many were killed as they did not have weapons. The *ribalts* would have been dead and defeated had it not been for Baldwin coming to the rescue. Many sword blows were rained on the Saracens, and many feet, hands and heads cut off; the battlefield was strewn with dead and wounded. King Godfrey brandished his sword of tempered steel, urged Capalu on with his golden spurs, met Cornumarant and landed a great blow down on the middle of his helmet of beaten gold, sending the jewels and floral decorations flying. The sword glanced to one side as it smashed down on the left side of the shield. Everything the other side of the blow was cut off, and if the blow had been straight it would have cut Cornumarant right in half. When Cornumarant realised his assailant was Godfrey, not all the treasure of Cahu would have been enough to make him wait around for a further blow; he spurred off as fast as the horse would carry him. King Godfrey headed for Malargu and struck him; he was the nephew of the *algolant* and son of the *amiral*. He cut him in half through his chest. His thick-maned horse galloped off with one half and would not be stopped all the way to the army of the Sultan. Many Saracens were terrified when they saw this blow, and fled like the cowardly infidels they were; they would not soon be seen in battle again and nobody would be spurring after them. The King retreated, having won the day on the battlefield, but not so much as a finger was laid on the treasure. They were highly upset about lord Peter the Hermit. 'Alas', said the King, 'this is a real loss I have suffered. I will not be happy again without him'.

197

The atmosphere in Jerusalem was sombre. 1,000 fainted away in sheer grief for Peter the Hermit, and the King of the Tafurs was beside himself, lamenting and calling himself the most unfortunate of wretches. However King Godfrey bolstered their morale: 'My lords, for the love of God, do not lose heart like this. If he met his end for God he is likely to be blissfully happy. Let me tell you all this one thing for you to hear – as long as I live this city will not be taken. Take it from me: I would rather be torn limb from limb than have the Devil served and worshipped there any longer. If you hold fast to your faith God will be your Defender: and if he comes to your aid you have nothing to fear'. When the King had reassured them in this way, he shouted to his brother Eustace: 'Heat me some water – my hand is so swollen that I cannot put down my sword'. 'I shall do as you ask', said Eustace. The hand and wrist of the King were so swollen that it was extremely difficult to prise the sword from his grip.[175] Then Eustace ordered: 'Let a guard of 7,000 armed men be set over the city'. This order was carried out. Now I am going to leave there our men beloved of God and talk instead about Peter [the Hermit], who was backed up against a dark-coloured rock. He was hard pressed by Turks and Persians, and wounded all over by the Turkish bows of horn. But he was under the protection of Jesus and will not suffer any more wounds. Imagine Cornumarant coming spurring up in a great lather. 'Your end has come, old man!' he yelled at the top of his voice. If you do not defend yourself I am going to strike you! See this sharp pike – you will find it sticking in your chest and sides! Surrender now or you are a dead man! By his grey moustache, you will be handed over to the Sultan!' 'You will do no such thing if God is with me', said Peter the Hermit.

---

[175] Robert of Normandy had a similar problem in laisses 17 and 18.

'You will pay a high price before you can take me. You will be a really valiant and capable man if you can lay a finger on me'. He leapt forward, sword at the ready; running at Cornumarant like a madman [he was about to strike him with his gold-hilted sword; Cornumarant was furious when he saw this and] swung his square-headed pike at him.[176] He struck Peter the Hermit in his left side; the weapon went right through his trunk and knocked him flying with the force of the blow. 'Come and take this old man captive for me', shouted Cornumarant. The Saracens seized Peter, swarming over him from 100 directions. They tied his hands and blindfolded him. Lifting him onto a horse, they brought him back to their army and presented him to the Sultan in the main royal tent. The emir ordered him disarmed; this was done and his helmet taken off. The hermit was very tall, burly and well built;[177] he had a long stiff beard, luxuriant moustaches, and his hair stood out in tangles: it was a good year since he had had a wash or done any laundry or had a bath or [even] combed his hair. His face was filthy and stained with dirt. He had a wide forehead and aquiline nose. He was prouder than a provoked lion. Peter ground his teeth, raised his eyebrows and stared the *almacours* and kings full in the face. He rolled up his sleeves and braced himself four times. He seized the emir when he was released. Canabel shouted to him, 'Calm down, my friend. If you as much as move a muscle your head will be cut off straight away'. 'My friend, where were you born; what is your family and ancestry?' the Sultan asked Peter. 'Do not try and hide anything: tell me who you are'. 'My lord, I shall tell you exactly that', said the hermit.

198

The emir Sultan addressed Peter, 'Tell me your name, noble friend'. 'My lord, I shall not try and hide it', said the hermit. 'I am known as Peter on both sides of the ocean. I was born in Armenia and that is where I live'.[178] But before he could finish the sentence he found himself fainting away right in the middle of the tent. When the emir saw this he called for Lucion, the most skilled doctor anyone had ever seen. 'Go and make a potion straight away', said the Sultan. 'Get this Frank back on his feet immediately'. Lucion unlocked a chest and pulled out some *marabiton* – this is a very holy herb from Simon Magus who threw the seven sages into a prison dungeon.[179] As soon as he could get it between Peter's teeth he set about treating his wound, which was so deep that you could see his lungs: in a trice he was healthier than any hawk or falcon. The Sultan had him seated on an ivory bench with golden sides. Next to Rubion, sending Tahon to sit on his other

---

[176] Thorp's emendation faced with significant scribal variation.
[177] Not in reality: he was small. Jean Flori, *Pierre l'Ermite et la première croisade* (Paris, 1999) p. 24.
[178] Peter was in fact from Amiens, which sounds not dissimilar.
[179] 'Marabiton' is attested as an Arabic gold coin but not as a herb: T-L V.1112.

side. Corsubles sat on the ground with the *aupatris* Macon, the emir, the *amustan* and Noiron; the noble *amulaine* sat on a barrel-shaped stool all worked with pure gold in the time of Solomon. The other kings disposed themselves round and about. The tent was thickly strewn with rushes and wild mint, filled with the sweet fragrance of honeysuckle, and with balm and incense scattered on the floor; 30 candles flickered in front of [the image of] Mahomed. 150 Persian and Esclavon kings were seated in front of the tent, all looking at Peter to see what he looked like and what his face was. 'He looks like a nasty piece of work', they muttered to each other. 'He's one of those who grill our people and eat them. His teeth are sharper than a bradawl or a punch. Look at him champing and chomping. He looks like a devil and his expression is like a dragon's. If he was left alone in the tent he would have gulped a Turk down his throat quicker than a lion would devour quarter of a sheep!' The Saracens were all quivering in front of the hermit, and he was under a great deal of Turkish and pagan scrutiny.

199

When Peter the Hermit saw the pagans muttering he became very concerned, terrified that they intended to kill him. He rolled up his sleeves and made for one of the kings: he landed such a heavy blow on his neck that he smashed his brain stem to smithereens and knocked him dead in front of the Sultan's feet. The pagans rushed on him, Saracens and Esclers, determined to cut off his head with their steel swords. At this the emir Sultan issued immediate orders: 'Anyone who dares attack him will regret it!' The Sultan had him seized and brought in front of him. He started to quiz Peter in his own language as to whether he was willing to serve and worship Mahomed and renounce and forswear the Christian religion. 'If you do, Peter, I am willing to grant you Damascus, and then you can accompany me to fight France. You shall have this whole great army to lead. We shall start by taking passage across the sea: that is what I intend to do in order to destroy the Christians. I shall have you crowned at Aix-la-Chapelle!'[180] When Peter heard this he shook his head and said to the emir, 'I am willing to consider your proposal, but show me your religion and tell me about it. If it is to my taste you will see me convert'. 'By Mahomed', said the Sultan, 'you are a truly noble man. Nothing could be better than the qualities you display'. 'You should hear me speak then', said the hermit. 'I can give a truly rousing speech from the back of my donkey. There would be no need to send a Caliph rather than me'. When the Sultan heard this, he bowed to Peter and said to the Saracens: 'I want to grant this man my favour. Go straight away and have Mahomed brought. I shall show Peter the god who can give him salvation and find out whether he is able to accept him'. 'Indeed', said Lord Peter, 'if he wants to hear me out. I intend to reduce him to tears before he leaves'.

---

[180] Charlemagne was crowned at Aix-la-Chapelle on Christmas Day 800; Peter is implicitly compared with him.

200

[The image of] Mahomed was brought into the emir's tent. The glitter of its gold and the rock crystal on it glanced off the walls of the royal tent all the way round. More than 1,000 candles burned in front of it. Lord Peter bowed down in front of it, but did not mean it. Then they brought a high metal tower. A Saracen went up into it and made a huge din. Peter bowed down to it again – but not sincerely. Under his breath he invoked God, the spiritual father, to help him again to escape the clutches of that wicked race. The Sultan instructed that he should be offered an ivory horn, and a sceptre of pure gold set with coral, and a richly enamelled cup. The Saracens were thrilled, capering and dancing with delight. They showered him with bezants and costly royal silks. They had Peter confirmed according to the rite of Marragal .He was dragged backwards to a small door and hit beneath his chin as part of the rite.[181] The Sultan and Corbadas could hardly contain their joy.

201

Once Peter the Hermit had worshipped Mahomed and the Turks had confirmed him according to the pagan rite, the Sultan gave him his command. He had Peter sat next to him on a folding stool, and asked him all about those in Jerusalem and about King Godfrey whom they had crowned – was it true that he was such a good swordsman as they said? 'He certainly is', said Lord Peter. 'He can cut an armed Saracen in half down the middle.[182] No pagan can withstand the power of his mighty blows, and he is so brave that he fears no king or emir. And he is more generous than I can possibly say'. Now imagine them bringing in Sucaman, who had lost his right arm and right side. Next came the horse he had been riding, which Duke Godfrey had cut in half; the saddle and saddlebow were dripping with blood. Sucaman saw the Sultan and begged his mercy. 'My God, who has done that to you?' said the emir. 'By Mahomed', replied Sucaman, 'it was that Frankish infidel Baldwin of Edessa with his sharp sword, to whom the Old Man of the Mountains has given his daughter as a wife. He is the brother of that Godfrey who has caused us so much trouble, destroyed our religion and put Mahomed to shame. See the sort of blows he has landed on this king: he sliced him as easily as a stripped reed. And they have taken away my son and imprisoned him in chains in the Tower of David. By the great loyalty I have shown you, avenge me or I shall see myself as a dead man'. The Sultan was very upset when he heard this. He swore solemnly by Mahomed Gomelin that if [the Christians] did not surrender the city the following day they were facing certain death: 'I shall have them flayed alive and all burnt at

---

[181] The *Antioche* has similar accounts of imaginary rites e.g. laisses 113, 223. It is not entirely clear what is happening here, though the *Gran Conquista* describes a broadly similar ritual to gain entrance to the Holy Sepulchre (I.186–8).

[182] Recounted in *Antioche* laisses 162–3; also described in sources such as OV vol.V pp. 84–5, RC 79, RM IV.20.

the stake. All the gold in the world would not be enough to buy their lives!' The Sultan soon had an interpreter brought along and praised Peter the Hermit to the skies in front of him. He sent the interpreter to Jerusalem with instructions to tell Godfrey to come to him immediately, and not to delay if he valued his life. He was to have his hair cut off according to pagan rites. Once he had renounced and foresworn his God, the Sultan would make him his heir and give him his lands. He was not going to get any help from his fellow Christians: it was at least a month since they had departed across the sea. If he refused to do this, he should be quite clear that his body would be eaten by bears and lions.

202

Once the emir Sultan had sent off his message, his wisest Turks advised him to have his white charger from Aragon brought up. It was covered with a rich silken cloth worked in Carthage. The emir's saddle was worked of gold and covered with pictures, enamelled images of birds and fish from the sea. The saddle was a splendid example of pagan workmanship. A man could have travelled over all the earth and sea, field and home, sea and forest, before he could have found a better one no matter how far he travelled. 'Emir', said the Caliph, 'send your shield as well. It has a magnificent carbuncle on top of it. The French are covetous by nature. If they once start throwing envious glances at it, you can be sure any proclamation will not last long; and it will impair their ability to fight because those who are covetous are often led to act shamefully'. 'By Mahomed, that is good advice', said the Sultan. He immediately sent for his white charger from Aragon; Marin l'Aigage equipped it splendidly for the king's use.

203

The emir had the charger magnificently harnessed. The bridle and saddle were made entirely of pure gold; the stirrups were hung with gold ornaments; and all was thickly studded with emeralds and priceless topazes. The chestplate had an amazing property: there was no man in France rich enough to buy it at its proper worth because anyone who had it could not be killed by poison. The horse was whiter than snow in a snowstorm and its head as red as coals in a brazier. It was covered by a vermilion silk coat with a chequered pattern, very delicately worked so that you could see the white shimmer through the red. The bridle it wore was worth the entire fief of Pithiviers: there was hardly a man in the world who would not have coveted it. The emir entrusted the horse to the messenger and sent them off to Jerusalem to try out the effect on King Godfrey. He gave instructions to the messenger to tell Godfrey to be very afraid: he would have him eaten alive and devoured by lions along with both his brothers if they refused to deny and foreswear God; and the other captives would all be bound and tied to targets to give his archers some shooting practice. The messenger turned and left straight away, carrying an olive branch. He had the horse on a leading rein to his right, a splendidly proud animal. He spurred all the way to Jerusalem without stopping. The King was up on the walls and saw him coming. 'Look, a messenger is coming', he said to his men, 'I have no idea what he is going to tell us. That horse with him is worth all the gold in Montpellier. I want you to be absolutely clear about my orders: you are not to take as much as a *denier* of his. Anyone who lays a finger on him will regret it, because I know full well he has been sent to spy on us'.[183] 'My lord, we shall obey your orders', said the knights. The messenger reached the gate and started shouting [for admission]. King Godfrey had him let in. There was a rich palace opposite the Holy Temple: they had the messenger taken there and the horse attached to a ring. King Godfrey summoned his interpreter and ordered his men to be well armed.

204

There was a noble palace right in front of the Holy Temple. That was where they took the Persian messenger. King Godfrey summoned his interpreter Morant, who talked to the infidel in fluent Saracen, then relayed the replies to the King in his own tongue – not secretly but out loud so that everyone could hear. King Godfrey was to go to the noble Sultan; he was to put his faith in Mahomed and to worship Tervagant; and if he did not he could be sure that he would be eaten alive by lions whilst his brothers would be killed by flaying and the other [Christians] tightly bound and tied to archery targets to be shot with arrows by some of his men. 'You cannot expect any help from the armies of France', he said, 'and Peter the Hermit has become an emir. If you are willing to submit to his religion, he will make you his heir and you will hold all of the Orient'. King Godfrey replied: 'Let it not be the pleasure of Almighty God that I should relinquish my faith as long as I live, and I have no intention either of giving up Jerusalem. As long as I am capable of striking out with my sharp sword, I would rather lose my head than give any pagan grounds for triumphing over me'. Then he said to the interpreter: 'Tell him that I give him this message. By rights it should be pagans subject to Franks, bowing their heads and taking their orders. And this I can tell him for certain because I am absolutely sure of it: if God, in Whom I put my faith and the true judge in Whom I believe, protects me I shall carry on the fight as long as I live. I shall go conquering my way all the way to the kingdom of Persia. I will not stop until I reach the ancient city of Mecca and see its towers and marble palaces topple; I will place the huge candlesticks which burn to Mahomed in the Holy Sepulchre where God rose from the dead; and I shall hand over the god they believe in, Mahomed Gomelin, to the *ribalts* to do with as they will – they will smash his arms and his ribs and wrench off the jewels and Arabic gold. As for the emir himself, if he does not renounce Tervagant, I will have his two eyes gouged out or chop off his head myself with my sharp sword. I do not rate him or give

---

[183] A further attempt to distract the Christians with the prospect of rich pickings.

him the worth of even a bezant'. The King had the messenger relay everything he had said publicly. Now picture his men coming in two by two, all richly dressed in buckram. With them were the *ribalts* strutting along proudly. They all filed in front of the messenger, although not one allowed his glance as much as to rest on the horse. They went out through a door and then came back in again in front, wearing different clothes so they could not be recognised. Each of them went past a good ten times.[184] Then they took off the silken coats and put on rags and tatters which they tore to pieces; they carried hefty clubs and looked thoroughly thuggish. They stared at the messenger aggressively and bared their teeth at him. The King of the Tafurs rolled his eyes, snapped his jaws and gnashed his teeth; he could barely restrain himself from hitting the messenger in the name of God the Redeemer, and was prevented only by the presence of the King, whose man he was, and because the man was an envoy from the noble royal Sultan. On seeing this, the messenger was weak-kneed with fear, and would have given all the gold of Bocidant not to be there. He was positively writhing with terror of imminent death and his limbs and body were giving way beneath him: what he would have given to be back in the tent of the Emir of Persia!

205

The Turk was terrified when he saw the *ribalts*; he would have given all the gold which ever existed to be elsewhere. His whole body trembled as if in the grip of a fever. He asked repeatedly for leave to depart, saying 'I have heard more than enough'. He made as if to flee, but Raymond held him back. When Godfrey saw the state the Turk was in, he spread gold on the floor in front of him, more than 20,000 bezants all the way down the marshy ground. The nobles were passing back and forth rapidly by it. The messenger watched all this closely. He took careful note of it all to be able to tell the Sultan, if he could, as someone who had seen it with his own eyes. The King sent for Marbrin, and he was brought in a state of high emotion. Godfrey implored him earnestly to place his trust in Christ. The pagan replied: 'Your request is ridiculous. Not even for all the treasure of Cahu would I renounce my god and his power or Tervagant or Apollon for your lout of a God. There is no way I will ever have faith in a God Whom the human race put to death'. When King Godfrey heard the Turk say he would not believe in God, he was furious. He had his arms given back to him and saw the pagan armed and prepared to fight. Then he had a sword of tempered steel buckled at his side, and a pointed green-sheened helmet laced on his head. They brought him his thick-maned charger. Marbrin mounted, shield slung round his neck, and the King had him given a sharply tempered spur. The French were watching all agog: they had no idea what this was all about. They thought they were probably in for a considerable disappointment, but they were about to see the King try his strength. He is going to strike such a massive blow – that was clear to everyone –

---

[184] This repeats the episode at laisse 184.

that nobody will see a bigger one struck this century; all those who saw it were amazed. He put on his hauberk with its finely meshed rings. On his head he put the helmet he had from King Malagu, the worst pagan between here and Arthur's Wood. He asked for his steel sword and it was brought to him. He pulled it out of the scabbard and brandished the naked blade. 'Ah, my blessed sword!' he said. 'I have dealt many blows with you and been the victor in many battles, and sliced numerous Turks and Persians in half right down the middle. May God reward your good service by ensuring that no infidel gains possession of you after my death'. He hung his shield of beaten gold round his neck. Then they brought his charger Capalu.

206

Once King Godfrey had prepared himself to fight, they brought him his charger Capalu. The King leapt into the saddle with no need for the stirrup. However he did not take either a lance or a niello-inlaid spear because that would have been rather like cheating if he was jousting with a Turk. They all made their way to the Mount of Calvary. The horse was led along after the messenger, who was petrified by everything he was seeing. They all stopped in a large square, and the crowds climbed up to upper stories and onto ramparts. King Godfrey addressed Marbrin. 'My friend, place your trust in the holy majesty of Jesus. Have yourself baptised and embrace the Christian faith. You shall be my close associate and be given large holdings of land'. 'By Mahomed', said Marbrin, 'there is absolutely no question of me believing in that God who was put to death. Look at the Mount of Calvary, where His body was hung. I am not going to believe in Jesus. He has no power'. 'That was just what I expected', said the King. 'Since you have blasphemed against Jesus in my hearing, I would not let you live as long as this evening for all the gold in the world – that is how much I hate you. But I am going to give you a signal advantage. I am going to wait until you have charged at me and landed a great blow from your steel sword. If you can kill me you will have done well: you can leave safe and sound. But if you have not managed to kill or injure me, I will give you one blow from my steel sword'. 'I agree these terms, by Mahomed, and am grateful to you'. The Turk went to the upper end of the lists. He spurred his horse into a gallop and set his direction with a great deal of skill. Brandishing his spear with its sharp four-square head, he landed a blow on King Godfrey's gold-striped shield. He splintered and smashed it above the golden buckler, tore and ripped his mailed hauberk and grazed Godfrey's side with the spear: God protected him so that he was not wounded and did not lose his stirrups or knotted reins. 'On my head, that was a good blow you landed', said the King. 'Now land your other blow and then you will have played your turn'. Marbrin drew his sword, eyed the King appraisingly, and landed a huge blow right on his gem-studded helmet: however he did not do as much as a *denier*'s worth of damage. 'You have had your turn', said King Godfrey. 'Now it is my turn to strike and I have raised the stakes against you. I shall avenge Jesus Whom you have insulted in my hearing'. He put his hand to his sword and whipped it out of its scabbard; once drawn it glittered brightly. He galloped with great determination towards the Turk. The pagan protected himself with his striped shield: King Godfrey raised his sword on high, gripping and brandishing it so hard that he broke out in a sweat. As he drew the sword he swung it down and struck the Turk a massive blow, aiming it carefully at the middle of the shield. He slashed through the wood and the steel with which it was edged, cutting down through the helmet so that it fell into four quarters. The mailed hood was no more use than a peeled egg; the sword swung down as viciously as a wind in a storm and cut him in half all the way down to the felt pad of the saddle. God performed an extraordinary miracle because [Godfrey] cut the swift horse into two halves. He left horse and rider utterly destroyed on a hillock. His sword was exceptional and was not even damaged. All the Christians shouted as one at the sight, 'King, a blessing on the father who engendered you!' Baldwin and Eustace embraced the King, raining kisses on his blood-spattered arms. They bathed his fist in warmed wine and water because he had injured and paralysed it with the sheer strength of the blow. Once they had soothed the arm and hand, they wrapped them in a piece of silk and wrapped the whole thing in coarse grey cloth, covering it all with ointment. They lifted the Saracen onto two pack animals and tied [the remains of] his horse onto two others. The messenger swore solemnly to them that he would take him back to the emir Sultan. He left Jerusalem: picture him en route. He was overjoyed to have got away without the *ribalts* garrotting and eating him.

207

So off went the messenger without turning to right or left; he was so terrified that he was sweating all over. The whole area in front of the Sultan's tent was full of Turks and pagans, that race of infidels. The Sultan was busy having falcons released from their jesses. Picture the messenger pushing his way through the throng, with the pack animals leaving a trail of blood on the road. The messenger, in the grip of fear, cried out: 'Alas, lord emir, Godfrey with the help of his God has done something appalling to you. He cut this horse and this Turk – even though he was wearing a hauberk – in two with one blow as if he were cutting a hemlock stem. And the French are the least susceptible race to bribery you have ever seen: not one of them so much as tried to lay a finger on my horse, and when I saw pure gold flung down before me on the road they simply walked over it as if it were grass – they do not value gold or silver any more than the iron of a ploughshare. A race of devils has come with the King: their teeth are sharper than a tempered bradawl, and they gulp down our people without any seasoning of ground pepper. Noble lord emir, do not be deceived by appearances: nobody has ever seen knights as good as those the King has, and there is no way you will defeat him'. The Sultan's blood ran cold when heard this. By contrast Lord Peter, he of the white beard, laughed.

208

'Noble lord emir', continued the messenger, 'the forces in Jerusalem are so strong that I cannot tell you how many I saw with my own eyes. The King has instructed me to say that he will have all of you burnt in pitch and wax and sizzled in a cauldron and at the very least cut you about and put you to death. He is determined to kill and destroy your massive army. He will not leave a tower intact between here and the ancient city of Mecca, and I heard him say that he will take away the golden candelabrae. He will take his pick of your treasure and use it to make reliquaries for the Sepulchre'. The Sultan heaved a miserable sigh at hearing this. He seized his beard in his hand and tugged, pulled and tore at it; ripping out handfuls of hair before he stopped. Then he seized his hose, which were entirely made of Syrian cloth, ripping them apart from one end to the other. Peter sniggered covertly behind his Syrian cloak as he watched this.

209

When the Sultan heard what the messenger had to say, he foamed at the mouth with anger and rage. No pagan who saw him in this state could help trembling. He had Peter the Hermit chained up to a ring and ordered four pagan kings to mount guard over him to make sure he could not flee or escape. The emir had buglers sound 30 horns. At this you might have seen the pagans arming themselves, taking up their weapons, seizing their spears and mounting their horses, then coming together to assemble in front of the Sultan's tent. They stared at the Saracen cut in half and called down curses on the man who had proved himself capable of striking such a blow. The emir Sultan had the order to assemble shouted. Woe on any pagan, Saracen or Escler capable of wielding lance or dart or arrow who stayed behind: all were to go to Jerusalem to attack the city and break down the walls. 'Anyone who takes Godfrey must be careful not to get carried away: I want him brought to me alive so that I can pass sentence as I see fit'. The pagan kings drew up their battalions, of which there were 150. A good 100,000 Turks were in each. The Sultan had them put under the command of 150 kings. Then he sat down to play a game of chess with the noble emir from beyond the Red Sea. The army rode off and continued without stopping until it had reached Jerusalem. There you might have seen them surround the city on all sides; you would have heard bugles and brass horns sounded and the wicked pagans yelping and shouting. They made so much noise that the earth trembled from it and the city and walls and Temple shook. Now may Our Lord protect those inside because now there is going to be the fiercest attack ever heard of.

210

The Saracens and Persians attacked Jerusalem, whilst the King and his men defended it. They killed and slaughtered large numbers of the infidels; anyone they pursued could not escape death. But the people of the Devil had come in such large numbers that all the hills and slopes were swarming with them; indeed it looked to our leaders as though the numbers were actually growing. The attack was ferocious and the din huge. Those from Siglaie came scrambling up to the wall whilst the others attacked and mined beneath it, breaking apart the stones with picks and hoes and bringing it crashing down in more than 200 places. The Christians killed them and battered them down, plunging blades and lances into their bodies. But those from Siglaie just carried on scrambling up to the walls. If you ask me the city was on the point of being taken when the King and his brothers came riding up. They killed so many with their steel swords that they completely filled the ditches beneath the walls. The men from Siglaie came bounding down, baying like hounds hot on the chase; they ran around beneath the walls barking. When they found they could not get inside [the city], they foamed at the mouth with rage, devouring each other and baring their teeth. Elsewhere Cornumarant's men were assembling. He shouted commandingly at them and issued his orders; they gathered their forces ready to launch an attack. They knocked down a lance's length of the wall and swarmed in, jostling pell-mell. Imagine the King of the Tafurs and his *ribalts* bellowing as they ran at top speed to where the Turks had breached the wall. They disembowelled them with their sharp knives and smashed out the brains of many with their clubs. The King of the Tafurs himself displayed no mercy. They left the earth strewn with dead and injured in their wake and forced them back out of Jerusalem. They rained blows on them straight away, knocking them down with heavy iron maces and clubbing them to death with large lead weapons as they lay on the ground. So much Saracen blood was spilt that rivers of it flowed down into the ditch. But if you ask me all that effort was not worth as much as the value of a *denier* because the pagans were launching assaults in more than a hundred places. I reckon the city was on the verge of being taken had not night fallen and the sun gone down, quenching the Turkish ardour for attack. If the sun had still been high in the sky Jerusalem would have been taken, and that would have been appalling. The Saracens retreated as day faded; the Sultan's horns were being blown on the plains of Ramleh and the pagans rode back towards them. They dismounted outside their tents and disarmed; the majority were badly wounded and many injured. The Sultan went to his uncle Soliman and explained that Jerusalem would have been captured had night not fallen. . 'Tomorrow we shall have taken it before midday!' When the emir heard the news he summoned Roboant. 'Go and fetch Mahon, Malenidant and all the kings in my army; not a single emir is to remain behind'. Roboant turned and left to spread the word immediately to the 150 kings and emirs. He enjoined them all, starting with the *almustant*, to make an unbreakable vow to kill Godfrey; they were all to be ready at his command. The Turks had not caused as much grief by killing Roland as they were going to by killing our men – in fact more so. Once they had heard this exhortation the kings turned and left, each heading back to his pavilion. Now may God our All-Powerful Father turn his attention to our men, agitated and lamenting their plight in Jerusalem! Before prime tomorrow that will turn to joy and delight because the army of God is on the way and has already crossed the River Jordan. They are spoiling for a battle, desperate to fight; and they are going to have such a fierce one that there has truly never been anything like it since God made Adam.

211

Our Christian armies were inside Jerusalem. Every last one of them had taken a pounding, and many of them were hurt and badly wounded. The King counted up their numbers in the Temple of Solomon. Once they were all inside he addressed then as follows. 'My lords', said the King, 'your attention in God's name. The nobles have returned home; as far as I know they have all taken passage. I have remained here surrounded by Saracens. This city was on the verge of being taken yesterday, surrounded by an enormous force. Each man of you has stayed here for the love of God to protect His city where His body was tortured. He will not allow its walls to be broken down again. Tomorrow morning at sunrise we will ride out and, with your agreement, take on the Turks. A curse on anyone who remains shut up inside! If we do not do this, the Holy City will be captured. It is more honourable for us to have our heads cut off than to be led away into captivity. Happy the one who dies for God; he will be crowned in Heaven with the angels'. When our people heard this imagine them shouting, 'King Godfrey, our lord, you are our protector and not one of us will let you down even at the price of dismemberment. Every last one would rather have his head cut off than flee as much as four feet from the pagans'. 'My lords, go to your quarters', said the King. 'Once you have eaten, go to bed and sleep. You will all need to be well rested; so I will mount guard over you tonight. Tomorrow you must be up and dressed at dawn; put your hauberks on quickly as soon as you can and buckle your swords on your left sides. Once you are all armed and ready, I beg you for love of the God Who was hanged from the Cross to forgive one another your sins'. This put heart into all of them for the outcome of the battle. The count of St-Gilles said, 'It shall be as you say. There is no need to feel downcast: God will be your protector'. 'In faith', said Baldwin, 'I will not be disarming myself tonight or taking off my hauberk or helmet, and that is how I shall know the outcome of the battle. I do not know how that should be, but I am as confident as if we had enough people, or indeed more than enough. Let me tell you this for certain; believe me. Before three days of the week are past you will see so many pagans killed and beheaded that no man born of woman has ever seen more. Do you really think God has forgotten his friends? We are going to rout them with our steel swords. We have no need to worry whatever their numbers – if a good greyhound were released and there were 2,000 dogs together in these fields he would still defeat them; that is the fact of the matter. One of our noble warriors is worth 100 villains together'. Ah, God these words put heart back into them. Each one presented himself before the King offering to keep vigil with him, and he thanked them. Picture them all heading for the Sepulchre of God; there were candles and tapers in abundance but all were unlit with not a single one burning. Each laid himself down on the ground. Now listen to a great miracle, the most impressive you will every hear. Before the King had arisen from his prayers, light descended from the sky and in a flash the King's candle was alight.[185]

212

The Franks were deep in prayer all the way round the Sepulchre. Candles and tapers were all around. King Godfrey was on his knees. He had put his candle on the dais where God came back to life after His Passion. The noble King bowed down and prayed. 'Lord Father God' he said, 'by Your holy name, You are He Who created the heavens and the earth and the sea, animals, birds to fly, fresh water and fish, then made Adam from the clay and gave Paradise into his keeping. You created his wife, called Eve. You gave all creatures into Adam's keeping but forbade him to eat the fruit of an apple tree. Eve inveigled him into eating it through the offices of the wicked Satan, and they were thrown into deepest captivity for a long time with all their line, racked by pain and fear; there was no saint, male or female, brave enough to go down to their prison in Hell. But You took pity on them God and came into this world. You announced through the Angel Gabriel that the Word would become flesh in the Virgin Mary. The message came to her as a virgin girl in the Temple of Solomon, and she was unnerved. But she submitted to Your will with unswerving dedication; and You took on the incarnation of human form within her. The Virgin carried You in peace until You were born on Christmas Day. You were born in the guise of a child in Bethlehem. The three kings sought You out, each coming from his own kingdom. They offered gold, incense and myrrh into Your hands and You received them graciously. At the entrance to the Temple You were taken into the lap of one who was desperate for Your coming, St Simeon. We read that he was missing a hand. But when he said, 'Nunc dimittis a Deu servum tuum' – in other words, 'God, we are eager for your coming' – and lifted You onto his right knee, he suddenly found that he had hands and feet, the finest ever seen.[186] You were put on the altar alongside rich offerings. The tyrant Herod had large numbers of small children beheaded for You, and suffered the consequences. Those who died for You live in a mansion in Heaven wearing crowns and are known as the Innocents. Then, God, You spent 30 years on earth living like any other man. The Apostles prayed with You. You raised Lazarus from the dead in Bethany and then, God, took up residence in the house of Simon. The beautiful Mary Magdalen came so close to You beneath Your couch that she kissed Your feet and put them beneath her chin. She shed so many tears that she washed Your feet all over. Then she dried them with her hair and anointed them reverently with myrrh. She acted with good sense, and she was well

---

[185] A reminder of the miracle which identified Godfrey as king, and hence of his right to rule Jerusalem.

[186] This is to say the least not quite accurate as a translation of the 'Nunc Dimittis'.

rewarded because You forgave her all her sins. Lord, You suffered for us on the Holy Cross where Longinus stabbed wildly at You with the Lance. It is known for a fact that he was blind. The blood flowed down over his hands and, as he rubbed it on his eyes, he saw light. He begged You for mercy God, and was forgiven. You were laid in the Sepulchre and guarded by thieves. You rose on the third day and descended to Hell where with irresistible force You freed Adam, Noah and Aaron, Jacob, Esau and many other patriarchs. Then You rose to Heaven on the day of Your Ascension in majesty to where your mansion was. You entrusted the keys of Paradise to Peter. You gave the Apostles the responsibility of preaching the Holy Gospel throughout the world. Lord, if all this is true – and we believe it is – give me a clear sign, noble Lord, that I shall have victory over the race of Mahomed'. At this imagine a white dove flying up bringing a letter folded in four. It stirred the King's candle into flame followed by the other candles so that suddenly everyone could see.[187] They wept for sheer joy on all sides.

213

Once King Godfrey had finished his prayer, he confessed his sins to Our Lord. Picture a white dove fluttering up and lighting his candle in front of him; then it went to the other candles and lit those too. It gave a letter to the King. He undid it and passed it to a cleric from his region. The cleric was overjoyed when he read the letter and called to the King at the top of his voice: 'Noble and renowned King Godfrey, Our Lord sends word that his army has returned! They have already crossed the waters of the Jordan, and tomorrow they will be here before the heat rises!' When the King heard this his face lit up, and he and all the others were overjoyed. There was much embracing of the Sepulchre and tears of love and pity shed on all sides. They kept vigil all night until day rose. Nobody took off his hauberk or mailed hood and nobody unbuckled his sword: the army of Our Lord was armed all night. They kept vigil that night until dawn rose, then swung immediately into the saddle and rode out of Jerusalem, each with lance raised, whilst the count of St-Gilles guarded the city. The King spurred ahead at speed and came across the army of God very close to Jerusalem. Count Hugh of Vermandois was holding the fringed pennant; the brave Robert of Normandy, Tancred and Bohemond were riding along the valley; so was Count Robert of Flanders, no lover of boasting [unless it was aimed at the infidel race of pagans; count Thomas of Marle, an effective swordsman];[188] and Rotrou of La Perche on his bay from Valgree and all the other princes from the land of salvation were advancing in a line across the sandy ground and the road.[189] They immediately recognised the flag of Godfrey, a dragon which had a diagonal pattern on its

---

[187] Again reminiscent of the miracle of the Holy Fire in the Holy Sepulchre at Easter.
[188] Thorp supplies extra lines arguing that there has been eyeskip
[189] The lines in square brackets are omitted in A, most likely through eyeskip, and supplied from D.

tail. They pointed it out to each other: 'See, that is the golden standard of good King Godfrey – Ah, God, how destiny has favoured us'. Not a single other word was uttered. They spurred towards him as fast as possible and the King towards them, delighted at the reinforcements come to help. They rushed towards each other, arms raised. Ah God, what enormous joy was expressed and how many tears of love and pity shed. The army took up quarters over towards Bethlehem. Now the Holy City is safe. The news was brought to the noble Sultan that the Christian army had returned in full. When the emir heard this the colour drained from his face and his head jerked with rage and anger. The noble lords from the land of salvation called on the Sultan to give battle on the plains of Ramleh in beautiful countryside. The emir accorded this to the messenger, and they swore solemnly on both sides that the battle would take place on the long expanse of plain outside Ramleh: that was what was decided. They set it for Friday morning.[190] Now you are going to hear about a really fierce and painful battle, the worst anyone has ever heard of. The written source says – and this is absolutely true – that it could not be finished in two days. Battle was going to be given; there was no secret about it. The news spread down through the pagan army. Peter listened carefully to what was being said, and called secretly and repeatedly on God: 'Our Holy Lady Mary, queen of heaven, allow me to have this chain taken off my feet; I would strike the man who put it on me such a blow that his eyes would be knocked out of his head all the way over to that meadow. It will be a dark day for me if I am not in the battle. I would rather kill Turks than eat a dish with pepper'. He offered repentance for his apostasy.

214

Battle was joined on a Friday, with both sides pledging themselves to it. The army of Our Lord returned on the Saturday. It was nearly midday by the time they had found lodgings. The nobles, princes and clerics in full garb went to the Sepulchre and all made offerings. They kept vigil all night until day broke. The bishop of Mautran followed in procession with the other nobles – may Jesus' blessing be on them. Once Mass had been said our people left and ate their fill at their lodgings. On Monday they went to hear Mass at Bethlehem. They spent the three days polishing their arms and hauberks, strengthening their shieldstraps and burnishing their steel swords. Each prepared himself to fight to the utmost of his ability; the Turks and Saracens did likewise, and both sides were spoiling for a fight. The brave were keen to have a battle; the cowards and weaklings were terrified.

---

[190] Like the battle of Antioch. In reality the battle took place at Ascalon rather than Ramleh, and on a Wednesday. Placing it at Ramleh strengthens the link with St George. A pitched battle was a relatively rare occurrence, and agreeing the time and place was accepted custom; see G. Duby, *Le dimanche de Bouvines* (reprinted Paris, 1985) pp. 190–208 for the significance of battle: 'la bataille comme l'oracle appartient au sacré', p. 191.

215

The holy forces prepared minutely; they were not frightened by the coming battle. That evening God inspired an announcement that they should carry the Cross on which His body was wounded, and the holy stake to which It was tied and also the Lance with which It was pierced. The bishop of Mautran assembled our lords, the priests, abbots and other clergy; he led them to the Cross and pointed it out to them. The bishop of Mautran seized it first along with the Abbot of Fécamp, and they both embraced it; it was still watered and bathed with the blood of God. There were many heartfelt tears. The Counts, princes and other lords all ran to bow down in front of the Cross. Each of them worshipped it and bowed down in humble sincerity, putting his lips to the earth and kissing it repeatedly. They processed from there to the stake; the cords which had bound Our Lord were scattered abundantly round it. They sang the 'Te Deum' and then the litany. After all that the army of God was so determined and courageous that they feared death no more than a sorb apple. Every last one kept saying: 'Let us get on and fight the Persians!' 'My lords', said the barons, 'there is no need to be in such a hurry. We shall fight on Friday if God allows us to live that long. You should know that there is no boasting involved in this battle; it will be the fiercest anyone has ever seen or heard of'. Then Robert, count of Normandy, spoke. 'My lords, may it be God's pleasure, the Son of the Blessed Virgin Mary, that every last pagan were here; as the sky is above the earth and the sea bounds it round, they would all be dead before compline on Friday'. Godfrey was in no laughing mood when he heard all this. The other lords bowed down fervently. They were desperate for battle and could not wait.

216

The forces of Our Lord acted as they should. They got their helmets burnished and their hauberks rolled up, their swords polished and their helmets in good order, and their shields and spurs repaired and the laces of their green-sheened helmets tightened and properly attached. They made full confession every day. On the Friday morning as day broke they blew the great horn from the Tower of David. At that you might have seen our men arming and preparing, tying on their iron greaves and putting on their hauberks, lacing on their brightly glittering helmets, buckling on their swords and covering themselves with their shields. The bishop of Mautran went to sing Mass at the Sepulchre where God rose from the dead, and the noble barons went to listen. Once Holy Mass was finished, they embraced each other and exchanged the sign of the Peace. All stretched themselves on the ground to worship Jesus. You might have seen them bowing right down. Each went to kiss and embrace the Sepulchre. 'To horse! Come to our aid, Lord God!' they cried when they rose. They went to draw up ranks outside Jerusalem, ordering and arranging their squadrons. They had the True Cross carried in front of them, the Lance with which God allowed his body to be wounded, and the stake to which the Jews had him tightly bound, tying and contorting his noble body and arms.[191] You might have heard the holy clergy singing as they carried them. They marched out of the gate in ranks and lined up. Imagine the sight: pennants blowing in the wind, innumerable shields and helmets glittering and glinting. The nobles and princes had them led forward and stopped them in the middle of the fields. You might have heard bugles, horns and trumpets sound while the horses neighed, kicked and whinnied. God's army was well equipped and a redoubtable sight, but not one count or lord or peer had yet armed since they wanted to get ready at the last moment. Godfrey left the ranks to go and prepare along with the renowned princes and counts. Imagine the countless hauberks put on, the swords buckled at sides, the green-sheened helmets closed, the mounting of horses and protecting with shields, the flags and banners blowing in the wind. Nobody could have failed to find them an impressive sight. They sent the vanguard forward to Jaffa.

217

The noble King Godfrey was the first to arm. He put on his greaves and hauberk. Baldwin and Eustace laced up his helmet; then he buckled on his prized sword. Shield round his neck, he swung into Capalu's saddle. There were four dragons on the flag he carried. Once the King was armed he spurred his horse on so powerfully that it arched its back beneath him. Then he raised his hand and signed himself in the name of his God. He passed with his retinue in front of the True Cross. Weeping with emotion he worshipped it with all his heart. All his companions bowed in front of it. The bishop of Mautran commended them to God, then raised his hand, blessed them and made the sign of the Cross over them. Godfrey rode away nobly with his retinue, not stopping all the way to the plains of Ramleh. The emir Sultan was planted in front of his tent on a golden throne which sent glancing beams of light everywhere. He was attended by 50 kings from Arabia. Peter was seated in front of him. The Sultan addressed him: 'Tell me, Peter the Hermit, which squadron is that? If you know who they are do not keep me in ignorance'.[192]

---

[191] The True Cross was discovered in less than clear circumstances by Arnulf of Choques just before the battle of Ascalon: Asbridge, *First Crusade* pp. 322–3. AA VI.38 reports an earlier discovery of the Cross which was nothing to do with Arnulf; also FC I.30. See A. Frolow, *La rélique de la Vraie Croix: recherches sur le développement d'un culte*, (Institut français d'études byzantines, 1961). The Lance refers to the lance used by Longinus to wound Christ on the Cross and supposedly dug up in Antioch just before the battle of Antioch: Asbridge, *First Crusade* pp. 221–6 and see C. Morris, 'Policy and vision; the case of the Holy Lance found at Antioch', in *War and Government in the Middle Ages: essays in honour of J. O. Prestwich*, (eds) J. Gillingham and J. C. Holt (Woodbridge, 1984) pp. 33–45; S. Runciman, 'The Holy Lance found at Antioch', *Analecta Bollandiana* 68 (1950) pp. 197–205. The pillar to which Christ was tied is that portrayed in sculptures of the Ecce Homo and heads the list of relics for the taking in Constantinople in the supposed letter of Alexius to the West.

[192] Peter's role explaining the forces to the Sultan parallels that of Amedelis in the *Antioche* at laisses 315-28.

Peter responded truthfully: 'My lord, that is the king who cut the pagan and his horse in half with one single blow – those were the two halves brought in front of you. His name is Godfrey. His mother was the daughter of the Swan Knight who brought her to Nijmegen.[193] There has never been such a knight and never will be again'. When the Sultan heard this he flew into a rage. He foamed at the mouth like a wild beast with anger.

218

The next to arm was Count Robert of Normandy. He laced on his greaves with their interlocking mail rings. He pulled on his mailed shirt quickly and laced up a green-sheened helmet which glittered with gold. He buckled his burnished sword at his left side, and hung his gold-edged shield round his neck. He leapt from the ground onto his Nubian warhorse. Then he took his spear, brandishing it proudly, and swore by Lord God, the son of the Virgin Mary, that if he was lucky enough to meet the Emir of Persia neither helmet nor ornamented shield would be enough to save the pagan from having his head sliced open down to his ears. He commanded a horn to be blown resoundingly in front of him. He turned about with his squadron and got under way. He led his men in front of the True Cross. Count Robert worshipped it then kissed it; and every man in his squadron bowed down likewise. The Bishop signed them with the cross in the name of God, son of the Virgin Mary. 'Lord God, Holy Father, come to their aid', he said. Count Robert rode off with his knights. Imagine the sight of all those Nubian warhorses, all those hauberks and those helmets glittering with gold, all those luxurious shields and all those flags raised. Each one was looking down beneath the helmet. Their appearance made it clear that they meant business. Not one drew rein all the way to the plains of Ramleh; the Count's squadron lined up next to the King. The Sultan was watching this in no laughing mood. 'Don't try and mislead me', he said to Peter the Hermit. 'Whose is that squadron which has come over near us?' 'My lord', said the hermit, 'I shall tell you straight. The man leading them is Robert of Normandy who killed the Red Lion in a ferocious fight in the fields outside Antioch. There is no better knight between here and Urgalie'. 'By Mahomed', said the Sultan, 'I will certainly have heard of something strange if these bastards can defeat my men. Personally I wouldn't give as much as a rotten apple for them'.

219

The next one to prepare was Lord Robert the Frisian: he was lord of Flanders and the surrounding lands. He laced on greaves which shone more lustrously than

---

[193] This refers to the legend of the Swan Knight recounted elsewhere in the Cycle. It does not give any indication as to relative datings of the *Jérusalem* and the Godfrey texts since it was easy to insert allusions later in existing texts.

brass; then he pulled on a mailed hauberk and laced on a green-sheened helmet worked by Solomon, and buckled a sword at his left side. He hung round his neck a shield with a device of a lion, then leapt onto the horse more swiftly than a falcon. A spear with a square-headed tip was passed up to him. He turned and rode onto the sandy plains accompanied by his countrymen and rode past the True Cross to adore it in all sincerity. He kissed it rapturously 20 times in one go, and all his companions did likewise in silence and good order. The bishop of Mautran pronounced a blessing over them. They spurred on their chargers, heads bent beneath their helmets, and did not stop all the way to the plains of Ramleh. When the Sultan saw them he addressed Peter: 'Now who are these people, by the faith you owe Mahomed? They have a noble demeanour and an impressive reputation'. 'We shall explain this to you without delay', said Peter the Hermit. 'In his own country he is known as Lord Robert the Frisian, and he is lord of Flanders and the surrounding region. No better knight has ever donned spurs'. 'By Mahomed', said the Sultan, 'I wouldn't give a button for him. I have no doubt that I am going to lead them all off into captivity'. 'By my head and my white moustache, you won't be boasting like that by the time it comes for us to leave', said Peter.

220

Count Hugh of Vermandois hurried to prepare, and Lord Thomas of Marle rose to put on arms with him. They put on their hauberks and fastened their helmets; they hung their shields striped with gold from their necks; they swiftly mounted their warhorses which were champing at the bit, and seized spears with sharp four-square heads. Picture them sat together on their horses. Lord Hugh turned and led his people away. The noble lord passed in front of the True Cross, worshipped it and rained kisses on it. Thomas and the others turned their heads towards it and each bowed down complete with his shining helmet. The Bishop of Mautran blessed them in the name of God. Then they spurred on their horses; imagine them en route, not one drawing rein until the plains of Ramleh. The Emir Sultan watched them narrowly and said to Peter the Hermit: 'My friend, do not play games. Who are those people I can see gathered over there? They have a noble demeanour and are full of pride'. 'You shall know that straight away', said Peter the Hermit. 'The one who has led them over here is the brother of the King of France; he is called Hugh of Vermandois and is very well regarded. No better knight was ever born to any mother. He was the one who killed Soliman in the fields outside Antioch'. 'By Mahomed', said the Sultan, 'let me tell you something amazing. My gods had clearly forgotten them that day, since I wouldn't give as much as two *deniers* for them. I shall have them all led away in chains alongside me; they will repopulate the deserts of Abilant'. 'On my head', said Peter, 'if you ask me you won't be boasting about this when you leave here'.

221

Bohemond and Tancred of Apulia armed themselves. Antelme and Moran laced on their greaves; then they put on their mailed hauberks, laced their glittering green-sheened helmets on their heads, buckled their swords at their left sides and swiftly mounted their spirited chargers. Gold gleamed from the shields round their necks. They too raised their spears with their pennants attached. Each had 1,000 brave knights in his squadron. All of them passed before the True Cross, each of them bowing down to worship it. The bishop of Mautrans, an impressively shrewd cleric, blessed them in the name of God the All-Powerful. The cousins turned and spurred away with their sizeable force of cavalry. Bugles, horns and trumpets might have been heard sounding. Not one drew rein all the way to the plains of Ramleh. Both drew up their ranks in good order on the battlefield, all of them solemnly swearing that they would leave the pagans in a state of furious misery. The Emir Sultan watched them from his tent, surrounded by an entourage of 100 Turkish kings and emirs. 'Do you know who these are?' he said to Peter the Hermit. 'They are a pleasure to look at; they certainly have a proud demeanour. It would be a shame if they were not true believers'. 'I will tell you the truth', replied Peter. 'This one is Bohemond. His father was Norman. He is accompanied by numerous Lombards and Tuscans, who like nothing better than killing Saracens and Persians. The one in the other squadron, the proud-looking one, is called Tancred. He is an aggressive fighter: he likes battle more than any pure gold or bezants'. 'So what?' said the emir. 'I wouldn't give a glove for either. I am going to kill most of them and take the rest back to repopulate my desert of Abilant'. 'On my head', said Peter, 'you will not be left with much to boast about. A very poor remnant of your forces is going to survive'.

222

Count Rotrou of Perche hurried to prepare; so did his relative Stephen of Blois and the proud count of Vendôme.[194] Each was armed to a very high standard and between them they had four squadrons of exceptionally confident men. Imagine the sight of all those silver shields, and hauberks and helmets glinting with pure gold. The gold in the weapons sent beams of light everywhere. They marched in good order past the True Cross, each worshipping it with heartfelt sincerity. The bishop of Mautran made the sign of the Cross over them benevolently in the name of the glorious [lord] of Heaven who made the oceans and the winds. Then the princes turned and left with their forces, riding together in a tightly compressed formation. They rode without stopping all the way to the plains of Ramleh; the two

---

[194] The historical Stephen of Blois was certainly not there: he had abandoned the Crusade before the fall of Antioch. See Table of Names for references. His cowardice is a major feature in the *Antioche* which emphasises Stephen's cowardice mercilessly at laisses 62–72, 233–4 and 285; the compiler has overlooked this here.

squadrons marched together in an impressive formation. The Sultan was sitting in front of his tent in the breeze. He called to Peter the Hermit and asked him pressingly, 'Tell me who these people are; do not try and hide the truth'. 'I shall tell you honestly', said Peter the Hermit. 'That is Rotrou of la Perche, a very proud man; Stephen of Blois on that piebald charger; and the Count of Vendôme similarly on that dun-coloured one. Over there you can see Lambert of Liège on that bay from the East – that is someone who would rather kill Turks than drink spiced honeyed wine. Today they will inflict huge slaughter on the pagans: they will flee an acre and more to escape death'. When the Sultan heard this, he replied curtly: 'By Mahomed Gomelin, whose power extends over every land, I wouldn't give as much as a stinking dog for all of them together. I shall ensure they all die a horrible death'.

223

Stephen of Albemarle hurried to arm himself. Hugh of St-Pol did not wait, nor did his son Enguerrand who had the courage of a wild boar; the other princes did not exactly hang around either. The bishop of Mautran took up arms. He had a hauberk and a green-sheened helmet which gleamed brightly; he mounted his horse, which he had ordered to be saddled, with his stole round his neck under his bossed shield. The clerics and women were left to guard Jerusalem along with 200 knights; these were hardly in the first flush of youth, being old and white-haired, but redoubtable fighters none the less: they were hardly delighted at being left behind but did not dare refuse their orders. The bishop of Forez was ordered to stay with them. They shut and barred the gates of Jerusalem. The bishop of Mautran had two horns blown; at this you might have seen our people start to move forwards, the ranks keeping closely together. They put the King of the Tafurs in the lead with his fearsome *ribalts* and *tafurs*. The abbot of Fécamp was charged with carrying the Cross on which God allowed His body to be wounded and broken. The Bishop of Noble, whose name was Guy, carried the stake to which Jesus allowed himself to be bound fast, or so I have heard tell. An abbot was given the Lance of God to carry. So now they were all riding out together – may Jesus save them! They rode to the plains of Ramleh without stopping. At the point when the True Cross was about to be carried onto the battlefield, everyone in the squadrons began to weep; imagine all those heads bowed down again and again. The Emir Sultan watched them and said to Peter the Hermit: 'I now want to ask you who those people are that I see assembling. I have never seen any who gave me such pause for thought'. 'I will not hide the truth', said Peter the Hermit. 'That is the King of the Tafurs who used to be my companion. Have a look at his *ribalts*. They are truly terrifying: they eat your men without so much as a seasoning of salt or pepper. Over there you can see the True Cross being raised, and the Lance which God allowed to pierce His body, and here the stake to which He was bound. Take it from me, you have no chance of escaping. You are going to have to fight a battle, and soon'. The Sultan lost all wish to boast when he heard this. He began to sweat with anger and rage.

224

When the Sultan saw our men drawn up in ranks ready to fight, he felt ready to explode with anger and rage. He gave orders that his standard should be raised in double-quick time, and his men armed and prepared. You might have heard bugles being sounded and blown, 1,000 mountain horns all blown in unison, so that the earth rang from Ramleh to Jaffa. Imagine the Kenelius baying and barking, whilst the men of Siglaie howled like devils. They had the standard raised on a chariot made entirely of iron. It was a standard with a very long shaft and its base was made of medlar wood. Two men would have been hard put to it to get their arms round it. It was made of 10 separate pieces. The first was of olivewood; [the second of a tree known as wild cherry]; the third of oak; the fourth of hawthorn; the fifth of ebony; the sixth of applewood; the seventh of viburnum; the eighth of sorbus; the ninth of ivory taken from a most holy relic; and the tenth entirely of pure gold. The whole standard was anointed with balm from a balsam tree – the Sultan did this to make it smell sweet – and as a result it could not rot away nor be broken or pierced. You could throw it end over end some 300 feet.[195] Nobody had ever seen a bell tower that high. Apollon was sitting at the very top, holding a psalter in which the tenets of his religion were written from the time of Adam. Every so often the wind made him spin round on top of it. His finger moved as if he were teaching his religion. He held a golden stick with which to menace the French. Through necromancy he was made to announce that every Christian should submit to the Sultan.[196] A precious carbuncle was on his head which could be seen gleaming from 20 leagues off. That marked the spot where the Saracens would rally in battle. The Emir Sultan summoned Brehier, his middle son by his wife; he had another 14 who were all knights. He summoned them and implored them to take courage and avenge their brother Brohadas.

225

The wicked Saracens made a terrible din. The Emir Sultan summoned Sinagon; he was the son of the Sultan and had long flowing hair. The next one, his second, was called Brehier. There were another 13 and I am going to tell you their names. One

---

[195] The meaning is not clear. 'Bracoier' means to wave, but that is hardly practical here: something like tossing the caber may be intended. A fleece is roughly six feet long: the Old French says it could be thrown the length of 50 fleeces.

[196] For similar idols see *La Destruction de Rome: version de Hannovre* (ed.) L. Formisano and G. Contini (Florence, 1981) lines 227–30; *La Prise de Cordres et de Sébille* (ed.) M. del Vecchio-Drion (Paris, 2011) lines 2806–9.

was called Acéré; the second Glorion; the third Lucifer; the fourth Lucion; the fifth was called Aufage; the sixth Danemon; the seventh Corsuble; the eighth Fauseron; the ninth Esmeré; the tenth Clarion; the eleventh Sanguin; the twelfth Tahon; and the thirteenth brother was called Rubion. Each one had 20,000 Esclavons in his command. 'My noble sons, listen to what I have to say', said the Sultan. 'I beg you with everything in my power to avenge Brohadas'. 'We shall do as you wish', they replied. 'You will have Godfrey's head before evening. We shall slaughter the French nobility with our spears: counts and dukes, princes and barons. We shall carry them off with us to the kingdom of Persia and throw them into dungeons if such is your pleasure. Bohemond will be brought forcibly to the kingdom of the East and we shall send our noblest men with him. He will find himself bowing down to Tervagant and Mahomed. Lord emir, noble father, we beg your leave to depart: it is time for battle and we want to go'. 'Do so', said the emir. 'We commend you to Mahomed Gomelin with all your companions'. The sons of the Sultan mounted their Aragonese warhorses. Horns and bugles were blown resoundingly. They led 100,000 Turks: nothing could be further from our minds than lying about this. They stopped in the middle of the battlefield in front of the pavilions.

226

The pagans were making a huge racket, blowing horns and bugles and oliphants. The Turks and pagans were busy arming down from the army. The emir summoned the *aupatris* and Morgant, King Loquifer and his brother Morant; along with them he summoned his nephew the *amustant*, the elderly Calcatras and Canebalt the emir. 'I order you to draw up my squadrons for battle', he said. 'Your lightest wish is our command, my lord', they answered. Off they spurred through the middle of the pagan army. They formed themselves into 50 squadrons – yes really – with 100,000 Arabs in each. 50 kings led them in the name of Tervagant's religion. The first squadron was composed of men from Bocidant – they were blacker than ink made up, and had no white on them other than their eyes and teeth. They were led by Cornicas, the brother of Rubiant. The warhorse he rode had a horn on its forehead; you will never have seen a bull with one so sharp, and he did not carry any bird for that reason. It was covered with a scarlet cloth which swept all the way to the ground. In the second squadron were the Moors from Moriant: they were blacker than peppercorns and looked like devils.[197] There were 100,000 of them, led by Malquidant. In the third squadron were the Bulgars; in the fourth the Africans; in the fifth Syrians; in the sixth the Agolant; in the seventh Esclavons; in the eighth Samorgant; in the ninth Carbuncles; and in the tenth giants. The 10 squadrons advanced together baying; they were like mongrels barking at our men.

---

[197] See the Douce Apocalypse folios 51–2 for monstrous black devils: *The Douce Apocalypse*, presented Nigel Morgan (Oxford, 2007) pp. 76–7. For monstrous Saracens compare *Guillaume* lines 3170–74.

The Apostolic Caliph was busy blessing them in the name of Mahomed Gomelin and the great Apollon.

227

The emir drew up his squadrons. He had ten of them drawn up in textbook fashion on one side. In the first were pagans; in the second Esclers; in the third Persians; in the fourth Basques; in the fifth Indians; in the sixth Bomers, a fiendish people from the other side of the Red Sea, the only people capable of living there; in the seventh the Afars; in the eighth those from Oper; in the ninth people from Tabais with tusks like wild boars; and in the tenth those from the land of winter, a diabolical race who have never been known to wear shoes. So now there were 20 squadrons; that was how many could be counted. As they came together you might have seen them baying; anyone who was there would have been able to hear them clearly. They were just like devils and very fearsome; nobody had ever heard of such a hideous race. Now you will be able to hear all about the battle: nobody has ever seen one large enough to rival it.

228

It was a beautiful crystal clear morning. The pagans shouted and yelled and created an almighty din. The emir summoned Carcan, who came from overseas. He organised ten squadrons of Apollon's men. The first was of Sucomals; the second of men from Arbrin; the third of men from Majols and the fourth of [men from] Afain – these are a diabolical race who never drink wine. The rocks [there] are high with marble platforms. They all live under the ground in deep pits and eat peppercorns and cumin seed. Their teeth are sharper than steel razorblades and they run faster than fawns in the woods. They have never put on clothes of wool or linen; they have coats like greyhounds and bark like mastiffs. The lord in charge of them was called Alepantin and rode a horse called Cain who could swim in the sea better than any fish in the Rhine. That day he killed Baldwin of Clermont. Tancred in turn killed him with his ashwood spear, then flung down dead the noble *almustain*, the King of Valnuble and Sanguin's brother.

229

The *aupatris* had the other six squadrons drawn up. The first was of Indonesians; the second of Lutis; the third of Jalfres; the fourth of Norns; the fifth of Morans; and the sixth of Torins. Each carried a sharp-bladed knife; they were naked and unarmed and carried no other weapons. The swarthy Estonamon led this squadron. He rode a horse called Partridge which could cover hills and mountains better than any other moorland pony. Its head was redder than a hot coal, the rest of its body white and its chest black. It would belong to Bohemond before the day was out. The Apostolic Caliph blessed the Turks. Now there are 30 squadrons of those accursed cowards.

230

They divided up into another ten squadrons. In the first were Masan and Fransion – these last come from a land known as France named so by Mahomed Gomelin and situated beyond the Orient. The third was of Cops, the fourth of Asnoon, the fifth of Argales, the sixth of Arbolon, the seventh of Lalvages and the eighth of Arragon, and the ninth of Espies – this is what they look like. They have beaks like snipe and heads of mastiffs, and lions' claws on their hands and feet. When they howl in unison they make such a din that the earth rings with it for two leagues around. The *amustans* hits them with a stick to shut them up. The tenth squadron came from the mountains of Lucion – a diabolical race with horns like sheep. Each carried a leaden mace in his hand. These would have inflicted terrible damage on us had it not been for Godfrey and the other nobles. They slaughtered so many of them with their swords that the blood reached up as far as the fetlocks of their horses. Now it is nearly time for the battle: nobody has ever heard of a fiercer one.

231

The Emir Sultan kept ten squadrons with him. Some were composed of Persians and some of Guinebalts, Turks and Arabs with excellent horses; the Africans were there too, very noble and brave; pagans and Saracens who shoot at targets; and all those from the Orient led by Canabels. There were also Almoravids who had the most amazing horses, able to run faster than sparrowhawks or gerfalcons. All their weapons were of gold and enamel, and their shields were more lustrous than ivory or crystal; they had good swords which would deal heavy blows. With them were Esclavons, whom I rate the most impressive in appearance. They were richly armed with imperial weapons. So now there were 50 squadrons under the command of Lucabel.

232

Once the 50 squadrons were all drawn up in ranks, the Sultan retained 10 particularly well armed ones for his own use; the swords numbered 150,0000. The others turned and left; picture them en route. They put their numbers at two million. The squadrons took up position down on the plains. You might have heard the horns blown so emphatically that the mountains, peaks and valleys all rang with them; and war cries shouted proudly. The army of Our Lord raised their lances, the silken ensigns flapping in the wind. The green-sheened helmets and gilded shields glittered. They signed themselves on the head in God's name and confessed their sins. They knotted the reins of their horses and held their shields close, balancing them on the cantle of their saddles and pulling them in against their chests. Our squadrons separated and split. Picture them riding forward for battle. Their front extended more than the equivalent of 20 shots of a crossbow.

233

A great cry went up as the army came together. The bishop of Mautran raised the Cross on high and unwrapped it to show it to our people. With that words were at an end. They charged towards the Turks at high speed. Godfrey led the way, visor shut, and charged against Sinagon and his armed retinue – he was one of the sons of the Sultan by his senior wife. They sped towards each other like falcons in flight, and landed immense blows on each other. Sinagon's lance was shattered and broken. The King did not lose his seat on the golden saddle, and struck the pagan on his striped shield; piercing it below the buckler and ripping his hauberk he plunged the fringed pennant right into his heart and knocked him dead from his horse. His soul fled and was welcomed by devils into the stinking regions of Hell. King Godfrey shouted his war cry: 'Noble knights, attack those pagans who have refused to believe in the Blessed Virgin! The first blows in this affair are for us'. At that you might have heard a terrible din with much bellowing and shouting. Innumerable lances were shattered and shields buckled, feet and hands and heads cut off in profusion. The earth was soaked with the blood which flowed from the bodies. The Turks shot arrows more thickly than dew falls.

234

The battle was enormous and there was much bloodshed. The eldest of the Sultan's 15 sons was killed; this meant that the remaining 14 came spurring on with their blood up. Each had with him 20,000 heavily armed men. When they saw their brother dead they wept bitterly and lamented him loudly: 'What a terrible fate, noble friend! Sinagon, whoever it was that killed you has left us badly weakened. It was Godfrey with his shield coated with gold. If we happen across him he will suffer our vengeance!' With that they had their horns sounded and blew their instruments. Lucifer directed his Arab warhorse and spurred it on, shouting at the top of his voice: 'Where have you got to, Godfrey of Bouillon, you villainous coward?' He went to attack Anseïs in his rage, a noble young man from Paris. He punched through the shield above the buckler and smashed and ripped the hauberk on his back. The heart in his chest was slashed in two and he was knocked dead from his horse in the centre of a clearing. St Michael took his soul up into Paradise. Lucifer shouted out and turned back. Now the battle and the hacking down were getting under way. The noise and shouting could be clearly heard on all sides, from the plains all the way to Acre.

235

The battle was ferocious on the plains of Ramleh. Up spurred Acéré across the sandy ground; he was the Sultan's son by his first wife. He was richly armed on [his horse] Bondifer, who was covered with a rich silken cloth over his head, neck and crupper. He shouted at the top of his voice: 'Godfrey, you worthless man, you have killed my two brothers like the treacherous villain you are. If I can just lay hands on you you will regret ever having left Bavaria. I am going to make a new bier ready for you'. In his rage he attacked Eudes of Lanciere. His shield was no more use to him than a piece of bracken; he tore his hauberk with its unbroken rings, plunged the lance right into the middle of his chest and knocked him dead from his horse into a reedbed. Then he shouted 'Baudarie!' and turned and rode back, killing two of our men next to a patch of heather. At this the cries of the diabolical race grew louder, and more arrows flew than fine rain. The dust cloud flung up by horses and riders was enormous. Such a river of blood flowed down from the plains of Ramleh that the horses were wading through it up to the stirrup leathers.

236

There were ferocious skirmishes all the way down the plains of Ramleh. Picture Glorian and Brehier spurring up. Lucion and the emir, Danemon and Gorhier, Fauseron, Esmeré and the agile young Sanguin, Clarïel and Tahon, Rubin and Perelier. They had 100,000 pagans with them. They made a huge din as they lowered their lances. You might have heard bugles being sounded and blown, and those diabolical people baying and barking. However the noble lords whom God loves and cherishes did not have a moment's fear or dread of the Turks; on the contrary they went to attack them with iron and steel. Not since God came down to earth to preach from the mountain had so many brave knights been seen in battle. You might have seen King Godfrey riding to the rescue, he and his two brothers riding up and down the ranks with their swords killing and slaughtering Saracens and pagans; they left the earth strewn with dead and injured. At this point our men suffered a terrible setback, because Rainalt of Beauvais had his horse killed under him. Ah God! What a terrible effect when he found himself stumbling to the ground. The lord got to his feet, fiercely determined; he put his shield on his arm and drew his steel sword, and cut his way through the press of Turks. Anyone he attacked had no need of a doctor. If there was any chance of him staying alive he intended to sell himself at a high price. But Lucifer confronted him and struck him, plunging his sharp dart into his body. The lord staggered backwards and started to pray to God to take mercy on his soul: and he was in sore need of it. He broke off three blades of grass so that he could take Communion. With that the noble knight's soul left his body and God received him into Paradise. Eustace spurred forward, determined to avenge him.

237

Eustace of Boulogne saw Rainalt cut down by Lucifer and was grief-stricken. He directed his horse and spurred forward at high speed, brandishing his spear with its tempered blade. He struck Lucifer in front on his shield, breaking and splitting it beneath the golden buckler and ripping apart the links of his mailshirt. He plunged the tempered blade right into the middle of his chest and knocked him dead from his horse near an elder tree. 'Go to your death, coward!' he said. 'May you suffer horribly, you pagan. I have given you what you deserved for killing Rainalt'. He shouted, 'In the name of the Holy Sepulchre!' and drew his tempered blade. He made for Aceré and struck him on his pointed helmet. He sliced off the jewels and floral decorations and cut him in half all the way down to the chest. The lord pulled out his weapon and sent him sprawling in death. Then he killed Principle, the son of the emir. Picture King Godfrey spurring up on Capalu. Eustace cried, 'Brother, I have been watching you. With those great blows you are just like our ancestor, the Swan Knight, who overcame the Saxons. If I fail you, may my soul never find salvation. Let us spur forward together from here on, noble brother, me and you together! But by God, where is Baldwin? I am not sure whether we have lost him'. With that picture the count spurring across a grassy meadow on his Aragonese steed Prinsaut with its white head. He killed one of Malagu's sons and one of the Sultan's sons called Corsu in front of his brother. He chased Sanguin but could not manage to catch him up. He was furious that he couldn't. He encountered King Marcepelu in the middle of the path and sliced off his head as easily as a straw.

238

It was an enormous and hard fought battle. Now picture Robert, duke of Normandy, entering the fray with his proud retinue. He carried his lance upright with the pennant blowing. He set his horse as fast as it could go and flung himself into the middle of the Turks – may the body of God curse them! He struck King Atanas, lord of Almeria; he slashed and tore right through his large mailed hauberk, ripping the rings apart and slicing through his heart. His soul left his body and was welcomed to Hell by devils; the pagan tumbled to the ground off his warhorse from Orcanie. 'Come to my aid, Holy Lady Mary, Queen of Heaven!' cried Robert. He put his hand to his sword and pulled it from its scabbard, then cut a Turk in two down to his ears. Next he killed the emir of Nubia, then Clapamor and Carcan of Russia. The count landed blow after skilful blow in a paroxysm of rage, and the earth was strewn with the pagans he killed. The Turks fled from him faster than magpies fleeing a falcon, and the baron chased them vigorously for more than the distance of a good long bowshot. But if Jesus is not with him he will have gone too far. He had gone so far into the press of pagans that none of his men could see or hear him. The pagans had fallen back to the place known as Three Shadows. This was where the mother of God relaxed and rested; she paused there and prophesied that God would bring shade if she should so wish; and at that the earth was cast into darkness all around and the sun did not shine for a good league and a half.[198] This shade was over towards Jaffa beyond Calkerie. That was where Robert of Normandy was surrounded by Turks, who rained arrows down on him; he had so many sticking out of his arms and armour that if they had all been put into a bundle it would have been too big to put your arms round. The Saracens shot and shot, accompanied by a barrage of shouting. I don't know what to tell you about Count Robert – if God does not spare him a thought he is certainly not long for this world because he has more arrows in him than a full armload. There was so much shouting down across the plains of Ramleh, such a cacophony of horns and bugles and such damage being inflicted on hauberks and helmets that the whole earth shook with it all the way towards Acre. If the Lord Who rose from death to life does not turn His attention that way, our people are on the verge of being overcome and defeated; and our powerful knights will find themselves in a desperate position: there are so many Persians that the earth is groaning with them for a full seven leagues.

239

It was a hard fought battle with a fierce *mêlée*. The Persians had surrounded Robert of Normandy; they were shooting at him with their Turkish bows, taking aim from far off. They had killed his spirited charger beneath him. The brave-hearted lord leapt up, protecting himself with his shield and brandishing his unsheathed sword. He defended himself stoutly against the pagans; anyone he attacked was cut right down. The Turks were too scared to approach within a lance's length of him. His knights rode through the press of battle looking for him; they were very concerned at being unable to find him. Messengers went to Robert the Frisian in tears: 'My lord, in the name of God the Redeemer help us – the Persians are carrying off Robert of Normandy!' When the count heard this he was deeply concerned. 'Holy Sepulchre! Forward, gentlemen!' he cried. With that he had a horn sounded and turned about. His companions followed him, all eager for combat. Bohemond and Tancred of Apulia were informed that the Saracens were carrying off lord Robert of Normandy and that the count of Flanders was in hot pursuit. Bohemond heaved a great sigh when he heard this. Tancred yelled: 'Sound that olifant! The pagans will not find any refuge all the way to the east!' The cousins and their large retinue turned and spurred after Robert of Flanders, striking about them ferociously in the press of Turks. When they lowered their lances they killed so many that all those who watched were left marvelling. Then they drew their swords in a burst of rage and charged through cutting off heads, hands and feet. Many fled, dragging their bowels.[199] Our lords showed no mercy but struck and struck, not stopping anywhere and inflicting such damage with their good steel swords that a large

---

[198] This refers to the apocryphal gospel of the Birth of Mary and the Childhood of Our Lord: see Duparc-Quioc, *Cycle*, 35–7.

[199] Standard topos. Compare the graphic realism of *Guillaume* lines 495–99.

cart should have been dragged along behind them. They fought the Turks back to the Three Shadows. There they found Robert wounded and covered in blood, but even so inflicting massive blows which were hardly those of a child and /he was not scared of the pagans by as much as a *denier*. Bohemond brought him a spirited charger and Robert mounted it undaunted. Once he was on horseback he did not exactly hang back but killed a Turk as he rode past. The barons flung their arms round him and showered him with kisses, and Robert the Frisian embraced him warmly. Picture the proud Cornumarant in the midst of the battle with 30,000 Tervagant-worshipping Turks. He cut his way through the French inflicting a great deal of damage. 'Damascus and Tiberias!' he shouted repeatedly.

240

[The Christians] had landed many large blows as they rescued Robert, killing and decapitating numerous Turks and pagans. Now picture Esmeré spurring through the mêlée; he was the son of the Sultan of Persia and had been dubbed by Antan. He had 20,000 armed Turks in his retinue. He was carrying his lance upright with the pennant laced on. He kept shouting for Godfrey of Bouillon: 'You royal bastard, I am desperate to get my hands on you: it is time you paid for what you did in killing three of my brothers!' He came up against Roger in the middle of the press of battle; giving his horse its head, he charged him.[200] He pierced his shield, tore his hauberk and knocked him from his horse which was very badly wounded. When Roger of Rosoie found himself on the ground, he leapt up immediately and drew his steel sword. Before Esmeré could dodge Roger pursued him and landed such a blow of his sharp sword, carefully aimed for the top of his helmet, that he split it into quarters. His thrust went down between shield and body so that he cut off his arm and shieldstrap together; the force of the blow was such that it knocked the Saracen sprawling on the meadow. Roger of Rosoie grabbed his horse, seized the knotted reins in his left hand and leapt into the saddle with no need for the stirrup. The Saracens all raised a cry when they saw this. Esmeré's nine brothers were all appalled. They swore by Mahomed Gomelin that 20,000 Franks would be killed in revenge for their brother. With that all nine formed up for battle; they gave battle orders to their squadrons and ordered their horns to be blown; when they were all drawn up ready there were a good 100,000, all thoroughly diabolical in appearance. Now may God come to the aid of Holy Christianity, because they are going to suffer badly in this battle: God will certainly be their friend if they manage to escape.

241

It was a huge battle and the *mêlée* was hard fought. The land rang all around with the sound of horns and bugles. The infidel squadrons advanced to the tune of 50,

---

[200] Another character from the *Antioche*.

all pagan. Many of them were far blacker than pepper and some had horns; all carried lead clubs. One squadron was of sturdy black men, all far blacker than wet soot and each carrying an axe sharpened to a fine edge. This was the first squadron to engage our men. A huge din rose as the two clashed head on; innumerable feet, hands and heads were cut off and large numbers of our people killed and wounded. Picture Rotrou of la Perche and his armed companions, Lord Hugh of Vermandois carrying his standard, the Count of Vendôme with men from his region, and with them Count Lambert, an excellent swordsman. They drew up their men together in a well-organised formation, and then the Count had 10 horns sounded. Count Hugh spurred forward crying 'Montjoie!' With his horse galloping as fast as it could, the Count made for the pagans ready to strike. He lowered his lance so effectively that he disembowelled more than 20 of them before it broke; and when it did he drew his sword. Anyone he attacked was not long for this world. He slashed 30 Turks in two down to their entrails. Count Rotrou of La Perche laid about him furiously; the Count of Vendôme shouted at the top of his voice; and Count Lambert of Liège split numerous heads. Our people were intoxicated by the slaughter of the Turks. They killed and slaughtered and slashed their way through this squadron and forced it to retreat to the Three Shadows, the place where the Blessed Virgin Mary took refuge from the heat. You could have more than filled a ship with the dead Turks there.

242

It was a huge battle, the fiercest ever seen. The squadrons from the east came spurring on at top speed; there were more than 30,000 of those inky-black villains, led by Cornicas from the mountains of Rubion. The horse he rode was whiter than a dove and had two large horns on its forehead which were sharper and cut more than a punch. Its hooves were split from front to heel just like an ox. It had claws tougher than steel or brass and ran faster than a sparrowhawk or falcon could fly. The pagans had put a vermilion silk horsecloth over it, and it carried a banner with a dragon. Cornicas aimed it and spurred forward, protecting himself with his shield. The warhorse gave him more impetus than a merlin hawk. He struck Thomas of Marle on his shield with a device of a lion. He smashed and damaged it above the golden boss, but did not manage to pierce his mailed hauberk. Splinters went flying from the lance he carried, but Thomas was not dislodged; he stayed firmly in his saddle. He went for his sword to take his revenge, but the Turk swept past him, caring not as much as a button for him because his steed flew faster than an eagle. Thomas scowled at seeing this, and burnt with greater anger than any coal fire. In his rage he went for Clarion, one of the Sultan's sons and King of Monbrandon. His helmet and shield were of no help to him: Thomas cut him in half right down to the chin. Then he killed Clarion's two brothers Brehier and Lucion. Picture Enguerrand, son of Hugh of St-Pol, coming spurring up. He aimed for Tahon and struck him on the front of his shield; this was one of the Sultan's sons who held Persia in his name. Enguerrand struck him so vigorously that he pierced his shield and one of the panels of his hauberk; his mailshirt was of no more protection to him than an ermine mantle. Enguerrand plunged his spear right into his lungs and knocked him dead so cleanly that he had no time to say yes or no. Then he drew the sword hanging at his side and struck Tahon's brother Glorion in the middle of his helmet, cutting it in two and slicing him in half all the way down to the saddle. With another blow he killed Tahon's brother Rubion. There were only two others left alive worth naming to you, Sanguin and the emir, a pretty pair of villains. When they saw their brothers dead they invoked Mahomed, and the other pagans howled so loudly that the noise could be heard all the way to the Sultan's tent.

243

When the emir saw his brother die in this fashion, he was so enraged that he thought he would go mad. In a transport of anger he spurred on his horse and made for Enguerrand with a pike he was carrying. He smashed and broke the shield Enguerrand had at his neck, and tore and ripped the mailed hauberk; he cut his heart in two inside him and struck him such a deadly blow that he sent him flying. Enguerrand of St-Pol invoked the Holy Spirit, imploring Him if such be His will to have mercy on his soul and come to the aid of His people, not to let them die and not to let them be killed and slaughtered by the infidels. He raised his hand to sign his head with the Cross; God brought him death with his head to the east. As He made Enguerrand's soul leave his body He sent St Michael to receive it and take it up to a seat in Paradise, there to be waited on by saints and angels. Enguerrand had every right to expect this because he had given his body to be killed for God.[201] His father was overwhelmed with grief at seeing him lying dead. He wrung his hands so hard that blood spurted out, and trembled with grief and anguish. 'God, why have You allowed my son to die when he had come all this way to serve You?' he said. Imagine numerous princes and barons flocking round, all making it clear how sorry they were to lose Enguerrand. Hugh wrung his hands and snapped his joints in anguish. He wrenched his sword from its scabbard and was about to put an end to himself when Robert the Frisian seized it from his hands. The barons and princes could not bear [to watch] Hugh's misery, and were on the point of fainting.

244

There was a wave of grief at the death of Enguerrand, and numerous barons and princes wept that day. They laid the noble warrior on a shield and hastily carried

---

[201] Enguerrand in fact died from illness at Ma'arrat-an-Nu'man: AA V.30. The *Antioche* has a similar scene of a father lamenting his son Gosson of Montaigu at laisses 114–15.

him far from the mêlée. Then they returned to battle with their blood up, each brandishing his coloured sword in his right hand; they were all griefstricken at the death of Enguerrand, and that day 100 emirs breathed their last in revenge for his death. The forces of Our Lord were filled with courage; they bore themselves proudly and killed many that day. Lord Hugh of St-Pol did not hang back that day, his heart full of emotion at the death of his child. He sought out the emir amongst the pagans and ran him to earth amongst his vassals. Not his whole fief could have made him happier, or indeed the whole land of Greater Africa ruled over by the Emperor of Upper India.

245

Lord Hugh of St-Pol caught sight of the emir and spurred up to him brandishing his naked sword. He landed an enormous blow down through the middle of his helmet, sending the jewels and floral ornaments flying. The blow cut right down through him with tremendous force and cut him in half all the way down to the saddle; the lord pulled out his weapon and left him dead. 'Take that, pagan', he said, 'a curse be on you. I have paid you back for the death of Enguerrand!' The Saracens were totally dismayed at the sight. You might have heard them shouting and yelling and creating a huge din, with more than 100,000 flocking to the spot. The Especs were there, who have beaks; they have the heads of dogs and furry bodies, long talons and sharp teeth. In battle they snare people like birdlime. When they saw the *ribalts* they flung themselves on them, ripping off pieces of their flesh with their beaks and talons and ripping out their intestines from their bodies. The *ribalts* suffered severe losses that day.[202]

246

When the King of the Tafurs saw those savage beings inflicting such vicious damage on his men, he flew into a furiously angry rage. 'Don't lose heart', he shouted to the *ribalts*. 'Do not be cowed by these savages. They have no hauberks or helmets, shields, spears or protection. Remember God Who made the birds who fly'. When the *ribalts* heard this they made the sign of the Cross in front of their faces, and found new bravery and determination. They inflicted such damage with their knives and axes that a whole mound of slain was left lying down the meadow.

247

Once the *ribalts* had tracked down their beaked adversaries, they smashed off their heads and arms and chests with maces, axes and knives. They yelped piercingly through their beaks, barking and howling and yelling so much that they could be

---

[202] Compare Revelation 19:17–21.

heard all the way to St George at Ramleh. The King of the Tafurs easily killed 100, whilst the *ribalts* fought off their attacks with axes. They inflicted such slaughter on the plains of Ramleh that their fists were plunged into blood. The beaked enemies lost heart, and you can picture them falling back in disarray; they fled faster than any horse or nag and not one turned round all the way back to the standard. They finally came to a halt outside the main tent of the emir of Persia where he was playing at chess with his brother the emir.[203] When he saw the Beaked Ones all sitting down in front of him he threatened them horribly and mocked them mercilessly. However it was not long before his mood turned to bitter grief: he was about to hear about the fate of his 14 sons, each of whom had been cut into quarters.

248

It was a mighty battle, one made to be remembered: nobody had ever seen one like it. Had you been there you would have seen innumerable blows struck, shields pierced and mailed hoods torn, pagans and Saracens dead and dying, barking and baying and yelping like dogs, with the Kenelius neighing and bellowing. Picture Cornicans from the Red Sea spurring forward, seated on a horned horse which he urged to a speed faster than merlin falcons flying after a stork. He killed two of our men, Roger and Martin, in mounted combat. Baldwin nearly went mad when he saw this. He coveted the horse intensely; if he could once get his hands on it he would not surrender it for four measures of pure gold. He spurred Prinsaut and gave him his head. This meant that King Cornicas was completely unable to avoid the encounter. Baldwin made for him and landed such a blow down through the middle of his helmet that he sent the jewels and floral ornaments flying. He cut all the way down with his sword to the chest and, seizing the horse, sent the Turk flying. Baldwin turned about and rode back. He dismounted from Prinsaut and mounted [the Turk's] horned horse, ordering his own to be led well out of the mêlée and kept there. Baldwin urged on the horned horse faster than a sparrowhawk set to hunting birds. This meant he could come and go without being in danger, being able to attack the pagans when he pleased and ride in and out of the mêlée. The Turks would pay the price for losing this horse. On his first sally Baldwin killed 10, crying: 'By the Holy Sepulchre! This accursed people who refuse to love God are not going to hold out for long. Come on, my lords – watch how they fall! All of you are to advance as one'. At this you might have heard them shouting 'Montjoie!' at the tops of their voices, bellowing 'By the Holy Sepulchre!' and 'By St George!' They forced the Turks to retreat more than the length of a crossbow shot.

---

[203] Rather unlikely in mid-battle but mirrors *Antioche* laisse 299.

249

It was a huge battle, extraordinarily hard fought. There were shouts on all sides and the press got tougher. Picture the Moors of Moriaigne spurring up, Mincomans and Aufinds and men from Buriaigne; they were as hairy as mastiffs and horrible to look at. Anyone who fell into their hands was in for a rough time. But the noble lords from the deserted land laid about them valiantly with their steel swords, leaving the surrounding land covered with dead and wounded. There was not an inch of earth not strewn with intestines and entrails, and every single one of their horses was swimming in crimson blood. The Moors were completely routed and fled down across the plain.

250

After this squadron another set of people rode back: Gaufres and Bougres and the Kenelius who stink to high heaven: when a man has decomposed they eat him and leave the remains scattered round. Their chins and teeth are in their chests.[204] Alongside them were all the men from Bocidant who live ten days' travel beyond the tree which splits open once a year to renew itself. None of them has ever eaten bread or wheat, or indeed even heard of them and they know nothing of them. They live entirely on spices. They do not have permanent dwellings and spend all their time out in the sunshine and the wind. Their flesh is blacker than pitch or ink and they run faster than a bolt fired from a crossbow. They have the bodies of monkeys, the heads of serpents and bellow like bulls; they have no other language. Every single one was equipped with a mace or iron weapon. They are horribly hideous, and spoiling for a fight.[205] If God, glorious in the heavens and Ruler of the world, does not think about His divine plan, these people are going to cut a swathe right through our men.

251

Imagine the king of the donkeys spurring forward, with all his men advancing like braying asses. They made such a noise and commotion that the whole plain of Ramleh shook. The army of Our Lord quailed in agitation – had not God kept them there they would have turned and fled. The True Cross was immediately brought forward in response, the bishop of Mautran spurring up with it, whilst the abbot of Fécamp brought the Lance with its sharp blade and the bishop of Noble brought the stake at which the villains beat Jesus Christ, each wielding his rod until his

---

[204] These sound like Blemmies: Block Friedman, *Monstrous Races* p.12. The Hereford Mappa Mundi portrays two figures of this kind.
[205] Duparc-Quioc, *Cycle* 65–6 points out the close resemblance of this passage to the *Roman d'Alexandre*.

noble head and body streamed with blood. The bishop of Mautran shouted at the top of his voice: 'Come back here, noble and brave lords! Don't lose heart: take courage. Look, here is the True Cross which will protect us. The Saracens and Persians are not going to win against that! Make sure you do not retreat another step; instead you should be vying to lead in attacking these cowards. In the name of God the True Father I forgive you all the evil you have done in your lives. You can be sure that if you die in His name you will be taken up to Paradise singing'. When the Christians heard the bishop of Mautran and saw the True Cross being paraded in front of them, they were all cheered. Not one was cowardly enough not to be eager for battle, and they gave no more than a denier for the prospect of death. They rained blows on the race of the Devil. What more can I say? They killed so abundantly that nobody could say how many fell and no *jongleur* could do it justice in song. Their enemies were about to turn and run when the giants came on the scene, each carrying a great heavy iron mace. They launched an onslaught on the Christians and killed many of them. The bishop of Mautran came spurring up, came to a halt and held up the True Cross in front of him, steadying it on the neck of his horse. The giants looked at it and were all immediately plunged into confusion. They killed each other with their enormous maces, knocking each others' brains out. Snatching up Greek fire they flung it at each other with abandon. What more can I say? They burnt each other to death and only 200 escaped from the original 5,000. The wind turned the fire back on the remainder of that diabolical force and incinerated them all. Now picture Cornumarant spurring up. When he saw his army on fire he was appalled. He turned and spurred Plantamor, brandishing his naked sword; he struck Gerard of Gournay in the middle of his glittering helmet. Neither mailed hood nor visor was any help to him: he slashed through him right down to the chin, knocked him dead from his horse and rode off again. Count Baldwin spurred on the horned horse and pursued the Turk with drawn sword but could not catch him before he reached the Sultan's tent; he did not dare wait for Baldwin but dived into a pavilion. Baldwin saw Peter the Hermit sitting by the standard with 10,000 Arabs seated around him; he did not dare to stop but threw him a greeting as he rode past. He killed an emir in front of the royal tent, then urging on his horned horse he turned on a sixpence; the horse carried him faster than a bird in flight and he did not dismount all the way to the east. Meanwhile Cornumarant came running up to the royal tent shouting at the top of his voice: 'Where are you, my lord emir? All your men have been killed. Not a single pagan is left alive – Hungarians, Bulgars and Publicans, the Almoravids so distinguished by their bravery, and the Lombards and the tallest giants'. These words, as you can imagine, brought Sanguin running. He was accompanied by the Moors of Moriant, who tore their hair with both hands as they came, loudly invoking Apollon and Mahomed. Sanguin came in front of his father wringing his hands, the Moor with him, both hitting one hand into the other. Each fell to his knees in front of the Sultan. 'What in the name of the gods is the matter?' said the emir to them. 'By my god Tervagant, you look as though you have had a rough time'.

252

Sanguin, the son of the Sultan, cried out very loudly: 'My lord emir and father, you are in a terrible situation. You have lost your sons and you will never see them again. The French nobles have flung them down dead. All your men are killed and hardly any remain!' The Sultan fainted four times on hearing this. Then he got up again and shouted a command at the top of his voice: 'Bring me my arms straight away!' said the emir. 'We shall do as you command', replied his men. Corsaus and Salatrés brought him his arms. A carpet was thrown down in front of the main tent, and a coloured silken cloth placed on it: the emir sat himself down on it in great state. King Matusalés laced on his leg guards for him, made of a supple material whose like nobody had ever seen. The curved bits were of gold, crafted by a very skilful Jew well skilled in such arts called Salatrés; each link was fixed with silver nails. The emir Josué attached his spurs; no animal they were used on would ever suffer from swollen sides.[206] Then he put on a hauberk made by Antequités who was worshipped as a god for 25 years. Israel and the elderly Galans were his men – that was where they learnt the skills they each possessed. The hauberk was very richly decorated: each panel was gilded, with an interlacing pattern of pure gold and silver, and the whole of the body had stripes. The hood was made entirely of gold and very splendid: no man wearing it on his head could be stunned by a blow. The visor was decorated with brightly glistening jewels, and fastened with 30 laces of fine gold. Mahomed Gomelin was moulded in relief on it, along with Tervagant, Jubin and the first born Margos: anyone who looked at it would come to no harm on that day. The emir Esteflés brought him his sword. It had been forged by a devil called Barés in the mountains of Loquifer where he was imprisoned. The steel was tempered for a year and a half. When the sword was completed he killed two pagans with it because they had made fun of him at a trial in Hell. The sword was blacker than ink powder. Its name was Hideous and that is what it was called. It had no hilt, but letters were inscribed on the blade talking about the great majesty of the heavens. The scabbard was made of ivory studded with jewels, and the belt of silk with embroidered padding. The Sultan buckled it at his left side. It was getting on for six feet long and six inches wide, and sharper than a freshly honed razor. That day it took the head off many of our men. His uncle Bausumés hung his shield round his neck. It had 30 rivets impressively set in rows.[207] The wood of the shield itself was edged with pure gold. To ensure that it could not get even slightly damaged by any weapon, it was lined inside with elephant hide and protected outside with the pelts of deer and ermine. They brought him his horse, which had been splendidly saddled and had a rich bridle and chest-strap. Even if the emir Codröés had not chosen the harness, it could not have been bought

---

[206] In other words infected or damaged from clumsy application of spurs.

[207] It is less than clear what is meant. The manuscripts show a high degree of variation, suggesting that the scribes were also unclear. 'Boucle' is a boss but the shield would not have had 30 of them; 'bannes principees' can mean 'splendid banners' but the context is not clear.

for [the price of] half of Spain. The horse was equipped with four strong saddle girths. The stirrups were of thoroughly tanned deer hide with golden rings which measured 100 units. [The Sultan mounted from the left stirrup], with 20 crowned kings to hold the right one. He seized a spear with a square blade; it was a good sharp one and covered all over with poison so that nobody who had been injured by it stood any chance of recovery. It had a dragon on top decorated with 20 golden nails. The Sultan's beard spread out over his chest, as white as meadow flowers. He settled himself into the niello-decorated stirrups with Maigremor saddled beneath him. He was very strong and handsome. Take it from me, if he had been Christian nobody would ever have seen such a prince as him. (He was very strong and handsome.) A huge din went up once the Sultan was armed and the main horn was blown next to the standard. Imagine all those pagans assembling in one place, horns, drums and tabors and brass instruments being sounded and the noise being heard for a good five leagues.

253

Once the Sultan had armed himself, a great cry went up. Horns and bugles were blown and drums sounded; the whole country rang with the noise all the way down to the plains of Ramleh. Each of the emirs led his followers; those mad bastards numbered half a million. The rich emir, with a great display of confidence, was sitting on his white horse with chestnut croup – this was the noble horse which was used to test the resolve of our noble forces in Jerusalem. The Sultan was sitting on the marble[-white horse] with its chestnut croup; it could run 30 leagues at a go without its feet or legs getting tired. The emir Sultan swore on his beard that any pagan who fled would have his head cut off. Now may God come to the aid of our forces in their renowned valour. They are going to find themselves in a tough and hard fought battle; a harder one has never been heard of or listened to.

254

The squadrons rode out. The Sultan had them led, ordered and positioned by 30 emirs. He had his treasure carried out onto the plains of Ramleh [and laid out invitingly in front of our Christians] to see if they would make for it, load it up and lash it [onto their pack animals]. He thought this was a good stratagem for attacking and killing them, but not a single one so much as turned aside: they were a great deal keener on decapitating pagans. The emir ordered his forces to try their mettle. At this more than 100,000 Esclers rushed forward, and the Arabs gave their horses their heads. But the noble lords, God save them, were in no mood to refuse battle with the Turks. A massive shout went up as the two sides rushed together. Imagine all those vicious blows landed, and all those feet, hands and heads cut off, one Saracen tripping over another and sent flying, chests and entrails sliced open, helmets cut in quarters and sparks flying off the iron and steel. You might have heard war cries in a thousand places at once. Here and there you might see intestines dragging on the ground, one soldier attacking and retreating from others, the Turks with their horn bows repeatedly shooting and aiming, and swords smashing down on steel helmets. Anyone on the scene would have been amazed at the sight – and in my opinion a brave man if he lingered there.

255

Picture Corbadas spurring through the *mêlée*, well armed and riding Goliath. He killed an Auvergnat from Clermont in the Auvergne. Then he killed Berard, the cousin of Lord Thomas. He rained blows down on our Christians. 'By Mahomed', he said, 'you will avenge the loss of Jerusalem to the French, those sons of Satan. I shall have the noblest barons in my shackles, and I shall cart off Godfrey of Bouillon to Baghdad. They will find it no laughing matter as they are dragged away – none will escape, fat or thin. I am going to take them all away as wretched captives'. Bohemond of Sicily heard him boasting like this, and shouted at the top of his voice: 'You will be sorry you ever thought that, you coward. You will pay for it today if such be the pleasure of God and his mother'. He rushed towards the pagan at no small speed.

256

Bohemond aimed and spurred on his warhorse from Castile; he was brandishing his naked sword, a beautiful piece of workmanship but smeared all over with blood and brains. He struck Corbadas on his glittering gleaming helmet. The mailed hood was no more good to him than a piece of chervil; it cut straight through it like the panel of a tunic. As it reached the shield it cut and broke it. He sliced into the flesh below the breast, and the sword went all the way down to his pelvis cutting him in half all the way down to the saddle; his intestines spilled out over the saddle bow. 'That is what I call proper revenge!' cried out Bohemond. 'You will not get as much as a spoon off us!' This news was not exactly welcome to Cornumarant. Bohemond cried, 'By the Holy Sepulchre!' and rallied his troops.

257

Picture Lucabel spurring up through the press of battle. He was richly armed on his swift horse, his lance couched and his shield on the cantle of the saddle. He made for Mirabiel, whose ancestor was the King Charles Martel, and struck him on his shield. The shield round his neck was no more use to him than a coat. He ripped his hauberk as if it had been a piece of coarse cloth. He plunged his niello-decorated spear right into his body and knocked him dead from the horse into a little thicket. Then he drew his sharp-bladed sword and killed two of our men, Ralph and Guy of

Ponciel. He was inflicting considerable damage on our Christian forces. Tancred caught sight of him and was not happy. [He landed such a blow on him with his steel sword that he cut open his helmet and sliced through his brain. No shield or mailed hauberk was any good; he cut through him right down to where he held his spear and knocked him dead from the horse into a little meadow. Tancred spurred past him on Morel,] made for Piniel, and struck down onto his helmet so hard that he sliced open his body and the intestines spilled out.[208] He met the emir on the slope of a small valley and sent his head flying into it. 'Come on, young men, in the name of the Holy Sepulchre!' he cried. At this you might have heard much combat with swords and innumerable pagans knocked flying down near the small bridge. Everybody found their arms splattered with blood and brains. The Bishop of Mautran swore by St Daniel that never had there been such a race since God created Abel. The pagans and Saracens sounded their calls to battle on brass horns, drums and pipes. There had never been such a battle since the time of Israel for Christian suffering – it was hardly an occasion for enjoyment.

258

It was a massive battle, impressive and hard fought. The Saracens found the Christians resolute, and 100,000 of them fell – that was a good day's work. Picture Cornumarant spurring straight up. He found his father lying dead on the hard ground; this made him break out into a sweat of anguish and foam at the mouth with emotion. He aimed and spurred Plantamor, breaking out of an amble. He struck down onto Guy of Autemue's helmet and cut him in half all the way down to the pelvis, knocking him dead on a hillock with lush and refreshing grass. It is remarkable that God should tolerate a pagan striking such a blow without being defeated. But he will pay for it before nightfall because Count Baldwin is coming to exact his due.

259

It was a huge battle and bitterly fought. The proud Cornumarant was grief stricken on account of his father. He killed the brother of Drogo of Amiens right before his eyes, then killed Guinemant of the Valley of Rivere, Guerin of Aubefort and Guy of Monpère, Arnold the Poitevin and Arnold of Beaucaire. This was bitter news for Count Baldwin. He could not rest until the Turk had paid the price. The Sultan spurred on; he was not pleasant to look at. Makon the enchanter was riding next to him. Not much room there for a harp or a vielle player. The emir Sultan cut an imposing figure.

---

[208] The passage in square brackets is omitted in some manuscripts: Thorp suggests eyeskip is at fault.

260

The emir Sultan was an imposing sight. He arrived at the *mêlée* with his noble barons, more than 50,000 armed men in his force. Kings and emirs surrounded him as he rode. They made way for him and he spurred forward. 60,000 Turks followed behind him and mounted guard over him the whole day down from the battle. The Sultan confronted the Count of Blandas. He landed a massive blow on his striped shield, breaking right through it at the gold boss and tearing apart the hauberk on his back. He plunged the square-cornered blade right into the middle of his heart, pulling his spear out of the body once he had sent him sprawling dead. He swept past digging his spurs into the horse. He made for Tancred to launch an attack as fast as his horse could carry him. The spear struck the middle of his shield but did not shift the baron from stirrups or saddle. When Tancred saw the Sultan he sized him up and struck a huge blow with the sword he was carrying down through the middle of his helmet, leaving it completely buckled out of position. However he was wearing a strong mail hood and not a link was knocked out of position so that the emir Sultan's head remained undamaged. Maigremor swung away and the Sultan turned his attention to Guiré, cutting off his head at the shoulders. At this point the Arabs lifted a vessel and flung Greek fire down onto our men. Their armour and bossed shields all caught on fire, and their horses keeled over unconscious and dead beneath them: many Christians were seriously hurt and killed. Picture the bishop of Noble and the abbot of Fécamp throwing the Lance and the Stake into the fire: imagine how it immediately swung round onto the pagans, and set so many on fire that they could not be numbered by hundreds or thousands.

261

Picture Baldwin of Beauvais and Richard of Chaumont, no lover of villainy, in the midst of the battle. They spurred on their horses and drew their naked swords, and headed into the thick of things to engage in combat; anyone they attacked immediately found himself at peace. Lord Richard of Chaumont went to attack Encilais whilst Baldwin struck Bausumés of Folais. They sliced and shattered the green-sheened steel helmets and knocked them dead off their warhorses from Biais. Then they killed Corsuble and Tanas of Vavais. They put paid to 20 Turks who had eaten their last meal. It was an enormous battle with not an hour of respite. There was so much Saracen blood that the horses were in it up to their hocks.

262

It was a very heavy battle and much blood was shed. The Devil's race were full of vigour. Picture the emir spurring through the battle, seated on the white horse which was breathing hotly. He struck the Count of Vendôme on his shield from in front and cut right through it from one end to the other. The hauberk on his back was less use than a glove would have been. The emir plunged his pennant right into his body; this was not enough to kill him but he knocked him to the ground covered in blood. Godfrey of Bouillon came spurring up. He was appalled to see the Count had fallen, and chased after the emir so fast that he caught him up. He gave him such a heavy blow with his sharp sword that he drove the blade all the way down into his chest. He knocked him dead from his horse and triumphed over him. 'So much for you, you coward', he said, 'you pushed your pursuit too far'. He seized the white horse, which he coveted greatly. Then he spurred over to the Count at top speed He gave him Capalu, his favourite mount, and himself got onto the white horse which had belonged to the pagan. He flung himself into the press of pagans and slaughtered his way through them, landing massive blows with his steel sword and splattering blood and brains everywhere. But there were so many of the pagans that it felt to our lords as though their numbers just kept on increasing. Imagine the main squadron belonging to the emir Sultan; composed of Esclers from the east. They blew their horns so loudly that the earth shook beneath them, and killed swathes of our men with darts and javelins; they threw Greek fire at them which caught fire and plunged them into flames, and burnt innumerable shields on the warhorses. The men of Our Lord were beginning to fall back when the bishop came spurring up to them holding the True Cross out in front of him as he went and raising the morale of our troops as they fought. 'My lords, take courage! Do not act like cowards! You will all be crowned in eternal joy'. At these words they found fresh reserves of strength – something the Saracens and Persians would pay for that night. The bishop ran wherever the fire was burning and put it out completely with the True Cross. The Turks took aim at the bishop with their bows of horn but the arrows came out the wrong way and they could not harm him no matter what they did; he was under the protection of the True Cross. As the bishop passed by the pagans fell back and now it was the Christians striking the Turks, spattering the ground with blood and brains. Picture the proud Cornumarant in the battle. He spurred on Plantamor who was breathing spiritedly, and killed our men William and Pagan of Guillant. His war cry 'Damascus and Tiberias!' was heard everywhere. He spurred ferociously after our men, and they could not intercept him any more than they could a bird in flight. If Baldwin does not turn his mind to dealing with him, things will go badly.

263

When Count Baldwin saw the pagan busy killing our people, he flew into a rage. He urged on his great horse with his golden spurs towards the Saracen, raising his naked sword. Cornumarant saw him coming and did not exactly hang around. He fled more quickly than an antlered stag. Baldwin chased him at full speed on the horned horse which galloped swiftly. He followed Cornumarant for a good league, and caught up with him at the place known as the Three Shadows. Baldwin shouted to him, in a carrying voice: 'Saracen, if you do not turn round, I shall strike you full in the chest'. When Cornumarant saw he was the only one in pursuit he reined Plantamor in and turned his shield towards him. They landed huge blows on each other's shields. However it was Count Baldwin who was the first to strike down through his helmet of beaten gold, sending the jewels and floral ornaments flying. He cut through the hood of the mailshirt, good as it was. The sword cut its way down with irresistible power all the way to his chest. The Count pulled out his weapon and sent Cornumarant sprawling in death. 'So much for you, pagan!' he said. 'I curse you! Take that as your reward for the death of Pagan of Garland!'. He seized Plantamor, that great warhorse, and unbuckled Cornumarant's sword Murglaie from his body. Then he rode back at full gallop and handed Plantamor over to his brother Eustace, who would not have given him up for all of Montagu. Count Baldwin brandished his good sword. The Saracens were plunged into turmoil when they saw it. Such a din of horns and bugles went up that the noise could be heard all the way to Jerusalem.

264

The brave Cornumarant was dead.[209] The pagans were demonstrative in their grief. 100,000 lamented him, all saying, 'Alas, Cornumarant, great lord, your death is a major blow. There was no braver pagan in all of Persia nor anyone who could strike better blows with their burnished sword. My lord, may Mahomed's curse be on the man who killed you!' The emir Sultan heard the news. He had the rallying call blown in front of the standard; Saracens, Persians and pagans all flocked to it. There were more than 100,000, each in battle order. Now our men were in grave danger of being completely overrun. If God, the son of the Virgin Mary, does not remember them, it will be a black day for Christianity. The bishop of Mautran shouted at the top of his voice: 'God, come to the aid of your men and your knights who have suffered so much for you this day!' Now picture Robert of Normandy spurring up; Robert the Frisian, hardly a coward; and Count Hugh, may Jesus' blessing be on him. Tancred and Bohemond were with them, King Godfrey on the white horse from Alenie, his brother Baldwin on Cornu of Rousie, and Eustace riding Plantamor of Nubia. With them came Thomas lord of Marle, Gerard of Le Puiset and Raymond of St-Gilles, Stephen of Albemarle with the mailed hauberk, Gerard of Gournay and Everard of Pavia, and Lord Raimbaut Creton who inflicted serious punishment on the pagans; Count Rotrou of La Perche, whose shield had been holed; and Hugh of St-Pol, still in mourning for the loss of his son Enguerrand. Along with them came Thomas holding his sword boldly. Baldwin of Beauvais was part of this squadron with Richard of Chaumont, the brave Harpin and Lord John of Alis in their squadron, Drogo of Melé brandished his burnished sword; Ralph of Carembaut held his sword drawn; Fulcher from the port of Chartres grasped his in his hand, whilst the sword of Aicart of Montmerle

---

[209] Appropriately the next King of Jerusalem kills the prince who would have been king of Jerusalem.

was in a filthy state, crimson with blood all the way to the hilt. The King of the Tafurs grasped a sickle. The holy company all rode forward together, resolutely determined to attack the pagans. Now there is going to be a truly fierce battle.

265

When the Franks and Saracens clashed, blows rained down from swords and darts. The pagans squawked and shouted in abject concern; the plain was strewn with dead and wounded. Our barons shouted urgently, 'My lords, strike hard! The pagans have lived too long already!' They forced the Saracens back to the standard, where the Arabs turned and made a stand. At that point many warhorses were killed and disembowelled, innumerable hands and feet and limbs cut off. Our men were forced by sheer weight of numbers to retreat a good two acres back into the plains of Ramleh. All the pagans came together there in a mass of combat, more than 20,000 horns being blown at once. A massive force of Turks came up against them in tight ranks. That would have been enough to leave the Christians dead and defeated because by now they were exhausted by the fighting. The bishop of Mautran looked to the right and saw a company riding towards them in tight ranks: I estimate there must have been some 700,000 armed soldiers, all whiter than flowers opening in the meadow. St George was in front carrying a banner, the noble St Maurice on a swift white horse, St Denis, St Domitius and a multitude of others. Every one of them had his pennant raised on lances with a golden cross. They stormed through the tents and thus found Peter the Hermit. St George swept down and freed him; Peter leapt up, readying himself for action; [and St George and his other companions turned and rode away with Peter putting on a hauberk].[210] [St George] installed the noble [Peter] swiftly on his horse. Then he looked a little way down the valley and saw the Sultan's axe hanging at the door of the tent. Lord Peter seized it and cut the standard down. He saw a horse ready saddled in front of him; the hermit swung into the saddle from the niello-decorated stirrup and the Saracens, catching sight of him, pursued him. They turned and fled when they saw the angels. Peter came up against Sanguin, the Sultan's son, and hacked him with an axe all the way down to his waist. He shouted at the top of his voice invoking Jesus' name: 'Holy Lady Mary, come to the aid of your men!' The pagans saw the angels and turned and fled, leaving their backs exposed and totally defeated. The Sultan went completely mad when he saw this. He invoked Mahomed in ringing tones: 'Alas, Lord Mahomed! How I have adored you and served you and worshipped you with all my might. If ever in my life I get back to safety you will find your body and ribs smashed to smithereens. You won't be getting any more devotion or worship from me. A curse on the God who betrays his own people!'

---

[210] The lines in square brackets are omitted: eyeskip again. The reading is from C.

266

The Sultan saw the pagans spurring away in full retreat and the French chasing them with boundless enthusiasm. He invoked Mahomed at the top of his voice: 'Noble divine Apollon, what damage you are allowing my men to suffer – this is a terrible situation. I had your whole body fashioned in gold – I didn't put in any brass – and look at how you have rewarded me in return! I think Mahomed Gomelin is a complete criminal because he did not warn me about any of this when I was safe at home. If I can just manage to escape and avoid being killed or put in prison, I shall have you burnt to nothing in a coal fire! Apostolic Caliph, I shall never see you again, because I can see my men dying in huge numbers'. He called for the emir and the wicked Rubion, 'See how our men are being mercilessly cut down. Throw the Greek fire and let's make our escape. We are never going to get our standard back; I know full well it has been cut down by Peter the Hermit. I was a real fool when I took him into my household. Look at the appearance of those people spurring up – they are as white as snow and stronger than lions. I cannot see any other solution if we are to avoid anyone losing his life. Let us throw the Greek fire and save ourselves: anyone who saves his own skin is offering up a worthy prayer'. At that the wicked Saracens flung the [Greek] fire. The Caliph saw the flames from his pavilion and knew that the Saracens were defeated.[211] He spurred up to Mahomed Gomelin and chopped off his head under the chin; then he mounted his dromedary and made off at top speed. He did not wait for a single one of his peers or companions; he made his way all the way to Acre without stopping. He wrapped Mahomed's head in a piece of silk and wept bitterly over him. The noble lords – God pardon them – inflicted such slaughter on the Turks and pagans that the horses were in blood up to their fetlocks. The pagans turned and fled without stopping.

267

So now the pagans are in full flight with no hope of retrieving the situation. They were not looking for paths, roads or tracks: they were fleeing pell mell to save their lives. The French, those noble lords, were pursuing them and raining down blows with their steel swords. Picture Hugh of Vermandois spurring up on his warhorse; King Godfrey on his white charger and his brothers Eustace and noble Baldwin; Robert the Frisian, beloved friend of God; Robert of Normandy distinguished by so many noble acts; those excellent knights Tancred and Bohemond; Baldwin of Beauvais with his amazing feats; Richard of Chaumont and John of Alis; and the other noble lords, may Jesus come to their help. [All] these circled round in front of the forces of the Devil and forced them back with drawn swords. The pagans

---

[211] This is reminiscent of the fire which the Turks set towards the end of the battle of Antioch; AA makes the link to Greek fire. Compare *Antioche* laisse 359. See e.g. RM VII.14, AA IV.49.

were completely unable to get back to their bivouacs. The Sultan nearly lost his reason when he saw this. He made for Garnier and struck down on his helmet, sending the jewels and floral ornaments flying and slicing him all the way down to his seat; he struck a mighty blow and sent him reeling. God took his soul and carried it away to glory. Then the Sultan flung his large pure gold shield across his body and spurred away in an attempt to cheat death, with more than 30,000 pagans streaming after him. The spirited warhorses raised so much dust that the clear day was obscured.[212] The sun went down and night came on. The French had no idea where they should take refuge. The bishop of Mautran began a prayer to Jesus imploring God to make it his will for day to bring its light, and God granted his request immediately. The night fled away faster than a sparrowhawk can fly: the sun rose and God sent its beams shining out. The Christians on seeing this thought of nothing but launching an assault. The pagans by contrast were appalled and invoked Mahomed and Apollon at the tops of their voices.

268

God accomplished a huge miracle for the lords of France: he made night pass and day come, and the Turks and Saracens turned and fled. Each made shift as best he could to find safety, whilst the noble lords pursued them hotly. They rained down ceaseless blows on them and left the ground strewn with blood and brains so that it streamed down across the plains of Ramleh. Count Hugh of Vermandois pursued Mauquidant: he landed such a blow in the middle of his glittering helmet that he sliced him in half all the way down to his chest. King Godfrey slashed the emir in half with his sharp sword all the way down to his horse. Picture Peter the Hermit running up and meeting Salehadin next to a ravine. He landed a double-handed axe blow on him as he ran past: neither helmet nor shield sufficed to protect him and he cut him and his horse right in half. The French were delighted at the sight. Count Baldwin, riding his horned horse breathing spiritedly, pursued the Sultan accompanied by many noble knights. The Sultan fled on his great steed Maigremor with 30,000 Persians in his company. They made for two leagues beyond Acre. Baldwin shouted, 'You will not get away, sultan!' When the Sultan heard him he yelled to his men, 'My lord, turn and face your pursuers. There aren't many of them and most are injured. By our god Tervagant, not one will escape with his life!' When the Arabs heard the Sultan's words they turned back towards Baldwin with a very bad grace.

269

When the Saracens heard the Sultan shouting out, they turned their horses towards Count Baldwin. There was a hard fought skirmish, with numerous Arabs killed

---

[212] A similar description is found in the Crusaders' letter to the Pope.

and beheaded. But Count Baldwin found himself in a very difficult position because not one of his companions remained in action. Raimbaut Creton's horse was killed under him and the lord leapt to his feet as a brave knight should. Sword in his right hand, he pressed himself hard into the protection of the shield. He killed and decapitated so many Saracens that the pagans could hardly fail to be terrified at the sight. With that Raimbaut Creton shouted at the top of his voice: 'Baldwin of Edessa, where have you gone? Come and help me, noble lord's son that you are! Alas, lords of France, what a terrible thing it will be if you never see me or Baldwin alive again!' At that imagine Baldwin coming spurring up at speed on his horned horse which never grew tired. He came alongside Raimbaut Creton. 'Raimbaut', said the Count, 'get onto this horned horse. Take the news to the King and lords that I am surrounded by Turks before Acre'. 'You cannot stay here without me', said Raimbaut Creton. 'I should rather have my head cut off together with you than see you separated or cut off from me. Alas! What would the lords of France say if I were to leave you here in such mortal danger? I should never again be received honourably in any court. By my faith, I would not leave here even if I were to be dismembered as a result!' 'You will do as you are told, my noble sir', said Count Baldwin. He swung off the horned horse and the cry went up. The horse made a bid for freedom, knocking more than 20 Turks out of its way. The pagans made way for it as it stormed through, reins across its neck, going faster than a thunderclap when a storm has passed. It did not stop until it had reached our side. The Arabs surrounded both princes, aiming and shooting arrows and missiles at them. They pierced their shields and damaged their hauberks: each had wounds and injuries to his body. Now may He Who was hanged on the Cross come to their aid! If He does not help them – this is the plain truth – neither of them will be proof against death.

270

Baldwin of Edessa and Lord Raimbaut Creton were both fighting on foot in the middle of the wicked Turks. The Sultan came spurring up and addressed both barons in ringing tones. 'Well', said the Sultan, 'and what might your names be?' 'In faith', said Baldwin, 'we will tell you the truth: we are not going to hide it for any Saracen. My name is Baldwin and this is Raimbaut Creton. He has killed more than 1,000 Turks and Esclavons, and I have killed as many of those inky-black bastards'. The Sultan's expression was as black as coal when he heard this. 'By Mahomed', he said, 'Bouillon is a kingdom of the devil! Both you and your brother are from there and you are both dyed in the wool villains. You three are responsible for bringing my army to its knees and conquering Jerusalem with the Temple of Solomon. Godfrey is the king and holds the whole region. Our religion has been shamed utterly by him. But we are going to revenge ourselves on you for all of this. We shall have you flayed alive with very sharp knives and then sizzle you to a crisp in boiling lead. At the very least we shall cut off your heads, or perhaps take you off to suffer captivity in the middle of the desert where you will be eaten by bears or lions'. 'By God's will you will not!' said Count Baldwin. 'Come on Baldwin, let's fight', shouted Raimbaut Creton. 'As long as we are still alive let us kill enough to ensure we are not reproached after our death!' Imagine the two barons side by side slashing through Saracen and Persian chests and chins. The Turks did not dare to attack them any more than a mallard would attack a falcon. They dodged like willow-warblers fleeing sparrowhawks and taking refuge in the bushes, shooting at them with Turkish bows and creating a huge din.

271

The barons were hard pressed by the pagans. They struck Raimbaut down in front of Baldwin, wounding him with a sharp steel dart. Count Baldwin picked him up, then landed such a mighty blow on a Turk that he cut him in two. The emir Sultan cried to his Turks: 'Make sure these two wretches do not get away, because I am very upset indeed by them and their ancestry. They have killed my 16 sons and ruined my domains'. When the Arabs heard this they blew a horn and launched a massive fresh assault on the [two] barons. If God in His holy mercy does not remember them now, the princes will find themselves martyrs. However King Godfrey happened on the horned horse running across the plains of Ramleh with its reins over its neck. His heart gave a jolt when he did not see Baldwin. He chased it so hard on his spirited white horse that he and his companions caught up with it and seized it. At that you might have seen many hands wrung and hair torn. 'Noble brother', said the King, 'now I know for a fact that the pagans, those infidel cowards, have killed you. By that Lord to whom I have vowed myself, if you are taken alive, no matter where you have been carried off to, the Turks will not keep you under lock and key in any castle or city!' Picture Peter the Hermit spurring up in a great hurry, clasping his axe with which he had landed so many blows in both hands, including cutting the standard in two. He called to King Godfrey loudly, 'My lord, I saw your brother heading for Acre. He was chasing the emir with Raimbaut Creton and they had 100 armed knights with them'. When the King heard this he gave fervent thanks to God. Eustace took a horn and blew it loudly. All the lords headed for Acre: they will get a poor reception if the Turks are waiting for them.

272

So the princes rode off at full speed, heading straight for Acre. They were blowing so many horns and bugles that the plains, the mountains and the valleys all rang with it.[213] The Sultan heard the noise all too well, and saw a great cloud of dust rising towards Ramleh. 'The battle is over', he said to the Saracens. 'The French

---

[213] Reminiscent of RM's description in IX.24 citing Isaiah.

armies are coming: I can hear their horns. Let us make straight for Acre. Anyone they find in their way is a dead man'. When the pagans heard this they were terrified. They left the fight with Raimbaut and the Count and rode to Acre without drawing rein. They raised the bars and shut the gate. The Sultan was presented with a galley. The grey-bearded emir rode in with the Apostolic Caliph, keeper of their religion, and 500 Saracens of that misguided faith. They had wrapped Mahomed's head in a white silk cloth striped with gold embroidery. Then they shipped the anchor and raised the sail. Many tears were shed as they left. 30,000 were left behind to guard Acre under the capable command of Abrahan and Amise. Off sailed the galley across the salt sea; there were favourable winds and they had good conditions so that they reached the port of Siglaie without incident. The noble barons from the land of salvation [i.e. France] had ridden so far and so fast that they found Baldwin, who had a flesh wound, and lord Raimbaut Creton covered in blood. They were overjoyed to find the pair of them alive, and there was great embracing between lords and princes. Each mounted his horse with its golden saddle. The day was coming to its end and evening approached. Our men rode back without drawing rein all the way to the pagan tents, and that was where the army of God spent that night. They found abundant food and threshed oats, meaning that they spent a very pleasant evening.[214] After they had eaten they all took their rest; Bohemond mounted guard until dawn.

273

The following morning as day broke, the counts and princes all across the army got up, kings, barons and other knights. They had all the treasure sought out and put together. Pack animals carried the tents and the silks; they were counted as 15,000 without all the other animals too numerous to count: bullocks, camels, palfreys and warhorses. I would estimate the numbers at a good 100,000. They had the standard carried off along with the image of Mahomed made of pure gold: this last was carried by a sturdy elephant. The following day they had hammers taken to it. They decided to make straight for Jerusalem. The King and counts had the camp searched thoroughly: the wounded who were there were loaded onto shields along with any dead whom they held in particular regard. You can imagine how much they wept as they saw Enguerrand carried away, with the knights weeping and tearing their hair. [His father Count Hugh thought he might go mad with grief. Imagine the lord tearing his silk tunic] and slamming one fist into another, fainting and reviving and shouting at the top of his voice:[215] 'My sweet noble son Enguerrand, your father who held you so dear will live on as a miserable man. May it be the pleasure of God, Judge of all, that I should not live to see tonight'. He bent down over his son to embrace his corpse. Anyone who saw him kissing his eyes and mouth would have been worse than a devil not to feel pity for him.

---

[214] Reminiscent of the battle of Antioch.
[215] Thorp's emendation.

You might have seen many princes weeping griefstricken at the sight: even the death of Roland did not provoke such lamentation.[216] Count Hugh of Vermandois tried to console him. 'Alas, Lord Hugh of St-Pol, in God's name I implore you not to grieve like this. You should be glad. If your son is dead, it is because he died to avenge God. He has been taken up to heaven to live with the angels'. But the Count was unable to stem Hugh's grief by any attempts at consolation or chastisement; he grieved all the way to the church and in fact lamented more as he went.

274

There was great lamentation over Enguerrand and it lasted all the way to the church. The bishop of Mautran sang Mass. After Holy Mass they buried the body near a marble pillar close to the altar. At that you might have seen his father fainting across the tomb, embracing the ground and biting it. 'My noble son Enguerrand, now I have to tear myself from your body, my beloved – how can I want to live. May it not be God's pleasure that I see this evening fall before my heartstrings break in my body!' Hugh's grief made all the barons weep. 'My lord, let things be', said King Godfrey. 'You cannot change anything with all this mourning. It is true that your son was a very brave young warrior and nobody bore arms better than him. Now Jesus Christ has had him called to his service. [You should not be dismayed by the fact that God has taken him into his keeping. Be quite clear: if there was any chance of finding him] safe and sound and alive, I can assure you that we would seek him amongst the pagans all the way to the Red Sea.[217] But in time all of us will follow him'. The King had Hugh led into the tower and sent the Bishop to console him. Now the barons had all their spoils carried in front of the holy Temple and assembled. They had it equally split and shared out; neither rich nor poor wanted to miss out, and each [of them] received so much that he could claim himself a rich man: if he had had such riches at home in his lands he would have wanted to look after it carefully and if possible spend each day in an honourable state. One and another praised God; they had Jerusalem filled with incense from the censers and candles carried to the Sepulchre and the Temple. They began praising God fervently straight away. They stayed there two days to recover.

275

The company of God was in Jerusalem, in a terrible state after the battle. Hardly surprising that they were exhausted: they had gone through such a hard fight that nobody had ever seen or heard the like. The knights of God stayed there for three

---

[216] Enguerrand is given the same status as the legendary Roland in a deliberate linking to chivalric legend.

[217] Thorp's emendation.

days. On the Tuesday Robert of Normandy rose; so did Robert the Frisian, God's blessing be upon him; Count Hugh of Vermandois, without an ounce of malice in him; and the valiant King Godfrey. The counts of the joyous land assembled amidst the polished stone of the Temple of Solomon.

276

The assembly in the Temple of Solomon was massive. Hugh of Vermandois set out his thinking. 'My lords, by the love of God, say what we are to do. We have won the battle of Ramleh, praise be to God. If you are all in agreement we shall go to Cantari. We shall garrison the surrounding castles: let us go and capture Caesarea, Jaffa and Calençon. We shall take passage across the sea at Acre; and we shall clear the country along the coast of the accursed race who believe in Mahomed'. 'By faith, that is an excellent plan', said the lords. 'We certainly agree if that is what the King commands'. At this Godfrey of Bouillon responded courteously, 'My lords, that would be an excellent course of action. Our God who suffered for us will be grateful'. The princes left and went to their lodgings, equipping themselves with great splendour. The following morning when the rays of the sun appeared in Jerusalem above the main keep, they had two horns and a brass instrument sounded, and armed themselves swiftly down outside Jerusalem. You might have seen innumerable mailed hauberks put on, flags laced and pennons strapped on. Lord Hugh of St-Pol was desperate to seek vengeance for love of Enguerrand. He was up and armed on his black Aragonese steed in a trice, consumed with greed to kill Saracens. He was keener to kill them than to drink any potion.

277

Our barons armed themselves below Jerusalem. Every last one swiftly put on his hauberk and laced his green-sheened bejewelled helmet onto his head. Each buckled his sword at his left-hand side. They mounted their horses and took up their shields. They left Jerusalem in serried ranks, not however taking as much as half the army with them. They numbered 32,000. All the others stayed inside the city: most were wounded, some very seriously. They took their way over the plains of Ramleh, but found no Saracens or Esclers because devils had cleared the country of them. Meanwhile a lion had carried our Christian dead away, piling them up on top of each other outside its lair, as it was called. Cornumarant was the only one to be found in the middle of the battlefield. The princes and castellans were astonished. They signed themselves in the name of God as they went past. They made their way firstly to St George of Ramleh, but found no Turks or infidel pagans.[218] [They rode all the way to Caesarea without stopping] and spurred their way in. When they found nobody they turned and left, leaving 100 knights to

---

[218] Appropriately given the help received from St George.

guard the city. They scoured the countryside from top to bottom, coming and going between Jaffa and Calençon and not finding a single Saracen anywhere. When the princes saw this they worshipped God. Hugh of St-Pol though was filled with rage. He kept spurring out in front of the others, but did not meet a single pagan all day. He would have gone all the way to Acre but they stopped him.

278

When the princes saw that the Turks had fled, they found the castles all empty and without supplies. Not a single Arab remained from Jerusalem to Acre. They ensured that Calençon, Caesarea and Jaffa and the other castles along the coast had ample supplies laid in. This time they did not make for Acre. They did not forget the valiant Cornumarant: our brave knights carried him to Jerusalem. The princes, counts and marquis, bishops, abbots and holy clergy assembled in front of the holy Temple built by Solomon. 'My lords', said the King, 'listen to what I have to say. God has accomplished a great miracle: nobody has ever seen a more striking one. The Turks have been carried off the plains of Ramleh whilst all our Christians are nearby. A lion put them there by Jesus' mercy. Anyone who has fought a good fight can rejoice'. The people all quivered with joy when they heard this. The bishops and abbots hurried to put on their vestments and they processed to the lion's lair. There they found our lords whom God had blessed. The Bishop of Lutis sang Mass there.

279

The princes were overjoyed at what they had seen. They convened a council in front of the holy Temple. They decided that the following day the army would move on immediately; they would make for Acre and launch a determined assault, and would not leave a single infidel Saracen inside the walls. King Godfrey heard this and was delighted. He asked for Cornumarant. His brothers went running off, ordering four knights to go with them. They brought Cornumarant on a shield and put him down in front of the princes beneath a vaulted archway. 'A sad way for this Saracen to go', they said to each other. 'True', said the King. 'He was incredibly brave and struck many blows with his tempered sword. But the one who cut him in half struck a better one!' 'By the salvation of my soul', said Count Baldwin, 'I would rather have had all of Montagu than kill him. I never saw him falter or admit defeat in a skirmish. Strip him', he said to two knights, 'except for his breeches and undershirt. Take off his hauberk and his pointed green-sheened helmet and cut his body open with a sharp knife [because I want to see his heart which never despaired].

280

Baldwin had Cornumarant disarmed. They took a sharp knife and cut out his heart: it would have filled a helmet up to the top. All the barons assembled to look at the heart, saying to each other, 'That was a truly noble pagan! It was a sad thing that he did not turn to God; had he been Christian there would have been nobody like him'. 'True', said Baldwin, 'I can vouch for that. I never saw a knight better at single combat nor at turning and pursuing, dodging and manoeuvring. He knew just how to deal many ferocious blows with his sword, and to inflict slaughter left, right and centre in the thick of battle. He was a very skilled warrior when he chose to display it'. They had his heart wrapped in a cloth; then they had his body sewn up again, wrapped in a golden cloth and raised high on a bier.[219] They had him buried outside Jerusalem.

281

The battle was over and the field empty, and Cornumarant buried with honour, and the Sepulchre delivered from the pagans. Our Christian forces were inside Jerusalem. Each was well equipped at his lodgings. They polished their helmets and mended their hauberks.

That is the last you will hear of this song for the moment. This is where the story comes to an end: God be praised. You will be able to hear about Acre in another volume, and the great battle where the Turks were defeated, Acre taken and then Tyre and Tiberias.[220] And you will hear how the Temple was founded and the Hospital where God was consecrated. This is where I shall finish my book: I have said plenty. May all men who have listened and women on all sides be crowned up in Heaven when they reach the end of their days.

---

[219] This slightly gruesome procedure was employed elsewhere. Bertrand du Guesclin's heart was buried in Dinan and the rest of him in Paris: R. Vercel, *Du Guesclin*, (Paris, 1932) p. 250.

[220] This looks forward to the later texts in the Cycle, notably the *Prise d'Acre*. The reference to a book again points to a written rather than oral approach.

PART III
Appendices

Table of Rhymes by Laisse Number

Chanson des Chétifs

1: -i.e.	37: -é	73: -ans	109: -i.e.
2: -é	38: -ié	74: -on	110: -ant
3: -as	39: -ans	75: -a	111: -ee
4: -er	40: -ier	76: -is	112: -age
5: -i.e.	41: -é	77: -é	113: -er
6: -an	42: -és	78: -i.e.	114: -és
7: -ee	43: -or	79: -ent	115: -ir
8: -és	44: -i.e.	80: -ais	116: -er
9: -us	45: -és	81: -us	117: -us
10: -és	46: -ee	82: -ee	118: -ee
11: -ant	47: -iés	83: -i.e.	119: -és
12: -é	48: -ier	84: -ant	120: -ier
13: -er	49: -ant	85: -is	121: -és
14: -ier	50: -on	86: -ee	122: -is
15: -ant	51: -u	87: -on	123: -ors
16: -on	52: -ue	88: -és	124: -ee
17: -i	53: -i.e.	89: -ans	125: -iés
18: -on	54: -ee	90: -i.e.	126: -i.e.
19: -a	55: -iés	91: -ons	127: -é
20: -ent	56: -a	92: -és	128: -ent
21: -u	57: -és	93: -ier	129: -on
22: -ier	58: -ier	94: -ai	130: -és
23: -ois	59: -ee	95: -ee	131: -in
24: -in	60: -és	96: -és	131bis: -ant
25: -ans	61: -ais	97: -ir	132: -i.e.
26: -is	62: -i.e.	98: -us	133: -al
27: -é	63: -ai	99: -i.e.	134: -on
28: -ier	64: -ent	100: -i	135: -ue
29: -aille	65: -is	101: -al	136: -ee
30: -ent	66: -a	102: -ans	137: -ele
31: -és	67: -on	103: -é	138: -ier
32: -ee	68: -és	104: -ue	139: -in
33: -al	69: -és	105: -ant	
34: -i.e.	70: -ent	106: -ent	
35: -ant	71: -as	107: -és	
36: -i	72: -i.e.	108: -oi	

There are a few assonances, for example at laisse 74 where line 2472 assonances in –om rather than rhyme with –on, or laisse 112 where lines 3415–6 assonance in –ace rather than rhyme in –age. These are dictated by the sense of the text.

Chanson de Jérusalem

1: -on	49: -i	97: -is	145: -ue	193: -i.e.	241: -ee
2: -i.e.	50: -ons	98: -ier	146: -e	194: -ier	242: -on
3: -renr	51: -on	99: -ant	147: -on	195: -aille	243: -ir
4: -as	52: -ier	100: -i.e.	148: -é	196: -u	244: -or
5: -or	53: -ee	101: -on	149: -ent	197: -és	245: -u
6: -ans	54: -i.e.	102: -ee	150: -al	198: -on	246: -age
7: -ant	55: -ois	103: -al	151: -ois	199: -er	247: -is
8: -ier	56: -er	104: -ent	152: -ent	200: -al	248: -er
9: -es	57: -ant	105: -er	153: -on	201: -é	249: -aigne
10: -ant	58: -ir	106: -on	154: -i.e.	202: -age	250: -ent
11: -i	59: -i.e.	107: -é	155: -or	203: -ier	251: -ant
12: -ant	60: -és	108: -i.e.	156: -ee	204: -ant	252: -és
13: -ier	61: -is	109: -ier	157: -on	205: -u	253: -ee
14: -is	62: -ent	110: -aus/ls	158: -ant	206: -é	254: -er
15: -i.e.	6:3: -ier	111: -a	159: -és	207: -ue	255: -as
16: -on	64: -ant	112: -ee	160: -i.e.	208: -ire	256: -ele
17: -ee	65: -aus/als	113: -on	161: -iés	209: -er	257: -el
18: -i.e.	66: -on	114: -ans	162: -er	210: -ant	258: -ure
19: -aire	67: -is	115: -is	163: -é	211: -és	259: -ere
20: -os	68: -ain	116: -és	164: -üe	212: -on	260: -é
21: -el	69: -as	117: -é	165: -er	213: -ee	261: -ais
22: -on	70: -é	118: -ié	166: -i.e.	214: -i	262: -ant
23: -ier	71: -al	119: -i.e.	167: -ant	215: -i.e.	263: -u
24: -ure	72: -ee	120: -i	168: -ir	216: -er	264: -i.e.
25: -er	73: -able	121: -er	169: -i	217: -a	265: -et
26: -ant	74: -el	122: -ue	170: -i.e.	218: -i.e.	266: -on
27: -ier	75: -er	123: -u	171: -ue	219: -on	267: -ier
28: -és	76: -a	124: -ent	172: -ant	220: -és	268: -ant
29: -ié	77: -aille	125: -ee	173: -ier	221: -ans	269: -és
30: -i.e.	78: -aine	126: -ier	174: -és	222: -ent	270: -ons
31: -ié	79: -ans	127: -é	175: -is	223: -er	271: -et/é/és
32: -on	80: -i.e.	128: -ant	176: -i.e.	224: -ier	272: -ee
33: -é	81: -és	129: -i.e.	177: -al	225: -ons	273: -ier
34: -ee	82: -is	130: -és	178: -er	226: -ant	274: -er
35: -a	83: -er	131: -on	179: -ier	227: -er	275: -i.e.
36: -is	84: -ier	132: -é	180: -on	228: -in	276: -on
37: -ier	85: -és	133: -er	181: -i.e.	229: -is	277: -é/et
38: -iere	86: -i.e.	134: -is	182: -é	230: -on	278: -i/is
39: -i.e.	87: -on	135: -i.e.	183: -ons	231: -als	279: -u
40: -ons	88: -é	136: -ant	184: -ent	232: -ees	280: -er
41: -is	89: -ire	137: -er	185: -é	233: -ee	281: -és
42: -és	90: -ee	138: -ee	186: -i.e.	234: -is	
43: -one	91: -ent	139: -ier	187: -ee	235: -iere	
44: -ois	92: -ant	140: -on	188: -at	236: -ier	
45: -on	93: -és	141: -i.e.	189: -és	237: -u	
46: -as	94: -ies	142: -ier	190: -ainte	238: -i.e.	
47: -ai	95: -ue	143: -é	191: -on	239: -ant	
48: -i.e.	96: -er	144: -és	192: -a	240: -é	

Table of Names and Places

The tables below list:

- characters in the *Chanson des Chétifs*
- placenames in the *Chanson des Chétifs*
- characters in the *Chanson de Jérusalem*
- placenames in the *Chanson de Jérusalem*

They do not include names in the variants translated.

The borderline between history and fiction is frequently blurred. Fictional and probably fictional characters and places are italicised as are probably real people used in a fictional context. Biblical names are not.

References to God, the Christians, Franks, the French, Arabs, Turks and Saracens are ubiquitous and I have not listed them separately.

For characters I have used the forms in Riley-Smith's *First Crusaders* unless there is a more familiar modern variant.

For places with a familiar modern name such as Beirut, I have followed modern convention. For less well known places I have followed the gazetteer in Baldwin and Setton. For imaginary places I have retained the spelling in the text and cross-referred to Moisan. Places referred to only as part of a character's name will be found in the Index of Characters.

The tables draw on the following sources:

Baldwin and Setton: Gazetteer in *The First Hundred Years*, (ed.) M. Baldwin pp.626–66 in *A History of the Crusades* (ed.) M. Baldwin and K.Setton, second edition 6 vols (University of Wisconsin, Madison, 1969–89).
A. Moisan, *Répertoire des noms propres de personnes et de lieux cités dans les chansons de geste francaises et les oeuvres étrangères derivées*, 5 vols (Geneva, 1986): referred to as Moisan.
A. Murray, *The Crusader Kingdom of Jerusalem: a dynastic history 1099–1115; Prosopographica et Geneaologica* (Oxford, 2000): referred to as Murray.
Myers, Introduction, 'Développement' and 'Version fécampoise'.
J. Riley-Smith, *The First Crusaders 1095–1131* (Cambridge, 1997): referred to as Riley-Smith.

Other works referred to are cited in full in the tables.
All references are by laisse.

Table of Characters by Laisse:

Chanson Des Chetifs

Aalais of Beauvais: wife of Ernoul: 61 evoked by Ernoul.
Abbot of Fécamp: 25 sings Mass before battle; 28 prays before battle; 66 adds his counsel to that of Bishop of Forez; 67, 68 gives Baldwin document with the 99 Names of God; 68 his blessing sought by Baldwin; 73 evoked by Baldwin; 77 supports mission to find Baldwin; 81 blesses Saracens; 83 climbs Mount Tigris with Corbaran; 88 helps Corbaran rescue Baldwin; 89 marvels at dead Sathanas; 92 counsels against taking Sathanas' treasure; 93 encourages Corbaran; 94 exhorts him to seek baptism; 96 encourages Corbaran to fight; 130 asks Corbaran whether he intends to honour his pledge to convert.
Fécamp is the ancestral abbey of the Dukes of Normandy. Possibly the second abbot of Fécamp, Jean d'Alie: see Myers, 'Développement' 77–9.
Abel: 28 evoked in context of Harrowing of Hell; 115 evoked by Harpin in same context.
Abraham: 28 referred in context of Harrowing of Hell in Richard's prayer; 71 referred to in Harrowing of Hell in Baldwin's prayer; 115 evoked by Harpin in same context.
Adam: 1 expulsion from Paradise; 25 evoked; 28 evoked in Richard's prayer and referred in context of Harrowing of Hell; 71 the Fall and Harrowing of Hell evoked in Baldwin's prayer.
Aeneas, son of: 3 evoked in context of Brohadas' death. The reference is not clear.
Aimery of l'Aitrus: 129 evoked by Richard of Chaumont.
Angel Gabriel: 71 evoked in Baldwin's prayer at Annunciation and later at Sepulchre.
Apollon: 3 blamed by Sultan for loss of Brohadas; 89 Corbaran says God more powerful; 134 evoked by Saracens attacking *chétifs*; 139 evoked by Cornumarant's Saracens. Saracen deity, often part of trilogy with Termagant and Mahomed. See M. Zink, 'Apollin'. Numerous references: Moisan vol.1 pp. 167–8.
Apostolic Caliph: Saracen equivalent of the Pope: 4 preaches sermon against Franks.
Apostles: 71 evoked in Baldwin's prayer after the Resurrection; 76 evoked by Baldwin as Sathanas attacks.
Arfulans: son of Goliath and nephew of Red Lion: 40 tries to assassinate Richard of Chaumont at banquet; allies with Lyon de la Montagne; 50 seeks Richard in battle; attacks Corbaran; 51 loses, flees, and hung by Sultan; 92 Sultan's forces mistaken for his. Pagan leader at the battle of Antioch, *Antioche* laisse 356.
Baal: 115 evoked by Harpin.

Balan of Orcanie: 81 Saracen overwhelmed by storm created by Sathanas; 83 climbs Mount Tigris with Corbaran. Balant is a common Saracen name: Moisan vol.1 pp. 203–04.

Baldwin of Beauvais: 53, 54, 56: combat with serpent foretold; 57, 61 evoked by Ernoul; 60 hears Ernoul's screams; 61–3 seeks permission from Corbaran to climb mountain and fight the Sathanas; 64 given arms by Corbaran; 64–6 makes confession to Bishop of Forez; 67,68 Abbot of Fécamp gives him document with 99 Names of God; 68 arms for combat, seeks blessing from Bishop of Forez and Abbot of Fécamp and asks forgiveness from *chétifs* for any sins he has committed against them; 69, 70 climbs the mountain; 71 *prière du plus grand péril*; 72 challenges Sathanas; 73 momentarily loses heart; 74 begs for help finding Sathanas; 75 finds it; 76 takes it on; 77 attacks Sathanas; 79, 80 hard pressed by Sathanas and strikes miraculous blow with God's help; 81 faces up to it as Devil expelled; 83–5 desperate battle with Sathanas with help from angel; 86 kills Sathanas and faints from loss of blood; 87, 88 recovers from faint and addresses dead brother's head; 88 Corbaran and companions come to the rescue; 93 Corbaran blames him for apparently getting him into a sticky situation; 100 Corbaran describes his achievement to Sultan; 101 Sultan summons him. Defeat and captivity at Civetot is recounted at laisses 17–34 of the *Antioche*. Not attested outside the Cycle. It is noteworthy that he does not appear at all in the *Chétifs* until the start of the second episode.

Barabbas: 28 evoked in Richard's prayer.

Bishop of Forez: 23 confesses *chétifs*; 25 preaches sermon before battle; 28 prays before battle; 30 prays before battle; 64–6 asked by Baldwin to confess him before fight with Sathanas; 68 his blessing sought by Baldwin; 73 evoked by Baldwin; 77 supports mission to find Baldwin; 78 supports Corbaran in sending reinforcements up Mount Tigris; 81 greets Saracens; 83 climbs Mount Tigris with Corbaran; 88 helps Corbaran rescue Baldwin; 89 marvels at dead Sathanas; 94 addressed by Corbaran; 95 welcomes his proposed apostasy; 97 prepares to bless Corbaran and chétifs thinking they are about to be attacked by Saracens; 130 asks Corbaran whether he intends to honour his pledge to convert; 134 in clash with Saracens. In Calabra's dungeons at laisses 27–31 of the *Antioche*.

Bishop of Le Puy: 26 alluded to at battle of Antioch. Adhemar of Le Puy, Papal Legate and crucial stabilising influence on Crusade. See J. H. and L. L. Hill, 'Contemporary Accounts and the Later Reputation of Adhemar, Bishop of Le Puy', *Medieval History* 9 (1955) pp. 30–38; J. A. Brundage, 'Adhemar of Puy: the Bishop and his Critics', *Speculum* 34 (1959) pp. 201–12.

Blessed Virgin Mary: 28 evoked in Richard's prayer.

Bohemond: 2 cited by Sultan; 13 Corbaran plans to seek help from; 121 cited by Harpin; 129 evoked by Richard of Chaumont; 132 rumoured to be about to attack Jerusalem. See entry under *Chanson de Jérusalem* Table of Names.

Brohadas: 1 mourned over by Corbaran and Saracens; 2 Sultan angry over death of; 7, 8, 11, 26, 37 death alluded to; 42 Corbaran forgiven for his death. Son of the Sultan. His death at Godfrey's hands whilst under Corbaran's protection is recounted in laisses 347–51 of the *Antioche*.

Brudalans, Saracen: 7, 8 speaks up for Corbaran. At the battle of Antioch in the *Antioche* laisses 356, 365. Found elsewhere in *Anseis de Carthage* line 3676; *Anseis von Karthago*, (ed.) Johann Alton, Bibliothek des litterarischen Vereins 194 (Tübingen, 1892); Moisan vol.1 p. 263.

Bruiant of Orcanie: 78 Saracen ordered by Corbaran to lead forces up Mount Tigris; 93 Corbaran seeks his advice. Bruiant is a common Saracen name: Moisan vol.1 pp. 263–5.

Bulgars: 11 defeat at Antioch alluded to.

Cain: 24, 139 Turks and Saracens from line of.

Calabra: daughter of Josué and mother of Corbaran: 10 greets Corbaran on return to Oliferne and already knows what has happened; 11 suggests using captives for ordeal and goes to quarry; 14 tells Corbaran not to seek help from Antioch and advises using prisoners for judicial ordeal; 15 suggests he use Richard of Chaumont; 19 delighted at Richard's acceptance; 20 ensures he is well fed at supper; 22 takes Richard off for some rather dubious relaxation; 26, 35 allusion to sword she gave Richard; 52, 53 alluded to; 83, 89 allusion to her future attack on Corbaran when he converts to Christianity; 91 her foreknowledge of events alluded to; 94 her prophecy about Corbaran alluded to; 104 predictably delighted to see Richard of Chaumont; 106 makes *chétifs* very welcome indeed; 111 sets off in pursuit of Papion, who has kidnapped her great-nephew; 128 rewards Richard and Harpin; 130 rides part of the way with the *chétifs*. Not found outside Crusade *chansons de geste*. Foretells that Corbaran will receive help from the *chétifs* at laisse 33 of the *Antioche*; dialogue with Corbaran 277–83. She is found at *GF* 51–6 and in the derivatives based on it: RM VI.12, PT 93–6, GN 212–16. Her portrayal draws on stereotypes about Saracen women as magicians: see N. Hodgson, 'The role of Kerbogha's mother in the *Gesta Francorum* and other selected chronicles of the First Crusade', in *Gendering the Crusades* (ed.) S.Lambert and S. B Edgington (Cardiff, 2001) pp. 163–76.

Canon of St Peter's: 54 referred to as author of text. Unidentified.

Chapoés: 103 alluded to as brother of Goliath of Mecca. Saracen; not found elsewhere.

Charlemagne: 16, 50 evoked as ancestor of Richard of Chaumont; 50 evoked in battle cry; 129 ancestry evoked by Richard of Chaumont.

Corbadas, King of Jerusalem: 130 Corbaran gives *chétifs* letters of introduction to. 135, 136 receives news of defeat of Saracens in skirmish with *chétifs*. See entry under *Chanson de Jérusalem* Table of Names.

Corbaran: 1 runs away mourning Brohadas; 2 interview with very angry Sultan at Sarmasane; 4,5 Sultan says he must undergo judicial ordeal; 5–7 King of Nubia speaks up for; 7 condemned by Sultan; 8 defends himself in front of Sultan; 9 offers to set up single combat to prove innocence; 10 hands over hostages and returns to Oliferne; 11 defeat at Antioch alluded to; 12 upset at state of *chétifs*;

13 plans to seek help from Christians in Antioch; 15 unimpressed by *chétifs*; 16 talks to Richard of Chaumont; 17 offer reported to *chétifs*; 19 delighted at Richard's acceptance; 20 at supper; 21 gives Richard horse; 22 delighted at his prowess; 23 presents him with three splendid horses; 24,25 prepares to watch single combat; 26 takes Richard to Sultan and reminds him of how bravely he fought at Antioch; 29 refuses Sultan's offer to make peace; 30 alluded to; 37, 38 seeks leave from Sultan to depart having won ordeal; 39 dines with Sultan; 42 forgiven for death of Brohadas and given rich gifts; 42, 43 dreams of being attacked by wild beasts; 44 warns of Lyon of the Mountain; 45 gives chétifs horses; 45–7 attacked by Lyon of the Mountain; 48 presented with horse by Harpin; 49 encourages men; 51 honoured by Sultan, who executes Arfulans for attacking him; 52–4 rides away seriously injured towards Mount Tigris; 55 camps at Mount Tigris; 60 hears Ernoul's screams; 61–3 reluctantly persuaded to let Baldwin fight the Sathanas; 64, 68 gives him arms; 68 consternation at Baldwin's departure to fight Sathanas; 73 evoked by Baldwin; 77 initially cautious about going to save Baldwin but then persuaded and promises gifts and honour to the *chétifs*; 78 orders reinforcements to be sent up Mount Tigris; 81 overwhelmed by storm created by Sathanas; 82 acknowledges power of Christianity and pledges to reward Christians; 83 climbs Mount Tigris to rescue Baldwin; 83 reference to being prized by God and his future conversion to Christianity and attack by Calabra; 84 evoked; 88 rescues Baldwin; 89 marvels at Sathanas and says would be converted to Christianity if he did not fear attack from Calabra; 90–92 encourages Saracens to take Sathanas' treasure unaware of impending attack by Sultan; 93 seeks advice and blames Baldwin for his perceived predicament; 94, 95 says he will seek baptism if he survives; 96, 97 reaction on receiving reinforcements from Sultan; 98, 99 discovers they are friends, not foes; 100 reports back to Sultan; 101 sent to fetch Baldwin; 102 brings him to Sultan; 103 returns to Oliferne with *chétifs*; 104 arrives; 106 gives *chétifs* leave to depart; 107 offers them rich rewards; 111 receives news that his nephew has been snatched by Papion; 120, 122 referred to as having exiled robbers who attack Harpin; 121 cited by Harpin; 122 rides to the rescue of his nephew and Harpin, helped by saints in the guise of three white stags which is a miracle by Christ; 123, 124 attacks robbers in cave; 125, 126 agrees not to attack robbers in return for getting child back; 127 tribute handed over by robbers; 130 gives *chétifs* letters of introduction to King of Jerusalem; says he will convert to Christianity within next two years; rides part of the way with the *chétifs;* 131a takes leave of them at the River Jordan; Saracens coming to seek help from. Leading character in the *Antioche*. The fictional version of Kiwam (ed.) Daula Karbugha, atabeg of Mosul, who failed to defeat the Christians at Antioch: Ibn al-Athir, *Histoire des atabegs de Mosul, RHC.Or* II, part 2, pp. 28–31.

Corbaran's nephew (not named): 109 snatched by lion whilst relaxing next to river; 112, 113 taken from lion by monkey; 114 taken up a tree by the monkey with Harpin at the foot; 116–18 rescued by Harpin from monkey; 120 snatched by robbers; 121 cited by Harpin; 122 Harpin argues it would be a bad idea for the robbers to kill him.

Cornumarant, son of the King of Jerusalem: 130 Corbaran gives *chétifs* letters of introduction to; 136, 137 says will challenge *chétifs* in order to keep his kingdom; 138 arms for battle. Leading character in the *Jérusalem*, functioning as *jeune premier* and equivalent to Sansadoine in the *Antioche*.

Daniel: 71 evoked in Baldwin's prayer.

Devil: 28 evoked in Richard's prayer.

Dionas: 3 Saracen who uncovers Brohadas' body. Found only here.

Droon of Moncy: 16 at Antioch. Drogo I of Mouchy-le-Châtel (dépt. Oise). Attested elsewhere: Riley-Smith p. 203. Appears in the *Antioche* escorting Stephen of Blois (62), in Antioch (253) and rescuing Gerard of Melun (360–61); at 66, 157 of the *Jérusalem*.

Emir of Spain: 24 sees preparations for single combat. Unidentifiable Saracen.

Ernoul of Beauvais: 56, 57 story of how he was taken captive, made slave to a rich Turk then sent as envoy with gifts for the Sultan; 57 attacked by Sathanas; 58 prière du plus grand péril and communion with three blades of grass as appropriate to epic hero about to meet unpleasant end; 59, 60 carried off with his donkey by the Sathanas; 61 killed by Sathanas; 72, 75 head and ears conveniently left by Sathanas for purposes of identification; 87, 88 head addressed by Baldwin. Laisse 17 of the *Antioche* looks ahead to his consumption by the serpent. Not attested elsewhere.

Escanart son of Florent: 128 instructed by Calabra to set the *chétifs* on their way home. Found only in the Cycle. Possibly to be identified with the Eschignar at laisse 50 of the *Antioche*.

Esau: 28 evoked in context of Harrowing of Hell in Richard's prayer; 71 evoked in Baldwin's prayer in same context.

Eustace of Albemarle, son of Count Otto: 129 evoked by Richard of Chaumont. Probably refers to Stephen of Albemarle, who appears at laisses 50, 139 and 355 of the *Antioche*; also attested in AA II.23. Riley-Smith p. 223 identifies him with Stephen of Aumale.

Eve: 28 evoked in context of Harrowing of Hell in Richard's prayer; 71 Fall and Harrowing of Hell evoked in Baldwin's prayer.

Everard of Gournay: 16 at Antioch. Not attested elsewhere. Possibly to be identified with Gerard of Gournay-en-Bray (dépt. Seine-Maritime), who appears at laisses 72 and 355 of the *Antioche* and is attested elsewhere: Riley-Smith pp. 166, 208.

Fabus: 98 Saracen with Sultan of Persia. Common Saracen name: Moisan I.395–6. Faburs is found at laisses 82–3 and 136 of the *Antioche*.

Faramans: 102 seneschal of Sultan, ordered to reward Baldwin.

Faramon, vicious quarry master who has made life hard for the *chétifs*: 11 summons *chétifs* for Calabra to take her pick. Found as Saracen name in *Simon de Pouille* lines 1674, 1716, 4781: *Simon de Pouille* (ed.) D. Conlon (Frankfurt am Main/Bern/New York, 1987).

Florie: 109 sister of Corbaran and mother of his nephew. Saracen female name: also found in *Jehan de Lanson, Ami et Amiles* and *Lion de Bourges*; Moisan vol.1 pp. 414–15.

Fulcher of Melun, *chétif*: 11 so miserable that wants to die; 73 evoked by Baldwin; 83 climbs Mount Tigris with Corbaran. Defeat and captivity with the chétifs at laisses 17–34 of the *Antioche*. Not recorded outside the Cycle (Riley-Smith p. 234). Myers, 'Développement' 82–3 suggests he may be from Meulan (Yvelines) where Fulk was a common family name.

Galans (Wayland): 6, forger of Christian swords; also at *Jérusalem* 252. Referred to as master blacksmith in numerous chansons de geste despite Norse origin: see e.g. *Fierabras* lines 644–54 where he forges Floberge, Hauteclere and Joyeuse (*Fierabras: chanson de geste du XIIe siècle*, (ed.) Marc Le Person (Paris, 2003); and Moisan vol.1 p.442 for further references. Also at *Antioche* 177.

Gerard of the Donjon: 16 at Antioch; 129 evoked by Richard of Chaumont. Found at laisse 355 of the *Antioche* and laisses 1, 16, 66 of the *Jérusalem*; otherwise unattested.

Germans: 11 sing hymns in captivity; not clear why they should be singled out as not at the rhyme.

Gervais of Beauvais, son of Ernoul: 61 evoked by Ernoul.

Gillebert of Beauvais, son of Ernoul: 61 evoked by Ernoul.

Godfrey of Bouillon: 1 referred to as killing Brohadas; 2 cited by Sultan; 13 Corbaran plans to seek help from; 132 referred to as fighting ferocious battle. See under *Chanson de Jérusalem* Table of Names.

Goliath of Mecca, brother of Longinus: 26 one of Richard's two assigned opponents; 28 arms for battle; 30 wounds Richard then is killed by him; 54 referred to; 93, 103, 121 death referred to. Not found outside Crusade *chansons de geste*, though Golias is well attested as a Saracen name; Moisan vol.1 pp. 504–05.

Goliath's brother (?) and cousin: 40 dissuade Goliath's son from assassination of Richard.

Gor(h)ans of Esclavonia: 72, 73 wicked Saracen who built abandoned mosque on top of Mount Tigris. Gorhans is well attested as a Saracen name: Moisan vol.1 pp. 510–11.

Harpin of Bourges, *chétif*: 11 so miserable that wants to die; 18 bolsters Richard's resolve and would have volunteered himself to fight; 19 given robe by Richard; 20 at supper; 21, 22 encourages Richard; 26 goes to palace with Richard; 43 in Corbaran's dream; 45 begs and receives horse from Corbaran; 48 unhorses Lyon of the Mountain and presents horse to Corbaran; 55 encourages Corbaran; 63, 64 advises Corbaran to give Baldwin arms to fight Sathanas; 73 evoked by Baldwin; 83 climbs Mount Tigris with Corbaran; 88 helps Corbaran rescue Baldwin; 89 marvels at Sathanas; 96 encourages Corbaran to fight; 102 accompanies Baldwin to Sultan; 106 made welcome by Calabra; 107 accepts Corbaran's rewards on behalf of *chétifs*; 108 rides out for a change of scene; 110, 112 pursues giant lion Papion to rescue Corbaran's nephew; 113 sees nephew snatched by monkey; 114 sits at foot of tree where monkey has taken child, then attacked by four lions; 115 prays and lions do not attack; 116 prays in name of St Jerome and lions turn tail; child breaks free of monkey and Harpin defends him; 117, 118 defeats monkey and rescues child; 119 sets off back to Oliferne but attacked by armed men; 120 fights robbers; 121 summarises his story to robbers; 122 fights robber king; 123 Corbaran pleased he is alive; 127 put in charge of the robbers' tribute by Corbaran; greeted by Richard and suggests they should go to the Holy Sepulchre; 128 rewarded by Calabra for saving Corbaran's nephew; 129 argues that the *chétifs* should make their way to Jerusalem; 130 thanks Corbaran for letters of introduction; 131bis takes leave of Corbaran; 133 makes pre-battle speech to *chétifs*; 134 clash with Saracens; 139 facing unpleasant end at the hands of Cornumarant. Eudes Arpin, count of Bourges; sold his lands to go on Crusade, participated in the expedition of 1101 and taken captive, released at the initiative of the Emperor Alexius and later became a monk at Cluny; OV V.350–53. See J. Shepard, 'The 'muddy road' of Odo Harpin from Bourges to La-Charité-sur-Loire', in *The experience of Crusading* vol.2: *Defining the Crusader Kingdom*, (ed.) P. Edbury and J. Phillips, (Cambridge, 2003) 11–28; G. Constable, 'The three lives of Odo Arpinus: Viscount of Bourges, Crusader, monk of Cluny', *Crusaders and Crusading in the twelfth century*, G. Constable (Guildford, 2008) pp. 215–28.

Heliseum: 115 evoked by Harpin; Elisha the prophet.

***Hodefrin*:** 24 Corbaran has his house. Saracen. Found only here.

Holy Spirit: 30 intervenes to help Richard.

Hugh le Maisné, count of Vermandois: 2 cited by Sultan; 16 at Antioch; 121 cited by Harpin; 129 evoked by Richard of Chaumont; 132 rumoured to be about to attack Jerusalem. See under *Chanson de Jérusalem* Table of Names.

Hungarians: 6, 11 defeat at battle of Antioch referred to; classed with Saracens and heretics.

Innocents: 22 slaughter of evoked.

Jacob: 28 evoked in context of Harrowing of Hell in Richard's prayer; 71 evoked in same context in Baldwin's prayer.

Jesus: 14 possible apostasy from Islam; 16 invoked; 21 invoked as saving *chétifs*; 26 evoked with token for ordeal; 71 childhood evoked under name of Jesuiel.

John of Alis, *chétif*: 11 so miserable that wants to die; 19 given robe by Richard; 26 goes to palace with Richard; 45 Harpin of Bourges asks for horse for him from Corbaran; 73 evoked by Baldwin; 77 stirs up *chétifs* and Corbaran to go and rescue Baldwin; 83 climbs Mount Tigris with Corbaran; 108 apprehensive at Harpin riding out; 121 evoked by Harpin. Not recorded elsewhere. Myers, 'Développement' 77–9 suggests he was the second abbot of Fécamp.

John the Baptist: 131 alluded to.

John the Norman, *chétif*: same as John of Alis? 89 marvels at dead Sathanas.

Jonah: 71 evoked in Harrowing of Hell in Baldwin's prayer.

Jonas: 98 Saracen with Sultan of Persia. Common Saracen name; Moisan vol.1 pp. 625–26.

***Jonatas*:** Roman soldier who nailed Christ to the Cross: 71 evoked in Baldwin's prayer.

Joseph: 28 evoked in context of Harrowing of Hell in Richard's prayer; 71 evoked in same context in Baldwin's prayer.

Joseph of Arimathea: 28 evoked in Richard's prayer, described as soldier of Pilate; also at Jérusalem 35. In Gospel of Matthew 27:57–60; referred to in other *chansons de geste*, Moisan vol.1 p. 628.

Judas: 3 Saracens race of Judas; 25 treachery evoked; 71 evoked in Baldwin's prayer.

Jupiter: 24 evoked for single combat; 42 evoked; 134 evoked as Jupiter Baraton by Saracens attacking *chétifs*. Frequent Saracen deity; Moisan vol.1 pp. 630, 633–4.

***King Abraham*,** Saracen monarch: 52–4 Mount Tigris in his domain; 56 story of how he sought help from Sultan to defeat Sathanas and was killed by a Frenchman; 98, 102 with Sultan of Persia; 103 agrees to release his captives.

King Herod: 22 Calabra gives the sword he used for the Massacre of the Innocents to Richard for his combat; 71 evoked in Baldwin's prayer; 72, 73 time of alluded to.

***King of Antioch*:** 121 cited by Harpin. Unidentifiable Saracen.

***King of Beneventum*:** 64 maker of hauberk presented to Baldwin of Beauvais by Corbaran. Unidentifiable Saracen.

***King of Damascus*:** 3 mourns Brohadas. Unidentifiable Saracen.

King of Euffras (Euphrates): 3 picks up Sultan from faint. Unidentifiable Saracen.

***King of Falerne*:** 1 mourns Brohadas; 2 with Corbaran at Sarmasane. Unidentifiable Saracen.

***King of Nubia*:** 1 mourns Brohadas; 2 with Corbaran at Sarmasane; 5 -7 speaks up for Corbaran; 10 two kings of Nubia accompany him to Oliferne. Also found a number of times in the *Jérusalem*: see Table of Names.

***King Solins*,** son of Dinas: 3 picks up Sultan from faint. Found only here.

Lazarus: 67 alluded to; 74 evoked by Baldwin.

***Longinus*,** centurion who pierced Christ's side with a lance, lost his sight and was subsequently cured and converted: 25 miracle of his sight restored by Christ's blood; 28 evoked in Richard's prayer; 71 evoked in Baldwin's prayer; 74, 76 evoked by Baldwin; 115 evoked by Harpin; 122 evoked by Harpin. Referred to repeatedly in the Cycle; features in the *Vengeance de Christ* theme with which the central trilogy begins and which emphasises the place of the Crusade in the divine plan.

***Lyon of the Mountain*:** 40 allies with Arfulans, son of Goliath; 44 Corbaran warns of him; 45–7 Lyon attacks Corbaran; 48 unhorsed by Harpin of Bourges; 49 remounts and continues battle. Not found outside Crusade *chansons de geste*.

Mahomed: Saracen God. The Saracens frequently swear oaths by Mahomed and I have not included those here. 1 rejected by Corbaran for failure to protect Saracens; 3 invoked by Sultan; 6 to be invoked by Sultan; 9 invoked; 10 worshipped in Oliferne; 14 possibly renounced; 24, 25 evoked for single combat; 42 evoked; 89 Corbaran says God more powerful; 94 invoked by Corbaran; 139 evoked by Cornumarant's Saracens.

Malachi: 138 Jew who made Cornumarant's helmet, not favoured by God. Frequent Saracen name though no other reference in this context: Moisan vol.1 pp. 670–71.

Malcus, Roman soldier who nailed Christ to the Cross: 71 evoked in Baldwin's prayer.

Maragonde, elderly aunt of Corbaran: 52, 53 alluded to. Found only here, though as Saracen name in *Destruction de Rome* and *Fierabras*; Moisan vol.1 p. 682.

Margot: 134 Saracen deity evoked by Saracens attacking *chétifs*. Lesser member of the Saracen pantheon: Moisan vol.1 p. 686.

Mary Jacobi, mother of James: 71 visit to Sepulchre evoked in Baldwin's prayer.

Mary Magdalen: 66 alluded to; 71 visit to the Sepulcre and meeting with Jesus in garden evoked in Baldwin's prayer.

Mary Salome, mother of Salome: 71 visit to Sepulchre evoked in Baldwin's prayer.

Morehier: 78 Saracen told by Corbaran to lead forces up Mount Tigris; 81 overwhelmed by storm created by Sathanas; 83 climbs Mount Tigris with Corbaran; 93 Corbaran seeks his advice. Some references elsewhere: Moisan vol.1 p. 716.

Moses: 28 evoked in Richard's prayer; 49 evoked as example of battle; 71 evoked in context of Harrowing of Hell in Baldwin's prayer.

Noah: 28 evoked in context of Harrowing of Hell in Richard's prayer; 71 evoked in same context in Baldwin's prayer; 115 evoked by Harpin in same context.

Payen of Camelli: 16 at Antioch; 129 evoked by Richard of Chaumont. Found in the *Chétifs* and at laisse 355 of the *Antioche*. Not attested elsewhere; almost certainly the same as the Pagan of Camelia in the *Jerusalem*: see Table of Names.

Pallas (Athene): 3 evoked in context of Brohadas' death. Also evoked at 178, 187 of the *Jérusalem*.

Papion: 109 giant lion which seizes Corbaran's nephew; 110 pursued by Harpin; 112 child taken from him by large monkey. Not found elsewhere: see note to laisse 109 for discussion of reference in Jacques de Vitry.

Patriarch of Antioch: 54 given song on death of its author. See discussion in Introduction; likely to be Patriarch Aimeric of Limoges.

Persians: 6, 11 defeat at battle of Antioch referred to.

Peter the Hermit: 12, 16, 54, 56, 57, 72, 74, 121 defeat at Civetot referred to. See under *Chanson de Jérusalem* Table of Names.

Pharaoh: 28 evoked in Richard's prayer.

Pilate: 28 evoked in Richard's prayer; 71 evoked in Baldwin's prayer.

[Pirrus]: 7 betrayal of Antioch alluded to; not named in the text but called Pirrus in most sources; Datien in the *Antioche* and OV vol.5 pp.86–7.

Publicani: 11 defeat at Antioch alluded to. Saracens named after the sect of heretics known as Publicani.

Queen Eublastris: 4 mourns death of Brohadas and has captives summoned. Not found elsewhere.

Raimbaut Creton: 129 evoked by Richard of Chaumont. See under *Chanson de Jérusalem* Table of Names.

Raymond of Antioch: 54, 56 referred to as commissioner of poem. Raymond of Poitiers, son of Guilhem IX of Aquitaine; invited to come to Antioch as ruler in 1136, killed by Nureddin in 1149. See discussion in Introduction.

Raymond of Pavia, *chétif*: 83 climbs Mount Tigris with Corbaran. Probably to be identified with Richard of Pavia at *Antioche* laisse 31 and Rainald of Pavia at *Jérusalem* laisse 15. See Myers. 'Développement' p. 83, who argues that it is quite feasible someone from Pavia might have found themselves in Normandy.

Raymond of St-Gilles, Count of Toulouse: 16 at Antioch; 129 evoked by Richard of Chaumont; 132 rumoured to be about to attack Jerusalem. See under *Chanson de Jérusalem* Table of Names.

Red Lion: 7 decapitation at Antioch alluded to; 11, 16 defeat at Antioch alluded to. Saracen king who acts as Corbaran's informant at the battle of Antioch in the *Antioche* and is killed by Robert of Normandy at laisse 357. Not found outside Crusade *chansons de geste*, although in *Tristan de Nanteuil* line1298 Galafre d'Erminie is described as his son (*Tristan de Nantueil: chanson de geste inédite*, (ed.) K. Sinclair (Assen, 1971).

Richard of Chaumont, *chétif*: 11, so miserable that wants to die; 15 praised by Calabra; 16 talks to Corbaran; 17 discusses his offer with *chétifs*; 18 discusses with Harpin; 19 agrees to undertake combat; 20 at supper; 21 in rich robes; 22 demonstrates prowess; 23 given three horses by Corbaran; 25 spiritual preparations for battle; 26 taken to Sultan's palace by Corbaran and prepares for battle; 28 *prière du plus grand péril* before battle; 30 engages in battle killing Goliath but being wounded by both Saracens; 31–7 hard-fought duel with Sorgalé which ends up winning; 40 survives assassination attempt at supper by Golias' son; 41 referred to; 42 offered treasure by Sultan but refuses; 45 given horses for John of Alis and Harpin of Bourges and encourages Corbaran; 51, 52 trusted ally of Corbaran; 52 rides towards Mount Tigris with Corbaran; 54, 55 wounded and in pain; 63 Corbaran wants his advice; 73 evoked by Baldwin; 77 laments supposed death of Baldwin; 84 evoked; 89 marvels at dead Sathanas; 94 evoked by Corbaran; 95 prepares to fight; 96 reaction to reinforcements sent by Sultan; 102 accompanies Baldwin to Sultan; 103 Sultan commands him to be rewarded; 104 received in Oliferne by Calabra, his reaction not recorded; 105 enters Oliferne in triumph with *chétifs*; 106 his agreement with Corbaran referred to; 121 evoked by Harpin; 127 greets Harpin on his triumphant return; 128 rewarded by Calabra; 129 suggests that the *chétifs* should rejoin the crusader army but Harpin prevails on them to go to Jerusalem; 131bis takes leave of Corbaran; 132 hears mass with chétifs in garden of King Abraham and makes for Jerusalem, though will face difficulties on the way; 133 rides to Jerusalem with *chétifs*; 134 in clash with Saracens; 136, 138, 139 facing an unpleasant end at the hands of Cornumarant.

Appears a number of times in the *Jérusalem*. See Myers, 'Développement' pp. 79–82. Riley-Smith p. 231 suggests he is Richard of Chaumont-en-Vexin; see also Riley-Smith, *What were the Crusades?* pp.75–7 for discussion of role of Hugh of Chaumont-sur-Loire and related families.

Robert the Frisian, by mistake for Robert count of Flanders: 16 at Antioch; 129 evoked by Richard of Chaumont. See under *Chanson de Jérusalem* Table of Names.

Robert of Normandy: 13 Corbaran plans to seek help from; 16 at Antioch; 121 cited by Harpin; 129 evoked by Richard of Chaumont; 132 rumoured to be about to attack Jerusalem; evoked as of particular help to *chétifs*. See under *Chanson de Jérusalem* Table of Names.

Roger of Rosoie: 16 at Antioch; 129 evoked by Richard of Chaumont. Owes his fame to the soubriquet 'qui cloche du talon' for sake of rhyme rather than any particular achievement. Referred to a number of times in the *Antioche* and the *Jérusalem*. Roger of Rozoy (Aisne), castellan of Jaffa. Attested elsewhere on Crusade: Murray p. 227; Riley-Smith p. 222.

***Rogin*:** 24 assigned as steward to *chétifs*. Found only here.

St Barbara: 122 helps Corbaran in guise of a white stag. Only here in the Cycle. See under *Chanson de Jérusalem* Table of Names.

St Denis: 76 evoked by Baldwin as Sathanas attacks. Patron saint of Paris; here convenient for the rhyme. Also invoked in the *Antioche* and the *Jérusalem*. See under *Chanson de Jérusalem* Table of Names.

St Domitian: 122 helps Corbaran in guise of a white stag. See under *Chanson de Jérusalem* Table of Names.

St George of Ramla: 76 evoked by Baldwin as Sathanas attacks; 122 helps Corbaran in guise of a white stag. See under *Chanson de Jérusalem* Table of Names.

St Gervais: 80 evoked in miraculous blow against Sathanas. Early Christian martyr and also eleventh-century hermit; referred to in some *chansons de geste*; Moisan vol.1 p. 481.

St Gilles: 76 evoked by Baldwin as Sathanas attacks. Abbot in south of France; referred to in some *chansons de geste*; Moisan vol.1 p. 484.

St James: 76 evoked by Baldwin as Sathanas attacks.

St Jerome: 116 evoked by Harpin and lions attacking him turn tail. Highly appropriate given the well-known apocryphal legend of St Jerome and the lion he tamed.

St John: 2, Saracens celebrate feast of (24 June); 57 feast of occasion for sending gifts to Sultan. It is not clear why this should be observed by Saracens.

St Leonard: 76 evoked by Baldwin as Sathanas attacks. Patron saint of prisoners; his shrine at St-Léonard-de-Noblat was a place of pilgrimage, not least being visited by Bohemond in 1106 after his release from captivity. See A. Poncelet, 'Boémond et St Léonard', *Analecta Bollandiana* 31 (1912) pp. 24–2.

St Maurice: 76 evoked by Baldwin as Sathanas attacks. See under *Chanson de Jérusalem* Table of Names.

St Michael: 74, 75 appears in shape of dove sent by Jesus to help Baldwin find Sathanas; 80 evoked in miraculous blow against Sathanas; 81 helps Baldwin fight Sathanas; 84, 85 helps in fight (name of angel not given). See under *Chanson de Jérusalem* Table of Names.

St Nicholas: 57, 61 invoked by Ernoul; 63 invoked by Baldwin of Beauvais and Harpin of Bourges; 69, 71 invoked by Baldwin of Beauvais; 76 evoked by Baldwin as Sathanas attacks; 80 evoked in miraculous blow against Sathanas; 119 evoked by Harpin when attacked by robbers; 121 evoked by Harpin. See under *Chanson de Jérusalem* Table of Names.

St Peter: 67 alluded to; 76 evoked by Baldwin as Sathanas attacks. See under *Chanson de Jérusalem* Table of Names.

St Simeon: 18 body of invoked; the Simeon to whom Christ was presented in the Temple; here for the sake of the rhyme. See under *Chanson de Jérusalem* Table of Names.

Salatré: 24 assigned as steward to *chétifs*; 103 charged by Sultan with rewarding Richard of Chaumont. Referred to as skilled craftsman in *Jérusalem* 178, 252. Common Saracen name: Moisan vol.2 pp. 863–4.

Samaritans: 6 defeat at battle of Antioch referred to.

Sathanas, Saracen god: 3 blamed by Sultan for loss of Brohadas.

Sathanas the serpent: 53, 54 described; 57–61 attacks and kills Ernoul of Beauvais; 61–3 Baldwin seeks permission to attack; 71 alluded to; 72 description of how the serpent became possessed by the Devil; 73 apostrophised by Baldwin; 74 Baldwin prays to find it; 75 he finds a very replete Sathanas; 76 Sathanas attacks; 77 God drives out the Devil from the Sathanas, and its cries are heard all the way down the mountain; 79, 80 attacks Baldwin hard then suffers miraculous blow which leaves sword stuck in its throat; 81 Devil expelled by Jesus in the form of a crow; 83–5 desperate battle with Baldwin; 86 killed by Baldwin; 89 Saracens marvel at its corpse; 100 described by Corbaran.

Slavs: 18 invoked.

Solomon: 74 time of evoked.

Sorgalé of Valgris (of *Allier* in laisse 93): 26 one of Richard's two assigned opponents; 27 arms for battle; 30 wounds Richard; 31–7 single combat with Richard during which he offers him apostasy before being beheaded; 46, 77, 93, 103, 121 death referred to. Found only here; name Sorgalé also in *Chevalerie Ogier de Danemarche* and *Prise d'Orange*, Moisan vol.2 p. 901.

Sultan of Persia: 1 anger over death of Brohadas alluded to; 2 furious over death of Brohadas and throws dart at Corbaran; 3 grieves for Brohadas and asks to see body; 4,5, 7 blames Corbaran and says he must undergo judicial ordeal; 9 agrees to single combat to try Corbaran's innocence; 13, 17, 19 anger alluded to; 24, 25, 26 worried about combat; 26 receives Richard and Corbaran; 27 watches Sorgalé arm; 28 esteems Goliath; 29 makes last minute offer of peace to Corbaran; 30 makes preparations for ordeal; 31 maintains truce during ordeal; 32 receives report from ordeal; 37, 38 gives Corbaran leave to depart after ordeal; 39 dines with Corbaran; 41, 42 forgives him for death of Brohadas and gives him rich gifts; 51 hangs Arfulans for attacking Corbaran; 57 en route to Mount Tigris with 60,000 knights; 73 evoked by Baldwin; 89 Saracens fear he will attack if Corbaran apostatises; 92, 95 arrives at Mount Tigris and his army mistaken for a hostile one; 96 receives report that Corbaran has gone to fight Sathanas and orders reinforcements sent; 98, 99 his messengers reach Corbaran; 100 receives Corbaran's report; 101 sends Corbaran to fetch Baldwin; 102 rewards Baldwin; 103 releases *chétifs* and returns home; 121 cited by Harpin.

Susanna: 71 evoked in Baldwin's prayer.

Tancred: 2 cited by Sultan; 121 cited by Harpin, 129 evoked by Richard of Chaumont. See under *Chanson de Jérusalem* Table of Names.

Tervagant, Saracen God: 1 rejected by Corbaran for failure to protect Saracens; 4 Brohadas' body laid in state in front of statue; 6 to be invoked by Sultan; 11 invoked; 24 invoked for single combat; 89 Corbaran says God more powerful; 126 invoked by Corbaran. Important Saracen deity; Moisan vol.2 pp. 915–16 for numerous references.

Thomas of La Fère, lord of Marle: 2 cited by Sultan; 16 at Antioch; 121 cited by Harpin; 129 evoked by Richard of Chaumont; clearly seen as important Crusader. See under *Chanson de Jérusalem* Table of Names.

Thomas the Apostle: 71 his doubt of Christ evoked in Baldwin's prayer.

Three kings, Melchior, Jaspas and Balthasar: 71 evoked in Baldwin's prayer.

Turcopoles: 11 will use *chétifs* as target practice.

Table Of Places By Laisse:

Chanson Des Chétifs

Abilant: 35 Richard's sword, given to him by Calabra, forged by a Jew in the deserts of. All purpose Saracen name: Moisan vol. 2 pp. 997–8. See G. Paris, 'La chanson du *Pèlerinage de Charlemagne*', *Romania* 9 (1880) pp. 1–50 at p. 29 for identification of Abilant with Abila in the Anti-Lebanon.

Almeria: 90 silks from. Common all-purpose name: Moisan vol.2 pp. 1032–33.

Antioch: 1, 2 death of Brohadas at; 6 Sultan's loss of; 7 betrayal of; 11 Corbaran at; 13 plans to go to in order to seek mercy from Christians; 16, 26 Corbaran at; 29 Corbaran says Richard of Chaumont was not at Antioch but is in his service; 54 mourning at death of Raymond; 121 Corbaran's defeat at described by Harpin of Bourges; 132 garrisoned by Christians; 137 Cornumarant thinks Christians have come from.

Arabia: 23 horses from; 131a, 132 Saracens from.

Arm of St George at Constantinople: 88 Baldwin remembers crossing with brother.

Armenia: 131 *chétifs* ride past.

Asconie: 62 anonymous pagan from. Possibly to be identified with Lake Ascanius near Nicaea.

Bacar valley: 131 *chétifs* ride past. See discussion by Myers, Introduction xxvi-vii, who identifies the valley with Sem and says that the only other reference to this name is in Ernoul.

Beauvais: 57, 61 evoked by Ernoul; 77 French think Baldwin will not see again.

Beirut: 132 taken by Christians.

Besançon: 91 all the gold in (formulaic).

Betean Sea: 7 marker of Saracen territory. Commonly a synonym for remoteness: Moisan vol.2 p. 1062.

Bethlehem: 49, 79 Christ born in; 64 Christ King of; 71 Christ born in in Baldwin's prayer.

Biés, city of: 92 would not be enough to compensate for danger (formulaic). Saracen city found only in Cycle: Moisan vol.2 p. 1063.

Black Mountain: 1 Corbaran flees towards. See discussion by Myers, Introduction xxii-iv: classical range of Amanus, first named in the vernacular by William of Tyre.

Byzantium: 126 all the gold and silver of (formulaic).

Carcloie: 132 conquered by Christians. Form not found elsewhere: Myers suggests an identification with Kephalia: Introduction xxix-xxx.

Castile: 31 Sorgalés' horse from.

Civetot: 12 allusion to *chétifs* being taken captive at; 122 defeat at described by Harpin of Bourges. Classical port of Kibotos.

Confession: 129 Imaginary shrine in Jerusalem.

Cordie: 109 river where Corbaran's nephew captured.

Cordoba: 6 knife from.

Coroscane: 2 Turks from. Khurasan, a region of North-East Persia.

Damascus: 89 all the gold in.

Damascus Gate, Oliferne: 104 Corbaran and *chétifs* enter through.

Edessa: 1 Corbaran avoids; 80 even the fief of could not please Baldwin more than defeating the Sathanas.

Esclavonia: 90 fabrics from. Commonly found; country of the Esclavons or Slavs. Moisan vol.2 p. 1144.

Fondefle: 109 Corbaran's sister Florie lady of. Myers, Index to *Chétifs*, p.355 suggests this may be a distorted version of Philadelphia, modern Amman.

France: 22 evoked; 45 *chétifs* well reputed in; 53 Baldwin of Beauvais from; 63 Baldwin will not return to until Sathanas defeated.

Galicia: 76 St James of.

Garden of Abraham: 132 *chétifs* hear Mass in. FC III.364.

Gate of Blood at Sarmasane: 24 *chétifs* enter through.

Gate of the Ravine, Oliferne: 108 Harpin of Bourges leaves through.

Gibel: 132 taken by Christians. Latin Gibelum, modern Djablah.

Golden Gate, Jerusalem: 71 Christ entered through at Passion in Baldwin's prayer; 134 Saracen survivor enters Jerusalem through.

Golgotha: 28 Christ at in Richard of Chaumont's prayer; 71 Christ's death at in Baldwin's prayer.

Greece: 127 embroidered silk cloths made in.

Haleching: 131 *chétifs* ride past. Unidentified and no parallels.

Hamelech: 131 *chétifs* ride past. Unidentified and no parallels.

Holy Sepulchre: 9, 11 Corbaran seeks leave to go and find a champion at; 13 says will restore to Christians; 16 Richard of Chaumont had been on way to; 28 Christ's body laid at in Richard of Chaumont's prayer; 30 *chétifs* had been on way to; 36 Sorgalés alludes to Christ's body being laid in; 63 invoked by Baldwin of Beauvais; 71 Christ laid in in Baldwin's prayer; 76, 88 invoked by Baldwin; 77 Corbaran will reward *chétifs* when return from; 96 anyone who fails to fight well enough will not see; 121 invoked by Harpin of Bourges; 127 *chétifs* finally think they might be able to get there; 129 questioned by Richard of Chaumont but Harpin of Bourges wants to see. See C. Morris, *The Sepulchre of Christ in the Medieval West: from the beginning to 1600* (Oxford, 2005).

Hungary: 90 all the gold in (formulaic).

Jerusalem: 6 part of Sultan's kingdom; 13 Corbaran says will restore to Christians; 28 Christ at in Richard of Chaumont's prayer; 56 forward look to conquest of in the *Chanson de Jérusalem*; 94 Corbaran will go to; 131a *chétifs* make for; 132 Christians camped at mosque two and a half leagues from; 139 Saracens arming inside.

Joriam: 131 *chétifs* ride past. Myers identifies with Georgia: Introduction xxv.

Lutis: 26 Saracen domain. Moisan vol.2 p. 1227.

La Mahomerie: 132 Crusaders arrive there. Modern Ed-Bireh, about 15 km from Jerusalem.

La Marce: 132 taken by Crusaders. Vernacular name for Ma'arrat-an-Nu'man: Myers, Introduction xxix.

Margat: 132 taken by Christians. Castle of Marqab; Hospitaller fortress, too important for Saladin to attack: Myers, Introduction xxviii-ix.

Mount of Calvary: 28 Christ at in Richard of Chaumont's prayer; 36 invoked by Sorgalés; 58 Crucifixion invoked by Ernoul of Beauvais; 71 Crucifixion on in Baldwin's prayer; 129 Harpin of Bourges wants to see.

Mount Tabor: 71 scene of Ascension in Baldwin's prayer.

Mount Tigris, home of the Sathanas in the land of King Abraham: 52, 53, 54 Corbaran and *chétifs* find themselves at, hopelessly lost; 55 home of Sathanas; 56 Sultan sent Turks to without success; 57, 58 Ernoul attacked by Sathanas on; 63, 65 Baldwin will climb to attack Sathanas; 68 too steep for any horse; 69 Baldwin's hard climb up; 78 Corbaran agrees to climb; 96 has climbed. Generally situated in Armenia; not found outside Crusade epics. Moisan vol.2 p. 1424.

Oliferne, Corbaran's capital: 10 Corbaran returns to; 23 plains of; 26 horse from; 38 Corbaran asks leave to return to; 62 wants to make for rather than stay at Mount Tigris; 83, 89 allusion to Corbaran being besieged in; 91 Corbaran and *chétifs* plan to return to having defeated the Sathanas; 103, 104, 105 Corbaran

Table of Names and Places 375

and *chétifs* return to in triumph; 110 Saracens and Persians mount rescue mission of Corbaran's nephew from; 122 Corbaran's nephew captured outside; 127 Corbaran returns to; 130 *chétifs* finally leave with great honour. Commonly referred to, often in association with Corbaran: Moisan vol.2 p. 1297.

Orcanie: 62 horse from (formulaic); 78 Saracens left to guard deserts of. Commonly found Saracen country: Moisan vol.2 pp. 1300–01.

Orient: 11 marker of Saracen territory.

Pateron: 131 *chétifs* ride past. Myers suggests this may reflect the heretics known as Patarini, particularly in the Balkans: Myers, Introduction xxv.

Persia: 96 Sultan has marched from.

Pré Noiron: 67 St Peter buried in. Refers to the Gardens of Nero in Rome where St Peter was tortured and the Vatican built. Moisan vol.2 p. 1288; commonly found.

Provence: 76 St Gilles of.

Ramla, also Rama or Rames; Arabic ar-Ramlah: 76 St George of.

Red Cistern: 131a, 132 *chétifs* meet 140 Turks at on the way to Jerusalem; 135, 136 defeat of Saracens at. Also in Ernoul: Myers, Introduction xxviii.

River Euphrates, a river blessed by God: 1 Corbaran crosses; 2 Brohadas mourned at. Seldom referred outside Crusade epics: Moisan vol.2 pp. 1150–51.

River Jordan: 131 *chétifs* bathe in.

River Quinquaille: 29 river at Sarmasane. A few references elsewhere: Moisan vol.2 p. 1337.

Romania: 62 inhabitants of could not defeat Sathanas; 99 all the gold of (formulaic).

Russia: 90 silken cloths from. Russia in chansons de geste; here could also refer to valley of Rusia near Aleppo (Myers, Index to *Chétifs* pp.360–61).

Saphoria: 132 Christians have conquered March all the way to. Saffuriyah, classical Sepphoris, NW of Nazareth.

Saragossa: 26, 27 helmets from.

Sarmasane, the Sultan's capital: 2 Corbaran and entourage make for to report death of Brohadas to Sultan; 4 Saracen mourning in; 24 Corbaran and *chétifs* return to; 38, 40 families of those killed by Richard march out of to seek vengeance on Corbaran; 42 *chétifs* march out of. Modern Kermanchah in Iran. Little found outside Crusade epics Moisan II.1410. Variously identified with Kermanchah, Samosata, Hamadhan or even Samarkand: Myers, Introduction xxiv-v.

Sidon: 132 taken by Christians. Arabic Saida; port.

Silver Bridge: 2 Saracens pass on way to Sarmasane. Found only in the central trilogy: Moisan vol.2 p. 1024.

Spain: 40 all the gold in.

Syria: 1 Corbaran flees across; 62 helmet from; 90 mules from; 109 Corbaran's sister Florie lady of; 132 Christian conquests in.

Surrexion: 16 place of the Resurrection in Jerusalem: see Myers, Introduction xxxi.

Temple of Solomon: 4 captives brought to on order of Queen Eublastris; 16 Richard of Chaumont had been on way to; 16, 17 Corbaran offers him passage there in return for help; 74 St Michael tells Baldwin to release captives from;

94 Corbaran will go and serve in; 129 Harpin of Bourges wants to see. See Table of Places for the *Jérusalem*.

Tiberias: 62 inhabitants could not defeat Sathanas; 78 Saracens and Persians from. Arabic Tabariyah.

Tower of David: 135 Saracen survivor rides to to give news of defeat. See Table of Places for the *Jérusalem*.

Tudela: 137 three young men from bring Cornumarant's arms.

Turkey: 23 horses from; 109 Corbaran's nephew born in.

Valenie: 132 taken by Christians. Modern Arabic Baniyas, medieval Valania.

Valley of Josaphat: 132 where Virgin Mary died; *chétifs* will be helped by Robert of Normandy in.

Table Of Characters By Laisse:

Chanson De Jérusalem

Aaron, brother of Moses: 212 released from Hell in Godfrey's prayer.

Abbot of Fécamp:15 fighting in battle; 29, 30 gives thanks for victory in raid; 66 assembled outside Jerusalem; 215 shows Holy Cross to army; 223 carries Holy Cross into battle of Ascalon: 251 displays Holy Lance; 260 helps Bishop of Nobles extinguish Greek fire with holy symbols. See under *Chanson des Chétifs* Table of Names.

Abel, brother of Cain: 74 time of alluded to; 257 alluded to.

Abraham: 14 alluded to as giving sword to Baldwin of Beauvais.

Abraham of Rusa:129 with Sultan.

Abrahan: 272 left in charge of Acre. General Saracen. Found as Saracen name only in the Cycle: Moisan vol.1 p. 103.

Acéré: 225 son of Sultan; 235 kills Eudes of Lancière; 237 killed by Eustache. Garsion's son, also Acéré, is killed at laisse 120 of the *Antioche*. Common Saracen name: Moisan I.106–8. Interestingly *Theseus de Cologne* has numerous references to an Aceré d'Antioche: Moisan vol.1 p. 108.

Achard of Byzantium: 15 sees *chétifs* fighting Saracens. Common Christian name: Moisan vol.1 pp. 104–6.

Achard of Montmerle: 194 killed in skirmish; 264 in final attack, rather puzzlingly (assuming to be identified with Aicart of Montmerle). Recorded in all historical sources: Riley-Smith p.197; lord of Montmerle in Burgundy, killed at Jaffa leading knights of Raymond IV. In the *Gran Conquista de Ultramar* he is credited with being one of the founding leaders of the Crusade: I.186–8.

Adam: 68 alluded to; 185 alluded to; 188 alluded to; 210 alluded to; 212 in Godfrey's prayer both at Genesis and Harrowing of Hell; 224 time of.

Aerofle, uncle of Cornumarant: 188 with Caliph. Common Saracen name: Moisan vol.1 p. 113.

Aimeric Ailatrus: 1 splits from main army at Jerusalem; 8, 9 sent as messenger to get reinforcements. Possibly to be identified with Aimeric Garaton at laisse 50 of the *Antioche*. Not attested elsewhere.

Alepantin: 228 commands men from Afaine; kills Baldwin of Clermont and killed by Tancred. Common Saracen name: Moisan vol.1 pp. 136–7.

Alexander: 176 previous owner of Sultan's amazing tent. Also mentioned *Antioche* 177 as previous owner of splendid sword owned by Garsion's son. Frequently referred to in *chansons de geste*: Moisan vol.1 p. 132.

Amindab of Rodes: 188 with Caliph. Saracen: not found elsewhere.

Amise: 272 left in charge of Acre. Not elsewhere in this form.

Angel Gabriel: 71 invoked by Bishop outside Jerusalem; 212 in Godfrey's prayer. Frequent messenger in *chansons de geste*: Moisan vol.1 p. 436.

Anseis of Paris: 234 killed by Lucifer. Not attested elsewhere in this form though Anseis is a common name: Moisan vol.1 pp. 158–61.

Anselm of Avignon: 64 captured by Turks and rescued by Richard of Chaumont. Helps arm Godfrey in *Antioche* 161. Not attested on Crusade. However appears in a number of *chansons de geste*, notably many versions of the *Roland* as lord of Valence and as a traitor in *Tristan de Nanteuil*; Moisan vol.1 pp. 164–5.

Antan, son of the Sultan of Persia: 240 dubs Esméré. Not found elsewhere.

Antelme (of the Valley): 103 given command of squadron by Raymond; 221 helps arm Bohemond and Tancred. Not attested elsewhere. Possibly to be identified with Anselm of Avignon above. Antelme is a widely attested name in the chansons de geste; possibly to be identified with Antiaume d'Avallon in *Jehan de Lanson*; Moisan vol.1 pp. 162–5.

Antequités: 252 maker of Sultan's hauberk. Also found in *Aliscans* line 1443, where the king of Antiquité gives sword to his successor: *Aliscans* (ed.) Claude Régnier, 2 vols (Paris: Champion, 1990).

Apollon: 10 invoked; 60 invoked; 76, 78, 98,100, 104 evoked by Corbadas; 109 evoked by Cornumarant; 133 evoked by Corbadas; 140 evoked by Saracens in Jerusalem; 171 invoked by King Sucaman; 179 image on top of Sultan's tent, possessed by the Devil Sathanas; 205 invoked by Marbrin; 224 image on top of Sultan's standard; 226 invoked to bless squadrons for battle of Ascalon; 228 men of; 251 invoked; 266 blamed by Sultan; 267 invoked by Saracens. See entry under *Chanson des Chétifs* Table of Names.

Apostles: 35 evoked by Peter the Hermit on arrival at Jerusalem; 212 in Godfrey's prayer.

Apostolic Caliph, equivalent of Christian Pope: 179, 180 preaches virtues of polygamy; 180 suggests captives should be used to repopulate desert; 188 suggests tempting the Christians with treasure, reminiscent of ploy used by the Antichrist; 226, 229 blesses squadrons marching out for battle of Ascalon; 266 invoked by Sultan; beheads statue of Mahomed Gomelin and flees in defeat; 272 at Acre with head. Moisan vol.1 p. 285.

Arachne: 178 wove silk of which Sultan's tent made. Famous for losing a spinning contest with Athena, who turned her into a spider. See Ovid, *Metamorphoses* VI.1–145.

Arnold of Beaucaire: 259 killed by Cornumarant. Not attested elsewhere; numerous references however to the similarly named Hernaus de Beaulande, eldest son of Garin de Monglane: Moisan vol.1 p. 578.

Arnold of Melun: 104 given command of squadron by Bohemond and Tancred. Not attested elsewhere.

Arnold of Pavia: 104 given command of squadron by Bohemond and Tancred. Not attested elsewhere.

Arnold the Poitevin: 259 killed by Cornumarant. Also found in Orson *de Beauvais* and *Girart de Vienne*; Moisan vol.1 p. 580.

Ataignant of Monnoigte: 188 with Caliph. Saracen; not elsewhere in this form though *Elie de St-Gilles* has an Ataignant d'Oliferne; Moisan vol. 1 pp. 180–81.

Aufage: 225 son of Sultan. Found as Saracen name elsewhere and also more generally as meaning 'Saracen'; Moisan vol.1 p. 186.

Baldwin, son of Robert of Flanders: 39, 147 evoked. Later to become Baldwin VII of Flanders.

Baldwin of Beauvais: 14 kills Copatris with lance, Turk with a sword and another 14 Saracens; 66 assembled outside Jerusalem; 76 given command by Godfrey; 82 wounded in first assault on Jerusalem; 261 in battle; 264 in final attack; 267 pursues defeated Saracens. Hero of the central episode of the *Chétifs* but largely absent from the *Jérusalem*. See entry under *Chanson des Chétifs* Table of Names.

Baldwin of Boulogne; also Baldwin of Edessa: 10 reinforcements on way to; 15 sees *chétifs* fighting Saracens; 51 sets up camp at Lion's Cemetery; 57 scouts round walls of Jerusalem for weak points; 64 captured by Turks and rescued by Richard of Chaumont; 66 assembled outside Jerusalem; 121 happens across Cornumarant; 122–4 fights Cornumarant; 125 pursues Cornumarant and fights Turkish forces; 126 retreats with men and hides in a reed bed; 127 attacked by leeches then smoked out when reed bed set on fire by Turks; 128 pursued by Cornumarant and saved in the nick of time by arrival of Christians; 167 rides out to rescue Raymond of Saint-Gilles; 168 fights Cornumarant; 169 defeats him; 170 attacks King Sucamans; 172 fights; 185 tries and fails to get Cornumarant to apostatise; 186 fight with King Sucaman alluded to; 188 cursed by Cornumarant; 189 on walls looking at treasure; 192 helps Peter the Hermit arm; 194 rides to rescue Peter; 196 rescues *ribalts*; 201 Sucaman describes wounding by; 206 tends Godfrey after combat with Marbrin, dressing his swollen hand; 211 defies Saracens; 217 helps Godfrey arm for battle; 236 in battle; 237 Eustace worried about him but kills Saracens; 248 seizes miraculous horse from Cornicas; 251 pursues Cornumarant all the way into the Saracen camp; 258, 259, 262 forthcoming attack on Cornumarant alluded to; 263 attacks and kills Cornumarant; 264 in final attack; 267 pursues defeated Saracens; 268 pursues Sultan; 269 fights alongside Raimbaut Creton;

270 defies Sultan; 271 helps wounded Raimbaut; 272 rescued by Christians; 279, 280 praises Cornumarant's valour. Younger brother of Godfrey, first Latin Count of Edessa 1097–1100, and King of Jerusalem 1100–1118 (Murray, *passim*). Presence here ahistorical as he was not at the taking of Jerusalem.

Baldwin of Clermont: 228 killed by Alepantin. Not attested elsewhere.

Barès: 252 devil who made Sultan's sword. The demon Barré appears in the *Bataille de Loquifer*, (ed.) M. Barnett (Oxford, 1975) lines 2408, 2439 where he helps Loquifer against Rainouart; also referred to *Moniage Rainouart* I (ed.) G. A. Bertin (Paris, 1973) line 7364.

Bausumés, uncle of Sultan: 252 hangs Sultan's shield round his neck. Only here in this form; more commonly Bafumet and variants, Moisan vol.1 p. 202.

Bausumés of Folais: 261 killed by Baldwin of Beauvais. Only attested here.

Bedouin woman: 53 narrative looks forward to her encounter with Thomas of Marle; 139 fights Thomas and predicts that he will be killed by his lord.

Berard, cousin of Thomas: 255 killed by Corbadas. Riley-Smith p. 201 points to Berald Silvain; there is no evidence the two are the same.

Bernard of the Valley: 103 given command of squadron by Raymond. Not attested elsewhere.

Bishop of Forez: 15 fighting in battle; 16 kills Saracen Faraon despite being a clergyman; 17 credited with decisive blow in winning battle; 29, 30 gives thanks for victory in raid; 50 praises Bohemond and Tancred; 66 assembled outside Jerusalem; 223 stays in Jerusalem at battle of Ascalon. See under *Chanson des Chétifs* Table of Names.

Bishop of Lutis: 278 sings Mass at lion's cave.

Bishop of Mautran (Martirano): 52 pronounces blessing; 66 pronounces blessing, to the displeasure of an impatient King of the Tafurs; 68 displays Holy Lance and preaches a sermon outside Jerusalem; 72 pronounces pre-attack blessing outside Jerusalem; 73 determined to evict Saracens from Temple; 74 pre-battle blessing; 75 addresses troops before assault on Jerusalem and displays the Lance; 76 pronounces blessing on *chétifs*; 80 commends soul of Pagan of Beauvais; 82 reminds defeated Christians of heavenly reward for going on crusade; 85 prophecies Jerusalem will fall within nine days; baptises leader of Saracen prisoners; 93 reads intercepted letters and writes counterfeit ones; 94 repeats performance; 97 blesses Tafurs; 116 raises Christian morale; 129 consulted on setting up catapult, hardly a matter for clerical expertise; 130 sends Christians to look for a hermit on the Mount of Olives, initially without success; 134 blesses Christians and displays Holy Lance; 143 blesses Christians killed in assault on Jerusalem; 145 Mass of absolution; shares out collection; 146 nominates Godfrey to be King of Jerusalem; 147 nominates Robert of Flanders; 148 nominates Robert of Normandy; 149 nominates Bohemond; 150 nominates Hugh; 151 despairs of finding a ruler; 152 criticises leaders and seeks a miracle; 153 confesses Godfrey and other leaders; 154 administers Communion; 157 absolves Godfrey; 161 intercepts letter which says Godfrey under siege; 162 persuades army to go back to help; 214 in procession at Jerusalem; 215 shows Holy Cross to army; 216 sings Mass at Holy Sepulchre; 217 blesses army; 217 – 222 blesses forces about to ride out to battle of Ascalon; 223 arms for battle himself; 233 displays Holy Cross; 251 encourages army with Holy Cross; 257 praises Christian army and invokes Daniel; 262 runs around putting out Greek fire with Holy Cross; 264 rallies Christians for final attack; 265 sees saints riding to aid; 267 prays for daylight and miracle granted; 274 sings Mass for Enguerrand of St-Pol. Arnulf, Bishop of Martirano, Calabria.

Blessed Virgin Mary: 5 allusion to death and Dormition; 10 invoked; 35 Dormition evoked by Peter the Hermit on arrival at Jerusalem, who exhorts the Crusaders to pray to her; 212 Annunciation in Godfrey's prayer; 238, 241 reference to her being granted shade at Three Shadows; 265 invoked by Peter the Hermit.;

Bohemond of Sicily, lord of Taranto: 7 Godfrey sends messenger to for reinforcements; 8, 9 receives message and responds; 10 rides to the rescue; 17 army rejoins after skirmish; 18 arms at midnight and rides out looking for Godfrey; 21 lays siege to Caesarea with Tancred; 22 prays at Ramleh; pre-battle sermon; 23 takes command in battle; 24, 25 boosts morale; 27 hunts Saracens down; 28 returns to army with flocks he has captured in raid; 30 returns to quarters; divides spoils from raid amongst the army; 40 compares Jerusalem to Antioch; 41 criticised by Tancred for pessimism; 42 prepares to attack; 50 sets up camp with Tancred near Bethlehem and praised by bishop of Forez; 66 assembled outside Jerusalem; 71, 72 drawn up for attack outside Jerusalem; 82 mounts night watch after failed assault; 83 accompanies soldiers going to fetch water and sets ambush for Garsion of Acre; 84 successfully attacks him; 85 discussion with leader of Saracen prisoners, who apostasises; 104 sets up squadron; 112 attacks; 116 takes night watch; 121 summoned to help in pursuit; 127 alluded to; 135 attacks Jerusalem; 138 on walls of Jerusalem; 140 pursues Saracens in Jerusalem; 143 attacks Saracens; 149 nominated as King of Jerusalem, refuses and offers kingship to Raymond of Saint-Gilles; 152 criticised by bishop of Mautran; 162 confronts reluctance in army; 213 rides out of Jerusalem; 221 rides out with Tancred for battle of Ascalon; 225 Sultan's sons plan to take him captive; 229 to get Estonamons' horse; 239 joins rescue mission for Robert of Normandy; 255 challenges Corbadas; 256 cuts him in half; 264 in final attack; 267 pursues defeated Saracens; 272 keeps night watch after battle of Ascalon. Son of Robert Guiscard and lord of Taranto. One of the leaders of the Crusade and first Crusade ruler of Antioch; in captivity 1100–03; married Constance of France 1106; defeated by Alexius 1108 and forced to swear oath of fealty; died 1111. See Jean Flori, *Bohemond d'Antioche, chevalier d'aventure* (Paris, 2007); supersedes R. B.Yewdale, *Bohemond I, Prince of Antioch* (Princeton, 1924).

Bondifer, horse of Acére: 235 alluded to. Name found elsewhere e.g. *Florence de Rome*; Moisan vol.1 p. 250.

Bondifer the tyrant: 188 with Caliph. Found as Saracen name in *Moniage Rainouart* lines 4010, 6084.

Brehier: 224, 225 Sultan's son; summoned for battle of Ascalon; 236 spurs into battle; 242 killed by Thomas of Marle. Common Saracen name: Moisan vol.1 pp. 258–9.

Brohadas: 59 death of and revenge for alluded to by Corbadas; 164 alluded to by Cornumarant; 224, 225 death alluded to. Son of the Sultan. His death at Godfrey's hands whilst under Corbaran's protection is recounted in laisses 347–51 of the *Antioche*.

Bruiant of Almerie: 166 killed by Godfrey. Bruiant is a common Saracen name: Moisan vol.1 pp. 263–4.

Brunamont of Valterne: 166 killed by Godfrey. Also in the *Antioche* 137. Only in this form here, but Brunamont a common Saracen name: Moisan vol.1 pp. 265–6.

Butors (of Salorie): 119 leads Cornumarant's horse; 188 with Caliph. Butor, son of Soliman, appears in the *Antioche* 24, 103, 105, 122, 125. Very frequent Saracen name however (Moisan vol. I, pp. 273–5).

Butras: 69 with Corbadas at Jerusalem. Not elsewhere in this form but references to Butran as Saracen name; Moisan vol.1 p. 275.

Cahu: 196, 205 treasure of. Pagan god familiar in *chansons de geste*. Bancourt, *Musulmans* vol.1 p. 384 for suggested meaning of chaos.

Cain: 67 Saracens lineage of.

Cain: 228 horse of Alepantin.

Caiaphas: 4 Saracens referred to as race of.

Calcatras, the elderly: 180 leads Saracens to attack; 188 with Caliph; 226 helps draw up battle order. Uncommon name; Moisan vol.1 pp. 28–9.

Caliph: 185 estimates Saracen numbers; 202 suggests Sultan add shield to treasure to tempt Christians.

Caliph of Baghdad: 69 prophecy about Franks referred to.

Canabel, brother of Nubion: 180 raises Corbadas to feet; rides dragon and leads Mahommed's elephant; 185 estimates Saracen numbers; 186 raises Cornumarant to feet; 197 restrains Peter; 231 Saracen commander.

Canebalt: 91 summoned to help by bird; 188 with Caliph; 226 helps draw up battle order. Found in versions of *Roland* as Baligant's brother; otherwise only *Anseis de Carthage* line 4657: Moisan vol.1 p. 286.

Capalu, Godfrey's horse: 262. Some attestations as name of Saracen or monster; Moisan I.287. Name of monster with whom Renoart fights in the *Bataille Loquifer*.

Carcan: 228 leads Saracen squadron.

Carcan of Rousia: 166 killed by Godfrey; 238 killed (again) by Robert of Normandy.

Carcan of Syria appears at *Antioche* 132. Name found only in the Cycle.

Caucadras, emir: 91 summoned to help by bird. See Calcatras above.

Cernugle of Monnoigte: 188 with Caliph. Versions of the *Roland* have Chernuble de Munigre killed by Roland: Moisan vol.1 p. 301.

Charlemagne: 16 alluded to; 180 France as kingdom of. Also alluded to at *Antioche* 300 as distant ancestor of Godfrey; at *Chétifs* 16, 50, 129 as ancestor of Richard of Chaumont.

Charles Martel: 257 alluded to as ancestor. Frequently referred to in *chansons de geste* as Charlemagne's ancestor: Moisan vol.1 p. 300.

***Chevalier au Cygne*:** 217 referred to as Godfrey's ancestor; 237 Godfrey compared with. See the first texts in the Cycle.

***Clapamor*:** 238 killed by Robert of Normandy. Only in the Cycle in this form.

***Clariel*:** 236 spurs into battle. Killed by Rainalt Porcet at *Antioche* 173. Common Saracen name in various forms: Moisan vol.1 pp. 307–8.

***Clarion*:** 225 son of Sultan; 242 killed by Thomas of Marle. In *Antioche* 129. Common Saracen name: Moisan vol.1 pp. 308–9.

Clemence, wife of Robert of Flanders: 39, 147 evoked. Clementia of Burgundy, daughter of Count William I of Burgundy.

***Codroés*, emir:** 252 chose harness for Sultan's horse. Common Saracen name: Moisan vol.1 p. 314.

***Copatris son of Justamar*:** 14 Saracen killed by Baldwin of Beauvais. Found only here.

***[Corbadas] King of Jerusalem*:** 2 orders attack on Christians; 6 presses Christians hard; 14 alluded to; 54 looks out at Franks; 55 evokes Vengeance of Christ theme; 57 demoralised by the miracle of the three kites shot by Godfrey; 58 summons Lucabel of Montir to pronounce on it; 59 tells Saracens about the miracle and its meaning; 60 advised by Lucabel and Maucolon; 65 receives news of forthcoming siege; 69 at Jerusalem; 70 warns Cornumarant not to ride impetuously out of Jerusalem; 74, 75, 76 goes up tower with Lucabel to watch battle; 76 evokes Saracen gods; 78 curses Christians; 83 alluded to; 85, 86 distressed at sight of Tafurs butchering Turks; 87 foretells defeat; 88 orders Christian captives to be consigned to dungeon; 94, 95 has counterfeit letters read; 96 upset by turn of events; 98, 99, 100, 101, 102, 103, 104 curses Christians; 105 his obstetric plans for the squadron of women; 109 watches combat; 117–19 upset at prospect of Cornumarant's departure; 133 curses Christians; 140 in anguish at fall of Jerusalem; 144 hands over Tower of David in return for safe conduct; 163 meets Cornumarant at Barbais; 164 encouraged to fight by Cornumarant; 175, 176 laments Cornumarant's capture; 176 seeks out Sultan at his tent; 180 begs and is granted help; 186 delighted to see Cornumarant; 200 delighted at Peter's apparent apostasy; 255 in battle; threatens Godfrey; challenged by Bohemond; 256 cut in half by Bohemond. A garbled form of the Fatimid governor of Jerusalem Iftikhar ad-Daulah. Largely in Cycle but a few other references: Moisan vol.1 p. 318.

***Corbaran of Oliferne*:** 14 alluded to as giving helmet to Baldwin of Beauvais; 15 alluded to as giving mailshirt to John of Alis; 59 loss of Antioch referred to by Corbadas; 91 summoned to help by bird, referred to as powerful king; 93 name taken in vain in counterfeit letters. See under *Chanson des Chétifs* Table of Names.

Corbon: 188 with Caliph. Common Saracen name: Moisan vol.1 p. 319.

Cornicas, brother of Rubiant: 226 leads squadron of men from Bocidant; 242 attacks Thomas of Marle, who fails to fight back successfully; 248 Baldwin seizes his miraculous horse. Common Saracen name in various forms: Moisan vol.1 p. 321.

Cornu of Rousie: 264 Baldwin's horse.

Cornumarant, son of the King of Jerusalem: 2 rides out for attack on Christians; 6 presses them hard; 17 grieves at death of emir Faraon; 54 looks out at Franks; 55, 56 reassures Corbadas that can withstand siege; 57 demoralised by miracle of the three kites shot by Godfrey; 59 angry at Corbadas' defeatism; 60 prepares to fight; 61 detailed description of arming for battle; 62 slips out of Jerusalem with detachment; 63 attacked by Harpin; 64 rides back to Jerusalem pursued by Harpin and Richard, and attacked by Richard; 65 attacks Harpin, rides back to Jerusalem and prepares for siege rejecting Saracen gods; 69 defies Franks and asks Lucabel for interpretation of the miracle of the kites; 70 unimpressed by Lucabel's interpretation of kite miracle; 80 wounded by Godfrey and kills Pagan of Beauvais in revenge; 83 had sent message by dove to summon Garsion of Acre; 86 rides out in combat; 87 encourages Corbadas not to give up hope; orders captives to be mistreated in revenge for treatment of Turkish prisoners; 88 rides to attack; 89, 90 responds to Lucabel's suggestion of using birds to carry messages; 91 summons help; 93 name taken in vain in counterfeit letters; 94, 95 letters read to and reacts violently; 96 consoles Corbadas and prepares to fight back; 107 gives battle cry; 108 strikes Enguerrand and knocks him from ladder; curses Christians; 109 taunts Christians; 113 reaction to Maucolon and Ysabars being taken captive; 114 reaction to fight on battlements; 116 accepts ransom terms; 117–19 says he will go and seek help from the Sultan and comforts Corbadas; 120 rides out and intercepted by two knights; 121 escapes Godfrey but confronted by Baldwin of Edessa; 122–4 fights Baldwin; 125 finds Turkish forces; 126, 127 challenges Christians; 128 turns back when confronted by Christian reinforcements; 129 reaches Sultan and is granted help; 130 alluded to; 140 invoked by Saracens in Jerusalem; 160, 162 on march to Jerusalem; 163 meets Corbadas at Barbais; 164 encourages him; 165 rides to Jerusalem; 166 joins battle with Godfrey; 167 takes Raymond of Saint-Gilles prisoner; 168 fights Baldwin of Boulogne; 169 surrenders to Godfrey after defeat by Baldwin; 170 Saracens ride to rescue; 174 shackled as a captive in Jerusalem; 175,176 Corbadas laments his capture; 180 captivity alluded to; 183 to be ransomed; 184 frightened by parade of Tafurs; 185 exchanged for Raymond of Saint-Gilles; refuses to apostatise and professes undying hatred for Christians; 186 tells Sultan of position; 188 pennant bearer with Caliph; 191 leads attack; 192 threatened by Peter the Hermit; 195 concerned at damage inflicted by Tafurs; 196 attacked by Godfrey and flees; 197 attacks and captures Peter the Hermit; 210 breaches wall of Jerusalem but beaten back by Tafurs; 239 in battle; 251 appalled at fate of army; kills Gerard of Gournay; 256 angered at death of Corbadas; 258

kills Guy of Autemue in revenge; 259 kills more Christians; 262 in battle; 263 killed by Count Baldwin; 264 mourned by Saracens; 277 body discovered on battlefield; 278, 279 body carried to Jerusalem by Christians; 280 cut open and heart discovered to be enormous; 281 buried with honour. Leader of Saracen opposition in the *Jérusalem*, functioning as a counterpart of Corbaran in the *Antioche*.

Corsaus: 252 arms Sultan.
Common Saracen name: Moisan vol.1 p. 324.

Corsu: 237 killed by Baldwin. Found elsewhere only at *Aliscans* line 2173.

Corsubles: 198 at Peter's interrogation. 225 son of Sultan; 261 killed by Richard of Chaumont and Baldwin of Beauvais. Very commonly found Saracen, killed at some point by most epic heroes: Moisan vol.1 pp. 325–6.

Count of Blandas: 260 killed by Sultan. Also in *Antioche* 133 as Count of Baudas. Not identified.

Count of Vendôme: 222 rides out with Rotrou of Perche and Stephen of Blois for battle of Ascalon; 241 in battle; 262 injured by emir and rescued by Godfrey, who gives him his horse Capalu. At the time of the First Crusade Geoffrey de Preuilly was count of Vendôme; he is not attested elsewhere.

Damemont: 188 with Caliph.

Danemolt: 166 killed by Godfrey.

Danemons (the Diabolical): 111 attacks Eurvin of Creel on siege ladder; 180 leads Saracens to attack; 225 son of Sultan; 236 spurs into battle. Common Saracen name; Moisan vol.1 pp. 337–8.

Daniel: 74, 257 evoked by Bishop of Mautran.

Dodequin of Damascus: 129 Cornumarant writes to him seeking help; 160 attacks Christians and forced back to Tiberias. This sounds like a garbled combination of Duqaq of Damascus and Tughtekin.

Drieu of Monci: 66 assembled outside Jerusalem; 157 asks who should crown Godfrey. Also found in *Antioche* 62, 253, 360–61; *Chétifs* 16. Drogo I of Mouchy-le-Château (Oise). See Riley-Smith p. 203.

Drogo of Amiens, brother of: 259 killed by Cornumarant. Identity unclear.

Drogo of Melé: 264 in final attack. Not attested unless a garbled form of Dreux of Nesle, who is well attested on the Crusade: Riley-Smith p. 203.

Emir Ali, son of Barbais: 11 killed by John of Alis. Unidentifiable Saracen.

Emir Aupatris: 129 with Sultan. Tautology: both words mean the same.

Emir Cahu: 123 Cornumarant seeking help from. See Cahu above.

Emir Corbon: 180 leads Saracens to attack. Unidentifiable Saracen. See Corbon above.

Emir Fanios of Ascalon: 19,20 assembles reinforcements for the Turks of Caesarea; 22 attacks Bohemond and Tancred. Unidentifiable Saracen.

Emir Galie: 166 killed by Godfrey. Galie and Galien attested as Saracen names: Moisan vol.1 p. 446.

Emir Sucaman of Algeria: 129 with Sultan. Probably to be identified with King Sucaman, q.v.

Emir of Escaille: 195 concerned about damage inflicted by Tafurs. Unidentifiable Saracen.
Emir of Nubia: 238 killed by Robert of Normandy. Probably to be identified with King of Nubia.
Emperor of Upper India: 244 alluded to.
Encilais: 261 killed by Richard of Chaumont. Only here in this form.
Enguerrand of St-Pol: 66 assembled outside Jerusalem; 75 leads detachment in attack on Jerusalem; 98 in charge of squadron attacking at Jerusalem; 108 climbs ladder into Jerusalem but injured and knocked from ladder by Cornumarant; 223 arms for battle of Ascalon; 242 kills three of the Sultan's sons; 243 killed by an emir; 244, 245 avenged by father Hugh; 264 death alluded to; 273, 274 father mourns his death; 276 father determined to avenge death. Leading character in the *Antioche*. From St-Pol (Pas-de-Calais). See *Antioche* Introduction chapter 1; Riley-Smith p. 204; for the St-Pols see R. Fossier, *La terre et les hommes en Picardie*, 2 vols (Paris, 1968), vol.2 p. 483. His presence at Jerusalem is ahistorical: he died of illness at Ma'arrat-an-Nu'man. He is portrayed here to give continuity with the *Antioche*.
Ernais of Melun: 104 given command of squadron by Bohemond and Tancred. Not attested elsewhere.
Esau: 212 release from Hell in Godfrey's prayer.
Esmérés: 225 son of Sultan; 236 spurs into battle; 240 attacks and worsted by Roger of Rosoie. Some references as Saracen name: Moisan vol.1 p. 385.
Estatin: 101 leads squadron of men from Constantinople. Possibly a reminiscence of Taticius, Grand Primiceros of the Emperor Alexius, who is pilloried in the *Antioche* and most other Western sources. He had left the Crusade by this stage. Not found outside the Cycle. See A. G. C. Savvides, 'Varia Byzantinoturcica II: Taticius the Turcopole', *Journal of Oriental and African Studies* 3–4 (1991–92) pp. 235–38.
Esteflé, emir: 188 with Caliph; 252 brings Sultan's sword.
Elsewhere only in the *Guillaume* cycle: Moisan vol.1 p. 388.
Estonamons: 229 leader of Saracen squadron. Found only elsewhere in *Enfances Renier* 19942: *Enfances Renier* (ed.) D. Dalens-Marekovic (Paris, 2009).
Estorgan of Alie: 166 killed by Godfrey. Estorgant is a common Saracen name; versions of the *Roland* refer to Estorgant d'Allier; Moisan vol.1 pp. 388–9. Two different pagans bear the name in the *Antioche*: 23, and 184 where Estorgan is one of the eight pagans accursed by God who torture Rainalt Porcet.
Eudes of Lancière: 235 killed by Acéré.
Eufroi of Buison: 10 reinforcements on way to; 16 in battle.
Eurvin of Creel, the elderly: 100 put in charge of squadron at Jerusalem; 111, 112 climbs ladder and dragged up as captive; 113 turns tables and captures Ysabars; 114 fights on battlements; 116 returned to Christian army. Found only elsewhere in the *Antioche* in a memorable fight over a donkey with Pierre Postel, laisse 303. Possibly from Creil: Riley-Smith p. 234.

Eustace of Boulogne: 10 reinforcements on way to; 15 sees *chétifs* fighting Saracens; 51 referred to by Baldwin; 57 scouts round walls of Jerusalem for weak points; 66 assembled outside Jerusalem; 68 with Godfrey outside Jerusalem; 124 alluded to; 140 pursues Saracens in Jerusalem; 167 goes to rescue Raymond of Saint-Gilles; 169 with Godfrey at Cornumarant's surrender; 170 attacked by rescue mission; 172 fights; 185 involved in exchange negotiations; 189 on walls looking at treasure; 192 helps Peter the Hermit arm; 194 rides to rescue Peter; 197 brings water for Godfrey's swollen hand; 206 tends Godfrey after combat with Marbrin, dressing his swollen hand; 217 helps Godfrey arm for battle; 236 in battle; 236, 237 avenges Rainalt of Beauvais; 237 kills Saracens and worries about Baldwin, unnecessarily; 263 receives Cornumarant's horse Plantamor; 264 in final attack; 267 pursues defeated Saracens; 271 blows horn. Eustace III of Boulogne, brother of Godfrey. Widely attested: Riley-Smith p. 205.

Eve: 68 alluded to; 185 alluded to; 188 alluded to; 212 in Godfrey's prayer.

Everard of Pavia: 264 in final attack.

Fabur: 188 with Caliph. Common Saracen name: Moisan vol.1 pp. 395–96.

Fanon of Valdoree: 125 killed by Baldwin. Not found elsewhere.

Faraon son of Corbadel: 16 Saracen killed by bishop of Forez. Common Saracen name though without reference to Corbadel: Moisan vol.2 pp. 776–7. *Antioche* 356 also has Faraon.

Fauseron: 183 sent as envoy to negotiate exchange of prisoners; 225 son of Sultan; 236 spurs into battle. Very common Saracen name implying treachery; brother of Marsilie in the *Roland* and killed by Oliver: Moisan vol. 1 pp. 397–8.

Ferrals: 65 will help at siege of Jerusalem. Common Saracen name in various forms: Moisan vol.1 pp. 403–04.

Flanbaut of Orquenie: 129 with Sultan.

Flanbalt of Tornie: 166 killed by Godfrey. In these forms only here, but Flanbalt a common Saracen name: Moisan vol.1 p. 406.

Fulcher of Alençon: 66 assembled with *chétifs* outside Jerusalem. In *Antioche* at laisses 253, 300, 355. Not recorded elsewhere: Riley-Smith p. 234.

Fulcher of Chartres: 8 messenger sent for reinforcements; fights his way through; 16 in battle; 264 in final attack. Well attested on Crusade: Riley-Smith p. 206.

Fulcher of Melun, *chétif:* 15 in battle; 62 mounts night watch outside Jerusalem; 64 captured by Turks and rescued by Richard of Chaumont; 99 put in charge of squadron at Jerusalem; 109 climbs ladder. See under *Chanson des Chétifs* Table of Names.

Galafres: 188 with Caliph. Common Saracen name; King of Saragossa and father of Marsilie and Baligant. Moisan vol.1 pp. 441–2.

Galans (Wayland): 252 helped make Sultan's hauberk. See reference under *Chanson des Chétifs* Table of Names.

Garin of Pavia: 104 given command of squadron by Bohemond and Tancred.

Garnier: 267 killed by Sultan.

Garsion, ruler of Antioch: 40 alluded to.

Table of Names and Places 387

Garsion (of Acre): 83 Saracen unfortunate enough to arrive with large flocks when the Crusade army is looking for supplies; 84 attacked by Bohemond, defeated and apostatises with indecent haste; 87 defeat alluded to; 92 identifies doves as messengers; 115 intervenes in negotiations with Godfrey. As general Saracen name Moisan vol.1 p. 461.

Gaston, lord: 131, 132 castle of.

Gautier: 194 killed in skirmish. Another Gautier is killed at Nicaea at *Antioche* 56.

Gerard of Blois: 103 given command of squadron by Raymond. Not attested elsewhere.

Gerard of Gournay: 46 sets up camp with Thomas of Marle in valley of Josaphat; 47 praises Raymond of Saint-Gilles; 251 killed by Cornumarant; 264 in final attack despite demise. Also in the *Antioche* at Nicaea, 72 and the battle of Antioch, 355. Gerard of Gournay-en-Bray (Seine Maritime), who subsequently made a further pilgrimage. Attested in other sources; Riley-Smith pp. 166, 208).

Gerard of the Keep: 1 splits from main army at Jerusalem; 16 in battle; 66 assembled outside Jerusalem. Also in the *Antioche* 355 at the battle of Antioch. Not attested elsewhere.

Gerard of Le Puiset: 264 in final attack. Not attested. But Everard of Le Puiset is widely attested (Riley-Smith, p. 205) and also appears in the *Antioche* at 50, 158–61, 165, 253, 360–61. See J. L. La Monte, 'The Lords of Le Puiset on the Crusades', *Speculum* 17 (1942) pp. 100–18.

Glorion: 180 accompanies Corbadas to Sultan; 225 son of Sultan; 236 spurs into battle; 242 killed by Enguerrand of St-Pol. Common Saracen name: Moisan vol.1 pp. 499–500.

Godescal: 194 killed in skirmish. Also in the *Antioche* as brother of Hugh, duke of the Basques at 50, 126, 130. Not recorded elsewhere.

Godfrey of Bouillon: 1 splits from main army at Jerusalem; 4 swears to fight to the death; 6 hard pressed by Saracens when sees *chétifs* coming to the rescue; 7 sends for reinforcements thinking the *chétifs* are Saracens; 8 asks whom should be sent; 10 reinforcements sent to; meets up with *chétifs*; 11 inspires them to fight; 15 sees *chétifs* fighting Saracens; 16 in battle; 18 Bohemond rides in search of; 28 greets Bohemond as he returns from raid; 29, 30 mounts nighttime watch; 38 Thomas of Marle professes loyalty to; 44, 45 agrees with Hugh about need for siege engines; 45 sets up camp on Mount Sion; 51 referred to by Baldwin; 57, 58 miraculously shoots three kites with one arrow; 60 – 62 alluded to; 66 assembled outside Jerusalem; 68 with Eustace outside Jerusalem; 71, 72 drawn up for attack outside Jerusalem; 75 advises troops to wait for horn signal to attack; 75 present at Thomas's feat with spears; 76 gives command of first attack on Jerusalem to *chétifs*; rallies troops and sets up another squadron; 80 launches assault and wounds Cornumarant in fray; 83 agrees army should find water; 85 mounts night guard; 85 hands over Turks who refuse to apostatise to Tafurs, who (literally) butcher them; 92, 93 sets falcon on messenger doves; 93 suggests sending out counterfeit letters using the same doves; 97 urges attack on Jerusalem; 100 sets up squadron; 106 commands squadron of nobles with Robert of Flanders; 107, 108, 109 sounds horn for successive waves of attack then calls them off when pressure too great; 111 dismayed when Wicher and Eurvin captured; 112 sounds horn for general attack; 113 Maucolon seeks his protection; offers ransom terms; 114 captives taken to his tent; 115 offers them apostasy; 116 oversees negotiations with Cornumarant; 120 rides to intercept Cornumarant; 121 pursues Cornumarant; 124, 127 alluded to; 128 meets Baldwin; 130 follows advice of Bishop of Mautran; 133 blows horn as signal to arm; 135 attacks Jerusalem; 136 orders siege engines to be taken up to wall; extinguishes Greek fire with vinegar; 137 raises morale for assault on Jerusalem; in lead guarding breach of wall; 138, 139 in fight at taking of Jerusalem; 140 pursues Saracens in Jerusalem; 142 cleanses Holy Sepulchre; 143 occupies palace with Robert of Flanders and Thomas of Marle; restores sight to watchman of palace with miraculous cloth, who rewards them with key to treasure; 146 refuses to become King of Jerusalem; 151 weeps at prospect of no ruler; 152 criticised by bishop of Mautran; 153 confessed; 156 candle lit in miracle proclaiming him King of Jerusalem; 157 crowned by King of the Tafurs; 157–9 tries to persuade other leaders to stay; 161, 162 in danger from Saracens; 163 alluded to; 165 prepares to defend Jerusalem; first to ride out; 166 joins battle with Cornumarant; 167 upset at capture of Raymond of Saint-Gilles; 169 receives surrender of Cornumarant; 170, 171 attacked by rescue mission; 172 fights; 173, 174 in danger in battle, helped by St George and St Demetrius; 174 feasts back in Jerusalem; 180 threatened by Sultan; 182 asks Peter to guard Jerusalem; captures Marbrin; 183 negotiates exchange of prisoners; 184 stages parade of Tafurs to frighten his Saracen captives; 185 releases Cornumarant and accompanies him part of the way; 186 valour in battle alluded to; 188 cursed by Cornumarant; 189 orders Christians not to be tempted by treasure; 189, 190 begs help from God; 191 insists Christians must not be tempted and argues with King of the Tafurs; l92 helps Peter the Hermit arm; 193 rides out to attack; 194 rides to rescue Peter; 196 attacks Cornumarant then literally cuts Malargu in half; regrets loss of Peter; 197 raises morale; 201 praised by Peter the Hermit; Sultan decides to send envoy demanding his surrender; 203 receives Saracen envoy; 204 defies the Sultan; 205 takes on Marbrin; 206 cuts him in half in single combat despite giving him the advantage; 209 Sultan orders that he should be captured alive; 211 raises morale in Jerusalem; candle miraculously lit in Holy Sepulchre; 212 *prière du plus grand péril*; dove brings him letter; 213 receives message from dove that reinforcements on the way; rides out to attack; 215 grim mood before battle; 216 prepares for battle; 217 arms and rides out for battle of Ascalon; 225 Sultan's sons plan to kill him; 230 fights Saracens; 233, 234 kills Sinagon; 234, 235 threatened by assorted Saracens; 236 in battle; 237 joins with Eustace; 240 challenged by Esméré; 262 kills emir who attacked Count of Vendome, takes his horse and gives Count his own horse; 264 in final attack; 266 pursues defeated Saracens; 268 kills emir; 270 evoked by Sultan; 271 sees

Baldwin's horse and realises he is in danger; 274 comforts Hugh of St-Pol for Enguerrand's death; 275 in Temple of Solomon; 276 welcomes Hugh's suggestion to secure Christian position in Outremer; 278 announces miracle of lion moving corpses; 279 orders Cornumarant to be cut open to see the size of his heart. Son of Eustace II of Boulogne and Ida; held the county of Verdun and fief of Bouillon; invested with the duchy of Lower Lorraine in 1087. See J. C. Andressohn, *The Ancestry and Life of Godfrey of Bouillon* (Bloomington, 1947); H. Glaesener, 'Godefroid de Bouillon était-il un médiocre?' *Revue d'Histoire Ecclésiastique* 39 (1943), pp. 309–41.

Golias: 255 horse of Corbadas.

Gondris: 188 agrees with Caliph's proposition on treasure. As Saracen only elsewhere in *Moniage Rainouart* line 4252. In the *Antioche* as one of the torturers of Rainalt Porcet, 184.

Gontier of Aire: 81 climbs ladder to be first into Jerusalem but has hands cut off and falls to his death. Squire to Robert of Flanders. Hero of one of the anecdotes in the *Antioche* where steals the splendid Saracen horse Faburs 142–3; enters Antioch 253. Not recorded elsewhere.

Gorant son of Brehier: 63 killed by Harpin. Common Saracen name; Moisan vol.1 pp. 510–11.

Gorhier: 236 spurs into battle. Outside the Cycle only in the *Chevalerie Vivien*.

Gregory of Arras, siege engineer: 69 sets up mangonels outside Jerusalem; 77 preparations for use; 107 takes battering ram up to walls; 132, 133 builds siege engine from wood found near Jerusalem. Not attested elsewhere. Arras is near Douai, which may point to local knowledge or local pride by Graindor.

Guerin of Montfort: 259 killed by Cornumarant. Not attested elsewhere.

Guinemant of the Valley of Rivere: 259 killed by Cornumarant. Not attested elsewhere.

Guiré: 260 killed in battle. Unidentified; probably owes his posthumous existence to rhyme scheme.

Guy, bishop of Nole or Noble: 223 carries out to battle of Ascalon stake to which Christ tied; 251 displays it to army; 260 helps abbot of Fécamp extinguish Greek fire with holy symbols;

Guy of Aubefort: 194 killed in skirmish. Not attested elsewhere.

Guy of Autemue: 258 killed by Cornumarant. Not attested elsewhere.

Guy of Monpere: 259 killed by Cornumarant Not attested elsewhere.

Guy of Poitiers: 103 given command of squadron by Raymond. Not attested elsewhere.

Guy of Ponciel: 257 killed by Lucabel. Not attested elsewhere.

Harpin of Bourges: 6 rides to the rescue of Godfrey outside Jerusalem; 10 meets up with Godfrey; 13 kills one Saracen with a lance and another with a sword; 15 in battle; 16 in battle; 62 mounts night watch outside Jerusalem; 63 prays then leads attack on Cornumarant's detachment and kills Gorant son of Brehier; 64 sees companions captured and calls for help to release them; pursues Cornumarant; 65 attacked by Cornumarant; 66 assembled outside Jerusalem;

76 given command by Godfrey; 82 wounded in first assault on Jerusalem; 87 alluded to; 264 in final attack. See under *Chanson des Chétifs* Table of Names.

Henry, relative of Godfrey and of Robert of Flanders: 87 Christian prisoner mistreated by Cornumarant. Possibly to be identified with Henry of Esch, brother of Godfrey of Esch: Murray pp. 205, 209; AA II.1.

Herod: 88 time of; 163, 165, 167 horn of, blown by Cornumarant; 175 summoned to help (unlikely to be King Herod); 212 massacre of the Innocents in Godfrey's prayer. Frequently referred to in *chansons de geste*: Moisan vol.1 p. 581.

***Hideuse*:** 252 Sultan's sword. Also in *Bataille Loquifer* lines 1556, 2397 as one of Loquifer's three swords along with Dolerose and Recuite or Plorance.

Holy Innocents: 23, 25 evoked by Bohemond in battle with emir of Ascalon; 37 evoked by Peter the Hermit at Jerusalem; 212 in Godfrey's prayer. Frequently evoked in the *chansons de geste*: Moisan vol. 1 p. 606.

Hugh of St-Pol: 66 assembled outside Jerusalem; 223 arms for battle of Ascalon; 243 attempts suicide in grief at death of his son Enguerrand; 244, 245 avenges him in battle and kills the emir who killed him; 264 in final attack; 273 mourns Enguerrand and comforted, after a fashion, by Hugh of Vermandois; 274 comforted by Godfrey; 276, 277 determined to avenge Enguerrand. Leading character in the *Antioche*. Hugh II of St-Pol-en-Ternois (Pas-de-Calais); Riley-Smith p. 212.

Hugh of Vermandois: 28 greets Bohemond as he returns from raid; 42–5 restraining influence, pointing out that the attack will not succeed without siege engines; 52 suggests strategy for provisioning the army; 71, 72 drawn up for attack outside Jerusalem; 75 leads detachment in attack on Jerusalem; 80 blows horn for attack; 92, 93 sets falcon on messenger doves; 97 suggests tactics for attack on Jerusalem; 102 sets up squadron and gives command to Thomas of Marle; 112 attacks; 127 alluded to; 135 attacks Jerusalem; 141 chases Saracens out of Jerusalem; 150 refuses kingship of Jerusalem; 152 criticised by bishop of Mautran; 162 confronts reluctance in army; 180 threatened by Sultan; 213 rides out of Jerusalem; 220 rides out with Thomas of Marle for battle of Ascalon; 241 in battle with Rotrou of La Perche, Lambert (of Liège) and the Count of Vendôme; 264 in final attack; 267 pursues defeated Saracens; 268 kills Mauquidant; 273 comforts Hugh of St Pol; 275 in Temple of Solomon; 276 suggests securing Christian position in Outremer. Younger son of Henry I and Anne of Kiev. Given a more prominent role here than his achievements warranted on the Crusade. See M. Bull, 'The Capetian Monarchy and the Early Crusade movement: Hugh of Vermandois and Louis VII', *Nottingham Medieval Studies* 40 (1996) pp. 25–46.

***Israel*:** 252 helped make Sultan's hauberk. Found only here. Probably to be identified with the Irashels at *Antioche* 177 as forger of splendid Saracen sword along with Wayland.

Jacob: 212 release from Hell in Godfrey's prayer.

Jesus Christ: 35 incidents in his Passion evoked by Peter the Hermit on arrival at Jerusalem; 36 lords evoke the Passion of; 46 arrest alluded to; 53 body laid on marble slab in Sepulchre; 60 Passion evoked; 67 wedding at Cana evoked; 68 Passion evoked; 72 Passion briefly evoked; 107 Passion evoked; 160 supper with Apostles alluded to; 161 miracle of loaves and fishes alluded to; 171 Ascension alluded to; 212 life set out in Godfrey's prayer.

John of Alis, *chétif*: 11 kills emir Ali in combat with lance and takes his horse; 15 kills a Turk; in battle; 16 in battle; 62 mounts night watch outside Jerusalem; 66 assembled outside Jerusalem; 76 given command by Godfrey; 82 wounded in first assault on Jerusalem; 134 cousin has hands chopped off and falls from battlements; 264 in final attack; 267 pursues defeated Saracens. See under *Chanson des Chétifs* Table of Names.

John of la Flèche: 103 given command of squadron by Raymond.; Not attested elsewhere.

Joseph of Arimathea: 35 evoked by Peter the Hermit on arrival at Jerusalem. In Gospel of Matthew 27:57–60; referred to in other *chansons de geste*, Moisan vol. 1 p. 628.

Joserant: 99 in charge of squadron attacking Jerusalem; 109 climbs ladder.

Josué, emir: 252 laces on Sultan's spurs. Frequent Saracen name: Moisan vol.1 pp. 629–30. Also at *Antioche* 183.

Jubin, Saracen deity: 10 invoked; 252 on Sultan's helmet. Synonym for Jupiter: frequent Saracen deity; Moisan vol.1 pp. 630, 633–4.

Jupiter: 10 invoked as Saracen deity.

Judas Iscariot: 4 Saracens referred to as companions of; 35 evoked by Peter the Hermit on arrival at Jerusalem; 46 alluded to.

King Abraham of the Silver Bridge: 91 summoned to help by bird. See Abraham above.

King Atanas, lord of Almeria: 238 killed by Robert of Normandy. Common Saracen name: Moisan vol.1 p. 181.

King Bricebalt: 166 killed by Godfrey. Unusual name, found elsewhere only *Prise de Cordres et de Sebille,* (ed.) M. del Vechio-Drion (Paris, 2011) lines 2502, 2508, 2664, 2679. Previously killed by Godfrey at *Antioche* 263.

King Calcatras: 129 with Sultan. See Calcatras above.

King Carbuncle, brother of Red Lion: 183 sent as envoy to negotiate exchange of prisoners. Some references in other *chansons de geste*: Moisan vol.1 p. 294.

King Darien: 65 summoned to help at siege of Jerusalem. Only in the Cycle in this form. Derions is a Saracen leader at *Antioche* 356.

King Glorient: 91 summoned to help by bird; 188 with Caliph. See Glorion above.

King Loquifer: 226 helps draw up battle order. Giant Saracen king killed by Rainouart in the *Bataille Loquifer*; more generally as Saracen name Moisan vol.1 p. 651. One of the eight pagans accursed by God who torture Rainalt Porcet at *Antioche* 184.

King Malagu: 205 Godfrey has his helmet. Common Saracen name: Moisan vol. 1 pp. 669–70.

King Malcoué: 166 killed by Godfrey. Not found elsewhere.
King Marcepelu: 237 killed by Baldwin. Elsewhere only in *Aliscans* line 1341.
King Mariaglau: 65 summoned to help at siege of Jerusalem. Not found elsewhere.
King Matusalés: 252 laces on Sultan's leg armour. Methusaleh; found elsewhere; Moisan vol.1 pp. 697–98.
King Murgalant of Esclaudie: 166 killed by Godfrey. Common Saracen name; Moisan vol.1 pp. 720–21.
King Philip of France, brother of Hugh: 180 Saracens want to defeat.
King Sucaman: 169 encourages Saracens to rescue Cornumarant; 170 attacked by Baldwin; 171 injured; 172 alluded to; 174 brought out on horse; 186 fight with Baldwin alluded to; 201 tells Sultan about fight with Baldwin. Not found outside the Cycle. Summoned by Sultan at *Antioche* 217. Cousin of Cornumarant. Suqman ibn Artuq (d.1104) is a historical figure.
King of Caneloigne: 188 with Caliph. The land of the Canelius: Moisan vol.2 p. 1093.
King of Nubia: 15 alluded to as giving mailshirt to John of Alis; 59 two kings of Nubia amongst the few to survive defeat at Antioch; 129 with Sultan; 186 enthused by plans for Saracen domination. Not found in quite this form elsewhere.
King of the Asses: 91 summoned to help by bird; 251 in battle of Ascalon. Already killed by Rainalt Porcet at *Antioche* 173.
King of the Tafurs: 57 alluded to; 66 urges immediate attack on Jerusalem; reference to being treated with respect by other leaders; 67 urges attack and advised by Robert of Flanders to be patient; 71, 72, 75 drawn up for attack outside Jerusalem; 76 Robert of Flanders says he should be granted honour of first attack; 78 promised first attack on Jerusalem and swears to fight hard; 79 launches first assault unsuccessfully and is wounded; 97, 98 demands honour of first (?) attack despite injuries; 106 receives orders for launching attack; 107 leads in attack and badly wounded; 133 promises plunder in return for helping build wooden defence; 136 attacks walls; 136, 140 receives homage from Thomas of Marle; 137 wants to be first into Jerusalem; 138, 139 encourages Christians into the city; 139 helps Thomas of Marle open gate; 140 first in unaided; 157 crowns Godfrey king as the highest ranking there; 159 offers to stay and defend Jerusalem; 165 in charge of defence of Jerusalem with Peter the Hermit; 167 marches out to rescue Raymond of Saint-Gilles; 169 leads Cornumarant to Jerusalem; 170, 171 attacked by rescue mission; 172 fights armed with scythe; 184 helps frighten Tafurs; 189 on walls looking at treasure; 191 furious about treasure and argues with Godfrey; 192 voices doubts about Peter the Hermit's battle abilities; 195 inflicts terrible damage on Saracens; 197 regrets loss of Peter; 204 intimidates envoy with much gnashing of teeth; 210 beats back Cornumarant from breach in wall of Jerusalem; 223 leads in march to battle of Ascalon; 246, 247 defeats beaked Especs; 264 in final attack Found in *Antioche* at several points, generally in context of dubious activity: thus cannibalism at 174–5, truce-breaking at 183 and rape and murder at 262–3. For

further bibliography and discussion of how his role in the *Jérusalem* differs see my article, 'The Count and the Cannibals: the Old French Crusade Cycle as a Drama of Salvation' in *Jerusalem the Golden: the Origins and Impact of the First Crusade*, (ed.) S.B. Edgington and L. Garcia-Guijarro (Turnhout, 2014) pp. 307–28 at pp. 314–22.

King of Valnuble, brother of Sanguin: 91 summoned to help by bird; 228 killed by Tancred. Not found elsewhere.

Lambert of Liège: 76 given squadron by Godfrey; 222 rides out for battle of Ascalon; 241 in battle. At *Antioche* 355.

Longinus: 35 evoked by Peter the Hermit on arrival at Jerusalem; 212 in Godfrey's prayer. See under *Chanson des Chétifs* Table of Names.

Lucabel of Montir, elderly Saracen and stepbrother of Corbadas: 58 summoned to Corbadas to pronounce on Godfrey's miracle with the kites; 59 discusses miracle with Maucolon; 60 advises Corbadas and Cornumarant and says believes in miracles by God; 65, 66 declares willingness to withstand siege; 69 asked to interpret miracle of kites; 70 tells Cornumarant the miracle means Godfrey will become King of Jerusalem, to the former's derision; 74 goes up tower with Corbadas to watch battle;75 anxious Saracens will lose; 76 looks down on battle from window; 83 alluded to; 86, 87 encourages Corbadas not to lose hope; 88 says prophecies about advent of Christians have come true; 89, 90 suggests using birds to get messages out seeking help; 94, 95 receives and reads counterfeit letters, to disgust of Cornumarant; 96 watches events with Corbadas; 101 comments; 105 dissuades Corbadas from his plans for the squadron of women; 117 with Corbadas; 119 asks Cornumarant how he plans to leave city; 140 consoles Corbadas at fall of Jerusalem; 144 accompanies him from Tower of David; 176 consoles him on capture of Cornumarant; 180 accompanies him to Sultan; 231 commander of 50 Saracen squadrons; 257 kills several Christians then killed by Tancred. Not found outside the Cycle although *Anseis de Carthage* line 2510 refers to Lucabel King of Pinchenie.

Lucifer: 225 son of Sultan; 234 kills Anseis of Paris; 236, 237 kills Rainalt of Beauvais. Some references in *chansons de geste*: Moisan vol.1 p. 654.

Lucion, Saracen doctor: 198 cures Peter instantly.

Lucion: 225 son of Sultan; 236 spurs into battle; 242 killed by Thomas of Marle. Common Saracen name; Moisan vol.1 p. 654. *Antioche* 356.

Macon: 198 at Peter's interrogation. Not found elsewhere.

Mahomed: 10 invoked; 59 fails to support Saracens; 76, 87 evoked by Corbadas; 90 invoked by Lucabel; 95, 99, 100, 101, 103 invoked by Corbadas; 113 evoked by Maucolon; 114 evoked by Cornumarant; 140 invoked by Saracens in Jerusalem; 171 invoked by King Sucaman; 178 legend of his drunkenness and subsequent consumption by pigs; buried in levitating magnetic coffin; 180 leads Saracens to Jerusalem riding an elephant; 186 invoked by Saracens; 188 image brought by Saracens; 198, 199 image of at Peter's interrogation; 200, 201 Peter pretends to worship image; 204 Godfrey invited to worship;

225 Bohemond to be forced to worship; 242, 251 invoked; 265 renounced by Sultan; 267 invoked by Saracens; 273 golden image of taken by Christians.
Main god of the Saracens: Moisan vol.1 pp. 663–7 for numerous references.

Mahomed Gomelin (unclear whether to be identified with Mahomed): 176, 178 maker of Sultan's amazing tent; 179 has image of Apollon lowered; 180 alluded to; 201 invoked; 204 Godfrey threatens to hand to *ribalts*; 222, 225 invoked by Sultan; 226 invoked to bless Saracen forces; 230 alluded to; 240 invoked; 252 on Sultan's helmet; 266 blamed by Sultan and statue beheaded by Caliph; 272 head alluded to;

Mahon: 210 summoned by Roboant. Unidentifiable Saracen. Mahon brother of the emir is found at *Antioche* 139.

Maigremors: 252, 260, 268 horse of Sultan. Also found as name of horse in *Gerbert de Metz*, *Maugis d'Aigremont* and *Vivien de Montbranc*; Moisan vol.1 p. 667.

Makon the enchanter: 259 with Sultan. Unidentifiable Saracen, found only here.

Malagu, son of: 237 killed by Baldwin.

Malargu: 196 cut in half by Godfrey.

Malcoué, son of: 182, 183 suggests exchanging Raymond of Saint-Gilles. See Malcoué above.

Malenidant: 210 summoned by Roboant. Found only here.

Malquidant: 226 leads Moors from Moriant; 268 killed by Hugh of Vermandois. Common Saracen name: Moisan vol.1 pp. 672–3. Already killed by Rainalt Porcet at *Antioche* 173.

Marbrin, son of King Sucaman: 174 with father; 183 captured by Godfrey; 183 to be ransomed; 184 frightened by parade of Tafurs; 185 consigned to dungeon but well treated; 186, 201 captivity alluded to; 205 Godfrey fights him when refuses to apostatise; 206 cut in half in combat by Godfrey.

Marbrin of Salorie: 166 killed by Godfrey. Common Saracen name: Moisan vol. pp. 682–3.

Margot, Margos, Saracen deity: 10 invoked; 252 on Sultan's helmet. Some references in other *chansons de geste*: Moisan vol.1 p. 686.

Margot: 183 sent as Saracen envoy to negotiate exchange of prisoners. Common Saracen name: Moisan vol.1 p.687. Also found at *Antioche* 206 at the court of the Sultan.

Marin l'Aigage: 202, 203 equips Sultan's horse. Found only here.

Marmoire: 188 with Sultan. Found only here.

Martin: 111 climbs ladder and knocked off but not killed; 248 killed by Cornicas. Unidentifiable.

Mary Magdalen: 78 invoked by Tafur king; 212 in Godfrey's prayer.

Masarie: 188 with Caliph. Found only here.

Maucoé, brother of Solimant: 188 with Caliph. Found only here.

Maucolon: 59 discusses miracle with Lucabel; 60 advises Corbadas and Cornumarant, taken aback by Lucabel's acceptance of Christian miracles; 65 with Corbadas; 69 with Corbadas at Jerusalem; 87 reassures Corbadas; 94

assembles to hear counterfeit letters; 113 taken captive by Wicher and seeks protection from Godfrey; 115 offers exchange of prisoners; 140 killed by Robert of Flanders. Found only in the Cycle.

Mirabiel, descendant of Charles Martel: 257 killed by Lucabel. Found only here; identity unclear.

Moor of Moriant: 188 with Caliph. Unidentifiable Saracen.

Morant: 204 Godfrey's interpreter; 221 helps prepare Bohemond and Tancred for battle.

Morant, brother of King Loquifer: 226 helps draw up battle order. Common Saracen name: Moisan vol.1 pp. 714–15.

Morel: 257 Tancred's horse. Very common name for horses: Moisan vol.1 p. 716. Enguerrand's horse is thus named at *Antioche* 56.

Morgan la Fée: 187 helped Pallas make Sultan's robe. Sister of King Arthur; referred to in various *chansons de geste*; Moisan vol.1 pp. 717–18; referred to as magician at *Antioche* 218.

Morgant: 188 with Caliph; 226 helps draw up battle order. Common Saracen name: Moisan vol.1 p. 717.

Murgalant of Audierne: 91 summoned to help by bird. Common Saracen name; Moisan vol.1 pp. 720–21.

Murglaie: 263 Cornumarant's sword, taken by Baldwin. Name of Ganelon's sword in the *Roland* lines 346, 607 and of Elyas' sword in the *Béatrix* line1662.

Nicolas of Duras, siege engineer: 69 sets up mangonels outside Jerusalem; 77 preparations for use; 107 takes battering ram up to walls; 132, 133 builds siege engine from wood found near Jerusalem. Companion engineer to Gregory of Arras. See entry in Table of Places under Duras for possible origin.

Noah: 212 release from Hell in Godfrey's prayer.

Noiron: 180 leads Saracens to attack; 198 at Peter's interrogation. Common Saracen name evoking the Emperor Nero: Moisan vol.1 pp. 735–6. At battle of Antioch, *Antioche* 356.

Old Man of the Mountains: 201 marriage of daughter to Baldwin alluded to. Main character in Baudouin de Sebourc; found outside the Cycle only in *Entrée d'Espagne* 11976. Summons Baldwin to Edessa at *Antioche* 110. See Murray, *Crusader Kingdom* pp. 124–5; 'The Old Man of the Mountains', C. E.Nowell, *Speculum* 22 (1947) pp. 497–519.

Orquenais: 125 carries oriflamme for Turks; 127 sets reed bed on fire as ordered by Cornumarant. Attested in some *chansons de geste*: Moisan vol.2 p. 751; lookout for Soliman at *Antioche* 65.

Pagan of Beauvais: 80 killed by Cornumarant. Attested elsewhere; see Riley-Smith p. 216. Rescues Gerard of Melun at *Antioche* 360–61 in a passage translated from Robert.

Pagan of Camelia: 1 splits from main army at Jerusalem; 16 in battle; 64 captured by Turks and rescued by Richard of Chaumont (if to be identified with Pagan the Norman); 111 attacks Turk and knocked off siege ladder but not killed. Not recorded elsewhere but at battle of Antioch *Antioche* 355.

Pagan of Guillant: 262 killed by Cornumarant. Probably to be identified with Gilbert Payen of Garland, seneschal of the King of France, who is well attested on Crusade; Riley-Smith pp. 88, 208. Also appears in the *Antioche* 126 in the first attack on Antioch.

Pallas Athene: 178 allusion to her turning Arachne into a spider; 187 helped Morgan la Fée make Sultan's robe. Referred to only in the Cycle; Moisan vol.2 p. 767 suggests she is identified as a pagan deity.

Partridge: 229 horse of Estonamons.

Pereliers: 236 spurs into battle. Found only here.

Peter the Hermit: 35 addresses army on arrival at Jerusalem evoking incidents of Christ's life; 36, 37 addresses army promising a place in Paradise to those who die fighting for Jerusalem; 113 alluded to; 165 in charge of defence of Jerusalem with King of Tafurs; 167 encourages Godfrey; 168 fights; 170, 171 attacked by rescue mission; 172 fights armed with axe; 174 night watch; 182 guards Jerusalem at Godfrey's request; 183 suggests only exchanging one Saracen; 184 helps frighten Saracens; 189 on walls looking at treasure; 191 threatened by Cornumarant; 192 arms for battle; 193 successfully kills 500 Saracens despite his unconventional techniques but is cut off; 194 holds off Saracens; 196, 197 loss lamented; 197 fights Cornumarant and captured by him; 198 faints and miraculously cured by Saracen doctor; under intense Saracen scrutiny; 199 attacks Saracens; Sultan asks him to apostatise; 200 pretends to; 201 discusses Christians with Sultan and praises Godfrey; 204 apostasy referred to by messenger; 207, 208 laughs at news of Marbrin's death and Godfrey's defiance; 209 chained up by order of the Sultan; 213 regrets apostasy; 217 – 223 describes Christian forces to Sultan; 251 Baldwin sees him in Saracen camp; 265 liberated by St George kills Sanguin; 266 evoked by Sultan; 268 kills Salehadin; 271 knows where Baldwin and Raimbaut Creton are. Presented by the *Antioche* as the key instigator of the Crusade; whilst he was undoubtedly a key figure, this overstates his role. See E. O. Blake and C. Morris, 'A hermit goes to war: Peter and the origins of the First Crusade', *Studies in Church History* 22 (1985) 79–107; Jean Flori, *Pierre l'Ermite et la première Croisade*, (Paris, 1999). It is striking that the *Jérusalem* often portrays him as fighting in concert with the King of the Tafurs, another outsider enjoying high status.

Pilate: 46 alluded to. Numerous references in *chansons de geste*: Moisan vol.2 p. 783.

Piniel: 257 killed by Tancred. Pinel is a common Saracen name: Moisan vol.2 p. 786. The *Antioche* has a Pinel at the battle of Nicaea.

Plantamor, Cornumarant's horse: 258, 262; 263 taken by Baldwin and given to Eustace; 264 ridden by Eustace in final attack. Name not found elsewhere.

Principle: 237 killed by Eustache. Only found in the Cycle. At *Antioche* 138, 175, where he is killed by Rainalt Porcet.

Prinsaut, horse of Baldwin of Bouillon: referred 121, 122, 125; 128 attacked by leeches; referred 167, 169, 237; 248 Baldwin dismounts and rides horned horse he has captured;

Quinquenas, nephew of Corbadas: 69 with Corbadas at Jerusalem. Found in the *Chevalerie Vivien* and variants common in the *chansons de geste*; Moisan vol.2 p. 801.

Radimans of Valerie: 59 Turk who reported defeat of Antioch to Corbadas. Found only here.

Raimbaut Creton: 66 assembled outside Jerusalem; 75 leads detachment in attack on Jerusalem; 100 put in charge of squadron at Jerusalem; 106 looks forward to battle; 111 climbs ladder and knocked off but not killed; 134 climbs siege ladder but has to retreat down; 140 pursues Saracens in Jerusalem; 157 nominates King of Tafurs to crown Godfrey; 264 in final attack; 269 fights Sultan alongside Baldwin; 270 defies Sultan; 271 wounded; 272 rescued by Christians. Hero of the *Antioche*, where laisses 167–9 recount his single-handed slaughter of hundreds of Turks on a bridge and rescue by St Michael; also at 50, 253, 355. Widely attested on Crusade: Riley-Smith p. 218. In reality a somewhat thuggish figure who had to do 14 years penance for castrating a monk: Riley-Smith pp. 155–6.

Rainald of Pavia, *chétif*: 15 in battle. Probably to be identified with the *chétif* Richard of Pavia, *Antioche* 31.

Rainalt of Beauvais: 236, 237 killed by Lucifer. Well attested on Crusade; Riley-Smith p. 218. At Nicaea and battle of Antioch in *Antioche* 50, 355. Gilo pp. 190–93 suggests he was part of the *iuventus* of Hugh of Vermandois.

Rainier, brother of Guy of Aubefort: 194 killed in skirmish. Not attested elsewhere.

Ralph of Carembaut: 264 in final attack. Not attested elsewhere.

Ralph of Pevier: 194 killed in skirmish. Not attested elsewhere.

Ralph (of Ponciel?): 257 killed by Lucabel. Not attested elsewhere.

Randol of Aleppo: 166 in attack on Jerusalem. Not attested elsewhere.

Raymond of Saint-Gilles, Count of Toulouse: 7 Godfrey sends messenger to for reinforcements; 8, 9 receives message and responds; 47 sets up camp on Mount of Olives and praised by Gerard of Gournay; 66 assembled outside Jerusalem; 72 squadron ready to attack outside St Stephen's Gate; blessed by Bishop of Mautran; 103 sets up squadron; 141 criticised for allowing Turks to buy themselves safety at fall of Jerusalem; 149 offered kingship of Jerusalem by Bohemond; 159 offers to stay to defend Jerusalem; 165 with Godfrey; 167 taken prisoner outside Jerusalem; 170 hostage for negotiations; 174 mistreated by Saracens; 180 threatened by Sultan; 183 to be exchanged for Saracen prisoners; 185 exchanged for Cornumarant; 186 exchange alluded to; 189 on walls looking at treasure; 191, 192 sounds horn for attack; 205 prevents envoy leaving; 211 supports Godfrey; 213 guards Jerusalem; 264 in final attack. One of the main leaders of the Crusade. Second son of Pons of Toulouse and Almodis of La Marche. Became ruler of Tripoli until his death in 1105. See J.H. and L. L. Hill, *Raymond IV* (New York 1962).

Red Lion: 218 killing by Robert of Normandy alluded to. Not found outside Crusade *chansons de geste*, although in *Tristan de Nanteuil* line 1298 Galafre d'Erminie is described as his son. Killed by Robert of Normandy at *Antioche* 357; key adviser to Corbaran.

Richard of Chaumont, *chétif*: 1 rides towards Jerusalem with Chétifs; 6 rides to the rescue of Godfrey outside Jerusalem; 10 meets up with Godfrey; 11 alluded to; 12 kills a Turk in combat with lance; 15 in battle; 17 he and *chétifs* credited with winning the day; 62 mounts night watch outside Jerusalem; 64 rides to the rescue of companions captured by Turks; pursues Cornumarant and strikes him but not fatally; 66 assembled outside Jerusalem; 76 given command by Godfrey; 82 wounded in first assault on Jerusalem; 87 alluded to; 140 kills Ysabars; 261 in battle; 264 in final attack; 267 pursues defeated Saracens. See under *Chanson des Chétifs* Table of Names.

Richard of Melun: 64 captured by Turks and rescued by Richard of Chaumont.

Robert the Frisian, Count of Flanders: 1 splits from main army at Jerusalem; 4 swears to fight to the death; 7 confers with Godfrey mistaking *chétifs* for Saracen reinforcements; 10 reinforcements on way to; 15 sees *chétifs* fighting Saracens; 16 in battle; 39 underlines commitment to taking Jerusalem; 49 sets up camp at the Gate of David; 66 assembled outside Jerusalem; 67 advises King of Tafurs to be patient; 71, 72 drawn up for attack outside Jerusalem; 75 present at Thomas's feat with spears; 76 says King of Tafurs should have honour of first attack; 81 upset at death of Gontier of Aire; 83 discusses with Godfrey what army should do; 92, 93 sets falcon on messenger doves; 106 commands column of nobles with Godfrey; 112 attacks; 140 kills Malcolon; 142 cleanses Holy Sepulchre; 143 occupies palace with Thomas of Marle and Godfrey; 147 refuses kingship of Jerusalem; 152 criticised by bishop of Mautran; 159 refuses to stay to defend Jerusalem; 162 volunteers to return to Jerusalem; 180 threatened by Sultan; 213 rides out of Jerusalem; 219 rides out for battle of Ascalon; 239 leads rescue of Robert of Normandy; 243 restrains Hugh of St-Pol from suicide at death of his son Enguerrand; 264 in final attack; 267 pursues defeated Saracens; 275 in Temple of Solomon. The *Jérusalem* like the *Antioche* persistently confuses father and son; by the early thirteenth century exact details could get blurred. Robert the Frisian is Robert I, count of Flander, second son of Baldwin V of Lille and Adela of France, married to Gertrude countess of Holland. He went on pilgrimage to the Holy Land in 1085. The apocryphal letter of Alexius is addressed to him: for text and references see my discussion in *Robert the Monk*, pp. 217–22. See C. Verlinden, *Robert Ier le Frison* (Ghent, 1935). Robert of Flanders, who actually went on the First Crusade, was his son: M. M. Knappen, 'Robert II of Flanders in the First Crusade', in *The Crusades and other historical essays* (ed.) L. J. Paetow (New Tork, 1928) 79–100. The *Canso d'Antioca* lines 10–12 comments waspishly that some authors cannot be trusted to tell the difference.

Robert of Normandy: 1 splits from main army at Jerusalem; 10 reinforcements on way to; 15 sees *chétifs* fighting Saracens; 17, 18 has fought so hard that his hand is clamped round the hilt of his sword; 30 leads the way to Jerusalem; 42 prepares to attack; 44 agrees with Hugh about need for siege engines; 48

sets up camp at St Stephen; 66 assembled outside Jerusalem; 72 ready to attack outside Jerusalem; 99 sets up squadron to attack Jerusalem; 112 attacks; 119 on night watch; 120 night attack; 127 alluded to; 129 has catapult set up outside Jerusalem; 130 calls council; 135 attacks Jerusalem; 141 distinguishes himself at fall of Jerusalem; 148 refuses kingship of Jerusalem; 152 criticised by bishop of Mautran; 160 pursues Dodequin to Tiberias; 162 confronts reluctance in army; 180 threatened by Sultan; 213 rides out of Jerusalem; 215 keenness to fight; 218 rides out for battle of Ascalon; 238, 239 carried away by enthusiasm for killing Saracens, gets surrounded and has to be rescued; 264 in final attack; 267 pursues defeated Saracens; 275 in Temple of Solomon. Son of William the Conqueror; defeated at Tinchebrai 1106 by his younger brother Henry and spent the rest of his life in captivity: W. M. Aird, *Robert Curthose: Duke of Normandy* (Woodbridge, 2008). His reputation was ambiguous: WM IV.389, vol. 1 pp. 702–3 suggested that his loss of the English throne was a punishment for refusing to accept the throne of Jerusalem. It is interesting that the *Jérusalem* singles him out more than once as an example of heroism: this reflects later accretions compared to the largely contemporary material on which the *Antioche* is based. A persistent tradition credited him with attacking Corbaran at the battle of Antioch: WM IV.389, vol.1 pp.702–3.

Robert of Tiois: 44 agrees with Hugh about need for siege engines. Not attested elsewhere: name likely to meet demands of rhyme scheme.

Robert the Seneschal: 103 given command of squadron by Raymond.

Roboant: 210 sent by Sultan to summon kings to fight. Common Saracen name: Moisan vol.2 p. 841. Killed at *Antioche* 23 and again at 173.

Roger: 248 killed by Cornicas. Unidentifiable.

Roger of Etampes: 194 killed in skirmish.

Roger of Rosoie: 1 splits from main army at Jerusalem; 16 in battle; 64 captured by Turks and rescued by Richard of Chaumont; 240 attacked by Esméré, beats him and takes his horse. Roger of Rozoy (Aisne), castellan of Jaffa. Attested elsewhere on Crusade: Murray, *Crusader Kingdom* p. 227; Riley-Smith p. 222. Referred to at *Antioche* 50, 147 and 355.

Roland: 210 death of alluded to; 273 mourning for his death compared to mourning for Enguerrand of St-Pol. Eponymous hero of the *Chanson de Roland*. Also cited at *Antioche* 337 and 358 at the battle of Antioch.

Rotrou of La Perche: 66 assembled outside Jerusalem; 74 leads attackers towards Jerusalem; 135 attacks Jerusalem; 212 rides out of Jerusalem; 222 rides out with Count of Vendôme and Stephen of Blois for battle of Ascalon; 241 in battle; 264 in final attack. Count of Perche and Mortagne (Cher); later to become confrater at Cluny. Well attested on Crusade: see Riley-Smith pp. 136, 144–5, 166. Referred to a number of times in the *Antioche* at Nicaea, Dorylaeum and Antioch.

Rubent (brother of King of Caneloigne): 91 summoned to help by bird; 188 with Caliph. Only found here.

Rubin: 236 spurs into battle. Only found here.

Rubion: 198 at Peter's interrogation; 225 son of Sultan; 242 killed by Enguerrand of St-Pol; 266 summoned by Sultan. Common Saracen name: Moisan vol.2 p. 854. Appears as Calabra's father Rubiant, *Antioche* 218; Rubiant, a clerk at the Persian court, *Antioche* 213; and as Yaghi-Sian's nephew Rubion *Antioche* 126.

St Andrew of Patras: 4 evoked by Godfrey. Also referred to at *Antioche* 291 in Peter Bartholomew's vision; similarly in *GF* 59–60, BB 67–68, and RA *passim*. His presence here is likely to reflect a generalised memory that he was associated with the Crusade.

St Archideclin: 67 wedding at Cana evoked. Bridegroom at the wedding of Cana: various references; Moisan vol.1 p. 174; Du Cange III p. 250. The name is a misunderstanding of 'architriclinum'.

St Demetrius: 173 helps Godfrey in battle; 174 accompanies Christians back to Jerusalem. Byzantine warrior saint, fourth-century military martyr and defender of Thessaloniki. See C. Walter, *The Warrior Saints in Byzantine Art and Tradition* (Aldershot, 2003) pp. 67–93. Appears a number of times at crucial moments in the *Antioche*: at Dorylaeum (100), fighting off attack by Soliman (124) and the battle of Antioch (358). Appears alongside saints George and Mercurius in the *Chanson d'Aspremont* lines 8586–7, 8599–600, 9393–4: *La Chanson d'Aspremont: chanson de geste du XIIe siècle. Texte du manuscript de Wollaton Hall*, (ed.) L. Brandin, 2 vols (Paris, 1919).

St Denis: 26 intervenes in battle with emir of Ascalon; 265 helps in final battle. Patron saint of Paris. Alluded to in *Antioche* 210.

St Domin (Domitian, Domitius): 26, 27 intervenes in battle with emir of Ascalon; 265 helps in final battle. In a number of *chansons de geste*: Moisan vol.1 p. 348. In *Aspremont* fights alongside saints George and Mercurius: lines 8586–7, 8599–600, 9393–4.

St George: 22 invoked by Bohemond and Tancred at Ramleh; 25 invoked by Bohemond; 26 intervenes in battle and kills emir of Ascalon; 27 helps kill Saracens; 173 helps Godfrey in battle; 174 accompanies Christians back to Jerusalem; 248 invoked in battle of Ascalon; 265 helps in final battle and liberates Peter the Hermit. Frequently cited in *chansons de geste*: Moisan vol.1 p. 627. See Walter, *Warrior Saints* 109–44; Pringle, *Churches* vol.2 pp. 9–27 for his cult in Syria. Referred to in other sources at the battle of Antioch e.g. *GF* 69; in visions by RA 112–13. Helps at a number of key points in the *Antioche*: Dorylaeum (100), fighting off attack by Soliman (1124) and the battle of Antioch (358).

St Jonah: 4 invoked by Godfrey. Frequently cited in *chansons de geste*: Moisan vol.1 p. 625.

St Lazarus: 1 alluded to as raised from the dead in Bethany; 66 invoked by bishop of Mautran; 191 evoked by King of Tafurs; 212 in Godfrey's prayer. Gospel of John 11. Frequently cited in *chansons de geste*: Moisan vol.1 p. 642. Invoked a number of times in the *Antioche*: 184, 253, 364.

St Maurice of Angers: 26 intervenes in battle with emir of Ascalon; 174 accompanies Christians back to Jerusalem; 265 helps in final battle. St Maurice was a Byzantine military saint, martryed with his company: he appears at the battle of Antioch at *Antioche* 358.

St Michael the Archangel: 71 evoked by Bishop outside Jerusalem; 80 receives soul of Pagan of Beauvais; 135, 136 receives souls of knights killed at Jerusalem; 234 receives soul of Anseis of Paris; 243 receives soul of Enguerrand of St-Pol. Frequently found in *chansons de geste* as receiving souls of dead knights, most famously in *Roland* lines 2393–6; Moisan vol.1 p. 705.

St Nicholas: 4 evoked by Robert of Flanders. Bishop of Myra. Frequently evoked in *chansons de geste*: Moisan vol.1 p. 733; also in the *Jeu de St Nicolas*, (ed.) F. J. Warne (Blackwell: Oxford, 1951). Not evoked in the *Antioche*.

St Peter: 46 evoked by Gerard of Gournay and Thomas of Marle; 113 evoked by Godfrey; 212 in Godfrey's prayer. In vision at *Antioche* 288–9. First bishop of Antioch, where the principal church was dedicated to him: Cahen, *Syrie du Nord* p.130.

St Simeon: 101 evoked by bishop (of Mautran); 104 evoked by Godfrey and Robert the Frisian; 191 body of evoked by King of Tafurs; 212 in Godfrey's prayer. Frequently referred to in *chansons de geste*: Moisan vol.1 p. 890. Gospel of Luke 2: 25–35. Referred to at *Antioche* 185, 253.

St Thomas: 4 evoked by Stephen of Albemarle. Frequently referred to in *chansons de geste*: Moisan vol.2 p. 933. *Antioche* laisse 13 puzzlingly says he was sent to Hell for his doubting of Christ.

St Veas: 4 invoked by Robert of Flanders. St-Vaast, the bishop of Arras; the main abbey there is consecrated to him.

St Barbara: 26, 27 intervenes in battle with emir of Ascalon; 174 accompanies Christians back to Jerusalem. Early Christian martyr. A church was dedicated to her in Antioch: Cahen, *Syrie du Nord* p. 131.

Salatré: 178 Jew who made Mahomed's floating coffin; 252 arms Sultan; maker of his leg armour. Very common Saracen name: Moisan vol.2 pp. 863–4.

Salehadin: 268 killed by Peter the Hermit. Used as general Saracen name: Moisan II.864–5. Killed twice over in the *Antioche* 57, 97.

Sanguin: 188 with Caliph; 225 son of Sultan; 236 spurs into battle; 237 escapes Baldwin; 242 upset (understandably) at slaughter of six of his brothers; 251, 252 tells Sultan the bad news; 265 killed by Peter the Hermit. Found in some *chansons de geste*: Moisan vol.2 p. 871. As Sanguis one of the eight pagans accursed by God who tortures Rainalt Porcet: *Antioche* 184.

Satan: 212 temptation of Eve in Godfrey's prayer.

Sathanas: 69 *chétifs* referred to as sons of; 179 devil occupying image of Apollon who prophesies downfall of Christians. *Antioche* 223 similarly has him as the devil inside an idol of Mahomed.

Seong Oain the Fat: 188 with Caliph. A splendidly named character found only here. Evokes Seon, King of the Amorites. There is considerable variation in the manuscripts suggesting uncertainty over the reading; the majority omit.

Simon, relative of Godfrey and of Robert of Flanders: 87 Christian prisoner mistreated by Cornumarant; 194 killed in skirmish. A similarly unidentified

Simon is found with the Duke of Brittany at *Antioche* 50, 126 and 130; he is likely to owe his fleeting existence to the rhyme scheme.

Simon Magus: 198 alluded to as having holy herb and throwing the seven sages into prison. Acts 8:9-24 for his confrontation with Peter: many legends circulated about him,

*Sinagon***:** 225 son of Sultan; 233, 234 killed by Godfrey. Common Saracen name: Moisan vol.2 p 895.

*Soliman, uncle of the Sultan***:** 210 Sultan explains to him why called off attack; 220 killing by Hugh of Vermandois alluded to. Based on the historical Qilij Arslan I, sultan of Rum 1092–1107; nicknamed Soliman reflecting his patronymic ibn Suleyman. He is in fact killed by Godfrey at *Antioche* 357.

Solomon: 101 alluded to; 198 time of.

Solomon: 219 maker of Robert of Flanders' helmet. Common Saracen name reflecting the Old Testament: Moisan vol.2 pp. 65–7.

Stephen of Albemarle son of Count Otto: 1 splits from main army at Jerusalem; 4 swears to fight to the death; 62 mounts night watch outside Jerusalem; 135 attacks Jerusalem; 223 arms for battle of Ascalon; 264 in final attack. Attested on Crusade as Stephen, count of Aumale; Riley-Smith p. 223. Mentioned in *Antioche* 50, 139, 355.

Stephen of Blois: 222 rides out with Rotrou of Perche and the Count of Vendôme for battle of Ascalon. The much maligned count of Blois and Chartres, famous for bravely beating a retreat at Antioch and convincing the Emperor Alexius that the Crusade was a lost cause; son-in-law of William the Conqueror. The *Antioche* criticises him repeatedly and venomously: 62–72, 233–4, 284–5. His death on the Crusade of 1101 did nothing to redeem his reputation. See J. A. Brundage, 'An Errant Crusader: Stephen of Blois', *Traditio* 16 (1960) pp. 380–95; K. B. Wolf, 'Crusade and narrative: Bohemond and the Gesta Francorum', *Journal of Medieval History* 17 (1991) pp. 207–16, at pp.214–15 for suggestion that Stephen was deliberately blackened by Bohemond; my article 'The Count and the Cannibals' for fuller references and argument that Stephen's role in the Cycle is to show that failure to complete a Crusade is the only sin which cannot be redeemed by Crusade.

Stephen the Black: 91 summoned to help by bird.

Stephen of Lucuel: 108 climbs ladder into Jerusalem and killed by Ysabars of Barbais.

*Sultan of Persia***:** 66 will be asked to come and help defend Jerusalem; 91 summoned by bird; 94 name taken in vain in counterfeit letters; 105 Corbadas plans to offer him captured Christian women as breeding stock; 108 alluded to as emir of Persia; 117, 121 Cornumarant decides to seek his help; 128 alluded to; 129 Cornumarant begs his help, which is granted; 167 alluded to; 176 Corbadas comes to find him at his amazing tent; 179 watches image of Apollon prophesy; 180 orders to procreate; Corbadas arrives; promises help to regain Jerusalem; 181 description as rides to Jerusalem; 185 army of; 186 briefed by Cornumarant; 187 description of; 192 threatened by Peter the Hermit; 197

Table of Names and Places 403

Peter brought to him; 198 interrogates Peter and orders his cure; 199 asks Peter to apostatise; 200 delighted that he apparently does; 201 interrogates Peter and sends envoy demanding Godfrey's surrender; 202 horse described; 206 two halves of Marbrin and his horse sent back to; 207 receives news of Marbrin's death and Christian refusal of treasure; 208 upset; 209 has Peter chained up and calls for attack on Jerusalem; 210 calls off attack on Jerusalem at nightfall; 213 horrified at news of reinforcements; agrees with Christians to give battle on plains of Ramleh; 217 – 223 reaction to Christian forces riding out for battle of Ascalon; 224 prepares for battle; 225 urges sons to avenge Brohadas; 226, 227 draws up squadrons for battle; 232 retains 10 squadrons for himself; 247 playing chess with his brother mid-battle when defeated Especs arrive; 251, 252 told most of his sons dead; faints four times then arms elaborately for battle; 253, 254 rides out for battle; 259, 260 at head of forces; 260 attacks and is attacked by Tancred; 264 launches attack to avenge Cornumarant; 265 renounces Mahommed; 267 kills Garnier then flees; 268 pursued by Baldwin and confronts him; 270 threatens Baldwin and Raimbaut Creton with some very nasty treatment indeed; 272 escapes to Acre. Also a main character in the *Antioche*.

Suspirant: 188 with Caliph. Found only here.

Tafurs (also referred to as *ribalts*): 66 described outside Jerusalem; 92 shoot messenger doves with catapults; 85 butcher Turks who refuse to apostatise; 97 blessed by bishop of Mautran before attack; 108, 109, 110 praised; 174 fight; 183, 184 dressed in rich clothes to frighten Saracen captives; 246, 247 defeat beaked Especs. See 'Count and Cannibals' for argument that their role is to demonstrate the power of the Crusade to redeem, and note 28 for bibliography on Tafurs.

Tahon: 198 at Peter's interrogation; 225 son of Sultan; 236 spurs into battle; 242 killed by Enguerrand of St-Pol.

Tanas of Vavais: 261 killed by Richard of Chaumont and Baldwin of Beauvais. Found only here.

Tancred: 7 Godfrey sends messenger to for reinforcements; 8, 9 receives message and responds; 10 rides to the rescue; 21 lays siege to Caesarea with Bohemond; 22 worships at St George of Ramleh; 30 returns to quarters; 41 urges Crusaders to make an immediate attack on Jerusalem; 42 prepares to attack; 50 sets up camp near Bethlehem with Bohemond, praised by Bishop of Forez; 66 assembled outside Jerusalem; 71 drawn up for attack outside Jerusalem; 85 mounts night guard; 104 sets up squadron; 107 launch first wave of attack on Jerusalem; 112 attacks; 116 takes night watch; 127 alluded to; 135 attacks Jerusalem; 138 on walls of Jerusalem; 140 pursues Saracens in Jerusalem; 152 criticised by bishop of Mautran; 180 threatened by Sultan; 213 rides out of Jerusalem; 221 rides out with Bohemond for battle of Ascalon; 228 kills Alepantin; 239 joins rescue mission for Robert of Normandy; 257 kills Lucabel and Piniel; 260 unsuccessfully attacks Sultan; 264 in final attack; 267 pursues defeated Saracens. Son of Odobonus Marchisus; later prince of Galilee and, during Bohemond's captivity, regent of Antioch. We know a fair amount about him thanks to Ralph of Caen's *Gesta Tancredi*. See also R. L. Nicholson, *Tancred* (Chicago, 1940).

Tervagant: 10 invoked; 57 invoked; 76, 99 evoked by Corbadas; 114, 128 invoked by Cornumarant; 172 Saracens race of; 184 invoked by Saracen captives; 188 image brought by Saracens; 204 Godfrey invited to worship and defies; 205 invoked by Marbrin; 225 Bohemond will be forced to worship; 226, 239 religion and worship of; 251 invoked; 252 on Sultan's helmet; 268 invoked by Sultan. See under *Chanson des Chétifs* Table of Names.

Thomas, cousin of Joserant: 99 put in charge of squadron at Jerusalem; 109 climbs ladder.

Thomas of Marle: 1 splits from main army at Jerusalem; 8 suggests two messengers to Godfrey; 10 reinforcements on way to; 15 sees *chétifs* fighting Saracens; 16 in battle; 28 greets Bohemond on his return from raid; 38 speech to army emphasising difficulty and importance of conquering Jerusalem; 42 prepares to attack; 46 sets up camp with Gerard of Gournai in valley of Josaphat; 53 narrative looks forward to his entry into Jerusalem at spearpoint and encounter with Bedouin woman; 57 scouts round walls of Jerusalem looking for weak points; 66 referred to twice at Jerusalem, once as Thomas of La Fère and once as Thomas of Marle; 75 leads detachment in attack on Jerusalem; his entry at spearpoint alluded to; 102 given lead of squadron by Hugh of Vermandois; 128 cures Baldwin with miraculous letter; 135 attacks Jerusalem; 136, 140 does homage to King of Tafurs; 137–9 thrown over walls into Jerusalem from points of spears *à la* bed of nails; 139 fight with Bedouin woman who foretells his death at the hands of his lord; helps open gate to let Christians in; 140 first into Jerusalem with help of others; 142 cleanses Holy Sepulchre; 143 occupies palace with Robert of Flanders and Godfrey; 212 rides out of Jerusalem; 220 rides out with Hugh of Vermandois for battle of Ascalon; 242 attacked by Cornicas and kills three of the Sultan's sons in pique; 264 in final attack. Thomas of Coucy, lord of La Fère and Marle. Well attested on Crusade: Riley-Smith pp. 99, 156–7, 223. Famous with contemporaries for his violence, extreme by even the standards of the time and which ultimately led to his execution: see Suger's *Vie de Louis VI le Gros* ch.7 pp.31–3 for eviction from his castle of Montaigu; ch.24 pp. 173–9 for his condemnation at the Council of Beauvais; ch.31 pp. 251–3 for his death and inability to receive Communion; 'virum omnium quos novimus hac aetate nequissimum' according to Guibert of Nogent, *Autobiographie* 328–9.

Titus Vespasian: 55 evoked by Corbadas as part of Vengeance of Christ theme. Emperor Titus CE 79–81; here confused with his father Vespasian. Also referred to at *Antioche* 12 as part of the Vengeance de Christ theme: Titus ordered the destruction of the Temple at Jerusalem.

Tort the son of Aresne: 188 with Caliph. Found only here.

Wicher the German: 10 reinforcements on way to; 100 put in charge of squadron at Jerusalem; 111, 112 climbs ladder and hauled up at the point of a hook, taken captive; 113 takes Maucolon captive; 114 fights on battlements; 116 returned to Christian army. Ministerialis of Fulda (Hessen). Widely attested on 1101 Crusade: Riley-Smith p. 224. According to the *Antioche* 362–3 he was killed at the battle of Antioch by Claras de Sarmazane; apparently resurrected here.

William (of Guillant): 262 killed by Cornumarant.

***Ysabars of Barbais*:** 108 kills Stephen of Lucuel on ladder; 111 attacks Wicher on siege ladder; 113 taken captive by Eurvin of Creel and seeks protection from Robert of Flanders; 115 refuses to apostatise; 116 returns to Jerusalem to offer ransom terms to Cornumarant; 140 killed by Richard of Chaumont. Only found here.

***Ysabras the giant*:** 188 with Caliph. Monster sent by Desramé to capture Rainouart and killed by him: *Bataille Loquifer*.

***Ysoré*:** 93 Saracen in whose house doves take refuge. Common Saracen name: Moisan vol.2 pp. 971–2. Garsion's nephew at *Antioche* 175.

Table of Place Names by Laisse:

Chanson De Jérusalem

In and around Jerusalem

Bethany: 1, 212 Lazarus raised from dead in.

Gate of David: 49 Robert of Flanders sets up camp at; 62 Cornumarant slips out from; 62, 63 Harpin of Bourges watches; 63 Cornumarant attacks outside; 64, 65 reenters Jerusalem through; 80 Godfrey fights at; 116 site of negotiations over hostages; 119, 120 Saracens ride out through; 132 Crusaders build siege machinery in front of; 172 battle outside. Gate near the Tower of David.

Gate of St Stephen: 1, 7, 8; 72 Raymond of St Gilles takes stand at; 80, 81 breached but Christians unable to take the city; 86 reinforced by Turks; 119, 120 Saracens ride out through; 132, 133, 134 Crusaders install siege engine in front of; 135, 136 Christians smash through but beaten back when a gate dropped on them; 189 Saracens lay out treasure in front of. Faces East to the Mount of Olives; gives access to St Stephen's chapel.

Golden Gate: 2; 35 pointed out by Peter the Hermit; 47 Raymond of St-Gilles to watch; 62 Fulcher of Melun and John of Alis watch; 77 siege engine set up at; 92 Christians outside; 142 Hugh chases Saracens to and massacres at. Identified with the Beautiful Gate by which Christ entered for the Passion; Pringle, *Churches* vol.3 pp.103–9; Ezekiel 44:1–3 for Messiah entering the city through it.

Golgotha: 35 alluded to by Peter the Hermit.

Holy Sepulchre: Invoked and/or described 4, 7, 8, 13, 23 25, 63, 85, 103, 104, 115, 120, 122, 135, 137 139, 147, 166, 170, 172, 237, 239, 248; 256 by Cornumarant; 257, Object of pilgrimage and worship; 10, 63, 79, 98, 101, 105, 121, 147, 216; Cleansing of and restoration of worship at; 84, 103, 142,

189 Godfrey, Thomas of Marle prospect of losing again; Godfrey, Thomas of Marle and Robert of Flanders cleanse 142; 35 pointed out by Peter the Hermit; 41 Tancred foretells taking of; 60 Corbadas describes resurrection of Christ; 72 allusion to Resurrection; 73 Turks using as a stable; 75 Thomas of Marle, Robert of Flanders and Godfrey go to find; 118 Corbadas curses; 157 Godfrey crowned at; 204 Godfrey will place candlesticks of Mahomed in; 211, 212, 213, 214 Christians keep vigil in; 212 Christ laid in; 216 Mass said at on the day of the battle of Ascalon; 274 candles carried to. Founded by Helena, who identified the site as Calvary; dedicated in 335, destroyed by Caliph al-Hakim in 1009, rebuilt in part by the Byzantines and extensively by the Crusaders. See Pringle, *Churches*, vol.3 pp. 6–72; Morris, *Holy Sepulchre*.

House of Simon: 212 Christ in.

Hospital (of St John): 281 another song will talk about founding of.

Jerusalem: *passim*

Josaphat, Valley of: 1, 2; 3–6, 9, 18 battle in; 2, 5 where the Blessed Virgin Mary died; 35 pointed out by Peter the Hermit as deathplace of the Virgin; 46 Gerard of Gournay and Thomas of Marle set up camp there; 165, 166, 167 Saracens mass for attack in; 169 Plantamors captured by Arabs in; 175 Cornumarant captured in; 182 Marbrin captured in; 186 Cornumarant describes capture in. Valley between the Temple Mount and the Mount of Olives: site of the Day of Judgement and death place of the Virgin Mary, marked by the church of St Mary in Jehosaphat: Pringle, *Churches* vol.3 pp. 287–306.

Lion Cemetery: 1; 51 Baldwin sets up camp at.

La Mahomerie: 2, 8, 17, 18. Around 15km from Jerusalem; Wilkinson p. 310.

Mount of Caiaphas: 35 Peter the Hermit describes Jerusalem from.

Mount of Calvary: 11; 35 pointed out by Peter the Hermit; 60 Corbadas describes death of Christ; 70 pagans assemble on; 206 Godfrey fights duel with Marbrin at to impress Saracen messenger.

Mount of Olives: 1; 6 *chétifs* appear on; 35 pointed out by Peter the Hermit; 47 Raymond of St-Gilles sets up camp on; 92 falcons pursue doves near; 93 doves released from on second flight; 130–32 home of initially elusive hermit who tells the Crusaders where to find wood for the siege. Separated from Jerusalem by the Valley of Josaphat; identified by Zechariah 14:4–5 as the place where God will start to redeem the dead on the Day of Judgement.

Mount Sion: 1; 35 pointed out by Peter the Hermit; 45 Godfrey sets up camp there. South of Jerusalem; site of the Last Supper and the Dormition of the Virgin.

Pool of Siloam: 1 Crusaders approach; 33–4 Crusaders drink from despite brackishness; 46 Gerard of Gournay and Thomas of Marle to have water from. At the bottom of Mount Sion.

St Mary in the Valley of Josaphat: 2 Christians retreat to.

St Peter of Galilee: 46 near valley of Josaphat.

St Stephen: 42 Crusaders make first contact with Jerusalem; 48 Robert of Normandy sets up camp at; 62 Richard of Chaumont watches; 71 Tafurs halt at; 76 Christian assault launched from; 181 Turks ride to Jerusalem via.

Table of Names and Places 407

Temple of Solomon: 35 pointed out by Peter the Hermit; 40 inhabitants of Jerusalem gather there; 41 Tancred foretells slaughter there; 65 inhabitants gather there; 73 Bishop of Mautran to sing Mass at; 86, 87 inhabitants throng near; 87 captives driven to; 88 pagans assemble near; 94, 95, 96 pagans assemble; 98, 100, 102, 103, 104, 105 Christians look up at; 115 Saracens unwilling to surrender; 117 Saracens assemble at; Corbadas evokes destruction of; 118 Corbadas curses; 140 Ysabars killed as flees to; 142 Godfrey, Thomas of Marle and Robert of Flanders cleanse; 143 caretaker of has sight restored miraculously by Godfrey; 144 women go to; 145, 146 Christians assemble at; 147 Robert of Flanders worships at; 148 and following scene of Bishop of Mautran's attempts to nominate a King of Jerusalem; 154 – 157 miracle of candle to designate King of Jerusalem; 157 Godfrey holds court in; 158, 159 attempts to persuade others to stay in Outremer in front of; 203, 204 Sultan's messenger taken to; 209 shakes with noise of Saracens; 211 Christians assemble in; 212 Annunciation in and Christ presented in; 270 alluded to; 274 treasure shared out in front of; candles carried to; 275, 276, 278 victorious Christians assemble in front of; 279 council of war in front of; 281 another song will talk about founding of Order of. Built by Solomon, destroyed by Nebuchadnezzar II, rebuilt by Herod and destroyed again by the Romans in AD 66. The Crusaders believed the al-Aqsa mosque on the Temple Mount was Solomon's Temple. Pringle, *Churches*, vol.3 pp. 397–417.

Tower of David: 1, 33; 57 three kites shot above; 70 Saracens sound horn from; 75 Lucabel watches from; 76 with Corbadas; 85, 86 Corbadas in; 96 Corbadas and Lucabel in; 105, 109 Corbadas in; 115 Saracens unwilling to surrender; 116 captives released from; 117 Corbadas evokes destruction of; 119 Saracens take up position in front of; 134 Christians raise ladder against; 137 Saracens play loud music from; 140 Corbadas sees fall of Jerusalem from; 141 Raymond of St-Gilles grants Saracens safety in for a mule loaded with bezants; 141 Saracen women flee towards and raped; 143 siege engine in front of; Corbadas in; 157 Godfrey's residence in; 163 Corbadas describes loss of; 165 messenger finds Godfrey in; 169 Cornumarant to be hung in front of; 180 Cornumarant imprisoned in; 186 Marbrin imprisoned in; 189 Godfrey goes up into to pray; 201 Marbrin captive in; 216 horn blown from to give signal for battle of Ascalon. Originally Herod's citadel; rebuilt by Byzantines and Muslims over the years

Elsewhere in Outremer

Acre: 51 Baldwin will send expedition to; 86 Christian threat to; 157, 158 needs to be conquered to assure future of Outremer; 175 Turks send letters to but to little avail as inhabitants have fled; 181 news of Sultan's arrival; 234, 238 din of battle can be heard all the way to; 266 Caliph flees to; 268 Sultan flees towards; 269 Raimbaut Creton and Baldwin fight near; 271, 272 lords head for his rescue at; 22 Saracens set sail from in defeat leaving a garrison; 276 Christians will take ship from; 277 Hugh would seek vengeance all the way to; 278 no Arabs left between it and Jerusalem; 279 decide to make for and attack Saracens; 281 another song will talk about taking of. Classical Ptolemais. Capital of Outremer after the fall of Jerusalem; finally lost in 1291 to the Mameluks.

Anatolia: 41 ride through evoked by Tancred.

Antioch: 40 Bohemond alludes to suffering at and conquest of; 42 Hugh's horse taken at; 43 Jerusalem stronger than; 59 taking of alluded to; 59, 70 Godfrey's domain will stretch as far as; 146 Holy Lance of; 149 Bohemond holds but says willing to cede to Raymond of St-Gilles; 164 Turks intend to win back; 218 allusion to Robert of Normandy killing Red Lion at; 220 allusion to Hugh of Vermandois killing Soliman at.

Armenia: 198 birthplace of Peter the Hermit (by mistake for Amiens).

Ascalon: 18 messengers sent to; 20, 22 send reinforcements; 43 Jerusalem stronger than; 86 Christian threat to; 157, 158 needs to be conquered to assure future of Outremer. Biblical Ashkelon.

Avalon: 43 Jerusalem stronger than. Possibly medieval Avlona, modern Vlone in Albania.

Banyas: 158 needs to be conquered to assure future of Outremer; 175 Saracens send letters to but to little avail as inhabitants have fled. Classical Caesarea Philippi, medieval Belinas, Arabic Baniyas.

Bethlehem: 50 Tancred and Bohemond set up camp on road to; 92 Christian army at; 131–3 Crusaders told they will find timber there and do; 149 Bishop of Mautran suggests Bohemond should hold; 152 taken by Crusaders; 167 Jesus from; 212 Christ born in; 213 army takes up quarters in; 214 hear Mass at before battle.

Bilbais, Barbais: 69 loss of evoked; 125 Cornumarant makes for; 129 Dodequin of Damascus to provision castle at; 144 Corbadas rides to having lost Jerusalem; 158 needs to be conquered to assure future of Outremer; 163 Cornumarant meets Corbadas at; 175 Saracens have sent wealth to for safe keeping; 175 Corbadas there; 176 battle at; 180 Saracens head for. Arabic Bilbis.

Caesarea: 18 – 28 Crusaders attack and fight near; 175 Saracens send letters to but to little avail as inhabitants have fled; 181 news of Sultan's arrival; 276 Christians will capture; 277 Christians ride to; 278 leave stocks in. Arabic Qaisariyah. Taken by the Crusaders in 1101, lost and recaptured, then retaken by Louis IX in 1251; lost to Baybars 1261.

Calençon: 51 Baldwin will send foragers to; 175 Saracens send letters to; 276 Christians will capture; 277 Christians ride between it and Jaffa; 278 leave stocks in. Unidentified: found only here. Moisan vol.2 p. 1090.

Cantari: 276 Hugh suggests Christians go to. Unidentified: found only here. Moisan vol.2 p. 1093.

Carkarie: 175 inhabitants have fled. A number of variants.

Castle of Lord Gaston: 131, 132 Crusaders told they will find timber there and do.

Damascus: 63 evoked by Cornumarant; 69 loss of evoked; 86 Christian threat to; 89 letters sent to; 94 letters from inhabitants of forged by Bishop of Mautran;

Table of Names and Places 409

158 needs to be conquered to assure future of Outremer; 166, 171 invoked; 175 Saracens have sent wealth to for safe keeping; 181 news of Sultan's arrival; 196, 239, 262 evoked by Cornumarant; 199 Sultan promises to Peter the Hermit if he apostatises.

Dead Sea: 155 as part of Outremer.

Duras: 43 Jerusalem stronger than. Modern Durres in Albania, classical Dyrrachium.

Galilee: 155 Godfrey to be lord of; 160, 161 Crusaders set up camp at Lake of Galilee.

Garden of St Abraham: 148, 149, 158 Crusaders have gathered palms in before return to the West; 157 branch brought from to crown Godfrey. Pringle, *Secular Buildings* 19, 99–101, identifies with Ain Duq and Tawahin as-Sukkar near Jericho.

Golfier's castle near Caesarea: 23.

Jaffa: 23, 24 Turks from; 51 Baldwin will send foragers to; 216 vanguard of army sent to; 224 earth rings all the way to; 276 Christians will capture; 277 ride between it and Calencon; 278 leave stocks in. Port dating back to Solomon; suburb of Tel Aviv.

Le Colant: 158 needs to be conquered to assure future of Outremer. Unidentified: found only here. Moisan vol.2 p. 1115. Variants suggest the scribes were uncertain about this name.

Merle: 18. Fortress between Caesarea and Haifa: found only here: Moisan vol.2 p. 1245. Pringle, *Secular Buildings* identifies this as Tantura (no.218 p. 99) some 12km north of Caesarea on the coast.

Mirabel: 21, 28 Crusaders ride past on way to and from battle. Pringle, *Secular Buildings*, identifies as castle of Mahdal Yaba about 25km inland from Jaffa (no 144, pp.67–9).

Montjoie: 31–3 first sight of Jerusalem for Crusade army. See Wilkinson pp. 90, 310. Pringle, *Churches*, vol. 2 p. 44: 'the term is commonly used in other medieval contexts both of hills on which there were saints' tombs and of stone cairns piled up by pious pilgrims'.

Mount Sinai: 14 where Baldwin of Beauvais' sword forged.

Nablus: 51 road of. Classical Neopolis, Arabic Nabulus.

Nazareth: 21 Syrians of serve at St George of Ramleh; 51 Baldwin will march towards.

Nicaea: 59 taking of alluded to; 164 Turks intend to win back.

Persia: 121 for comparison.

Qualquere: 175 Saracens send letters to. Unidentified: found only here. Moisan vol.2 p. 1336. Possibly to be identified with Calkerie.

Ramla, also Rama or Rames; Arabic ar-Ramlah: 165 Christian army to be driven to plains of; 174 pagans flee to; 175 pagans defeated on; 181 Turks come from; 185, 186 Sultan's army camped 10 leagues from; 187, 189 Saracens ride towards; 210 Saracens retreat to plains of; 213 battle arranged on plains of; 217, 218, 219, 220, 221, 222, 223 Christians ride to plains of; 224 earth rings all the way to; 235, 236, 238 ferocious battle on; 251 plains shake with force of battle; 253 noise of Sultan's army heard all the way to; 254 Sultan lays out treasure on to tempt Christians; 265 Christians forced back to plains of; 268 plains stream with blood; 271 Godfrey catches Baldwin's horse on; 272 cloud of dust over; 277 Christians ride to; 278 Christian corpses carried off plain of by lion.

Red Sea: 162 far-flung part of Saracen territory; 248 Cornicas from.

River Jordan: 158 pilgrims not able to bathe in if Outremer not secure; 187, 210, 213 Christian army has crossed returning to Jerusalem.

River Robanos: 20. Most manuscripts read Libanos.

St George of Ramla: 20, 21: army assembles there and does penance; 25 take stand at; 27, 28 battle at; 247 din of beaked adversaries can be heard all the way to; 277 Christians ride to. The Cathedral Church of St George was at Lydda, some 4 km from Ramla. It was built on the spot where the saint was supposedly martyred and in its original form dated back to the sixth century; Pringle, *Churches*, vol.2 pp. 9–27.

Sinai: 39 alluded to by Robert of Flanders.

Spring of the Dead: 51 Baldwin will bring water from.

Syria: 135 Stephen of Albemarle's horse from; 155 fief of.

Three Shadows: 238 Virgin rested there in the heat and prayed for shade, which was granted by God; Robert of Normandy surrounded there; 239, 241 Saracens pushed back to; 263 Baldwin kills Cornumarant at. The Abbey of St Mary of the Three Shades was situated between Lydda and Ramla: Pringle, *Churches* vol.2 p. 258.

Tiberias: 48 Robert of Normandy sends foragers to; 69 loss of evoked; 86 Christian threat to; 89 to send reinforcements; 129 Dodequin of Damascus to provision castle at; 158 needs to be taken to assure future of Outremer; 160 Crusaders attack Dodequin of Damascus at but abandon assault; 166 invoked; 181 news of Sultan's arrival; 239, 262 invoked by Cornumarant; 281 another song will talk about taking of. Founded by Herod Antipas; taken 1099 and subsequently lost to Saladin.

Tower of Flies: 18. Pringle, *Secular Buildings* pp. 16–17: tower at the east end of the mole of Acre.

Tyre, Arabic Sur: 51 Baldwin will send foragers to; 86 Christian threat to; 89 to send reinforcements; 157, 158 needs to be conquered to assure future of Outremer; 181 news of Sultan's arrival; 281 another song will talk about taking of.

Saracen places

Abilant: 187 Sultan's tent made in deserts of; 220, 221 Sultan will send Christian captives to repopulate. All-purpose Saracen location: Moisan vol.2 pp. 997–8. See under Table of Places for *Chanson des Chétifs*.

Afain: 228 Saracen forces from. Found in some other sources: Moisan vol.2 p. 1032.

Alenie: 264 Godfrey's horse from. A few references elsewhere: Moisan vol.2 p. 1007.

Almeria: 119 Saracen territory; 181 cloth from. Common Saracen name: Moisan vol.2 pp. 1032–3.

Arabia: 178, 187 gold of.

Arbrin: 228 Saracen forces from. One other reference in *Foucon de Candie*: Moisan vol.2 p. 1021.

Arthur's Wood: 205 marker of Saracen territory. Moisan vol.1 p. 178 for similar references.

Babylon: 91 Sultan in.

Baghdad, Baudarie: 235 evoked by Acéré; 255 Godfrey will be taken to as captive.

Betean Sea: 90 marks extent of Saracen lands. Moisan vol.2 p. 1062; frozen or Arctic sea.

Beton, valley of: 66 evoked. Moisan vol.2 p. 1441; one other reference as a Saracen name in *Maugis d'Aigremont* but more often site of battle between Girart de Roussillon and King Charles.

Bocidant: 226 black Saracens from; 250 men from described. In Persia: Moisan vol.2 p. 1069.

Buriaigne: 249 Saracens from. All-purpose Saracen name: Moisan vol.2 p. 1084.

Carthage: 202 silk coat of Sultan's horse worked in.

Dry or Withered Tree (Arbol Sec): 93, 119 Saracen boundary. Some other references; held by Saracens. Moisan vol.2 p. 1400. Jean Bodel's *Jeu de St Nicolas* has the Amiraus d'outre l'Arbre Sec as a character: *Le Jeu de Saint Nicolas*, (ed.) Warne, note to line 333: the legend was that an oak was blighted when Christ was crucified and would bear fresh leaves only when Mass was said under it by a Western prince once the Holy Land had been freed.

Esclavonia: 181 Sultan's army from. Country of the Slavs. Commonly found: Moisan vol.2 p. 1144.

France: 230 rather unlikely Saracen kingdom of.

Greater Africa: 244 Hugh more pleased to find his son's killer than if given lordship over.

Guinesbals: 65 Saracen empire will extend to. Found only here: Moisan vol.2 p. 1187.

Loquifer: 252 Sultan's sword forged in mountains of by a devil.

Land of the giant Loquifer: Moisan vol.2 p. 1223.

Lucion: 230 Saracens from mountains of. As Saracen name only here and in *Maugis d'Aigremont*: Moisan vol.2 p. 1225.

Luitis: 115 Saracen city marking bounds of territory. Commonly found: Moisan vol.2 p. 1227.

Majols: 228 Saracen forces from.

Mecca: 118 far point of Saracen territory; 178 Mahommed put in coffin there; 204 Godfrey aims to conquer; 208 Saracen messenger passes on his threat to conquer.

Moriaigne: 249 Saracens from; also Moriant 226, 252. Country of the Moors: Moisan vol.2 pp. 1272–3.

Nubia: 265 Plantamor the horse from.

Oliferne: 6 Saracen city, commonly associated with Corbaran: Moisan vol.2 p. 1297.

Oper: 227 Saracen forces from. Found only here: Moisan vol.2 p. 1298.

Orcanie: 2, 238 Saracen horse from. Commonly found: Moisan vol.2 pp. 1300–01. Possibly distorted version of Hyrcania.

Orfeis, island of: 61 Cornumarant's sword forged on. Found only here: Moisan vol.2 p. 1302.

Orient: 204 offered to Godfrey by Sultan; 231 Saracen forces from.

Persia: 204 Godfrey threatens to conquer.

Pré Noiron: 66 evoked; 147, 148 as marker of Saracen territory; 180 all the gold of. The Gardens of Nero at Rome, where St Peter was tortured and the Vatican built. Commonly referred to. Moisan vol.2 pp. 1288–9.

Quenelongne: 91 Saracen territory. Caneloigne, land of the Kenelius: Moisan vol.1 p. 286, vol.2 p. 1093.

Red Sea: 209 emir from beyond; 227 Bomers from beyond; 274 killer of Enguerrand of St-Pol to be sought as far as.

Rubion: 242 Saracens from mountains of. Identity unclear.

Rusia: 166 Plantamor Cornumarant's horse, from; 176 Corbadas' mule from; 264 Baldwin's horse Cornu from. Russia, seen generally as pagan land: Moisan vol.2 p. 1359.

Sarmasane: 129 Cornumarant finds court of Sultan at. Modern Kermanchah in Iran; found largely in Crusade epics. Moisan vol.2 p. 1410.

Siglaie: 210 ferocious soldiers from attack Jerusalem; 224 forces from; 272 Saracens sail to. Byblos, modern Djebail in Lebanon. Moisan vol.2 p. 1405.

Silver Bridge: 91 King Abraham from; 129 Cornumarant rides past on his way to Persia; 184 marker of Saracen territory. Found only in the central trilogy: Moisan vol.2 p. 1024. Thorp suggests this may echo the Pons Ferreus at Antioch.

Split Tree (l'Arbre qui Fent): 91 Saracens come to once a year to be rejuvenated. Fantasy location in the East: Moisan vol.2 p. 1020.

Tabais: 227 Saracen soldiers from. Unidentified.

Urgalie: 218 marker of Saracen territory (formulaic). A few references: Moisan vol.2 p. 1438. Variants suggest the scribes were uncertain about the name.

Places in the West

Aix-la-Chapelle: 199 Peter the Hermit will be crowned at by Sultan once France successfully invaded.

Apulia: 129 Sultan threatens to invade; 149 Bohemond's fief; 221 Bohemond and Tancred from.

Aragon: 22 horse from; 113 mule from; 121, 125, 128, 237 Count Baldwin's horse Prinsaut from; 180 mules from; 202 Sultan's horse from; 225 Sultan's sons' warhorses from; 276 Hugh of St-Pol's horse from.

Table of Names and Places 413

Arie, wood of: 39 evoked by Robert of Flanders.
Arras: 4; 39, 147 evoked by Robert of Flanders; 68 engineer Gregory from.
Arthur's Wood: 123 Saracens will invade as far as.
Bavaria: 235 Godfrey will regret having left.
Beneventum: 62 gold of (formulaic).
Bouillon: 87 captives from.
Brittany: 181 Sultan's robe worth as much as.
Calabria: 149 Bohemond's fief.
Castile: 256 Bohemond's horse from.
Clermont in the Auvergne: 255 Corbadas kills Christian from.
Cornwall: 77, 195 evoked (formulaic).
Dijon: 87 captives from.
Duras: 69, 107, 132 engineer Nicolas from. Attested as Durres in modern Albania. It is not clear why Nicolas would come from here. The first reference has Dinas in the base manuscript, suggesting some confusion. There is a small village called Dury some 10km from Arras, where his co-engineer Gregory was from: possibly a garbled form of that?
Flanders: 147 evoked by Robert of Flanders.
France: 129, 180 Saracens threaten to invade; 186, 187 Saracen domination of threatened; 189 nobility of invoked; 199 Sultan threatens to invade; 203 nobody there rich enough to buy breastplate with amazing qualities; 204, armies of; 268, 269 lords of.
Hungary: 181 Sultan's robe worth as much as.
Montagu (?): 279 Baldwin would rather have gained than kill Cornumarant.
Montpellier: 203 fief of (formulaic).
Niepe, hunting grounds of: 39 evoked by Robert of Flanders.
Nijmegen: 217 mentioned in connection with Swan Knight.
Pavia: 80, 108 helmets from (formulaic); 129 Sultan will launch attack on Europe from; 181 Sultan's hood worth more than.
Pithiviers: 203 fief of (formulaic).
River Rhine: 67 evoked; 228 Saracen horse swims better than any fish in.
Rouen: 67 coin of; 148 evoked by Robert of Normandy.
Romania: 100 formulaic; 129 Sultan threatens to invade.
Sainteron: 87 captives from. Possibly St-Trond in Belgium: Moisan vol.2 p. 1386.
Saragossa: 55 Cornumarant's sword from; 61 his helmet from.
Slavonia: 108 formulaic.
Spain: 252 Sultan's armour could not be bought for half the price of.
Valenciennes: 87 captives from.
Valgree: 213 horse of Rotrou of la Perche from (formulaic). Found only here: Moisan vol.2 p. 1449.

Bibliography

A full bibliography can be found in the companion volume, *The Chanson d'Antioche*. This bibliography includes only works cited in this book.

Editions in chronological order

La Chanson des Chétifs:
La Chanson du Chevalier au Cygne et de Godefroid de Bouillon, (ed.) Célestin Hippeau, 2 vols (Paris: Aubry, 1874–77)
The Chanson des Chétifs: an Old French Crusade Epic, Lucy Wenhold (University of Chapel Hill, North Carolina, 1928)
Les Chétifs, (ed.) Geoffrey Myers, *The Old French Crusade Cycle* vol. 5 (Tuscaloosa: University of Alabama, 1981)
La Chanson de Jérusalem:
La Conquête de Jérusalem, faisant suite à la Chanson d'Antioche, composée par le Pèlerin Richard et renouvelée par Graindor de Douai au XIIIe siècle, (ed.) Célestin Hippeau, 2 vols (Paris, 1868; reprinted Geneva 1969)
La Chanson de Jérusalem, (ed.) Nigel Thorp, *The Old French Crusade Cycle* vol. 6 (Tuscaloosa: University of Alabama, 1992)

Reference works

Baldwin and Setton: Gazetteer in *The First Hundred Years*, (ed.) Marshall Baldwin pp.626–66 in *A History of the Crusades* (ed.) Marshall Baldwin and Kenneth Setton, second edition, 6 vols, (Madison: University of Wisconsin, 1969–89)
Du Cange, Charles, *Glossarium mediae et infimae latinitatis*, 6 vols (Paris, 1840–48)
Hindley, Alan; Langley, Frederick; and Levy, Brian, *Old French-English Dictionary* (Cambridge: Cambridge University Press, 2000)
Moisan, André, *Répertoire des noms propres de personnes et de lieux cités dans les chansons de geste francaises et les oeuvres étrangères dérivées*, 5 vols (Geneva: Droz, 1986)
Murray, Alan, *The Crusader Kingdom of Jerusalem: a dynastic history 1099–1115* Prosopographica et Genealogica (Oxford: Unit for Prosopographical Research, 2000)
Pringle, Denys, *Churches of the Crusader kingdom of Jerusalem: an archaeological gazetteer*, 4 vols, (Cambridge: Cambridge University Press, 1993–2009)

_____ *Secular buildings in the Crusader kingdom of Jerusalem: an archaeological gazetteer*, (Cambridge: Cambridge University Press, 1997)

Riley-Smith, Jonathan, *The First Crusaders, 1095–1131* (Cambridge: Cambridge University Press, 1997)

Robert, Paul and Rey, Alain, *Le Grand Robert de la langue française*, 9 vols, (Paris: Le Robert, 1985)

Seigneuret, Jean-Charles, *Dictionary of literary themes and motifs*, (ed.) Jean-Charles Seigneuret, 2 vols, (New York, Westport, London: Greenwood, 1988)

Tobler, Adolf, *Altfranzösisches Wörterbuch: Adolf Toblers nachgelassene Materialien/ bearbeitet und herausgegeben von Erhard Lommatzsch; weitergeführt von Hans Helmut Christmann*, 11 vols (Berlin: Weidmann, 1925–2002) [T-L]

Wilkinson, John with Joyce Hill and W. F. Ryan, *Jerusalem Pilgrimage 1099–1185*, (London: Hakluyt Society, 1988)

The Old French Crusade Cycle

The Old French Crusade Cycle, (ed.) Jan A. Nelson and Emanuel J. Mickel, 10 vols (Tuscaloosa: University of Alabama, 1977–2003)

I: *La Naissance du Chevalier au Cygne* and *Elioxe*, (ed.) Emanuel J. Mickel; *Beatrix*, (ed.) Jan A. Nelson (1977)

II: *Le Chevalier au Cygne* and *La Fin d'Elias*, (ed.) Jan A. Nelson (1985)

III: *Les Enfances Godefroi* and *Retour de Cornumarant*, (ed.) Emanuel J. Mickel (1999)

IV: *La Chanson d'Antioche*, (ed.) Jan A. Nelson (2003)

V: *Les Chétifs*, (ed.) Geoffrey M. Myers (1981)

VI: *La Chanson de Jérusalem* (ed.) Nigel R. Thorp (1992)

VII: *The Jerusalem continuations*: Part 1: *La Chrétienté Corbaran*, (ed.) Peter R. Grillo (1984); Part 2, *La Prise d'Acre, La Mort Godefroi* and *La Chanson des Rois Baudouin*, (ed.) Peter R. Grillo (1987)

VIII: *The Jerusalem continuations: the London-Turin version*, (ed.) Peter R. Grillo (1994)

IX: *La Geste du Chevalier au Cygne*, (ed.) Edmond A. Emplaincourt (1989)

X: *Godefroi de Bouillon*, (ed.) Jan B. Roberts (1996)

There are two modern editions of the *Chanson d'Antioche*:

La Chanson d'Antioche, (ed.) Suzanne Duparc-Quioc, 2 vols (Paris: Geuthner, 1976, 1978); vol. I, *Edition*; vol. II, *Etude*.

La Chanson d'Antioche: chanson de geste du dernier quart du XIIe siècle, (ed.) and transl. Bernard Guidot (Paris: Champion, 2011)

English translation: *The Chanson d'Antioche: an Old French account of the First Crusade, Crusade Texts in Translation* 22, transl. Susan B. Edgington and Carol E. Sweetenham (Farnham, Burlington: Ashgate, 2011)

Primary sources: Latin

The nineteenth century *Recueil* remains a useful if by now elderly resource:
Recueil des historiens des croisades: historiens occidentaux, 5 vols (Paris, 1844–96): abbreviated as *RHC.Occ*
Albericus Trium Fontium, (ed.) P. Scheffer-Boïchorst, *Monumenta Germaniae Historica, Scriptores* XXIIII
Albert of Aachen, *Historia Ierosolimitana: History of the Journey to Jerusalem*, (ed.) and transl. Susan B. Edgington (Oxford: Oxford University Press, 2007)
The Douce Apocalypse, presented Nigel Morgan (Oxford: Bodleian Library, 2007)
Baldric of Bourgueil, Historia Jerosolimitana, (ed.) Steven Biddlecombe (Woodbridge: Boydell and Brewer, 2014)
Bestiary: Manuscript Bodley 764, presented Richard Barber (Woodbridge: Boydell and Brewer, 1999)
Fulcher of Chartres, *Historia Hierosolymitana (1095–1127)*, (ed.) Heinrich Hagenmeyer (Heidelberg: Carl Winter, 1913)
Gesta Francorum et aliorum Hierosolimitanorum, (ed.) Rosalind Hill (Nelson, 1962)
Geoffrey of Vigeois, *Chronica Gaufredi coenobitae*, (ed.) Philippe Labbé, *Novae Bibliothecae Manuscript librorum: Rerum Aquitanicarum praesertim Bituricensium uberrima collectio*, II, 1657, 279–342
Gilo of Paris, Historia Vie Hierosolimitanae, ed. and transl. Chris W Grocock and J. Elizabeth Siberry (Oxford: Oxford University Press, 1997)
Guibert of Nogent, *Autobiographie* (ed.) and transl. Edmond-René Labande (Paris: Champion, 1981)
_____*Dei gesta per Francos* (ed.) Robert B. C. Huygens, CCCM 127A (Turnhout: Brepols, 1996)
Historia de expeditione Friderici imperatoris (*MGH SRG* 5 (Berlin, 1928)
Jacques de Vitry, *Histoire orientale: historia orientalis*, (ed.) and transl. J. Donnadieu (Turnhout: Brepols, 2008)
Lambert of Ardres, *Chronique de Guines et d'Ardres*, (ed.) D. C. Godefroy-Ménilglaise (Paris, 1855); transl. Leah Shopkow, *The History of the Counts of Guines and Lords of Ardres* (Philadelphia: University of Pennsylvania, 2001)
Metellus of Tegernsee, *Expeditio Hierosolymitana*, (ed.) Peter C. Jacobsen (Stuttgart: Hiersemann, 1982)
The Ecclesiastical History of Orderic Vitalis, (ed.) and transl. Marjorie Chibnall, 6 vols (Oxford: Clarendon Press, 1969–80)
Otto of Freising's *Chronica sive Historia de Duabus Civitatibus*, (ed.) A. Hofmeister, *MGH Scriptores rerum Germanicorum* 45 (Hannover,1912); *The Two Cities: a chronicle of universal history to the year 1146 AD by Otto, Bishop of Freising*, transl. Charles Christopher Mierow (New York: Octagon, 1966)
Ovid, *Metamorphoses* VI.1–145, (ed.) Donald E. Hill, 4 vols (Warminster: Aris and Phillips, 1985–2000)

Peter Tudebode, *Historia de Hierosolymitano Itinere*, (ed.) John H. and Laurita L. Hill (Paris: Paul Geuthner, 1977)

Radulphi Cadomensis Tancredus (ed.) Edoardo d'Angelo (Turnhout: Brepols, 2011)

Le 'liber' de Raymond d'Aguilers, (ed.) John H. and Laurita L. Hill (Paris: Paul Geuthner, 1969)

The Deeds of Count Roger of Calabria and Sicily and of his brother Robert Guiscard, transl. Kenneth B. Wolf (Ann Arbor: University of Michigan Press, 2005)

Robert the Monk: *The 'Historia Iherosolimitana' of Robert the Monk*, (ed.) Damien Kempf and Marcus Bull (Woodbridge: Boydell and Brewer, 2013); transl. Carol Sweetenham, *Robert the Monk's History of the First Crusade* (Aldershot: Ashgate, 2005)

Suger: *Vie de Louis VI le Gros*, (ed.) Henri Waquet (Paris: Champion, 1964)

Walter the Chancellor's 'The Antiochene Wars': a translation and commentary, Thomas S. Asbridge and Susan B. Edgington (Guildford: Ashgate, 1999)

William of Malmesbury, *Gesta Regum Anglorum*, (ed.) and transl. Roger Mynors, completed Rodney M. Thomas and Michael Winterbottom, 2 vols (Oxford: Clarendon Press, 1998–99)

William of Tyre, *Chronicon*, (ed.) Robert B. C. Huygens, CCCM63, 2 vols (Turnhout: Brepols, 1986)

See also the collection of Crusade letters translated by Malcom Barber and Keith Bate: *Letters from the East: crusaders, pilgrims and settlers in the twelfth and thirteenth centuries*, (Aldershot: Ashgate, 2010). Latin texts in Heinrich Hagenmeyer, *Die Kreuzzugsbriefe aus den Jahren 1088 – 1100* (Innsbruck: Verlag des Wagner'schen Universitätsbuchhandlung, 1901).

Other relevant source material:

Two fifteenth century cookery books, (ed.) Thomas Austin, (Oxford: Oxford University Press, 1888; reprinted Woodbridge: Boydell and Brewer, 2000)

Anglo-Norman Lapidaries (ed.) Paul Studer and Joan Evans (Paris: Champion, 1924)

French and Occitan vernacular texts

Alexandre de Paris: le Roman d'Alexandre, (ed.) Laurence Harf-Lancner (Paris: Champion, 1994)

Aliscans, (ed.) Claude Régnier, 2 vols (Paris: Champion, 1990)

Ambroise, *The History of the Holy War*, transl. Marianne Ailes and Malcolm Barber (Woodbridge: Boydell and Brewer, 2003)

Anseis de Carthage: Anseis von Karthago, (ed.) Johann Alton, Bibliothek des litterarischen Vereins 194 (Tübingen, 1892)

Bataille de Loquifer, (ed.) Monica Barnett (Oxford: Blackwell, 1975)

Canso d'Antioca: an Occitan epic chronicle of the First Crusade, (ed.) and transl. Linda Paterson and Carol Sweetenham (Aldershot: Ashgate, 2003)

Canso de la Crozada: La Chanson de la Croisade Albigeoise, (ed.) Eugène Martin-Chabot, 3 vols, (Paris: Champion, 1931–60); reprinted and transl. Henri. Gougaud, *Chanson de la Croisade Albigeoise* (Paris: Livre de Poche, 1989)

La Chanson d'Aspremont: chanson de geste du XIIe siècle. Texte du manuscrit de Wollaton Hall, (ed.) and transl. Louis A. Brandin (Paris: Champion, 1919)

Cligès, (ed.) and transl. Charles Mela and Olivier Collet in *Chrétien de Troyes: romans*, intro. Jean-Marie Fritz (Paris: Livre de Poche, 1994) 291–494

Couronnement de Louis, (ed.) Ernest Langlois (Paris: Champion, 1925)

La Destruction de Rome: version de Hannovre (ed.) Luciano Formisano and Gianfranco Contini (Florence: Sansoni, 1981)

Enfances Renier, (ed.) Delphine Dalens-Marekovic (Paris: Champion, 2009)

Eracles, RHC.Occ 1–2.

Fierabras, (ed.) Marc Le Person (Paris: Champion, 2003)

The Romance of Flamenca, (ed.) Marion E. Porter, transl. Merton J. Hubert (Princeton: Princeton University Press, 1962)

La Chanson de Girart de Roussillon, (ed.) Winifred M. Hackett, transl. Micheline du Combarieu de Grès and Gérard Gouiran (Paris: Livre de Poche, 1993)

La Chanson de Guillaume, (ed.) and transl. Philip Bennett (London: Grant and Cutler, 2000)

La Gran Conquista de Ultramar, (ed.) Louis Cooper, 4 vols (Bogotá: Institute Caro y Cuervo, 1979)

Guerra de Navarra: Guilhem Anelier de Tolosa: Guerra de Navarra: Nafarroako Gudua, (ed.) Maurice Berthe, Ricardo Cierbide, Xavier Kintana and Julián Santale, 2 vols (Pamplona: Gobierno de Navarra, 1995)

Jeu de St Nicolas, (ed.) Frederick J. Warne (Oxford: Blackwell, 1951)

Jordan Fantosme's Chronicle, (ed.) Ronald C. Johnston (Oxford: Clarendon Press, 1981)

Le Roman de Mahomet, (ed.) and transl. Yves G. Lepage (Louvain/Paris: Peeters, 1996)

Les poésies du Moine de Montaudon, (ed.) Michael Routledge (Montpellier: Université Paul Valéry, 1977)

Le Moniage Guillaume: chanson de geste du XIIe siècle, (ed.) and transl. Nelly Andrieux-Reix (Paris: Champion, 2003)

Moniage Rainouart I (ed.) Gérard A. Bertin (Paris: A. & J. Picard, 1973)

La Prise de Cordres et de Sébille, (ed.) Magali del Vechio-Drion (Paris: Champion, 2011)

Raoul de Cambrai, (ed.) and transl. Sarah Kay (Oxford: Clarendon Press, 1992)

Robert de Clari, *La Conquête de Constantinople*, (ed.) and transl. Peter Noble (Edinburgh: Société Rencesvals, British Branch, 2005)

La Chanson de Roland, (ed.) Ian Short (Paris: Livre de Poche, 1990)

Jean Bodel, *Chanson des Saisnes*, (ed.) Annette Brasseur, 2 vols (Geneva: Droz, 1989)

Simon de Pouille, (ed.) Denis Conlon (Frankfurt-am-Main/Bern/New York: Lang, 1987)

Tristan de Nanteuil: chanson de geste inédite, (ed.) K. V. Sinclair (Gorcum: Assen, 1971)

Geoffroi de Villehardouin, *La Conquête de Constantinople*, (ed.) Edmond Faral, 2 vols (Paris: Belles Lettres, 1961)

The Poetry of William VII, Count of Poitiers, IX Duke of Aquitaine, (ed.) Gerald A. Bond (New York: Garland, 1982)

Other texts

Digenis Akritas: the Grottaferrata and Escorial versions, (ed.) and transl. Elizabeth Jeffreys (Cambridge: Cambridge University Press 1998)

The Damascus Chronicle of the Crusades, selected and transl. H. A. R. Gibb (London: Luzac & Co, 1932)

Ibn al-Athir, *Histoire des atabegs de Mosul, Recueil des Historiens des Croisades: Historiens orientaux*, 5 vols .1872–1906, vol. II, part 2

Secondary works

Aird, William M., *Robert Curthose: Duke of Normandy* (Woodbridge: Boydell and Brewer, 2008)

Alonso, Dámaso 'Estilo y creación en el Poema del Cid', *Ensayos sobre poesía espanola* (Buenos Aires, 1946) pp. 69–111

Andressohn, Joseph C., *The Ancestry and Life of Godfrey of Bouillon* (Bloomington: University of Indiana, 1947)

Asbridge, Thomas, *The First Crusade: a new history* (London: Simon and Schuster, 2004)

―――― *The creation of the Principality of Antioch 1098–1131* (Woodbridge: Boydell and Brewer, 2000)

―――― 'Alice of Antioch: a case study of female power in the twelfth century', in *The Experience of Crusading*, (ed.) Peter Edbury and Jonathan Phillips, 2 vols (Cambridge: Cambridge University Press, 2003), vol. 2 pp. 29–47

Bachrach, David S., *Religion and Conduct of War c.300 – 1215* (Woodbridge: Boydell and Brewer, 2003)

Bancourt, Paul, *Les Musulmans dans les chansons de geste du Cycle du Roi*, 2 vols (Aix-en-Provence: Université de Provence, 1982)

Barber, Peter and Harper, Tom: *Magnificent Maps: Power, Propaganda and Art* (London: British Library, 2010)

Bartlett, Robert, *Trial by Fire and Water: the medieval judicial ordeal*, (Oxford: Clarendon Press, 1986)

Bellos, David, *Is that a fish in your ear? The amazing adventure of translation* (London: Penguin, 2012)

Bennett, Matt, 'The First Crusaders' images of Muslims: the influence of vernacular poetry?' *Forum for Modern Language Studies* 22 (1986) pp. 101–22

Benvenisti, Meron, *The Crusaders in the Holy Land,* (Jerusalem: Israel Universities Press, 1970)

Besamusca, Bart et al., (ed.) *Cyclification: the development of narrative cycles in the chanson de geste and the Arthurian romance*, (Amsterdam: North Holland, 1994)

Blake, E. O. and Morris, Colin, 'A hermit goes to war: Peter and the origins of the First Crusade', *Studies in Church History* 22 (1985) pp. 79–107

Boutet, Dominique, *La chanson de geste* (Paris: PUF, 1993)

Bresc-Bautier, Geneviève, *Le cartulaire du chapitre de St-Sépulchre de Jérusalem* (Paris: Paul Geuthner, 1984)

Brown, Elizabeth and Cothren, Michael 'The twelfth century crusading window of the Abbey of St Denis: *Praeteritorum Enim Recordatio Futurorum Exhibitio*', *Journal of the Courtauld and Warburg Institute* 49 (1986) pp. 1–40

Brundage, James A., 'Adhemar of Puy: the Bishop and his Critics', *Speculum* 34 (1959) pp. 201–12

_____ 'An Errant Crusader: Stephen of Blois', *Traditio* 16 (1960) pp. 380–95

Bull, Marcus, 'The Capetian Monarchy and the Early Crusade movement: Hugh of Vermandois and Louis VII', *Nottingham Medieval Studies* 40 (1996) pp. 25–46

Burnett, Charles, 'Antioch as a Link between Arabic and Latin Culture in the Twelfth and Thirteenth Centuries', in *Occident et Proche-Orient: contacts scientifiques au temps des croisades*, (eds) A. Tihon, I. Draclants & B. van den Abeele, (Louvain-la-Neuve, 2000) pp. 1–78

Cahen, Claude, *La Syrie du Nord à l'époque des croisades et la principauté franque d'Antioche*, (Paris: Paul Geuthner, 1940)

Ciggaar, Krijnie, 'Manuscripts as intermediaries: the Crusader states and international cross-fertilisation', *East and West in the Crusader states: context – contacts – confrontations*, (ed.) Krijnie Ciggaar, Adelbert Davids and Herman Teule, Orientalia Lovaniensia Analecta 75 (Leuven: Uitgeverij Peeters, 1996) pp. 131–51

Clanchy, Michael, *From Memory to Written Record: England 1066- 1307*, second edition, (Oxford: Clarendon, 1993)

Clark, Alan, *Diaries: In Power 1983–92*, 3 vols, (London: Phoenix, 1994)

Constable, Giles, 'The three lives of Odo Arpinus: Viscount of Bourges, Crusader, monk of Cluny', *Crusaders and Crusading in the twelfth century*, G. Constable (Guildford: Ashgate, 2008) pp. 215–28

Cook, Robert, *Chanson d'Antioche, chanson de geste: le cycle de la croisade est-il épique?* (Amsterdam: Benjamins, 1980)

_____ 'Crusade propaganda in the epic cycles of the crusade', in *Journeys towards God: pilgrimage and crusade,* (ed.) Barbara N. Sargent-Baur (Kalamazoo:

Medieval Institute Publications University of Western Michigan, 1992) pp. 157–75

Cowdrey, Herbert E., 'Martyrdom and the First Crusade', *Crusade and settlement: papers read at the first conference of the SSCLE and presented to R. C. Smail*, (ed.) Peter Edbury (Cardiff: University of Cardiff Press, 1985) pp. 46–56

Damian-Grint, Peter, *The New Historians of the Twelfth-Century Renaissance: Inventing Vernacular Authority* (Woodbridge: Boydell and Brewer, 1999)

Daniel, Norman, *Heroes and Saracens: an interpretation of the chansons de geste* (Edinburgh: Edinburgh University Press, 1984)

_____ *Islam and the West: the making of an image* (Oxford: Oneworld, 1993)

Duby, George, *Le dimanche de Bouvines* (Paris: Gallimard, 1985, reprinted Folio histoire)

Duggan, Joseph, 'The manuscript corpus of the Medieval Romance epic', in *The medieval Alexander legend in Romance epic: essays in honour of David J. A. Ross*, (ed.) Peter Noble, Claire Isoz and Lucie Polak (New York: Kraus, 1982)

Dunbabin, Jean, *Captivity and Imprisonment in medieval Europe c.1000 – c.1300* (London: Palgrave McMillan, 2003

Duparc-Quioc, Susanne, *Le Cycle de la Croisade* (Paris: Champion, 1955)

Edgington, Susan B., 'Antioch: Medieval City of Culture', in *East and West in the Medieval Eastern Mediterranean I: Antioch from the Byzantine Reconquest until the End of the Crusader Principality*, (eds) K. Ciggaar & M. Metcalf (Leuven, 2006) pp. 247–59

_____ 'The doves of war: the part played by carrier pigeons in the crusades', *Autour de la première croisade: Actes du colloque du SSCLE, Clermont-Ferrand 22–25 juin 1995*, (ed.) M. Balard (Paris: Sorbonne, 1996) pp. 167–75

Emmerson, Richard, *Antichrist in the Middle Ages: a study of Medieval Apolacypticism, Art and Literature*, (Manchester: Manchester University Press, 1981)

Farnsworth, William, *Uncle and Nephew in the Old French chansons de geste* (New York: Columbia University Press, 1913)

Flori, Jean, 'Lexicologie et société médiévale: les "barons" de la première croisade (Etude des termes "baron", "barnage", "barné", baronie" dans la *Chanson d'Antioche*)', *Actes du XIe congrès international de la Société Rencesvals, Barcelone, 22–27 août 1988*, (Barcelona: Real Academia de Buenas Letras, 1990) pp. 245–73

_____ 'Un problème de méthodologie; la valeur des nombres chez les chroniqueurs du Moyen Age (A propos des éffectifs de la première croisade)', *Moyen Age* 99 (1993) pp. 399–422

_____ *Bohemond d'Antioche, chevalier d'aventure* (Paris: Payot, 2007)

_____ *Pierre l'Ermite et la première Croisade*, (Paris: Fayard, 1999)

Fossier, Robert, *La terre et les hommes en Picardie*, 2 vols (Paris: Béatrice-Nauweaerts, 1968)

France, John, 'An unknown account of the capture of Jerusalem', *English Historical Review* 87 (1972) pp. 771–83
_____ 'The Crisis of the First Crusade: from the defeat of Kerbogha to the departure from Arqa', *Byzantion* 40 (1970) pp. 276–308
_____ *Victory in the East: a military history of the First Crusade* (Cambridge: Cambridge University Press, 1994)
Frantz, Alison, 'Akritas and the dragons', *Hesperia* X.i (1941) pp. 9–13
Friedman, John Block, *The Monstrous Races in Medieval Art and Thought*, (New York: Syracuse University Press, 2000)
Friedman, Yvonne, *Encounter between Enemies: captivity and ransom in the Latin kingdom of Jerusalem* (Leiden/Boston/Cologne: Brill, 2002)
Frolow, Anatole, *La rélique de la Vraie Croix: recherches sur le développement d'un culte*, (Institut français d'études Byzantines, 1961)
Gally, Michèle 'Poésie en jeu: des jeux-parties aux fatras', in *Arras au Moyen Age: Histoire et Littérature*, (ed.) M-M. Castellani and J-P Martin (Arras: Presses Universitaires d'Artois, 1994) pp. 71–80
Glaesener, Henri, 'Godefroid de Bouillon était-il un médiocre?' *Revue d'Histoire Ecclésiastique* 39 (1943) pp. 309–41
Grillo, Peter, 'Les rédactions de la *Chrétienté Corbaran*, première branche des continuations du Cycle de la Croisade', *Au Carrefour des routes d'Europe: la chanson de geste. Xe congrès international de la société Rencesvals, Strasbourg 1985* (Aix-en-Provence, 1987) pp. 585–600
Hamilton, Bernard, *The Latin Church in the Crusader States; the secular church* (London: Variorum, 1980)
_____ 'Aimery of Limoges Patriarch of Antioch, ecumenist scholar and patron of hermits', in *The Joy of Learning and the Love of God: studies in honor of Jean Leclercq*, (ed.) F. Rozanne Elder, *Cistercian Studies* series 160 (Kalamazoo, Michigan and Spencer, Massachusetts, 1995) pp. 269–90
_____ 'Ralph of Domfront, Patriarch of Antioch (1135–40)', *Nottingham Medieval Studies* 28 (1984) pp. 1–21
Hammond, Peter, *Food and Feast in medieval England* (Stroud: Alan Sutton, 1993)
Harvey, P. D. A., *Mappa Mundi: the Hereford World Map*, (Hereford: Hereford Cathedral, 2010)
Hatem, Anouar, *Les poèmes épiques des croisades: génèse–historicité–localisation* (Paris: Paul Geuthner, 1932)
Heintze, Michael 'Les techniques de la formation de cycles dans les chansons de geste' in *Cyclification*, (ed.) Besamusca, pp. 21–58
Hibbard-Loomis, Laura, 'L'oriflamme de France et le cri Munjoie au douzième siècle', *Moyen Age* 14 (1959) pp. 469–99
Hiestand, Rudolph, 'Un centre intellectual en Syrie du Nord? Notes sur la personnalité d'Aimeri d'Antioche, Albert de Tarse et Rorgo Fretellus', *Moyen Age* series 5 vol. 8 (1994) pp. 7–36
John H. and Laurita. L. Hill, 'Contemporary Accounts and the Later Reputation of Adhemar, Bishop of Le Puy', *Medieval History* 9 (1955) pp. 30–38

_____ *Raymond IV* (New York, 1962)

Hodgson, Natasha, 'The role of Kerbogha's mother in the *Gesta Francorum* and other selected chronicles of the First Crusade', in *Gendering the Crusades* (ed.) S.Lambert and S. B Edgington (Cardiff: Cardiff University Press, 2001) pp. 163–76

Holmes, Urban T. and Mcleod, Wendell M. 'Source problems of the *Chétifs*, a Crusade chanson de geste', *Romanic Review* 28 (1937) pp. 99–108

Jacoby, David, 'Society, Culture and the Arts in Crusader Acre', in *France and the Holy Land: Frankish Culture at the end of the Crusades*, (ed.) Daniel H. Weiss and Lisa Mahoney (Baltimore and London: Johns Hopkins University Press, 2004) pp. 97–137

Janet, Magali, 'Les scènes de cannibalisme aux abords d'Antioche dans les récits de la première croisade: des chroniques à la chanson de croisade', *Bien dire et bien aprandre* 22 (2004) pp. 179–91

Jeffreys, Elizabeth, 'The Comnenian background to the "romans d'antiquité"', *Byzantion* 50 (1980) pp. 455–86

Kedar, Benjamin, 'The Jerusalem Massacre of July 1099 in the Western historiography of the Crusades', *Crusades* 3 (2004) pp. 15–75

Keen, Maurice F., *Chivalry* (New Haven and London: Yale University Press, 1984)

Knappen, Marshall M., 'Robert II of Flanders in the First Crusade', in *The Crusades and other historical essays* (ed.) Louis J. Paetow (New York, 1928) pp. 79–100

Knoch, Peter, *Studien zu Albert von Aachen* (Stuttgart: Klett 1966)

Koch, Sister Marie Pierre, *An analysis of the long prayers in Old French literature with special reference to the Biblical – Creed – Narrative prayers* (Catholic University of America, 1940)

Kostick, Conor, *The Siege of Jerusalem: Crusade and Conquest in 1099* (London: Bloomsbury, 2009)

La Monte, John L., 'The Lords of Le Puiset on the Crusades', *Speculum* 17 (1942) pp. 100–118

Linder, Amnon, 'The liturgy of the liberation of Jerusalem', *Medieval Studies* 52 (1990) pp. 110–31

Lobrichon, Guy, *1099: Jérusalem conquise* (Paris: Seuil, 1998)

Magdalino, Paul, 'Byzantine literature: the twelfth century background', in *Digenes Akritas: new approaches to Byzantine heroic poetry*, (ed.) Roderick Beaton and David Ricks (Aldershot and Vermont: Variorum 1993) pp. 1–14

Loutschitskaya, Sonia, 'L'image des musulmans dans les chroniques des croisades', *Moyen Age* 105 (1999) pp. 717–35

Mabey, Richard, *Food for Free* (reprinted HarperCollins: London, 2012)

Mickel, Emanuel J., 'Imagining history in the Enfances Godefroi' in *Echoes of the epic: studies in honor of Gerard J. Brault*, (eds) David P. and Mary. J. Schenck (Birmingham, Alabama: Summa, 1998) pp. 175–87

Morris, Colin, *The Sepulchre of Christ in the Medieval West: from the beginning to 1600* (Oxford: Oxford University Press, 2005

_____ 'Policy and vision; the case of the Holy Lance found at Antioch', in *War and Government in the Middle Ages: essays in honour of J. O. Prestwich*, (eds) John Gillingham and J. C. Holt (Woodbridge: Boydell and Brewer, 1984) pp. 33–45

Myers, Geoffrey '*Les Chétifs*: étude sur le développement de la chanson', *Romania* 105 (1984) pp. 63–87

_____ 'Le Développement des *Chétifs*: la version Fécampoise', *Les Epopées de la Croisade: première colloque internationale, Trêves 6–11 août 1984, Zeitschrift für Französische Sprache und Literatur* Beiheft 11 (Stuttgart, 1987) pp. 84–90

Nicholson, Robert L., *Tancred: a study of his life and work* (Chicago: AMS Press, 1940)

Nicolle, David, 'Armes et armures dans les epopées de croisade', *Les epopées de la croisade: première colloque internationale, Trêves, 6–11 août 1984, Zeitschrift für Französische Sprache und Literatur*, Beiheft 11 (Stuttgart: Franz Steiner, 1987) pp. 17–34

Northup, George T., 'La *Gran Conquista de Ultramar* and its problems', *Historical Review* 2 (1934) pp. 287–302

Nowell, Charles E., 'The Old Man of the Mountains', *Speculum* 22 (1947) pp. 497–519

Paris, Gaston 'La *Chanson d'Antioche* provencale et la *Gran Conquista de Ultramar*', *Romania* 17 (1888) pp. 513–41; 19 (1890) pp. 562–91; 22 (1893) pp. 345–63

_____ 'La chanson du *Pèlerinage de Charlemagne*', *Romania* 9 (1880) pp.1–50

Partington, James R., *A History of Greek Fire and Gunpowder* (Cambridge: Heffer, 1960)

Paterson, Linda, 'Occitan literature and the Holy Land', in *The World of Eleanor of Aquitaine: literature and society in Southern France between the eleventh and thirteenth centuries*, (ed.) Marcus Bull and Catherine Leglu (Woodbridge: Boydell and Brewer, 2005) pp. 83–99

_____ 'Syria, Poitou and the *reconquista* (or Tales of the undead)', in *The Second Crusade*, (ed.) Jonathan Phillips and Martin Hoch (Manchester: Manchester University Press, 2002) pp. 133–49

_____ *The World of the Troubadours: medieval Occitan society, c. 1100 – c.1300* (Cambridge: Cambridge University Press, 1993)

Paul, Nicholas, 'Crusade, Memory and Regional Politics in twelfth-century Amboise', *Journal of Medieval History* 31 (2005) pp. 127–41

Phillips, Jonathan, *Defenders of the Holy Land: relations between the Latin East and the West 1119–87* (Oxford: Clarendon Press, 1996)

Poncelet, A., 'Boémond et St Leonard', *Analecta Bollandiana* 31 (1912) pp. 24–44

Powell, James M., 'Myth, legend, propaganda, history: the First Crusade 1140 – ca. 1300', *Autour de la première Croisade: actes du colloque de la SSCLE, Clermont-Ferrand, 22–25 juin 1995*, (ed.) Michel Balard (Paris: Sorbonne, 1996) pp. 127–41

Powell, John Wesley, *The Exploration of the Colorado River and its Canyons*, (reprinted London: Penguin, 2003)

Prawer, Joshua, *The Crusaders' Kingdom: European Colonialism in the Middle Ages*, (republished London: Phoenix, 2001)

Purkis, William, 'Crusading and Crusade memory in Caesarius of Heisterbach's *Dialogus miraculorum*', *Journal of Medieval History* 39 (2013) pp. 100–127

Reuter, Timothy, 'Episcopi cum sua militia: The Prelate as Warrior in the Early Staufen era', *Warriors and Churchmen in the High Middle Ages: essays presented to Karl Leyser*, (ed.) Timothy Reuter (London and Rio Grande: Hambledon Press, 1992) pp.79–94

Richard, Jean 'L'arrière-plan historique des deux cycles de a croisade', *Les Epopées de la Croisade: première colloque internationale, Trêves 6–11 août 1984, Zeitschrift für Französische Sprache und Literatur* Beiheft 11 (Stuttgart, 1987) pp. 1–16

_____ 'La confraternité de la croisade: à propos d'un episode de la première croisade', *Mélanges offerts à Edmond-René Labande à l'occasion de son depart à la retraite et du XXe anniversaire du CESCM par ses amis, ses collègues, ses élèves* (Poitiers: CESCM, 1974) pp. 617–22

Riley-Smith, Jonathan, *The First Crusade and the Idea of Crusading*, (London: Athlone, 1986)

_____ *What were the Crusades?* fourth edition, (Basingstoke and New York: Palgrave McMillan, 2009)

Rosewell, Roger, *Medieval Wall Paintings in English and Welsh Churches*, (Woodbridge: Boydell and Brewer, 2008)

Rubenstein, Jay, 'Putting History to Use: Three Crusade Chronicles in Context', *Viator* 35 (2004) pp. 131–68

_____ *Armies of Heaven: the First Crusade and the quest for Apocalypse*, (Philadelphia: Perseus, 2011)

Runciman, Sir Steven, *A History of the Crusades* vol. 1, 3 vols (Cambridge: Cambridge University Press, 1951)

_____ 'The Holy Lance found at Antioch', *Analecta Bollandiana* 68 (1950) pp. 197–205

Rychner, Jean, *La chanson de geste: essai sur l'art épique des jongleurs*, (Geneva: Droz, 1955)

Savvides, A. G. C.,Varia Byzantinoturcica II: Taticius the Turcopole', *Journal of Oriental and African Studies* 3–4 (1991–92) pp. 235–8

Schein, Sylvia, *Gateway to the Heavenly City: Crusader Jerusalem and the Catholic West (1099–1187)*, (Guildford: Ashgate, 2005)

Scully, Terence, *The Art of Cookery in the Middle Ages* (Boydell: Woodbridge, 1995)

Shepard, Jonathan, 'The 'muddy road' of Odo Harpin from Bourges to La-Charité-sur-Loire', in *The experience of Crusading* vol. 2: *Defining the Crusader Kingdom*, (ed.) Peter Edbury and Jonathan Phillips, (Cambridge: Cambridge University Press, 2003) pp. 11–28

Söhring, Otto, 'Werke bildender Kunst in altfranzösischen Epen', *Romanische Förschungen* 12 (1900) pp. 491–640

Spencer, Colin, *British Food: an extraordinary thousand years of history* (London: Grub Street, 2002)

Spiegel, Gabrielle, *Romancing the Past: the Rise of Vernacular Prose Historiography in Thirteenth-Century France,* (Berkeley and Los Angeles: University of California Press, 1993)

Suard, François, *La Chanson de Geste,* (Paris: PUF, 1993)

Sweetenham, Carol, 'The Count and the Cannibals: the Old French Crusade Cycle as a drama of salvation' in *Jerusalem the Golden: the Origins and Impact of the First Crusade*, (ed.) Susan B. Edgington and Luis Garcia-Guijarro (Turnhout: Brepols, 2014) pp. 307–28

Sylvester, Walter, 'The communions, with three blades of grass, of the knights-errant', *Dublin Review* 121:23 (1897) pp. 80–98

Tannahill, Reay, *Food in History,* (London: Penguin, 1973; revised 1988)

Thorp, Nigel, '*La Chanson de Jérusalem* and the Latin chronicles', *Epic and Crusade: Proceedings of the Colloquium of the Société Rencesvals British Branch held at Lucy Cavendish College, Cambridge, 27–28 March 2004*, (ed.) Philip Bennett, Anne Cobby and Jane Everson (Edinburgh: Société Rencesvals, British Branch, 2006) pp. 153–71

_____ 'La *Gran Conquista de Ultramar* et les origines de la *Chanson de Jérusalem*', *Les épopées romanes, GRLMA* II.1.2 fasc.5 (1986) pp. 76–85

Tolan, John, 'Muslims as Pagan Idolators in Chronicles of the First Crusade', in *Western Views of Islam in Medieval and Early Modern Europe: Perception of Other*, (eds) David R. Blanks and Michael Frassetto (New York: St Martin's, 1999) pp. 97–117

Tyerman, Christopher, *God's War: a new history of the Crusades* (London: Penguin 2007)

_____ *The Invention of the Crusades* (Basingstoke and London: McMillan, 1998)

Venckeleer, Theo, 'Faut-il traduire VASSAL par "vassal"? Quelques réflexions sur la lexicologie du francais médiéval', *Mélanges de linguistique, de littérature et de philology offerts à J. R. Smeets*, (Leiden, 1982) pp. 303–16

Vercel, Roger, *Du Guesclin,* (Paris: Albin Michel, 1932)

Verlinden, Charles, *Robert Ier le Frison,* (Antwerp: De Sikkel; Gravenhage: Martinus Nijhoff; Paris: Champion, 1935)

Walter, Christopher, *The Warrior Saints in Byzantine Art and Tradition* (Aldershot: Ashgate, 2003)

Weitenberg, Jos J. S., 'Literary contacts in Cilician Armenia' in *East and West in the Crusader States: context – contacts – confrontation*, (eds) Krijnie Ciggaar, Adelbert Davids and Herman Teule, *Orientalia Lovaniensia Analecta* 75 (Leuven: Uitgeverij Peeters, 1996) pp. 63–72

Vikings: life and legend, (ed.) Gareth Williams, Peter Pentz and Matthias Wemhoff, (London: British Museum, 2014)

Wolf, Kenneth B., 'Crusade and narrative: Bohemond and the Gesta Francorum', *Journal of Medieval History* 17 (1991) pp. 207–16

Yewdale, Ralph B., *Bohemond I, Prince of Antioch,* (Princeton: [n.p.], 1924)

Zink, Michel, 'Apollin', *Mélanges René Louis: la chanson de geste et le mythe carolingien* (St.Père-sous-Vézelay: Musée Archaéologique Regionale, 1982) pp. 503–09

Index

The index refers to major characters and their main appearances, places, nationalities, themes and events. Minor characters, innumerable fictional Saracens and fleeting appearances are listed only in the Table of Names and Places. References to the chief players and places – Christians, Franks, Turks, Saracens, Persians, Arabs, infidels, pagans, the *chétifs* themselves, Antioch and Jerusalem – are ubiquitous and not listed. Places referred to only for the sake of the rhyme are also not listed. Neither are commonly used terms such as *chanson de geste* and crusade.

99 Names of God 110
Abraham, maker of sword 181
Adhemar, bishop of Le Puy 28
Agolant 323
Albericus Trium Fontium 16–17 and 17n, 18
Albert of Aachen 4, 18, 27, 30, 40
Alexander 285
Angevins 200
Antichrist 45–6
    Bribery by 45
    Defeat by Christ and end of days 44
Apocalypse
    Pseudo-Methodius 44
Apollon, image of 322
Apulia, men from 235, 241, 257
Arachne 286
Arfulans
    Revenge for death of kinsmen 92–98
Armenians 200
Arras, literary experimentation in 36
Athene 286, 294
Azoparts 296

Baldwin of Beauvais, *chétif* 7, 9, 12, 22, 41, 46, 60, 64
    Persuades Corbaran to let him avenge brother 106–8
    Climbs mountain and defeats Sathanas 111-
Baldwin of Boulogne 24, 29, 63

    Attacked by leeches 25, 62, 251–254
    Captures Cornumarant 280
    Injures Sucaman 281
    Wrongly placed at taking of Jerusalem 45
    Kills Cornumarant 64, 343
Baudry of Bourgueil 17n, 27, 44
Bavarians 191
Berry, men of 257
Bishop of Forez, *chétif* 8, 64
    Gives Baldwin penance 108–09
    Prays for Richard ahead of ordeal 81, 86
Blood up to knees of horses 263 and n137, 325, 327, 341, 345
Bocidant, men from 323, 335
Bohemond 24, 29, 61, 63, 64
    Argues with Raymond of St-Gilles over Antioch 40
    Captivity 20
    Divides spoils 190
    Kills Corbadas 64
    Leads successful ambush at Caesarea 184–190
    Refuses crown of Jerusalem 268–269
    Wrongly placed at taking of Jerusalem 45
Boulogne, men from 232, 237
Brabant, men from 257
Bretons 200, 231, 239–40,

430   *The* Chanson des Chétifs *and* Chanson de Jérusalem

Brohadas, death of 7, 16, 18, 42, 59,
    67—69, 71, 74, 277, 322, 323
Bulgars 74, 323, 336
Burgundy, men from 232, 240, 263

Caesarius of Heisterbach 17
Calabra, mother of Corbaran 7, 16, 41, 59
    Miracle involving 99
    Penchant for Richard of Chaumont
        79—80
    Rewards *chétifs* 140—141
    Suggests candidates for ordeal by
        battle 73—74, 76
    Variant involving magic cloth 147-8
Calabria, men from 235, 241
Candelabrae from Temple 306, 310
Candles, miracles with 271—272, 314
Canon of St Peter's at Antioch and St
    Peter's 9, 11, 14, 16
Canso d'Antioca 11n, 31
Canso de la Crozada 11n, 55
Chanson d'Antioche 3, 21, 23
    Earlier versions of 47
    Parallels to *Jérusalem* 23—27
Chanson de Guillaume 31
Chanson de Roland 32, 41
Charles Martel 339
Charlemagne 48, 76
    Ancestor of Richard of Chaumont 76,
        97
    France kingdom of 141, 288
Chrétienté Corbaran 8 and 8n, 16
Christ
    Baptism 142
    Forty days in wilderness 143
    Miracle of loaves and fishes 275
Civetot and defeat of Peter the Hermit 7,
    16, 22, 43, 75, 137
Communion with three blades of grass
    By Ernoul of Beauvais 105
    By Rainalt of Beauvais 327
    By Sorgalé 90
Confraternity at Jerusalem 199
Conventions of *chanson de geste* 30, 37, 43
    Description of 46
    Early material on Crusade 47
    Portrayal of Saracens 30
Corbadas 61, 62

    Killed by Bohemond 64, 339
    Leans at window 200, 201, 204, 213,
        214, 216, 222, 229, 231, 265
Corbaran 7, 8, 16, 18, 41, 42, 59, 60
    Allows Baldwin to avenge brother
        106—108
    Arrives and camps at Mount Tigris
        98—102
    Attacked by family of Golias and
        Sorgalé 92—98
    Chooses and prepares Richard as
        champion 77—83
    Conversion 8, 22, 41, 75, 125—126,
        142
    Disagreement with Sultan 67, 68–72
    Nephew 18, 60
        Kidnapped, rescued by Harpin
            131—135
    Reconciled to Sultan 91—92
    Reinforced by Sultan's arrival
        124—129
    Releases *chétifs* 142
    Rescues Baldwin 117—118, 119—120,
        122
    Returns to Oliferne 130—131
Cornumarant, son of the King of Jerusalem
    8, 61, 62
    Captured by Baldwin 63, 280; released
        292
    Killed by Baldwin 64
    Prepares for arrival of Christians
        144—146
    Size of heart 30, 65, 352—353
Crusade of 1101, failure of 10, 20
Cyclification of *chansons de geste* 36

Digenis Akritas 14—15 and 14n,
Dinas 43
Doves
    And candle 314
    And kites 202—203
    And St Michael 115
    As postal service 225—228
Dreams
    Corbaran 93—94

Editions 51
English 200

Eracles 32
Ernoul of Beauvais 7, 46, 60
    Attacked and eaten by Sathanas 103–6
Esclavons 290, 298, 323, 325 347
Escler(s) 229, 276, 278, 287, 303, 324, 338 351
Espccs, beaked monsters 333–334
Eurvin of Créel 24, 62
    Captured and escapes 241–244
Exempla and exemplary function 3–4

Faramon the jailer 73–74
Field of Blood 13, 14, 20
Flamenca, Le Roman de 31
Flanders, men from 232, 237, 240–241, 257, 263
Formulaic style 4, 21, 52
Fulcher of Chartres 20, 27, 40
Fulcher of Melun, *chétif*
    Identity 19
    In despair 74

Gascons 200, 234, 257
Genoese 200
Georgians 200
Germans 74, 191
    Calabra as German 148 variant 4
Gesta Francorum et aliorum Hierosolimitanorum 18n, 27
    Possible poetic material in 47

Giants, turn on each other in confusion 336
Girart de Roussillon 31
Godfrey of Bouillon 25, 29, 61, 62, 63
    Attacks Cornumarant 217
    Becomes King of Jerusalem 271–272
    Begs leaders not to leave Jerusalem 273–274
    Bisects Turk 64
    Cleans Holy Sepulchre 264–265
    Cuts Marbrin in half in combat 308–309
    Dove lights candle 314
    First ruler of Jerusalem 28, 63
    Greets *chétifs* 179
    Kills son of Sultan 64, 67
    Legendary origins and texts describing 5
    One of the Nine Worthies 36
    Restores sight of custodian of Temple 265
    Shoots three kites 201–203, 210
    Unable to put sword down 301
Gontier of Aire 24, 62
    Death in first attack on Jerusalem 218
Graindor de Douai and the *Antioche* 35–36, 39, 41
La Gran Conquista de Ultramar 22
    Parallels with *Jérusalem* 31–32
Greek fire 82, 125, 127, 215, 218, 229, 237, 245, 256, 258, 260, 341, 342, 345
Greeks 200
Guibert of Nogent 18, 27, 44

Harpin of Bourges, *chétif* 8, 9, 17, 21, 60–61, 62
    Argues for going to Holy Sepulchre 141
    Captures Lyon's horse 96
    Defeats robbers 135–140
    Encourages Baldwin to avenge Ernoul 108
    Encourages Richard to fight for Corbaran 78
    Fights Chainan in variant 148–56
    Identity 18–19, 20
    In despair 74
    Rescues Corbaran's nephew 132–135
    Rescues John of Alis and tames mother of Sathanas in variant 156–72
    Service in Temple 109
Harrowing of Hell 42
Herod 80, 114, 225
    Horn of 246
Hideous, Sultan's sword 337
Historiography, vernacular verse and prose 47
Holy Innocents 80, 114, 187, 194, 313
Holy Lance 209, 214, 215, 276, 316, 321, 335
    Turns fire back on Saracens 341
Holy Sepulchre
    Importance of 42
Horses
    Capalu, horse of Godfrey 300

Given to Count of Vendôme 342
Ridden to combat 308
Cornicas, horse of 331, 334
Captured by Baldwin 334
Maigremor, horse of Sultan
Described 294, 305 (?), 338
Sultan flees on 346
Morel, horse of Tancred 340
Mulberry, horse of Robert of Flanders 227
Partridge, Saracen horse captured by Bohemond 324—325
Plantamor, Cornumarant's horse 204, 246, 247, 248, 249, 250, 253—254
Briefly captured by Baldwin 251
Captured by Baldwin and given to Eustace 343
Escapes when Cornumarant captured 280—281
Prinsaut, horse of Count Baldwin 248, 249, 250
Recognisable by spiritedness 280
Attacked by leeches 253—254
Hugh of Vermandois 24, 29, 61, 63
Gives sound advice 196—197, 199, 230, 351
Refuses crown of Jerusalem 269
Wrongly placed at taking of Jerusalem
Hungarians 74, 336

Iftikhar ad-Dawla 28

Judas Maccabeus 93
Joseph of Arimathea 193

Kenelius 322, 335
King Abraham
Lands of 98, 102
King(s) of Nubia 59, 67, 72
Defends Corbaran 70—71
Kings of Jerusalem 14

Laisses 21, 52
Length as marker of age 37
Letter of Alexius to Robert of Flanders 44, 45
Lion, takes away Christian dead at Ascalon 351

Liturgy of Jerusalem 33
Lombards 320, 336
Longinus 81, 84, 90, 113, 115, 116, 133, 138, 193, 314
Lotharingians 234, 257
Lyon of the Mountain
Revenge for death of kinsmen 92—98

Mahomed
Image of 303, 304, 345
Destroyed by Christians 349
Killed by pigs 286
Magnetic coffin of 286—287
Malachi, Jew who made helmet 145
Manuscript tradition 3, 9, 21—22,
Marseille, men from 234
Metaphors
Angels like falcons 188
Celestial forces white as snow and stronger than lions 345
Chétifs like oxen 103
Franks:
Like dogs attacking boar 187—188
Like lions 186
like sparrow-hawk 205
like wild boars 188, 248, 278
Garsion like mongrel 223
Godfrey like wild boar 214
Godfrey and Saracen like falcons 326
Horses faster than falcon chasing stork and sparrowhawk attacking birds 334
Night flees like sparrowhawk 346
Richard of Chaumont like goshawk attacking lambs 206
Saracen killed
Like hemlock stem 309
like slaughtered piglet 180
like stripped reed 304
Turks and pagans:
like flock of ewes 300
like larks fleeing sparrowhawk 283
like magpies fleeing falcon 328
like mallard not attacking falcon 348
like mongrels 263, 323
like straw in the wind 300

like willow-warblers fleeing sparrowhawks 348
Montjoie 191 n34
Morgan la Fée 294
Moses 84—85, 6
Mount Tigris, home of the Sathanas 7

Nicolas and Gregory, siege engineers 25, 26, 30, 62, 210, 215, 237, 256, 257
Nine Worthies 4n, 36
Normans 231, 237, 239—40, 257, 263

Old French Crusade Cycle 3, 5, 6, 23, 35—37
Oliferne, Corbaran's city 7, 8
Oliver 47
Orderic Vitalis 18, 20, 27
Otto of Freisingen 44

Patarins 200
Patriarch of Antioch 11—12, 13, 14, 15, 16
Paulicians 74
Performance of *chansons de geste* 47—48
Peter the Hermit 61
    Defeat at Civetot, see Civetot
    Describes columns to Sultan 64, 317—321
    Describes Jerusalem to crusaders 192—194
    Genesis of Crusade 40
    Kills Salehadin 64
    Rescued by St George 64
    Taken prisoner and apostasies 63, 301—304
    Unorthodox fighting technique 299
Peter Tudebode 27
Picardy 3–4 and 3n, 16
    Picard origins of Cycle 36
Pisans 200
Poitevins 234, 257
Polygamy and procreation 70, 287
Ponthieu, men of 257
Prières du plus grand péril
    By Baldwin of Beauvais 112—113
    By Ernoul of Beauvais 104—105
    By Godfrey 313—314
    By Harpin of Bourges 133
    By Richard of Chaumont 84—85

Provencals and men from South of France 200, 234, 237
Publicans 336

Queen Eublastris 69—70
Queen of Sheba 93

Raimbaut Creton 24, 28, 64
    Cut off with Baldwin, attacked and wounded 347—348
Ralph of Caen, *Gesta Tancredi* 27
Raymond of Aguilers 20, 25, 27
Raymond of Poitiers, Prince of Antioch 9—11, 13, 16, 21, 32
    Commissioner of song 100—01, 102
Raymond of St-Gilles 28, 29, 61, 63
    Argues with Bohemond over Antioch 40
    Taken captive 283—284
    Released 292
Red Lion, death of 71, 74
Rhyme and metre 4, 21, 52
Ribalts 54—55
    Defeat Especs 333—334
    Kill Turks who refuse to apostatise 222
    Intimidate Saracen envoys 291; and again 307
Richard le Pèlerin 30, 32
Richard of Chaumont, *chétif* 7, 9, 16, 21, 42, 59
    Fights Golias and Sorgalé and wins 86—89
    In despair 74
    Negotiates with Corbaran 76—78
    Possible identity 17—18
    Prepares for ordeal 78—81
    Suggests rejoining army 141
Richard of Pavia, *chétif*
    Identity 19
Ripoll manuscript 33
Robert of Flanders 29, 61, 63
    Cleans Holy Sepulchre 264—265
    Refuses crown of Jerusalem 267
Robert of Normandy 29
    Hand frozen to sword 184
    Killed Red Lion at Antioch 318
    Suggests consulting hermit 255
    Refuses crown of Jerusalem 268

Rescued by Bohemond and Tancred 329—330
Robert the Monk 4, 27, 30, 40, 44
Roland 47, 311, 350
Romania, men from 257

St Andrew of Patras 175
St Barbara 15, 61, 138, 188, 189, 283
St Daniel 340
St Demetrius 283
St Denis 116, 188, 344
St Domitian 61, 138, 188, 189, 344
St George 61, 116, 138, 188, 189, 283, 284
    Rescues Peter the Hermit 344
St Gervais 118
St Gilles 116
St James 116
St Jerome 60, 134
St John, feast of 68
St Jonah 175
St Lawrence 116
St Lazarus 297, 314, 115
St Leonard 15, 116
St Maurice 116, 188, 283, 344
St Michael 46, 74, 115, 118, 119, 217, 326, 332, 359
St Nicholas of Myra 15, 108, 111, 112, 116, 118, 135, 175
St Peter 116, 242
St Simeon 297
St Thomas 175
St Vaast 175
St-Pol, Enguerrand and Hugh of 24, 26, 27, 36, 46
    Death of Enguerrand 45, 47, 64, 332
    Enguerrand leads squadron at Jerusalem 231
    Hugh avenges Enguerrand 332—333
    In second wave attack on Jerusalem 238
    Mourning for Enguerrand 349—350
Salvation and the divine plan 4, 38—39, 43—46
Sathanas 7, 14, 22, 42, 46, 60
    Attacks and eats Ernoul of Beauvais 103—6
    Description of 98—100
    Fights and is killed by Baldwin 116—122
Saxons 257
Scots 200
Sicily, men from 235
Siglaie, Saracens from 311, 322
Slavs 78, 183
Sorgalé and Goliath 7, 17, 59, 82
    Fight and defeated by Richard 83—89
    Golias dispatched with speed 86
    Son of Golias attempts revenge 92
    Sorgalé converts and begs death from Richard 90
Stake to which Christ tied, relic of 192—193, 316, 321, 335
    Turns fire on Saracens 341
Stephen of Blois 24, 29
    Flees at Antioch 26—27, 45
    Wrongly placed at Jerusalem 64
Structure
    Of *Chétifs* 21—22
    Of *Jérusalem* 23–4
Sultan of Persia 7, 59, 60, 62
    Anger and grief at death of son 67—72
    Description of 289, 24
    Frees captives 129
    Furious at revenge attack on Corbaran 98
    Reconciled to Corbaran 91—92
    Reinforces Corbaran at Mt Tigris 124—129
    Tries to negotiate with Corbaran 85
Swan Knight, Godfrey's ancestor 318, 328
Syrians 200

Tafurs and king of Tafurs 26, 27, 29, 30, 46, 62, 63
    Described 208
    First attack on Jerusaem 216, 230, 238
    Injured 216
    Invites those without a lord to join him 257
    King crowns Godfrey ruler of Jerusalem 272—273
    Redeemed by Crusade 45
    And *ribalts* 55
    Tempted by Saracen treasure 297
    Urges attack on Jerusalem 209

Tancred 61
    Kills Lucabel 64, 340
Taticius (Estatin) 233
Tents 101, 285–286, 287
Thomas of Marle 25, 26, 27, 29, 61, 62
    Boosts morale at Jerusalem 194
    Cleans Holy Sepulchre 264–265
    Cures Baldwin from effect of leeches with talisman 253–254
    Flung into Jerusalem from spearpoints and attacked by Bedouin woman 63, 199–200, 214, 261–262
    Prepares to attack Jerusalem 234
    Purifies Holy Sepulchre 63
    Redeemed by Crusade 45
    Swears fealty to King of Tafurs 263
Titus Vespasian 200
Treasure
    Of Sathanas 124
    Used to tempt Christians 295–297, 299, 338
    Used to tempt Saracens by Godfrey 307
True Cross, relic of 29, 316, 326, 335, 336

Christian squadrons ride past at Ascalon 317–321
    Protects bishop of Mautran from Saracens 342
Turcoples 74
Tuscans 320

Variants 9, 22, 51
    Calabra and the magic cloth 59, 147–148
    Chainan 59, 148–156
    Sathanas mère 60, 156–172
Venetians 235

Walter the Chancellor 13, 14, 20
Wayland the Smith 71
Welsh 257
William VII, Count of Poitiers 10, 11n, 13, 20
Women
    Carry water 178, 179, 239–240, 258, 260
    Lamenting 177
    Squadron to attack Jerusalem 236